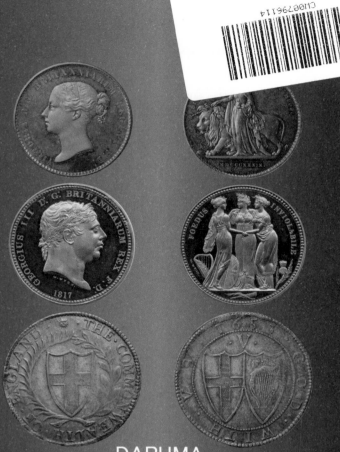

ENGLISH SILVER COINAGE

from 1649

ENGLISH
SILVER COINAGE
from 1649

BY

MAURICE BULL

Based on the original work by

P. ALAN RAYNER

SPINK

LONDON

English Silver Coinage 1649-1949 by H. A. Seaby
First Edition 1949
English Silver Coinage from 1649 by P. A. Rayner
Second edition 1957
Third (Revised) Edition 1968
Fourth (Revised) Edition 1974
English Silver Coinage from 1649
Fifth (Revised) Edition by P. A. Rayner 1992
Sixth (Revised) Edition by Maurice Bull 2015

Printed by Gutenberg Press Ltd., Tarxien, Malta

ISBN 978-1-907427-50-3

© 2015
Spink & Son Ltd.
69 Southampton Row
London WC1B 4ET

www.spink.com

CONTENTS

CONTENTS

(continued)

vi

CONTENTS

CONTENTS

PREFACE TO THE SIXTH EDITION

This completely revised edition of *The English Silver Coinage* came about as a result of a talk with Philip Skingley (Spink Numismatic Publications), when he asked if I would consider a long overdue update of the work by Alan Rayner. The last update was in 1992 when letter suffixes were used to record new additions. He suggested I re-number everything in order to remove the confusing letter suffixes. After a few unsuccessful attempts with new formats etc., this is the result.

In his fifth Edition Alan Rayner was undecided whether to re-number, in order to eliminate the use of letter suffixes, and to change the format by monarch rather than denomination. After consultation with other collectors I have decided to make those changes and to cross-reference each with the old ESC numbers.

Another major decision was what to include that had not been recorded before. After consultation with numerous collectors and knowledgeable persons I decided that this work should be a reference of ALL known silver coins both available and unavailable to collectors, i.e. a record of proofs and patterns of the greatest rarity. Thanks to the computer, the opportunity to profusely illustrate specimens and enlargements of die varieties has been possible. Unfortunately, some varieties, especially on smaller coins, are not photogenic taken from publications. I decided to list, as many as possible, every recorded coin at the back of the book under 'Provenances' to show where an illustration is available. This has the added benefit of proving the existence of many rare examples. A small number have not been located either because of rarity, or being too common to have been illustrated in publications.

Prior to 1816, when the reducing machine was introduced and dies were copied from a master die, they were individually made by hand, and no two dies were truly identical. This is not intended to be a finite record, but simply to show the major, and, some minor recognised varieties. Some, so-called, varieties have been delisted where they are considered to be the result of striking, damaged or filled dies and not true die-sinker's errors, i.e. missing stops, un-barred letters and edge inscriptions caused by slippage of the collar segments.

When re-numbering this series I decided to leave appropriate gaps in the sequence between reigns for a number of reasons; firstly to enable late additions to be incorporated easily and secondly to help future additions to be made in the next edition, if necessary, without the need to re-number the whole series again.

Maurice Bull
2013

ACKNOWLEDGEMENTS

The first edition of *English Silver Coinage 1649-1949* was published by H.A. Seaby in 1949. P.A. Rayner published a Second Edition in 1957, a Third in 1968, a Fourth in 1974 and the Fifth (Revised) in 1992 (over two decades ago).

Finally I must confess this sixth Edition (revised and updated in a new format) would not have been possible without the knowledge and dedicated work of Alan Rayner, to whom I am deeply grateful, and for the input by a number of collectors in their specialised fields.

My most sincere thanks are to Philip Skingley (Spink Numismatic Publications) for giving me the opportunity to tackle such an important task, and for backing the project from start to finish together with immense encouragement and assistance along the tortuous way.

I must give a very special thanks to Steve Hill for privately taking the time to proof read and correct my many mistakes and for his valuable suggestions to improve the text and imagery.

I wish to thank the following people for their contributions, suggestions, and permission to copy illustrations and notes from their various publications and collections, for without their generosity this publication would not have been possible, and my apologies to anyone I may have missed;

  Andrew Wide (private collector)
  Chris Webb, Director at D.N.W Auctions
  Dave Tisbury (private collector)
  Douglas Saville (Rare book seller),
  Ian Hunter (private collector)
  Lloyd Bennett (Coin dealer),
  Leon Juckett (private collector)
  Malcolm Lewendon (private collector)
  Mark Rasmussen (Coin dealer)
  Marvin Lessen (private collector)
  Mike Shaw (private collector)
  Nick Haddad (private collector)
  Nigel Prevost (private collector)
  Paul Cattermole (private collector)
  Roderick Farey (private collector)
  Roderick Richardson (Coin dealer)
  Seth Freeman & Steve Hill at Baldwin's, and last, but not least, thank you to all my friends with whom I bounced many new ideas; Alan Hawkins, Barry Allen, Mick Martin, Mark Rasmussen, Ray Bayford etc..

ACKNOWLEDGEMENTS

I am especially indebted to the following people for supplying wonderful images and helping me to unravel many complicated series; Roderick Farey and Nigel Prevost (shillings), Malcolm Lewendon (Gothic Florins etc.), David Tisbury (Commonwealth varieties), and to the anonymous collectors who allowed me to see their private collections.

Finally I am very grateful to all the famous named numismatists of the past whose collections were illustrated in the many auction and sales catalogues: Spink, D.N.W, Glendining, Seaby, St. James's, Bonham's etc., through which they were sold over the years (in no particular order); Hyman Montagu, Paul W. Karon, R.C. Lockett, Herman Selig, Colonel Morrieson, Lord Hamilton, H.M. Lingford, Jackson-Kent, E.D.J. Van Roekel, The Slaney collection, Dr Bruno Mantegazza, Frederick Willis, Dr D. Rees-Jones, J.C.S. Rashleigh, La Riviere and Kaufman, The Magnus collection, R. Henry Norweb, T.H. Paget, Alfred Bole, H.A. Parsons, H.E. Manville, G. Sommerville,, J.F. Rowlands, Martin Hughes, A.H. Whetmore Alan Barr and the publication by Alex Wilson & Mark Rasmussen *Trials and proofs in gold'*. (See under 'Provenances')

A special thanks to the auction houses, dealers and collectors who graciously waived copyright for me to use some of their images when actual specimens were unavailable, and to Nigel Prevost, John Howie and Roderick Farey for allowing me to reprint their published die studies of Anne Shillings.

Maurice Bull
2015

HISTORY OF MILLED COINAGE

(Reproduced from E.S.C. Fifth Edition by P. Alan Rayner)

ELIZABETH I

First use of the mill and screw press in England

It is usual to refer to all coins struck by machinery as 'milled' but this is a misnomer. The term 'mill money' was originally applied to coins made at the Paris Mint about 1552, when the metal was rolled to the required thickness, a cutting press stamped out the blanks, and a screw press was used to strike the coins. The power for these operations was supplied by horse or water (mill).

Despite the coins being technically and artistically superior to those made by hand, years of bitter opposition from mint workers who feared for their jobs finally drove the machine's inventor, Eloye Mestrelle, to seek employment at the Tower Mint in London in 1561. There he was allowed to set up and demonstrate his machinery, being paid the rather miserly salary of twenty-five pounds per annum. During the period from 1561 to 1572 he struck the following denominations. In gold: half-pound, crown, and halfcrown: and in silver: shilling, sixpence, fourpence, threepence, twopence and three-farthings.

Mestrelle's shilling

The gold coins are extremely rare and it is doubtful if they circulated in any quantity. The silver shillings were struck only in small numbers, but the sixpences, struck nearly every year between 1561 and 1571, are relitively common and display such numerous variations in the style of portraiture, mint-mark and diameter that a considerable number of dies is indicated. The fourpence, threepence and halfgroat are considerably scarcer than the sixpences and only a very few specimens of the three-farthings are known. In all, a very considerable number of coins must have been struck. Also known are several superb patterns in gold and silver from dies engraved by Derick Anthiony.

HISTORY OF MILLED COINAGE

Despite the obvious superiority of his coins, Mestrelle fell foul of strenuous opposition to his machinery and in 1572 was deprived of his emoluments, probably because he was related to a certain Philip Mestrelle who was hanged at Tyburn in 1569 for forgery. An attempt to restore his position resulted in completely false acccusations as to the speed and quality of stiking being made by the Warden of the Mint, Richard Martin. Mestelle was discharged and six years later he was hanged at Norwich together with several accomplaces for striking and passing false money.

CHARLES I

Further experiments with mill machinery by Nicholas Briot

It is to Charles' fine artistic taste and his intense desire to improve the poor quality of portraiture and striking of coins that we owe the employment in London of Nicholas Briot, one of the most brilliant artists and die cutters of his time. Like Mestrelle, he was of French origin, having spent some years working at the Paris Mint amid continuous hostility towards the mill and screw machinery, of which he was a staunch advocate. In 1628 he was allowed to set up machinery in the Tower Mint, and at once began to make a number of superb pattern pieces of an artistic and technical standard not previously achieved.

Apart from his outstanding qualities as an artist, his refinement over the machinery used by Mestrelle consisted of a circular collar which prevented the blank from spreading unevenly when struck, thus producing coins of a neater and rounder appearance bearing a fuller impression of the dies than had hitherto been possible. Portraiture on the hammered coins improved under his influence, although coins were still struck in a disgracefully shoddy fashion.

N. Briot's
1ˢᵗ milled
Crown
(D.J. Van Roekel 42)

xiii

HISTORY OF MILLED COINAGE

Briot's first milled issue consisted in gold of an angel, unite, double crown and crown, and in silver of a crown (see illustration above), halfcrown, shilling, sixpence, halfgroat and penny. These were struck between July 1631 and July 1632, some coins having in addition to the mintmark B, a flower or rose, the mark in use on the hammered coins at this time.

In August 1635 he was appointed Master of the Scottish Mint, and although he held this post until 1646, when he was succeeded by his son-in-law John Falconer, most of the coins for which the Scottish series is justly proud were struck in 1637. Doubtless under his influence, the use of the mill and screw press in Scotland pre-dates the general use of this machinery in London by several years. Briot's second milled issue in London, struck in 1638-9 with the anchor mintmark consisted only of a silver halfcrown, shilling and sixpence, although hammered halfcrowns and shillings were also made from his dies at this time. While continuing to work at the Tower Mint for the Parliamentary forces during the Civil War, he surreptitiously made dies for the King's coins at York and Oxford. He died at Oxford in 1646.

N. Briot's
Halfcrown
struck at York
c. 1643
(Bull 557)

COMMONWEALTH OF ENGLAND
1649-1660

In 1642, at the beginning of the Civil War, Parliament seized the Tower. It continued to strike coins in the name of Charles I and with his portrait. After the king's execution Parliament ordered coins to be made in the name of the Commonwealth and for the first time the inscriptions in English tongue. The types of all the denominations were uniform, except for the half-penny, and were very commonplace: the three smallest pieces bear no legend. The only variation is a change in the mintmark: until 1657 it was a sun, after that date an anchor; all pieces with this latter mintmark are rare.

The authorities having heard of the great advancements made in the manufacture of coins on the continent, sent to Paris for Peter Blondeau who had invented a new machine. He came over and in a house in the Strand erected a machine on the mill and screw principle, from which he struck the finely executed patterns of 1651. His halfcrown patterns were the first pieces made in this country with an inscription on the edge. His position at the Mint was, however, much opposed by the 'old brigade' and resulted in the issue of a series of patterns by David Ramage to show that a foreigner was not required. These pieces are of inferior workmanship to those of Blondeau. However, he held on for a time, but by 1658 the opposition was so strong that he was forced to resign leaving his machine behind. He returned to Paris with a pension of £100.

A proclamation of 7 September 1661 demonetised the *Commonwealth Coinage,* but the date was extended until 1 May 1662 for payment of taxes (Craig *The Mint, p. 157*)

The following recorded die varieties demonstrate how large the production must have been during this period. No doubt quantities of Charles I coins were melted down to augment the demand for silver.

1

COMMONWEALTH, 1649-60
CROWNS

Inverted N

Standard obverse

Blundered E A

Standard reverse

Thin wire-line inner circle
Inverted N in ENGLAND

6 over 4

Very large 2 over 1

Large 6 over small over 4

6 over 4

Small 6 over 4

Both Ns over inverted Ns

A for V in VS

Normal & inverted Ns

2

COMMONWEALTH, 1649-60
CROWNS

Standard design with value shown as • V •

Obv.	Cross of St George on a shield between; palm branch left and laurel branch right, with the mintmark above
Leg.	THE COMMONWEALTH OF ENGLAND
mm.	SUN
Rev.	Value • V • above conjoined shields; the cross of St George left and the Irish harp right with date above in the legend
Leg.	GOD WITH VS

Spink 3214

ESC	Date	Varieties, remarks, etc	R	(Old ESC)
1	1649	All Ns over inverted Ns	R^4	1
2	—	Thin wire-line inner circle, and inverted N in ENGLAND	R^5	2
3	1651	All Ns over inverted Ns	R^4	3
4	1652	All Ns over inverted Ns Many subtle die varieties	R	4
5	—	All Ns over inverted Ns Very large 2/1	R^3	5
6	1653	All Ns over inverted Ns Many subtle die varieties	N	6
7	—	All Ns over inverted Ns *Rev.* A for V in VS	R^3	6A
8	1654	All normal Ns	R^3	7
9	—	All normal Ns *Rev.* A for V in VS	R^3	7A
10	1656	Large round 6 possibly over 4 *Rev.* A for V in VS Blundered E A in COMMONWEALTH 2nd N inverted in ENGLAND	R^2	8
11	—	Small 6/4 All normal Ns	R^2	8A
12	—	Small 6/4 All normal Ns *Rev.* A for V in VS	S	9
13	—	Small 6/4 2nd N over inverted N in ENGLAND *Rev.* A for V in VS	S	9
14	—	Large 6 over small 6 over 4 *Rev.* A for V in VS 2nd N over inverted N in ENGLAND	R^3	8A

Note
There are many sub-varieties of these crowns; most notable in the size of the numerals, alignment of the legends and spacing of the date relative to the value etc. This is inherent in individually handmade coinage.

A challenge to make a full die study awaits someone with time and patience

3

CROWNS

FABRICATION

Caveat
There are many contemporary and modern forgeries of this series,
including some with a copper core, e.g., 1653 (Baldwin's cabinet)

"The re-cutting of the inscription on genuine coins
(All Commonwealth denominations) *to produce new or rarer readings*
was the particular line of the notorious 19th century forger, John White"

Typical example
(*Provenance* Spink Auction 147, lot 531)

ANCHOR

xxx	1660	Tooled to alter date from **1652** to **1660** and *mintmark* **Sun** to **Anchor** Normal **N** in **COMMONWEALTH** Ns over inverted Ns in **ENGLAND** *(Unique?)*		

HALFCROWNS

OBVERSES

Obverse A

All Ns over inverted Ns

Only stops by *mm*

COMMONWE·ALT·H

2nd N over inverted N

2nd N over inverted N

No stop after THE

Extra stop in TH·E·

E over ?

All Ns inverted

First O over M

Inverted Ns

N over G

·OF·F

Reverse B

Missing T

5

COMMONWEALTH, 1649-60
HALFCROWNS

Standard reverse with value shown as
• II • VI •   • II VI •   II VI
(Pattern **1651** shows value as **II • VI**)

All stops	Only stops by value	Only stops by value
No central stop in value	No stops by value	1655
5 over 4	2 over 1	3 over 1
3 over 2	4 over 3	6 over 4
6 over 5	All stops	8 over 7

6

HALFCROWNS

1659

Normal 2
Low central stop

Large 2
Centralised middle stop

Normal N

N over inverted N

Re-entered N

	A.	*mm.* SUN	Spink 3215	
ESC	Date	Varieties, remarks, etc	R	(Old ESC)
15	**1649**	No central stop in mark of value	R^3	425
16	—	All Ns inverted No central stop in mark of value		425
17	**1651**	With regular central stop in value	R^2	426
18	—	2nd N over inverted N in **ENGLAND** No central stop in mark of value	R^2	425A?
19	—	Mule; 1/- *obv.* with 2/6 *rev.* on a shilling flan All Ns over inverted N. No central stop in value (This coin is duplicated under shillings) *(2 known)*	R^7	428
20	—	No stops by value	R^2	425B?
21	—	No stop between **GOD WITH**	R^4	426A
22	—	No central stop in mark of value	R^4	426B
23	—	*Proof,* see note [1]	R^5	427
24	**1652**	Low central stop in value	R	429
25	—	Large figure **2** in date. Centralised stop in value	$R^?$	429A?
26	—	**2** over **1**	R^2	430
27	—	No stops after **THE OF** Extra stop in **COMMON·WEALTH**	R^4	430A
28	**1653**		N	431
29	—	Reads **·OF·F** *(due to double strike?)*	R	
30	—	2nd N over inverted N in **ENGLAND**	S	431A
31	—	Re-entered 2nd N in **ENGLAND**	S	431A

HALFCROWNS

32	1653	No stop after **THE**		*S*	431A
33	—	Only stops on obverse by mintmark (with all stops on reverse)		*R*	431C?
34	—	Only stops on obverse by mintmark Only stops on reverse by value		*R*	431C?
35	—	**5 over 4** All stops on obverse Only stops on reverse by value		*R*	431D?
36	—	Only stop in reverse legend after date		*R*	431B
37	—	**3 over 1**		*R*	432
38	—	**3 over 2**		*R*	433
39	—	**65 over 56** (i.e. altered from 1563)		*R⁴*	433A
40	1654			*S*	434
41	—	Only stops by mintmark		*R*	434A?
42	—	Only stops on reverse by value		*R*	434A?
43	—	**4 over 3**		*R*	435
44	—	Error; **E over I** in **COMMONWEALTH**		*R²*	?
45	—	Error; first **O** struck over **M** in **COMMONWEALTH**		*R³*	435A
46	—	Reads **COMMONWEALH** (note missing **T**)		*R⁴*	435B
47	—	Error; first **N** of **ENGLAND** over **G**		*R³*	?
48	1655		*(4 known. 2 in B.M.)*	*R⁵*	436
49	1656			*S*	437
50	—	Proof-like appearance		*R⁶*	437B
51	—	Only stops on obverse by mintmark		*R⁴*	437F
52	—	No stop after **THE**		*R⁴*	437E
53	—	Extra stop in **TH·E·**		*R⁴*	437A
54	—	**6 over 4**		*R*	437B?
55	—	**6 over 5**		*R⁴*	438
56	—	**6 over 5** and extra stop in **TH·E·**		*R⁴*	438A
57	1657		*(2 known)*	*R⁷*	438B?

B.		*mm.* **ANCHOR**		Spink 3216	
58	1658			*R⁵*	439
59	—	**8 over 7**		*R⁴*	440
60	1659		*(2 known)*	*R⁷*	441
61	1660			*R⁴*	442

HALFCROWNS

PATTERNS

Simon
C & D

Flaw?

62	C	By **Simon and (Blondeau)**[2], **1651**	R^3	443
	1651	Obverse similar to the current halfcrown, but much neater workmanship, and struck in a mill *Rev.* Value with central stop only *(13 harp strings)* *Edge,* **IN · THE · THIRD · YEARE · OF · FREEDOME · BY · GODS · BLESSING · RESTORED · 1651**		

63	D	Similar, but with different edge reading	R^2	444
	1651	*Edge,* **TRVTH : AND : PEACE : 1651** (olive branch) **: PETRVS : BLONDÆVS : INVENTOR : FECIT ·** (palm branch)		
64	—	Similar. *In copper,* on thin flan, *edge,* plain *(unique?)*	R^7	444A

Simon
E

65	E	By **Simon, 1651**	R^7	444B
	1651	Similar in design to the current halfcrown, but with a hair-line within a beaded border both sides, and leaves on inside of the palm branch; not machine made [3]		

HALFCROWNS

Ramage
F

66	F	By **Ramage, 1651**	R^5	445
	1651	*Obv.* Cross of St George on a smaller shield within twin laurel branches, with berries		
		Leg. ★ ˙ **THE ▪ COMMON ▪ WEALTH ▪ OF ▪ ENGLAND** Star at the top with lozenge stops in both legends		
		Rev. Small conjoined shields with cross of St George left and Irish harp right, in front of a guardian Angel. Inner beaded circles both sides		
		Leg. ★ **GAVRDED ▪ WITH ▪ ANGELES ▪ 1651**		
		Edge, **TRVTH** ★ **AND** ★ **PEACE** ★ **1651**		
		between two beaded lines *(9 examples*) wt. 17.312g*		
67	—	Similar. *Edge,* plain *(8 examples*) Slaney 364, wt. 15.23g*	R^7	445B³

*Numbers listed by Bergne (Numismatic Chronicle vol. XVII, 1855) - Slaney 364

Ramage
G

68	G	By **Ramage (?), 1651**	R^7	445D
	1651	*Obv.* Similar to current coin, but of finer style Shields are more square-shape and smaller		
		Rev. No mark of value. Plain edge		
		Leg. **GOD · VVITH · VS ·** (note **V V** for **W**)		

COMMONWEALTH, 1649-60
HALFCROWNS

Notes

1   This, in the British Museum, may be just an exceptionally well struck ordinary coin. Also in the B.M. is a halfcrown of this date with a milled edge; it is not as well struck as might be expected of a proof, so may be an experimental piece or have had the milling added unofficially

Old ESC 434a, with double TT error viz. 1654 COMMONWEALTTH, is almost certainly due to double-striking, and removed from listing.

2   In order to clear up a misconception; *"Blondeau did not make dies, but hardware; Simon made dies"* (Marvin Lessen)

3   For old ESC 445A & 445C see under Shillings

Variations in size, spacing and alignment of dates and legends are ignored unless significant. Specimens in high grades are much rarer than indicted (This applies to all denominations)

Because of the hammered coinage's hand-made nature it is prone to much variety between dies and lacks the uniformity of the milled coinage. (Steve Hill)

SHILLINGS

Standard design as crown with value shown on *rev.* as **• XII •** or **XII**

Mm. Sun

All stops
Normal Ns

All stops &
Ns over inverted Ns

Only stops by *mm.*
Ns over inverted N

No stop after THE

No stops
N over inverted N in
COMONWEALTH

Only stops by *mm.*
Normal Ns

All stops, extra stop in
COMMON·WEALTH

No stops
All Ns over inverted Ns

COMMMONWEALTH
Double-striking error

SHILLINGS

No stop after THE

No stop after OF

F over D

Extra stop in
COMMON·WEALTH
But not after N
nor after OF

O over M, 2nd M over O

No stop after ENGLAND

No stops by *mm.*

Stop in O·F

Single M

ENGLND (minus A)

COMMON•WEALTH

COMMONWEATH
(minus L)

COMMONWEALH
(minus T)

E over E

Re-entered T

D over P?

No stop after WEALTH

2nd N inverted

No stop after OF

SHILLINGS

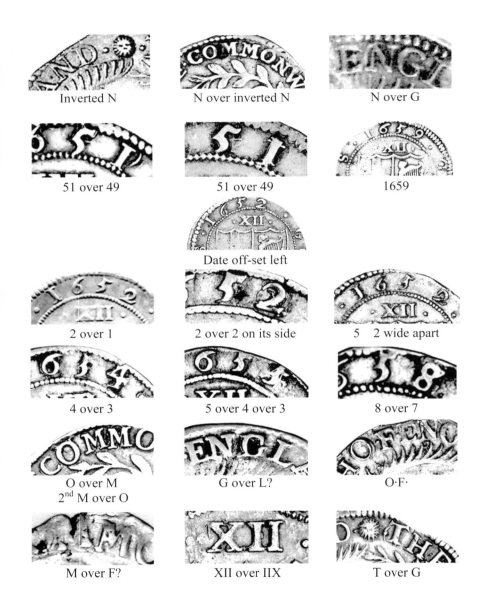

Inverted N   N over inverted N   N over G

51 over 49   51 over 49   1659

Date off-set left

2 over 1   2 over 2 on its side   5   2 wide apart

4 over 3   5 over 4 over 3   8 over 7

O over M
2nd M over O   G over L?   O·F·

M over F?   XII over IIX   T over G

COMMOMWEALTH, 1649-60
SHILLINGS

Mm. **Anchor**

| All stops | No stops by *mm*. | No stops |

No stop after THE   No stop after THE and ENGLAND   Stop in COMMMON·WEALTH but not before or after OF

All stops   No stops by value   No stops

Only stops by value   No stop after date   V over O

COMMOMWEALTH, 1649-60
SHILLINGS

A.   *mm.* **SUN**   Spink 3217

ESC	Date	Varieties, remarks, etc	R	(Old ESC)
69	**1649**		R	982
70	—	F over **D** in **OF**	R^3	982B
71	—	No stop after **OF**	R	982A
72	—	No stop after **ENGLAND**	R	982A
73	—	2nd **N** inverted in **ENGLAND**	R	
74	—	1st **N** over **G** in **ENGLAND**	R	982C?
75	—	All **Ns** over inverted **Ns**	R	
76	—	No stops after **THE** and by value	R	982D?
77	—	No stops after **OF** or **ENGLAND**	R	982B
78	—	Inverted **N** in **COMMONWEALTH**	R^2	
79	**1651**		N	983
80	—	Inverted **N** in **COMMONWEALTH**	R^2	
81	—	**N** over inverted **N** in **COMMONWEALTH**	R^2	
82	—	1st **N** over inverted **N** in **ENGLAND**	R^2	
83	—	2nd **N** over inverted **N** in **ENGLAND**	R^2	
84	—	No stops on obverse	R^2	
85	—	No stops on obverse. All **Ns** over inverted **Ns**	R^2	
86	—	No stops on obverse. **N** over inverted **N** in **COMMONWEALTH**	R^2	
87	—	**51** over **49** All **Ns** over inverted **Ns**	R^2	983A
88	—	**51** over **49** and only stops on obverse at mintmark	R^2	983A
89	—	**51** over **49** and no stops on obverse	S	983B
90	—	No stop after **THE**	R	984
91	—	*Proof.* No stop after **THE**	R^5	
92	—	Only stops on obverse at mintmark	R^2	984A
93	—	Only stops on obverse at mintmark All **Ns** over inverted **Ns**	R^2	984A
94	—	No stop after **OF** over **D** and **ENGLAND**	R^2	
95	—	No stop after **ENGLAND**	R	984B
96	—	No stops after **ENGLAND** and **COMMONWEALTH**	R	984B
97	—	Error, one **M** in **COMONWEALTH**	R^3	984C
98	—	Struck from shilling obverse die and a halfcrown reverse die [1]	R^7	984D
99	—	No stops at mintmark **N** over inverted **N** in **COMMONWEALTH**	R^2	984E

16

SHILLINGS

100	**1651**	Extra stop in **COMMON·WEALTH** No stop before or after **OF** and **F** in **OF** over **D**	R^2	984F
101	—	Mark of value over inverted value **XII** over **IIX**	R^4	?
102	—	Re-entered **T** in **WITH**	R	?
103	**1652**		N	985
104	—	Date off-set left	R	
105	—	Extra stop in **COMMON·WEALTH**	R^2	
106	—	No stops on obverse **N** over inverted **N** in **COMMONWEALTH**	R	986D
107	—	No stop after date	R	986A
108	—	No stop after **THE** and **N** over inverted **N** in **COMMONWEALTH**	N	986
109	—	No stop after **ENGLAND**	R	986B
110	—	No stop after **ENGLAND** and Extra stop in **COMMON·WEALTH**	R^3	986G
111	—	Extra stop in **COMMON·WEALTH** but No stops by mintmark	R^2	986H
112	—	**2** over **1** and no stop after **THE**	R	985A
113	—	**2** over **1** and no stop after **ENGLAND**	R	985A
114	—	Extra stop in **COMMON·WEALTH** **2** over **2** No stops on reverse including by value	R^2	985B
115	—	**2** over **1** and extra stop in **COMMON·WEALTH**	R^3	986C
116	—	**2** over **2** on its side, and no stop after **THE**	R^3	985C
117	—	**2** over **2** on its side, and no stop after **THE** and an extra stop in **COMMON·WEALTH**	R	986H
118	—	**2** over **1**? Error **V** over **O** in **VS**	R^2	986E
119	—	Large **2** and **N** over inverted **N** in **COMMONWEALTH**	R^2	
120	—	**5 2** in date wide apart	R^2	
121	—	No stops at mintmark	R^2	986F
122	—	No stops at mintmark and Extra stop in **COMMON·WEALTH**	R	986G
123	—	Colon (?) in **COMMON:WEALTH**	R^3	986I
124	**1653**		N	987
125	—	All **N**s over inverted **N**s	R	988C
126	—	Reads **COMMONWEALH** in error (minus T) [2]	R^3	988C
127	—	**D** over **P**? in **ENGLAND**	R^3	987A
128	—	**T** over **G** in **THE**	R^2	
129	—	No stop after **THE**	R	988A

17

SHILLINGS

130	**1653**	No stop after **THE** and Reads **COMMONWEALH** in error (minus T)^2	R^4	988B
131	—	No stop after **COMMONWEALTH**	R^2	
132	—	No stop after **ENGLAND**	R	988
133	—	No stops at mintmark	R	989B
134	—	**3 over 2**	R^2	989C
135	—	Only stops on obverse flanking mintmark	R	989E
136	—	Only stops on reverse after date	R	989D
137	1654		S	990
138	—	All stops and **N**s over inverted **N**s	R	
139	—	**4 over 3** All stops and **N**s over inverted **N**s	R	991
140	—	No stop after **ENGLAND**	R	990A
141	—	**4 over 3** and re-entered **E** in **COMMONWEALTH**	R	?
142	—	Reads **ENGLND** (minus letter A)	R^4	992
143	—	No stop after **OF**	R^2	992A
144	—	**N** over inverted **N** in **COMONWEALTH** Only stops on reverse flanking value		
145	1655		R^2	993
146	—	No stop after **OF**	R^2	
147	—	No stop after **ENGLAND**	R^2	993A
148	—	**5 over 4**	R^2	994
149	—	**5 over 4 over 3**	R^3	994A
150	1656		N	995
151	—	Reads **EGLAND** (minus letter N)	R	995D
152	—	No stop after **ENGLAND**	R	995A
153	—	No stops at mintmark	R	995B
154	—	Extra stop in **O·F·** but no stop after **COMMONWEALTH** and the 2nd **M** over **F**?	R^3	995C
155	—	No stops on obverse	R^2	995D
156	—	No stops on obverse or by value	R^2	995E
157	—	Only stops on reverse flanking value	R^2	995F
158	1657		R^5	996
159	—	No stop after **OF** and **7 over 6**? (B.M.)	R^5	996A
160	—	No stops on obverse	R^5	997

Errors; caused by striking have been delisted; e.g. Old ESC 989, 989a & 990b (illustrated as an example). Sub-varieties, due to the alignment of legends and size of lettering etc, are also generally ignored to avoid complication. The general quality of striking and size of flans in this period varies a great deal, especially with the smaller denominations.

The letter **N** is regularly found struck over an inverted **N** and recorded as much as possible.

SHILLINGS

	B.	mm. **Anchor**		Spink 3218
161	**1658**	With stops by mintmark	R^2	998
162	—	No stops by mintmark	R^3	
163	—	No stops on obverse	R^3	
164	—	No stop after **THE**	R^3	
165	—	No stop after **ENGLAND**	R^3	998A
166	—	No stop after **ENGLAND**. 1st **O** over **M** and 2nd **M** over **O** in **COMMONWEALTH**	R^3	
167	—	**8** over **7** no stop after **ENGLAND**	R^3	999A
168	—	**G** over **L** in **ENGLAND**	R^3	999
169	**1659**	*(2 known)*	R^7	1000
170	**1660**		R^3	1001
171	—	No stops by mintmark	R^3	
172	—	No stop after **ENGLAND**	R^3	

PATTERNS

Blondeau
C

	C.	By **Blondeau, 1651**		
173	**1651**	Similar to the ordinary shilling Much neater workmanship. Struck in a mill No stops by mintmark and mark of value Milled edge	R^3	1002
174	—	Similar, with plain edge (B.M. Collection)	R^6	1003

175	**1651**	By **Ramage, 1651** His halfcrown dies used on a shilling flan [3] Milled edge (See under halfcrown earlier)	R^6	445A
176	—	Similar with a plain edge *wt. 6.123g.*	R^6	445C

1	See 1651 halfcrown (*struck on a shilling flan*), note by P.A. Rayner
2	The error; COMMONWEALH (minus T), looks very convincing, so is retained
3	These were thought to be halfcrowns on thin flans, but now transferred to shillings; *Really a shilling struck from a halfcrown reverse die and a shilling obverse die. Only two examples are known, 1 in the British Museum. Some authorities consider these to be shillings but I am still inclined to regard them as halfcrowns struck on a thin flan* (P.A.R.)

19

COMMONWEALTH, 1649-60
SIXPENCES

Standard design as crown with value shown as • **VI** •

All stops	No stops by *mm.*	Only stops by *mm*

Colon after ENGLAND:	COM<u>MM</u>ONWEALTH (Not double struck)	Anchor

All stops	Only stop after date	1657

No stop after COMMONWEALTH	Letters NGLAN over GLAND	Inverted N and no stop after COMMONWEALTH

SIXPENCES

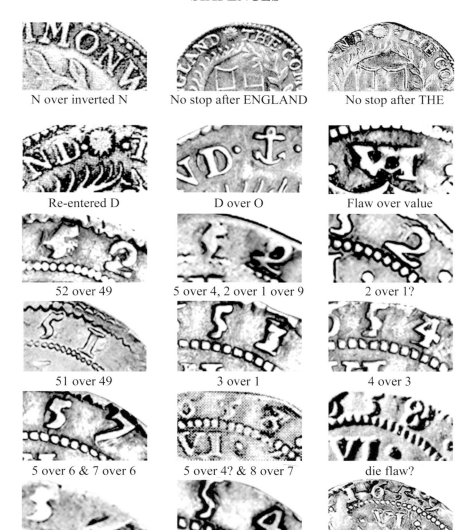

N over inverted N	No stop after ENGLAND	No stop after THE
Re-entered D	D over O	Flaw over value
52 over 49	5 over 4, 2 over 1 over 9	2 over 1?
51 over 49	3 over 1	4 over 3
5 over 6 & 7 over 6	5 over 4? & 8 over 7	die flaw?
7 over 6	Small 4 no serifs	1659

SIXPENCES

A.   *mm.* SUN   Spink 3219

ESC	Date	Varieties, remarks, etc	R	(ESC)
177	**1649**		*S*	1483
178	—	No stop after **ENGLAND**	*S*	1483A
179	**1651**		*N*	1484
180	—	N over inverted N in **COMMONWEALTH**	*R*	
181	—	No stops at *mm.*	*R*	1484A
182	—	No stops after **ENGLAND**	*R*	1484B
183	—	**51** over **49** No stops after **ENGLAND**[1]	*R*	1485
184	—	**51** over **49** and no stops at mintmark	*R*	1485A
185	—	**51** over **49** No stop after **COMMONWEALTH**[2]	*R*	1485B
186	**1652**		*N*	1486
187	—	Inverted N in **COMMONWEALTH**	*N*	1486C
188	—	Inverted N and No stop after **COMMONWEALTH**		1486C
189	—	Re-entered **D** in **ENGLAND**	*R*	1486A
190	—	No stops by mintmark	*R*	1486A
191	—	Only stop in reverse legend after date[2]	*R*	1486B
192	—	**52** over **49**?	*R*	1487
193	—	Large **2** over **1**?	*R*	1487A
194	—	**52** over **49** extra **M** in **COMMMONWEALH**[2]	*R*[5]	1487B
195	—	**52** over **1** over **49** and an extra **M** in **COMMMONWEALH**[2]	*R*[5]	1487D
196	—	Mark of value punched over lower placed **I**	*S*	1487C
197	**1653**		*S*	1488
198	—	No stop after **THE**	*R*	1488A
199	—	**3** over **I**	*R*	1488C
200	**1654**		*R*	1489
201	—	**4** over **3**	*R*[2]	1490
202	—	Small **4** without serifs	*R*[2]	1490
203	**1655**		*R*[4]	1491
204	**1656**		*S*	1492
205	—	Only stops on obverse are at mintmark	*R*	1492A
206	—	No stop after **ENGLAND**	*R*	
207	**1657**		*R*[5]	1493
208	—	**5** over **6** & **7** over **6** and letters **NGLAN** over **GLAND**	*R*[5]	1493A

COMMONWEALTH, 1649-60
SIXPENCES

B.		*mm.* **ANCHOR**	Spink 3220	
209	**1658**		R^3	1494
210	—	8 over 7	R^3	1495
211	—	D over O in ENGLAND	R^4	1495A
212	—	No stop after COMMONWEALTH	R^3	?
213	**1659**		R^6	1496
214	—	No stop after COMMONWEALTH	R^6	1496A
215	**1660**		R^3	1497
216	—	No stop after THE	R^4	1497A

PATTERNS

Blondeau
C

C.		By **Blondeau, 1651**		
217	**1651**	As the ordinary sixpence, but of much neater workmanship and struck in a press. No stops by value and mintmark. *Edge,* milled	R^2	1498
218	—	Similar. Thinner flan, plain edge *(Not traced)*	R^6	1498A

23

SIXPENCES

Ramage
D

D.   By **Ramage, 1651**

219	**1651**	Dated **1651** on the edge only As the ordinary sixpence, but of much neater workmanship and struck in a press	R^5	1499
	Leg.	★ **TRVTH** ★ **AND** ★ **PEACE** (both *obv. & rev)*		
	Edge	★ **TRVTH** ★ **AND** ★ **PEACE** ★ **1651** between two rows of beading		
220	—	*In gold* *wt. 13·94g*	R^6	1500
221	—	*In copper. Edge,* plain.	R^6	1501
222	—	*Edge,* ★★★★★★ between two rows of beading[3]	R^7	1502
223	—	*In copper, plated*	R^7	1503

Notes
The general standard of striking is poor with a large number of sub-varieties due to their hand-made nature. Specimens in high grades are very much rarer than indicated

1   This obverse die occurs paired with reverse dies dated 52 over 49, and what appear to be 52 over 51 over 49

2   Two examples of 3Ms spelling error recorded. Each is from a different reverse die, one clearly reading 1652/1/49, the other 1652/49 but it's unclear if also over a 1. The obverse die was also used for a half unite in gold (ex R.C. Lockett Collection)

3   This is probably not in silver, but silver-plated copper, i.e. 1502 and 1503 are the same coin. Both are in the B.M. and only a specific gravity test could determine their metal content if permitted

TWOPENCE, PENNY & HALF-PENNY
No legend, date or mintmark
HALFGROAT (TWOPENCE)
Standard design showing value · **II** · above conjoined shields

(x1.5)   Spink 3221

ESC	Varieties, remarks, etc	R	(Old ESC)
224	Caveat; crude dies are contemporary forgeries	C	2160
225	Shields transposed	R^3	2160A
226	Mark of value reads **H** due to die flaw	R	
227	Mark of value reads **III** due to double striking	R	

PENNY
As Halfgroat but showing value · **I** · above conjoined shields

(x1.5)   Spink 3222

228	Caveat; crude dies are contemporary forgeries	C	2263
229	No stops at mark of value	R^2	2263A

HALF-PENNY
Not showing any value above single reverse shield

(x2)   Spink 3223

230	Caveat; crude dies are contemporary forgeries	C	2363

Note: After 1672 the half-penny was only struck in copper!

OLIVER CROMWELL, 1656-58
INTRODUCTION

A set of coins with the Protector's portrait was issued by his order and with the consent of the Council. These pieces are of the finest workmanship, the dies having been executed by that greatest of engravers, Thomas Simon, and the striking done by means of Blondeau's machine. Most authorities consider that these pieces were never put into circulation and must therefore, be classed as patterns. In the writer's view, however, the rare halfcrowns of 1656 appear to have circulated as they nearly alwas turn up in worn condition. The coins of 1658 were struck in large quantities, except for the sixpence, and were probably intended for circulation: the majority were not issued owing to Cromwell's death in September of that year.

Some of Simon's puncheons for the Cromwell coinage were sold in the Low Countries and an imitation crown was made there, known as the *'Dutch crown'*. Other Durch dies were prepared and some of these found their way back to the Mint, and in 1738 it was decided to strike a set of Cromwell's coins. Shillings and sixpences were struck from Dutch dies; and John Tanner, the Engraver at the Mint, made a crown from new dies.[1] Although not originals, these pieces always realise a good price as they are all rare. (P.A. Rayner, 1949)

---

1   D.F. Allen. *The Coinage of Cromwell and its imitations.* B.N.J. xxiv, p. 191

OLIVER CROMWELL 1656-58
CROWNS

Leaf to A

Thomas'

8 over 7

Inverted N
(Dutch)

8

Tanner

Standard obverse and reverse by Thomas Simon

Obv.   Draped and laureate bust, left

Leg.   **OLIVAR · D · G · R · P · ANG · SCO · HIB &c PRO**
Oliver by the Grace of God Protector of the Republic of England Scotland and Ireland

OLIVER CROMWELL 1656-58
CROWNS

Rev. Large English crown above the quartered arms, left to right: - England, Scotland, Ireland and England. Superimposed in the centre is Cromwell's rampant lion.
The date above is divided by the cross on top of the crown

Leg. **PAX · QVÆRITVR · BELLO** *Peace is sought through war*

Edge **HAS · NISI · PERITVRVS · MIHI · ADIMAT · NEMO ★**
Let no-one remove these (letters) from me under penalty of death

Spink 3226

ESC	Date	Varieties, remarks, etc	R	L&S	(Old ESC)
240	**1658**	By **Thomas Simon**	*S*	1	10
		8 over **7** *(Only known with date altered from 1657¹)* Top leaf of laurel to left of right foot of **A** Lettered edge as above			
241	—	*In gold* *(2 known; wts. 716grs-46.39g & 758 grs-49.12g)*	*R⁷*	1A	10A
242	—	*In pewter* *(Contemporary cast with a very pronounced flaw across the neck)*	*R⁷*	1B	10B

Spink 3226A

243	**1658**	*'Dutch copy'* (Artist unknown) Similar, but top leaf of laurel to first limb of inverted letter **N**. Not an over-date Lettered edge as above *wt.32.58 g*	*R³*	2	11
244	—	*Silver gilt* *wt. 30.28 g*	*R⁶*	2A	11A
245	—	*In pewter. Edge rough, may have been lettered but now plain.* *(In British Museum Collection)*	*R⁷*	2D	

Spink 3226B

246	**1658**	**J.S. Tanner's copy** (struck in 1738) Similar, but slightly different features, top leaf of laurel between **A** and **N**, the **N** not inverted and leaf not so pointed; The beading of the border is wider; *wt. 31.47 g* Flaw in all **P**s Stops after **HIB·** and **PRO·** Lettered edge as above	*R³*	3	13
247	**1658**	Similar. *Edge*, plain *wt. 28.31 g*	*R⁵*	3A	14

OLIVER CROMWELL 1656-58
CROWNS

ESC	Date	Varieties, remarks, etc	R	L&S	(Old ESC)
248	**1658**	**Simon / Tanner** Simon's obverse muled with Tanner's reverse *Edge,* plain; on a thick flan *wt. 638 grains- 41.34g*	R^7	3B	14A

| 249 | **1658** | **Tanner / Simon**
Similar, but muling reversed;
Tanner's obverse muled with Simon's reverse | R^7 | 4 | 14B |

PATTERNS
(Imitation)

250	**1843**	Imitation Pattern Crown by **L.C. Wyon**	R^7	5	14C
	Obv	Similar to Simon's bust of Cromwell, but with different spacing and style of lettering			
	Leg	**OLIVAR·D·GR·P·ANG·SCO·HIB&c PRO**			
	Rev	Bust of Louis XVIII left, with long hair tied with a ribbon			
	Leg	**W WYON R . A .** **CUDI JUSSIT** *"W. Wyon R.A. ordered this to be struck"* **LEONARD.C.WYON 1843** below truncation			
	Edge	Plain. *In pewter*, on a 38 mm flan *wt. 32.46gm*			

Notes

1	At a very early stage a flaw started in the obverse die near the **O** in **OLIVAR** and slowly stretched right across the bust. They can be obtained with all the stages of the flaw showing. Some of the later strikings from this die show an attempt was made to repair the flaw. The frosting is achieved by tiny punch marks. This process is called *Mezotinto*
2	Leonard Wyon was only 16 years of age upon executing this piece
3	Tin, pewter or white metal are descriptions for the same metal
	Linecar & Stone list some other variations on pages 3-6 which are dubious and ignored

OLIVER CROMWELL, 1656-58
HALFCROWNS

By **Thomas Simon**

HI

Spurious fabrication 1657

HIB

Obv.	As crown, with two readings of legend
Leg.	**OLIVAR · D · G · RP · ANG · SCO · HIB (HI) &c PRO**
Rev.	As crown
Leg.	**PAX · QVÆRITVR · BELLO**
Edge	**HAS · NISI · PERITVRVS · MIHI · ADIMAT · NEMO +**

Spink 3227

ESC	Date	Varieties, remarks, etc	R	(Old ESC)
251	**1656**	Legend reads **HI &c PRO**	R^3	446

Spink 3227A

252	**1658**	Legend reads **HIB &c PRO**	*S*	447
253	—	*Proof in gold* *(6 known)*	R^5	447A
		Caveat		
xxx	**1657**	*Fabrication. Genuine 1658 coin altered to 1657*		

OLIVER CROMWELL, 1656-58
SHILLINGS

HIB &c PRO

Small swan countermark (unofficial)

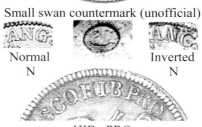

Normal N   Inverted N

HIB · PRO

Obv.	As crown, with two readings of legend
Leg.	**OLIVAR · D · G · RP · ANG · SCO · HIB & PRO**
Rev.	As crown
Leg.	**PAX · QVÆRITVR · BELLO**

Spink 3228

ESC	Date	Varieties, remarks, etc	R	(Old ESC)
254	**1658**	By **Thomas Simon**. Always a flaw below the **P** in front of laurel wreath. Reads **HIB &c PRO**. *Edge,* plain	S	1005
255	—	*In gold. Edge,* milled	R^7	1005A

Spink 3228A

256	**1658**	*Dutch copy* Similar but slightly different features and *Leg.* reads **HIB · PRO** (&c omitted) No flaw Inverted **N** in ANG. *Edge,* plain *Weights vary by ± 1g*	R^6	1006
257	—	On a thick flan. **8** of date over a smaller **8**	R^6	1006A
258	—	*Edge,* grained	R^6	1006B
259	—	*In copper*	R^6	1007
Unofficial fabrication (Possibly a Trader's mark)				
xxx	**1658**	*Genuine coin countermarked with a swan below bust*		

31

OLIVER CROMWELL, 1656-58
SIXPENCES

Thomas Simon

HIB &c PRO

Obv.		As the crown
Leg.	**1**	**OLIVAR · D · G · RP · ANG · SCO · HIB &c PRO**
Rev.		As crown
Leg.		**PAX · QVÆRITVR · BELLO**
Edge		Plain or milled

(Official issue by Simon)   Spink 3229

ESC	Date	Varieties, remarks, etc	R	(Old ESC)
260	**1658**	Laurel leaf points to left limb of **A** 4 berries in wreath. **HIB &c PRO** *Edge,* milled *(4 known)*	R^6	1504
261	—	Similar. *Edge,* plain. *In pewter*	R^7	1504A

Dutch copy by Tanner
As before, but legend reads **HIB · PRO**

HIB PRO

Liberty cap
(Cast)

OLIVER CROMWELL, 1656-58
SIXPENCES

		(Dutch copy by Tanner)		Spink 3229A
262	**1658**	Similar, but reads **HIB · PRO** (minus &c) Laurel leaf points to **P**, no berries in wreath *Edge*, milled[1] *Heaviest noted 6.24g (Norweb 48/432)*	R^5	1505
263	—	*Edge*, plain	R^4	1506
264	—	*In bronze* *(Not traced)*	R^6	1506A

Unofficial fabrication

xxx	**1658**	*Cast copy with the liberty cap below bust*[2]

Notes

1   These are on flans varying greatly in weight and thickness. The heavier pieces were at one time regarded as ninepences. Only four genuine Cromwell sixpences are believed to exist, although rather more of the copies were executed in the Low Countries by Tanner c. 1738.

2   *"The portrait of Cromwell with the liberty cap beneath may relate to the Netherlands, where the cap was an emblem of political freedom" "This piece is controversial and is possibly a later cast"* (Wilson & Rasmussen, p. 76) (St James's Auction 2, lot 157)

INTRODUCTION
CHARLES II
1660-85

At the beginning of this reign, Thomas Simon, who had been Chief Engraver at the Mint under the Commonwealth, applied for reinstatement, and although the King had already promised the position to Thomas Rawlins, he did in fact on May 31st 1661, grant *'to Thomas Simon ...... the office of one of the engravers of the King's Arms shields and stamp'.* It would appear that Simon shared the position with Rawlins, but most of the work devolved upon the former, although the two men may have co-operated to some extent in the production of dies for the three hammered coinages of 1660 to 1661 (The indenture, dated 20th July 1660, authorises silver crowns, but none are known). These hammered coinages consist of three main issues, the first having no mark of value or inner circles. The second has the mark of value added behind the King's head, as instructed by a warrant of 28th November 1661. The third issue, much the largest or at any rate the most common today, has an inner circle on both sides as well as the mark of value. There is practically no doubt that Simon was soley responsible for the dies of the undated Maundy and similar pieces, as in April 1665 he claims £35 in payment for *'altering the stamps of the fourpenny, threepenny, tuppeny and penny by way of the mill'.* As this claim is of later date than that on which Simon was displaced by John Roettier, it shows clearly that he worked on dies for minor coins almost until his death during the Great Plague of 1665. John and Joseph Roettier, two brothers whose family had rendered services to Charles during his exile, were appointed engravers in 1661 and in January of the following year were directed to prepare all the neccessary dies for the new 'milled' coinage. Shortly afterwards they were instructed *'to engrave a trial crown in competition with Simon, and all three men to cease all other work until the task be completed'.* The results were the famous 'petition crown' by Simon, and the pattern (E.S.C. 68-71) by the Roettiers: the sequel is of course well known; John Roettier was appointed Chief Engraver in May 1662 and was assisted by his brother Joseph in the production of dies for milled coinage. Joseph left the Mint and went to France in 1672. In April 1662 Peter Blondeau was recalled from France, appointed Engineer, a new post and was instructed *'to furnish all mills, rollers, presses and other instruments, to cut, flatten, make round and size the pieces; the engine to make the edges of money with letters and grainings, the great presses for coining of moneys and all other tools and engines for the new way of coining'.*

George Bower was appointed an Engraver in Ordinary in 1664, but worked mainly on the production of medals. He is not known to have engraved any coin dies for Charles II or James II.

INTRODUCTION
CHARLES II
1660-85

The first 'milled' halfcrowns and shillings were issued in 1663, the dated twopence in 1668, the dated fourpence, threepence and penny in 1670, and the sixpence in 1674. Thus four major and four minor denominations were struck in silver, the former having on their reverse four shields of arms in the form of a cross, and the small coins their value represented by one to four Cs. The crown and halfcrown have an inscribed edge; on this are the words **DECVS ET TVTAMEN** which translated means *'An ornament and a safeguard'*, followed by the monarch's regnal year, which in this reign was reckoned from the death of Charles I. This practice was continued on the crown with a few breaks until 1935, and on halfcrowns until the end of the reign of George II. The regnal year does not correspond to the calendar year, and for this reason we usually find coins of the same date with two different regnal years on the edge. Another custom previously only adopted for Welsh silver was extended in this reign, that is, the custom of marking some of the coins with a symbol to denote the source of metal from which they were struck:

Elephant, or *Elephant and Castle,* the Africa ('Guinea') Co.,
the symbol used on its badge
Plumes, silver from mines in Wales.
Rose, silver from mines in the West of England   (P.A. Rayner, 1949)

Charles II began the tradition whereby the portrait of each monarch faced in the opposite direction to his or her predecessor; Cromwell left - Charles II right – James II left etc. (The only exception; Edward VIII faces left and not right)

35

CHARLES II, 1660-85
FIRST HAMMERED ISSUES

Variants of the obverse legend found in this series

	CAROLVS	II	D	G	MAG	BRIT	FRAN	ET	HIB	REX
1	CAROLVS	II	D	G	MAG	BRIT	FRAN	ET	HIB	REX
2	—	—	—	—	—	—	FRA	—	—	—
3	—	—	—	—	—	—	FR	—	—	—
4	—	—	—	—	—	—	—	—	H	—
5	—	—	—	—	—	BRI	FRA	—	HIB	—
5E	CAROLV	—	—	—	—	—	—	—	HIB	—
6	CAROLVS	—	—	—	—	—	FR	—	—	—
6E	CARLVS	—	—	—	—	—	—	—	—	—
7	CAROLVS	—	—	—	—	—	—	—	HI	—
8	—	—	—	—	—	BR	—	—	HIB	—
9	—	—	—	—	—	—	—	—	HI	—
10	—	—	—	—	—	B	FR	ET	H	—
11	—	—	—	—	—	B	F	ET	HIB	—
12	—	—	—	—	MA	BR	—	—	HI	—
13	—	—	—	—	M	—	FR	ET	HIB	—
14[1]	—	—	—	—	M	—	—	ET	HI	—
16	—	—	—	—	—	—	F	ET	H	—
17	—	—	—	—	—	B	—	ET	H	—
18	—	—	—	—	—	B	—	ET	HIB	—
19[2]	CAPOLVS	—	—	M	BP	F	FT	H	PFX	
20	CPOLVS	—	—	M	BP	F	—	HI	PFX	(sic No ET)
21	CROLVS	—	—	MA	B	F	ET	HI	REX	

Charles II by the Grace of God King of Great Britain, France & Ireland

Standard reverse legend

CHRISTO AVSPICE REGNO
I reign under the auspice of Christ

Notes

1   Some specimens are found with legend reading M PR FR ET HI REX, since this is almost certainly the result of filled dies they are delisted

2   This peculiar legend is most likely due to a filled die. Large numbers of dies were used in this series, as proven by the variations in the alignment of legends etc. Unfortunately these differences are not significant enough to warrant inclusion as major varieties in this work.

FIRST HAMMERED ISSUES

Type A

No mark of value or inner circles

Undated, *mm.* Crown

HALFCROWN

| Reverse 1 | BRIT FRAN | Reverse 1a |

Obv.		Crowned and draped bust, left. King with long hair falling over his shoulders. Mintmark Crown (on obverse only)
Leg.	1	**CAROLVS•II•D•G•MAG•BRIT•FRAN•ET•HIB•REX**
Rev.		Square-topped shield over a long forked cross
Leg.		**CHRISTO • AVSPICE • REGNO**
	1	No stop above shield and no *edge* legend
	1a	With a stop above shield

Spink 3307

ESC	*Leg.*	Varieties, remarks, etc	*R*	(Old ESC)
270	1	Reverse 1	*R³*	448
271	1	Reverse 1a	*R³*	448A

FIRST HAMMERED ISSUES

SHILLING

Reverse 1   BRIT FR   Reverse 1a

			Spink 3308	
272	3	Reverse 1	R	1010
273	3	Reverse 1a	R	1009

SIXPENCE

BRIT FRAN

			Spink 3309	
274	1	Reverse 1a	R	1507

HALFGROAT
(TWOPENCE)

BRIT HIB   BRIT H   MAG B H

38

FIRST HAMMERED ISSUES

Leg. 3   **CAROLVS . II . D.G. MAG . BRIT . FR . ET . HIB . REX**
      4   **CAROLVS II D G MAG BRIT FR ET H REX**
    10   **CAROLVS . II . D:G: MAG : B : FR : ET . H . REX**

Spink 3310

ESC	*Leg*	Varieties, comments etc.		*Robinson*	*R*	(Old ESC)
275	3	With stops both sides	*5 harp strings*	*p. 143,2(i)*	*S*	2161
276	4	No stops obverse *5 harp strings* Minute stops flanking mintmark		*p. 143,2(ii)*	*S*	2162
277	4	No stops obverse, reads **RFX** (filled die?) Reverse: no stop after **REGNO** *5 strings*		*p. 143,2(iii)*	*S*	2162A
278	10	Reverse with stops	*5 harp strings*	*p. 143,2(iv)*	*S*	2163

PENNY
Type A^1
With crown *mintmark*

MAG BRIT HIB   (x1.5)

Leg. 3   **CAROLVS . II . D.G. MAG . BRIT . FR . ET . HIB . REX**
      4   **CAROLVS II D G MAG BRIT FR ET H REX**
    21   **CROLVS . II . D.G. MA . B . F . ET . HI . REX**
    C.

Spink 3311

ESC	*Leg*	Varieties, comments etc.	*Robinson*	*R*	(Old ESC)
279	3	With stops both sides	*p. 143,1 (i)*	R^2	2264
280	4	No stops both sides. Reads **ET H REX**	*p. 143,1 (ii)*	R^2	2264A
281	21	Reads **CROLVS** (minus A)	*p. 143,1 (iii)*	R^2	2264B

39

FIRST HAMMERED ISSUES

PENNY
Type A^2
No *mintmark*

M BR F HI   BR F ET H   CAPOLVS

Leg. 17   **CAROLVS II D G M BR F ET H REX**
20   **CAPOLVS II D G M BP F HI PEX** (minus **ET**)
21   **CROLVS . II . D.G. MA . B . F . ET . HI . REX** (minus **A & ET**)

Spink 3312

ESC	*Leg*	Varieties, comments etc.	*Robinson*	*R*	(Old ESC)
282	17	No stops on reverse	*p. 143,3 (ii)*	*R^3*	2265
283	20	Note: Ps for Rs. (minus ET)	*p. 143,3 (i)**	*R*	2266
		Stop above King's head *5 harp strings*			
284	21	(minus **A & ET**)			

*Robinson quotes this legend as reading CPOLVS (although not traced, numbered)

40

SECOND HAMMERED ISSUES

Type B
With mark of value
(No inner circles)

HALFCROWN - XXX

S over S

BRIT FRAN

Reverse 1a

BRIT FRA

Large XXX

BRI FRA

Mm.　　　　On *obv.* only, with or without stops left and right
Rev.　1a　With a stop above the shield

Spink 3313

ESC	*Leg.*	Varieties, remarks, etc	*R*	(Old ESC)
285	1	**BRIT FRAN**	R^4	449
286	2	**BRIT FRA**	R^5	450
287	5	**BRI FRA**　with small **xxx**	R^4	451
288	5	**BRI FRA**　with large **XXX**	R^4	451A
289	5	**BRI FRA**　S over S in **CHRISTO**	R^4	451B

SECOND HAMMERED ISSUES

SHILLING - XII

BRI HIB   Reverse 1a   BRI HI

BR HIB   BR HI

Spink 3314

290	6	**BRI FR ET HIB**	R^2	1011
291	7	**BRI FR ET HI**	R^5	1012
292	8	**BR FR ET HIB**	R^2	1013
293	9	**BR FR ET HI**	R^2	1014

SECOND HAMMERED ISSUES

SIXPENCE – VI

BRI HIB   Reverse 1a

				Spink 3315
294	6	**BRI FR ET HIB**	R^5	1508
295	7	**BRI FR ET HI**	R^5	1509

HALFGROAT - II
(TWOPENCE)

B FR ET H   Obverse B   Reverse 1a   (x1.5)

				Spink 3316
296	10	**MAG B FR ET H REX**	R^5	2164

43

THIRD HAMMERED ISSUES

Type C
With mark of value and inner circles

HALFCROWN – XXX

mm. between stops

| BR FR | V over R   A over R | Reverse 2 |

| CAROLV | BRIT FRA | BRI FRA |

Spink 3321

ESC	*Leg.*	Varieties, remarks, etc	*R*	(Old ESC)
297	2	**MAG BRIT FRA**	*S*	452
298	5	**MAG BRI FRA**	*S*	453
299	5E	**MAG BRI FRA** *Error,* **CAROLV**	*R*	454
300	6	**MAG BRI FR :**	*R*	455
301	8	**MAG BR FR :**	*N*	456
302	8	**MAG BR FR :** Obverse mintmark between stops	*N*	?
303	8	**MAG BR FR :** A over **R** in **CAROLVS**	*R³*	?
304	8	**MAG BR FR :** V over **A** in **CAROLVS**	*R³*	?
305	8	**MAG BR FR :** Bust to lower edge of coin	*R⁵*	456B
306	12	**MA BR FR HI?**	*R²*	456A

THIRD HAMMERED ISSUES

SHILLING - XII

BRIT FR	BRI FRA	CARLVS	2

		Rev. 2; with; *mm.* crown, usually a stop each side	Spink 3322	
307	2	**BRIT FRA ET HIB**	R^2	1015
308	3	**BRIT FR ET HIB** and no stops at mintmark	R^3	1016
		Large letters on reverse		
309	5	**BRI FRA ET HIB** Large **XII**	R^2	1019
310	6	**BRI FR ET HIB**		1018
311	6	**BRI FR ET HIB** Small **XII**		1019A
312	6E	**BRI FR ET HIB** *Error,* **CARLVS**	R^3	1019B
313	7	**BRI FR ET HI**	R	1021A
314	8	**BR FR ET HIB**	R	1020
315	9	**BR FR ET HI**	R	1021

SIXPENCE - VI

Reverse 2

3 - large crown

Reverse 3   Obverse 1   Reverse 2?   3- small crown

		BRI FRA ET HIB	Spink 3323	
316	5	Obverse (1) no stops by mintmark	S	1510
317	5	Obverse (1) no stops by mintmark	S	1510C
		Large mintmark on reverse		
318	5	Obverse (2) mintmark with a stop left	S	1510A
319	5	Obverse (3) mintmark between stops	S	1510B
320	5	On thicker flan (B.M.) *(Possibly a shilling blank)*	R^6	1511

THIRD HAMMERED ISSUES

Type A

SET OF FOUR COINS
GROAT, THREEPENCE, HALFGROAT & PENNY
(These were never issued in sets but collectors like to assemble them)

321		CAROLVS II D G M BR FR ET HI REX	*N*	2364

The following denominations are listed and numbered to highlight varieties

THIRD HAMMERED ISSUES

GROAT – IIII
(FOURPENCE)

BR FR ET HIB

Reverse 1

Spink 3324

ESC	Varieties, comments etc.	Robinson	R	(Old ESC)
322	**D. G. MAG. BR. FR. ET. HIB. REX.** All stops in reverse legend *(5 strings)*	*p. 144,12(i)*	R	1839
323	As before but no stop before **CHRISTO** and after **REGNO** *(5 strings)*	*p. 144,12(ii)*	R	
324	As before but no stop before **CAROLVS** and after **REX** *(5 strings)*	*p. 144,12(iii)*	R	

THREEPENCE – III

M BR FR HI

Reverse 3

Spink 3325

325	**D. G. M. BR. FR. ET. HI. REX.** *(4 strings)*	*p. 144,11*	R	1957

THIRD HAMMERED ISSUES

HALFGROAT – II
(TWOPENCE)

Obverse C   Reverse 3
BRI FRA   BR FR

Spink 3326

ESC	Varieties, comments etc.	Robinson	R	(Old ESC)
326	**D: G: MAG: BRI: FRA: ET. HIB. REX**	*p. 144,10(i)*		
327	As above, with stop before **·CAROLVS** and after **REX·**	*p. 144,10(ii)*		
328	**D. G. MAG: BRI: FRA: ET. HIB. REX** Reverse: **CHRISTO – AVSPICE □ REGNO;**	*p. 144,10(iii)*		
329	**D: G: MAG: BRI: FR: ET. HIB. REX** No stops on reverse	*p. 144,10(iv)*		
330	**D: G: MAG: BR: FR: ET. HIB. REX**	*p. 144,10(v)*		
331	King's name miss-spelt **CAROLLVS**	*p. 144,10(vi)*		

PENNY - I

Obverse E   Reverse 2
M B F ET HIB   (x1.5)

Spink 3327

ESC	Varieties	Robinson	R	(Old ESC)
332	**D G MAG: BR: FR: ET. HIB REX**	*p. 143,9(i)*	R^2	2267
333	**D. G. M. BR. FR. ET. HIB. REX**	*p. 143,9(ii)*		
334	**D: G: M B F ET HIB REX**	*p. 143,9(iii)*		
335	**D G M. B. F. ET. HIB REX**	*p. 143,9(iv)*		
336	**D. G: M:B: F: ET. HIB: REX**	*p. 144,9(v)*		
337	**MAG BR FR RT HIB**	*p. 144,9(vi)*		
338	**MAG B F ET HIB**	*p. 144,9(vii)*		

CROWNS

OBVERSES
Four of the
many different
positions of ties
by Alan Broad[1]

Both from top curl

Both from
between curls

Upper from top
curl, lower from
between curls

Both from lower curl

A, B & C – 1ˢᵗ bust – GRA•
Stop above - Rose below

D – 1ˢᵗ bust var. (larger)
II above - Rose below

E, G, H & I - 1ˢᵗ bust var.
(No rose) Stop after II •
Upper tie to R

J (E variety) GRATIA
No stop after II
Upper tie to O

Type F - see below - 𝒥ℛ & extra curl on neck

K – 2ⁿᵈ bust
Twisted ties

D¹ – Crooked ties

D – Twisted ties

L & N – 2ⁿᵈ bust variety
Crooked ties

CHARLES II, 1660-1685
CROWNS

OBVERSES

Type M – 2nd bust
Elephant below. Ties D¹

E – Elephant

F – Short ties
curve outwards

Type O – 3rd bust
Short ties

Type P – 4th bust
Longer ties

G – Longer ties
slant downwards

Elephant
& castle

Type Q – 4th bust
Elephant & castle below

Type F (as E, with)
𝓙𝓡 & extra curl on neck

Normal pellet frosting
Mezotinto

Striped frosting
With rose below

50

CROWNS

REVERSES

Reverse 1

Frosted Cs

Line below
crown

Reverse 2

No stops in legend

No line
below crown

RE·X

Garter star

T over R

R over B

B over R

T over G

ET over FR

Only stop before date

A over G in FRA

CHARLES II, 1660-1685
CROWNS

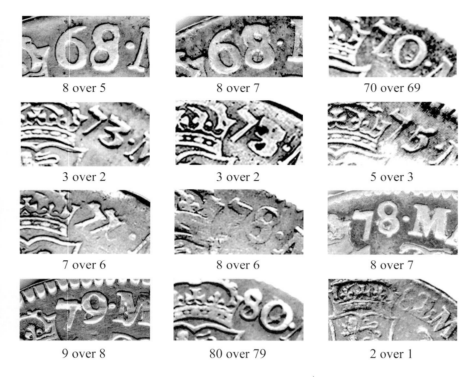

8 over 5	8 over 7	70 over 69
3 over 2	3 over 2	5 over 3
7 over 6	8 over 6	8 over 7
9 over 8	80 over 79	2 over 1

Type **A.**
(Old ESC - A)

First bust, right, **with a rose** ❀ below[1], stop above head, position of ties to wreath varies, bust divides legend after **CAROLVS**
Pellet frosting on the cloak, no regnal date on edge

Leg. **CAROLVS • II • DEI • GRA •**

(Old ESC - B) **B.**
Edge

As before, but edge dated in Arabic numerals
DECVS · ET · TVTAMEN ★✚★· 1662 · ★✚★·

C.

As before, but striped frosting on the cloak; vertical at the front and diagonal on the shoulder

D.

First bust variety; slightly larger, **rose below**, numeral **II** above King's head, upper tie from top curl, lower from between curls

Leg. **CAROLVS • II • DEI • GRA •**
Edge **DECVS · ET · TVTAMEN ★** (No regnal date)

52

CROWNS

Type _(Old ESC - C)	**E.**	First bust variety as 'D', but <u>no rose</u> below and bust divides new legend; **CAROLVS • II • DEI • GRATIA** (no stop) No regnal date on the edge, upper tie generally to **R**
	F.	As 'E', but frosted cloak and an extra curl on neck, initials **JR** (John **R**oettier) to the rear of lower curls, no regnal date
	G.	As 'E', but edge dated in Arabic numerals, with first reverse
	H.	As 'E' – no date on edge, but with second reverse
_(Old ESC - E)	**I.**	As 'G', but edge dated in Roman numerals, with second reverse
	J.	Similar to 'I', but no stop after **CAROLVS • II** cloak frosted, straighter ties, upper to **O** edge dated in Roman numerals
_(Old ESC - F)	**K.**	Second bust; smaller with larger drapery, the twin ties are twisted and the ends curve upwards, edge dated in Roman numerals
	L.	Second bust variety; similar to 'J', but different hair curls, the ties are only <u>crooked</u> and the ends curve outwards
_(Old ESC - G)	**M.**	Second bust variety with an Elephant below (Badge of the Africa Company, supplier of the bullion)
_(Old ESC - H)	**N.**	As 'K', but the regnal date in Roman words (not numerals)
Edge		**DECIMO NONO** etc
_(Old ESC - I)	**O.**	Third bust; much larger and broader than second (20 mm from tie to tip of nose), different hair curls, shorter ties curve outwards.
_(Old ESC - J)	**P.**	Fourth bust; older features, different hair style; three distinct long curls hang down over neck, twin crooked ties slant downwards
_(Old ESC - K)	**Q.**	Fourth bust with an Elephant and castle below
Rev.	**1.**	Crowned cruciform shields, top and bottom quartered (England and France), Star of the Garter in the centre and a pair of interlinked **C**s in the angles (**C**harles son of **C**harles)
Leg.		**16 ♛ 62•MAG• ♛ BR•FRA• ♛ ET•HIB• ♛ REX•**

CROWNS

Rev.   **2.**   Similar to reverse 1, but individual shields, clockwise; England, Scotland, France and Ireland. The number of harp strings varies, Given in brackets, and either with or without a stop after **HIB** Normal punctuation in reverse legend, unless stated;
         MAG• BR•FRA• ET•HIB• REX•

A/1.   First bust, **stop** above, **rose** below, *leg.* **GRA•**, no date on edge
       Rev. 1 - top and bottom shields quartered   Spink 3350

ESC	Date	Varieties, comments etc		R	(Old ESC)
339	1662	No stop after **HIB** [1]	*(10 strings)*	C^2	15
340	—	Edge lettering closely spaced		C^2	15A
		Note; with stop after **HIB•**	*(7,8,9,10 strings)*		
341	—	*Proof*		R^5	15B
342	—	Struck *en medaille* ↑↑	*(9 strings)*	S	
343	—	*Proof,* plain edge (RRSC4) *(7 strings)* (L&S 4)		R^5	16

RR = Roderick Richardson[7]; L&S = Linecar & Stone

B/1.   As before, but edge dated in Arabic numerals   Spink 3351

ESC	Date	Edge year	Varieties, comments etc	R	(Old ESC)
344	1662	1662	*(6,7,8,9,10 strings)*	S	17

C/1.   As before, but cloak with striped frosting   Spink 3351

345	1662	1662	*(7,10,12 strings)*	S	17

D/1.   First bust variety, **rose** below, but numeral **II** above King's head
       Rev. 1 – As before. No date on edge   Spink cf.3350

346	1662	*(Unique?) (9 strings)*	R^7	16A

E/1.   First bust variety, <u>no rose below</u>, bust divides new legend;
       CAROLVS • II •   **DEI • GRATIA** (no stop)
       Rev. 1 – As before. No date on edge   Spink 3353

347	1662	*(7,8,10,12 strings)*	S	19
348	—	Struck *en medaille* ↑↑ *(8 strings)*	R^5	19
349	—	Cloak wreath and tie frosted *(8 strings)*	S	20

F/1.   As before, but cloak frosted and an extra curl on neck shaped as initials *JR ('extra curl')* below curls.
       No regnal date on edge.   Spink 3353

350	1662	*(11 strings)*	R^5	20A

CHARLES II, 1660-1685
CROWNS

G/1. First bust variety, as type E, but edge dated in Arabic numerals
Rev. 1 – As before   Spink 3352

ESC	Date	Edge year	Varieties, comments etc		R	(Old ESC)
351	**1662**	**1662**		*(8 strings)*	R^2	18

H/2. As type G, but with second reverse and no regnal date on edge
Rev. 2 – Individual arms   Spink 3354?

352	**1663**			*(9 Strings)*	R^6	22A

I/2. As type G, but edge dated in Roman numerals   Spink 3354

353	**1663**	XV	(15)		*(8,9,10 strings)*	N	22
354	—	—	—	*Proof or pattern*		R^5	23
				Cloak & **C**s frosted *(10,11 strings)*			
355	—	—	—	*Proof* ^(RRSD5) *(11 strings)* (L&S 5)		R^6	24
356	—	—	—	*Proof in gold* ^(RRGD5) *(7 strings)* (L&S 5A)		R^6	25
357	—	—	—	Cloak only frosted		R^3	26
				No stop after **FRA** *(7 strings)*			
358	—	—	—	Initials ***JR** (extra curl)* below curls		R	27
				(7,9 strings)			
359	—	—	—	Initials ***JR** (extra curl)* below curls		R^3	27A
				No stops on reverse *(9 strings)*			

J/2. Similar to type I, but no stop after **CAROLVS • II**
Rev. 2 – Without stops except   Spink 3354

360	**1663**	XV	(15)		*(9 strings)*	R^2	26A
361	—	—	—	Stop before date • **1663**	*(8 strings)*	R^2	Cf.26

K/2. Second bust; smaller, with ends of <u>twisted ties</u> curving upwards
Rev. 2 - Edge dated in Roman numerals   Spink 3355

362	**1664**	XVI	(16)	Struck on a small flan *(6,7,8,9,10 str)*	N	28
363	—	—	—	*Proof* *(7 strings)* (L&S 10)	R^6	29

L/2. Second bust variety; different curls, <u>crooked ties</u> curve outwards
Rev. 2 - Edge dated in Roman numerals   Spink 3355

364	**1665**	XVI	(16)	Flaws in *rev.* field *(8 strings)*	R^6	30
365	—	XVII	(17)	Flaws in *rev.* field *(8 strings)*	R^3	31
366	**1666**	XVIII	(18)	*(6,7 Strings)*	S	32
367	—	—	—	Extra stop in **RE·X** *(6 strings)*	R^6	32A

55

CROWNS

M/2. Second bust variety with Elephant below
Rev. 2 - Edge dated in Roman numerals   Spink 3356

ESC	Date	Varieties, comments etc		R	(Old ESC)
368	**1666**	**XVIII** (18)	*(9 strings)*	R	33
369	—	— — Extra stop in **RE·X**	*(6 strings)*	R^2	34

L/2. Second bust variety; different curls, <u>crooked ties</u> curve outwards
Rev. 2 - Edge dated in Roman numerals   Spink 3355

370	**1667**	**XVIII** (18)	*(6 strings)*	R^7	34A

N/2. Second bust variety, as before, but
Rev. 2 - Edge date in Roman words   Spink 3357

371	**1667**	**D. NONO** (19)	*(5 strings)*	S	35
372	—	— —	**AN.˙REG.˙on edge** *(5,6 str)*	S	35A
373	**1668**	**VICESIMO** (20)	**ANNO·REGNI·** *(5,6 strings)*	N	36
374	—	— —	**TVTAMEN·ET·DECVS** Inverted half section of collar [3] *(7or8? strings)*	R^4	36A
375	—	— —	No stop after **MAG** *(6 strings)*		
376	—	— —	**8 over 7** *(5,6,7,9 strings)*	R^2	37
377	—	— —	**8 over 5**	R^4	37A
378	**1669**	**V. PRIMO** (21)	*Blundered edge* *(7,9 strings)*	R^3	38
379	—	— —	**9 over 8** *(7 strings)*	R^3	39
380	**1670**	**V. SECVNDO** (22)	*(9 strings)*	R	40
381	—	— —	**70 over 69** *(6,10 strings)*	R^2	41

N/2ns. Second bust variety as before, but
Rev. 2 - No stop after **HIB**   Spink 3357

382	**1671**	**V. TERTIO** (23)	*(6,7,8,10,11 strings)*	N	42
383	—	— —	**T over R in ET** *(7,10 strings)*	R^4	42A
384	—	— —	**ET over FR** *(7 strings)*	R^6	42B
385	—	— —	**R over B in FRA** *(9 strings)*		

O/2ns. Third bust; larger and broader, different curls and shorter ties
Rev. 2 - No stop after **HIB**   Spink 3358

386	**1671**	**V. TERTIO** (23)	*(6,7,8,9 strings)*	N	43
387	—	**V. QVARTO** (24)	Note [4] *(3-4 known)* *(7 strings)*	R^5	44
388	**1672**	— —	Note [5] *(7,8,9? strings)*	N	45
389	**1673**	**V. QVARTO** (24)		R^5	46

CROWNS

O/2. Third bust as before, but
Rev. 2 – With stop after **HIB•**   Spink 3358

ESC	Date	Varieties, comments etc		R	(Old ESC)
390	**1673**	**V. QVINTO** (25)	*(6,7,8,9 strings)*	N	47
391	—	— —	**B over R in BR** *(6,8 strings)*	R	47A
392	—	— —	**I over O in VICESIMO**$^{(7sr)}$	R	47B
393	—	— —	**3 over 2** *(6,7 strings)*	R	48
394	**1674**	**V. SEXTO** (26)	*(2-3 known)* *(8 strings)*	R^6	49

O/2ns. Third bust as before, but
Rev. 2 - No stop after **HIB**   Spink 3358

395	1675	**V. SEPTIMO** (27)	*(6 strings)*	R^4	50
396	—	— —	**5 over 3 and** **T over G in ET?** *(6,7 strings)*	R^5	50A
397	1676	**V. OCTAVO** (28)	*(6,7,8 strings)*	C	51
398	1677	**V. NONO** (29)	*(5,6,7,8 strings)*	S	52
399	—	— —	**7 over 6** *(6,7,8 strings)*	R^2	53
400	—	— —	**7 over 6 and** **A over G in FRA** *(7 strings)*	R	53A
401	1678	**TRICESIMO** (30)	**8 over 6** *(7 strings)*	R^2	55A
402	—	— —	**8 over 7** *(7 strings)*	R^2	55

O/2. Third bust as before, but
Rev. 2 – With normal stop after **HIB•**   Spink 3358

403	1679	**T. PRIMO** (31)	*(6,7,8,9,10 strings)*	C	56
404	—	— —	**9 over 8** *(6 strings)*	R^5	

P/2. Fourth bust; older features, three distinct long curls over neck
Rev. 2 - Stop after **HIB•** edge date in Roman words   Spink 3359

405	1679	**T. PRIMO** (31)	*(7 strings)*	N	57
406	—	— —	**HIB˙ R·EX** error	R	57A

O/2ns. Third bust as before, but
Rev. 2 - No stop after **HIB**   Spink 3358

407	1679	**T. PRIMO** (31)	*(6,7 strings)*	N	57
408	1680	**T. SECVNDO** (32)	*(7 strings)*	R^2	58
409	—	— —	**80 over 79** *(6 strings)*	R	59

CHARLES II, 1660-1685
CROWNS

O/2. Third bust as before, but
Rev. 2 – With normal stop after **HIB** •   Spink 3358

ESC	Date	Varieties, comments etc		R	(Old ESC)
410	1680	T. SECVNDO (32)		R^2	58
411	—	—	— **80 over 79** *(6 strings)*	R	59

P/2ns. Fourth bust as before / *Rev.* 2 - No stop after **HIB**   Spink 3359

412	1680	T. SECVNDO (32)	*(7,8 strings)*	S	60
413	—	—	— **80 over 79** *(6,7 strings)*	R^2	61
414	1681	T. TERTIO (33)	*(6,8,9 strings)*	S	64

Q/2ns. Fourth bust with **Elephant and castle** below
Rev. 2 - No stop after **HIB**   Spink 3360

415	1681	T. TERTIO (33)	*(6,8 strings)*	R^4	63

P/2ns. Fourth bust as before
Rev. 2 - No stop after **HIB** Larger edge letters   Spink 3359

416	1682	T. QVARTO (34)	*(See note 9)* *(5,6,7 strings)*	R^4	65
417	—	—	— **2 over 1** *(6,7,8 strings)*	N	65A
418	—	T. QVRRTO (34)	**2 over 1** and **QVARTO** over **TERTIO** *(6,7 strings)*	R^2	65B
419	1683	T. QVINTO (35)	*(6,7 strings)*	R^2	66
420	1684	T. SEXTO (36)	*(7,8 strings)*	R	67

1   Large numbers of dies were made, especially for **1662** with **rose** below bust, judging by the subtle differences in the alignment of the ties with legend. See the published result of an in depth die study (fully illustrated) by A. J. Broad (Seaby March 1981, pp. 60-65) and the article by Alan Bond (Seaby March 1989, pp. 41-44). Unfortunately most of these differences are not significant enough to warrant inclusion as major varieties. Although this is a very common coin, no crowns of Charles II are common in first class condition. (P.A.R) See illustrations of 3 variations (MB) Many rare high grade specimens have frosting on; lettering, face, wreath, cloak, Cs, shield edges and have a sharper design indicative of proofs or having been struck from proof dies.

2   The reverse is the same for the pattern die for ESC 71 (see flaw by letter X). Some suggest this should be classified as a pattern not proof, but since these are so rare it is purely academic.

3   On this variety, a section of the collar has been used inverted in error with cross pattée edge stops *(11-20 known)*

4   An example is in the B.M. (ex Clark Thornhill collection) and is rather interesting as it has the wrong edge for this year. The other edge if there were two, should be **VICESIMO SECVNDO**

5   In the years 1664, 1671 and 1672 the dies are not all made from the same working-punches so there are two or three slight varieties of busts.

CROWNS

PATTERNS

$\mathcal{JR}$| shape curls

Type R   Type S

No stop after 2
Frosted Cs &
No stop after date, with flaw   shield edges   With stop after date, no flaw

Type T

CROWNS

ESC	Date	Varieties, comments etc	R	L&S	(Old ESC)
421	1662	By **Roettier**, dated **1662** Type **R** - *Obv.* Similar to type C, but laureate bust and lettering frosted, *JR* shaped lower curls (initials), long thin loose curl on neck, thick ties to letter **R** *Rev.* **1** - As current coin, but interlinked Cs, shield edges and lettering all frosted, crown with interiors; see triangles above shields No stop after date, and characteristic flaw above **X**, *Edge. Plain* (RRSB2)[7] *(11 strings)*	R^6	3	21
422	—	Type **Ra** - (undated edge) (RRSB3)[7] **DECVS · ET · TVTAMEN ★＋★**	R^7		
423	—	Type **Rb** - No frosting (RRSB3A)[7] *(8 strings)* **DECVS · ET · TVTAMEN 1662**	R^7		18A
424	1662	Type **S** - *Obv.* Similar, but undraped bust with a pointed truncation. No initials or loose curl, thin ties to letters **AR** *Rev.* **1** - As before (without flaw) *wt. 29.82g* **DECVS · ET · TVTAMEN ★＋★** (undated edge) (RRSA1)[7] *(10 strings)*	R^6	2	68
425	—	Type **Sa** - *Edge,* plain (RRSA2)[7]	R^6	2A	70
426	—	Type **S** - *In gold (4 known)* (RRGA1)[7] *wt. 51.67g*	R^5	1A	69
427	—	Type **Sa** - *In gold. Edge,* plain *(9 strings)* *(3 known)* (RRGA2)[7] *wt. 58.01g - 58.77g*	R^5	1	71

| 428 | 1663 | By **Roettier**, dated **1663**
Type **T** - *Obv.* 1st laureate bust, right, draped
Cloak frosted
Leg. **CAROLVS · II · DEI · GRATIA**
Rev. **1** - As current coin, but the interlinked Cs are frosted
Edge. Plain. *Struck in pewter* | R^6 | | |

CHARLES II, 1660-1685
CROWNS

Simon's
'Petition Crown'

Type U

Simon's petition on the edge

(Upper line) **THOMAS SIMON · MOST · HVMBLY · PRAYS · YOUR ·
MAJESTY TO · COMPARE · THIS · HIS · TRYALL · PIECE · WITH ·
THE · DVTCH · AND · IF · MORE** (Lower line) **TRVLY · DRAWN & ·
EMBOSS'D · MORE · GRACE : FVLLY · ORDER'D · AND · MORE ·
ACCVRATELY · ENGRAVEN · TO · RELIEVE · HIM ·**
Two interlinked **C**s between palm branch and a branch of laurel,
with a crown above, separate the end of the lines from the beginning

Spink 3354A

ESC	Date	Varieties, comments etc	R	L&S	(Old ESC)
429	1663	*'Petition Crown'* by **Thomas Simon** Type **U** - As illustration* *(circa 15 known)* *In silver* *wt. 33.09g-34.73g (12 strings)*	R^4	6	72
430	—	*In pewter with a plain edge* *(unique)*	R^7	8	72A

Beware of electrotype copies unless stated as such

61

CROWNS

ESC	Date	Varieties, comments etc	R	L&S	(Old ESC)
431	1663	**'Reddite crown'** by **Thomas Simon** Type **V** - As before, but edge reading in Latin; **REDDITE · QVÆ · CÆSARIS · CÆSARI · & CT · POST** followed by the sun appearing out of a cloud. *"Render to Caesar the things which are Caesar's"* **CT · POST = POST NUBILA PHOEBUS** *"after the storm the sun shines"* an allusion to the Restoration of Charles II after the dark days of the Commonwealth *(9 known) wt. 32.88g*	R^5	7	73
432	—	*In pewter* *(3 known) wt. 21.49g*	R^6	7A	74

Spink 3354B

433	1663	**'Render to Caesar'** by **Thomas Simon** Type **W** - As before Edge reading in English; **RENDER · TO · CAESAR · THE · THINGS · WHICH · ARE · CAESARS &c ·★** In *Silver*	R^6	7B	74A
434	—	*In Pewter with a plain edge*	R^6	7C	74B

La Riviere
26
Silver cliché

A proof in thin silver of the finest coin ever engraved in England by J. Simon.

435		Silver cliché		L&S 9	

436		Lead obverse uniface undated		L&S 9A	

CHARLES II, 1660-1685
CROWNS

La Riviere
27
Lead cliché

| 437 | Uniface lead squeeze. Very thick flan [10] | L&S 9B |

See *Bibliography* for more information of Simon's patterns

6   There are a number of unique (?) uniface trial strikings of the Petition crown in various metals; La Riviere Collection *"Patterns of Charles II"* Spink Auction 166, lots 23, 26 & 27

7   Die study number by Roderick Richardson published in his circular Summer 1998.
J. ROETTIER PATTERNS & PROOFS OF CHARLES II CROWNS - NOTES - BY RODERICK RICHARDSON

8   *"Considered by some to be a proof* (with triangles above shields)*, but it is definitely struck from regular dies"* Mark Rasmussen - See Barr 69, good VF-EF

9   1682 variety *"the V in CAROLVS, an inverted A"* is not so. When the V and A are compared in high magnification the angle of the crossbars differ, therefore a die flaw. (M.B.)

10   See Linecar & Stone pages 12-13 for an interesting story and the detective work regarding the origin of this example

The following sub-varieties are not significant enough to warrant inclusion as major varieties (See Lingford collection for many examples);-
1. The variable number of strings on the Irish harp.
2. Missing stops, e.g. **HIB** is found both with and without a stop after.
3. Edge legends, where they are inverted in relation to the obverse or not.
4. Edge legend errors caused by collar slippage..
5. Flaws in striking, e.g. ESC 54 'Boar's head' *(7 strings)*→ removed from listing
6. Die axis variations.

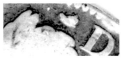

2 examples of the so-called *'Boar's head'* flaw
My thanks to Malcolm Lewendon for most of the illustrations of over dates and letters (M.B.)

HALFCROWNS

OBVERSES

Type D
1st bust

Type E
2nd bust

Type F
3rd bust

Type G
Elephant below 3rd bust

Type H
3rd bust variety

Type I
4th bust

Type J
Plume below 4th bust

Type D
No stops

Type D
V over S in CAROLVS

HALFCROWNS

Error **GRATTA**

Type I
Error GRATTA

Elephant & castle
Below 4th bust

Type L
E & C below 4th bust

Plume in centre

Error MRG for MAG

B over R

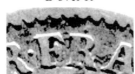

A over R

1666 over 4 over 3?

F over H?

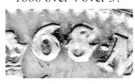

7 over 4

8 over 4

9 over 4

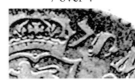

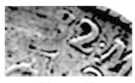

1 over 0

4 over 3

82 over 79

65

HALFCROWNS

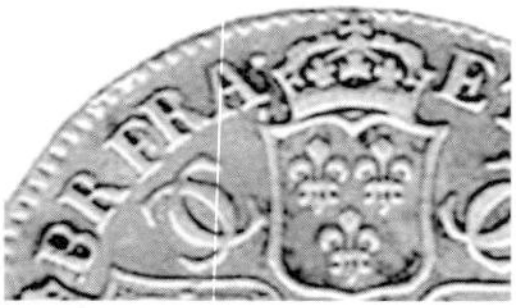

Edge errors

DECNS

DNCVS

No stop after BR

PRICESIMO

Retrograde 1

R of BR over F

4 over 3

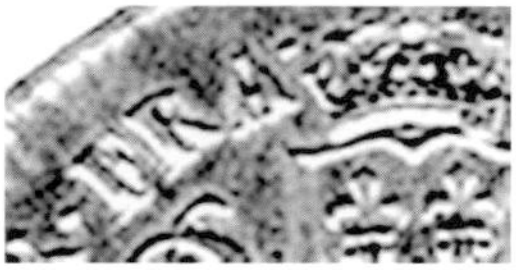

F over M

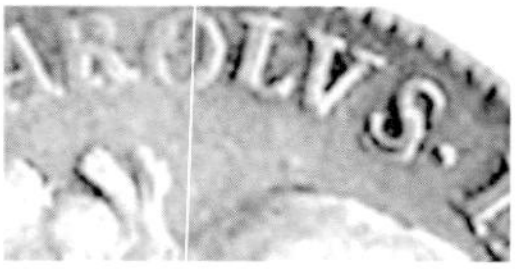

Re-entered S

R over B (die flaw?)

V over S

For types A-C See Charles II hammered coinage

Types **D.** **First bust,** laureate and draped, right, as illustration
Leg. **CAROLVS • II •   DEI • GRATIA**
Top laurel leaf protrudes above the others
Top tie; straight and pointing downwards to letter **O**
Rev. Standard crowned cruciform shields, as crown, with individual arms, clockwise; England, Scotland, France and Ireland. Star of the Garter in the centre and interlinked **C**s in the angles (Charles son of Charles) (With stops in legend unless stated)
Edge **DECVS · ET · TVTAMEN** followed by the regnal year

E. Similar, but **second bust**; broader, used only in **1664**
Three leading laurel leaves, tips almost in line
Top tie, wavy and pointing downwards to between **R O**

F. Similar, but **third bust**; smaller than 'D' & 'E'. Tips of the laurel leaves shorter, inside line of legend. Both ties wavy, sticking straight out, top one points to between letters **R O**

HALFCROWNS

Types **G.** **Elephant** below third bust, similar to 'F', but subtle differences; twin laurel leaves protruding above hairline, a pellet between tips

H. Similar to 'F' & 'G' but **third bust variety**; tips of laurel leaves similar to **'G'** but without the pellet, top one points to letter **O**

I. **Fourth bust**; much larger with more hair over forehead. Three prominent laurel leaves above. Ties curve downwards and point to letter **R**

J. Similar to 'I' but with a **Plume** below bust and the ties point between letters **A R**

K. As **J** with a plume on both sides

L. As **I** with an elephant and castle below bust

Normal punctuation in reverse legend, unless stated;
MAG• BR•FRA• ET•HIB• REX•

Type
D. First bust – Regal year in **Roman numerals** Spink 3361

ESC	Date	Edge year	Varieties, remarks, etc.		R	(Old ESC)
438	**1663**	**XV** (15)		*(6,8 strings)*	N	457
439	—	—		*(7 strings)*	N	457
440	—	—	V over S in **CAROLVS**	*(7 strings)*	R^2	457A
441	—	—	R over B in **CAROLVS** (flaw?)	*(6 strs)*		
442	—	—	A over T? in **GRATIA**	*(6 strings)*	R^2	457B
443	—	—	*Proof*		R^6	458
444	—	—	No stops *obv.*	*(6,8 strings)*	R	459

E. Second bust – regal year as before Spink 3362

445	**1664**	**XVI** (16)		*(6 strings)*	R^2	460

F. Third bust – regal year as before Spink 3363

446	**1666**	**XVIII** (17)	Last **6** over **4**	*(7 strings)*	R^5	461

G. Third bust, **Elephant below**, regal year as before Spink 3364

447	**1666**	**XVIII** (18)	Last **6** over **4**	*(6,7 strings)*	R^3	462

HALFCROWNS

Type

H. Third bust – regal year in **Roman words**   Spink 3365

ESC	Date	Edge year		Varieties, remarks, etc.	R	(Old ESC)
448	1667	**DECIMO**		**7 over 4** in date *(5 strings)*	R^6	463
		NONO	(19)	Edge **AN REG**		
449	1668	**VICESIMO**	(20)	**8 over 4** in date *(7,10 strings)*	R^2	464
450	1669	**V. PRIMO**	(21)	*(7,8 strings)*	R^5	465
451	—	—		Error **R over I** in **PRIMO** *8s*	R^5	465A
452	—	—		**9 over 4** in date *(8,9 strings)*	R^3	466
453	1670	**V. SECVNDO**	(22)	No stop after **HIB** *(7,8,9 strs)*	N	467
454	—	—		Error **E over R** in **ET**	$R^?$	
				No stop after **HIB** *(8 strings)*		
455	—	—		Error **MRG** for MAG	R^3	467A
				No stop after **HIB** *(8 strings)*		
456	—	—		**LV over SV** in **CAROLVS**	R^3	467B?
				No stop after **HIB** *(8 strings)*		

H¹. Third bust variety – regal year as before   Spink 3366

457	1671	**V. TERTIO**	(23)	No stop after **HIB***(7-10strings)*	N	468
458	—	—		**1 over 0** No stop after **HIB***8s*	R	469
459	1672	**V. QVARTO**	(24)	No stop after **HIB** *(6 strings)*	R	471

I. Fourth bust, plain below – regal year as before   Spink 3367

460	1672	**V. QVARTO**	(24)	*(7 strings)*	R^3	472

J. Fourth bust **Plume below**
Regal year as before, no stop (?) after **HIB**   Spink 3368

461	1673	**V. QVARTO**	(24)		R^5	466

K. Fourth bust, **Plume both sides**, regal year as before   Spink 3369

462	1673	**V. QVINTO**	(25)	*(4 known) (7 strings)*	R^6	475

I. Fourth bust, plain below – regal year as before
No stop after **HIB**   Spink 3367

463	1673	**V. QVINTO**	(25)	*(5,6,8 strings)*	N	473
464	—	—		**A over R** in **FRA** *(6 strings)*	R^5	473A
465	—	—		**F over M** in **FRA** *(6 strings)*	R^3	473B
466	—	—		**B over R** in **BR** *(5 strings)*	R^3	473C

(continued)

HALFCROWNS

ESC	Date	Edge year	Varieties, remarks, etc.	R	(Old ESC)
466	**1674**	**V. SEXTO** (26)	*(6,7 strings)*	R^2	476
467	—	—	**4 over 3** *(6,7 strings)*	R^4	476A
469	**1675**	**V. SEPTIMO** (27)	*(6 strings)*	R	477
470	—	—	Retrograde **1** *(6,7 strings)*	R^2	477A
471	**1676**	**V. OCTAVO** (28)	*(4,5,6,7 strings)*	S	478
472	—	—	Retrograde **1** *(5,6,7,8 strings)*	N	478A
473	**1676**	**V. OCTAVO** (28)	S over low S in **CAROLVS** *(6 strings)*	R^2	478B
474	—	—	Retrograde **1** *(8 strings)* **F** over **H** in **FRA** and **R** over **T** in **BR**	R^2	478C
475	**1677**	**V. NONO** (29)	*(6,8 strings)*	N	479
476	—	—	No stops after **BR HIB** *(6 str)*	N	479
477	—	—	**F** over **H** in **FRA** *(6 strings)*		
478	**1678**	**TRICESIMO** (30)	*(5,6 strings)*	R^4	480
479	—	—	No stops after **BR HIB** *(5 st)*	R^4	480A
480	**1679**	**T. PRIMO** (31)	*(6,7 strings)*	C	481
481	—	—	**GRATTA** *(6,7 strings)*	R^3	481A
482	—	—	No stops after **FRA HIB** *(6s)*		481?
483	—	—	Error **P** over **I** in **PRIMO**	R^3	480B
484	—	—	Edge error **REGЯI** 2nd **R** inverted *(6,7strings)*	R^6	482
485	—	—	Edge error **DECNS** *(6,7 strgs)*	R	483
486	—	—	Edge error **DNCVS** *(5 strings)*	R^6	483A
487	—	—	Edge error **PRICESIMO** *(6,7s)*	R^3	484
488	—	—	Edge error Inverted **A**s in **DECⱯS TⱯTAMEN**[1] *(6,7s)*	R^3	484A
489	**1680**	**T. SECVNDO** (32)	*(7 strings)*	R^3	485
490	**1681**	—	Reversed **D** in **SECVNꓷO**[2] *(5,7 strings)*	R^3	485A
491	—	**T. TERTIO** (33)	*(5,7 strings)*	R	486

L.   Fourth bust, **Elephant & Castle below**
Regal year as before, no stop after **HIB**   Spink 3370

492	**1681**	**T. TERTIO** (33)	*(6,7,8 strings)*	R^4	488

1   Uncertain if a die flaw rather than the use of an inverted 'A'. The Adams collection contained two specimens (lots 351 & 352) so this variety is retained.

CHARLES, II, 1660-85
HALFCROWNS

Type

I. Fourth bust, plain below
Regal year as before, no stop after **HIB**   Spink 3367

ESC	Date	Edge year	Varieties, remarks, etc.	R	(Old ESC)
493	1682	T. QVARTO (34)	*(6,7,8 strings)*	R^2	489
494	—	—	2 over 1 *(6 strings)*	R^4	489A
495	—	—	82 over 79 *(7 strings)*	R^4	489B

J. Fourth bust **Plume below**
Regal year as before, no stop after **HIB**   Spink 3368

496	1683	T. QVINTO (35)	*(Possibly unique)* *(5 strings)*	R^7	491

I. Fourth bust, plain below
Regal year as before, no stop after **HIB**   Spink 3367

497	1683	T. QVARTO (34)	*(5,6,8 strings)*	S	490
498	—	—	E over D in DEI *(5 strings)*		
499	1684	T. SEXTO (36)	4 over 3 *(6 strings)*	R^4	492

Notes

2   The Adam collection contained two specimens (lots 355 & 356) Adams 301; "inverted A in CAROLVS" is probably a flaw (Spink) Adams 326; "1675/4" not convincing so are disregarded. The numbers of strings on the Irish harp varies, but do not warrant inclusion as major varieties (Refer to Colin Adam's Collection of halfcrowns. Spink Auction 177, 2005/12/01for numerous examples). A few coins in the Adams collection are recorded with various letters being over-struck, but many are not convincing enough to warrant inclusion as major varieties and are disregarded, e.g. Lot 262, *'1663,* R of CAROLVS die flawed giving impression of an overstrike'; Lot 290, '1663, first A of GRATIA over T or inverted A'; Lot 291, '1663, V of CAROLVS with an interior bar'; Lot 298, '1666, over 4 over 3'; Lot 314, '1672, G of GRATIA over indeterminate letter'; Lot 320, '1673, no R in REGNI on edge'; Lot 326, '1675, 5 possibly over 4' and Lot 330, 1676, no R in REGNI on edge, where a segment of the collar has slipped.

SHILLINGS

BUSTS

D - 1ˢᵗ bust: **1663,** distinguishing features are:
(a) the top two leaves of the wreath seem to be thinner
(b) the gap between the hair ties seems smaller the forelock of hair over the forehead could be
(c) two locks of hair curl upwards
(d) **a circular lock of hair most obvious difference**
(e) there is a clear S-shaped curl
(f) missing lock of hair
(g) two curls at the bottom of the wreath
(h) the forelock of hair over the forehead seems to be shorter but this could be the effect of die filling

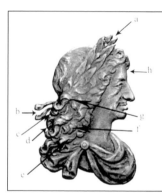

E - 1ˢᵗ bust variety: 1663 & 1668-9
(a) the top two leaves of the wreath are wider
(b) there is a marked gap between the hair ties ending in a straight upright section
(c) the two curls below the hair ties curl to the side rather than upwards
(d) **this curl does not form a circle**
(e) there is no S-shaped curl
(f) an extra lock of hair
(g) a single lock of hair curling downwards at the bottom of the wreath
(h) the forelock is longer

M - the guinea head: 1666 only

the absence of drapery is a sufficient distinguishing feature

CHARLES II, 1660-85
SHILLINGS

G - 2nd bust: 1666-73 & 1676-83

(a) there is a single prominent leaf to the top of the wreath
(b) the lines of the hair are different to those on the 1st bust
(c) there is an extra curl of hair
(d) the top hair tie is straighter
(e) the bottom hair tie shows a well developed kink with a clear vertical line
(f) the lips seem to be more closed
(g) the hair over the forehead is different

I - 2nd bust variety A: 1674-5

(a) the top leaf to the wreath is different
(b) the upper hair tie is straight and appears to have a void possibly due to die filling of a section in low relief
(c) the lower hair tie is straight and points downwards and the upper part could have part missing due to design or possible die filling
(d) totally different void under lower tie – lack of hair here

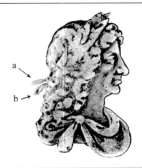

J - 2nd bust variety B: 1681 only

Similar to 2nd bust and variety 'A' but, the ties and outline are different; see hair over forehead and back of neck, and shape of lower truncation

a the upper hair tie has parallel sides
b lower tie shows a loop

72

SHILLINGS

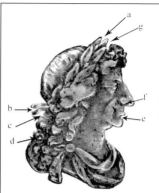

K - 3rd bust (large): 1674-5

(a) two clearly defined top leaves to the wreath
(b) very narrow gap between the hair ties
(c) large gap under the lower hair tie
(d) complete curl
(e) more pronounced dip under the lower lip
(f) nostrils more pronounced
(g) clear gap between wreath and hair over forehead

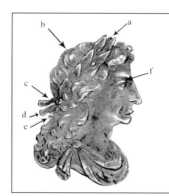

L - 4th bust (large): 1683-4

(a) different leaves at the top of the wreath
(b) clearer hair lines in an upwards direction
(c) thicker upper hair tie
(d) stubby lower hair tie
(e) different hair curl
(f) straight upper eye lid

The above images and descriptions courtesy of Roderick Farey and Nigel Prevost

TIES

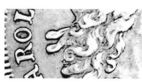

D - 1st bust
(both tie-ends up)

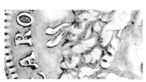

E - 1st bust variety
(c.f. curls)

SHILLINGS

G	I	J
2 bust	2 bust variety A	2 bust variety B

G
2nd bust
(top tie straight lower up)

I
2nd bust variety A
(lower tie down)

J
2nd bust variety B
(looped lower tie)

K - 3rd (larger) bust
(ties close & 3 curls)

L - 4th bust
(both ties curve up)

D
1st bust
2 top leaves

E
1st bust variety
Different hair curls

F
as type E with
1st elephant below

SHILLINGS

G - 2nd bust
Single top leaf

H - 2nd bust
Plume below

I - 2nd bust variety A
(lower tie down)

J - 2nd bust var. B
Elephant & castle

K - 3rd (larger) bust
(ties close & 3 curls)

L - 4th bust
(Both ties curve up)

SHILLINGS

1
Star in centre

M - Guinea die
(no drapery)

2
Plume in centre

A over G

3. Scot & Irish
shields transposed

E over R

No stop after HIB

Stop after II moved to
before DEI

Error GARTIA

SHILLINGS

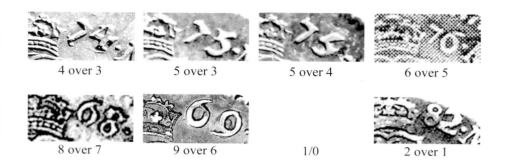

4 over 3	5 over 3	5 over 4	6 over 5

8 over 7	9 over 6	1/0	2 over 1

Type   **D.**   First bust, laureate and draped, right, two top leaves in wreath, two wavy ties with both ends curving upwards

Leg.   **CAROLVS • II •**   **• DEI • GRATIA** (2nd stop before **• DEI**)

E.   First bust variety; very similar in size and general style, but has a varied arrangement of the hair, which is particularly noticeable below the tie at the back of the head, with extra stop before **• DEI**

F.   As type E, but with an **Elephant below** bust, no stop before **DEI**

G.   Second bust, similar to first, but with a single top leaf in wreath, slightly different ties; top one almost straight and bottom wavy with upturned end, and no stop before **DEI**

H.   As type G, but with a **Plume** below bust

I.   Second bust variety A; similar to 'G', but lower tie straight and angled downwards 45°, and no stop before **DEI**

J.   Second bust variety B, similar to type G, but a narrower upper tie and loop to lower tie, with **Elephant & castle** (howdah) below

K.   Third bust, much larger, with three distinct ringlets hanging almost straight down, two top leaves in wreath close to outer beading, the two ties are shorter and closer together with round ends, and no stop before **DEI**

SHILLINGS

Type **L.** Fourth bust, large, similar to third, but not such fine work, the laurel leaves are larger and more prominent especially the top two, three distinct ringlets are more angled backwards and extend below the drapery, twin ties curve upwards, no stop before **DEI**

M. *"Guinea bust"* [1]; undraped bust, right, ten laurel leaves in the Wreath, three distinct tie ends, a lovelock over his left shoulder and more hair down over his brow, an **Elephant** below a deeply indented truncation, with an extra stop before · **DEI**

Rev. **1.** Standard crowned cruciform shields, as crown. Star of the Garter in centre and interlinked **C**ˢ in the angles

2. As before, but with a **plume** in the centre
Note In 1669 the upright edge milling was changed to oblique

D/1. First bust; with two top leaves in wreath, stop before • **DEI**
Rev. 1 - with star of the Garter in centre   Spink 3371
Leg. punc. – **MAG• BR•FRA• ET•HIB• REX•**

ESC	Date	Varieties, remarks etc		R	(Old ESC)
500	**1663**		*(6,7 strings)*	C	1022
501	—	*Struck en medaille ↑↑*	*(6 strings)*	C	1022
502	—	*Proof* in copper, plain edge		R^6	1022A
503	—	Error, reads **GARTIA**	*(5 strings)*	R^4	1023
504	—	Scottish and Irish shields transposed	*(8 strings)*	R^3	1024
505	—	**A** of FRA struck over **G**		R^5	1024A

E/1. First bust variety; varied arrangement of hair, stop before • **DEI**
Rev. 1 - *Leg. punc.* as before   Spink 3372

506	1663		*(7 strings)*	C	1025

Note; 1666, 1ˢᵗ bust variety is listed as old ESC 1025A – but it remains unseen so de-listed

F/1. First bust variety, **Elephant below**, but no stop before **DEI**
Rev. 1 - as before   Spink 3373

507	1666	No stop after **HIB**	*(5 strings)*	R^2	1026

G/1. Second bust, with a single top leaf in wreath, no stop before **DEI**
Rev. 1 - *Leg. punc.* as before   Spink 3375

508	1666		R^6	1028

78

SHILLINGS

Type **M/1.** *"Guinea head"* [1], **Elephant below**, with a stop before • **DEI**
Rev. 1 - Leg. punc. as before   Spink 3374

ESC	Date	Varieties, remarks etc	R	(Old ESC)
509	**1666**		R^4	1027

E/1. First bust variety; varied arrangement of hair, stop before • **DEI**
Rev. 1 - Leg. punc. as before   Spink 3372

510	**1668**		R^4	1029

G/1. Second bust, with a single top leaf in wreath, no stop before **DEI**
Rev. 1 - Leg. punc. as before   Spink 3375

511	**1668**	Stop after **II** • *(4,6,7 strings)*	C	1030
512	—	Stop after **II** re-positioned before • **DEI** *(6 strings)*		
513	—	**8** of date over **7** (or more likely **3**) *(6 strings)*	R^2	1030A
514	—	Large **66** & smaller **8** in date	R^2	

Note; new ***oblique milling*** from now onward

E/1. First bust variety; varied arrangement of hair, stop before • **DEI**
Rev. 1 - Leg. punc. as before,   Spink 3372

515	**1669**	**9** over **6**	R^6	1031

G/1. Second bust, with a single top leaf in wreath, no stop before **DEI**
Rev. 1 - Leg. punc. as before   Spink 3375

516	**1669**		R^7	1032
517	**1670**	*(8 strings)*	R^2	1033
518	**1671**	No stop after **HIB** *(8 strings)*	R^3	1034
519	—	No stop after **MAG**	R^3	1034A

H/2. Second bust, **plume** below, no stop before **DEI**
*Rev. 2 - **Plume*** in centre (not Garter star)   Spink 3376

520	**1671**	No stop after **HIB** *(5 strings)*	R^2	1035

G/1. Second bust, with a single top leaf in wreath, no stop before **DEI**
Rev. 1 - Leg. punc. as before   Spink 3375

521	**1672**	*(5 strings)*	R	1036
522	**1673**		R^2	1037
523	—	**3** over **2**	R^3	1037A
524	—	No stop after **HIB** and **E** over **R** in **ET** *(5? strings)*	R^3	1037B

CHARLES II, 1660-85
SHILLINGS

Type **H/2.** Second bust, **plume** below, no stop before **DEI**
Rev. 2 - **Plume** in centre (not Garter star) Spink 3376

ESC	Date	Varieties, remarks etc		R	(Old ESC)
525	1673		*(6 strings)*	R^3	1038
526	1674	No stop after **HIB**	*(6,7 strings)*	R^2	1040

I/1. Second bust variety A, single top leaf, no stop before **DEI**
Rev. 1 - as before Spink 3375

527	1674	4 over 3 No stop after **HIB**	*(6 strings)*	R^2	1039A

I/2. Second bust variety A, single top leaf, no stop before **DEI**
Rev. 2 - **Plume** in centre (not Garter star) Spink 3377

528	1674	Probably a mule of **H/I** No stop after **HIB** *(6 strings)*	R^4	1041

K/1. Third bust larger, three distinct ringlets hanging down, two top leaves in wreath close to outer beading, ties are shorter and closer together, no stop before **DEI** / *Rev.* 1 - as before Spink 3380

529	1674			R^6	1042
530	1675	No stop after **HIB**	*(5 strings)*	R^6	1043
531	—	5 over 3 No stop after **HIB**	*(5 strings)*	R^3	1043A

H/2. Second bust, **plume** below, no stop before **DEI**
Rev. 2 - **Plume** in centre (not Garter star) Spink 3376

532	1675		R^3	1046

I/1. Second bust variety A, single top leaf, no stop before **DEI**
Rev. 1 - as before Spink 3375

533	1675		*(5 strings)*	R^4	1044
534	—	5 over 4 No stop after **HIB**	*(5 strings)*	R^6	1045
535	—	5 over 3	*(5 strings)*	R^4	1045A

G/1. Second bust, with a single top leaf in wreath, no stop before **DEI**
Rev. 1 - *Leg. punc.* as before Spink 3375

536	1676	No stop after **HIB**	*(6 strings)*	S	1047
537	—	With stop after **HIB** *Clashed dies*	*(6 strings)*	S	1047
538	—	6 over 4		R^5	1048A
539	—	6 over 5 No stop after **HIB**		R	1048

80

SHILLINGS

Type	**H/2.**	Second bust, **plume** below, no stop before **DEI**		
		Rev. 2 - **Plume** in centre (not Garter star)		Spink 3376
ESC	Date	Varieties, remarks etc	R	(Old ESC)
540	**1676**	No stop after **HIB** *(5 strings)*	R^2	1049

	H/1.	Second bust, **plume** below, no stop before **DEI**		
		Rev. 1 - as before		Spink 3378
541	**1677**	Probably a mule of I/H	R^4	1051

	G/1.	Second bust, with a single top leaf in wreath, no stop before **DEI**		
		Rev. 1 - as before		Spink 3375
542	**1677**	No stop after **HIB** *(6 strings)*	R	1050
543	**1678**	No stop after **HIB** *(5 strings)*	R^2	1052
544	—	**8** over **7** *(Not traced)*	R^6	1053
545	**1679**	No stop after **HIB** *(5,6 strings)*	S	1054
546	—	**9** over **7**	R^2	1055

	H/1.	Second bust, **plume** below, no stop before **DEI**		
		Rev. 1 - as before		Spink 3378
547	**1679**	No stop after **HIB** A mule of I/H ? *(6 strings)*	R^3	1057

	H/2.	Second bust, **plume** below, no stop before **DEI**		
		Rev. 2 - **Plume** in centre (not Garter star)		Spink 3376
548	**1679**	No stop after **HIB** *(7? strings)*	R^3	1056
549	**1680**		R^5	1059
550	—	**80** over **79** *(Not traced)*	R^6	1060

	G/1.	Second bust, with a single top leaf in wreath, no stop before **DEI**		
		Rev. 1 - as before		Spink 3375
551	**1680**		R^6	1058
552	—	**80** over **79** *(Unique?)*	R^7	1058
553	**1681**	A over A & L over I in **CAROLVS** *(all with errors)*	R^3	1061
		No stop after **HIB** *(4? strings)*		
554	—	**1** over **0**	R^5	1061A

	J/1.	Second bust variety B, **Elephant and Castle** below,		
		No stop before **DEI** / *Rev.* 1 - as before		Spink 3379
555	**1681**	2nd **1** of date over **0**	R^5	1062

SHILLINGS

Type **G/1.** Second bust, with a single top leaf in wreath, no stop before **DEI**
Rev. 1 - as before   Spink 3375

ESC	Date	Varieties, remarks etc		R	(Old ESC)
556	1682	2 over 1	*(5 strings)*	R^4	1063
557	1683			R^6	1064

L/1. Fourth bust, large, not quite such fine work, laurel leaves larger
and more prominent especially the top two, three distinct ringlets
are more angled backwards and extend below the drapery, the
twin ties curve upwards, no stop before **DEI**
Rev. 1 - as before   Spink 3381

558	1683	No stop after **HIB**	*(5 strings)*	R^2	1065
559	1684	No stop after **HIB**	*(5 strings)*	S	1066

1 It has been suggested that the normal dies were lost in the Great Fire of London
and the guinea die had to be used

Patterns[2]

Type N   Type O

560	1663	N	By **Peter Blondeau**	R^6	1067
		Obv.	As currency type E		
		Leg.	**CAROLVS · II · · DEI · GRATIA**		
		*Rev.*1	A rose, thistle, lis and harp, each crowned and arranged cruciformly. Four interlinked Cs at the centre. Legend interrupted at intervals by crowns. The date **1663** is divided by the crown at top centre		
		Leg.	16 ♛ 63 ·MAG· ♛ BR·FRA· ♛ ET· HIB· ♛ REX·		
		Edge	Straight grained (Peck 486)		
561	—		*In copper* (Peck 487)	R^6	1067A

SHILLINGS

562	1663	O Rev.2	Similar, but reverse has the date **1663** wholly between two crowns, and reads **HI** instead of HIB	R^4	1067B
		Leg.	**MAG·BR·** ♕ **FRA·ET·** ♕ **HI·REX·** ♕ **1663** ♕ *In copper* (Peck 488)		
563	—		*In copper-nickel* Plain edge	R^6	1067A
564	—	Mule	Plain edge *Rev.* 1 with *Rev.* 2 (Peck 489)	R^6	

Mule of
two reverses

Q   R

565	1676	P/Q Mule	As type N & O , but dated **1676** Two reverses, thought to determine the best placing for the date. Plain edge *Struck in pewter.* *(6 known)* (Peck 490)	R^5	

2   *It's uncertain whether these are patterns for shillings or farthings*

SIXPENCES

| 5 over 4 | 6 over 5 | 8 over 7 | 2 over 1 |

Type **D.**   One type only; laureate and draped bust, right
Leg.   **CAROLVS · II ·**   **DEI · GRATIA**
Rev.   Standard crowned cruciform shields, as the crown
        Star of the Garter in the centre and interlinked **C**'s in the angles
        (**C**harles son of **C**harles)
Edge   Milled
Leg.   *Punctuation –* **MAG• BR•FRA•   ET•HIB   REX•**

Spink 3382

ESC	Date	Varieties, comments etc.		R	(Old ESC)
566	1674		*(4 strings)*	N	1512
567	1675		*(3 strings)*	N	1513
568	—	5 over 4	*(3 strings)*	R	1514
569	1676			R^5	1515
570	—	6 over 5		R	1515A
571	1677		*(3 strings)*	N	1516
572	—	G over O or D? of MAG		$R^?$	1516A
573	1678	8 over 7 G over O or D? of MAG	*(3 strings)*	R	1517
574	1679			R	1518
575	—	9 over 7		R^5	1518A
576	1680		*(3 strings)*	R^2	1519
577	1681			N	1520
578	1682			R^2	1521
579	—	2 over 1	*(3 strings)*	R^2	1522
580	1683		*(3 strings)*	N	1523
581	1684		*(4 strings)*	S	1524

"Sixpences of Charles II, James II and William and Mary are not uncommon in average condition. In EF or better grades they are much rarer than indicated here." (P.A. Rayner)

CHARLES II, 1660-85
MACHINE MADE MAUNDY

The story of Maundy Money is very complicated and its origin goes back many centuries. For a full history refer to *'Silver Pennies & Linen Towels'* *(Robinson)* the story of *the Royal Maundy* by Brian Robinson, Spink, London 1992. Variously called *'Daily Arms'*, *'Royal Gate Alms'* or *'The King's Dole'* until in the late Stuart periods this donation, to the needy, took place annually on or around Maundy Thursday, and thus became known as *'Maundy Money'*

In the past these small coins were erroneously and collectively known as 'Maundy Money'. For centuries the penny had been the popular denomination struck for circulation, and although the Groat, Threepence and Halfgroat had been introduced by previous monarchs, only the Penny and Halfgroat were used in the early Maundy Ceremonies. The regular annual ceremony is thought to have begun in the reign of William & Mary. In the opinion of P.A. Rayner (old ESC, p. 201-2) it was not until the reign of George III that sets of true Maundy Money (4d, 3d, 2d & 1d) were struck specifically for the Ceremony, until then they are treated as separate denominations.

Type C
With value but no inner circle and **undated**
Bust inside legend & *mm.* both sides

TWOPENCE

C.
Leg. 17 **CAROLVS · II : D : G : M : B : F : ET · H : REX·**

Spink 3317

ESC	Leg	Varieties, comments etc.	Robinson	R	(Old ESC)
582	17	No stop before **CAROLVS** *(4 harp strings)*	*p. 143,6 (i)*	R	2167A
583		Reads **M., F.** and **HI** and value **II.**	*p. 143,6 (ii)*		

MACHINE MADE MAUNDY

PENNY

AVSPCE

C.

Leg. 17 **CAROLVS · II : D : G : M : B : F : ET · H : REX·**

Robinson   Spink 3319

ESC	Leg	Varieties, comments etc.	Robinson	R	(Old ESC)
584	17	Reverse legend correct *(5 harp strings)*	*p. 143,5 (i)*	R^2	2271
585	17	Reverse legend error: **AVSPCE**, minus **I**	*p. 143,5 (ii)*	R^4	2271A

Type D
As before **with value** but no inner circle and **undated**
Bust to lower edge of coin & *mm. rev.* **only**
Usual **single arched crown**

TWOPENCE

D.   **CAROLVS.II.D.G ·M.B ·F.& ·H. REX.**   Spink 3318

586			*p. 143,8*	*S*	2168

PENNY

D.

Leg. 17 **CAROLVS · II : D : G : M : B : F : & · H : REX·**   Spink 3320

587	17	*(4 harp strings)*	*p. 143,7*	*S*	2272

MACHINE MADE MAUNDY

Type F
As before, but rather better struck and **undated**
Smaller second bust with **double-arched crown**

TWOPENCE

F.   Spink 3387

ESC	Varieties, comments etc.	*Robinson*	R	(Old ESC)
588	**CAROLVS.II. D. G. M. B. F. &. H. REX**	*p. 144,14*	*C*	2169
	No stop after **REGNO** (*7 harp strings*)			

PENNY

Type **F.**   Spink 3389

589	**CAROLVS.II D. G. M. B. F &. H. REX**	*p. 144,13*	*C*	2273
	No stop after **REGNO** (*6 harp strings*)			

Type B
SET OF FOUR COINS
First milled issue '*Undated Maundy*'
With value but no inner circles & *mm.* on reverse only
GROAT, THREEPENCE, HALFGROAT & PENNY
(These were never issued in sets but collectors like to assemble them)

MACHINE MADE MAUNDY

	As second hammered issue but machine made;
	Inferior workmanship to milled issues and no obverse mintmark
Obv.	Bust left, as before to edge of coin. King with long hair falling over his shoulders. Crown with double-arches
Leg.	Starts at 7 o'clock **CAROLVS II D G M B F & H REX**
Rev.	As before; square-topped shield over long cross within inner circle
Leg.	**CHRISTO • AVSPICE • REGNO •**

Type **B.**	Set of four coins		Spink 3391
590		*N*	2365

B.	Groat or fourpence		Spink 3383		
ESC	Varieties, comments etc.	*Robinson*	*R*	(Old ESC)
591	**CAROLVS.II D G. M B F & H REX** No stop after **REGNO** *(6 harp strings)*	*p. 144,16* *(i, ii, iii)*	*N*	1840
B.	Threepence		Spink 3385		
592	**CAROLVS.II. D. G. M. B. F. &. H. REX** No stop after **REGNO** *(4,5,6 harp strings)*	*p. 144,15* *(i, ii, iii)*	*N*	1958
B.	Halfgroat or two-pence. As type F		Spink 3387		
See F (588)	**CAROLVS.II. D. G. M. B. F. &. H. REX** No stop after **REGNO** *(7 harp strings)*	*p. 144,14*	*C*	2169
B.	Penny. As type F		Spink 3389		
See F (589)	**CAROLVS.II D. G. M. B. F &. H. REX** No stop after **REGNO** *(6 harp strings)*	*p. 144,13*	*C*	2273

MACHINE MADE MAUNDY

Type C
'Dated milled Maundy'
Second milled issue with value but no inner circles
GROAT, THREEPENCE, HALFGROAT & PENNY

SETS OF THE FOUR DENOMINATIONS
(Usually assembled by collectors and so numerated)

(R.B. 46)

Type	C.	New bust; laureate and draped facing, right, dividing legend
Leg.		**CAROLVS • II • DEI • GRATIA**
Rev.		Value indicated by the number of intertwined **C**s crowned
		The groat (only) has a rose, thistle, lis and harp in the angles
Leg		**16 ♔ 70 • MAG • BR • FRA • ET • HIB • REX**

Type   **C.**   Spink 3392

ESC	Date	Comm.	R	(Old ESC)	ESC	Date	Comm.	R	(Old ESC)
593	**1670**		*R*	2366	601	**1678**		*R²*	2374
594	**1671**		*S*	2367	602	**1679**		*R*	2375
595	**1672**	2 over 1²	*R*	2368	603	**1680**		*S*	2376
596	**1673**		*S*	2369	604	**1681**		*R²*	2377
597	**1674**		*S*	2370	605	**1682**		*R*	2378
598	**1675**		*R²*	2371	606	**1683**		*S*	2379
599	**1676**		*S*	2372	607	**1684**		*R*	2380
600	**1677**		*S*	2373					

The following denominations are listed and numbered to highlight varieties
Maundy coins are generally too small to illustrate many varieties clearly

MACHINE MADE MAUNDY

GROAT or FOURPENCE

Rev. Rose, thistle, lis and harp in the angles formed by the 4 interlinked **C**s
C.
Spink 3384

ESC	Date	Varieties, comments etc.	*Robinson*	R	(Old ESC)
608	**1670**		*p.147,21*	R^2	1841
609	**1671**		*p.147,25*	R	1842
610	**1672**	**2 over 1**	*p.147,29(i)*	S	1843
611	**1673**		*p.147,33*	S	1844
612	**1674**			S	1845
613	—	**4** of date over **4** on its side *(Not traced)*		R^5	1845A
614	—	**7 over 6**		R	1845B
615	—	**4 over 6**	*p.147,37(i)*	R	1845C
616	**1675**			R^4	1846
617	—	**5 over 4**		R^3	1846A
618	**1676**			S	1847
619	—	**7 over 6**	*p.147,45(i)*	S	1847A
620	—	**Second 6 over 5**	*p.147,45(ii)*	S	1847B
621	—	Large lettering and figures	*p.147,45(iii)*	S	1847C
622	—	Reads **CAROLVS:I.I**	*p.147,49(i)*	S	1847D
623	—	**A** partly over **R** in **CAROLVS**	*p.147,49(ii)*	S	1847E
624	**1677**			N	1848
625	**1678**	*(Not traced)*		N	1849
626	—	**8 over 7**	*p.147,53(i)*	S	1850
627	—	**8 over 6**	*p.147,53(ii)*	R	1850A
628	**1679**			C^2	1851
629	—	Fine lettering	*p.148,57(i)*	C^2	1851A
630	—	Heavy lettering	*p.148,57(ii)*	C^2	1851B
631	—	No stop after **CAROLVS** or **DEI**	*p.148,57(iii)*	C^2	1851C
632	**1680**		*p.148,61*	C	1852
633	**1681**			C	1853
634	—	**B** of **HIB** over **R**		R^3	1853A
635	—	**1 over 0**	*p.148,65(i)*	S	1854
636	**1682**			N	1855
637	—	**2 over 1**	*p.148,69(i)*	S	1856
638	—	**2 over 1.** No stop after **CAROLVS**	*p.148,69(ii)*	S	1856A
639	**1683**		*p.148,73*	C	1857

(continued)

90

MACHINE MADE MAUNDY

ESC	*Leg*	Varieties, comments etc.	*Robinson*	*R*	(Old ESC)
640	**1684**	*(Not traced)*		*R³*	1858
641	—	**4** over **3**	*p.148,77(i)*	*N*	1859

THREEPENCE

Normal 3d size flan

O over A   Struck on a 4d flan   6 over 5

C.   *Rev.* 3 interlinked **C**s (plain in angles)   Spink 3386

ESC	*Leg*	Varieties, comments etc.	*Robinson*	*R*	(Old ESC)
642	**1670**		*p.147,20*	*S*	1959
643	**1671**			*N*	1960
644	—	Error, **GRATIA** (Vs for As)	*p.147,24(i)*	*R*	1961A
645	—	Error, **GRV TIA** (inverted A)	*p.147,24(ii)*	*R*	1961
646	—	Error, **GRATIV** (inverted 2ⁿᵈ A)	*p.147,24(iii)*	*R*	1961B
647	**1672**	**2** over **1**	*p.147,28(i)*	*N*	1962
648	**1673**		*p.147,32*	*N*	1963
649	**1674**		*p.147,36*	*N*	1964
650	—	**7** over **4**		*N*	1964A
651	**1675**		*p.147,40*	*S*	1965
652	—	**5** over **4**		*S*	1965A
653	**1676**			*N*	1966
654	—	**6** over **5**	*p.147,44(i)*	*N*	1966A
655	—	Reads **ERA** instead of **FRA**	*p.147,44(ii)*	*S*	1967
656	—	Struck on a fourpence flan		*R⁹*	1967A
657	**1677**		*p.147,48*	*S*	1968
658	**1678**	Small letters on obverse			1969
659	—	Large letters on obverse	*p.147,52(i)*		1969A

(continued)

MACHINE MADE MAUNDY

660	1679			C	1970
661	—	O of CAROLVS over A	p.148,56(i)	R	1971
662	—	Broken die	p.148,56(ii)	R	1971A
663	1680			N	1972
664	—	Double cut 6 in date	p.148,60(i)		1972A
665	—	Very badly cracked die	p.148,60(ii)		1972B
666	1681			N	1973
667	—	1 over 0	p.148,64(i)	R^3	1974
668	1682			N	1975
669	—	2 over 1	p.148,68(i)	R^3	1976
670	1683			N	1977
671	—	Large 3 in date	p.148,72(i)	N	1977A
672	—	Large flan of 4d diameter	p.148,72(ii)	R	1977B
673	1684	*(Not traced)*		R^3	1978
674	—	4 over 3	p.148,76(i)	S	1979

HALFGROATS or TWOPENCES

1679 both types at double magnification

Large size flan   Normal size flan

Rev. As before but with 2 interlinked Cs

Type **G.**   Spink 3388

ESC	Date	Varieties, comments etc.	*Robinson*	R	(Old ESC)
675	1668	*Probably a Pattern, en medaille* ↑↑	p.147,17	S	2170
676	1670		p.147,19	N	2171
677	1671		p.147,23	N	2172
678	1672	2 over 1	p.147,27(i)	N	2173
679	—	With a clear cut date	p.147,27(ii)	R^4	2173 A
680	1673		p.147,31	S	2174

(continued)

MACHINE MADE MAUNDY

ESC	Date	Varieties, comments etc.	Robinson	R	(Old ESC)
681	**1674**		*p.147,35*	*N*	2175
682	—	**7** over **4**		*N*	2175A
683	**1675**		*p.147,39*	*S*	2176
684	**1676**		*p.147,43*	*N*	2177
685	**1677**			*S*	2178
686	—	Reads **CAROLVS II.**	*p.147,47(i)*	*S*	2178A
687	**1678**	*(Not traced)*		*R³*	2179
688	—	**8** over **6** and **CAROLVS II.**	*p.147,51(i)*	*N*	2180
689	—	**8** over **6** and **CAROLVS. II.**	*p.147,51(ii)*	*N*	2180A
690	**1679**			*C*	2181
691	—	Blundered **HIB**	*p.147,55(i)*	*R*	2181A
692	—	Error **HIB** over **FRA**	*p.147,55(ii)*	*R*	2181B
693	—	Blundered **DEI**	*p.148,55(iii)*	*R*	2181C
694	—	On large flan *(2 known)*	*p.148,55(iv)*	*R*	2181D
695	**1680**	*(Not traced)*		*R³*	2182
696	—	**80** over **79**	*p.148,59(i)*	*N*	2183
697	**1681**		*p.148,63*	*N*	2184
698	**1682**	*(Not traced)*		*R³*	2185
699	—	**2** over **1**	*p.148,67(i)*	*R²*	2186
700	—	**2** over **1** and error **ERA** for **FRA**	*p.148,67(ii)*	*R²*	2187
701	**1683**	*(Not traced)*		*R³*	2188
702	—	**3** over **1**	*p.148,71(i)*	*R³*	2189A
703	—	**3** over **2**	*p.148,71(ii)*	*N*	2189
704	**1684**	*(Not traced)*		*S*	2190
705	—	No stop after **CAROLVS** or **DEI**	*p.148,75(i)*	*S*	2190A

PENNY

Rev.   Single crowned letter **C**

ɔRATIA

MACHINE MADE MAUNDY

Type	**G.**				Spink 3390
ESC	Date	Varieties, comments etc.	*Robinson*	*R*	(Old ESC)
706	**1670**			*S*	2274
707	—	With a blundered date **0** like **9**	*p.147,18(i)*	*S*	2274A
708	**1671**		*p.147,22*	*S*	2275
709	**1672**	2 over 1	*p.147,26(i)*	*S*	2276
710	**1673**		*p.147,30*	*S*	2277
711	**1674**	*(Not traced)*		R^3	2278
712	—	Error; inverted **G** in Ɔ **RACIA**	*p.147,34(i)*	*S*	2279
713	—	Error; inverted **G** in Ɔ **RATIA**	*p.147,34(ii)*	*S*	2279A
714	**1675**		*p.147,38*	R^2	2280
715	—	Error **ERA** for **FRA**		R^2	2280A
716	—	Error; inverted **G** in Ɔ **RATIA**		R^3	2280B
717	**1676**			*R*	2281
718	—	Error; inverted **G** in Ɔ **RATIA**	*p.147,42(i)*	R^3	2281A
719	**1677**			*S*	2282
720	—	Error; inverted **G** in Ɔ **RATIA**	*p.147,46(i)*	*R*	2283
721	—	Reads **GRATIA.RE.X**	*p.147,46(ii)*	*R*	2283A
722	**1678**	*(Not traced)*		*R*	2284
723	—	Error; inverted **G** in Ɔ **RATIA**	*p.147,50(i)*	*R*	2285
724	**1679**			*R*	2286
725	—	No stop after **DEI** or **CAROLVS**	*p.147,54(i)*	*R*	2286A
726	**1680**			*S*	2287
727	—	On a 2d size flan, thinner [1] *(5-10 known)*	*p.148,58(i)*	R^5	2287A
728	**1681**		*p.148,62*	R^3	2288
729	**1682**			R^2	2289
730	—	2 over 1	*p.148,66(i)*	R^2	2290
731	—	Large lettering on obverse	*p.148,66(ii)*	R^2	2289B
732	—	Error **ERA** for **FRA**	*p.148,66(iii)*	R^2	2289A
733	**1683**			*S*	2291
734	—	No stop after **CAROLVS**	*p.148,70(i)*	*S*	2291
735	—	3 over 2	*p.148,70(ii)*	*R*	2291A
736	**1684**			*R*	2292
737	—	4 over 3	*p.148,74(i)*	R^3	2292A
738	—	No stop after **CAROLVS**	*p.148,74(ii)*	R^3	2292A

JAMES II, 1685-88
CROWNS

There is little to be said about this reign, as the coinage continued with but few changes. The dies were again engraved by Roettier and the only variety is two slightly differing busts on the crown and halfcrown. The only difference in the larger denominations is that the interlinked Cs for Carolus in the angles of the shields on the reverses are omitted. On smaller coins, 4d to 1d, the former *'linked Cs'* design on Charles II is replaced by one to four Roman Is: this serves both as an indication of denomination, and also, by a useful coincidence, the initial letter of the King's Latin name.

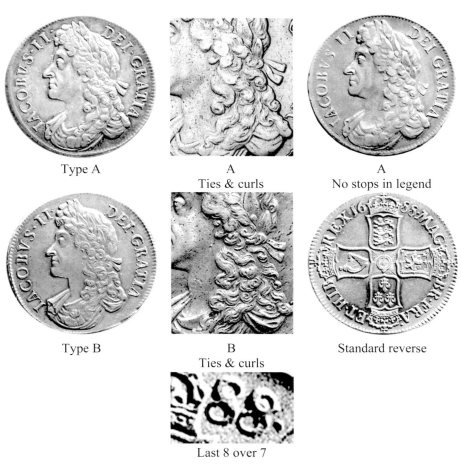

Type A	A Ties & curls	A No stops in legend
Type B	B Ties & curls	Standard reverse
	Last 8 over 7	

JAMES II, 1685-88
CROWNS

Type **A.** First bust[1]
Obv. Laureate and draped, left
Short lock of hair below ear curves towards the chin
Leg. **IACOBVS • II • DEI • GRATIA**
James second by the Grace of God

B. Second bust[2], similar but narrower than last, neater looking
arrangement of the curls, short lock curls towards back of head

Rev. Crowned cruciform shields to outer beading, clockwise;
England, Scotland, France and Ireland
Star of the Garter in the centre and plain in the angles
Leg. **16 ♛ 86 •MAG• ♛ BR•FRA• ♛ ET•HIB ♛ REX•**
Punc. The pellet stops may be high or low and usually not after **HIB**
Edge **DECVS ET TVTAMEN ANNO REGNI SECVNDO**

	A.	First bust		Spink 3406	
ESC	Date	Edge year	Varieties	R	(Old ESC)
740	**1686**	**SECVNDO** (2)	*(5,6 strings)*	R^2	76

	A.	First bust, without any stops in legend		Spink 3406	
741	**1686**	**SECVNDO** (2)	*(6,8 strings)*	S	77
742	—	—	Unbarred **H** in **HIB** *(6,8 strings)*	R^3	77A

	B.	Second bust		Spink 3407	
743	**1687**	**TERTIO** (3)	*(5,6,7 strings)*	C^2	78
744	—	—	Edge: **E** over **R** in **ET** *(6 strings)*	R	79
745	—	—	Edge lettering smaller *(7 strings)*	R	79A
746	**1688**	**QVARTO** (4)	See note [3] *(6,7,8 strings)*	C	80
747	—	—	Last **8** over **7** [2] *(7 strings)*	N	81

Notes

1 This type is rarer than stated in first class condition

2 Second bust crowns are often found with the hair above the forehead not properly struck up

3 Unbarred 'A' occurring in the legends of some coins, particularly 1688 are almost certainly
due to die-filling and are therefore ignored

HALFCROWNS

Obverse A	Standard reverse	Obverse B

Ties down		Ties up

Last 6 over 5	7 over 6	6 over 8

V over B die flaw	V over S	A over R

Type   **A.**   First bust, similar to the crown, but ties curve downwards

         B.   Second bust, similar to the crown but with different hair arrangement, ties curve upwards

HALFCROWNS

A.   First bust, with ties downwards
Rev. 1 - No stop after **HIB**   Spink 3408

ESC	Date	Edge year		Varieties		R	(Old ESC)
748	**1685**	**PRIMO**	(1)		*(6,7 strings)*	*N*	493
749	**1686**	**SECVNDO**	(2)		*(6,7 strings)*	*N*	494
750	—	—	—	**6** over **5**	*(6,7 strings)*	*R³*	495
751	—	**TERTIO**	(3)		*(6,7 strings)*	*R*	496
752	—	—	—	**V** over **S** in **IACOBVS**	*(6,7 strings)*	*R³*	496A
753	**1687**	—	—		*(6,7,8 strings)*	*N*	498
754	—	—	—	**7** of date over **6**	*(7 strings)*	*R*	499
755	—	—	—	**6** of date over **8**	*(6 strings)*	*R⁴*	499A

B.   Second bust, with ties upwards
Rev. 1 - No stop after **HIB**   Spink 3409

756	**1687**	**TERTIO**	(3)		*(6-8 strings)*	*R²*	500
757	—	—	—	1ˢᵗ **A** over **R** in **GRATIA**	*(6 strings)*	*R²*	500A?
758	—	—	—	*Proof*	*(Not traced)*	*R⁶*	501
759	**1688**	**QVARTO**	(4)		*(6,7,8 strings)*	*S*	502

Note; ESC 498 V/B in IACOBVS is considered a die flaw and de-listed.
The other specimens; V/S & A/R are retained although also possible die flaws

ALL James half-crowns are scarce in first class condition and are prone
to weak striking especially around the date and lower drapery

SHILLINGS

One bust similar to crown with two reverses; A & B

Reverse A with   No stops   Standard obverse   Reverse B with
Garter star   Plume in centre

Large Garter star rays in centre   Smaller Garter star rays in centre
Heavy-looking shield devices   Finer looking shield devices

7 over 6   6 over 5   8 over 7

E over T & T over?   V over S   G over A

SHILLINGS

A/1. **Garter star** in the centre of *reverse* Spink 3410
Leg. punc. – **MAG˙ BR•FRA˙ ET•HIB REX•**

ESC	Date	Varieties	R	(Old ESC)
760	**1685**	*(4,5,6 strings)*	S	1068
761	—	Larger Garter Star at centre of reverse	R^2	1068A

A/1. **Garter star** in the centre of *reverse* Spink 3410
Leg. punc. – **MAG BR FRA ET HIB REX**

762	**1685**	Note; no stops on *rev.* and shield devices smaller *(5 strings)*	R^3	1069

B/2. **Plume** in the centre of *reverse* Spink 3411
Leg. punc. – **MAG˙ BR•FRA˙ ET•HIB REX•**

763	1685	*(4 known)*	R^6	1069A

A/1. **Garter star** in the centre of *reverse* Spink 3410
Leg. punc. – **MAG˙ BR•FRA˙ ET•HIB REX•**

764	1686	E over T in ET	R^2	1070C

A/1. **Garter star** in the centre of *reverse* Spink 3410
Leg. punc. – **MAG BR•FRA˙ ET•HIB REX•**

765	1686	*(6,8 strings)*	S	1070
766	—	V over S in **IACOBVS**	R^2	1070A
767	—	6 over 5	R^2	1070B

A/1. **Garter star** in the centre of *reverse* Spink 3410
Leg. punc. – **MAG˙ BR•FRA˙ ET•HIB REX•**

768	1687	*(4 strings)*	R^2	1071
769	—	7 over 6 *(4,6,7 strings)*	S	1072
770	—	7 over 6 and G over A in **MAG** B over V in **IACOBVS** *(7 strings)*	R	1072A
771	1688		R	1073
772	—	Second 8 over 7	R^2	1074

Note
The subtle variations in the Garter Star and devices on the shields are ignored to avoid complications

First class examples are scarcer than the rarity indicated

SIXPENCES

Reverse A	Early	**SHIELDS**	Late	Reverse B

Early shields	late over early	Late shields

7 over 6	6 over 6	8 over 6	B over R

Type **A.** Similar to crown, *rev.* with early shields; indented tops

B. Similar, but *rev.* with late shields; pointed tops,

A. Early shields / *Rev.* No stop after **HIB** Spink 3412

ESC	Date	Varieties		R	(Old ESC)
773	**1686**		*(4,5 strings)*	S	1525
774	—	1ˢᵗ **6** over lower **6** & **8** over **6**?	*(4 strings)*	R	1525A
775	**1687**		*(5?strings)*	R	1526
776	—	**7** over **6**		R	1526A

B. Late shields / *Rev.* No stop after **HIB** Spink 3413

777	**1687**		*(4 strings)*	S	1526B
778	—	Late shields, altered from early		R²	1526C
779	—	**7** over **6**	*(Not traced)*	R	1527
780	**1688**	Late shields, altered from early **B** over **R** in **BR**	*(4 strings)*	R²	1528

"Sixpences of Charles II, James II and William and Mary are not uncommon in average condition In EF or better grades they are much rarer than indicated" (P.A. Rayner)

MAUNDY SETS

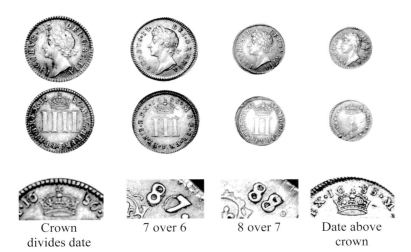

| Crown divides date | 7 over 6 | 8 over 7 | Date above crown |

Type	A.	Only the one type
Obv.		Laureate bust, left, dividing the legend
Leg.		**IACOBVS · II · DEI · GRATIA**
Rev.		Crowned value in Roman numerals.
		It is thought the numeral **I** is the initial letter for **IACOBVS**
Date		Usually divided by crown above the value, except on the
		threepence where it is normally above the crown

A.   Spink 3418

ESC	Date	Varieties	R	(Old ESC)
781	**1686**		*N*	2381
782	**1687**	4d always **7 over 6**	*N*	2382
783	**1688**		*S*	2383

MAUNDY

GROAT – IIII

A.   Spink 3414

ESC	Date	Varieties, comments etc.		Robinson	R	(Old ESC)
784	**1686**				S	1860
785	—	Date above crown	*(Not traced)*	*p. 150,83(i)*	R	1861
786	**1687**	7 over **6** *(on all coins)*		*p. 150,87(i)*	N	1862
787	**1688**				S	1863
788	—	With a threepence obverse die			R^5	1863A
789	—	No stop after **FRA**		*p. 150,91(ii)*	R^3	1863B
790	—	**1** over **8**			R^3	1863C
791	—	**8** over **7**		*p. 150,91(i)*	S	1864

THREEPENCE – III

A.   Spink 3415

ESC	Date	Varieties, comments etc.		Robinson	R	(Old ESC)
792	**1685**				S	1980
793	—	On flan for the groat [1]	*(5-10 known)*	*p. 150,79(i)*	R^5	1980A
794	—	Reversing sideways		*p. 150,79(ii)*	R	1980B
795	**1686**	*(Die flaw on some specimens)*		*p. 150,82(ii)*	S	1981
796	—	**IACoBVS** with a small **o**		*p. 150,82(i)*		1981A
797	—	Mule with groat obverse			R^4	1981B
798	**1687**				S	1982
799	—	**7** over **6**		*p. 150,86(i)*	S	1983
800	—	**7** over **6** on a 2.4 cm diameter flan		*p. 150,86(ii)*	S	1983A
801	**1688**				S	1984
802	—	**8** over **7**		*p. 150,90 (i)*	S	1985

MAUNDY

TWOPENCE or HALFGROAT – II

A.   Spink 3416

ESC	Date	Varieties, comments etc.	*Robinson*	R	(Old ESC)
803	**1686**			*N*	2191
804	—	**IACoBVS** with a small **o**	*p. 150,81(i)*		2191A
805	—	**IACoBVS** with a small **o** and inverted **V** for A	*p. 150,81(ii)*	*R*	2192
806	**1687**			*N*	2193
807	—	Last **7** over **8**		R^2	2193A
808	—	**ERA** for FRA	*p. 150,85(i)*	R^2	2193B
809	**1688**	Last **8** over **7**	*p. 150,89(i)*	*S*	2195

PENNY – I

A.   Spink 3417

ESC	Date	Varieties, comments etc.	*Robinson*	R	(Old ESC)
810	**1685**		*p. 150,78*	*S*	2293
811	**1686**		*p. 150,80*	*N*	2294
812	—	**E** over **I** in **REX**		R^3	2294A
813	**1687**			*S*	2295
814	—	**7** over **8**	*p. 150,84(i)*	R^2	2295A
815	—	**7** over **6**	*p. 150,84(ii)*	R^2	2295B
816	**1688**	Last **8** over **7**	*p. 150,88(i)*	*S*	2297

(See B. Robinson; *Story of Maundy Money*, p. 150)
"Groats are not scarce in fair or fine condition" (P.A. Rayner)
"Threepences are only scarce in very fine condition or better" (P.A. Rayner)

See Charles II for introduction to Maundy money, notes 1 & 2

WILLIAM & MARY
1688-94

Many engravers had a hand in the production of the various coinges for this interesting reign and it is a matter of no little difficulty to attribute certain coins to any particular artist, as some records, especially those appertaining to dies, are no longer in existance.

In 1688-9 John Roettier, still Chief engraver, became ill with some kind of muscular disease which affected him in both hands, thus causing him to delegate most of his work to his two sons, James and Norbert, who were appointed engravers about this time. Henry Harris, who had served at the Mint in a junior capacity during the reign of Charles II, was appointed as one of the chief engravers in August 1689, but his work seems to have been concerned chiefly with medals and seals, the Roettier brothers having carried out most of the engraving of coin dies under their father's direction. Norbert Roettier was reported to have stated that he engraved the Coronation Medal (which is usually attributed to John Roettier) 'with his assistance', and indeed this may be so, as the elder Roettier was disabled at that time. Belonging to this year also were the first and second issue halfcrowns and the fact that their high relief busts are so very like those on the Coronation Medal leads one to suppose that these also were the work of Norbert Roettier. The reverse design of the first and second issue halfcrowns of 1689-90 was a crowned square-topped shield. The third issue halfcrowns with the other silver were more likely to have been the work of James Roettier who always appears to have preferred working in lower relief than his brother. The reverse design of these coins consisted of four crowned shields in the form of a cross with the monogram WM interlinked in each angle. The sixpence however seems to have some similarity to the early halfcrown punches, but exact attribution is not possible. The reverse of the small silver, from the fourpenc down to the penny, now shows a crowned modern numeral, a design which continues unchanged on the Maundy coins until the present day. (P.A. Rayner, 1949)

WILLIAM & MARY, 1688-94
CROWNS

As are inverted Vs
stop after GRATIA

No stop after GRATIA   Lion with billets   1691

I over E

1692   2 over inverted 2   1692 over inverted 2

Obv.	Conjoined busts, right, laureate and draped (Only the one bust)
Leg.	**GVLIELMVS • ET • MARIA • DEI • GRATIA**
	William and Mary by the Grace of God
Rev.	Crowned cruciform shields quartering the legend, with rampant lion of Nassau in the centre, **W/M** monogram in the angles
Leg.	♛ **MAG•BR** ♛ **FR•ET•HI•** ♛ **REX•ET•** ♛ **REGINA•**
	King and Queen of Great Britain France and Ireland
Date	Separate numeral below each monogram arranged in two lines left to right around the central Lion of Nassau, surrounded by varying numbers of billets (lozenges)
Edge	Regnal year in Roman words
Leg. & edge	As before

Note; number of harp strings and billets abbreviated to *(s-b)*

106

CROWNS

No stop after **BR**   Spink 3433

ESC	Date	Edge year	Varieties, comments etc *(strings-billets)*	R	(Old ESC)
820	**1691**	**TERTIO** (3)	*(8s-10b; 8s-8b; 6s-13b)*	*N*	82
821	—	—	Re-entered **G** *(8 billets)* **I** over **E** in **GVLIELMVS** [1]	*N*	82B
822	**1692**	**QVARTO** (4)	*(8s-9b)*	*N*	83
823	—	—	**2** over inverted **2** *(10s-9b, 6s-9b; 9s-9b)*	*R³*	84
824	—	**QVINTO** (5)	**2** over inverted **2** and a stop after **GRATIA·** *(9s-9b)*	*S*	85
825	—	—	**2** over inverted **2** and **G** over **R** in **REGNI** [3]	*R*	85A

Note; 1692 QVINTO without the 2 over inverted 2 believed not to exist *(Not traced)*

1   Similar error on William III half-crown, dated 1696
2   This error is unlikely to be the result of collar slippage so allocated its own number

3   Uncertain if this error is on all 1692 QVINTO.

WILLIAM & MARY, 1685-94
HALFCROWNS

OBVERSES

First bust

No stops in legend

Second bust

REVERSES

First

Second

Third

First shield

Second shield

HALFCROWNS

VARIETIES OF THE CROWN ABOVE SHIELD
(Often indistinct due to weak striking or wear)

Caul   Leather cap inside the crown, visible below arches
Band   Lower part of the crown with or without pearls
Interior   Oval area showing inside the band

Frosted Caul & interior

With pearls   No pearls

Frosted Caul Plain interior

With pearls   No pearls

Plain Caul Plain interior

With pearls   No pearls

(Size of the 3 lions varies from large to small but ignored to avoid complications)

THREE VARIATIONS OF 1689
Frosted caul, plain interior, with pearls

Regular caul   Defined top of caul   No stop after date

HALFCROWNS

2nd L over M

1st V over A or Λ

2nd V over S

GRETIA

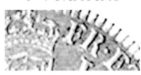

FR over A

FRA

No stop after date

Normal stop after date

Stop after GRATIA˙

No stop after BR

No stop after ET

Stop after HI before REX

In two lines L-R

2nd L over lower L
Date in two lines
with 1692 exception

Date clockwise

Inverted 3

3 over inverted 3

3 correct

110

HALFCROWNS

Type	**A/1.**	**First bust** with **first shield**
Obv.		Conjoined draped busts right; William's laureate bust over Mary's, V-shape ties at the back of hair
Leg.		**GVLIELMVS • ET · MARIA • DEI · GRATIA**
		William and Mary by the Grace of God
Rev.		Crowned square-topped shield with quarterly arms clockwise; England, Scotland, France and Ireland
		The rampant Lion of Nassau superimposed in the centre, surrounded by varying numbers of billets (lozenges)
Leg.		**16 ♔ 89•MAG•BR•FR•ET•HIB•REX•ET•REGINA•**
		King and Queen of Great Britain France and Ireland
Edge		**DECVS·ET·TVTAMEN·ANNO·REGNI·PRIMO**

Type	**A/2.**	**First bust** with **second shield**
Obv.		As before
Rev.		Crowned square-topped shield with arms of England & France quartered in 1st & 4th, Scotland in 2nd and Ireland in 3rd quarters
		Lion of Nassau superimposed in the centre, surrounded by varying numbers of billets (lozenges)
Leg.		As before
Edge		As before with regnal years; **PRIMO, SECVNDO & TERTIO**

Type	**B/3.**	**Second bust** with **third shield**
Obv.		Similar conjoined busts right as before but finer style and portraits in lower relief
Rev.		Third reverse similar to the crown; crowned cruciform shields quartering the legend, with the rampant lion of Nassau in centre
		W/M monogram in the angles. Arms clockwise; England, Scotland, France and Ireland
		Date **16 91** in two lines, surrounding the shield of Nassau, the Lion surrounded by varying numbers of billets (lozenges)
Leg. & edge		As before

Note; number of harp strings and billets abbreviated to *(s,b)*

HALFCROWNS

A/1.   First busts, with first shields   Spink 3434

ESC	Date	Edge year	Varieties, comments etc *(strings-billets)*	R	(Old ESC)
826	**1689**	**PRIMO** (1st)	Caul & interior frosted, with pearls *(9s-7b;9s-6b;8s-?b;7s-7b; 7s-6b)*	C^2	503
827	—	—	Caul & interior frosted, with pearls 2nd **L** over **M** in **GVLIELMVS** *(7&8s-6b)*	R	503A
828	—	—	Caul & interior frosted, with pearls *(7s-8b)* 1st **V** over **A** or **Λ** in **GVLIELMVS**	R	503B
829	—	—	Caul & interior frosted, with pearls Reads **FRA** *(8s-6b;7s-6b)*	R^2	507B
830	—	—	Caul & interior frosted (no pearls)*(9s-7b)*	S	504
831	—	—	Caul only frosted, with pearls*(6s.7b;7s.6b)*	C^2	505
832	—	—	Caul only frosted, with pearls Inverted **N** in **REGINA**	S	505A
833	—	—	Caul only frosted, with pearls *(7s-8b)* 1st **V** over **A** or **Λ** in **GVLIELMVS**	R	505B
834	—	—	Caul only frosted (no pearls)*(9s-6b;6s-5b)*	N	506
835	—	—	No frosting, with pearls *(7s-6b;8s-6b)*	N	507
836	—	—	No frosting, with pearls No stops on obverse *(7s-3b)*	R	507A

A/2.   First busts, with second shields   Spink 3435

837	**1689**	**PRIMO** (1st)	Caul & interior frosted, with pearls *(6s-8b)*	N	508
838	—	—	Caul & interior frosted, no pearls *(7s-8b)*	N	509
839	—	—	Caul only frosted, with pearls *(6-8b;7s7b;8s-7b;8s-8b)*	N	510
840	—	—	Caul only frosted, with pearls Inverted **N** in **REGINA**	R^2	510A
841	—	—	Caul only frosted, with pearls No stop after date *(8s-?b)*		
842	—	—	Caul only frosted, with pearls Well defined top to the caul with stop after date *(6s-?b)*		
843	—	—	Caul only frosted, no pearls *(7s-8b)*	R	510B
844	—	—	Interior only frosted, no pearls *(Not traced)*	R	510A
845	—	—	No frosting, with pearls*(8s-8b;7s-7b;6s-8b)*	N	511
846	—	—	No frosting, no pearls *(7s-8b)*	N	512

(continued)

HALFCROWNS

A/2. First busts, with second shields   Spink 3435

847	1690	SECVNDO (2nd)	No frosting, no pearls 2nd **L/L** in **GVLIELMVS** No stop after date *(5s-8b)*	R	513
848	—	—	Caul & interior frosted, with pearls Error; **GRETIA** No stop after date 2nd **V/S** in **GVLIELMVS** *(5s-8b)*	R³	514
849	—	TERTIO (3rd)	No frosting & no pearls 2nd **L/L** in **GVLIELMVS** *(6s-5b)*	R²	515

B/3. Second busts, with third shields   Spink 3436

850	1691	TERTIO	Date in two lines, edge normal *(6s-8b)*	N	516
851	1691	— (3)	Date in two lines. Edge error; First part of edge inscription right way up as opposed to second half	R⁵	516A
852	—	—	No stop after **BR** Note; full orbit in the crown *(6s-12b)*		516B
853	1692	QVARTO (4)	Date reads clockwise *(6s-8b)*	N	517
854	—	—	**R/G** in **REGINA** & **H/R** in **HI** Unbarred As in **MARIA** *(5s-8b)*	R³	517A
855	—	QVINTO (5)	*(6s-8b)*	R⁴	518
856	1693	—	**3** of date upside down Reads clockwise **1636** *(5s-11b)*	R²	520
857	—	—	**3** over **3** upside down *(5s-12b;5s-11b)*	N	521
858	—	—	**3** over **3** upside down, last A in **MARIA** overlaps Mary's forehead hair, no stop after **GRATIA**	R	521A
859	—	—	**3** over **3** upside down and **F** over **E** in **FR²**	R	521B
860	—	—	**3** of date correct *(6s-14b)* With a stop after **GRATIA˙** Stop after **HI** moved to before **˙REX**	C	519A
861	—	—	**3** of date correct *(5s-16b)* Stop after **GRATIA˙** No stop between **ET REX**	C	519
862	—	QINRTO (5)	Error **QINRTO** letters **FR** over **A** No stop after **GRATIA** *(5s-16b)*	R⁹	519A?

WILLIAM & MARY, 1685-94
HALFCROWNS

Notes

1   One common error die sinkers made was the selection of a wrong letter punch, usually by missing out a letter or putting it in upside down. Usually the sinker quickly realised and immediately corrected it by simply over-striking with the correct letter or letters. Spelling errors often went un-noticed until production was well under way. Most easily seen overstrikes are recorded, but a few less obvious ones remain to be discovered.

2   F/8 according to David Seaman

Old ESC records a number of so-called inverted letters; F in place of E, but since this is not possible, and is almost certainly the result of filled dies, they are deleted. The following are also considered too insignificant to warrant separate ESC numbers; harp strings, billets surrounding the Lion of Nassau, variable sizes of lions, lis and stars or crosses in the edge

The fleur de lis vary in size, e.g. 1691-2 large and 1693 smaller

See *Variations on a theme – ESC 510,* an article by Malcolm Lewendon, published in S.N.C. Vol. CXVI, № 6, December 2008, p. 300. Quote; *"The William & Mary series of halfcrowns is short in date lengthwise, but of great interest to variety collectors"* (Unfortunately many of which are beyond the remit of this publication. (M.B.)

SHILLINGS
Only one type
As the crown but with oblique milling on the edge

A
No stop after GRATIA

B
GRATIA with stop

Irregular size lettering

Normal 9

RE over ET

9 over 0?

Flawed F

A.	No stop after **GRATIA**			Spink 3437	
ESC	Date	Edge	Varieties, comments etc	R	(Old ESC)
863	**1692**	Milled	Irregular size reverse lettering *(7 strings)*	S	1075
864	—	—	Inverted **1** in date	R	1075A
865	—	—	No stop after **BR**, flawed **F** in **FR** and **RE** over **ET** in **REX** *(6s-12b;7s-12b)*	R	1075B
866	—	—	**AT** over **TI** in **GRATIA**	R	1075C
867	**1693**	—	No stop after **BR** *(5s-8b)*		

B.	With a stop after **GRATIA•**			Spink 3437	
868	**1693**	—	No stop after **REGINA** *(6s-10b;6s-11b)*	R^4	1076

115

SIXPENCES

As the shilling
Only one type

Inverted 3

4/?

Spink 3438

ESC	Date	Edge	Varieties, comments etc	R	(Old ESC)
869	**1693**	Milled	*(3s-10b;4s-9b;4s-10b)*	N	1529
870	—	—	**3** of date upside down	R^3	1530
871	**1694**	—	*(4 strings-10? billets)*	R^2	1531

Note
The figures 9 & 6 in the date often look more like 0
*"The average condition of shillings of this reign is poor and really first class examples are scarcer than the rarity indicated. Sixpences are not uncommon in average condition.
In EF or better grades they are rarer than indicated here"* (P.A. Rayner)

MAUNDY SETS

Type A.   Large lettering, **ET** central above busts / Date above crown

Type B.   Medium size lettering, **ET** offset left above King's head
Date above crown

Type C.   Small lettering, wide space in legend above busts
Date divided by crown

MAUNDY MONEY

Spink 3446

ESC	Date	Type	Varieties, comments etc	R	(Old ESC)
872	**1689**	A		R^3	2384
873	**1691**	B		R	2385
874	**1692**	C		R	2386
875	**1693**	B		R^2	2387
876	**1694**	C		R	2388

True sets are very much rarer than indicated, made up ones are usually obvious

The following denominations are listed separately to highlight varieties [1]

GROATS

No stop before & after G

A
No tie to wreath
Large lettering

Small crown

1 over 0

Stop before • G

6 over 5

GV below bust

B
With ties to wreath
Small lettering

Wide crown

2 over 1

Flaw over I in MARIA

3 over 2

118

MAUNDY MONEY

GROATS

Type	**A.**	**First busts**; crude style usually without ties to the wreath	
Obv.		Conjoined busts, right. King laureate (only)	
		Legend continuous above heads in large lettering with variable stops and alignment with busts.	
		No uniformity with denominations	
Leg.		**GVLIELMVS · ET · MARIA · D · G**	
Rev.	1	Date above small crown above numeral **4** within legend	
Leg.		**· MAG·BR·FR·ET·HIB·REX·ET·REGINA·**	

	B.	**First busts** variety. Similar to '**A**' but, medium lettering not continuous above heads; space between **ET · MARIA ·**

	C.	**Second busts**; neater style, ties to the wreath and small lettering
Obv.		Taller conjoined busts, right. King laureate with two long ties Queen's hair nearer to outer beading dividing legend
Leg.		**GVLIELMVS · ET · MARIA · D · G ·**
Rev.		Date divided by a wider and flatter crown above numerals

A.   First busts, no ties, large lettering / *Rev.* 1   Spink 3439

ESC	Date	Below bust	Varieties, comments etc.	*Robinson* [1]	R	(Old ESC)
877	**1689**	**GV**	Threepence *obv.* die used in error. Stop after **G •** (only)		C	1865
878	—	**G**	Stop before **• G** (only)		C	1866
879	—	**G**	Stop before **• G** and after **G•**		R	1867
880	—	**G**	No stops before or after **G**s		R	1867
881	—	**G**	with berries in wreath		R	1868
882	—		Error **GVLEELMVS (I/E)**		R[3]	1868A
883	**1690**		No stop after date	*p. 151,98(i)*	N	1869
884	—		No stops after **D** and date	*p. 151,98(ii)*	N	1869
885	—		**6 over 5**, no stop after **D·G**		R	1869A

B.   First busts variety, no ties, medium lettering
     Reversed Z-type 1[s] in date   Spink 3439

886	**1691**	**G**	Stop after **G •**	*p. 151,102(i)*	R	1870
887	—-		**1 over 0**	*p. 151,102(ii)*	S	1871
888	**1694**		Small lettering both sides	*p.152,114(i)*	R	1878A

MAUNDY MONEY

GROATS

C. Second busts with ties, small lettering both sides
Rev. 1 - Date above crown   Spink 3440

ESC	Date	Below bust	Varieties, comments etc.	*Robinson*[1]	R	(Old ESC)
889	**1692**	GV	Stop after **G •**		*S*	1872
890	—	G	Stop after **G •** **2** over **1** *(The so-called stop in MAR•IA is a flaw)*		*R⁴*	1873
891	—		Small lettering on obverse & large lettering on reverse, with all stops Inverted **V** in **MARIA**	*p.152,106(iii)*	*S*	1874
892	—		Small lettering on obverse & reverse,	*p. 151,106(i)*		
893	—		Small lettering on obverse & reverse, no stop after date & **2** over **1**	*p. 152,106(ii)*		
894	—		Large lettering on obverse & reverse, with all stops	*p. 152,106(iv)*		

C. Second busts with ties, large lettering both sides
Rev. 1 - Date above crown   Spink 3440

895	**1691**			*p.151,102(iii)*		
896	**1692**			*p.151,102(iii)*	*R*	1875

C. Second busts with ties in wreath
Rev. 1. – Date above crown   Spink 3440

897	**1693**				*R²*	1876
898	—	GV	**3** over **2** stop after **G •**	*p.152,110(i)*	*R*	1877
899	**1694**			*p.152,114(ii)*	*R²*	1878
900	—		Smaller lettering both sides		*R²*	1878A
901	**1694**		Inverted **V** in **MARIA**		*R²*	1879

THREEPENCES

A
No ties to wreath Large lettering

GVL below bust

Stop before
Roman I

No stop before
Arabic 1

Date above crown

LMV over MVS

Type B
Large ties to wreath
Small lettering

GVL below bust

G below bust

Crown divides date

Type	**A.**	**First busts;** similar to groat crude style and virtually no tie
		Legend continuous above heads in large lettering
Rev.		Small crown above numeral **3** within legend
	B.	**Second bust;** similar to groat finer style and with ties
		Legend divided by the taller heads in smaller lettering
Rev.		Larger crown above numeral **3** within legend, small lettering

MAUNDY MONEY

THREEPENCES

A. First busts, no ties, large lettering / *Rev.* 1   Spink 3441

ESC	Date	Below bust	Varieties, comments etc.	*Robinson*	R	(Old ESC)
902	**1689**	GVL	Roman **I** in date Stop after **G** •			1986
903	—	GVL	Stops before and after **G**s • and before but not after date	*p. 151,95(i)*		1986
904	—	GV	Stops only after **G** • and before but not after date	*p. 151,95(ii)*		1986
905	—	GVL	Stops only after **G** • and before but not after date	*p. 151,95(iii)*		1986
906	—	GV	Stops only after **G** • and only after date	*p. 151,95(iv)*		1986
907	—	GVL	No stops before and after **G**s but a stop before date	*p. 151,95(v)*		1986
898	—	GVL	No stops before and after **G**s but a stop before date and with berries in hair	*p. 151,95(vi)*		1986
909	—	GVL	No stops before and after **G**s but stops before and after date without berries in hair	*p. 151,95(vii)*		1986
910	—	GVL	No stops before and after **G**s but stops only after date without berries in hair	*p. 151,95(viii)*		1986
911	—	GVL	No stops before and after **G**s but stops only after date with berries in hair	*p. 151,95(ix)*		1986
912	—	G		*p. 151,95(x)*		1986
913	—	G	Stop before **G**	*p. 151,95(xii)*		1986
914	—	G	with berries in wreath	*p. 151,95(xiii)*		1986
915	—	GV		*p. 151,95(xi)*		1986
916	—	GVL	Arabic **1** in date. Stop after **G** •			1986A
917	—	GVL	Roman **I** in date Hyphen stops on reverse			1987

(continued)

122

MAUNDY MONEY

THREEPENCES

A. First busts, no ties, large lettering / *Rev.* 1   Spink 3441

ESC	Date	Below bust	Varieties, comments etc.	Robinson [1]	R	(Old ESC)
918	**1689**	**GVL**	Arabic **I** in date Hyphen stops on reverse **LMV** over **MVS** in **GVLIELMVS**	*p. 151,94(v)*	*S*	1987A
919	—		No stop after date	*p. 151,94(i)*		
920	—		No stop before or after date	*p. 151,94(ii)*		
921	—		No stops on reverse	*p. 151,94(iii)*	*S*	1988
922	—		Hyphen stops on reverse	*p. 151,94(iv)*	*S*	1988
923	**1690**		No stop after **D** and date	*p. 151,97(i)*	*N*	1989
924	—		No stop after **D** With a stop after date	*p. 151,97(ii)*	*N*	1989
925	—		No stop after **GVLIELMVS** With a stop after **D·** No stop after date **9** over **6**	*p. 151,97(iv)*	*N*	1989
926	**1691**		*(No ties)*	*p.151,101(iii)*	*N*	1989

B. First busts variety, with ties, medium lettering
Reversed Z-type 1s in date   Spink 3441

927	**1691**	**GVL**	• Stop over heads & after **G**	*p.151,101(iv)*	*R³*	1990

C. Second bust, small lettering
Rev. 1. – Date above crown   Spink 3442

928	**1691**		Long space between **REGINA** and date	*p. 151,101(i)*	*R*	1990A
929	**1691**		Reads **ETREGINA**	*p. 151,101(ii)*	*R*	1990A
930	**1692**	**G**		*p. 151,105(i)*	*R*	1991
931	—	**GV**		*p. 151,105(ii)*	*R*	1992
932	—	**GV**	Stop after **G** •		*R*	1992
933	—	**GV**	Stop before **G**	*p.151,105(iv)*	*R*	1992
934	—	**GVL**		*p.151,105(iii)*	*R³*	1993
935	**1693**	**G**	Stop after **G** •	*p.152,109(iii)*	*R*	1994
936		**G**	**3** over **2**	*p.152,109(i)*	*S*	1994A
937	—	**GV**	**3** over **2**	*p.152,109(ii)*	*R³*	1995
938	—	**GV**		*p.152,109(iv)*	*R³*	1995

(continued)

THREEPENCES

C.   Second bust, small lettering

Rev. 1. – Date above crown   Spink 3442

ESC	Date	Below bust	Varieties, comments etc.	*Robinson* [1]	R	(Old ESC)
939	**1694**	G		*p.152,113(i)*	S	1996
940	—	G	Reads **MARIA**	*p.152,113(ii)*	S	1997
941	—	GV		*p.152,113(iii)*	S	1998
942	—	GVL		*p.152,113(iv)*	R^2	1999

TWOPENCES

Type A
No ties to wreath
• GV below bust   Large lettering   Date above crown

3 over 2

Type B
No ties to wreath
Small lettering
GVL below bust   Crown divides date

Type   **A.**   **First small busts**; similar to groat crude style and no ties.
Legend continuous above heads in large lettering

      B.   **Second larger busts**, small legend broken by the heads
Rev.   Small crown above numeral **2** within legend

MAUNDY MONEY

TWOPENCES

A. First busts, large lettering and Roman date / *Rev.* 1   Spink 3443

ESC	Date	Below bust	Varieties, comments etc.	*Robinson* [1]	R	(Old ESC)
943	**1689**		Legend continuous above heads	*p. 151,93(i)*	C	2196
944	—	**GV**	No stop after **D G** or **REGINA 1629** (date error)	*p. 151,93(ii)*		2196A

Note   From 1691 to 1694 lettering is smaller than 1689

B.   First busts variety, no ties, medium lettering   Spink 3443

945	**1691**	**GVL**	No stop after **G**		C	2197
946	—	**GVL**	No stop after date	*p. 151,100(i)*	C	2197

C.   Second bust, small lettering
         Rev. 1. – Date above crown   Spink 3443

947	**1692**	**GVL**	No stop after **G** small date	*p. 151,104(i)*	N	2198
948	**1693**	**GV**		*p.152,108(iii)*	N	2199
949	—	**GVL**	**3 over 2** in date Stop after **G·**	*p. 152,108(i)*	S	2200A
950	—	**GVL**	**3 over 2** in date No stop after **G**	*p. 152,108(ii)*	S	2200A
951	**1694**		*(Not traced)*		S	2201
952	—		**4 over 3**	*p. 152,112(i)*	R	2201A
953	—	**GVLI**	**HIBREXET** with stops after **D.G.**	*p.152,112(iii)*	S	2202
954	—	**GVLI**	**HIBREXET** No stop after **G** of **D·G**	*p.152,112(ii)*	S	2202
955	—	**GVLI**	**HI.REX.ET** (with stops) With stop after **G** of **D·G**	*p.152,112(iv)*	S	2203
956	—	**GVLI**	**HI.REX.ET** (with stops) With stop after **G** of **D·G** Reads **MARIA**	*p.152,112(v)*	S	2203
957	—	**GVL**	**HI.REX.ET** (with stops) With stop after **G** of **D·G** Reads **MARIA**	*p.152,112(vi)*	S	2203
958	—	**GVL**			S	2204

(continued)

WILLIAM & MARY, 1688-94
MAUNDY MONEY

TWOPENCES

C. Second bust, small lettering
Rev. 1. – Date above crown   Spink 3443

ESC	Date	Below bust	Varieties, comments etc.	*Robinson* [1]	R	(Old ESC)
959	**1694**		**HI.REX.ET** (with stops) With stop after **G** of **D·G** Reads **MARLA**	*p.152,112(vii)*	S	2205
960	—		**HI.REX.ET** (with stops) With stop after **G** of **D·G** Reads **MARIA**	*p.152,112(ix)*	S	2205

PENNIES

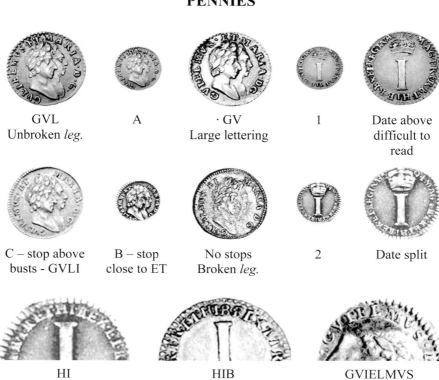

GVL Unbroken *leg.*	A	· GV Large lettering	1	Date above difficult to read
C – stop above busts - GVLI	B – stop close to ET	No stops Broken *leg.*	2	Date split
HI		HIB		GVIELMVS

PENNIES

Type **A.** **First busts**; similar to Halfgroat; crude style and no ties
Legend continuous over heads

B. **First busts variety**; similar to 'A' but, legend broken by busts
Stop after **ET** • close, behind king's head

C. **Second busts**; larger with legend broken by busts
Stop after **ET** • central above head

Rev. **1.** **Small crown** above Roman **I**, date above, difficult to read
2. **Large crown** dividing date above Roman **I**

A/1. First busts / *rev.* 1. – Small crown, date above   Spink 3444

ESC	Date	Below bust	Varieties, comments etc.	*Robinson* [1]	R	(Old ESC)
961	**1689**		Reads **ETREGINA6** (Figure 1 of date not visible)	*p. 151,92(i)*		
962	—	G	Stop after **G** • See note [1]		R^2	2298
963	—		Reads **GVIELMAS**	*p. 151,92(ii)*	R^5	2299
964	—		Reads **GVIELMAS**	*p. 151,92(iii)*	R^5	2299
965	—	G	Stop after **G** • Reads **GVIELMVS**	*p. 151,92(iv)*	R^5	2299
966	—	G	No stops before and after Gs		R^3	2299A
967	—		Reads **MARIA**		R^3	2299A
968	—	GVL	*(Not traced)*			
969	—	GV	Stop before • **G** and after **G** •			

B. First busts variety, stop above heads, no ties, medium lettering
Note: all pennies of this date have 2nd **1** over **0**   Spink 3445

970	**1691**	GVL	Stop after **G** •	*p. 151,99(i)*	C	2301
971	—	GVL	Stop after **G** • and Stop before date only	*p. 151,99(ii)*	C	2301
972	—	GVL	No stop after **D** and Stop before date only	*p. 151,99(ii)*	C	2301
973	—	GVL	No stops before / after date	*p. 151,99(iv)*	C	2301
974	—	GVL	No stop after date	*p. 151,99(v)*	C	2301

MAUNDY MONEY

PENNIES

C/1. Second busts / *rev.* 1. – Small crown, date above   Spink 3445

ESC	Date	Below bust	Varieties, comments etc.	*Robinson* [1]	R	(Old ESC)
975	**1690**		No stop after **D** and date	*p. 151,96(i)*	R	2300
976	**1692**	**GVL**	Stop after **G** •		R^2	2302
977	—		**2 over 1**	*p. 151,103(i)*	R^2	2303
978	—		**2 over 1** no stop after **G**	*p. 151,103(ii)*	R^2	2303
979	**1693**	**GVL**	Stop after **G** •		S	2304
980	—		Stop after **ET** • (close to it)	*p. 151,107(i)*	S	2304
981	—		Stop after **ET** above head	*p. 151,107(ii)*	S	2304

C/2. Second busts / *rev.* 2. – Large crown dividing date   Spink 3445

982	**1694**		Stop above head	*p. 152,111(i)*	R^2	2305
983	—		Stop after **ET** •	*p. 152,111(i)*	R^2	2305
984	—		No stops on obverse	*p.152,111(iii)*	R	2306
985	—		Reads **HI** not usual HIB	*p.152,111(iv)*	S	2306A
986	—		**9 over 1** *(Not traced)* Reads **HI** not usual HIB		R^3	2306B

Note
The varieties found during this reign are considerable

[1] *"At the time of editing this edition, Brian Robinson's commendable detailed study of the varieties of Maundy money, published over two decades ago, was the only one available, and has been copied in detail. Additional varieties, recorded in various other sources, have been added, even though many details are often incomplete, with the inevitable result of duplication in many instances, for this I apologise."* (M.B.)

This whole series of small money requires a detailed study by a dedicated numismatist with considerable patience, knowledge and time. My hope is this publication, with its short-falls, will encourage someone to undertake such a challenge.

WILLIAM III
1694-1702

On the death of Mary, from smallpox on 28th December 1694, no great change occured in the silver coinage although the designs of the four larger silver coins are more similar to those of James II. The crown, shilling and sixpence were struck in 1695 but not in very large quantities.

Up to this date the old hammered money was still in existance as it had never been withdrawn from circulation. Owing to the rise in the value of silver, much of the full weight coinage had been exported to the Continent and the hammered currency that still circulated here was worn out and much clipped. Also there was a large number of counterfeit hammered coins mixed up with it.

In 1695 the Government decided on a complete recoinage and laws were passed for the prohibition of all clipped coins, for the prevention of clipping and forgery and for the issue of a new coinage to replace the old and light money. The old coins were mostly accepted at their face value and not by the weight so that the Government sustained the loss and not the owner. The famous *'Window tax'* was levied on dwelling houses to raise £1,200,000 to make good this deficiency and to pay for the new coinage. In order to hasten this large undertaking, branch mints were opened at Bristol, Chester, Exeter, Norwich and York, the coins being marked B, C, E, N, y (or Y) below the bust. These mints opperated for over two years with dies prepared mainly in London and dated 1696 and 1697. No crowns are known of these provincial mints. That there were millions of coins struck during this reign is obvious as today many of the pieces are still relatively common, especially the crowns and sixpences of the first first three years and the halfcrowns of 1698.

The King's bust was changed frequently during the reign and one of these needs a few words of comment. This is the one known as the *'second bust'* on the higher denominations, and is readily distinguished by two large curls coming forward right across the chest. The sixpence of 1697 with this bust is only moderately rare, but all the other pieces are of exceptional rarity and must be patterns, but they have all been in circulation. Furthermore, there are two distinct varieties of this bust, one in lower relief of heavy style and the other with a rather narrower bust in higher relief, and with more hair more deeply engraved. At the time the first edition was written, the shilling of the second bust was still unknown, but was included in the table on the assumption that it might exist. A shilling with this bust in lower relief did eventually come to light c. 1949 and is now in a private collection.

WILLIAM III
1694-1702

Once again, symbols are used to denote the source of the silver in the case of some of the coins of the later dates. Most are rare.

With regard to the engravers, Norbert Roettier, having been involved in some form of scandal, due possibly to his Jacobite sympathies, fled to France before the middle of the year 1695, thus leaving the entire responsibility for the engraving of coinage dies in the hands of his brother James; and it is to this artist that one can with some certainty attribute all the early coins of this reign; the first bust on the halfcrown, shilling and sixpence in particular. James Roettier also fell into disgrace as he was found guilty at a Mint enquiry in 1697 of having smuggled dies of coinage for James II and Charles II out of the Tower to France; he was therefore dismissed from his post. Harris, who was still Chief Engraver, although not active on coinage dies, was directed to *'carry on the service'*, which he did with the help of John Croker. This later, by far the most important of the engravers of the period, was a German who came to England in 1691 and was appointed an Engraver in 1697. After the death of Harris in 1705, Croker became Chief Engraver, and it was stated at that time that Harris was *'only a seal cutter and employed by Mr Croker to do the business of the mint'*. To Croker then must be attributed most of the dies made after those engraved by James Roettier were worn out. He was later assisted by one James Bull, appointed Assistant Engraver or Probation Engraver in Christmas 1698. Turning now to the coinage and design of the coin, by far the most important event during the reign was the great re-coinage. Manuscript records at the Mint show the opperating periods of the various provincial mints as follows:

Exeter	August	1696 to July 1698
York	September	1696 to April 1698
Bristol	September	1696 to September 1698
Norwich	September	1696 to April 1698
Chester	October	1696 to June 1698

It will thus be seen that even reckoning dates according to the old style, at any rate in the case of Bristol, Exeter and Chester, one would expect to see coins dated 1698. The fact that none exist lends colour to T.B. Graham's theory that the late dies of 1697 were prepared so late in that year as to serve until the closing down of the mints in 1698.

There seems to be little doubt, due to the uniformity of design on the obverses, that Roettier was responsible for the engraving of most of the dies that were used in the provincial mints. In Treasury Papers of May 21st 1697, appears a

WILLIAM III
1694-1702

petition by Roettier, after his dismissal, for payment in respect of *'500 pairs of Dyes for Country Mints.....'*. Later we see that *'Mr Neale* (the then Master) *intends to pay him, his demand of sixty pounds tenn* (sic) *shillings, and with your Lordship's approbation, to give him fifty pounds more being the summ he desired for ye five hundred pair of Dyes for Country Mints'*. An Assistant Engraver was appointed for each mint *'to polish the Dyes in each country mint at a reasonable sallary to be allowed by ye K. (King) not exceeding forty (pounds) a year'*.

Turning once more to the engravers Roettier and Croker, and the attribution to one or the other of the first and third bust coins, let us consider two possibilities. Firstly, as Roettier asserted that his designs, and only his, had been used until July 1697, did he produce the third bust coins for provincial and Tower mints prior to his dismissal? If it could be proved that the third bust existed more frequently than only on rare coins (probably mules) dated 1696, then this could well be so, for as we have seen, he is known to have engraved five hundred pairs of dies for the provincial mints. However, it seems much more likely that Croker was responsible for the third bust silver coins as the shilling is almost identical with the second type guinea, usually ascribed to him. It is natural also that Croker would as nearly copy the general style of the Roettier coins as possible, particularily as the authorities desired uniformity of design for the provincial coinage. It is almost certain that due to the length of time the country mints operated, Roettier's dies would have been exhausted before the mints ceased working.

It seems quite likely that after the provincial mints closed down, Croker adopted a more individual style, typified by the fourth bust or *'flaming hair'* shilling of 1698.

The correct attribution of the *'fine work'* gold and silver of 1700-1701 has presented a great problem. Let us first consider the existing contemporary records concerning this last period: In Mint MS. records appears an *'account of all dyes for gold and silver defaced and left good in the hands of ye Engravers April 13th 1700'*. This account is an order for certain dies in stock at the time to be destroyed in the presence of the Warden and states *'eight heads, five 'armes', six 'paires' of Bull's dies for the shilling should be defaced with exception of one reverse die which should be 'left good'*. The dies for gold are not ascribed.

Another manuscript of January 7th 1701/2, gives *'tryall dyes of Mr Bulls ..... armes left goode formerly 01'*. This is most probably the reverse die referred to in 1700, and it is interesting to note that it was apparently only a trial die.

131

WILLIAM III
1694-1702

There is also a list of puncheons delivered into the Warden's custody on 13 January 1702, which include puncheons for five-guineas, guineas, half-guineas, halfpence and farthing, all by Bull.

As to whom the fine work coinage may be attributed, there are three possibilities. Firstly, Croker and Bull may have each produced a series of dies for all denominations as there was a great demand for gold due to very large imports from the Continent. Secondly, Bull's dies may never have been used, and have all been defaced due to William's death. Thirdly, we can attribute the whole issue to Bull alone. It is interesting to note that no two guineas is shown in the list of puncheons by Bull, and if this coinage were his work, he could not have completed this puncheon before the list was made (January 9th 1701/2). These puncheons cannot be for the gold issues of 1699 as they were not in stock in the earlier list of April 1700, where only the dies for a shilling were stated to be by Bull. Obviously therefore, Croker must have been responsible for the 1699 coinage. One can also see how nearly the bust on this gold resembles that on the fourth bust flaming hair shilling.

Returning to the 'fine work' coinage of 1700-01, it seems far more likely that these dies were the work of Croker than of Bull. Bull, although he must have been a very competent artist, as is shown by the reverses of some of Croker's medals of Queen Anne, had, at this time, been at the Mint only for about eighteen months, and it is not likely that such a large task as a completely new coinage would have been given to him; also the dies appearing in manuscript mint records are mentioned as being only trial dies. The style of the fine work coinage is also very typical of Croker's medallic work. The obverse of the State of Britain medal, and that of the fifth bust shilling are very similar in style. It would appear much more likely that this last issue of gold, including a Two-Guineas dated 1701, and silver represents Croker's later and more mature style with the *'flaming hair'* shilling and the 1699 gold coinage forming a transition in style between the *'Roettier copies'* and these later coins. With regard to the second bust coins referred to earlier, it is possible that these were patterns made by Croker to obtain the post of Engraver when Roettier was dismissed in February 1696/7. The workmanship of the coins is far better than that shown on the other unique crown of the hair across the breast, which is much flatter relief and not such fine style. This coin is similar to the scarce second bust sixpence which occurs dated 1697 and very rarely 1696. The portaiture on these coins differs so greatly from the style of Roettier or Croker that one wonders if it could not be the work of Harris when he was working alone after Roettier's disgrace, or perhaps one of his junior

WILLIAM III
1694-1702

assistants. Finally, it is interesting to note that the portrait on the halfcrowns shows hardly any variation throughout the reign although new reverse designs or modifications are used from the beginning of 1698 onwards. It is quite likely that Roettier had made sufficient obverse dies for the whole reign before he quitted the Mint, as the reverse dies always tend to wear out more rapidly than do the obverses. (P.A.Rayner, 1949)

Spink published a detailed study of this reign by E.R. Jackson Kent in the Numismatic Circular May 1961, pp. 108-20 *Some notes and observations on the Silver Coinage of King William III, 1695-1701* (crowns, halfcrowns, shillings & sixpences)

OBVERSES

Curved breastplate

Type A - 1st bust

Type A (no stops)

Type B – 2nd bust (See Patterns)

Straight breastplate

Type C – 3rd bust
short ties

Type E – 3rd bust variety
longer ties

133

WILLIAM III, 1694-1702
CROWNS

Error GEI (not DEI) and G over O in GRΛ

G over D

Unbarred A in GRΛ

REVERSES

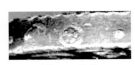  

Cinquefoil

Last 6 over 5

1st rev. – harp 1 – shield 1

7 with straight leg

7 with curved leg

2nd rev. – harp 2 – shield 3

3rd rev. – harp 3 – shield 3

Harps & Shields

Harps	1	Large female bust at front, higher than plain back
	2	Small female bust at front, level with scroll back
	3	Scrolls, large at front, smaller at back, both level
	4	Small female bust at front, higher than scroll back (pattern?)
Shields	1	Same width as crown above, top middle pointed
	2	Wider than crown above, top middle pointed
	3	Wider than crown above, top middle indented

134

CROWNS

Harp 1	Harp 2	Harp 2	Harp 3	Harp 4
Shield 1	Shield 2	Shield 3	Shield 3	Shield 3

Type	**A.**	**First bust with first reverse** - 1st harp - 1st shield
Obv.		Laureate and draped with curved breastplate or drapery, right, hair breaking legend.
Leg.		**GVLIELMVS • III • DEI • GRA •**
		William third by the Grace of God
Rev.	**1**	Crowned cruciform shields to outer beading, clockwise; England, Scotland, France and Ireland
		Star of the Garter in the centre and plain in the angles
		1st harp with large female bust, left end higher then right
Leg.		**16 ♔ 95•MAG• ♔ BR•FRA• ♔ ET•HIB• ♔ REX•**
Edge		**DECVS ET TVTAMEN ANNO REGNI SEPTIMO**
	B.	**Second bust** (See patterns[4])
	C.	**Third bust with first reverse** - 1st harp - 1st shield
		Similar to first bust, with a distinctive straight breastplate
	D.	**Third bust with second reverse** - 2nd harp - 2nd shield
	E.	**Third bust variety with third reverse** - 3rd harp – 3rd shield
		Similar, but recut die; longer ties and hair varied a little

A/1. First bust / *Rev.* 1 - 1st harp & 1st shield Spink 3470

ESC	Date	Edge year		Varieties, comments etc *(strings-billets)*	R	(Old ESC)
990	**1695**	**SEPTIMO**	(7)	Cinquefoil stops on edge *(6s-9b;7s-9b;8s-9b)*	N	86
991	—	**OCTAVO**	(8)	+ stops on edge *(6s-9b,8 strings)*	C	87
992	—	**OCAVO**	—	Sic. *(Is this due to a slipped collar?)*	R	87B
993	—	**OCTAO**	—	Sic. *(Is this due to a slipped collar?)*	R	87C

(continued)

WILLIAM III, 1694-1702
CROWNS

ESC	Date	Edge year		Varieties, comments etc _(strings-billets)_	R	(Old ESC)
994	**1695**	None		_Proof en medaille_ ↑↑ (L&S 1) Unbarred **A** in **GRA** Plain edge _(8s-10b)_	R^4	88
995	**1696**	**OCTAVO**	(8)	_(6s-9b;7s-9b;8s-11b)_	C	89
996	—	—	—	No stops on obverse **G** over **D** in **GRA** _(6s?-9b)_	R^3	89A
997	—	—	—	Unbarred **A** in **GRA** _(7s-9b)_	R^2	89C
998	—	—	—	Last **6** over **5** _(6s-9b;6s-10b;7s-9b 8s-?b)_	R^3	90
999	—	—	—	Last **6** over **5** **E** over ? in **DEI** _(8 strings)_		
1000	—	—	—	Error **GEI** for **DEI** and **G** over **O** in **ORA** _(6s-?b;7s-9b)_	R^5	91
1001	—	—	—	**CT** over **TC** in **OCTAVO**	R^4	91A
1002	—	**OCCTAVO**	—	Sic. Last **6** over **5** _(7 strings)_		
1003	—	None		_Proof,_ plain edge [2] _(8str)_ (L&S 2)	R^4	92

C/1. Third bust / _Rev._ 1 - 1st harp & 1st shield   Spink 3472

1004	**1696**	**OCTAVO**	(8)	_(6s-9b;7s-9b)_	C	94
1005	—	—	—	No stops on obverse _(6 strings)_	R^3	
1006	—	—	—	No stops on reverse _(7s-9b)_	R^3	
1007	—	**TRICESIMO**	(30)	Error edge of **1678** _(Not traced)_	R^6	94A

C/4. Third bust / _Rev._ 4 – 4th harp - 3rd shield, plain edge [2] Spink 3472

1008	**1696**	None		_Proof or pattern,_ _(8s-9b)_ _Struck en medaille_ ↑↑ (L&S 4)	R^4	95

D/2. Third bust / Second reverse - 2nd harp & 2nd shield   Spink 3473

1009	**1697**	**NONO**	(9)	No stops after **FRA HIB** _8s.7b_ Flaw stop inside **G** of **MAG**	R^3	96

E/3. Third bust variety /_Rev._ 3 – 3rd harp & 3rd shield   Spink 3474

1010	**1700**	**DVODECIMO**	(12)	_(4s-7b;7s-7b;8s-7b;9s-7b)_	N	97
1011		**D. TERTIO**	(13)	**D** over ꓷ in **DECIMO** _(9s-7b;8s-?b;6s-?b)_	R	98

Many edge errors are the result of slipped collars

136

CROWNS

PATTERNS [3]

Spink 3471

ESC	Date		Varieties, comments etc _(strings-billets)_	R	(Old ESC)
1012	**1696**	_Obv._ **B1**	Laureate and draped bust, right, hair breaking legend, two locks of hair across the breast, not below truncation[4]	R^7	93
		Rev. 2	with 2nd harp & 2nd shield _(7s-9b)_		
		Edge	**OCTAVO** (8) _(L&S 3)_		

Spink 3471

1013	**1696**	_Obv._ **B2**	Similar, but, narrower bust in higher	R^7	93A
		(variety)	Relief, the hair more deeply engraved		
		Rev. 2	with 2nd harp & 2nd shield _(7s-9b)_		
		Edge	**OCTAVO** (8) _(L&S 3)_		

2   _"The harp on these two proofs is a variety, not quite like the first or second.The shields are the same design as that shown containing the third harp. Perhaps we should class them as patterns rather than proofs"_ (P.A. Rayner)

3   _"These are the only two known examples with the second bust, both in the B.M. collection, from completely different obverse dies.------ Both these coins are patterns."_ (P.A. Rayner)

4   Type B; retained from old ESC classification

HALFCROWNS

LONDON MINT
As the crown but, with varieties of shields
Proofs - Characteristically have distinctive beaded borders
(London, being the parent mint, required no identification letter)
OBVERSES

| Standard bust | *Proof* | Elephant & castle below |

1	3	4
Small shields	Large shields	Large shields
Small early harp	Large early harp	Large late harp

Rev. 2; medium shields, small late harp. See Bristol & Norwich mints

| 5i - Lion's tail curves in | 6 - Plumes in angles | 5o - Lion's tail curves out |

HALFCROWNS

Scottish arms at date   Lion of Nassau inverted   No stops

Frames around central lion of Nassau

1 - Circular frame   2 - Curved frame   3i - Oval frame   3o - Oval frame
Tail **i**nwards   Tail **o**utwards

Shields & Irish harps

1   Small shields; same width as crowns, pointed tops and bottoms
    Early harp; small female bust at front, higher than back scroll

2   Medium (intermediate) shields; wider than crowns, pointed tops and
    bottoms with late harp; slightly larger than early, front and back level

3   Large shields; wider than crowns, indented tops, pointed bottoms
    Large early harp; large female bust at front, higher than plain back

4   As 3, but with a large late harp, front and back level

5   As 4, but shields more square shaped

1   2   3   4   5

WILLIAM III, 1694-1702
HALFCROWNS

7 over 6   Error GRR   8 over 7

G over A   Elephant & castle   Unbarred A in GRΛ

M·AG   No stop after   I over E
           GVLIELMVS

M over higher M

LONDON MINT
Normal punctuation in reverse legends, unless stated
MAG• BR•FRA• ET•HIB• REX•

L/1.   *Rev.* 1 - **small shields & small early harp**   Spink 3475

ESC	Date	Edge year		Variety, comments etc		R	(Old ESC)
1014	**1696**	**OCTAVO**	(8)		*(5s-9b)*	C	534
1015	—	—	—	Reads **DECɅ S**	*(5s-9b)*	R³	534A

L/3.   *Rev.* 3 - **large shields & early harp**   Spink 3481

1016	**1696**	**OCTAVO**	(8)	The bust varies slightly [1]	*(7s-9b)*	N	522
1017	—	—	—	**I over E in GVLIELMVS***(7strs)*		R⁴	523
1018	—	None		*Proof, plain edge*	*(8s-9b)*	R⁴	523A
1019	—	—		*Proof, plain edge.* Thicker flan		R⁶	523B

HALFCROWNS

L/4 *Rev.* 4 - **large shields** & **late harp** Spink 3487
Leg. punc. – No stops after **MAG FRA HIB**

ESC	Date	Edge year		Variety, comments etc		R	(Old ESC)
1020	**1696**	**OCTAVO**	(8)		*(8s-7b)*	R^3	530
1021	**1697**	**NONO**	(9)	Note^2 *(6s-5b;7s-6b; 8s-6b;9s-6b;9s-7b)*		C	541
1022	—	—	—	**I** over **E** in **GVLIELMVS**		R^2	541
1023	—	—	—	**M** over **M** in **GVLIELMVS**		R^3	
1024	—	—	—	**7** over **6**	*(7s-6b)*	R^2	541A
1025	—	—	—	Error reads **GRR**	*(8 strings)*	R^5	541B
1026	—	—	—	2nd **N** over **O** in **NONO**	*(6s-5b)*	R^3	541C
1027	—	—	—	Inverted **N**s on edge **ANNO**		R^2	541C
1028	—	—	—	Unbarred **A** in **GRA**	*(8s-6b)*	R^3	541D
1029	—	—	—	**GRA** no stop. Stop in **M·AG** *(7s)*		R^3	541E
1030	—	—	—	No stop after **GVLIELMVS** *(7s)*		R^3	541F
1031	—	—	—	**G** over **A** in **MAG** Stop after **FRA**	*(9 strings)*	R^5	541G
1032	—	None		*Proof, plain edge (15.52g) (10s-8b)*		R^5	542

L/5.   *Rev.* 5i & 5o - **modified large shields** and harp
Leg. punc. – No stops after **MAG FRA HIB**   Spink 3494

1033	**1698**	**OCTAVO**	(8)	**5i** Wrong edge year	*(7s-6b)*	R^6	553
1034	—	**DECIMO**	(10)		*(7s-7b)*	C^2	554
1035	—	—	—	**8** over **7**	*(6 strings)*	R^3	554A
1036	—	**UNDECIMO**	(11)		*(5s-?b;6s-7b;7s-7b)*	R^5	555

L/5.   *Rev.* 5i & 5o - **modified large shields** and harp   Spink 3494

1037	**1699**	**UNDECIMO**	(11)	**5i**	*(5s-5b)*	R	556
1038	—	—	—	Some **N**s in legend inverted All **N**s on edge inverted		R^3	557
1039	—	—	—	**DEC∀S ET ∀ TAMEN** *7s*		R^3	557A
1040	—	—	—	Unbarred **A** in **GRA**	*(5s-7b)*	R^3	558
1041	—	—	—	Arms of Scotland at date* *(5s)*		R^4	559
1042	—	—	—	Lion of Nassau inverted* *(5s)*		R^3	560
1043	**1700**	**DVODECIMO**	(12)		*(5s-7b)*	N	561

*Engraver's error caused by rotation of legend

Note
In 1701 the figure 1 changed from the regular reversed Z to a J type

HALFCROWNS

L/5. *Rev.* 5i & 5o - **modified large shields** and harp
Leg. punc. – No stops after **MAG FRA HIB**   Spink 3494

ESC	Date	Edge year		Variety, comments etc	R	(Old ESC)
1044	**1700**	**D. TERTIO**	(13)	**5o** See note ^{3} *(8s-6b;6s-6b;7s)*	N	562
1045	—	—	—	Reads **DE𝒴 S** *(6s-7b; 6s-8b)*	R^2	563
1046	**1701**	—	—	**J** type 1s. See note^1 *(7s-6b)*	N	564
1047	—	—	—	**J** type 1s. Extra **R** on edge before **DECVS**	R^3	564A
1048	—	—	—	**J** type 1s.**E** over **N** in **DECVS**	R^6	564B
1049	—	—	—	**J** type 1s. No stops on reverse	C^2	565

LE/5.   **Elephant & Castle** below bust ^{4} /   *Rev.* 5o – **square shields**
Leg. punc. – No stops after **MAG FRA HIB**   Spink 3495

1050	**1701**	**D. TERTIO**	(13)	**5o J** type 1s. *(7s-6b)*	R^4	566
1051	—	—	—	**J** type 1s. Broader Elephant with taller castle than before^4	R^5	566A

L/6.   *Rev.* 6 – **Plumes in angles, square shields**   Spink 3496

1052	**1701**	**D. TERTIO**	(13)	**5i J** type 1s. *(7s-7b)*	R	567

ESC 541c; DECVS·EMEN·AMEN·ANNO·REGINONO (Ex MB collection) de-listed
because blundered edge legend caused by a segment of the collar slipping

Note; All provincial dies were supplied by the Tower mint

PROVINCIAL MINTS

BRISTOL MINT - B below bust
September 1696 to September 1698 = 24 Months production
Leg. punc. – **MAG• BR•FRA•   ET•HIB•   REX•**

1 – Small shields	Standard obverse	2 – Medium shields
Early harp	B below bust	Late harp

HALFCROWNS

B/1.   *Rev.* 1 – **small shields & small early harp**   Spink 3476

ESC	Date	Edge year		Variety, comments etc		R	(Old ESC)
1053	**1696**	**OCTAVO**	(8)		*(5s-9b)*	*R*	535
1054	—	—	—	*Proof* [9]		*R⁶*	535B

B/2   *Rev.* 2 – **medium shields & small late harp**   Spink ?

1055	**1696**	**OCTAVO**	(8)	No stop after **HIB** *(6s-8b)*	*R³*	535A
				(Note; medium or intermediate shields)		

B/3.   *Rev.* 3 – **large shields & large early harp**   Spink 3482

1056	**1696**	**OCTAVO**	(8)	Angle of letter **B** varies *(6;7s-9b)*	*S*	524
1057	—	—	—	Error on edge reads **REGNE**	*R⁴*	
1058	—	—	—	Thick flan, *wt. 328.5 grs (Not traced)*	*R⁶*	524A

B/4.   *Rev.* 4 – **large shields & late harp**
No stops after **MAG FRA HIB**   Spink 3488

1059	**1696**	**OCTAVO**	(8)		*R⁴*	530A
1060	**1697**	**NONO**	(9)	*(No strings-6b⁵;11s-7b;2,5,6, strings)*	*N*	543
1061	—	—	—	*Proof on a thick flan.* **B** below bust partly erased on die *wt. 21.3g*	*R⁶*	543A
1062	—	—	—	No stops on reverse *(5s-7b)*	*R*	544
1063	—	—	—	**E over?** re-entered **I**, No harp strings⁵	*R²*	

CHESTER MINT – C below bust
October 1696 to June 1698 = 20 Months production
Leg. punc. – **MAG• BR•FRA• ET•HIB• REX•**

Small c

large C

HALFCROWNS

C/1. Small letter **c** below bust
Rev. 1 – **small shields & small early harp**　　Spink 3477

ESC	Date	Edge year		Variety, comments etc		R	(Old ESC)
1064	1696	OCTAVO	(8)		*(5s-9b)*	R^2	536

C/3. Large letter **C** below bust
Rev. 3 – **large shields & large early harp**　　Spink 3483

1065	1696	OCTAVO	(8)		*(6s-9b)*	R	525

C/4. Large letter **C** below bust
Rev. 4 – **large shields & large late harp**　　Spink 3489

1066	1696	OCTAVO	(8)	No stop after **MAG?**[*]	*(7s-8b)*	R^3	531
1067	—	—	—	No stop after **BR**	*(7s-8b)*	R^3	531
1068	1697	NONO	(9)	No stop after **MAG FRA HIB**		S	545
				(6s-5b;6s-8b;9s-5b;5 strings)			

[*]The grade of examples studied leaves room for doubt concerning the stops

EXETER MINT - E below bust
August 1696 to July 1698 = 23 Months production
Leg. punc. – MAG• BR•FRA• ET•HIB• REX•

E over C　　　　　　　　E　　　　　　　　E over B

E over c　E over C　　　　Inverted A　　　　E over B　Stop after G

E/1.　*Rev.* 1 - **small shields & small early harp**　　Spink 3478

1069	1696	OCTAVO	(8)		*(5s-8b)*	R^4	537

HALFCROWNS

E/3.   *Rev.* 3 - **large shields & large early harp**   Spink 3484

ESC	Date	Edge year		Variety, comments etc	R	(Old ESC)
1070	**1696**	**OCTAVO**	(8)	*(6s-9b;7s-?b)*	R^2	526

E/4.   *Rev.* 4 - **large shields & late large harp**, all stops   Spink 3490

1071	**1696**	**OCTAVO**	(8)	*(7s-8b)*	R^3	532
1072	—	**NONO**	(9)	Error; wrong edge year *(?s-8b)*	R^5	532A
1073	**1697**	**OCTAVO**	(8)	Error; wrong edge year *(8s-8b)*	R^5	546
1074	—	**NONO**	(9)	*(5s-8b;6s-7b)*	N	547
1075	—	—	—	Reads Ⱥ **TAMEN**[*]	R^5	547
1076	—	—	—	No stop after **MAG** (only)*(9s-5b)*	R^3	547A

E/4.   *Rev.* 4 - **large shields & late large harp**
No stops after **MAG FRA HIB**   Spink 3490

1077	**1697**	**NONO**	(9)	*(6s-7b)*	N	547
1078	—	—	—	E over small **c** under bust Stop in **G·RA·** [*] *(9s-6b)*	R^4	548
1079	—	—	—	E over large **C** under bust Edge reads Ⱥ **TAMEN**[*] *(7s-7b)*	R^4	548A
1080	—	—	—	E over **B** under bust *(5s-8b)*	R^4	548B
1081	—	—	—	E over **B** under bust *(7s-6b)* Edge reads Ⱥ **TAMEN**[*]	R^4	548C
1082	—	—	—	Reads **GVLIELMⱯ S** *(7 strings)*	R^3	548D

*These may not be true errors but simply flaws

NORWICH MINT - N below bust
September 1696 to April 1698 = 19 Months production
Leg. punc. – **MAG• BR•FRA• ET•HIB• REX•**

Small N   Arms of Scotland at date   Normal N

HALFCROWNS

Unbarred A
Medium shields

N/1. Small letter N below bust
Rev. 1 - **small shields & early harp**   Spink 3479

ESC	Date	Edge year		Variety, comments etc	R	(Old ESC)
1083	**1696**	**OCTAVO**	(8)	*(5s-9b)*	R	538

N/2. Small letter N below bust
Rev. 2 - **medium shields & smaller late harp**   Spink 3479

1084	**1696**	**OCTAVO**	(8)		R^5	538A

N/2. Normal letter N below bust
Rev. 2 - **medium shields & smaller late harp**   Spink 3479

1085	**1696**	**OCTAVO**	(8)	No stops after **FRA HIB** *(9s-8b)*	R^4	538B
1086	—	—	—	No stops after **MAG FRA HIB** Unbarred **A** in **FRA**	R^4	538C
1087	—	—	—	Inverted **A** for **V** in **OCTAVO**	R^3	538D

N/3. Normal letter N below bust
Rev. 3 - **large shields & large early harp**   Spink 3485

1088	**1696**	**OCTAVO**	(8)	8th	R^4	527

N/4. Normal letter N below bust
Rev. 4 - **large shields & large late harp**   Spink 3491

1089	**1696**	**OCTAVO**	(8)	*(Not traced)*	R^5	533
1090	**1697**	—	—	Error; wrong edge year *(6s-7b)* No stop after **MAG** (only)	R^6	549
1091	—	**NONO**	(9)	No stop after **MAG FRA HIB** *(6s-5b)*	S	550
1092	—	—	—	Arms of Scotland at date No stop after **FRA HIB** *(6s-6b)*	R^5	550A
1093	—	—	—	No stop after **MAG FRA** *(7s-8b)*	S	550B

HALFCROWNS

YORK MINT - Y below bust
September 1696 to April 1698 = 19 Months production
Leg. punc. – MAG• BR•FRA• ET•HIB• REX•

Y over inverted A

Normal Y

Y over inverted A

Y/1. *Rev.* 1 - small shields & early harp   Spink 3480

ESC	Date	Edge year		Variety, comments etc	R	(Old ESC)
1094	**1696**	**OCTAVO**	(8)	*(5s-9b)*	R^2	539

Y/3. *Rev.* 3 - large shields & large early harp   Spink 3486

1095	1696	OCTAVO	(8)	*(6s-9b)*	R	528
1096	—	—	—	No stops after MAG FRA *(5s-9b)*	R	528B
1097	—	—	—	Arms of Scotland at date	R^5	528A
				(Not traced)		
1098	—	—	—	Y over E looks like inverted A	R^5	529
				(6s-9b)		

Y/4. *Rev.* 4 - large shields & late harp   Spink 3492
Leg. punc. – No stops after MAG FRA HIB

1099	1697	OCTAVO	(8)	Error; wrong edge year *(7s-9b)*	R^6	550B
1100	—	NONO	(9)	*(0s-5b;4s-5b;7s-5b) (4,8 strings)*	N	551
1101	—	—	—	More a capital Y than Y^7 *(5strings)*	R^5	552

Notes
1   The majority of the reverse varieties are illustrated in the superb Colin Adam's collection
Spink Auction 177, 1 December 2005.
2   *"The size of the lions on the English shield varies very considerably on coins of this year.*
Some could be called 'large lions' and some 'small lions'. Also there are differences in the
size of the harp. (P.A. Rayner)
3   Some of these have slightly larger lettering on reverse and larger harps

HALFCROWNS

Pattern [8]

| P. | | | | Second bust / second reverse? | | Spink 3493 | |

ESC	Date	Edge year		Variety, comments etc	R	(Old ESC)
1102	**1696**	**OCTAVO**	(8)	Laureate and draped, right, hair breaking legend, two locks of hair across the breast	R^7	540

4   There is a variety with the provenance mark larger, i.e. the castle is much taller, and the elephant broader and of different style (R^5) as explained in the notes of Charles II; the edge legend can be upright or inverted in relation to the obverse, and some collectors regard this as a variety and try to collect both, but since the legend was put on the blank flan prior to striking, it could be either way

5   The die sinker was left to add the strings to the Irish harp, and occasionally forgot. This is evident on high grade coins but suspect on lower, see 'E4' graded GEF. E.R. Jackson Kent lists a few other specimens. Although they may be of interest to a specialist collector, they do not warrant inclusion as major varieties. Neither do missing pellets in the legends unless out of the ordinary; **MAG FRA HIB** are found both with and without pellets. The harp strings, and billets surrounding the lion of Nassau, also vary in numbers, but do not warrant inclusion as major varieties. See the Colin Adam's sale for many examples.

6   Previously wrongly described as **Y** over **E**

7   This '**y**' is sometimes called a capital **Y**, as it is without the usual tail of the normal **y**, but it is not such a definite capital **Y** as is found on the shillings and sixpences and is probably a badly cut small **y**. One common error found on all denominations of William III coins is the accidental use of an inverted 'A' punch for the letter 'V'(P.A. Rayner)

8   This unique coin (in the B.M.) is in the same style as the second bust crown, and therefore re-classified as a pattern also. Uncertain if both types exist matching the crowns

WILLIAM III, 1694-1702
SHILLINGS

Legends and style as the crown and halfcrown
My grateful thanks to Roderick Farey for supplying the following
portaits with descriptions, and many of the enlarged images. (M.B.)

	**A.** **FIRST BUST**	
	(a) hair turns outwards above and below the crown of the head	
	(b) broad ties with a clear gap	
	N.B. the ties can be absent due to die filling	

B - Bristol

Small D in DEI

C - Chester

E - Exeter

Standard reverse

N - Norwich

y - York

Y over inverted Y

Y - York

SHILLINGS

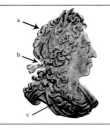

B. SECOND BUST

(a) hair over the crown of the head consists of curls
(b) long thin ties show a clear gap and there is an extra curl of hair at the right hand end
(c) the most recognisable feature is the hair across the breast

2nd bust - London

C. THIRD BUST

(a) there is a gap between the top two laurel leaves of the wreath
(b) the hair at the back of the head turns downwards and inwards
(c) the ties are thinner and lack a clear gap between them
(d) the curl under the bust is narrower
(e) the front of the drapery has a long narrow fold

B - Bristol   C - Chester

3rd bust - London

150

SHILLINGS

E - Exeter

N - Norwich

Y - York

Y - York

D.   THIRD BUST VARIETY

(a)   the hair at the back of the head turns downwards and inwards like the 3rd bust
(b)   the ties are wider and have no gap between them
(c)   the hair curl under the bust is larger
(d)   the profile is thought to be more aquiline and the features somewhat coarser

B - Bristol

3rd bust variety - London

C - Chester

E.   FOURTH BUST
'Flaming hair'

(a)   the hair on the top of the head resembles flames, hence the description *'flaming hair'*
(b)   the hair at the back of the head consists of curls somewhat similar to those on the 2nd bust
(c)   the ties are joined together and have a hair curl at the right hand end similar to the 2nd bust but curling downwards rather than upwards

SHILLINGS

Flaming hair

4th bust - London

'J' type 1 in date

F. **FIFTH BUST**   **G. – Plume below bust**
     'High hair'

(a) the hair on the top of the head is higher obscuring one of the laurel leaves, hence the description *'high hair'*

(b) the hair at the back of the head turns downwards and inwards like the 3rd bust and 3rd bust variety

(c) there is a distinct gap between the ties

(d) there is an extra curl of hair on the shoulder

(e) the fold at the front of the drapery is shorter

5th bust - London

Plume below

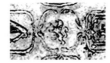

No billets

Small

Lions

large

Plume below

SHILLINGS

REVERSES

1	2	3	4
Plain in angles	Roses in angles	Plumes in angles	Plumes in angles
Small lions	Small lions	Small lions	Large lions

ARRANGEMENT OF ARMS
(Clockwise from date)

(Halfcrown illustrated)

5	6	7	8
Normal with	arms transposed	arms transposed	Scottish arms
small lettering	Scottish ↔ Irish	French ↔ Irish	at date
E-S-F-I	E-I-F-S	E-S-I-F	S-F-I-E

Small lettering	Large lettering	No stops

LM/M	Error 1669	Tall 00s & no stops

153

SHILLINGS

E over A

EL over M & colon (?)

Error GRI

GⱯLIELMVS

GVLIEMVS

GVLELMVS

GVLIELMⱯS

Error MAB

R over V or inverted A?

Obv. **A.**   **First bust**, distinctive dent in hair at the back of head and the hair turns outwards above and below it. Note; small **D** in **DEI**

      B   **Second bust** with hair across the breast; see *Patterns*

      C.   **Third bust**, right, similar to first bust but no dent and the hair at the crown all turns downwards and inwards
Note; Letter **L** aligns with the bottom end of top tie

      D.   **Third bust variety**, right, very similar to third bust, but ties closer to hair, more aquiline profile, coarser features and the back of his hair and forehead is noticeably closer to the legend

      E.   **Fourth bust,** known as the *'flaming hair'* type on account of the appearance of the hair at the top of the head

      F.   **Fifth bust**, known as the *'high hair'* type. A narrower bust and with hair at top somewhat between that on the earlier busts and the fourth bust, V-shape ties stick straight out

      G.   **Fifth bust** with a **plume** below

SHILLINGS

LONDON MINT
(No letter below bust)

L.A/1. First bust, dent in hair at the back / *Rev. 1*   Spink 3497
Leg. punc. – **MAG⦁ BR•FRA⦁   ET•HIB⦁   REX•**

ESC	Date	Variety, comments etc	R	(Old ESC)
1103	**1695**	*(5s-7b;5s-8b;5s-9b)*	N	1077
1104	**1696**	*(5s-9b; 6s-9b)*	C	1078
1105	—	No stops on reverse *(Not traced)*	R^3	1078A
1106	—	Error; reads **MAB** for MAG	R^5	1078B
1107	—	*Proof* on heavy flan	R^5	1079
1108	—	Error reads; **GVLIEMVS**	R^4	1080
1109	—	Error reads; **GVLIELMⱯ S** 2nd **V** inverted **A**	R^4	1080A
1110	—	Error reads; **Ɐᵢ LIELMVS** 1st **V** inverted **A** *(5s-9b)*	R^4	
1111	—	**EL** over **M** in **GVLIELMVS:** Note, colon (flaw?)	R^5	1080B
1112	—	Colon after **BR:**	R^4	1080B
1113	—	second **L** over **E** in **GVLIELMVS**	R^5	1080C
1114	—	Error, date reads **1669**	R^6	1080D
1115	—	*Struck in copper on a thick flan[1]*	R^6	

L.B/9. Second bust / *Rev. 9* - shields with pointed tops   Spink 3504
Leg. punc. – **MAG   BR•FRA   ET•HIB   REX•**

1116	**1696**	See note [3] *(Unique with matching 5/- & 2/6)* *(5?s-6b)*	R^7	1088A

L.A/1. First bust, dent in hair at the back / *Rev. 1*   Spink 3497
Leg. punc. – **MAG   BR•FRA   ET•HIB   REX•**

1117	**1697**	*(4s-7b;6s-8b)*	C	1091
1118	—	Transposed arms of Scotland ↔ Ireland. E-I-F-S	R^4	1091A
1119	—	Error; Irish shield at date *(Not traced)*	R^5	1091B
1120	—	2nd **L** over **M** in **GVLIELMVS**	$R^?$	1091C
1121	—	Error reads; **GVLIELⱯI S** (2nd **V** Inverted **A**)	R	1091D
1122	—	No stops on reverse *(6s-7b)*	R	1092
1123	—	Error reads; **GVLELMVS** *(4s-5b)*	R^5	1093
1124	—	Error **E** of **DEI** struck over **A**	R^3	1094A
1125	—	Error reads; **GRI** not GRA *(6s-8b)*	R^5	1094
1126	—	*Struck in copper with a plain edge, wt. 9.66grs[1]*	R^7	1094B

SHILLINGS

L.A/1. First bust, dent in hair at the back / *Rev.* 1   Spink 3497
Leg. punc. – **MAG BR FRA   ET HIB REX**

ESC	Date	Variety, comments etc	R	(Old ESC)
1127	**1697**	No stops visible on reverse *(possible weak strike?)* *(6s-7b)*	R	1092

L.C/1. Third bust, no dent in hair at the back / *Rev.* 1.   Spink 3505
Leg. punc. – **MAG BR•FRA   ET•HIB REX•**

1128	**1697**	Large lettering *(6s-7b)*	N	1102
1129	—	No billets around lion of Nassau *(5 strings-no billets)*	R$^?$	1102B
1130	—	Small lettering	N	1102A
1131	Undated	Double obverse mule *(3 known)*	R^6	

L.D/1. Third bust variety, hair closer to the legend / *Rev.* 1. Spink 3511
Leg. punc. – **MAG BR•FRA   ET•HIB REX•**

1132	**1697**	*(6s-6b)*	N	1108
1133	—	Error reads; G∀ LIELMVS 1st V inverted **A**	R^5	1108A
1134	—	Error reads; GVLIELM∀ S 2nd V inverted **A**	R^5	1108B
1135	—	Second **L** over E(?) in GVLIELMVS	R$^?$	1108C?
1136	**1698**	*(6s-6b)*	S	1112
1137	—	*Proof* with plain edge *(Usual reverse die flaws)* *(5s-7b)*	R^5	1113

L.D/4. Third bust variety, hair close to legend
Rev. 4 - **plumes** in angles, large lions   Spink 3514
Leg. punc. – **MAG BR•FRA   ET•HIB REX•**

1138	**1698**	*(6s-6b)*	R^4	1114

L.E/1. Fourth bust *'flaming hair'* / *Rev.* 1.   Spink 3515
Leg. punc. – **MAG BR FRA   ET HIB REX**

1139	**1698**	No stops on reverse *(6s-7b)*	R^3	1115B

L.E/1. Fourth bust *'flaming hair'* / *Rev.* 1.   Spink 3515
Leg. punc. – **MAG BR•FRA   ET•HIB REX•**

1140	**1698**	*Proof* with plain edge *(6s-7b)*	R^6	1115A

L.E/1. Fourth bust *'flaming hair'* / *Rev.* 1.   Spink 3515
Leg. punc. – **MAG˙ BR•FRA˙   ET•HIB˙ REX•**

1141	**1698**	*(6s-7b)*	R	1115
1142	**1699**	*(5s-7b)*	R	1116

(continued)

156

SHILLINGS

ESC	Date	Variety, comments etc	R	(Old ESC)
1143	**1699**	Edge grained, struck on a thick flan, wt. 128.8grs	R^7	1116A
1144	—	Edge plain *(Reverse die flaw over* **REX·16***)* *(c.6-9s-6b)*	R^7	1116B

L.F/1. Fifth bust *'high hair'* / Rev. 1. Spink 3516
Leg. punc. – **MAG⁺ BR•FRA⁺ ET•HIB REX•**

1145	**1699**	*Note; no stop after* **HIB** *(5s-6b)*	R	1117
1146	—	*Proof* with plain edge *(5s-6b)*	R^5	1118
1147	—	*Note; with stop after* **HIB•** *(5s-6b)*	R	1117

L.F/3. Fifth bust / *Rev. 3* - **Roses** in angles, small lions Spink 3518
Leg. punc. – **MAG⁺ BR•FRA⁺ ET•HIB⁺ REX•**

1148	**1699**	*(5s-7b)*	R^3	1120

L.F/4. Fifth bust / *Rev. 4* - **Plumes** in angles, large lions Spink 3517
Leg. punc. – **MAG⁺ BR•FRA⁺ ET•HIB⁺ REX•**

1149	**1699**	*(5s-7b;5s-8b?)*	R^2	1119

L.F/1. Fifth bust *'high hair'* / Rev. 1. Spink 3516
Leg. punc. – **MAG⁺ BR•FRA⁺ ET•HIB⁺ REX•**

1150	**1700**	Tall **0**s in date ² *(5s-7b)*	S	1121
1151	—	Smaller and circular **oo**s in date ² *(6s-6b)*	S	1121A

L.F/1. Fifth bust *'high hair'* / Rev. 1. Spink 3516
Leg. punc. – **MAG⁺ BR FRA⁺ ET•HIB⁺ REX•**

1152	**1700**	Large linked circular **O**s in date ²	R	1122
		Note; no stop after BR *(5s-6b)*		

L.F/1. Fifth bust *'high hair'* / Rev. 1. Spink 3516
Leg. punc. – **MAG BR FRA ET HIB REX**

1153	**1700**	Tall **0**s in date ¹ *Note; no stops on rev.* *(7s-7b?)*	R	1122A

L.G/1. Fifth bust, with **plume** below / Rev. 1. Spink 3519

1154	**1700**	*(5 known) (6s-?b)*	R^5	1123

L.F/1. Fifth bust *'high hair'* / Rev. 1. Spink 3516
Leg. punc. – **MAG⁺ BR•FRA⁺ ET•HIB⁺ REX•**

1155	**1701**	*(5s-6b)*	R	1124
1156	—	No stop after **DEI** *(5s-7b)*	R	1124

SHILLINGS

L.F/4. Fifth bust / *Rev.* 4 - **Plumes** in angles, large lions   Spink 3517
Leg. punc. – **MAG˙ BR•FRA˙ ET•HIB˙ REX•**

ESC	Date	Variety, comments etc	R	(Old ESC)
1157	**1701**	*(7s-8b)*	R^2	1125

BRISTOL MINT - B below bust

B.A/1. First bust, **B** below / *Rev.* 1 - Large lettering   Spink 3498
Leg. punc. – **MAG˙ BR•FRA˙ ET•HIB˙ REX•**

1158	**1696**	See note [3] *(5s-9b)*	R	1081
1159	—	Small **x** in **REx**	S	
1160	—	Error; **G∀ LIELMVS** , large **G** in **MAG**	S	

B.C/1. First bust, **B** below / *Rev.* 1 - Large lettering   Spink 3506
Leg. punc. – **MAG BR•FRA ET.HIB REX•**

1161	**1697**	*(5s-6b;6s-6b)*	$R^{4?}$	1095

B.C/1. Third bust, **B** below / *Rev.* 1 - Large lettering   Spink 3506

1162	**1697**		R^5	1103

B.C/5. Third bust, **B** below / *Rev.* 5 - Small lettering   Spink 3506

1163	**1697**		R	1103A

B.D/1. Third bust var. **B** below, hair close to leg. / *Rev.* 1.   Spink 3512
Leg. punc. – **MAG BR•FRA ET.HIB REX•**

1164	**1697**	*(6s-6b?)*	R^3	1109

CHESTER MINT - C below bust

C.A/1 First bust, **C** below / *Rev.* 1.   Spink 3499
Leg. punc. – **MAG˙ BR•FRA˙ ET•HIB˙ REX•**

1165	**1696**	*(5s-9b)*	S	1082
1166	—	**R** of **GRA** over **V?** See note [3] *(6s-11b?)*	R^4	1082A
1167	—	*Proof* on heavy flan *(Not traced)*	R^5	1083
1168	**1697**	*(5s-9b;6s-8b)*	S	1096

158

SHILLINGS

C.C/1. Third bust, **C** below / *Rev.* 1 - Large lettering   Spink 3507

ESC	Date	Variety, comments etc	R	(Old ESC)
1169	**1696**	Probably a mule	R^3	1089
1170	—	No stops on *obv.*	S	1104A

C.C/5. Third bust, **C** below / *Rev.* 5 - Small lettering   Spink 3507

1171	**1696**		R^3	1089

C.A/1 First bust, **C** below / *Rev.* 1.   Spink 3499

1172	**1697**	*(5s-9b;(6s-8b)*	S	1096

C.D/1. Third bust var. **C** below, hair close to leg. / *Rev.* 1.   Spink 3512

1173	**1697**	No stops after **MAG FRA HIB** *(6s-6b)*	R	1109

C.A/6 First bust, **C** below
Rev. 6 - Transposed Arms of Scotland ↔ Ireland   Spink 3499

1174	**1697**		R^4	1097

C.C/1. Third bust, **C** below / *Rev.* 1 - Large lettering   Spink 3507
Leg. punc. – **MAG˙ BR•FRA˙   ET•HIB˙ REX•**

1175	**1697**	*(6s-7b; 6s-8b)*	S	1104
1176	—	Reads **FR·A · ET** in error *(Not traced)*	R^4	1104C

C.C/8. Third bust, **C** below
Rev. 8 - Arms of Scotland at date   Spink 3507

1177	**1697**	*(Not traced)*	R^5	1104B

C.D/1. Third bust var. **C** below, hair to close leg. / *Rev.* 1.   Spink 3513
Leg. punc. – **MAG BR•FRA   ET.HIB REX•**

1178	**1697**	*(6s-6b)*	R^3	1110
1179	—	Thick flan, *wt. 10.2g, 157.5grs*, *(halfcrown blank) (2 known)*	R^5	1111

EXETER MINT - **E** below bust

E.A/1 First bust, **E** below / *Rev.* 1   Spink 3500
Leg. punc. – **MAG˙ BR•FRA˙   ET•HIB˙ REX•**

1180	**1696**	*(5s-9b;6 strings)*	S	1084

E.C/1. Third bust, **E** below / *Rev.* 1- Large lettering   Spink 3508

1181	**1696**	*Probably a mule*	R^7	1089A

WILLIAM III, 1694-1702
SHILLINGS

E.A/1 First bust, **E** below / *Rev.* 1   Spink 3500

ESC	Date	Variety, comments etc		R	(Old ESC)
1182	**1697**		*(Not traced)*	R^3	1098

E.C/1. Third bust, **E** below / *Rev.* 1- Large lettering   Spink 3508
Leg. punc. – **MAG˙ BR•FRA˙ ET•HIB˙ REX•**

1183	**1697**	*(Uncertain if punctuation correct)*	*(5 strings)*	R	1105

NORWICH MINT - N below bust

N.A/1 First bust, **N** below / *Rev.* 1   Spink 3501
Leg. punc. – **MAG˙ BR•FRA˙ ET•HIB˙ REX•**

1184	**1696**		*(5s-9b)*	S	1085
1185	**1697**		*(5 strings)*	S	1099
1186	—	No stops on obverse		R^4	
1187	—	Small **7** in date		S	

N.C/1. Third bust, **N** below / *Rev.* 1- Large lettering   Spink 3509

1188	**1697**		*(7 strings)*	R	1106

YORK MINT
Capital **Y** or script **y** below bust

Y.A/1 First bust, capital **Y** below / *Rev.* 1.   Spink 3503
Leg. punc. – **MAG˙ BR•FRA˙ ET•HIB˙ REX•**

1189	**1696**		*(5 strings)*	R	1087
1190	—	**Y** over Λ upside down (die flaw?)	*(5s-9b;6s-9b)*	R^4	1088

y.A/1 First bust, script **y** below / *Rev.* 1.   Spink 3502
Leg. punc. – **MAG˙ BR•FRA˙ ET•HIB˙ REX•**

1191	**1696**		*(5s-9b)*	S	1086
1192	—	No stop after **GVLIELMVS**		S	1086

y.C/1 Third bust, script **y** below/ *Rev.* 1.   Spink 3510

1193	**1696**	Probably a mule		R^6	1090

SHILLINGS

Y.A/1   First bust, capital **Y** below / *Rev.* 1.   Spink 3503

ESC	Date	Variety, comments etc		R	(Old ESC)
1194	**1697**		*(5s-9b)*	R	1101
1195	Undated	Double obverse **Y** below busts erased	*(2 known)*	R^7	1101A

Y.A/1   First bust, script **Y** below / *Rev.* 1.   Spink 3502
         Leg. punc. – **MAG   BR•FRA˙   ET•HIB˙   REX•**

1196	**1697**	Note; no stop after **MAG**	*(4s-5b)*	S	1100

Y.A/7   First bust, script **Y** below / *Rev.* 7.   Spink 3502

1197	**1697**	Transposed Arms of Scotland ↔ Ireland	R^7	1100B

Y.A/8   First bust, script **Y** below / *Rev.* 8.   Spink 3502

1198	**1697**	Transposed Arms of France ↔ Ireland	*(unique?)*	R^7	1100A

Y.C/1   Third bust, script **Y** below/ *Rev.* 1.   Spink 3510

1199	**1697**		*(5s-8b; 7s-7b)*	R^2	1107

PATTERN

(No illustration)

L.E var./9. Fourth bust variety / *Rev.* 9 - shields with pointed tops
         Leg. punc. – **MAG   BR•FRA   ET•HIB   REX•**Spink 3504

ESC	Date	Variety, comments etc		R	(Old ESC)
1200	**1699**	*		R^7	1127

*In the British Museum there is a shilling dated 1699 as those of the fourth bust, but the hair is more wiry and the bust broader; hair on top is more like that on the early busts. It is in high relief. (P.A. Rayner)

1	See Spink Auction 140, lots 637-640 Shillings struck on copper flans, with explanation; lions vary in size on the English arms, but to simplify things they are either small or large
2	There seems to be at least three differing types of 0 used in the date 1700. Type 1 has slightly avoid figures and is the normal variety, type 2 has smaller, almost circular figures, and type 3 very elongated 0's. This exists both with and without stops on *rev.*
2	Two specimens were noted in March 1990 both from the same die and VAS
3	This bust, although known for other denominations, was not believed to exist on the shilling, and, in fact, did not appear in the first edition of this work. Seaby purchased a specimen in 1949 and this unique coin was sold by Spink & Son in Auction 3, 1979, the Lord Hamilton of Dalziel collection lot 236, £13,000

Some of the inverted Vs for As may be due to filled dies or weak strikes

WILLIAM III, 1694-1702
SIXPENCES

Legends and style as the halfcrown & shilling
Edge diagonally milled. Struck at all provincial mints

First bust (A)
(Note; 3 long curls hang almost vertically below ear)

B over E

B - Bristol

B over E

E over B

E - Exeter

Capital

Y - York

(x2)

No stops in legend

C

C - Chester

E over Y

N

N - Norwich

script

Y - York

Second bust (B)
Two locks of hair across breast; B^1 thick, B^2 thinner, cf. *Patterns* later

B^1 - GVLELMVS

B^1 - GVLIELMVS
(x2)

B^2 - GVLIELMVS

162

SIXPENCES

Third bust (C)
(Note; curls above shoulder almost diagonal)

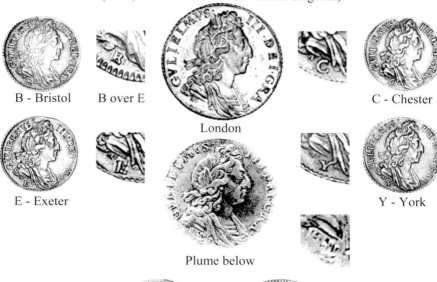

B - Bristol   B over E

London

C - Chester

E - Exeter

Y - York

Plume below

Struck on a shilling flan
REVERSES (x1·5)
Harps – crowns

1 (i)
Early - large

2 (ii)
late - large

3 (iii)
late - small

SIXPENCES

7
Plumes

9
Roses

No stops
Plain

Errors due to rotated legend

4
Scottish arms at date

6a
Irish arms at date

6
Irish arms at date

5
French arms at date

8
Irish & French arms
transposed

10
Lion inverted

GⱯLIELMVS

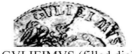

GVLIEIMVS (filled die)

GVLIEMVS

164

WILLIAM III, 1694-1702
SIXPENCES

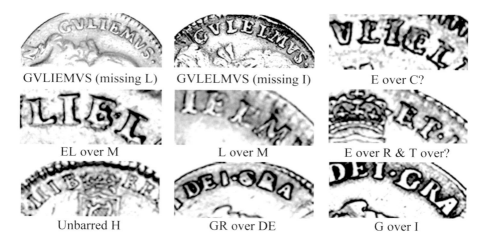

GVLIEMVS (missing L)	GVLELMVS (missing I)	E over C?
EL over M	L over M	E over R & T over?
Unbarred H	GR over DE	G over I

Bust   **A.**   **First bust**, right, with distinctive hair turned outwards above and below the crown of the head (Note; 3 long curls hanging below ear)

Rev.   **1.**   **Early harp** - Front higher than back
           Large crowns - same width as shield

       2.   **Late harp** - both front and back level
           Large crowns - same width as shield

       3.   **Late harp**
           Small crowns – narrower than shield

       B[1].   **Second bust**, large broad head with thick curls and two locks of hair spread right across breast, in very low relief [1]

       B[2].   Similar, but narrower bust with "wiry" hair, in higher relief
       3.   **Late harp - Small crowns**

       C.   **Third bust,** with hair at the back turning down and inwards (Note; curls above shoulder almost diagonal), longer ties
       2.   **Late harp - Large crowns**
       3.   **Late harp - Small crowns**
       4.   **Late harp - Large crowns - Roses** in the angles
       8.   **Late harp - Large crowns - Plumes** in the angles
       D.   **Third bust** with a small **plume below**
       2.   **Late harp - Large crowns**

WILLIAM III, 1694-1702
SIXPENCES

LONDON MINT

L.A/1. First bust / *Rev.* 1 – Early harp, large crowns   Spink 3520
         Leg. punc. – **MAG˙ BR•FRA˙   ET•HIB˙   REX•**

ESC	Date	Varieties		R	(Old ESC)
1201	**1695**		*(4 strings-7 billets)*	R	1532
1202	**1696**	See note [2]	*(3s-8b; 4s-8b)*	C^2	1533
1203	—	2nd **V** in **GVLIELMVS** is inverted **A**		R^3	
1204	—	**D** of **DEI** over **I**	*(Not traced)*	R^4	1533B
1205	—	No stops on *obv.*		R	1533A
1206	—	No stops on *rev.*		R	
1207	—	2nd **6** over **5**		R^2	1534
		E over **C?** in GVLIELMVS	*(3 strings)*		
1208	—	2nd **L** over **M** in GVLIELMVS and **E** over **R** in **ET**		R^2	1534?
1209	—	Large **As** on reverse thick flan *wt. 4.91g*	*(4 strings?)*	R^5	1534A
1210	—	*Proof in copper,* heavy flan, plain edge	*(3 strings)*	R^5	1534C

L.A/2 First bust / *Rev.* 2 – Late harp, large crowns
         Leg. punc. – **MAG   BR•FRA   ET•HIB   REX•**   Spink 3527

1211	1696	No stop after **GRA**	*(5s-6b)*	R^3	1543
1212	—	No stops on *rev.*	*(5s-6b)*	R^4	1544

L.A/3 First bust / *Rev.* 3 – Late harp, small crowns   Spink 3531

1213	1696			R^3	1545

L.A/4. First bust / *Rev.* 4 – Arms of Scotland at date   Spink 3520
         Leg. punc. – **MAG˙ BR•FRA˙   ET•HIB˙   REX•**

1214	1696		*(3 strings)*	R^4	1534B

L.A/5. First bust / *Rev.* 5 – Arms of France at date   Spink 3520

1215	1696		*(4s-8b)*	R^7	1534C

L.A/10 First bust / *Rev.* 10 – <u>Inverted lion</u> of Nassau
         Leg. punc. – **MAG   BR•FRA   ET•HIB   REX•**   Spink 3520

1216	1696			R^3	1545

SIXPENCES

L.B/3 Second bust, larger head, two locks of hair spread across the
breast, very low relief / *Rev.* 3 – Late harp, small crowns
Leg. punc. – **MAG BR•FRA   ET•HIB   REX•** Spink 3537

ESC	Date	Varieties		R	(Old ESC)
1217	**1696**	*Pattern or proof?* No stop after **GRA** *(4s-5b;7s-7b?)*		R^4	1550
1218	**1696**	Second bust. Error **GVLELMVS** *(3 known) (3 strings)*		R^5	1551

L.A/3 First bust / *Rev.* 3 – Late harp, small crowns   Spink 3531
Leg. punc. – **MAG˙ BR•FRA˙   ET•HIB˙   REX•**

1219	1697		*(5s-7b)*	C	1552
1220	—	Struck en medaille ↑↑	*(6 strings)*	R^3	1553
1221	—	**GVLIELM∀ S**		R^3	1553

L.A/3 First bust / *Rev.* 3 – Late harp, small crowns   Spink 3531
Leg. punc. – **MAG BR•FRA   ET•HIB   REX•**

1222	1697	Struck on a shilling blank	*(5s-5b)*	R^6	1552A

L.A/8 First bust / *Rev.* 8 – France ↔ Ireland <u>arms transposed</u>
Leg. punc. – **MAG BR•FRA   ET•HIB   REX•** Spink 3531

1223	1697		*(4s-6b?)*	R^5	1552B

L.B/3 Second bust, larger head, two locks of hair spread across the
breast, very low relief. No stop after **GRA**
Rev. 3 – Late harp, small crowns
Leg. punc. – **MAG BR•FRA   ET•HIB   REX•** Spink 3537

1224	1697	See note [2]	*(5s-7b)*	R^2	1564
1225	—	No stop after **GVLIELMVS**		R^5	1564B?
1226	—	Untidy *rev. leg.*	*(4 strings-7 billets)*	R^5	1564C?
1227	—	Neat *rev. leg.*	*(4s-7b; 6?str-7b)*	R^5	1564D?
1228	—	**GR** in **GRA** over **DE**		R^4	1564A
1229	—	**GR** in **GRA** over **DE GVLIEMVS** *(4 strings)* Blundered letters **H** over? & **R** over? in *rev. leg.*		R^4	1565
1230	—	**G** over **I**? in **GRA**	*(4 strings)*	R^4	1565B
1231	—	**G∀ LIELMVS**		R^4	1565C
1232	—	**GVLIELM∀ S**		R^4	1565A

2   *"I have increased the rarity of ESC 1564 to R^2. This coin is quite scarce even in poor state,
and notoriously difficult to find in VF or better, when the rarity would perhaps be R^2.
There are a great number of error readings on sixpences of this reign"* (P.A. Rayner)

SIXPENCES

L.C/2   Third bust, back hair turning downwards and inwards, longer ties
         Rev. 2 – Late harp, large crowns   Spink 3538
         Leg. punc. – **MAG   BR•FRA   ET•HIB   REX•**

ESC	Date	Varieties		R	(Old ESC)
1233	**1697**		*(4s-6b)*	C^2	1566
1234	—	**D** over **E** in **DEI**			
1235	—	**G** over **D** in **GRA**			
1236	—	**GⱯLIELMVS** Large lettering obv. & rev.	*(4s-6b)*	R^4	1566B
1237	—	**GVLIEIMVS** *(due to filled die?)*	*(4s-6b)*	R^4	1566C

L.C/3   Third bust / *Rev.* 3 – Late harp, small crowns   Spink 3542

1238	1697		R	1567
1239	—	Larger lettering on reverse		
1240	—	**D** over **E** in **DEI**	R	1567A
1241	—	**G** over **D** in **GRA**	R^3	1567B
1242	—	**G** over **I** in **GRA**	R	1567C

L.C/2   Third bust, back hair turning downwards and inwards, longer ties
         Rev. 2 – Late harp, large crowns
         Leg. punc. – **MAG   BR•FRA   ET•HIB   REX•** Spink 3538

1243	**1698**		*(4s-7b)*	N	1574

L.C/7   Third bust / *Rev.* 7 – **Plumes** in the angles
         Leg. punc. – **MAG   BR•FRA   ET•HIB   REX•** Spink 3546

1244	**1698**		*(4s-6b)*	R	1575

L.C/7   Third bust / *Rev.* 7 – **Plumes** in the angles   Spink 3546
         Leg. punc. – **MAG•   BR•FRA•   ET•HIB•   REX•**

1245	**1699**	Large lettering obverse & reverse	*(4s-6b)*	R^2	1577

L.C/8   Third bust as before / *Rev.* 8 – **Roses** in the angles   Spink 3547
         Leg. punc. – **MAG•   BR•FRA•   ET•HIB•   REX•**

1246	**1699**		*(3s–?b)*	R^2	1578
1247	—	No stop after **GRA**		R^2	1578A

Note; the following three varieties have been de-listed;
Old ESC 1534d, DFI; *"from an F. Punch with both serifs, not a broken E punch or from a clogged die."* (P.A.R.) The illustration shows the error to be caused by striking
Old ESC 1566c GVLIEIMVS looks convincing, but is probably a filled die not an error
Old ESC 1568a; DNW 16, 2011 lists lot 126 as IRA for FRA but this is due to striking

SIXPENCES

L.C/2 Third bust, back hair turning downwards and inwards, longer ties
Rev. 2 – Late harp, large crowns Spink 3538
Leg. punc. – **MAG˙ BR•FRA˙ ET•HIB˙ REX•**

ESC	Date	Varieties		R	(Old ESC)
1248	1699		*(3s–6b;4s–?b;5s-7b)*	R^3	1576
1249	—	**G Ɐ LIELMVS**	*(4s–7b?)*	R^5	1578A
1250	1700		*(4s-6b; 4s-7b;5s-7b)*	N	1579
1251	—	**G Ɐ LIELMVS**		R^4	1579A
		Large lettering obverse & reverse	*(5s-7b)*		
1252	1701		*(5s-7b)*	S	1581

L,D/2. Third bust with a small **plume** below
Rev. 2 – Late harp, large crowns Spink 3548
Leg. punc. – **MAG˙ BR•FRA˙ ET•HIB˙ REX•**

1253	1701		*(5 strings)*	R^6	1580

BRISTOL MINT

B.A/1. First bust, **B** below / *Rev.* 1 – Early harp, large crowns
Leg. punc. – **MAG˙ BR•FRA˙ ET•HIB˙ REX•** Spink 3521

1254	1696	Over-size As	*(3s-8b;4s-9b)*	N	1535
1255	—	**B** altered from **E** and over-size As	*(3s-8b;3s-9b)*	S	1535A

B.A/2. First bust, **B** below
Rev. 2 – Late harp, large crowns Spink 3528

1256	1696			R^3	1546
1257	—	No stops on obverse	*(Not traced)*	R^5	1546A

B.A/3. First bust, **B** below
Rev. 3 – Late harp, small crowns Spink 3532

1258	1696		*(4 strings, 7 billets)*	R^2	1547
1259	—	No stops on obverse		R^2	1548

B.A/2. First bust, **B** below / *Rev.* 2 – Late harp, large crowns
Leg. punc. – **MAG BR•FRA ET•HIB REX•** Spink 3528

1260	1697	9 over 9?	*(4s-6b)*	R	1554

Many varieties are generally too small to illustrate clearly

SIXPENCES

B.A/3. First bust, **B** below / *Rev.* 3 – Late harp, small crowns
Leg. punc. – **MAG BR•FRA   ET•HIB   REX•** Spink 3532

ESC	Date	Varieties	R	(Old ESC)
1261	**1697**	*(4 strings-6 billets?)*	*N*	1555
1262	—	*Struck en medaille* ↑↑ *(5s-6b?)*	*R³*	
1263	—	**B** altered from **E** *(4s-7b)*	*N*	1555A
1264	—	**B** altered from **E** Reads **M•AG** *(4s-7b)*	*N*	1555C
1265	—	Inverted lion of Orange in centre *(? strings-6 billets)*	*N*	1555B

B.C/2. Third bust, **B** below / *Rev.* 2 – Late harp, large crowns
Leg. punc. – **MAG BR•FRA   ET•HIB   REX•** Spink 3539

ESC	Date	Varieties	R	(Old ESC)
1266	**1697**	*(4 strings)*	*R*	1568
1267	—	**B** altered from **E** Large lettering obverse & reverse *(4 strings)*	*R*	1568A

CHESTER MINT

C.A/1. First bust, **C** below / *Rev.* 1 – Early harp, large crowns
Leg. punc. – **MAG˙ BR•FRA˙   ET•HIB˙   REX•** Spink 3522

ESC	Date	Varieties	R	(Old ESC)
1268	**1696**	Over-size **As** *(3 strings-9 billets)*	*S*	1536

C.A/3. First bust, **C** below / *Rev.* 3 – Late harp, small crowns
Leg. punc. – **MAG BR•FRA   ET•HIB   REX•** Spink 3533

ESC	Date	Varieties	R	(Old ESC)
1269	**1696**	*(6s-7b)*	*R⁴*	1548A

C.A/2. First bust, **C** below / *Rev.* 1 – Late harp, large crowns Spink 3529

ESC	Date	Varieties	R	(Old ESC)
1270	**1697**	*(Not traced)*	*R⁴*	1556

C.A/3. First bust, **C** below / *Rev.* 3 – Late harp, small crowns
Leg. punc. – **MAG BR•FRA   ET•HIB   REX•** Spink 3533

ESC	Date	Varieties	R	(Old ESC)
1271	**1697**	*(4s-7b;5s-6b)*	*N*	1557
1272	—	Plain edge, struck without a collar *(5s-7b)*	*R*	1557B
1273	—	No stops after **MAG FRA HIB**	*R⁵*	1557A

C.A/6. First bust, **C** below / *Rev.* 6/ – Irish arms at date and inverted lion
Leg. punc. – **MAG BR•FRA   ET•HIB   REX•** Spink 3533

ESC	Date	Varieties	R	(Old ESC)
1274	**1697**	Note; Inverted lion of Orange in centre Mixed size lettering on reverse *(4s-7b)*	*R⁵*	1558

SIXPENCES

C.C/2. Third bust, **C** below / *Rev.* 2 – Late harp, large crowns
Leg. punc. – **MAG BR•FRA   ET•HIB   REX•**   Spink 3540

ESC	Date	Varieties		R	(Old ESC)
1275	**1697**	See note	*(4 strings)*	R^3	1569

C.C/3. Third bust, **C** below / *Rev.* 3 – Late harp, small crowns
Leg. punc. – **MAG BR•FRA   ET•HIB   REX•**   Spink 3543

| 1276 | **1697** | Large lettering obverse & reverse | *(6s-6b)* | R^3 | 1570 |

EXETER MINT

E.A/1. First bust, **E** below / *Rev.* 1 – Early harp, large crowns
Leg. punc. – **MAG˙ BR•FRA˙   ET•HIB˙   REX•** Spink 3523

| 1277 | **1696** | | *(3s-8b)* | R | 1537 |

E.A/3. First bust, **E** below / *Rev.* 3 – Late harp, small crowns
Leg. punc. – **MAG BR•FRA   ET•HIB   REX•** Spink 3534

| 1278 | **1696** | | *(6s-7b)* | R^3 | 1548B |

E.C/1. Third bust, **E** below /
Rev. 1 – Early harp, large crowns   Spink 3537A
Leg. punc. – **MAG˙ BR•FRA˙   ET•HIB˙   REX•**

| 1279 | **1696** | *A mule* | *(?s-7b)* | R^7 | 1542A |

E.A/2. First bust, **E** below / *Rev.* 2 – Late harp, large crowns
Leg. punc. – **MAG BR•FRA   ET•HIB   REX•** Spink 3530

| 1280 | **1697** | | *(4s-6b)* | R | 1559 |

E.A/3. First bust, **E** below / *Rev.* 3 – Late harp, small crowns
Leg. punc. – **MAG BR•FRA   ET•HIB   REX•** Spink 3534

1281	**1697**	*Rev.* mixed size lettering	*(4s-6b)*	S	1560
1282	—	**E** over **B** below bust		R^4	1560A
1283	—	Small **7** in date (from Maundy?)		R^2	1560C

SIXPENCES

E.A/3. First bust, **E** below
Rev. 3 – Late harp, small crowns   Spink 3534
Leg. punc. – **MAG· BR·FRA· ET·HIB· REX·**

ESC	Date	Varieties		R	(Old ESC)
1284	1697	E over M in **GVLIE·LMVS**	*(3s-6b)*	R^2	1560B
		Note; the stop is underlying remnant of letter M			
1285	—	E over C in **GVLIELMVS**		R^3	1560B
		Over-size **A**s obverse & reverse	*(3s-6b?)*		

E.C/2. Third bust, **E** below / *Rev.* 2 – Late harp, large crowns
Leg. punc. – **MAG BR·FRA ET·HIB REX·**   Spink 3541

1286	1697	Large lettering obverse & reverse	*(4s-6b)*	R^3	1571

E.C/3. Third bust, **E** below / *Rev.* 3 – Late harp, small crowns
Leg. punc. – **MAG BR·FRA ET·HIB REX·** Spink 3544

1287	1697		*(4s?-7b)*	R	1572

NORWICH MINT

N.A/1. First bust, **N** below / *Rev.* 1 – Early harp, large crowns
Leg. punc. – **MAG· BR·FRA· ET·HIB· REX·** Spink 3524

1288	1696		*(3s-8b)*	S	1538

N.A/3. First bust, **N** below / *Rev.* 3 – Late harp, small crowns
Leg. punc. – **MAG BR·FRA ET·HIB REX·** Spink 3535

1289	1696		*(4s-7b)*	R^3	1549
1290	1697	Unbarred **H**	*(4 strings) (4s-8b)*	N	1561
1291	—	No stop after **BR**		N	1561
1292	—	Larger lettering on reverse	*(4s-6b)*	R^2	1561
1293	—	Error reads **GVLIEMVS** Stop after **FRA·**	*(4s-6b)*	R^5	1561A

YORK MINT
Capital **Y** or script **y** below bust

Y.A/1. First bust, capital **Y** below / *Rev.* 1 – Early harp, large crowns
Leg. punc. – **MAG· BR·FRA· ET·HIB· REX·** Spink 3526

1294	1696		*(4 strings)*	R	1540
1295	1696	No stops on obverse	*(3s-8b)*	R^2	1541

SIXPENCES

Y.A/1. First bust, script **Y** below / *Rev.* 1 – Early harp, large crowns
Leg. punc. – **MAG˙ BR•FRA˙ ET•HIB˙ REX•** Spink 3525

ESC	Date	Varieties		R	(Old ESC)
1296	**1696**	Mixed size lettering on reverse	*(3s-9b)*	C	1539

Y.C/1. Third bust, capital **Y** below
Rev. 1 – Early harp, large crowns   Spink 3537B
Leg. punc. – **MAG˙ BR•FRA˙ ET•HIB˙ REX•**

1297	**1696**	*A mule* [3]	*(4s-9b)*	R^6	1542
		Mixed size lettering on reverse	*(3 known)*		

Y.A/3. First bust, script **Y** below / *Rev.* 3 – Late harp, small crowns
Leg. punc. – **MAG BR•FRA ET•HIB REX•** Spink 3536

1298	**1697**	*(2s-6b; 3s-7b;4s-7b;5s-7b)*	R	1562

Y.A/6a. First bust, script **Y** below
Rev. 6a – Irish arms at date and lion of orange sideways
Leg. punc. – **MAG BR•FRA ET•HIB REX•** Spink 3536

1299	**1697**	*(5s-6b)*	R^5	1563

Y.C/1. Third bust, capital **Y** below
Rev. 1 – Early harp, large crowns   Spink 3537B

1300	**1697**	A mule *(struck in 1697, with an old reverse of 1696 in error)*	R^6	?

Y.C/3. Third bust, capital **Y** below / *Rev.* 3 – Late harp, small crowns
Leg. punc. – **MAG BR•FRA ET•HIB REX•** Spink 3545

1301	**1697**	Large lettering obverse & reverse	*(5s-7b?)*	R^2	1573

PATTERNS
By **James Roettier, 1696 & 1697**

Second bust - B[1]

SIXPENCES

PATTERNS

Second bust - B²

Bust   **B¹.**   **Second bust**, large broad head, laureate and draped, thick curls, two locks of hair spread right across breast, in very low relief [1]

       B².   **Second bust**, similar, but with "wiry" hair, in higher relief and more finely engraved. Note alignment of legend closer to top hair

L.B¹/3.   Second bust, low relief [1]
Rev. 3 – Late harp, small crowns

ESC	Date	Varieties	R	(Old ESC)
1302	**1696**		R^5	
1303	**1697**		R^7	

L.B²/3.   Second bust "wiry" hair, in higher relief
Rev. 3 – Late harp, small crowns

1304	**1696**	*(3 known, 2 in private hands)* *7 harp strings, wt. 2.80g*	R^6	

1   There is a matching second bust crown and halfcrown in the National Collection,

MAUNDY MONEY

MAUNDY SETS
(The four denominations with uniform dates and toning)

Spink 3553

ESC	Date	Varieties	R	(Old ESC)
1305	**1698**		R	2389
1306	**1699**		R^2	2390
1307	**1700**		R^2	2391
1308	**1701**		R	2392

GROATS
Only one type, as illustration

1702

MAG

Spink 3549

ESC	Date	Varieties, comments etc.	*Robinson*	R	(Old ESC)
1309	**1697**	(Unique?)	*p. 153,115*	R^7	1880
1310	**1698**	MAG		R	1881
1311	**1699**		*p. 153,123*	S	1882
1312	**1700**	No stop after date	*p. 153,127(i)*	R	1883A
1313	**1701**		*p. 153,131*	R	1884
1314	**1702**	**J** type 1 in date. See note [1]		N	1885

WILLIAM III, 1694-1702
MAUNDY MONEY

THREEPENCES
Only one type, as illustration

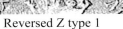

Reversed Z type 1   J type 1

Spink 3550

ESC	Date	Varieties, comments etc.	Robinson	R	(Old ESC)
1315	**1698**		p. 153,118	N	2000
1316	**1699**		p. 153,122	S	2001
1317	**1700**		p. 153,126	N	2002
1318	**1701**	**Z**-type **1**s in date Small lettering	p. 153,130(i)	N	2003
1319	—	**J**-type **1**s in date Large lettering	p. 153,130(ii)	N	2004
1320	—	**GBA** for GRA	p. 153,130(iii)	S	2003A

HALFGROATS or TWOPENCES
Obverse as groats and threepences with *reverses* 1, 2 & 3

1   A   2   3

Type   **A/1**   *Rev.* 1. - crown to edge of coin dividing date, large figure **2**

      A/2   *Rev.* 2. - crowned numeral smaller than 1 but larger than 3

      A/3   *Rev.* 3. - crown within inner circle of legend, date above, smaller **2**

WILLIAM III, 1694-1702
MAUNDY MONEY

A/1. *Rev.* 1. - crown to edge of coin, large figure **2**   Spink 3551

ESC	Date	Varieties, comments etc.	*Robinson*	*R*	(Old ESC)
1321	**1698**			*R*	2206

A/2. *Rev.* 2, - crowned numeral smaller than '1'   Spink ?

1322	**1698**	Date partly above the crown	*p. 153,117(i)*		

A/3. *Rev.* 3. - crown within inner circle of legend   Spink 3551A

1323	**1699**		*p. 153,121*	*S*	2207
1324	**1700**		*p. 153,125*	*S*	2208
1325	**1701**		*p. 153,129*	*N*	2209

PENNIES
Only one type, as illustration

Spink 3552

ESC	Date	Varieties, comments etc.	*Robinson*	*R*	(Old ESC)
1326	**1698**			*S*	2307
1327	—	**6** of date above crown	*p. 153,116(i)*	*S*	2308
1328	—	**9** of date above crown	*p. 153,116(ii)*	R^2	2309
1329	—	Reads **IRA** for FRA	*p. 153,116(iii)*	*S*	2310
1330	—	Reads **HI· BREX**	*p. 153,116(iv)*	*S*	2311
1331	—	Reads **HI BREX**	*p. 153,116(v)*	*S*	2311
1332	**1699**		*p. 153,120*	R^2	2312
1333	**1700**	1st **0** partly over the crown	*p. 153,124(i)*	*R*	2313
1334	**1701**		*p. 153,128(i)*	*S*	2314
1335	**1701**	No stop after **MAG** or **ET**	*p. 153,128(ii)*	*S*	2314

---

1   This date, 1702, does not occur upon any other coins of this reign and should not correctly occur upon this. At this period the New Year commenced on the 25th March, whilst the king died on 8th March

ANNE
1702-14

No great change occured in the coinage of this reign but the Union with Scotland in 1707 affected the design of the Royal arms on the shield. Heretofore the arms of England and Scotland had been placed in separate shields, but after the Act of Union they were impaled on two shields. Two new provenance marks appear on the coins of Anne. Some coins from the crown to sixpence have VIGO below the queen's head – this commemorates the capture of the Spanish treasure at Vigo Bay in 1702 and it is from the metal captured that the coins were struck. Also we find for the first time the use of roses and plumes together on the same coin. An Order in Council of the 5th April 1706 directed the money coined from silver brought into the Mint by the *'Company for smelting down Lead with Pitcoale and Seacoale should 'have the mark of distinction on each piece as represented in their petition'.*

Before the Act of Union the coinage of Scotland was quite separate from that of England, the Sottish denominations being equivalent to only 1/12th of the English. For this reason the Anne 10 shilling piece struck in Scotland in 1705 weighed only 71grains compared with the English shilling of 92 grains. As from the Union, the United Kingdom of England and Scotland used the same coinage, but during the years 1707-9, the Mint in Edinburgh continued to strike coins. These were the same design as those struck in London and were for the most part from London made dies and puncheons, but had an E or E★ below the queen's bust. As these coins were circulating in both coutries it seems reasonable to include them in this book especially as some of them are almost the commonest coins of the reign.

At the beginning of the reign the engravers upon whom the work of engraving the coin dies rested were Croker and his apprentice Bull. James Roettier had been dismissed in 1697 as mentioned earlier, and his brother Norbert, who had been accused of 'playing tricks' with William III's portrait on the halfpence of William and Mary in 1694, had taken little active part in coinage ever since.

The sketches from which the coinage of Anne was engraved were probably the work of Sir Godfrey Kneller as a portrait in oils by this artist is very similar to that on the first coins. A newspaper of that period (*The Postman*) mentioned in April 1702 that *'..... the Queen had lately had her picture drawn by Sir Godfrey Kneller in order to grave an impress for her coronation medals and coin'.*

ANNE
1702-14

Croker was responsible for the engraving of most of the coinage dies, but his apprentice Bull and also one Gabriel Leclerk were appointed Assistant Engravers in 1705 and the former may have been responsible for some of the reverses as the task was often performed by an under-engraver at this time. Bull in fact engraved many of the reverses for Croker's medals of Anne. Little is known of Leclerk and he is not thought to have played an active part in the engraving of coinage dies – he left the Mint in 1709. It is, as in the previous reign, almost impossible to differentiate between the work of Bull and Croker due to the lack of contemporary records, but the former may have been responsible for the portrait on the 5 guineas of 1711, which differs in style from the other coins.

After the Union in 1707, it became the task of the Mint in Edinburgh to call in and convert into United Kingdom coin all the old Scottish money.

Puncheons for the making of dies were supplied by the Tower Mint and in a Warrant of June, the Master of the Edinbugh Mint was ordered to *'cause the .... engraver to make new dyes' from these Tower Puncheons and ' ...... to make new puncheons and to use them for making dyes' which should be 'perfectly lyke the monies coined in .... the Tower'.* Over half the bullion was coined into shillings and sixpences and this naturally caused more wear and tear on the dies for these denominations than those for the crown and halfcrown. This most probably accounts for the *'Edinburgh'* bust on the small coins; this was undoubtedly an effort on the part of James Clerk, the then Scottish engraver, after Croker's puncheons for the second and third bust shillings and the ordinary sixpences had become exhausted.

An extract from Treasury papers of 1711 states that Clerk and his assistant Cave *'did .... make puncheons .... for small coynes, viz. foure pence, three pence, two pence and one penny, etc.'* They were asking for an increase in salary in respect of their *'extraordinary trouble during the great coinage'*. Little is known of the Maundy coins. There is however a slight change in portaiture on the small coins of 1706-7, but one cannot ascribe these with any certainty to the Mint at Edinburgh. (P.A.Rayner, 1949)

ANNE 1702-14
CROWNS

OBVERSES

First bust
VIGO below

First bust
Plain below

Second bust
Plain below

Second bust
E below

Third bust
Plain below

CROWNS

REVERSES

Reverse 1
Plain in angles

Before union
crowns with
interiors

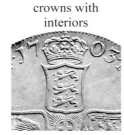

J type 1
Straight 7

Reverse 2
Plumes in angles

Reverse 3
Roses & plumes in angles

After union
crowns without
interiors

Script 1 & 7

Reverse 4
Plain angles

Reverse 5
Plumes in angles

Reversed Z type 1
Smaller O8

Large O & 8 over 7

Reverse 6
Roses & plumes in angles

CROWNS

BEFORE UNION WITH SCOTLAND

LONDON MINT
Leg. BR FRA

Type	**A.**	First bust, the two stray curls on top are low, **VIGO•** below
Leg.		**ANNA • DEI • GRATIA .**
Rev.	**1.**	Single crowned cruciform shields as before, with the Star of the Garter in the centre. Plain in angles
Leg.	1p	17♛ 03•MAG ♛ BR•FRA ♛ ET•HIB ♛ REG• (pellets) (Note; no stops after **MAG FRA HIB**)
Edge		**DECVS ET TVTAMEN ANNO REGNI TERTIO**
Type	**B.**	As before, but, without VIGO below bust
Rev.	**2.**	As before, but with **Plumes** in the angles
Type	**C.**	As type B
Rev.	**3.**	As before, but with **Roses** and **Plumes** alternately in the angles

A/1. First bust, **VIGO•** below / *Rev.* 1 – plain in angles
   Leg. punc. – **MAG BR • FRA ET • HIB REG •** Spink 3576

ESC	Date	Edge year		Varieties		R	(Old ESC)
1340	**1703**	**TERTIO**	(3)		*(7 strings)*	*N*	99

B/2. First bust, plain below / *Rev.* 2 – **Plumes** in angles
   Leg. punc. – **MAG BR • FRA ET • HIB REG •** Spink 3577

1341	**1705**	**QVINTO**	(5)		*(7 strings)*	R^2	100

C/3. First bust, plain below / *Rev.* 3 – **Roses** and **Plumes** in angles
   Leg. punc. – **MAG BR • FRA ET • HIB REG •** Spink 3578

1342	**1706**	**QVINTO**	(5)		*(6 strings)*	*R*	101
1343	**1707**	**SEXTO**	(6)		*(7,8 strings)*	*C*	102

CROWNS

AFTER UNION WITH SCOTLAND
Leg. **BRI FR**

Type	**D.**	Second bust, the two stray curls on top are taller, the head is also at least 1 mm. broader. Letter **E** (*Edinburgh mint*) below bust
Rev.	**4.**	*'After Union' reverse;* Cruciform shields, but the top and bottom shields have the English and Scottish arms impaled, and the shield on the right bears the French arms (3 lis) and the left one the Irish harp. Plain in the angles
Leg.	2	Reads **BRI FR**
Type	**E.**	Second bust as before, but without the letter E below (*Tower*)
Rev.	**4.**	As before, plain in angles
Type	**F.**	As type E
Rev.	**5.**	As before, with **plumes** in the angles
Type	**G.**	Third bust, hair more wiry, plain below
Rev.	**6.**	As before, but **roses and plumes** in the angles

LONDON MINT
Reverse punctuation as shown

E/4. Second bust, plain below / *Rev.* 4 - plain in angles
Leg. punc. – **MAG BRI : FR • ET • HIB : REG :** Spink 3601

ESC	Date	Edge year		Varieties	R	(Old ESC)
1344	**1707**	**SEPTIMO**	(7)	*(9 strings)*	N	104

E/4. Second bust, plain below / *Rev.* 4 - plain in angles
Leg. punc. – **MAG BRI : FR ET HIB : REG :** Spink 3601

1345	**1707**	**SEPTIMO**	(7)	*(9 strings)*	N	104

E/4. Second bust, plain below / *Rev.* 4 - plain in angles
Leg. punc. – **MAG : BRI : FR • ET • HIB : REG :** Spink 3601

1346	**1708**	**SEPTIMO**	(7)	*(8,9 strings, some with twin ends)*	N	105

F/5. Second bust, plain below / *Rev.* 5 - **plumes** in the angles
Leg. punc. – **MAG : BRI : FR • ET • HIB : REG :** Spink 3602

1347	**1708**	**SEPTIMO**	(7)	*(8,9 strings)*	S	108

CROWNS

F/5var. Second bust, plain below / *Rev.* 5 - **plumes** in the angles
Error with before Union legend reads **BR • FRA**

ESC	Date	Edge year		Varieties	R	(Old ESC)
1348	**1708**	**SEPTIMO**	(7)	*(Recorded by Rayner but not traced)*	R^7	108A

G/6. Third bust, wiry hair, plain below / *Rev.* 7 - **roses** and **plumes**
Leg. punc. – **MAG : BRI • FR • ET • HIB • REG •** Spink 3603

1349	**1713**	**DVODECIMO**	(12)	*(8 strings)*	N	109

EDINBURGH MINT

D/4. Second bust, **E** below / *Rev.* 4 - plain in angles
Leg. punc. – **MAG : BRI : FR • ET : HIB : REG :** Spink 3600

1350	**1707**	**SEXTO**	(6)	*(10 strings)*	C^2	103

D/4. Second bust, **E** below / *Rev.* 4 - plain in angles
Leg. punc. – **MAG : BRI : FR • ET • HIB : REG :** Spink 3600

1351	**1707**	**SEXTO**	(6)	*(9,13 strings)*	C^2	103

D/4. Second bust, **E** below / *Rev.* 4 - plain in angles
Leg. punc. – **MAG : BRI : FR : ET • HIB : REG :** Spink 3600

1352	**1707**	**SEXTO**	(6)	*(? strings)*	C^2	103

D/4. Second bust, **E** below / *Rev.* 4 - plain in angles
Leg. punc. – **MAG : BRI : FR   ET   HIB : REG :** Spink 3600

1353	**1707**	**SEXTO**	(6)	*(13 strings)*	C^2	103

D/4. Second bust, **E** below / *Rev.* 4 - plain in angles
Leg. punc. – **MAG : BRI : FR : ET • HIB : REG :** Spink 3600

1354	**1707**	**SEPTIMO**	(7)	*(11 strings)*	R^6	103A
1355	**1708**	**SEPTIMO**	(7)	**8 over 7** *(9,11,12 strings)* **M over E** in **SEPTIMO**	S	107

D/4. Second bust, **E** below / *Rev.* 4 - plain in angles, Z-type 1 in date
Leg. punc. – **MAG   BRI • FR   ET • HIB   REG •** Spink 3600

1356	**1708**	**SEPTIMO**	(7)	Straight **7,** small **08** *(7 strings)*	N	106

HALFCROWNS

As crowns

(A) 1st bust

(B) 1st bust VIGO •

(C) 1st bust E

(D) 2nd bust

REVERSE - BEFORE UNION

(1) Plain

(2) Plumes

(3) Rose & plumes

REVERSES - AFTER UNION

(4) Plain

(5) Plumes

(6) Rose & plumes

J type 1 in date

Z type 1 in date

4 over 3

ANNE, 1702-14
HALFCROWNS

Obv.	**A.**	First bust, left, short length of dress showing over her right shoulder, square top end to ribbon, tied in a bow, plain below
Leg.		As the crown, with letters in **GRATIA** widely spaced

B. As before, with **VIGO•** below bust

C. As before, with letter **E** (*Edinburgh Mint*) below bust

D. Second bust, with subtle changes to hair style, longer length of dress showing over her right shoulder, bevel top end to ribbon blends with the hair above, a small butterfly shape curl protrudes above the hair line, V-shape ties

Leg. As before, but the letters in **GRATIA** closer together

Before Union types

Rev. **1.** As the crown, with individual arms in each shield, plain in angles
Leg. Reads **BR FRA**

2. As before, but with **plumes** in the angles

3. As before, but with **roses and plumes** alternately in the angles

After Union types

4. English & Scottish arms impaled in the top and bottom shields, French on the right and Irish left. Plain in angles
Leg. As the crown, reading **BRI FR**

5. Similar, but with **Plumes** in the angles

6. Similar, but with **Roses & Plumes** in alternate angles

J type figure 1s in date for London dies
A reversed Z type 1s in date for Edinburgh dies
Note; some rare Edinburgh dies have a J type 1 in date

ANNE, 1702-14
HALFCROWNS

BEFORE UNION WITH SCOTLAND
LONDON MINT
BR : FRA

A/1. First bust, plain below / *Rev.* 1 - Plain in angles, colons in *leg.*
Leg. punc. – **MAG: BR:FRA• ET•HIB: REG:**   Spink 3579

ESC	Date	Edge year		Varieties		R	(Old ESC)
1357	1703	TERTIO	(3)		*(7 strings)*	R^4	568

B/1. First bust, **VIGO** below / *Rev.* 1 – As before
Leg. punc. – **MAG: BR:FRA• ET•HIB• REG:**   Spink 3580

| 1358 | 1703 | TERTIO | (3) | **VIGO** below bust | *(6,7 strings)* | N | 569 |

A/2c. First bust, plain below / *Rev.* 2 - **Plumes** in angles, colons in *leg.*
Leg. punc. – **MAG: BR:FRA• ET•HIB• REG:**   Spink 3581

| 1359 | 1704 | TERTIO | (3) | | *(7 strings)* | R^2 | 570 |

A/2s. First bust, plain below / *Rev.* 2 - **Plumes** in angles, stops in *leg.*
Leg. punc. – **MAG• BR•FRA• ET•HIB• REG•**   Spink 3581

| 1360 | 1705 | QVINTO | (5) | | *(8 strings)* | R | 571 |

A/3. First bust, plain below / *Rev.* 2 – **Roses & plumes** in angles,
Leg. punc. – **MAG• BR•FRA• ET•HIB• REG•**   Spink 3582

1361	1706	QVINTO	(5)	See note [1]	*(8,9 strings)*	S	572
1362	1707	SEXTO	(6)		*(6,8 strings)*	N	573
1363	—	—	—	No stops on reverse		R^4	

A/3. First bust, plain below / *Rev.* 2 – **Roses & plumes** in angles,
Leg. punc. – **MAG• BR:FRA• ET•HI B• REG:**   Spink 3582

| 1264 | 1707 | SEXTO | (6) | Wide colon after **REG:** | *(6 strings)* | N | 573 |
| 1265 | — | — | — | Narrow colon after **REG:** | *(8 strings* | N | 573A |

187

HALFCROWNS

AFTER UNION WITH SCOTLAND
LONDON MINT
BRI • FR
Standard punctuation; **MAG BRI•FR ET•HIB REG•**

D/4. Second bust, plain below / *Rev.* 4 - Plain in angles   Spink 3604

ESC	Date	Edge year		Varieties		R	(Old ESC)
1366	**1707**	**SEPTIMO**	(7)		*(8 strings)*	N	574
1367	—	—	—	Extra **T** on edge before **TUTAMEN**		R^4	574A
1368	—	—	—	*Piedfort* wt. 20.63g	*(8 strings)*	R^6	574B

A/5. First bust , plain below / *Rev.* 5 - **Plume**s in angles   Spink 3606

1369	**1708**	**SEPTIMO**	(7)		*(8 strings)*	R	578

D/4. Second bust, plain below / *Rev.* 4 - Plain in angles   Spink 3604

1370	**1708**	**SEPTIMO**	(7)		*(7,8 strings)*	C	577
1371	**1709**	**OCTAVO**	(8)		*(7,8 strings)*	N	579

D/6. Second bust, plain below
    Rev. 4 - **Roses & plumes** in alternate angles   Spink 3607

1372	**1710**	**NONO**	(9)	++++ in edge *leg.*	*(7 strings)*	S	581
1373	—	—	—	Inverted **A**s for **V**s on edge		R^2	581A
1374	**1712**	**UNDECIMO**	(11)	++++ in edge *leg.*	*(7 strings)*	C	582
1375	—	**DVODECIMO**	(12)	Inverted **A**s for **V**s on edge		N	584

D/4. Second bust, plain below / *Rev.* 4 - Plain in angles   Spink 3604

1376	**1713**	**DVODECIMO**	(12)		*(7,8 strings)*	S	583

D/6. Second bust, plain below
    Rev. 4 - **Roses & plumes** in alternate angles   Spink 3607

1377	**1714**	**D. TERTIO**	(13)		*(7 strings)*	N	585
1378	—	—	—	4 over 3 [4] + cross on edge	*(6 strings)*	R^4	585A

ANNE, 1702-14
HALFCROWNS

EDINBURGH MINT

		C/4. First bust, **E** below / *Rev.* 4 - Plain in angles			Spink 3605	
1379	**1707**	**SEXTO**	(6)	*(6,7 strings)*	C^2	575
1380	—	*Reading unclear*	**T★TAMEN** (Note ★ for V) *(7 strgs)*		R^4	
1381	—	**SEPTIMO**	(7)	*(7 strings)*	R^5	575A

		C/4. First bust, **E** below / *Rev.* 4 - Plain in angles				Spink 3605	
1382	**1708**	**SEPTIMO**	(7)	**J** type figure 1	*(6,7,9 strings)*	R^2	576
1383	—	—	—	**J** type figure 1	*(6,7,9 strings)*	R	576A
1384	**1709**	**OCTAVO**	(8)	**Z** type 9 stars on edge *(7 strings)*		R^3	580

1	The style of the crowns above the shields on 1706 and 1707 roses and plumes varies.
2	On Edinburgh halfcrown's of 1707 the figure 1 in date is always a J-type, as on all coins of the London mint. Edinburgh coins of 1708 usually have a local *rev.* die with a Z-type 1. Tower die with a J-type figure 1 on coins of 1708 are rare
3	On this coin the 1 in the date appears to be J over Z or Z over J.
4	This over date is very difficult to discern.

189

SHILLINGS

BUSTS

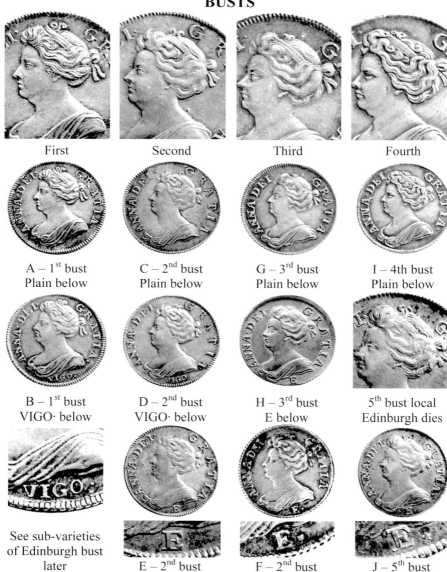

First	Second	Third	Fourth

A – 1st bust	C – 2nd bust	G – 3rd bust	I – 4th bust
Plain below	Plain below	Plain below	Plain below

B – 1st bust	D – 2nd bust	H – 3rd bust	5th bust local
VIGO· below	VIGO· below	E below	Edinburgh dies

See sub-varieties of Edinburgh bust later	E – 2nd bust	F – 2nd bust	J – 5th bust
	E below	E ★ below	E ★ below

190

ANNE, 1702-14
SHILLINGS

REVERSES

BEFORE UNION
BR • FRA

1	2	3
Plain	Roses & Plumes	Plumes

AFTER UNION
BRI • FR

4	5	6
Plain	Roses & Plumes	Plumes

Blundered crown over B	3 over 2

Obv. **A.** First bust, draped, left, plain below, similar to the half-crown, square top ended wide ribbon tied in a large bow with long outward curving ties, two thick round curls above ribbon

B. First bust with **VIGO·** below

191

SHILLINGS

C.   Second bust, subtle changes to hair style, thinner ribbon, with a bevelled top end, blending with the hair above, two thin wispy curls protrude above the hair line, smaller bow with shorter ties

D.   Second bust with **VIGO·** below, the letters in **G R A T I A** are more widely spaced than on the first bust

E.   Second bust with **E** *Edinburgh Mint* below

F.   Second bust with **E ★** below

G.   Third bust with changes to hair style; wider ribbon cutting into the hair creating a distinctive notch above, large front curls conceal the top end and one curl half crosses the middle, tied in a large bow with v-shape downward curving ties

H.   Third bust with letter **E** below

I.   Fourth bust, plain below, similar to third bust, but more changes to hair style; curls are more snake-like, especially above the ribbon and the ties are together

J.   Fifth bust with **E ★** below, Edinburgh mint, local dies

Rev.   **1.**   Before Union; *Leg.* reads **BR FRA**
                As the crown, with individual arms in each shield, plain in angles

    2.   As before, but with **plumes** in the angles

    3.   As before, but with **roses and plumes** alternately in the angles

    4.   After Union; *Leg.* reads **BRI FR**
                English & Scottish arms impaled in the top and bottom shields, French on the right and Irish left. Plain in angles

    5.   Similar, but with **plumes** in the angles

    6.   Similar, but with **roses & plumes** in alternate angles

SHILLINGS

BEFORE UNION WITH SCOTLAND

LONDON MINT
BR • FRA
Standard *legend* & *punctuation* unless stated
MAG   BR•FRA   ET•HIB   REG•

A/1.   First bust, plain below / *Rev.* 1 – Plain in angles   Spink 3583

ESC	Date	Varieties, comments etc.	R	(Old ESC)
1385	**1702**	*(6 strings)*	S	1128

A/2.   First bust, plain below / *Rev.* 2 – **Plume**s in angles   Spink 3584

1386	**1702**	*(6 strings)*	R	1129

B/1.   First bust, **VIGO•** below / *Rev.* 1 – Plain in angles   Spink 3585

1387	**1702**	*(6 strings)*	S	1130

D/1.   Second bust, **VIGO•** below / *Rev.* 1 – Plain in anglesSpink 3586

1388	**1703**	*(5,6 strings)*	S	1131

C/1.   Second bust, plain below / *Rev.* 1 – Plain in angles   Spink 3587

1389	**1704**	*(6 strings)*	R^5	1132

C/2.   Second bust, plain below / *Rev.* 2 – **Plume**s in angles. Spink 3588

1390	**1704**	*(6 strings)*	R^2	1133

C/1.   Second bust, plain below / *Rev.* 1 – Plain in angles   Spink 3587

1391	**1705**	*(6 strings)*	R^2	1134

C/2.   Second bust, plain below / *Rev.* 2 – **Plume**s in angles Spink 3588

1392	**1705**	*(6 strings)*	S	1135

C/3.   Second bust, plain below
     Rev. 3 – **Roses & plume**s in angles   Spink 3589

1393	**1705**	*(6 strings)*	S	1136
1394	**1707**	*(6 strings)*	R	1137

SHILLINGS

AFTER UNION WITH SCOTLAND

LONDON MINT
BRI • FR
Standard *legend* & *punctuation* unless stated
MAG   BRI•FR   ET•HIB   REG•

G/4.   Third bust, plain below / *Rev.* 4 – Plain in angles   Spink 3610

ESC	Date	Varieties, comments etc.	R	(Old ESC)
1395	**1707**	*(8 strings)*	N	1141

G/5.   Third bust, plain below / *Rev.* 5 – **Plumes** in angles   Spink 3611

1396	**1707**	*(6 strings)*	S	1142

C/4.   Second bust, plain below / *Rev.* 4 – Plain in angles   Spink 3613A

1397	**1708**		R^7	1146A

C/6.   Second bust, plain below
            Rev. 6 – **Roses & plume**s in angles   Spink 3613

1398	**1708**	*(6 strings)*	R^3	1146

G/4.   Third bust, plain below / *Rev.* 4 – Plain in angles   Spink 3610

1399	**1708**	*(6 strings)*	C^2	1147

G/5.   Third bust, plain below / *Rev.* 5 – **Plumes** in angles   Spink 3611

1400	**1708**	*(7 strings)*	N	1148

G/6.   Third bust, plain below
            Rev. 6 – **Roses & plume**s in angles   Spink 3614

1401	**1708**	*(6 strings)*	R^2	1149

G/4.   Third bust, plain below / *Rev.* 4 – Plain in angles   Spink 3610

1402	**1709**	*(6,7 strings)*	C^2	1154

G/6.   Third bust, plain below
            Rev. 6 – **Roses & plume**s in angles   Spink 3614

1403	**1710**	No stops after **MAG FR HIB** *(6 strings)*	N	1155

SHILLINGS

I/4. Fourth bust, plain below / *Rev.* 4 – Plain in angles   Spink 3618

ESC	Date	Varieties, comments etc.	R	(Old ESC)
1404	**1710**	*Pattern or Proof.* Plain edge, wt. *123grs* *(7 strings)*	R^7	1155A

I/6. Fourth bust, plain below
Rev. 6 – **Roses & plume**s in angles   Spink 3617

1405	**1710**		*(6 strings)*	R^2	1156
1406	---	*Proof* with plain edge *(Punctuation & strings uncertain)**	R^6	1156A
		*Listed but not traced		

G/4. Third bust, plain below / *Rev.* 4 – Plain in angles   Spink 3610

1407	**1711**	*(Mule? late use of 3rd bust die?)* *(6 strings)*	R^4	1157

I/4. Fourth bust, plain below / *Rev.* 4 – Plain in angles   Spink 3618

1408	**1711**		*(5,6 strings)*	C^3	1158
1409	---	Plain edge	*(Punctuation & strings uncertain)*		

I/6. Fourth bust, plain below
Rev. 6 – **Roses & plume**s in angles   Spink 3617

1410	**1712**		*(6 strings)*	N	1159
1411	**1713**	3 over 2	*(6 strings)*	S	1160
1412	**1714**		*(6 strings)*	N	1161
1413	**1714**	4 over 3	*(6 strings)*	R^3	1161A

EDINBURGH MINT

The following images and data are reproduced courtesy of
Roderick Farey, Nigel Prevost and John Howie
Taken from their in-depth die study:
"A Guide to the Die Varieties of Edinburgh Shillings 1707-9"
Published in S.N.C. Sept. 2013, pp. 79-81 "and January 2014, p. 125
See also
"Local bust Edinburgh Shillings of Queen Anne"
By Roderick Farey in Coin News April 2014, pp.35-36
In view of their generosity all recorded varieties are listed verbatim

All coins struck at the Edinburgh Mint were distinguished by the addition
of **E** or **E★** under the Queen's effigy, although dies, puncheons and other stamps,
including letters, had been supplied from the Mint in the Tower of London.
Permission was granted for the engravers, James Clark and Joseph Cave, to

SHILLINGS

produce further puncheons and dies and in a petition dated 17th January 1711 they
included a claim for payment in respect of one shilling obverse and reverse.
The authors are of the opinion that this is the Edinburgh bust, which continued to
be used in 1709 after the departure of the supervising moneyers from London.
After an examination of many Edinburgh shillings, the authors believe that they
have identified five local dies which seem to have used existing puncheons and
have then had the top curls modified on individual dies. It is proposed that these
varieties are classified as Edinburgh local die varieties 1 to 5, as follows:-

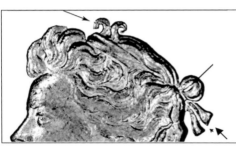

(Fig. 1) Second bust;

Two tall fine curls on top of head,
pointing in opposite directions; the hole
in the hair knot being high and the ties
to the fillet curving upwards at the ends

(Note; this bust also appears on coins
struck at the London Mint)

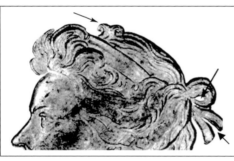

(Fig. 2) Third bust;

Two low curls still pointing in the
opposite directions on top of the head;
The hole in the hair knot is low and the
ties to then fillet are thicker and point
downwards at the ends

(Note; this bust also appears on coins
struck at the London Mint)

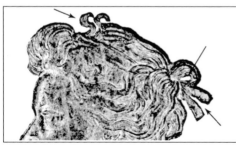

(Fig. 3) Edinburgh bust;

Two taller curls on the top of the head
but which both point back in the same
direction, the hole in the hair knot is
low and the ties to the fillet are slightly
shorter and both point downwards at the
ends (Note; this bust only appears on
coins struck at the Edinburgh Mint)

SHILLINGS

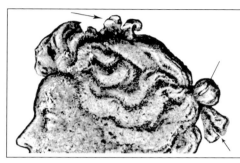

KA - (Fig. 4) Edinburgh local variety 1;

This seems to be modified from the 2nd bust, where the two top curls have been recut, producing the appearance of two much bushier less clearly defined curls with what might be a tiny third curl in the centre, the hole in the hair knot and the ties to the fillet match those for the 2nd bust

Fig. 9
G and D on E below coins

Fig. 16
I for one in date

Fig. 17
ſ for one in date

Fig. 10
Narrower G and D on Eʳ below coins

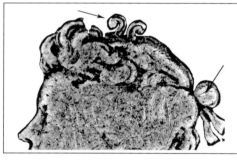

KB - (Fig. 5) Edinburgh local variety 2;

This is also similar to the 2nd bust, with the two top curls being more globular at the ends and showing an incuse line in the middle of each. The hole in the hair knot and the ties to the fillet again match the 2nd bust

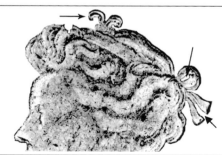

KC – (Fig. 6) Edinburgh local variety 3;

Similar to variety 2, but the front curl lacks the globular end associated with that variety and the incuse line in the front curl is more pronounced and wider towards the end

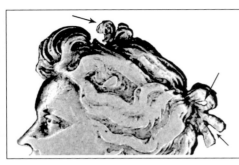

KD - (Fig. 7) Edinburgh local variety 4;

Bushier less clearly defined curls over the fillet, facing left and right with the right hand curl having a cone like appearance, the hole in the hair knot is low and the ties to the fillet curve downwards in the manner of the 3rd bust

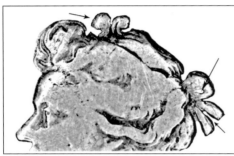

KE - (Fig. 8) Edinburgh local variety 5;

Bushier less clearly defined curls over the fillet, facing left and right but the right hand curl lacking the cone like appearance of variety 4, the hole in the hair knot is low and the ties curve downwards

Fig. 11
Wide zero (O) in date for London reverses

Fig. 12
Narrow zero (0) in date for local reverses

Fig. 13
Q for zero in date

Fig. 21
One over faint seven in date

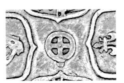

Fig. 20
No rays to the Garter Star

Fig. 18
Eight over seven in date

ANNE, 1702-14
SHILLINGS

Fig. 14	Fig. 15	Fig. 19
Wide shield	Narrow shield	Wider French and Irish shields

No stops on *rev.* slanting date London *rev.* die axis 45°

Reversed Z-type 1, narrow 0 & large 9

Note; all the Edinburgh local varieties KA-KD (figs 1-5) have the **E★** mintmark and appear to have the D of DEI and the G of GRATIA, in particular, of slightly narrower aspect than on coins bearing the **E** mintmark (see fig. 9 & 10). Using the technique of overlaying transparencies, the 1709 Edinburgh bust shilling with the **E** below has been found to be from the same die as that with **E★** below, the missing ★ being due to die filling.

EDINBURGH LOCAL REVERSES

7.   Date with **J** type 1 unless stated

8.   Date with reversed **Z** type 1

ANNE, 1702-14
SHILLINGS

Standard *legend* & *punctuation* unless stated
MAG˙ BRI•FR˙ ET•HIB˙ REG•

E/4. Second bust, **E** below
London *rev.* wide **O** & **J** type 1 in date   Spink 3608

ESC	Date	Varieties, comments etc.	R	(Old ESC)
1414	17O7	Wide shields. No stops after **G, R** and **B** *(6,7 strings)*	S	1138
1415	—	Narrow shields *(6 strings)*		1138C
1416	—	*Proof with plain edge* (All stops) *(6 strings)*	R^6	1139

E/7. Second bust, **E** below
Edinburgh local *rev.* narrow **0** & **J** type 1 in date   Spink 3608A

ESC	Date	Varieties, comments etc.	R	(Old ESC)
1417	1707	Narrow shields. No stops *rev.*, faint stops *obv.* Crescent shaped harp in Irish shield *(6 strings)* Narrow slanting figures in date	R^4	1138A
1418	—	Narrow shields. Slanting one in date Irish shield with harp of 1695-1696 No stops after **G, R** and **B** *(5 strings)*	R^2	1138B

F/4. Second bust, **E ★** below
London *rev.* wide **O** & **J** type 1 in date   Spink 3609

ESC	Date	Varieties, comments etc.	R	(Old ESC)
1419	17O7	Wide shields. No stops after **G, R** and **B** *(6 strings)*	R^2	1140
1420	—	Wide shields. *Rev. die axis 45° (All stops)* *(6 strings)*	R	1140iv
1421	—	Narrow shields. Possibly no stop after **G**	R	1140i
1422	17O7	Narrow shields. Flawed **0** in date like a **Q**	R	1140ii
1423	—	Narrow shields. No stops *obv.*	R^3	1140iii

KA/4. Edinburgh local bust variety 1, **E ★** below
London *rev.* wide **O** & **J** type 1 in date   Spink 3609

ESC	Date	Varieties, comments etc.	R	(Old ESC)
1424	17O7	Wide shields. No stops after **G, R** and **B** *(6 strings)* *(An apparent variety with a saltire in place of Garter star rays is due to die filling)*	R^2	1140A

F/7. Second bust, **E ★** below
Edinburgh local *rev.* narrow **0** & **J** type 1 in date   Spink 3609A

ESC	Date	Varieties, comments etc.	R	(Old ESC)
1425	1707	Narrow shields. No stops after **G, R** and **B** Crescent shaped harp in Irish shield Slanting one and seven in date *(5,6 strings)*	R^2	1140iv

SHILLINGS

H/4. Third bust, **E** below
London *rev.* wide **O & J** type 1 in date   Spink 3612

ESC	Date	Varieties, comments etc.	R	(Old ESC)
1426	**17O7**	Wide shields. No stops after **G, R & B** *(5,6,7 strings)*	*N*	1143
1427	—	Narrow shields. No stops after **G, R** and **B**	*R*	1143i
1428	**17O7**	Narrow shields. Flawed **0** in date like a **Q** *(6 strings)*	*R*	1143ii

H/7. Third bust, **E** below
London *rev.* wide **O & J** type 1 in date   Spink 3612A

1429	**1707**	Narrow shields. No stops after **G, R** and **B** Crescent shaped harp in Irish shield Slanting one and seven in date *(5 strings)*	*N*	1143iii

F/7. Second bust, **E★** below
Edinburgh local *rev.* narrow **0 & J** type 1 in date   Spink 3609A

1430	**1708**	Narrow shields. No stops after **G, R** and **B** Thinner one and seven in date. One over faint **7** and **8** over **7** *(5,6 strings)*	*R*	1145A

KB/8. Edinburgh local bust variety 2, **E★** below   Spink 3609A
Edinburgh local *rev.* narrow **0** & reversed **Z** type 1 in date

1431	**1708**	Narrow shields. No stops after **G, R** and **B** *(6 strings)*	R^2	1145B

F/8. Second bust, **E★** below   Spink 3609A
Edinburgh local *rev.* narrow **0** & reversed **Z** type 1 in date

1432	**1708**	Narrow shields. No rays to Garter star No stops after **G, R** and **B** *(5 strings)*	R^5	1145C
1433	—	As before with rays to Garter star	R^2	1145E

F/7. Second bust, **E★** below   Spink 3609A
Edinburgh local *rev.* narrow **0 & J** type 1 in date

1434	**1708**	Narrow shields. No rays to Garter star No stops after **G, R** and **B** *(5 strings)*	R^4	1145D

KC/8. Edinburgh local bust variety 3, **E★** below   Spink 3609A
Edinburgh local *rev.* narrow **0** & reversed **Z** type 1 in date

1435	**1708**	Narrow shields. No stops after **G, R** and **B** *(6 strings)*	R^2	1145F

Coins showing un-barred letters, are not true varieties but due to the 'filled dies'

SHILLINGS

H/4.
Third bust, **E** below
London *rev.* wide **O** & **J** type 1 in date — Spink 3612

ESC	Date	Varieties, comments etc.	R	(Old ESC)
1436	17O8	Wide shields. No stops after **G, R** and **B** *(6 strings)*	R	1150

H/8.
Third bust, **E** below — Spink 3612A
Edinburgh local *rev.* narrow **0** & reversed **Z** type 1 in date

1437	1708	Narrow shields. No stops after **G, R** and **B** **8 over 7** *(6 strings)*	*N*	1150A
1438	—	As before but seven in date is longer	*N*	1150B

J/4.
Fifth ('Edinburgh') bust, **E★** below — Spink 3615
London *rev.* wide **O** & **J** type 1 in date

1439	17O8	Wide shields. No stops after **G, R** and **B** *(5,6 strings)*	R^2	1151

J/8.
Fifth ('Edinburgh') bust, **E★** below — Spink 3615A
Edinburgh local *rev.* narrow **0** & reversed **Z** type 1 in date

1440	1708	Narrow shields. No stops after **G, R** and **B** *(6 strings)*	R	1151A
1441	—	Narrower split shields, with wider borders especially the wider French & Irish shields *(7 strings)*	R^2	1151D

KD/4.
Edinburgh local bust variety 4, **E★** below — Spink 3615B
London *rev.* wide **O** & **J** type 1 in date

1442	17O8	Wide shields. No stops after **G, R** and **B** Faint or no stop after **ANNA**. Note that all known specimens have a doubled row of pearls to French shield and **B** of **BRI** is over a lower **B** *(5 strings)*	R^2	1145B

KE/8.
Edinburgh local bust variety 5, **E★** below — Spink 3615C
Edinburgh local *rev.* narrow **0** & reversed **Z** type 1 in date

1443	1708	Narrow shields. No stops after **G, R** and **B** No stop after **ANNA** *(6 strings)*	R^2	1151C

J/8.
Fifth ('Edinburgh') bust, **E★** below — Spink 3616
Edinburgh local *rev.* narrow **0** & reversed **Z** type 1 in date

1444	1709	Narrow shields. No stops after **G, R** and **B** *(6 strings)*	R	1152
1445	—	As before but, appears to be only **E** below bust due to the filling of ★	R	1153

1708E (without star) second bust formerly ESC 1144 R^2 has been delisted because all specimens studied indicate a filled die by showing traces of the star

ANNE, 1702-14
SIXPENCES

Similar to the other denominations
BUSTS

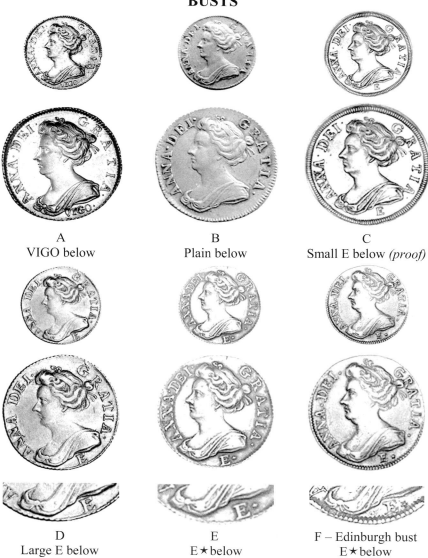

A
VIGO below

B
Plain below

C
Small E below *(proof)*

D
Large E below

E
E★below

F – Edinburgh bust
E★below

SIXPENCES

REVERSES

1
Plain in angles
early shields

2
Plumes in angles
early shields

3
Plumes in angles
late shields

4
Rose & Plumes
in angles with
late shields

5
Plain in angles with
wide shields
BR FRA

6
Plain in angles with
wide shields
BRI FR

SIXPENCES

REVERSES

High stop after 17·

HI·B

7	8	8 over 7
Plumes in angles with wide shields	Roses & plumes in angles with wide shields	

Shield tops

Indented (1703-5)

Convex (1705-7)

Indented After Union

French lis

Small with a gap below

Large no gap below

205

SIXPENCES

OBVERSES

A.   First bust, left, with **VIGO•** below
hair tied with ribbon, curls above lean forward

B.   As before, but plain below

C.   As before with **E** *Edinburgh mint* below

D.   As before with a larger **E** below

E.   As before with **E** ★ below

F   *'Edinburgh bust'* taller than first with **E** ★ below, subtle changes
in hair style; top twin curls above ribbon stand upright, etc

REVERSES
BEFORE UNION - BR • FRA

1.   Standard crowned cruciform shields with individual arms, plain
in angles, early shields; same width as crowns, with indented tops

2.   As before with **plumes** in angles, early shields

3.   Similar with **plumes** in angles, but late shields; same width as
crowns, with convex tops

4.   As before, but **roses & plumes** in alternate angles, late shields

AFTER UNION - BRI • FR
Arms of England & Scotland impaled on top and bottom shields

5.   As '1', but wide shields to accommodate the impaled arms and
Before Union leg. **BR FRA** (error)

6.   As before, but with correct *After Union leg.* **BRI FR**

7.   As before, but with **plumes** in angles, wide shields

8.   As before, but with **roses & plumes** in alternate angles

ANNE, 1702-14
SIXPENCES

BEFORE UNION WITH SCOTLAND
LONDON MINT – Legend reads BR • FRA

A/1. VIGO• below bust / *Rev.* 1 - Plain in angles with early shields
Leg. punc. – **MAG BR•FRA ET•HIB REG•** Spink 3590

ESC	Date	Varieties etc	R	(Old ESC)
1446	**1703**	*(4,5 strings)*	C	1582

B/1. Plain below bust / *Rev.* 1 - Plain in angles with early shields
Leg. punc. – **MAG BR•FRA ET•HIB REG•** Spink 3591

1447	**1705**	*(5 strings)*	R^2	1583

B/2. Plain below bust / *Rev.* 2 - **Plumes** in angles with early shields
Leg. punc. – **MAG BR•FRA ET•HIB REG•** Spink 3592

1448	**1705**	*(5 strings)*	N	1584

B/3. Plain below bust / *Rev.* 3 - **Plumes** in angles with late shields
Leg. punc. – **MAG BR FRA ET•HIB REG•** Spink 3593

1449	**1705**	*(5 strings)*	R	1584A

B/4. Plain below bust
Rev. 4 – **Roses & plumes** in angles with late shields
Leg. punc. – **MAG BR•FRA ET•HIB REG•** Spink 3594

1450	**1705**	*(4,5 strings)*	S	1585
1451	**1707**	*(4 strings)*	S	1586

AFTER UNION WITH SCOTLAND
LONDON MINT - Legend reads BRI • FR

B/5. Plain below bust / *Rev.* 5 – Plain in angles with wide shields
Leg. punc. – **MAG˙ BR•FRA• •ET•HIB• REG•** Spink 3619

1452	**1707**	Error; *Before Union leg.* & extra stop •ET• *(5 strings)*	R^2	1587A

B/6. Plain below bust / *Rev.* 6 – Plain in angles with wide shields
Leg. punc. – **MAG˙ BRI•FR˙ ET•HIB˙ REG•** Spink 3619

1453	**1707**	Correct *After Union leg.* & extra stop •17˙ *(5,6 strings)*	N	1587

ANNE, 1702-14
SIXPENCES

B/6. Plain below bust / *Rev.* 6 – Plain in angles with wide shields
Leg. punc. – **MAG BRI•FR ET•HIB REG•** Spink 3619

ESC	Date	Varieties etc	R	(Old ESC)
1454	**1707**	*(5,6 strings)*	*N*	1587

B/7. Plain below bust / *Rev.* 7 – **Plumes** in angles with wide shields
Leg. punc. – **MAG˙ BRI•FR˙ ET•HIB˙ REG•** Spink 3619

1455	**1707**	*(5,6 strings)*	*S*	1590

B/6. Plain below bust / *Rev.* 6 – Plain in angles with wide shields
Leg. punc. – **MAG BRI•FR ET•HIB REG•** Spink 3619

1456	**1708**	*(5,7 strings)*	*S*	1591

B/7. Plain below bust / *Rev.* 7 – **Plumes** in angles with wide shields
Leg. punc. – **MAG BRI•FR ET•HIB REG•** Spink 3619

1457	**1708**	*(5,6 strings)*	*R*	1593
1458	**1709**	*(6 strings)*	*R*	1594

B/8. Plain below bust /
Rev. 8 – **Roses & plumes** in angles with wide shields
Leg. punc. – **MAG BRI•FR ET•HIB REG•** Spink 3623

1459	**1710**	See note [1]	*(6 strings)*	*R*	1595

B/6. Plain below bust / *Rev.* 6 – Plain in angles with wide shields
Leg. punc. – **MAG BRI•FR ET•HIB REG•** Spink 3619

1460	**1711**	Small lis 2.2 mm	*(6 strings)*	C^2	1596
1461	—	Large lis 2.6 mm	*(5 strings)*	C^2	1596A

AFTER UNION WITH ENGLAND
EDINBURGH MINT - E or E ★ below bust

C/6. E below bust / *Rev.* 6 – Plain in angles with wide shields
Leg. punc. – **MAG: BRI:FR: ET•HIB: REG:** Spink 3620

1462	**1707**	*(7 strings)*	*S*	1588

C/6. E below bust / *Rev.* 6 – Plain in angles with wide shields
Leg. punc. – **MAG˙ BRI•FR˙ ET•HIB˙ REG•** Spink 3620

1463	**1707**	*(6 strings)*	*S*	1588

SIXPENCES

C/6. E below bust / *Rev.* 6 – Plain in angles with wide shields
Leg. punc. – **MAG˙ BRI•FR˙ ET•HIB˙ REG:** Spink 3620

ESC	Date	Varieties etc		R	(Old ESC)
1464	**1707**	*(6 strings)*		S	1588
1465	**1707**	*Proof,* with plain edge *wt. 3.15g (7 strings)*		R^4	1589

D/6. E <u>larger than normal</u> below bust
Rev. 6 – Plain in angles with wide shields
Leg. punc. – **MAG BRI•FR ET•HIB REG•** Spink 3620

1466	**1707**	Note; letter **E** as used on larger denominations *(7str)*		R	1588A

C/6. E below bust / *Rev.* 6 – Plain in angles with wide shields
Leg. punc. – **MAG BRI•FR ET•HIB REG•** Spink 3620

1467	**1708**	*(5,6 strings)*		R	1592

E/6. E ★ below bust / *Rev.* 6 – Plain in angles with wide shields
Leg. punc. – **MAG˙ BRI•FR• ET•HIB˙ REG•** Spink 3622

1468	**1708**	*(6 strings)*		R	1593

E/6. E ★ below bust / *Rev.* 6 – Plain in angles with wide shields
Leg. punc. – **MAG˙ BRI•FR• ET•HIB˙ REG•** Spink 3622

1469	**1708**	*(6 strings)*		R	1593

E/6. E ★ below bust / *Rev.* 6 – Plain in angles with wide shields
Leg. punc. – **MAG˙ BRI•FR• ET•HI•B REG•** Spink 3622

1470	**1708**	Note; stop after **HI•** but not **B** *(5 strings)*		R	1593

E/6. E ★ below bust / *Rev.* 6 – Plain in angles with wide shields
Leg. punc. – **MAG BRI•FR ET•HIB REG•** Spink 3621

1471	**1708**	J type 1 in date and **8** over **7** *(Uncertain if no stops on obverse)* *(4? strings)*		R^2	1593A

F/6. *'Edinburgh bust'* taller than normal first bust with **E★** below,
Rev. 6 – Plain in angles with wide shields
Leg. punc. – **MAG BRI•FR ET•HIB REG•** Spink 3622

1472	**1709**	Z type 1 in date *(5 strings)*		R	1593B

"Coins of 1705 occur mainly weakly struck. It is difficult to find well struck coins in better than fine condition. (P.A. Rayner)

1   This coin is notoriously difficult to obtain in good condition and is usually weakly struck: a piece in better than 'VF' would be at least R^2. (P.A. Rayner)

MAUNDY

SETS
True sets are very much rarer than indicated
Made up ones are usually obvious

ESC			Spink 3599	
1473	**1703**		R^2	2393
1474	**1705**		R^2	2394
1475	**1706**		S	2395
1476	**1708**		R^3	2396
1477	**1709**		R	2397
1478	**1710**		R	2398
1479	**1713**		R	2399

GROATS or FOURPENCES

A	B	C
Small face	Larger face	Re-engraved hair

MAUNDY

GROATS

1c	1b	1a	2a
BR FR	BR FRA	BRI FR	BRI FR

Obv. **A.** First bust, small face, curls at back of head point downwards

B. Second bust, larger face, curls point upwards

C. As before, but with re-engraved hair

Rev. **1.** Small crown with decorated arches above the figure **4**
2. Larger crown with pearls on arches, large serifs on figure **4**

Variations of *rev.* legend
Leg. **a.** **MAG · BRI · FR · ET · HIB · REG**
b. — **BR FRA** — — —
c. — — **FR** — — —

A/1c. First bust, small face
Rev. 1c - Small crown, decorated arches, **BR FR** Spink 3595

ESC	Date	Varieties, comments etc.	*Robinson*	R	(Old ESC)
1480	**1703**		*p. 155,136*	R	1886
1481	**1704**			N	1887
1482	—	No stop on obverse	*p. 155,139(i)*	N	1887A

(continued)

MAUNDY

GROATS

B/1c. Second bust, larger face
Rev. 1c - Small crown, decorated arches, **BR FR** Spink 3595A

ESC	Date	Varieties, comments etc.	*Robinson*	R	(Old ESC)
1483	**1705**		*p. 155,143*	R	1888

B/1b. Second bust
Rev. 1b - Small crown, decorated arches, **BR FRA** Spink 3595A

| 1484 | **1706** | | *p. 155,147* | N | 1889 |

B/1a. Second bust
Rev. 1a - Small crown, decorated arches, **BRI FR** Spink 3595A

| 1485 | **1708** | | *p. 155,153* | N | 1890 |
| 1486 | **1709** | | *p. 155,157* | N | 1891 |

B/2a. Second bust
Rev. 2a - larger crown, pearls on arches, **BRI FR** Spink 3595B

| 1487 | **1710** | | *p. 155,161(i)* | R^2 | 1892 |

C/2a. Re-engraved hair (Second bust)
Rev. 2a - larger crown, pearls on arches, **BRI FR** Spink 3595C

| 1488 | **1710** | | *p. 155,161(ii)* | N | 1892A |

B/2a. Second bust
Rev. 2a - larger crown, pearls on arches, **BRI FR** Spink 3595B

| 1489 | **1713** | *(This may well be one of the following two varieties)* | | N | 1893 |

C/2a. Re-engraved hair (Second bust)
Rev. 2a - larger crown, pearls on arches, **BRI FR** Spink 3595C

| 1490 | **1713** | | *p. 155,166(i)* | N | 1893A |
| 1491 | **1713** | Very close date | *p. 155,166(ii)* | N | 1893B |

PATTERNS of GROATS

E. Edinburgh bust with letter **E** below

| 1492 | **1711** | *In silver* | *(Unique)* | *p. 155,162* | | |
| 1493 | **1711** | *In copper* | *(Unique)* | *p. 155,162* | | |

ANNE, 1702-14
MAUNDY

THREEPENCES

a	b	c
BRI FR	BR FRA	BR FR

Obv. **A.** Bust 1, broad bust, top tie points slightly outwards

B. Bust 2, taller and narrower, ties point more downwards

C. Bust 3, similar to 'A', larger, hair more finely engraved

Rev. **1.** One type, but with three different abbreviations of legend (See groats) and subtle differences in alignment

MAUNDY

THREEPENCES

A/1c. First bust / *Rev.* 1c – *leg.* **BR   FR**   Spink 3596

ESC	Date	Varieties, comments etc.	*Robinson*	*R*	(Old ESC)
1494	**1703**	7 of date above edge of crown	*p. 155,135(i)*	*R*	2005
1495	—	7 not above edge of crown *(Not traced)*	*p. 155,135(ii)*	*R³*	2006

B/1c. Second bust / *Rev.* 1c – *leg.* **BR   FR**   Spink 3596A

1496	**1704**		*p. 155,138*	*S*	2007
1497	**1705**		*p. 155,142*	*S*	2008

B/1b. Second bust / *Rev.* 1b – *leg.* **BR   FRA**   Spink 3596A

1498	**1706**		*p. 155,146*	*N*	2009

C/1c. Third bust / *Rev.* 1c – *leg.* **BR   FR**   Spink 3596B

1499	**1707**		*p. 155,149*	*N*	2010

C/1a. Third bust / *Rev.* 1a – *leg.* **BRI   FR**   Spink 3596B

1500	**1708**		*p. 155,152*	*N*	2011
1501	—	8 over 7		*R*	2011A
1502	**1709**			*N*	2012
1503	—	No stop after date	*p. 155,156(i)*	*N*	2012A
1504	**1710**		*p. 155,160*	*N*	2013
1505	**1713**	Much larger bust	*p. 155,165(i)*	*N*	2014
1506	—	Two distinct curls over head	*p. 155,165(ii)*	*N*	2014A
1507	—	Mule with fourpence obverse die		*R*	2014B

ANNE, 1702-14
MAUNDY

HALFGROATS or TWOPENCES

1b	Only obverse	2a
BR FRA		BRI FR

Obv.	**A.**	One type only, as groat and threepence, *legs.* as before
Rev.	**1.**	Crown to edge of coin, small figure 2
	2.	Crown within inner circle of legend, large figure 2

A/1b *Rev.* 1b – small figure 2, *leg.* **BR   FRA** Spink 3597

ESC	Date	Varieties, comments etc.	*Robinson*	R	(Old ESC)
1508	**1703**		*p. 155,134*	R	2210
1509	**1704**			N	2211
1510	—	All date well above crown *(Not traced)*	*p. 155,137(i)*	R	2212
1511	—	No stops on obverse *(Not traced)*	*p. 155,137(ii)*	R	2213
1512	**1705**		*p. 155,141*	N	2214
1513	**1706**			S	2215
1514	—	No stop after **DEI**	*p. 155,145(i)*	S	2215A
1515	**1707**		*p. 155,148*	S	2216

A/2a *Rev.* 2a – large figure 2 & crown, *leg.* **BRI   FR** Spink 3597A

1516	**1703**			R^4	2210A
1517	**1708**		*p. 155,151(i)*	N	2217
1518	**1709**		*p. 155,155(i)*	R	2218
1519	—	No stop after **DEI**	*p. 155,155(ii)*	R	2218A
1520	**1710**		*p. 155,159*	N	2219
1521	**1713**		*p. 155,164*	N	2220
1522	—	**3 over 0**		R	2220A

MAUNDY

PENNIES

Obv. /rev. & legs. as groat

Rev.	**1a**	**MAG · BRI · FR · ET · HIB · REG**
	1b	— **BR** **FRA** — — —
	1c	— — **FR** — — —

A	B	C
BRI FR	BR FRA	BR FR

A/1b   *Rev.* 1b –*leg.* **BR FRA**   Spink 3598

ESC	Date	Varieties, comments etc.	Robinson	R	(Old ESC)
1523	**1703**		*p. 155,133*	R	2315

A/1c   *Rev.* 1c –*leg.* **BR FR**   Spink 3598

ESC	Date	Varieties, comments etc.	Robinson	R	(Old ESC)
1524	**1705**		*p. 155,140*	S	2316
1525	**1706**			S	2317
1526	—	**0** of date above crown	*p. 155,144(i)*	S	2318

A/1a   *Rev.* 1a –*leg.* **BRI FR**   Spink 3598

ESC	Date	Varieties, comments etc.	Robinson	R	(Old ESC)
1527	**1708**		*p. 155,150*	R^3	2319
1528	**1709**			S	2320
1529	—	**M A G** all three letters widely spaced	*p. 155,154(i)*	S	2320A
1530	—	**M AG** only wide space between M A	*p. 155,154(ii)*	S	2320B
1531	**1710**		*p. 155,158*	R^2	2321
1532	**1713**	**3** of date over **0**	*p. 155,163(i)*	R	2322
1533	—	**3** of date over **0**. No stop after **DEI**	*p. 155,163(ii)*	R	2322A

Note
Some of the Robinson's numbers may be wrongly allocated, if so I apologise (M.B.)
See William & Mary Maundy notes

GEORGE I
1714-1727

With the accession of House of Brunswick the coinage remained the same except for the changes to the Royal titles and the Royal arms. The titles were abbreviated to; **D . G . M . BR . FR . ET . HIB . REX . F . D . BRVN . ET . L . DVX . S . R . I . A . TH . ET . EL**, which stands for DEI GRATIA MAGNAE BRITANNIAE FRANCIAE ET HIBERNIAE REX FIDEI DEFENSOR BRUNSVICENSIS ET LUNEBURGENSIS DUX SACRI ROMANI IMPERII ARCHI-THESAURIUS ET ELECTOR, or translated, *'By the Grace of God, King of Great Britain, France and Ireland, Defender of the Faith, Duke of Brunswick and Lüneburg, Arch-Treasurer and Elector of the Holy Roman Empire'*. Note; the *Fidei Defensor* title now appears on the coinage for the first time though it had been enjoyed by British sovereigns ever since it was conferred by the Pope on Henry VIII. We now find the arms of Brunswick Lüneburg in one of the shields. In this reign the bulk of the silver came from importation of very large quantities from the South Sea Company, notorious for the *'South Sea Bubble'*. Lesser amounts were supplied by the 'Company for smelting down lead' and a very small amount by the Welsh Copper Company. All the silver obtained from this latter source was coined into shillings, which are fairly rare, and these pieces have the letters WCC below the king's bust and a Welsh plume and interlinked letter Cs in the angles of the shields on the reverse.

With regard to the designers and engravers of this reign, Croker and Bull, who had together been responsible for the greater part of the coinage of Queen Anne, continued in office during this reign, although Bull may have not played a very large part in the engraving the coinage dies. Treasury papers of 1726 suggest that he may have been inactive for a number of years prior to this date, for in dealing with the appointment of John Rollo, an engraver of seals, they state that the Chief Engraver (Croker) had *'lacked the services of a skilful artist for many years'*. Bull must therefore have died some long time before 1726 and a petition by Croker dated January 30th 1728-9 asking that *'Sigismund Tanner should serve as his apprentice states that Croker 'his Mat.s first engraver............. being advanced in years' was ' the only one now living who has hitherto made puncheons for heads on the coins'*. The same document mentions that one Johann Rudolf Ochs, a Swiss engraver, also aged at that time, had been responsible for the reverse dies on the coins of George I. It seems therefore fairly reasonable, in view of these two pieces of contemporary evidence, to attribute the obverse dies of this coinage to Croker and the reverses to Ochs. (P.A.Rayner, 1949)

CROWNS

SOLE BUST

Obverse A

Large rose in angles
1716-20 over-date

Small rose
1720 &1726

Reverse 1 - 1716

Reverse 1- 1718
Large rose

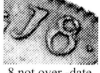

8 not over -date

8 over 6

Reverse 1 – 1718 over 6
Large rose

Reverse 1 – 1720 over 18
Large rose

20 over 18

Not over-date

Reverse 2 – 1720
Small rose

218

CROWNS

Small rose
1726

Reverse 2
Small rose

Reverse 3
SS C in angles

(All dates illustrated to show subtle differences)

Obv.	**A.**	Laureate bust, right, wearing armour (cuirassed)
Leg.		**GEORGIVS·D˙G·M·B·BR·FR·ET·HIB·REX·F·D·**
		George by the Grace of God King of Great Britain,
		France and Ireland, Defender of the Faith
Rev.	**1.**	Small crowns above cruciform shields, quartering legend,
		Garter star in the centre and large **rose** and **plumes** in the angles
		Clockwise from the top; the arms of England and Scotland
		conjoined, France, Ireland and the new Hanover Arms; the arms
		of the Duchy of Brunswick & Lüneburg with the Crown of
		Charlemagne in the centre
Leg.		**17♛16 •BRVN♛ET·L·DVX♛S•R•I•A•TH♛ET•EL•**
		*(**BRUNSVICENSIS ET** LUNEBURGENSIS **DUX SACRI ROMANI**
		IMPERII ARCHI-THESAURARIUS ET ELECTOR)*
		Duke of Brunswick and Lüneburg, Arch-Treasurer of the Holy
		Roman Empire and Elector
Edge		As before, regnal year in words **1716-1720/18**
	2.	Similar, but *reverse* with letters **SS C** alternately in the angles
		(South Seas Company) **1723** only
	3.	Small **Rose** and **Plumes** in the angles, most noticeable in the
		size of the centre of the roses **1720** and **1726**

CROWNS

A/1.   *Rev.*1 – large **Rose** and **Plumes** in angles   Spink 3639

ESC	Date	Edge year		Varieties		R	(Old ESC)
1540	**1716**	**SECVNDO**	(2)		*(11s-6hts)*	S	110
1541	**1718**	**QVINTO**	(5)		*(11s-6hts)*	R^4	111
1542	—	—	—	**8** over **6**	*(11s-6hts)*	R	111A
1543	**1720**	**SEXTO**	(6)	**20** over **18**	*(11s-6hts)*	R	113

A/3.   *Rev.*3 - small **Rose** and **Plumes** in angles   Spink 3639A

1544	**1720**	**SEXTO**	(6)	Not over-date	*(10s-6hts)*	R^2	112

A/2.   *Rev.*2 - **SS C** alternately in angles   Spink 3640

1545	**1723**	**DECIMO**	(10)		*(8s-6hts)*	S	114

A/3.   *Rev.*3 - small **Rose** and **Plumes** in angles   Spink 3639A

1546	**1726**	**D. TERTIO**	(13)		*(9s-7hts)*	R^2	115
1547	—	—	—	No R in **REGNI** on edge		R^4	115B
1548	—	—	—	All **N**s on edge inverted	*(9 str)*	R^2	115A

GEORGE I, 1714-27
HALFCROWNS

Similar to the crowns
(Sole obverse)

(*Proof*)

Obv. A

Rev. 1

Rev. 2

Rev. 3

Rev. 4

J-type 1 & Z type 7

Z-type 1 & 7

1720 over 17, Z-type 17

1720 Z-type 1 & 7

Z-type 1 & 7

Retrograde 1 & plain 7

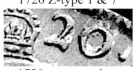

1720 not over-date

1720 over 17

221

GEORGE I, 1714-27
HALFCROWNS

Obv. **A.**   As the crown

Rev. **1.**   Plain in the angles

      2.   **Roses** and **plumes** in alternate angles

      3.   **SS C** alternately in the angles

      4.   As '2', but smaller **roses** and **plumes**

A/1.   *Rev.* 1 – plain in angles   Spink 3641

ESC	Date	Edge year	Varieties & comments	R	(Old ESC)
1549	**1715**	None	*Pattern* with Plain edge *(9s-6hts)*	R^5	586

A/2.   *Rev.* 2 – large **Roses & plumes** in angles   Spink 3642

1550	**1715**	**SECVNDO**	(2)	**J**-type **1** & **Z** type **7** *(8s-6h;9s-6h)*	R	587
1551	—	—	—	Minus **A** in **ANNO** on edge	R^3	588B
1552	—	—	—	Edge *leg.* in wrong order*(8s-7hts)*	R^2	588C
1553	—	None		Plain edge *(total collar slippage)* *(8s-6hts)*	R^6	588A
1554	**1717**	**TIRTIO**	(3)	Error **TIRTIO** for TERTIO **Z**-type **1** & **7** *(8s-7hts)*	S	589
1555	**1720**	**SEXTO**	(6)	**20** over **17** **Z**-type **1** & **7** *(9s-6hts)*	S	590
1556	—	—	—	Date not altered **Z**-type **1** & **7** *(9s-6hts)*	R^3	591

A/3.   *Rev.* 3 – **SS C** alternately in the angles   Spink 3643

1557	**1723**	**DECIMO**	(10)	**Z**-type **1** & **7** *(7s-6hts)*	S	592
1558	—	—	—	Minus **A** in **ANNO** on edge	R^2	592A

A/4.   *Rev.* 4 – smaller **roses** and **plumes** in angles   Spink 3644

1559	**1726**	**D.TERTIO**	(13)	Retrograde **1** & plain **7** in date *(6s-5hts)*	R^5	593

All George I halfcrowns are difficult to find in high grades, and 1726 in any grade

GEORGE I, 1714-27
SHILLINGS

Obverse A   Obverse B   Obverse C

No stops on obverse   No stops on reverse   Rev. 1 – plain in angles

SHILLINGS

Rev. 2 – roses and
plumes in angles

Rev. 3 – plumes and
roses in angles

Rev. 4 – SS and C in
alternate angles

Rev. 5 - Plume and two
interlinked **C**s alternately
in angles

Rev. 6
French arms at date

GEORGE I, 1714-27
SHILLINGS

C over SS

20 over 19

1 over 0

21 over 19

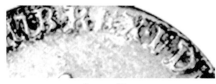
Large D

O over G

Slanting colon between A·.TH

Normal upright colon between A:TH

Type   **A.**   First bust, two ends to tie of wreath

         B.   Second bust, similar, but bow and one end to tie

         C.   **W.W.C.** (Welsh Copper Co.) below second bust

Rev.   **1.**   Plain in the angles

         2.   **Roses** and **plumes** in alternate angles (clock-wise) R-P-R-P

         3.   **Plumes** and **Roses** in alternate angles (wrong order) P-R-P-R

         4.   **SS C** alternately in the angles (clock-wise) SS-C-SS-C

         5.   **Plume** and two interlinked **C**s alternately in angles P-Cs-P-Cs

SHILLINGS

A/2. First bust / *Rev.* 2 - **Roses** and **plumes** in angles Spink 3645

ESC	Date	Varieties, comments etc.	R	(Old ESC)
1560	**1715**	*(10 strings)*	*S*	1162
1561	—	Colon after **D:G·**	*R²*	1162A
1562	**1716**	*(8 strings)*	*R³*	1163
1563	—	**V over L in GEORGIVS**	*R³*	1163A
1564	**1717**	*(7 strings)*	*S*	1164
1565	—	Obverse lettering larger	*S*	1164A
1566	**1718**	*(7s-6hts)*	*N*	1165
1567	**1719**	*(7s-6hts)*	*R²*	1166
1568	**1720**	See note ¹ *(6,7 strings)*	*S*	1167
1569	—	Large **O** in date	*R²*	1167A
1570	—	Large **O** in date **20** over **18**	*R⁴*	1167B
1571	—	Large **O** in date **20** over **19** *(7s-6hts)*	*R⁴*	1167C

A/1. First bust / *rev.* 1 – Plain in angles Spink 3646

1572	**1720**	Plain edge *(6s-6hts;8s-7hts;7s-6hts)*	*N*	1168
1573	—	Larger **O** of date and lettering on reverse *(6 strings)*	*N*	1169
1574	—	Larger **O** of date / **O over G in GEORGIVS** *(6s-5hts)*	*R*	1169A
1575	**1721**		*R⁴*	1170
1576	—	**O** of **GEORGIVS** over zero	*R²*	1170A

A/2. First bust / *Rev.* 2 - **Roses** and **plumes** in the angles (R-P-R-P) Spink 3645

1577	**1721**	*(8 strings)*	*R*	1171
1578	—	**1** over **0** *(7,9 strings)*	*S*	1172
1579	—	**21** over **19** *(9s-7hts)*	*R*	1173

A/3. First bust / *Rev.* 3 - **Plumes** and **Roses** in wrong order P-R-P-R Spink 3645

1580	**1721**	**21** over **19** or is it **18**? / *(Note Plumes & Roses in different order)*	*R⁴*	1171A

1 The so-called 'plain edge' variety is really a coin struck without going through the edging machine. It is very rare. No circulation coins were struck in collars until later in the eighteenth century

SHILLINGS

A/2. First bust
Rev. 2 - **Roses** and **plumes** in the angles (R-P-R-P)   Spink 3645

ESC	Date	Varieties, comments etc.		R	(Old ESC)
1581	**1722**		*(6s-6hts;6s-7hts)*	*S*	1174
1582	—	No stop after **HIB**		*R*	1174A
1583	**1723**	Usual slanting colon between **A·.TH**	*(7 strings)*	*S*	1175
1584	—	No colon between **A TH**	*(6 strings)*	*S*	1175A
1585	—	Large **D** in **F·D**	*(7 strings)*	*R*	1175B

A/4. First bust
Rev. 4 - **SS C** alternately in angles (SS-C-SS-C)   Spink 3647

1586	**1723**		*(6s-6hts ;8s-6hts;7s-6hts)*	*C²*	1176
1587	—	Reads **E:T BRVN**		*R*	1176A
1588	—	Small **v** above **V** Reads **B:RVN**		*R*	1176B
1589	—	Arms of France at date [2]		*R²*	1177
		No colon between **A TH**	*(7 strings)*		
1590	—	**C** over **SS** under **DVX** in 2nd angle [3]	*(7 strings)*	*R*	1176A

B/4. Second bust
Rev. 4 - **SS C** alternately in angles (SS-C-SS-C)   Spink 3648

1591	**1723**		*(7 strings)*	*N*	1178

C/5. Second bust with **W.C.C.** below
Rev. 5 - **Plume** and **Cs** (P-Cs-P-Cs)   Spink 3650

1592	**1723**	Mixed sized lettering in reverse legend	*(7s-6hts)*	*R²*	1180

B/2. Second bust
Rev. 2 - **Roses** and **plumes** in angles (R-P-R-P)   Spink 3649

1593	**1723**		*(7 strings)*	*S*	1179
1594	**1724**	**FR** re-entered	*(6,7 strings)*	*S*	1181

C/5. Second bust with **W.C.C.** below
Rev. 5 - **Plume** and **Cs** (P-Cs-P-Cs)   Spink 3650

1595	**1724**		*(7s-6hts)*	*R²*	1182
1596	**1725**		*(6 strings)*	*R³*	1185

2   These pieces mostly turn up in a very worn state; the rarity of a really fine example is perhaps R[5]
3   **C** over **SS** is very difficult to discern

SHILLINGS

B/2. Second bust
Rev. 2 - **Roses** and **plumes** in angles (R-P-R-P)   Spink 3649

ESC	Date	Varieties, comments etc.		R	(Old ESC)
1597	**1725**		*(6 strings)*	*S*	1183
1598	—	**5** of date over **4**		*R²*	1183A?
1599	—	No stops on obverse	*(6 strings)*	*R*	1184
1600	—	No stops on reverse		*R*	1184A
1601	**1726**			*R⁵*	1186
1602	—	No stops on obverse		*R⁵*	1186A
1603	—	No stops on reverse	*(Not traced)*	*R⁵*	1186B

C/5. Second bust with **W.C.C.** below
Rev. 5 - **Plume** and **C**s (P-Cs-P-Cs)   Spink 3650

1604	**1726**		*(6 strings)*	*R²*	1187
1605	—	No stops on reverse		*R³*	1187A

B/2. Second bust
Rev. 2 - **Roses** and **plumes** in angles (R-P-R-P)   Spink 3649

1606	**1727**	*(Not traced with stops in obverse legend)*		*R⁵*	1188
1607	—	No stops on obverse	*(7 strings)*	*R⁵*	1188A
1608	—	No stops on reverse		*R⁵*	1188B

GEORGE I, 1714-27
SIXPENCES

General type as larger denominations

Large   lettering   small

Rev. 1   Rev. 2   Rev. 3

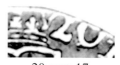

3 over 0   R over B   20 over 17

Rev.	**1.**	**Roses** and **Plumes** in alternate angles
	2.	**SS C** alternately in the angles
	3.	As '1' but smaller **Roses** and **Plumes**

229

SIXPENCES

A/1. *Rev.* 1 - **Roses** and **Plumes** in angles   Spink 3651

ESC	Date	Varieties		R	(Old ESC)
1609	**1717**		*(7s-6hts)*	R	1597
1610	—	See note [1]		R^5	1598
1611	**1720**	**20** over **17**	*(7s-7hts)*	R	1599

A/2. *Rev.* 2 - **SS C** alternately in angles   Spink 3652

1612	**1723**	Lettering; small on obverse and large on reverse *(5s-5hts;5s-6hts;6s-6hts)*		C	1600
1613	—	**3** over **0**. Lettering; small on obverse and large on reverse *(6s-6hts;6s-7hts)*		R	1601
1614	—	Larger lettering both sides	*(6s-6hts)*	R	1601A
1615	—	Larger lettering both sides **B** over **R** in **BR** *(5s-6hts)*		R	1601B

A/3. *Rev.* 2 - smaller **Roses** and **Plumes** in angles   Spink 3653

1616	**1726**		*(7 strings)*	R	1602

---

1   Sixpences of 1717 with a plain edge are currency coins which were not put through the edging machine. See Dyer and Gaspar, *Plain-Edged Sixpences* of 1717, SNC 1983, pp. 6-7

GEORGE I, 1714-17

MAUNDY

Obv.	As larger denominations
Rev.	Crown above large Roman numeral indicating value

MAUNDY SETS

Spink 3658

ESC	Date	Varieties, comments etc.	*Robinson*	R	(Old ESC)
1617	**1723**			R	2400
1618	**1727**			R	2401

GROATS or FOURPENCES

Large lettering   Small lettering

Spink 3654

1619	**1717**		*p. 157,170*	S	1894
1620	**1721**		*p. 157,175*	S	1895
1621	**1723**		*p. 157,179*	S	1896
1622	**1727**	Smaller letters and date on reverse	*p. 157,186(i)*	R	1897

231

MAUNDY

THREEPENCES

| Large 3 | | Smaller 3 |
| Large lettering | | Small lettering |

Spink 3655

ESC	Date	Varieties, comments etc.	Robinson	R	(Old ESC)
1623	**1717**		*p. 157,169*	N	2015
1624	**1721**		*p. 157,174*	S	2016
1625	**1723**			S	2017
1626	—	Reads **F.R**	*p. 157,178(i)*	S	2017A
1627	**1727**	Smaller letters and date on reverse		S	2018
1628	—	Obverse legend finishes nearer the bust	*p. 157,185(i)*	S	2018A

There are many subtle variations in the crowns above the numeral
Some of Robinson's numbers may be wrongly allocated
See William & Mary Maundy notes

Comments regarding Maundy; see Charles II earlier

GEORGE I, 1714-17
MAUNDY

HALFGROAT or TWOPENCE

Large 2
Large lettering

Small 2
Small lettering

Spink 3656

ESC	Date	Varieties, comments etc.	Robinson	R	(Old ESC)
1629	**1716**		*p. 157,168(i)*	*N*	2223
1630	**1717**	No stop after **GRA**	*p. 157,168(i)*	*N*	2224
1631	**1721**		*p. 157,173(i)*	*C*	2225
1632	**1723**		*p. 157,177*	*R*	2225A
1633	**1726**		*p. 157,182*	*C*	2225B
1634	**1727**	Reads **GEOrGIVS** large **O**	*p. 157,184(i)*	*S*	
1635	—	Reads **GEORGIVS** normal **O**	*p. 157,184(ii)*	*S*	
	—	Smaller letters on reverse		*S*	

GEORGE I, 1714-17
MAUNDY

PENNIES

1716[1]
Note the
alignment of
date & legend
with crown
and value

Type A
With stop after date

Type B
No stop after date

PEX

Crown divides date
Z type 1
Large lettering
BR FR ET HI PEX

Date above crown
J type 1
Small lettering
BRI FR ET HIB

Spink 3657

ESC	Date	Varieties, comments etc.	*Robinson*	*R*	(Old ESC)
1636	**1716**	Variety A - reads • **1716** • (with stop after date)	*p. 157,167(i)*	*C*	2323
1637	—	Variety B - reads • **1716** (no stop after date)	*p. 157,167(ii)*	*C*	2323A
1638	**1718**	No stop after **GRA**	*p. 157,171(i)*	*C*	2324
1639	—	No stops after **GRA** or **GEORGIVS**	*p. 157,171(i)*	*C*	2324A
1640	**1720**		*p. 157,172*	*C*	2325
1641	—	Reads **HIPEX**	*p. 157,172(i)*	*C*	2326
1642	**1723**		*p. 157,176(i)*	*S*	2327
1643	—	**GEORGIVS.** (with stop after)	*p. 157,176(i)*	*S*	2327A
1644	—	Large **V** in **GEORGIVS** (no stop after)	*p. 157,176(ii)*	*S*	2327B
1645	**1725**	Reads **FR.ET.** (note size of letters)	*p. 157,180(i)*	*C*	2328
1646	—	Reads **FR.ET.** (note size of letters)	*p. 157,180(ii)*	*C*	2328A
1647	**1726**		*p. 157,181*	*R*	2329
1648	**1727**	No stop after **GRA**	*p. 157,183(i)*	*R*	2330
1649	—	Reads **BRI·FR** in smaller letters		*R*	2330A

1   See *TWO VARIETIES OF THE 1716 MAUNDY PENNY* by B. Robinson in
Spink Numismatic Circular September 1981, pp. 275-6

GEORGE II
1727-1760

During the first part of this reign Croker, although very old, was still Chief Engraver, and responsible for the young head portrait of this monarch. As mentioned previously, Johann Sigismund Tanner worked at the Mint as apprentice to Croker from January 1728-9 onwards, and on the death of Croker in March, 1741, succeeded him as Chief Engraver.   The task of engraving the reverse dies of this coinage was now the duty of the assistant engraver; and from the beginning of 1729 until he became Chief Engraver this work probably occupied all Tanner's time. The name of Ochs, who had probably performed a similar task during the previous reign is again mentioned, but as he was an old man in 1728, according to Croker's petition mentioned in the last reign, it seems very unlikely that he, George II's engraver, was the same person who is mentioned by Hawkins as being on the Mint books in 1757 as Third Engraver. Hawkins even suggested that the same Ochs engraved for George III, but as Ochs senior had a son of the same name it seems almost certain that this son worked for George II and his successor and that Hawkins is in error.

We have definite documentary evidence that Tanner engraved some reverse dies in the form of an undated manuscript in the British Museum, which is an estimate by Croker of the expenses for making dies, etc. An extract reads as follows: *'In keeping accounts i doo propose to allow Mr Tanner for making ye reverse Dyes ... twelve shillings, and for ye remainder part of ye money I will make the dyes for ye heads ... '*

Tanner probably made the reverses for all the coins from 1729 until he became Chief Engraver, after which time they were probably engraved by Ochs junior. The old head coinage was undoubtedly Tanner's work, though the so-called intermediate head which appears on the gold may be Croker's work, as he did not die until 1741. Tanner, however, may have done the engraving under Croker's guidance.

Croker's dies for the obverse of the Maundy were used throughout the reign. Possibly there was no necessity for new dies to be made after Croker's death, as complete sets were issued during this time only in 1743, 1746 and 1760.

The source of the silver is still marked by provenance marks during this reign as follows:
Roses — silver from mines in the West of England.
Plumes — silver from the Welsh Copper Company.
Roses and plumes — silver from the Company for Smelting down Lead.

CROWNS

Obv. A
GEORGIVS (letter V)

Obv. B
GEORGIUS (letter U)

Obv. C
LIMA. Below (letter V)

Obv. D
GEORGIVS (letter V)

Rev. 1
Roses & plumes in angles

Rev. 2
Roses in angles

CROWNS

Rev. 3
Plain in angles

Obv.	**A.**	Young head, left, laureate, draped over armour with the face of a young lion on his shoulder epaulette
Leg.	**1.**	**GEORGIVS · II · DEI · GRATIA ·** (Some without stop after **II**) *George second by the Grace of God*
	B.	Old-head; mature bust, left, wearing more armour with the face of a mature lion on his shoulder epaulette
Leg.	**2.**	**GEORGIUS · II · DEI · GRATIA·** Note; U in **GEORGIUS**
	C.	**LIMA·** below old-head, with regular **V** in **GEORGIVS** LIMA; provenance of Spanish silver captured by Admiral Anson during his round the world voyage; 1740-44.
	D.	As 'B', but **GEORGIVS** spelt with regular **V**
Rev.	**1.**	Crowned cruciform shields with **roses** and **plumes** in the angles
Leg.		♛ **32·M·B·F·ET·** ♛ **H·REX·F·D·B·** ♛ **ET·L·D·S·R·I·**♛ **A·T·ET·E·17** *King of Great Britain, France and Ireland, Defender of the Faith, Duke of Brunswick and Lüneburg, Arch-Treasurer of the Holy Roman Empire and Elector*
	2.	As before, but with **Roses** in angles
	3.	As before, but plain in angles

GEORGE II, 1727-60
CROWNS

A/1. Young head *leg. punct.* **GEORGIVS · II · DEI · GRATIA ·**
Rev. 1 - **Roses** and **Plumes** in angles   Spink 3686

ESC	Date	Edge year		Varieties		R	(Old ESC)
1660	1732	SEXTO	(6)	(All stops)	*(10s-7hts)*	R	117
1661	—	—	—	*Proof*[1] L&S 6 No stop after **II** *(10s-7hts)*		R³	118
1662	1734	SEPTIMO	(7)	No stop after **II**	*(10s-8hts)*	R	119
1663	1735	OCTAVO	(8)	No stop after **II** *(12,13, strings) (14s-7hts)*		S	120
1664	1736	NONO	(9)	(All stops)	*(12s-7hts)*	S	121

A/2. Young head / Rev. 2 - **Roses** in angles   Spink 3687

1665	1739	DVODECIMO	(12)	*(10 strings) (9s-7hts)*		N	122
1666	1741	D. QVARTO	(14)	*(8s-6hts;8s-7hts)*		N	123

B/2. Old head, plain below. Note; **U** in **GEORGIUS**
Rev. 2 - **Roses** in angles   Spink 3688

1667	1743	D. SEPTIMO	(17)	*(10s-6hts)*		N	124

C/3. **LIMA** below old-head. Note; **V** in **GEORGIVS** again
Rev. 3 - plain in angles   Spink 3689

1668	1746	D. NONO	(19)	*(10s-6hts;10s-7hts)*		N	125

D/2. Old head, plain below. Note; **V** in **GEORGIVS**
Rev. 3 - plain in angles   Spink 3690

1669	1746	VICESIMO	(20)	*Proof* *(9s-7hts)* L&S 7		R	126
1670	1750	V. QVARTO	(24)	*(8s-8hts)*		S	127
1671	1751	—	—	*(8s-7hts)*		R	128

ENIGMAS
Lineacar and Stone list two Crowns on pages 16-17; **1728 Plumes** in angles (L&S 1) & **1731 plain** in angles (L&S 5) both of which are unknown today but recorded by Martin Folkes in his publication in1745 and illustrated on Plates XL. 1731 is more likely to exist since a proof five guineas and halfcrown exist of this date so is allocated a number in case

1672	1731	Edge unknown	Plain in angles *(Not traced)* (L&S 5)	R⁷	116

1   The obverse of this coin is distinctly convex with a plain edge

238

HALFCROWNS

Obverse and reverse types as crown

V over U

Obv. A

Obv. B

Obv. C

Obv. D

Obv. E

Rev. 1

Rev. 2

Rev. 3

41 over 39

45 over 45

6 over 5

HALFCROWNS

Obv. **A.** Young head, left, laureate, draped over armour with the face of a young lion on his shoulder epaulette

Leg. **1.** **GEORGIVS II   DEI GRATIA**

B. Old-head; mature bust, left, wearing more armour with the face of a mature lion on his shoulder epaulette, **GEORGIUS** with **U**

C. **LIMA** below old-head, **GEORGIUS** spelt with **U**

D. As before, but **GEORGIVS** with regular **V**

E. As 'B', but **GEORGIVS** spelt with regular **V**

Rev. **1.** Plain in angles

2. **Roses** and **plumes** in angles

3. **Roses** in angles

A/1   Young head / *Rev.* 1 – Plain in angles   Spink 3691

ESC	Date	Edge year		Varieties	R	(Old ESC)
1673	**1731**	None		*Pattern*, plain edge [1] *10s-7hts)*	R^4	594

A/2   Young head / *Rev.* 2 – **Roses & Plumes** in angles   Spink 3692

1674	**1731**	**QVINTO**	(5)	*(10s-7hts)*	N	595
1675	**1732**	**SEXTO**	(6)	*(10s-8hts)*	N	596
1676	**1734**	**SEPTIMO**	(7)	*(7s-8hts)*	S	597
1677	**1735**	**OCTAVO**	(8)	*(8s-6hts)*	S	598
1678	**1736**	**NONO**	(9)	*(12s-6hts)*	R	599

A/3   Young head / *Rev.* 3 – **Roses** in angles   Spink 3693

1679	**1739**	**DVODECIMO**	(10)	*(7s-7hts)*	N	600
1680	—			Inverted **Ns** in **ANNO REGNI**	N	N
1681	**1741**	**D. QVARTO**	(14)	*(8s-7hts)*	S	S
1682	—	—	—	**41** over **39** *(7s-7hts)*	R	R
1683	—	—		Larger obverse lettering *(7s-7hts)*	R	R

HALFCROWNS

B/3 Old head, plain below, **GEORGIUS** spelt with a **U**
Rev. 3 – **Roses** in angles   Spink 3694

ESC	Date	Edge year		Varieties		R	(Old ESC)
1684	**1743**	**D. SEPTIMO**	(17)	See note [2]	*(8s-7hts)*	*N*	603A
1685	**1745**	**D. NONO**	(19)		*(8s-9hts)*	*N*	604
1686	—	—	—	45/45 *(numerals re-entered)*	*(8s-9hts)*	*R²*	604A

C/1 Old head, **LIMA** below bust, **GEORGIUS** spelt with a **U**
Rev. 1 – Plain in angles [3]   Spink 3695

1687	**1745**	**D. NONO**	(19)		*(8s-7hts)*	*C²*	605

D/1 Old head, **LIMA** below bust, **GEORGIVS** spelt with regular **V**
Rev. 1 – Plain in angles [3]   Spink 3695A

1688	**1746**	**D. NONO**	(19)	*(7s-7hts;8s-7hts;9s-7hts;9s-9hts)*		*C³*	606
1689	—	—	—	**6 over 5**	*(8s-7hts;9s-7hts)*	*R*	607
1690	—	—	—	**V** over **U** in **GEORGIVS**	*(8 strings)*	*R³*	607A

E/1 Old head, plain below, **GEORGIVS** spelt with regular **V**
Rev. 1 – Plain in angles   Spink 3696

1691	**1746**	**VICESIMO**	(20)	*Proof only*	*(8s-7hts)*	*R*	608
1692	**1750**	**V. QVARTO**	(24)		*(7s-7hts)*	*S*	609
1693	**1751**	—	—		*(7s-6hts)*	*R²*	610

1   This pattern has a slightly convex obverse

2   ESC 603; V in GEORGIVS (De-listed. Does this variety of spelling exist?)

3   The design of the Scottish arms varies slightly on different specimens of
         1745 &1746 with the LIMA *obv.*; we have noted at least three varieties. (P.A.R.)

4   See proof article in SNC 1993 pp. 156-7 (2 specimens recorded by M. Faintich)

GEORGE II, 1714-60
SHILLINGS

Obverse and reverse types as crowns and halfcrowns
Note; **1743** and **1745**, with letter **U** in **GEORGIUS**

| Obv. A – small lettering | Obv. B – larger lettering | Obv. C |
| Ties to small AT | Ties to larger T | Ties to larger I |

Obv. D	Obv. E	Obv. F
Ties to A	O.H. GEORGIUS	O.H. GEORGIUS
Extra large Gs	(letter U)	(letter U) LIMA below

242

GEORGE II, 1714-60
SHILLINGS

Note; only variations in size of lettering and alignment of ties with GRATIA are noted. There are many more subtle variations which are ignored to avoid complication; these are left to the specialist collector to discover

| Obv. G | Rev. 1 - Plumes | 2 - Roses & plumes |
| O.H. GEORGIVS | Small legend | Small legend |

| 3 – Plain, small legend | Rev. 4 - Roses | Rev. 5 - Roses |
| 6 – Plain, larger legend | Small legend | Larger legend |

GEORGE II, 1714-60
SHILLINGS

5 over 5?

6 over 5

41 over ?

43 over 41

45 over 34

50 over 46

Thin 0

O over 7

Small cross

Normal cross

S - Single pearls
on crown band

Small 9
Crown – S

Regular 9
Crown - D

D - Double pearls
on crown band

T over E

4 over 4

V over U

Obv.

A. Young-head, left, small legend, GEORGIVS with **V**, ties to **A T**

B. As 'A', but larger lettering, ties to **T** and sometimes with an extra stop before **·DEI** (stop often very weak or not visible)

C. As 'A', but ties to **I** (Note; wider space after **GRATIA·**)

D. As 'C', but with extra large G's in legend, ties to **A**

E. Old-head, left, large lettering, GEORGIUS with a **U**

F. As 'E' with **LIMA** below

G. As 'D, but GEORGIVS with a **V**

244

SHILLINGS

REVERSES in order of issue

Rev. **1.** **Plumes** in angles, small lettering

2. **Roses** and **Plumes** in angles, small lettering

3. Plain in angles, small lettering

4. **Roses** in angles, small lettering

5. **Roses** in angles, large lettering

6. Plain in angles, large lettering

A/1. Young head, small lettering, ties to **A T** & **GEORGIVS** with a **V**
Rev. 1 - **Plumes** in angles.
Crowns with single pearls in bands — Spink 3697

ESC	Date	Varieties		R	(Old ESC)
1694	**1727**		*(8? strings)*	*S*	1189

A/2. As before with ties to **A T** / *Rev.* 2 – **Roses & Plumes** in angles
Crowns with single pearls in bands — Spink 3698

1695	**1727**		*(7s-6hts)*	*N*	1190
1696	**1728**		*(7 strings)*	*R*	1192
1697	—	**E over R in GEORGIVS**		*R*	1192A

A/3. As before but, ties to **-T-** / *Rev.* 4 - Plain in angles
Crowns with single pearls in bands — Spink 3699

1698	**1728**		*(7s-6hts)*	R^2	1191

A/2. As before with ties to **A T** / *Rev.* 2 – **Roses & Plumes** in angles
Crowns with single pearls in bands — Spink 3698

1699	**1729**	Small **9** in date	*(8 strings)*	*R*	1193

A/2. As before with ties to **A T** / *Rev.* 2 – **Roses & Plumes** in angles
Crowns with double pearls in bands — Spink 3698

1700	**1729**	Regular size **9** in date	*(7 strings)*	*R*	1193

SHILLINGS

B/2. As 'A', but larger lettering and ties to **T**
Rev. 2 – **Roses & Plumes** in angles   Spink 3698

ESC	Date	Varieties		R	(Old ESC)
1701	**1729**	Weak extra stop before **·DEI**	*(8 strings)*	R	1193

A/1. As before with ties to **A T** / *Rev.* 1 - **Plumes** in angles.
Crowns with single & double pearls in bands   Spink 3697

1702	**1731**	Crowns - S over English & Irish shields *(9 strings)*		R^2	1195
		Crowns - D over French & Hanoverian shields			

A/2. As before with ties to **A T** / *Rev.* 2 – **Roses & Plumes** in angles
Crowns with double pearls in bands   Spink 3698

1703	**1731**		*(6 strings)*	S	1194

A/2. As before with ties to **A T** / *Rev.* 2 – **Roses & Plumes** in angles
Crowns with single pearls in bands   Spink 3698

1704	**1731**	A·T over E·ET·E·		S	1194
1705	**1732**		*(8 strings)*	R	1196

B/2. As 'A', but larger lettering and ties to **T**
Rev. 2 – **Roses & Plumes** in angles
Crowns with single pearls in bands   Spink 3698

1706	**1734**	Extra stop before **·DEI** *(9s-6hts)* *(10 strings)*		N	1197

A/2. As before with ties to **A T** / *Rev.* 2 – **Roses & Plumes** in angles
Crowns with single pearls in bands   Spink 3698

1707	**1735**		*(8 strings)*	N	1198
1708	—	**5 over 5?**	*(10 strings)*		1198A

A/2. As before, but larger lettering and ties to **T**
Rev. 2 – **Roses & Plumes** in angles
Crowns with single pearls in bands   Spink 3698

1709	**1736**		*(8s-5hts;10s-7hts)*	N	1199
1710	—	**6 over 5** No visible pearls in crowns *(10? strings)*		R^2	1199A

A/2. As before with ties to **A T** / *Rev.* 2 – **Roses & plumes** in angles
Crowns with single pearls in bands   Spink 3698

1711	**1737**		*(7strings) (8s-7hts)*	N	1200
1712	—	Both **A**s unbarred in **GRATIA**			1200A

SHILLINGS

A/4. As before, ties to **T I, I** in **GEORGIVS** to king's upper lip, but
Rev. 4 – **Roses** in angles
Crowns with single pearls in bands   Spink 3701

ESC	Date	Varieties		R	(Old ESC)
1713	**1739**		*(7s-7hts; 8s-7hts)*	C	1201
1714	—	**9 over 7**		R^5	1201A
1715	—	**A·T** over ? **·ET** over ? **·E** over ?	*(7,8 strings)*	R^4	1201B

B/4. As before but, larger lettering, **I** in **GEORGIVS** to king's nose
Rev. 4 – **Roses** in angles
Crowns with single pearls in bands   Spink 3701

1716	**1739**		*(8 strings)*	C	1201
1717	**1741**	Smaller Garter Star	*(7s-7hts)*	C	1202
1718	—	**41** over **39**		R^5	1202A

D/4. Young head. N.B. larger G's in large lettering
Rev. 4 – **Roses** in angles
Crowns with single pearls in bands   Spink 3701

1719	**1741**	**41** over **39**?	*(7 strings)*	C	1202B

E/5. Old-head, left, large lettering, GEORGIUS with a **U**
Rev. 3 – **Roses** in angles
Crowns with single pearls in bands   Spink 3702

1720	**1743**		*(6,7 strings) (8s-6hts)*	C	1203
1721	—	**43** over **41**	*(7s-6hts)*	R^3	1203A
1722	**1745**		*(8 strings)*	N	1204
1723	—	**45** over **34**	*(8 strings)*	R	1204A

F/6. Old-head, left, **LIMA** below, large lettering, GEORGIUS with **U**
Rev. 6 – Plain in angles, large lettering
Crowns with single pearls in bands   Spink 3703

1724	**1745**		*(6,9 strings)* *(7s-7hts ;8s-6hts)*	C^2	1205

Fvar. /6 Old-head, left, **LIMA** below, as before but, **V** over **U** in
GEORGIVS / *Rev.* 6 – As before   Spink 3703

1725	**1746**			R^2	1206
1726	—	**6 over 5**		R^2	1207

SHILLINGS

G/6. Old-head, left, plain below, large lettering, GEORGIVS with a **V**
Rev. 6 – Plain in angles, large lettering
Crowns with single pearls in bands   Spink 3704

ESC	Date	Varieties		R	(Old ESC)
1727	**1746**	*Proof only*	*(8s-7hts)*	R	1208

G/5. Old-head as before, but GEORGIVS with a regular **V**
Rev. 3 – **Roses** in angles. Crowns - S   Spink 3702

1728	**1747**		*(7s-6hts)*	N	1209

G/6. Old-head, left, plain below, large lettering, GEORGIVS with a **V**
Rev. 6 – Plain in angles, large lettering
Crowns with single pearls in bands   Spink 3704

1729	1750	Thin **0** in date & small legend	*(7s-7hts; 8s-8hts)*	N	1210
1730	—	Thin **0** in date over **6**		S	1210A
1731	—	Thin **0** in date over **7**		S	?
1732	—	Wide **O** and **50** over **47** or is it **46?**	*(7 strings)*	S	1211
1733	1751		*(7s-5hts)*	R^3	1212
1734	1758	*(Apparently struck for many years)*	*(8s-7hts)*	C^3	1213
1735	1758	Note, small **58** in date		$C^?$	1213A?

GEORGE II, 1727-60
SIXPENCES

OBVERSES
(Similar to shillings)

Obv. A
GEORGIVS

Obv. B
GEORGIUS

Obv. C
LIMA   GEORGIUS

Obv. D
LIMA   GEORGIVS

Obv. E
Plain   GEORGIVS

O over R

D over ?

GEORGIV (minus S)

249

SIXPENCES

REVERSES
(Similar to shillings)

Rev. 1
Plain in angles

Rev. 2
Plumes in angles

Rev. 3 – Roses &
Plumes in angles

Rev. 4
Roses in angles

5 over 3

5 over 3

5 over 3

6 over 5

SIXPENCES

| 6 over 5 | 8 over 7 | Large O | Small 2 |

Obv.   **A.**   Young head, left, plain below, with a **V** in **GEORGIVS**

      B.   Old head, left, plain below, with a **U** in **GEORGIUS**

      C.   Old head, **LIMA** below, with a **U** in **GEORGIUS**

      D.   Old head, **LIMA** below with a **V** in **GEORGIVS**

      E.   Old head, plain below, with a **V** in **GEORGIVS**

Rev.   **1.**   Plain in angles
      2.   **Plumes** in angles
      3.   **Roses** and **Plumes** in angles
      4.   **Roses** in angles

A/1.   Young head, **V** in **GEORGIVS**
       Rev. 1 – Plain in angles   Spink 3705

ESC	Date	Varieties		R	(Old ESC)
1736	**1728**	*(6 strings)*		R^2	1603
1737	—	*Proof,* with plain edge *wt. 3.46g (5s-5hts?)*		R^4	1604

A/2.   Young head, **V** in **GEORGIVS**
       Rev. 2 – **Plumes** in angles   Spink 3706

1738	**1728**	*(7s-7hts;8s-6hts)*		S	1605
1739	—	Plain edge *(Struck without a collar)* *(7s-8hts?)*		S	1605A

A/3.   Young head, **V** in **GEORGIVS**
       Rev. 3 – **Roses** and **Plumes** in angles   Spink 3707

1740	**1728**	*(6s-6hts;7s-7hts) (8 strings)*		N	1606
1741	**1731**	*(8 strings) (7s-5hts)*		N	1607
1742	**1732**	Some letters in obverse legend double-entered *(6s-7hts)*		N	1608
1743	—	Smaller **2** in date *(6s-6hts?; 8s-8hts?)*		N	1608

(continued)

SIXPENCES

ESC	Date	Varieties		R	(Old ESC)
1744	**1734**		*(7s-5hts?)*	R^2	1609
1745	**1735**			R^2	1610
1746	—	**5 over 4**	*(6s-4hts?)*	R^3	1610A
1747	**1736**		*(7 strings)*	R	1611
1748	—	**GEORGIV** (minus S)	*(7 strings)*	R^4	1610B?

A/4. Young head, **V** in **GEORGIVS**
Rev. 4 – **Roses** in angles   Spink 3709

1749	**1739**		*(7 strings)*	N	1612
1750	—	**O over R** in **GEORGIVS** and **D** over?	*(7s-7hts)*	R^3	1612A
1751	**1741**		*(6s-6hts;7s-6hts; 7s-7hts)*	N	1613

B/4. Old head, plain below, **U** in **GEORGIUS**
Rev. 4 – **Roses** in angles   Spink 3708

1752	**1743**		*(6s-5hts;6s-6hts) (7 strings)*	N	1614
1753	**1745**		*(6s-5hts?)*	S	1615
1754	—	**5 over 3**	*(6s-5hts?)*	R^2	1616
1755	—	**5 over 4**		R^2	1616A

C/1. Old head, **LIMA** below, **U** in **GEORGIUS**
Rev. 1 – Plain in angles   Spink 3710

1756	**1745**		*(7s-7hts)*	S	1617

D/1. Old head, **LIMA** below, **V** in **GEORGIVS**
Rev. 1 – Plain in angles   Spink 3710A

ESC	Date	Varieties		R	(Old ESC)
1757	**1746**		*(7 strings)*	C^2	1618
1758	—	**6 over 5**	*(7 strings)*	R^2	1618A

D/1. Old head, plain below, **V** in **GEORGIVS**
Rev. 1 – Plain in angles   Spink 3711

1759	**1746**	*Proof only*	*wt. 2.98g (6s-5hts)*	R^2	1619
1760	**1750**		*(5s-5hts)*	S	1620
1761	**1751**			R^2	1621
1762	**1757**		*(6 strings)*	C^3	1622
1763	**1758**		*(5,6 strings)*	C^3	1623
1764	—	**8 over 7**	*(6s-6hts)*	R^3	1624

Old ESC 1624A - Stop in centre of **DEI** is considered a flaw so de-listed

MAUNDY

ORIGINAL MAUNDY SETS
UNIFORM DATES

Spink 3716

ESC	Date	Varieties	R	(Old ESC)
1765	**1729**		R	2402
1766	**1731**		R	2403
1767	**1732**		S	2404
1768	**1735**		S	2405
1769	**1737**		S	2406
1770	**1739**		S	2407
1771	**1740**		S	2408
1772	**1743**		R^2	2409
1773	**1746**		S	2410
1774	**1760**		R	2411

THREE DISTINCT CROWNS

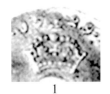  

1   2   3

Rev.   **1.**   Small crown, no interior, pearls on arches, date above

       2.   Wide crown, with interior, ornate arches, divides date

       3.   Large crown, with interior, pearls on arches, divides date

MAUNDY

The following denominations are listed separately to highlight varieties

GROAT or FOURPENCE

(X1.5)

A
Young head
Stop after II ·

Rev. 2

(X1.5)

A
1740 - 3d die used

Rev. 3

A/2. *Rev.* 2 - Wide crown, ornate arches, divides date   Spink 3712

ESC	Date	Varieties, comments etc.	*Robinson*	R	(Old ESC)
1775	**1729**	Stop after **II•**		S	1898
1776	**1729**	Stop after **II** above head •	*p. 159,190(i)*	S	1898
1777	**1731**		*p. 159,194*	S	1899

A/3 *Rev.* 3 - Large crown, pearls on arches, divides date Spink 3712A

1778	**1732**		*p. 159,198*	S	1900
1779	**1735**		*p. 159,202*	S	1901
1780	**1737**		*p. 159,206*	S	1902
1781	**1739**		*p. 159,210*	S	1903
1782	**1740**	Struck on a threepence obverse die	*p. 159,214*	S	1904
1783	**1743**			R	1905
1784	—	**3 over 0**	*p. 159,218*	R^3	1905A
1785	**1746**		*p. 159,222*	N	1906
1786	**1760**		*p. 159,237*	S	1907

GEORGE II, 1727-60
MAUNDY

THREEPENCE

Stop above head   Obv. B
Young head   Rev. 2

Stop after II ·   A
6 over3   Rev. 3

B/1.   *Rev.* 1 - Small crown, pearls on arches, date above   Spink 3713

ESC	Date	Varieties, comments etc.	*Robinson*	*R*	(Old ESC)
1787	**1729**	A or B *(Not traced)*		*S*	2019

B/2.   Stop above head
        Rev. 2 - Wide crown, ornate arches, divides date   Spink 3713A

1788	**1729**		*p. 159,189(i)?*	*S*	2019A
1789	**1731**			*S*	2020
1790	—	Small obverse lettering	*p. 159,193*	*S*	2021

B/3.   Stop above head
        Large crown with interior, pearls on arches   Spink 3713B

1791	**1732**			*S*	2022
1792	—		*p. 159,197(i)*	*S*	2023
1793	**1735**		*p. 159,201*	*S*	2024
1794	**1743**		*p. 159,217(ii)*	*N*	2028
1795	—	**3 over 0**		*R*	2028A
1796	—	Large letters both sides		*N*	2030

255

MAUNDY

THREEPENCE

A/3.   Stop after **II** ·
Large crown with interior, pearls on arches   Spink 3713B

ESC	Date	Varieties, comments etc.	Robinson	R	(Old ESC)
1797	**1737**		*p. 159,205*	N	2025
1798	**1739**		*p. 159,209*	N	2026
1799	**1740**	**40** over **39**	*p. 159,213*	?	2027
1800	**1743**	Large letters both sides	*p. 159,217(i)*	N	2029
1801	**1746**	**6** over **3** *(On all coins)*	*p. 159,221(i)*	R	2031
1802	—	**6** over **5**	*p. 159,221(ii)*	R	2031A
1803	**1760**		*p. 159,236*	S	2032

TWOPENCE or HALFGROAT

GRATIA

A
Young head

Rev. 1

GRATIA ·

Rev. 3

Small o in GEoRGIVS

A/1.   Small crown, no interior, pearls on arch   Spink 3714

1804	**1729**	Smaller figure **9**	*p. 159,188(i)*	N	2226
1805	**1731**		*p. 159,192*	N	2227

MAUNDY

TWOPENCE

ESC	Date	Varieties, comments etc.	Robinson	R	(Old ESC)
A/3.		Large crown with interior, pearls on arches			Spink 3714A
1806	**1732**	Small **o** in **GEoRGIVS**	*p. 159,196(i)*	*N*	2228
1807	**1735**		*p. 159,200*	*N*	2229
1808	**1737**		*p. 159,204*	*N*	2230
1809	**1739**	Cracked die	*p. 159,208(i)*	*S*	2231
1810	**1740**		*p. 159,212*	*R*	2232
1811	**1743**			*N*	2233
1812	—	**3** over **0**	*p. 159,216(i)*	*S*	2233A
1813	**1746**		*p. 159,220*	*N*	2234
1814	**1756**		*p. 159,229*	*N*	2235
1815	**1759**		*p. 159,233*	*N*	2236
1816	**1760**		*p. 159,235*	*N*	2237

PENNY

GRATIA

A
Young head

Rev. 1

GRATIA·

6 over 3

Rev. 3

GRATIA:

Colon after GRATIA:

Rev. 3

MAUNDY

PENNY

A/1. *Rev.* 1 - Small crown, no interior, pearls on arch   Spink 3715

ESC	Date	Varieties, comments etc.	*Robinson*	R	(Old ESC)
1817	**1729**			S	2331
1818	—	No stop after **GRATIA**	*p. 159,187(i)*	S	2331A
1819	—	*Proof?* Struck on a thick flan.	*p. 159,187(ii)*	S	2331B
1820	**1731**		*p. 159,191*	N	2332

A/3. *Rev.* 3 - Large double arched crown with pearls,
Value in larger numerals   Spink 3715A

ESC	Date	Varieties, comments etc.	*Robinson*	R	(Old ESC)
1821	**1732**			N	2333
1822	—	A slight variety of bust is used	*p. 159,195(ii)*	S	2334
1823	**1735**		*p. 159,199*	S	2335
1824	**1737**		*p. 159,203*	S	2336
1825	**1739**		*p. 159,207*	N	2337
1826	**1740**		*p. 159,211*	N	2338
1827	**1743**		*p. 159,215*	N	2339
1828	—	**3** over **0**		N	2339A
1829	**1746**			N	2340
1830	—	**6** over **3** or is it a **5**?	*p. 159,219(i)*	R	2341
1831	**1750**		*p. 159,223*	C	2342
1832	**1752**			C	2343
1833	—	**2** over **0**	*p. 159,224(i)*	S	2344
1834	**1753**			C	2345
1835	—	**3** over **2**	*p. 159,225(i)*	R	2345A
1836	**1754**		*p. 159,226*	C	2346
1837	**1755**	Colon after **GRATIA:**	*p. 159,227(i)*	C	2347
1838	**1756**		*p. 159,228*	C	2348
1839	**1757**	Colon after **GRATIA:**	*p. 159,230*	C	2349
1840	**1758**		*p. 159,231*	C	2350
1841	**1759**	Colon after **GRATIA:**	*p. 159,232*	C	2351
1842	**1760**			S	2352
1843	**1760**	Large second **G** in **GEORGIVS**	*p. 159,234*	S	2352A

Note
Some obverse dies vary slightly from those illustrated

GEORGE III
1760-1820

Although this was a long reign, the number of silver coins issued by the Mint in the first 55 years was small, due to the escalating value of silver in the latter half of the 18th century and the mint's reluctance to either pay more than the 60 shillings per troy pound or reduce the weight of coins. Nevertheless it's very interesting from a numismatic point of view. There was a small issue of shillings in 1763; threepences in 1762 and 1763, and Maundy money. The issue of shillings in 1763 was a special one and it is said that £100 worth were struck for distribution by the Earl of Northumberland when he entered Dublin as Lord Lieutenant. These are therefore known as *'Northumberland Shillings'*, though it seems certain that the total issue was considerably larger than the £100 worth[1] required for the Earl. In 1787 a great quantity of shillings and sixpences were issued. These were the last shillings to be issued for general circulation prior to the recoinage of 1816, if we discount the rare *Dorien and Magens shillings* of 1798 - In 1798 Mr Magens Dorien Magens and nine other banking firms sent (to the Mint) silver bullion for coinage to the amount of upwards of £30,000. This was partly coined into Shillings, but their issue was prohibited by order of the Lords of the Committee of Council. The name given above is so rendered in the book, but in Lowndes *London Directory* for 1798, the firm is described as Dorien, Magens, Mello, Martin and Harrison, 22 Finch Lane, Cornhill. After the authorities ordered the whole issue to be melted down, one of the bankers, Magens Dorien Magens, expressed his sentiments in no uncertain terms, in an anonymous publication of the same year entitled, *'Thoughts upon a new Coinage of Silver.'* Royal Mint Museum Catalogue, Vol. I, p. 158.

At this time Spain was mining vast quantities of bullion in her American colonies and coining from this silver 'pieces of eight' or eight reales, and also smaller denominations. These seem to have circulated in many parts of the world and as very considerable quantities were captured by the English, and owing to the shortage of regal silver in this country, they very readily passed as currency. This was technically illegal, but the government turned a blind eye and in fact legalised the position in 1797 by having them countermarked with the head of George III in a small oval. The puncheon used was that employed by the Assay Master at Goldsmith's Hall for stamping the duty mark on silver plate assayed after 1785. The dollars were then made current at 4/9d, and gave rise to the saying *'two King's heads not worth a crown'*. These oval-countermarked dollars circulated at 4/9d from 9th March to 21st October 1797. They did not, as mentioned by some writers, circulate for a second period up to 1804. Early in 1804 the stamp was changed, the king's head being larger and in an octagon. The punch used for the head was that

GEORGE III
1760-1820

for the Maundy penny 1795-1800. These octagonal-countermarked dollars circulated from 11th January to 2nd June 1804, and were current for five shillings.

In the same year, arrangements were made for Spanish dollars to be completely over struck, thereby removing all but traces of the original design. This was made possible by Boulton's powerful machinery recently installed at the Soho Mint in Birmingham. These pieces were struck for The Bank of England, and were called Bank of England Dollars (Crowns). They were really tokens but as they were an authorised issue, it appears proper that they should find a place in this work. The original patterns for the issue were engraved and dated as early as 1798. The dollars are all dated 1804, but they were struck until the year 1811, and occasionally on a coin restruck with insufficient pressure it is possible to detect dates later than 1804 of the original Spanish coin. There were three 'valuations' or periods of circulation for the Bank dollars, viz. 20th May 1804 to 10th March 1811 at five shillings; 11th March 1811 to 30th April 1817 at five shillings and sixpence (due to the shortage of silver prior to the recoinage); 1st May 1817 until demonetization on 25th March 1820 again at five shillings. Three shillings and 1/6d bank tokens were also issued: dies were prepared for a ninepence, but it was never put into circulation.

The Mint's old quarters in the Tower of London had been inadequate for many years past, and during the years 1810-12 the Royal Mint was built on Tower Hill and new steam-powered machinery was made and installed by Boulton and Watt. In 1816 it was resolved to issue a completely new coinage despite difficulties and expense. Halfcrowns, shillings and sixpences were struck during this year, Maundy in 1817 and the crown in 1818-20. The issue of silver is of reduced size and weight being now sixty-six shillings instead of sixty-two to the pound troy. All silver shillings from 1816 were still legally current until the withdrawal of the large decimal five pence coin. (Demonetized 1st January 1991)

On the crown as well as on the larger gold denominations, we find the St. George and the Dragon device for the first time since the reign of Henry VIII. The head of the halfcrown was changed in 1817, as the original design, showing the back of the shoulder to the spectator, was not popular. These early halfcrowns are often colloquially known as *'Bull Heads'*. The artist responsible for all theses designs was Benedetto Pistrucci, an Italian gem-engraver who had come to find employment in London and whose work came to the notice of William Wellesley Pole, the Master of the Mint.

GEORGE III
1760-1820

There were probably more changes of portraiture and design in this reign than in any other. Regarding the engravers, Tanner remained at the Mint holding the office of Chief Engraver until his death in 1775, but probably took little active part in preparing the new dies, as during his later years he suffered from approaching blindness and other infirmities. Most of the work was carried out by his Chief Assistant, Richard Yeo, who succeeded to the post of Chief Engraver on Tanner's death. Yeo died only four years later in 1779.

Among the obverse dies attributed to Yeo are those for the first three issues of guineas, half-guineas, quarter-guineas and the Northumberland shilling referred to earlier. Thomas Pingo, who was the Assistant Engraver from 1771 until his death in 1776, produced the dies for the fourth issue guineas and half-guineas. He was succeeded by his son Louis, who was responsible for the design and engraving of many of the dies in George III's middle period. Among these are the well-known 'Spade' guineas, the 1787 shillings and sixpences etc. He engraved the obverses for the later gold coins from models supplied by Nathaniel Marchant, Assistant Engraver from 1792-1815.

J.R. Ochs junior remained as Third Engraver until his retirement in 1786. The dies for the first issue of Maundy are usually ascribed to him.

Thomas Wyon junior was appointed Assistant Engraver in 1811 and became Chief Engraver in 1815. He died two years later. Although active for so short a time, he left his stamp on the coinage. He was responsible for the design and engraving of the reverses for the first *Bull Head* halfcrown, the shilling and the sixpence. He engraved the obverses of these coins from a model by Benedetto Pistrucci. After Wyon's death Pistrucci engraved the dies himself. The crown is perhaps the most widely known as the reverse bears his renowned portrayal of St. George and the Dragon; the second type halfcrown shows almost the same obverse as the crown and the modification of Wyon's reverse, which was used for the first type halfcrown.

William Wyon, cousin of Thomas Wyon junior, joined the Mint in 1816, and engraved the dies for the last issue of Maundy coins. (P.A.Rayner, 1949)

---

1   See John Craig's *The Mint* for total mintage. According to James O'Donald Mays, author of *The Splendid Shilling* (New Forest Leaves, Burley, Ringwood, Hampshire), p. 81 *'Mint records show that 48 pounds of the George III shillings were struck in 1763. At standard weight, this would have permitted 2,976 "Northumberland" pieces to be made.'*

GEORGE III, 1760-1820
COUNTERMARKED SPANISH DOLLARS & FRACTIONS

This is a very complex series as many examples are unique or nearly so. One major difficulty is trying to differentiate between the original Soho Mint strikings and the later restrikes by W.J. Taylor. Collectors are advised to refer to the die study by Michael Dickinson *"BANK OF ENGLAND DOLLAR VARIETIES"*, S.N.C. 1999, part I, pp. 275-277 & part II, pp. 310-314.

DOLLARS - Type A/1 & 2
OVAL PUNCH ON COMMON SPANISH DOLLARS (8 Reales)
Treasury Warrant dated 3 March 1797

Type   1   With a bust / *rev.* small crown above large shield (Spanish mints)
          2   With a bust / *rev.* pillar design (Spanish American mints)
          3   No bust (pillar design) / *rev.* large crown above squat shield
          4   No bust (circular shield) / *rev.* crowned square-topped shield

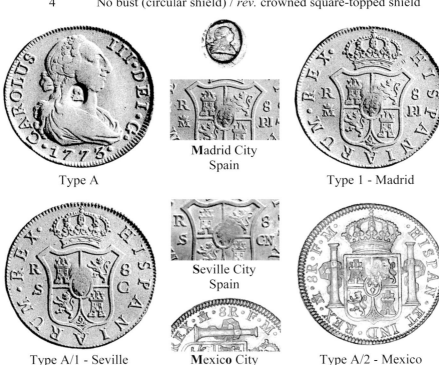

Type A

Madrid City
Spain

Type 1 - Madrid

Type A/1 - Seville

Seville City
Spain

Mexico City
Mexico

Type A/2 - Mexico

COUNTERMARKED SPANISH DOLLARS & FRACTIONS

DOLLARS

Santiago
Chile

Nueva Granada
Guatemala

Type A/2 - Santiago

Type A/2 - Guatemala

PoToSI
Bolivia

LIMÆ
Peru

Type A/2 - Potosi

Type A/2 - Lima

RARE SPANISH PILLAR DOLLARS

Mexico City
Mexico

Type A/3

Type A/3

COUNTERMARKED SPANISH DOLLARS & FRACTIONS

DOLLARS

LIMÆ
Peru

Type A/3 - Lima   **PoToSI** Bolivia   Type A/3 - Potosi

EXTREMELY RARE FRENCH COINS

Type A/4, 5 & 6

A

Toulouse (M)
France

5

A

Pau (cow)

5

COUNTERMARKED SPANISH DOLLARS & FRACTIONS

EXTREMELY RARE FRENCH COINS

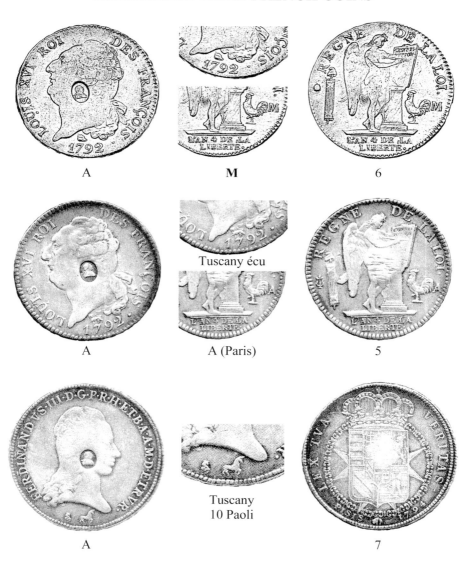

A   M   6

A   Tuscany écu   5

A (Paris)

A   Tuscany 10 Paoli   7

COUNTERMARKED SPANISH DOLLARS & FRACTIONS

DOLLARS
SNC 2012, MS9816 example of the oval countermark double struck (Mexico)
The following tables list possibilities see *Provenances* for known examples

ESC	Ob/rv.	Country	Mint	Mintmarks	R	(Old ESC)
1850	**A/1**	Spain	**M**adrid	**M**	R^3	135
1851	—	Spain	**S**eville	**S**	N	135
1852	**A/2**	Mexico	**M**exico City	M̥	C^2	129
1853	—	Chile	**S**antiago	S̥	R^3	134
1854	—	Guatemala	*Nueva Granada*	**NG**	R^2	132
1855	—	Bolivia	**P**o**T**o**SI**	**PTSI** monogram	S	131
1856	**A/3**	Mexico	**M**exico City	M̥ *Pillar dollar* [7]	R^5	131
1857	—	Bolivia	**P**o**T**o**SI**	**PTSI** *Pillar $*	S	131
1858	—	Peru	**LIMA**	**LIMÆ** *Pillar $*	N	133
1859	**A/5**	France	Bayonne 1784		R^6	136
1860	—	France	Pau 1786		R^6	136
1861	—	France	Toulouse 1784		R^6	136
1862	**A/6**	France	A (Paris) 1792		R^6	136
1863	—	France	M 1792		R^6	136
1864	**A/7**	France	Tuscany 1794		R^6	
1865	**A/8**	U.S.A.	*(1 known in B.M.)*	Small eagle	R^7	

RARE OCTAGONAL PUNCH ON
COMMON SPANISH DOLLARS (8 Reales)
Treasury Warrant dated 2 January 18047
Type B/1 & 2

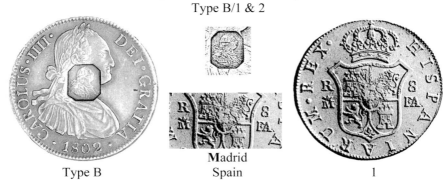

| Type B | Madrid Spain | 1 |

COUNTERMARKED SPANISH DOLLARS & FRACTIONS

DOLLARS

Santiag**o**
Chile

Sevill**e**
Spain

Mexic**o** City
Mexico

Po**T**o**SI**
Bolivia

Nueva **G**ranada
Guatemala

LIMÆ
Peru

USA
DOLLARS

Types B/3 & 4
Extremely rare

Small eagle

B

8

Large eagle

B

9

COUNTERMARKED SPANISH DOLLARS & FRACTIONS

DOLLARS

1866	B/1	Spain	Madrid	M	See note [3]	R^2	141
1867	—	Spain	Seville	S		R^2	141
1868	B/2	Mexico	Mexico City	M̥		S	138
1869	—	Chile	Santiago	S̥		R^3	134
1870	—	Guatemala	Nueva Granada	NG		R	140
1871	—	Bolivia	PotoSI	PTSI monogram		R	139
1872	—	Peru	LIMA	LIMÆ monogram		R^2	140A
1873	B/8	U.S.A.	(2 known)	Small eagle		R^7	143
1874	B/9	U.S.A.	(5 known)	Large eagle		R^5	143

HALF-DOLLARS (4 Reales)
(Currency 2s-4½d)
OVAL & OCTAGONAL COUNTERMARKS [6]
Types and mintmarks as dollars

Type A

Pillar obverse (early)
Mexico

Type B

Madrid
Spain - Type 1

Mexico City
Mexico – Type 3

Seville
Spain – Type 1

COUNTERMARKED SPANISH DOLLARS & FRACTIONS

HALF-DOLLARS

Mexico City
Mexico

PoToSI
Bolivia - Type 2

LIMÆ
Peru

Santiag**o**
Chile

inverted countermark

Madrid

Madrid
Spain

Type 4

Seville
Spain

COUNTERMARKED SPANISH DOLLARS & FRACTIONS

HALF-DOLLARS

1875	A/1	Spain	*Madrid*	**M**	*S*	611
1876	—	Spain	*Seville*	**S**	*S*	—
1877	A/2	Mexico	*Mexico City*	**M̊**	*S*	—
1878	—	Chile	*Santiago*	**S̊**	R^5	—
1879	—	Guatemala	*Nueva Grenada*	**NG**	R^5	—
1880	—	Bolivia	*Potosi*	**PTSI** monogram	R^2	—
1881	—	Peru	***Lima***	**LIMÆ** monogram	R^2	—
1882	A/3	Peru	***Lima*** (Pillar)	**LIMÆ** monogram	R^6	—
1883	A/3	Spain	*Madrid* (Pillar)	**M**	*R*	—
1884	A/4	Spain	*Madrid* (Circular)	**M**	*R*	—
1885	A/4	Spain	*Seville* (Circular)	**S**	*R*	—
1886	B/1	Spain	*Madrid*	**M**	R^5	—
1887	—	Spain	*Seville*	**S**	R^3	—
1888	B/4	Spain	*Seville* (Circular)	**S**	*R*	—
1889	B/2	Mexico	*Mexico City*	**M̊**	R^3	—
1890	—	Guatemala	*Nueva Granada*	**NG**	R^5	—
1891	—	Bolivia	*Potosi*	**PTSI** monogram	R^4	—
1892			USA Half dollar 1795		R^7	—

Doubts about the authenticity of the following fractions of the
Dollar is allayed by the remarks published by Glendining below*

2 Reales

Madrid   Mexico

1893	A/1	Spain	*Madrid*	**M**	R^4	
1894	A/2	Mexico	*Mexico City*	**M̊**	R^5	
1895			*(Number reserved for new discovery)*			

COUNTERMARKED SPANISH DOLLARS & FRACTIONS

2 Reales

Lima

1896	B/2	Spain,	M*adrid*	M	R^4	
1897	—	Peru,	*Lima*	LIMÆ	R^6	

1 Reale

Mexico   LIMÆ

1898	A/1	Spain	M*adrid*	M	R^4	
1899	A/2	Mexico	M*exico City* [8]	M̊	R^4	
1900	—	Peru	*Lima*	LIMÆ	R^5	

Half-Real

Mexico   Mexico

1901		*(Number reserved for new discovery)*				
1902	A/2	Mexico,	M*exico City*	M̊	R^6	
1903	A/3	Mexico,	*Pillar type*	M̊	R^6	

Note
For the specialist collector there are many varieties and dates

GEORGE III, 1760-1820
COUNTERMARKED SPANISH DOLLARS & FRACTIONS

Trial piece, octagonal countermark on a shilling-sized silver blank
(Another test strike is known on a copper halfpenny)

*My thanks to Glendining's Auction 1992/10/12, lot 507, for the following article
"Oval countermarks on Dollar fractions have for long aroused controversy, some authorities condemning them as bogus. E.M. Kelly has presented a countervailing view (Spanish Dollars & Silver Tokens, Spink. London 1976, p. 24)

A much more interesting set of figures, numismatically, is that showing the dollars going into the Current Cash Account for twenty eight out of sixty entries show half-dollars and one gives quarter dollars. As these were the totals for the day there were probably many more to make up a round figure in dollars. The Bank added half and quarter dollars to make up a bag to the standard weight of 1,000 ounces troy. Segments were also used and there was the occasional coin other than Spanish thrown in, all of which were complained of at a later date by the Military authorities, who preferred some uniformity. Having no precedents for counter-marking, the Mint would have considered it acceptable to strike fractional coins to make up the weights. *The doubts that are cast on the validity of these coins by numismatists would seem to have no foundation."*

1	Believed to be unique (in Bank of England collection)
2	Five genuine specimens are known; also 3 forgeries.
4	Many of these are known to exist, but rarity unknown.
5	Listed but, not all are known and if so are very rare; some collectors doubt if these are authentic
6	All colonial octagonal punch countermarks are very rare; most on this list are unrecorded.
7	A small number of non-portrait *'pillar dollars'* countermarked with an oval stamp exist. These appear to be genuine countermarks and may have been stamped in error.
8	False oval countermark but a good example of its type.

272

THE PATTERN CROWNS

1798 – Spade-shape shield
In the past ESC classified these patterns as *'Bank of England Dollars'*
Latest research by Michael Dickenson has proved them to be
Crowns from original documents of 1798
See Spink Numismatic Circular 1999, pp. 243-246
'Pattern Crowns Dated 1798' by Michael Dickenson
See also *'Bank of England Dollar Varieties'*
Part I, pp. 275-277 & part II, pp. 310-314

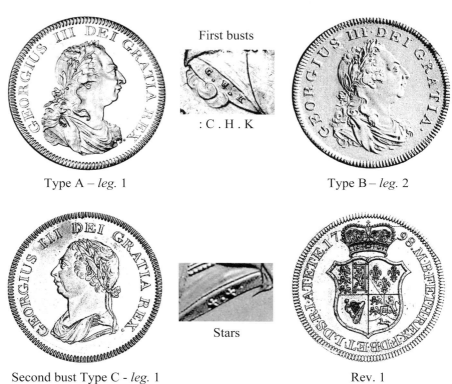

First busts

: C . H . K

Type A – *leg.* 1

Type B – *leg.* 2

Second bust Type C - *leg.* 1

Stars

Rev. 1

Caveat; W.J. Taylor, the London engraver and manufacturer, acquired many of the dies for these crowns and the following Bank of England Dollars at auction in 1850, and is known to have produced coins from them for collectors. Many of the mules found today are attributed to him and therefore not genuine. (No attempt has been made to differentiate re-strikes)

THE PATTERN CROWNS

Obv.	**A.**	**First bust, right**, laureate and draped, with a stop after **REX.** First leaf of laurel points to the upright of **E** in **DEI**; on the truncation, **· : C · H · K ·** or **: C · H · K** the stops before **C** are not always clear
Leg.	1	**GEORGIUS III DEI GRATIA REX .** (Only 1 stop)
	A¹	As 'A' but, leaf to centre of **E** in **DEI**
	A²	Leaf to centre of **E**, and **· · K** on truncation
	A³	As before but, leaf to upright of **E**
	B	First leaf to **D**, on truncation **: . C.K.H.**
Leg.	2	**GEORGIUS III · DEI GRATIA ·** (no REX and 2 stops)
	B¹	Similar to 'H' but **· : C.K.H.** on truncation
	B²	Similar to 'H' but either **· : K** or **. : K .** on truncation
	C⁵	**Second bust, left**, smaller laureate and draped, first leaf to upright of **D**; **✶·✶·** on truncation; five berries in wreath
Leg.	1	**GEORGIUS III DEI GRATIA REX .** (Only 1 stop)
Rev.	**1.**	Spade-shape shield, small crown above dividing date
Leg.		**98.M·B·F·ET·H·REX·F·D·B·ET·L·D·S·R·I·A·T·ET·E.17**

A/1.   **First bust right**, 1ˢᵗ leaf to upright of **E** in **DEI**
Leg. 1 - **GEORGIUS III DEI GRATIA REX .**   (1 stop)

ESC	Date	Obv	Varieties, remarks etc.	R	L&S	Davis	(Old ESC)
1904	**1798**	A	**· : C · H · K ·** or **: C · H · K** on truncation	R^2	33	D.3	171
1905	—	—	*In copper*	R^4	34	D.4	172

A¹/1   **First bust right**, 1ˢᵗ leaf to centre of **E** in **DEI** / *Rev.* as before

1906	**1798**	C	**: C · H · K** on truncation	R^4	29	D.1	168
1907	—	—	*In Gold* *W&R143* *wt. 38.55g*	R^7	30		169
1908	—	—	*In copper* *wt. 29.93g*	R^2	31	D.2	170
1909	—	—	*In copper thick flan* Plain edge *wt. 31.07g*	R^2	32		170A

THE PATTERN CROWNS

A²/1 First bust right, 1ˢᵗ leaf to centre of E in DEI / *Rev.* as before

ESC	Date	Obv	Varieties, remarks etc.	R	L&S	Davis	(Old ESC)
1910	**1798**	F	· · **K** on truncation	R^4	35	D.5	173
1911	—	—	*In copper*	R^3	36		174

A³/1 First bust right, 1ˢᵗ leaf to upright of E in DEI / *Rev.* as before

1912	**1798**	G	· · **K** on truncation	R^6	37		175
1913	—	—	*In copper*	R^6			175A
1914	—	—	*In copper gilt*	R^6			175B

B/1 First bust right, 1ˢᵗ leaf to D in DEI
Leg. 2 - GEORGIUS III · DEI GRATIA · (Minus REX)

| 1915 | **1798** | H | **: . C.K.H.** on truncation | R^7 | 38 | | 176 |
| | | | *In white metal (tin)*   *wt. 25.56g* | | | | |

B¹/1 First bust right, 1ˢᵗ leaf to D in DEI /
Leg. 2 - GEORGIUS III · DEI GRATIA · (no REX)

1916	**1798**	I	**· : C.K.H.** on truncation	R^4	39		177
1917	—	—	*On a flan ⅓ inch thick*	R^4	40		177A
1918	—	—	*In copper*	R^4	41		178

B²/1 First bust right, 1ˢᵗ leaf to D in DEI / *Rev.* as before

1919	**1798**	J	**· : K** or **. : K .** on truncation	R^6	42		178A
			In copper on a very thick flan *wt. 28.3g*				
1920	—	—	*In white metal (tin)* Plain edge *wt. 26.34g*	R^6		D.5	178B
1921	—	—	*In pewter, edge* plain	R^6			178C

C⁵/1 Second bust left, 1ˢᵗ leaf to D in DEI, five berries in wreath
Leg. 1 - GEORGIUS III DEI GRATIA REX .

1922	**1798**	K	★·★· on truncation	R^4	43		179
1923	—	—	*In copper*	R^4	44	D.29	180
1924	—	—	*In gold* *W&R 145, wt. 38.86g*	R^7			180A

"In spite of the fact that few collectors will ever be in the position to own a specimen of these very rare patterns, apart from, perhaps, the odd one or two, they are recorded for the sake of interest. Many are unique"

BANK OF ENGLAND DOLLARS

Matthew Bolton, of Birmingham, over-stamped Spanish Dollars [5] with a new design for the first issue of these Bank of England dollars. Later the Spanish dollars were melted down and the silver used to coin in the normal way.

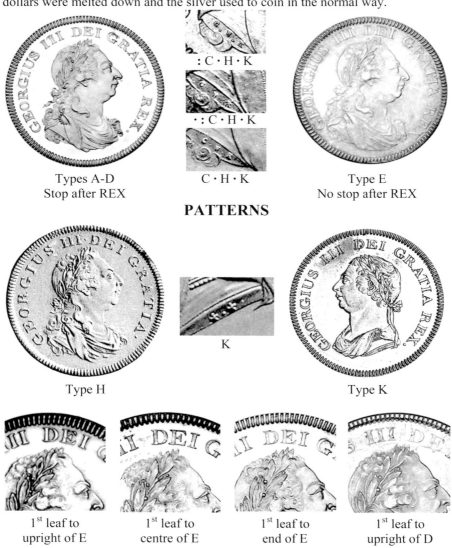

Types A-D
Stop after REX

: C · H · K
· : C · H · K
C · H · K

Type E
No stop after REX

PATTERNS

Type H

K

Type K

1st leaf to
upright of E

1st leaf to
centre of E

1st leaf to
end of E

1st leaf to
upright of D

BANK OF ENGLAND DOLLARS

Rev. 2

Rev. 3

Rev. 4

5

Rev. 5

Normal raised K

Inverted raised K

Inverted incuse K

BANK OF ENGLAND DOLLARS

Obv. **A.** **First bust, right,** laureate and draped. First leaf of laurel points to the upright of **E** in **DEI**; on the truncation, **· : C · H · K ·** or **: C · H · K** ; the stops before the **C** not always clear

Leg. **GEORGIUS III DEI GRATIA REX .** (Stop after **REX.**)

B. Similar, but only a colon before **: C H K** (no stops between)

C. As 'A' but, leaf to centre of **E** in **DEI**

D. As 'A' but, leaf to end of **E** in **DEI**, and **C.H.K.** close

E. As 'A' but, no stop after **REX**, leaf to centre of **E** in **DEI**

F. Leaf to centre of **E**, and **· · K** on truncation

G. As 'F' but, leaf to upright of **E**

H. First leaf to **D**, on truncation **: . C.H.K.**

Leg. **GEORGIUS III · DEI GRATIA ·** (minus REX)

I. Similar to 'H' but **· : C.H.K.** on truncation

J. Similar to 'H' but either **· : K** or **. : K .** on truncation

K. **Second bust, left,** smaller laureate and draped, first leaf to upright of **D**; ★·★ on truncation; five berries in wreath

Leg. **GEORGIUS III DEI GRATIA REX .**

L. Similar to 'K', but six berries

Rev. **2** Britannia seated facing left, in her left hand a spear, her arm resting on a shield above a cornucopia, in her right hand an olive branch, all within a crowned oval band with the words; **FIVE SHILLINGS DOLLAR** letter **K** in relief under shield

Leg. **BANK OF 👑 ENGLAND** date **1804** below

2a Similar, but **K** inverted thus ⋊ [3]

2b Similar, but the inverted ⋊ is incuse [3]

BANK OF ENGLAND DOLLARS

3.   **Royal arms within Garter** date **18   04** above **DOLLAR** below
Leg.   **BRITANNIARUM   REX   FIDEI   DEFENSOR**

4.   **Britannia seated left**, holding a spear in right hand and
    resting her left arm on a shield, large ground below.
Leg.   **BANK OF ENGLAND TOKEN.**
    In exergue, **FIVE SHILLINGS // & SIXPENCE // 1811.**

5.   **BANK //   TOKEN //   5s. 6d.   //   1811** within an oak wreath,
    stem slightly downwards, **I.P.** under tie

5a.   Similar, but stem slightly upwards, **I·P.** under tie

Type   **A/2.**   **1st bust right**, 1st laurel leaf points to the upright of **E** in **DEI**
                Leg. **GEORGIUS III DEI GRATIA REX.** (Only 1 stop)
                Rev. 2 – **Britannia** – **FIVE SHILLINGS DOLLAR** Spink 3768

ESC	Date	*Obv/rv*	Varieties, remarks etc.	R	L&S	Davis	(Old ESC)
1925	**1804**	**A/2**	*Rev.* **K** in relief under shield *Weights vary between 26.82-27.02g*	C^2	53	D.17	144
1926	—	—	*Proof*	R	54		145
1927	—	—	*Proof in copper*	R^3	55	D.18	146
1928	—	**A/2b**	Inverted **K** incuse under shield	R^4	56		147

    B/2.   **1st bust right**, 1st leaf to upright of **E** in **DEI**   Stop after **REX.**
                Rev. 2 – **Britannia** – **FIVE SHILLINGS DOLLAR** Spink 3768

ESC	Date	Obv/rv	Varieties, remarks etc.	R	L&S	Davis	(Old ESC)
1929	**1804**	**B/2**	**: C H K** (no stops between) *Rev.* **K** in relief under shield	R	57	D.16	148
1930	—	—	*Silver proof, en medaille* ↑↑	R	84		148A

    C/2.   **1st bust right**, 1st leaf to centre of **E** in **DEI**   Stop after **REX.**
                Rev. 2 – **Britannia** – **FIVE SHILLINGS DOLLAR** Spink 3768

ESC	Date	Obv/rv	Varieties, remarks etc.	R	L&S	Davis	(Old ESC)
1931	**1804**	**C/2**	**: C H K** (no stops between) *Rev.* **K** in relief under shield	S	58	D.10	149
1932	—	—	*Proof in silver*	S	59		150
1933	—	—	*Proof in silver gilt* *wt. 24.57g*	R^5	60		151
1934	—	—	*Proof in copper*	S	61	D.11	152
1935	—	—	*Proof in copper on a thick flan*	S	62	D.11	152
1936	—	—	*Proof in copper-nickel*	R^5			152B
1937	—	—	*Proof in nickel-silver* (restrike)	R^5			152A

(continued)

BANK OF ENGLAND DOLLARS

ESC	Date	Obv/rv	Varieties, remarks etc.	R	L&S	Davis	(Old ESC)
1938	**1804**	**C/2a**	Inverted **K** in relief under shield. *In silver*	R	63	D.19	153
1939	—	—	*Proof in silver*	R	64	—	154
1940	—	—	*Proof in copper*	R	65		155
1941	—	**C/2b**	Inverted **K** incuse under shield	S	66	D. 6	156
1942	—	—	*Proof en medaille* wt. 26.97g	R^7			156A
1943	—	—	*Proof in copper* (Not traced)	R^3	67	D. 7	157

D/2. **1st bust right,** 1st leaf to end of **E** in **DEI**   Stop after **REX.**
Rev. **2 – Britannia – FIVE SHILLINGS DOLLAR** Spink 3768

1944	**1804**	**D/2**	: C H K (no stops between) *Rev.* **K** in relief under shield	R^3	68		158
1945	—	**D/2a**	Inverted **K** relief under shield	R^2	69	D. 8	159
1946	—	—	*Proof in silver*	R	70		160
1947	—	—	*Proof in silver gilt*	R^5			160A
1948	—	—	*Proof in copper*	R^2	71	D. 9	161
1949	—	**D/2b**	Inverted **K** incuse under shield	R^2	72	D.12	162
1950	—	—	*Proof in copper*	R^2	73	D.13	163

E/2. **1st bust right,** 1st leaf to centre of **E** in **DEI**   No stop after **REX**
Rev. **2 – Britannia – FIVE SHILLINGS DOLLAR** Spink 3768

1951	**1804**	**E/2**	*Rev.* **K** in relief under shield	C	74	D.14	164
1952	—	—	*Proof in silver*	R	75		165
1953	—	—	*Proof on a thicker flan* wt. 35g	R^4	76		165A
1954	—	—	*Proof in copper*	R	77	D.15	166
1955	—	—	*Proof in silver.* **C.H.K.** recut *Very thick flan* wt.35.6-37.2g	R^4	78	—	167
1956	—	—	*Proof in copper.* Thicker flan	R^3	79		164A

E/3. **1st bust right,** 1st leaf to centre of **E** in **DEI**   No stop after **REX**
Rev. **3 – Royal arms within Garter - DOLLAR**   Spink 3768

1957	**1804**	**E/3**	Mule	R^6			167B

C/3. **1st bust right,** 1st leaf to centre of **E** in **DEI**   Stop after **REX.**
Rev. **3 – Royal arms within Garter - DOLLAR**   Spink 3768

1958	**1804**	**C/3**	*In copper* wt. 30.6 g	R^6			

BANK OF ENGLAND DOLLARS

G/3.   **1ˢᵗ bust right**, 1ˢᵗ leaf to upright of **E** in **DEI**   Stop after **REX**.
      Rev. 3 – **Royal arms within Garter - DOLLAR**   Spink 3768

ESC	Date	Obv/rv	Varieties, remarks etc.	R	L&S	Davis	(Old ESC)
1959	1804	G/3	*(Not traced)*	R^3	99	D.24	188
1960	—	—	*In copper*	R^5	100	D.25	189

H/3   **1ˢᵗ bust right**, 1ˢᵗ leaf to **D** in **DEI**
      Leg. **GEORGIUS III · DEI GRATIA ·** (No REX & 2 stops)
      Rev. 3 – **Royal arms within Garter - DOLLAR**   Spink 3768

1961	1804	H/3	**: . C.H.K.** on truncation	R	90	D.20	181
1962	—	—	*On a thick flan* *wt. 31.975g*	R^6			181A

I/3   **1ˢᵗ bust right**, 1ˢᵗ leaf to **D** in **DEI**
      Leg. **GEORGIUS III · DEI GRATIA ·** (No REX & 2 stops)
      Rev. 3 – **Royal arms within Garter - DOLLAR**   Spink 3768

1963	1804	I/3	**. : C.H.K.** on truncation	R	91	D.21	182
			(Under-type often apparent)				
1964	—	—	*In copper* *(Not traced)*	R^4	92	D.22	183
1965	—	—	*In white metal*	R^5	93		184

J/3   **1ˢᵗ bust right**, 1ˢᵗ leaf to **D** in **DEI**
      Leg. **GEORGIUS III · DEI GRATIA ·** (No REX & 2 stops)
      Rev. 3 – **Royal arms within Garter - DOLLAR**   Spink 3768

1966	1804	J/3	**· : K** or **. : K.** on truncation	R^3	95	D.23	185
1967	—	—	**. : K** on truncation²	R^4	97	—	186
1968	—	—	*In copper* ↑↓ *wt. 24.0g*	R^4	98	—	187

K/3.   **2ⁿᵈ bust, left**, 1ˢᵗ leaf to upright of **D**, five berries in wreath
      Leg. **GEORGIUS III DEI GRATIA REX .** (Only 1 stop)
      Rev. 3 – **Royal arms within Garter - DOLLAR**   Spink 3768

1969	1804	K/3	*In copper* *wt. 30.54 g*	R^6	101	D.24	189X

I/2.   **1ˢᵗ bust bust right**, 1ˢᵗ leaf to **D** in **DEI**
      Leg. **GEORGIUS III DEI GRATIA REX .** (Only 1 stop)
      Rev. 2 – **Britannia holding olive branch, within value**

1970	1804	I/2	**: . C.H.K.** on truncation	R^5	80		190
			Silver pattern				

BANK OF ENGLAND DOLLARS

J/2.   **First bust** right, 1st leaf to **D** in **DEI**
   Leg. **GEORGIUS III DEI GRATIA REX .** (Only 1 stop)
   Rev. 2 – **Britannia holding olive branch, within value**

ESC	Date	Obv/rv	Varieties, remarks etc.	R	L&S	Davis	(Old ESC)
1971	1804	J/2	**· : K** or **. : K.** on truncation *Silver pattern*	R^5	81		191

K/2.   2nd **bust, left,** 1st leaf to upright of **D**, five berries in wreath
   Leg. **GEORGIUS III DEI GRATIA REX .** (Only 1 stop)
   Rev. 2 – **Britannia holding olive branch, within value**

1972	1804	K/2	*Copper pattern*	R^3	83	D.41	193

L/2.   2nd **bust, left,** 1st leaf to upright of **D**, six berries in wreath
   Leg. **GEORGIUS III DEI GRATIA REX .** (Only 1 stop)
   Rev. 2 – **Britannia holding olive branch, within value**

1973	1804	L/2	*Copper pattern*	R^3	82	D.41	192

C/4.   1st **bust right,** 1st leaf to centre of **E** in **DEI**
   Leg. **GEORGIUS III DEI GRATIA REX .** (Only 1 stop)
   Rev. 4 – **Britannia holding spear on exergue line**

1974	1811	C/4		R^4	105	D.30	194
1975	—	—	*In bronzed copper on a thick flan* wt. 36.667g	R^7	107		194A
1976	—	—	*In copper a thick flan* [1]	R^3	106	D.31	195
1977	—	—	*In copper gilt*	R^6	108		195A

D/4.   1st **bust right,** 1st leaf to end of **E** in **DEI**
   Leg. **GEORGIUS III DEI GRATIA REX .** (Only 1 stop)
   Rev. 4 – **Britannia holding spear on exergue line**

1978	1811	D/4		R^4	109	D.32	196
1979	—	—	*In copper* (Not traced)	R^4	110	D.33	197

C/5a.   1st **bust right,** 1st leaf to centre of **E** in **DEI**
   Leg. **GEORGIUS III DEI GRATIA REX .** (Only 1 stop)
   Rev. 5 – **Wreath - BANK // TOKEN // 5s. 6d.**

1980	1811	C/5a		R^4	132	D.42	208
1981	—	—	*In copper*	R^2	133	D.43	209

BANK OF ENGLAND DOLLARS

K/2.   **2nd bust, left,** 1st leaf to upright of **D**, five berries in wreath
        Leg. **GEORGIUS III DEI GRATIA REX .** (Only 1 stop)
        Rev. 2 – **Britannia holding olive branch, within value**

ESC	Date	Obv/rv	Varieties, remarks etc.	R	L&S	Davis	(Old ESC)
1982	**1811**	**K/2**		R^4		$D.27/_{41}$	199B

K/4.   **2nd bust, left,** 1st leaf to upright of **D**, five berries in wreath
        Leg. **GEORGIUS III DEI GRATIA REX .** (Only 1 stop)
        Rev. 4 – **Britannia holding spear on exergue line**

1983	**1811**	**K/4**		R^3	111	D.26	198
1984	—	—	*In copper* [1]	R^2	112	D.27	199
1985	—	—	*In copper, thick flan* wt.44·28g	R^2			199A

L/4.   **2nd bust, left,** 1st leaf to upright of **D**, six berries in wreath
        Leg. **GEORGIUS III DEI GRATIA REX .** (Only 1 stop)
        Rev. 4 – **Britannia holding spear on exergue line**

1986	**1811**	**L/4**		R^4	113	D.28	200
1987	—	—	*In copper*	R^3	114		201
1988	—	—	*In white metal, thick flan*	R^7	115		202
1989	—	—	*Copper washed* (Looks plated)	R^6	116		202A

L/5.   **2nd bust, left,** 1st leaf to upright of **D**, six berries in wreath
        Leg. **GEORGIUS III DEI GRATIA REX .** (Only 1 stop)
        Rev. 5 – **Wreath - BANK // TOKEN // 5s. 6d.**

1990	**1811**	**L/5**		R^4	121	D.34	203
1991	—	—	*In copper*	R^4	122	D.35	204
1992	—	—	*In silver, thin flan* wt. 426grs	R^3	123		204A

K/5.   **2nd bust, left,** 1st leaf to upright of **D**, five berries in wreath
        Leg. **GEORGIUS III DEI GRATIA REX .** (Only 1 stop)
        Rev. 5 – **Wreath - BANK // TOKEN // 5s. 6d.**

1993	**1811**	**K/5**	*In silver* (2 known) wt. 31.2g	R^7			204
1994	—	**K/5a**	*In silver* wt. 445 grs-28.83g [6]	R^3	124	D.36	205
1995	—	—	*In silver, thick flan* wt. 32.01g	R^5	125	D.36	205A
1996	—	—	*In copper* wt. 24.94g-25.66g	S	126	D.37	206
1997	—	—	*In copper* Stop nearer to bust and different figures in date	R^3	127	D.37	206A
1998	—	—	*In copper, thin flan* wt .22.29g	S	128	D.37	206B

(continued)

GEORGE III, 1760-1820
BANK OF ENGLAND DOLLARS

ESC	Date	Obv/rv	Varieties, remarks etc.	R	L&S	Davis	(Old ESC)
1999	**1811**	**K/5a**	*Copper, thick flan* wt. 26.89g	S	129	D.37	
2000	—	—	*In copper on an extra thick flan* wt.42.25g	R	130	D.37	206B
2001	—	—	*In brass*	R^6	131	D.38	207

D/5a. 1st **bust right**, 1st leaf to end of **E** in **DEI**
Leg. **GEORGIUS III DEI GRATIA REX .** (Only 1 stop)
Rev. 5 – **Wreath - BANK // TOKEN // 5s. 6d.**

2002	1811	**D/5a**	*(Not traced)*	R^4	134	D.44	210

PATTERN

2003		Uniface trial striking of obverse used on the 1811 pattern by **W. Philip,** struck *in lead* *(Unique?)*	L&S 145	
	Obv.	Laureate and draped bust left, signature below		
	Leg.	**GEORGIUS III . PIUS DEFENSOR FIDEI.**		
2004	—	As before but minus the signature below bust	146	

The column headed; 'Davis №' is reference to;
'The Nineteenth Century Token Coinage' by W.J. Davis
L&S refers to the classification numbers by Linecar and Stone. Spink 1968
L&S 141 (uniface reverse), 142 (uniface reverse) & 143(uniface obverse) ignored

1	These coins are probably mules
2	Struck *over octagonal countermarked dollar*
3	2a & 2b listed as inverted **K** but is it an H for Halliday?
5	On many coins, part of the design/legend on the host coin is still visible
6	These are the weights recorded by Lingford, weights of others will vary

LAST OR NEW COINAGE
CROWNS

Type	Only the one
Obv.	Large laureate bust, right, **PISTRUCCI** below truncation
Leg.	Starting at 7 o'clock; **GEORGIUS III D : G : BRITANNIARUM REX F:D:** Date below truncation
Edge	**DECUS ET TUTAMEN ANNO REGNI** followed by the regnal year in Roman numerals, all in high relief and occupying the whole width of the edge.
Rev.	St George slaying the dragon, broken lance on the ground. In exergue **PISTRUCCI** all within the Garter with motto; **HONI · SOIT · QUI · MAL · Y · PENSE.** W (Wyon) on buckle

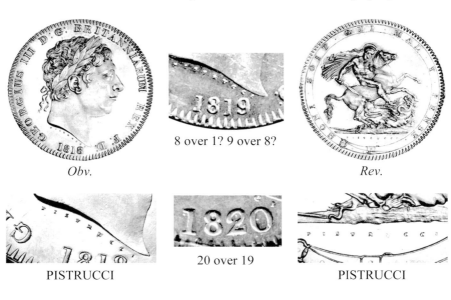

Obv.

8 over 1? 9 over 8?

Rev.

PISTRUCCI

20 over 19

PISTRUCCI

H   N

Double entered letters

M   Y

W on buckle

LAST OR NEW COINAGE
CROWNS

Spink 3787

ESC	Date	Edge	year	Varieties	R	L&S	(Old ESC)
2005	**1818**	**LVIII**	(58)		C		211
2006	—	—	—	*Proof* [1]	R^2	197	212
2007	—	—	—	*Pattern* (3 known) Edge incuse with star stops	R^6	198	213
2008	—	—	—	Edge in wrong order [4]	R^5		213A
2009	—	**LIX**	(59)		C		214
2010	**1819**	—	—	See note [2]	C^2		215
2011	—	—	—	No stops on edge	R^3		215A
2012	—	—	—	**8** over **1**? & **9** over **8**?	R^3		215B
2013	—	**LX**	(60)		N		216
2014	—	—	—	*Proof* [1]	R^2	203	217
2015	—	None		*Proof,* plain edge (Unique)	R^7	204	218
2016	**1820**	**LX**	(60)	See note [3]	C		219
2017	—	—	—	*Proof* [1]	R^3	206	220
2018	—	—	—	**20** over **19**	R^3		220A
2019	—	—	—	**S** over **T** in **SOIT**	R^3		220B

1   With some hesitancy these inscribed edge proofs have been included as they have been published previously and are generally considered to have been struck. This is confirmed by the other denominations of which there are undoubted proofs. The standard of the striking of these crowns was so high and they were issued, and are still found, in such perfect preservation that it is almost impossible to distinguish a proof from a perfect ordinary specimen

2   This coin exists with the date crudely re-engraved.

3   We have seen photographs of the reverse of a crown dated 1820, which clearly shows traces of certain letters in the Garter legend having been re-engraved on the die.

4   Reads; DECUS ANNO REGNI ET TUTAMEN LVIII

These two sub-varieties are considered insignificant; 1818 (Old ESC 214, Dr Rees Jones 204) unbarred A in TVTAMEN (filled die?) and 1819 (Old ESC 214, Dr Rees Jones 206) *rev.* garter ruled slightly thicker, different reverse die.

Note
The following unique (?) L&S numbers are omitted: 199-202; 205; 215-218

PATTERN CROWNS

Obv. M   W. WYON.   Rev. 6

ESC	Type	Varieties, remarks etc	R	L&S	(Old ESC)
2020	**M/6**	By **W. Wyon**, dated **1817**	R^2	152	223
	Obv	Bare, laureate bust, right			
		W. WYON. below a shorter truncation			
	Leg	**GEORGIUS III D:G: BRITANNIARUM REX F : D : — 1817**			
	Rev	**1.** Three figures emblematical of the three kingdoms (the 'Three Graces') with emblems and shield; **W. WYON.** to the left of harp; palm branch and quiver in exergue.			
	Leg	**FOEDUS INVIOLABILE** in smaller letters than obverse *'An unbreakable treaty'* Edge, plain *(50 struck) weights vary 24.6g-25.1g*			
2021	—	*In gold* *(3 known)* *wt. 52.45g*	R^6	153	224
2022	—	*In copper*	R^6	154	225
2023	—	*In white metal; or lead?* *wt. 33.88g*	R^5	155	226
2024	—	*In tin.* Heavily frosted, *Sealed in glass lunettes (2 known)* *wt. 44.80g*	R^6		226A
2025	—	*Uniface obverse in copper* *(Unique?)*	R^7	156	225

Note
In 1968 Linecar and Stone published a die study of all known examples of George III pattern crowns, and listed all the engraver's uniface trials, usually in soft metals. Usually these are unique strikings, rarely available to collectors, so most are omitted from this edition of E.S.C. The following is a list of the numbers omitted: L&S 45-48; 141-144; 164; 168-177; 189; 190; 199-202 & 205. Please refer to their publication for details.

PATTERN CROWNS

Rev. 7	Obv. N	Rev. 8
Small lion & thistle	*W. WYON*	Larger lion & thistle

ESC	Type	Varieties, remarks etc	R	L&S	(Old ESC)
2026	**N/7** *Rev* *Leg* *Edge*	Similar, but larger lettering on *obv*. No F:D:, signature *W. WYON* (script capitals) **2.** Small lion's head above a small thistle, artist's name in exergue in place of ornament. Smaller lettering than obverse **FŒDUS** spelt with **Œ** for **OE** Plain. *In lead* on a very thick flan	R^7	157	227
2027	—	Trial striking of the unfinished obverse die above, minus the artist's name Struck in lead with a copper coating, on the obverse only, on a thin flan	R^7	157A	228
2028	**N/8**	As before but with reverse **3.** - Similar to reverse 2, but larger lion's head and thistle *In lead* on a piedfort flan	R^7	158	228A

PATTERN CROWNS

W. WYON:

Obv. O   Rev. 9

ESC	Type	Varieties, remarks etc	R	L&S	(Old ESC)
2029	**O/9**	By **W. Wyon**, dated **1817**	R^4	159	229
	Obv	Broad bust, draped and laureate, right,			
		W. WYON: below truncation, date below			
	Leg.	**GEORGIUS III D:G:**			
		BRITANNIARUM REX			
	Rev.	**4.** Large crowned shield (somewhat similar			
		in design to Simon's Cromwell crown).			
	Leg.	**INCORRUPTA FIDES VERITASQUE**			
		'An untarnished faith'			
		Edge, plain *(25 struck)*			
2030	—	*In gold* *(7 known) wt. 48.61g- 50.34g*	R^5	160	230
2031	—	Uniface obverse as before	R^5	161	230A
		In silver on a thick flan wt. 617grs-39.98g			
2032	—	Trial striking of obverse die *in lead*	R^6	162	230B

Obv. P   Rev. 10a

ESC	Type	Varieties, remarks etc	R	L&S	(Old ESC)
2033	**P/10a** *Obv*	By **Pistrucci**, dated **1817** (unsigned) Laureate bust, right, tie with bow and two ends, rather like the adopted coin but broader and with slightly shorter neck	R^6	163	231
	Leg.	**GEORGIUS III DEI GRATIA BRITANNIARUM REX F: D: 1817** No beaded border either side			
	Rev.	**10a.** St George and dragon within the Garter with usual legend and ruled with fine horizontal lines, large wide buckle, with engraver's centring spot on the horse's body. Short ground line below horseman			
	Edge	Plain, thick flan *wt. 36.13g*			
2034	—	Trial striking of obverse die with plain edge *In lead on a large broad flan*	R^7	165	

Obv. Q   Rev. 10b

2035	**Q/10b** *Rev.*	As last but, reads **D.G. BRITANNIARUM** **10b.** Wider Garter, motto in larger letters No initials on small buckle, 3 buckle holes, engraver's centring spot on the horse's body. Short ground line below horseman *wt. 436 grs*	R^7	167	233
	Edge	**DECUS ET TUTAMEN · ANNO REGNI LVIII** (58) in raised letters between two fine cord borders *wt. 28.25g*			

PATTERN CROWNS

Obv. R

With centring spot
and short ground

Rev. 10c

ESC	Type	Varieties, remarks etc	R	L&S	(Old ESC)
2036	**R/10b**	By **Pistrucci**, dated **1817** (unsigned)	R^7	166	232
	Obv	Laureate bust, right, as before, wider space either side of date due to legend reading **BRITANNIAR:** (not BRITANNIARUM)			
	Rev.	**10c.** Similar to 10a, but narrower Garter, not shaded with lines, **W.W.P.** on small buckle, 5 buckle holes, with engraver's centring spot on the horse's body and short ground below Beaded borders both sides			
	Edge	Incuse reads; **DECVS ET TUTAMEN·ANNO REGNI QUINQUAGESIMO ⅄ SEPTIMO** (sic) *(fifty-seventh year)* wt. 28.19g; 435grains			

Obv. S

10d – with centring spot
and long ground

Rev. 10e – no spot
with long ground

PATTERN CROWNS

ESC	Type	Varieties, remarks etc	R	L&S	(Old ESC)
2037	**S/10d** *Obv* *Leg.* *Rev.*	By **Pistrucci**, dated **1818** Very large *'Bull-like'* bust, laureate, right, two ties (No bow) to wreath, PISTRUCCI in small letters below truncation. Small toothed border each side. **GEORGIUS III D: G:** **BRITANNIARUM REX F: D: — 1818** St George and dragon within narrow Garter ruled with fine horizontal lines, 3 buckle holes, with engraver's centring spot on the horse's body and long ground below **PISTRUCCI** in exergue. Plain edge	R^5	178	234
2038	—	*In lead on a larger flan*	R^7	179	235
2039	**S/10e** *Edge*	As before, but the engraver's centring spot on the horse's body has been removed Plain	R^5	180	234
2040	—	*In gold* (2 known?) *wt. 38.63g*	R^7	181	234A
2041	—	*In white metal*	R^7	182	234B
2042	**T/10d**	*In silver.* As type S/10d, but with edge legend: **DECUS ET TUTAMEN ANNO** **REGNI LVIII** (58) *(assumed full edge reading)*	R^7	179A	235A
2043	**T/10f** *Edge*	*In silver.* As type S/10e, but with edge inscribed in large letters as on current coin, filling the width of the edge **DECUS ET** **TUTAMEN ANNO REGNI LVIII** (58)	R^5	183	236
2044	**T/10g**	*In silver.* As type T/10f, but edge <u>incusely</u> inscribed in letters which do not occupy the whole width of the flan	R^5	184	238
2045	**T/10h**	*In silver.* As type T/10g, but edge inscribed in <u>raised letters</u> which do not occupy the whole width of the flan	R^6	185	237
2046	**T/10i**	*In lead.* As type T/10g, edge <u>incuse</u>, but reverse with a very heavy toothed border	R^7	186	239
2047	**T/10j**	*In silver.* As type T/10i, but the obverse is unpolished	R^7	187	239A

PATTERN CROWNS

Obv. S variety   Short ground ground   Rev. 10b variety

ESC	Type	Varieties, remarks etc	R	L&S	(Old ESC)
2048	**S/10b**	Obverse as type S, but the toothed border is coarser. The die is unpolished	R^7	188	240
	Rev.	Similar to 10b, but buckle holes indistinct and without a border			
	Edge	Plain. *In silver*			

Obv. U in Silver   Obverse U in Lead

2049	U	Uniface *obverse* by **Pistrucci**, dated **1818**	R^7	191	
		Laureate bust, right, ties hang down			
		very similar to currency issue			
		Signed **PISTRUCCI** below truncation			
	Leg	**GEORGIUS III D:G:**			
		BRITANNIARUM REX F:D: 1818			
	Edge	Plain. *Struck in silver from a broken die* [1]			
2050	—	*In lead*	R^2	192	244

PATTERN CROWNS

Obv. V

Centring spot removed
Long ground

Rev. 10h

PISTRUCCI

PISTRUCCI

ESC	Date	Varieties, remarks etc	R	L&S	(Old ESC)
2051	**V/10h**	Similar to 1818 currency coin, but lettering on obverse larger, back of the truncation of the neck is chamfered sharply, **PISTRUCCI** in fine letters below truncation	R^6	193	241
	Leg.	**GEORGIUS III D:G: BRITANNIARUM REX F:D: 1818**			
	Rev.	The Garter is narrow and ruled with fine horizontal lines. 3 buckle holes. **PISTRUCCI** in fine lettering in exergue			
	Edge	in raised letters with cinquefoil stops **DECUS ET TUTAMEN ANNO REGNI LVIII** (58) *wt. 28.25g*			
2052	—	*Edge,* incusely inscribed with star stops	R^7	194	241A
2053	—	*Edge,* plain	R^7	195	242
2054	**W/10i**	As before but, obverse lettering smaller, exactly as that on the coin for currency and the Garter on the reverse narrower and *not* ruled with horizontal lines. The borders are toothed*		196	242A
	Edge	Plain. *In white metal* (Unique?)			

*After Pistrucci slightly altered the amount cut off at the back of the neck and straightened the truncation line this was ready for currency production

PATTERN CROWNS

Obv. X   *Mills   Fecit*   Rev. 11

ESC	Type	Varieties, remarks etc	R	L&S	(Old ESC)
2055	**X/11** *Obv*	By **Webb and Mills for Mudie**, undated Tall bare, laureate bust, right, beneath, in script, *JM. D* and *TW. F.*	S	214	221
	Leg.	**GEORGIVS III DEI GRATIA**			
	Rev.	Four crowned cruciform shields, with the badge of the Garter, in the centre, in the angles, separately, a rose, thistle, shamrock and the Hanover horse. In the angle above the rose at 10 o'clock *Mills fecit*			
	Edge	Plain.			
2056	—	*In lead*	R⁵	215	222

1   "This is a most interesting piece in that it was Pistrucci's finest impression of
George III's head produced. Originally a note from the artist accompanied this coin,
(Now lost) which read; *"Enclosed is a proof of the head of the 5 Shilling piece of George
III, of extremely rarity, being unique, the die having broken as may be seen by the flaw in
the impression. This is different from all, and as regard the work it is the best head which
I ever did for that coin. I never succeeded in re-doing it as fine, notwithstanding the
innumerable times I had to repeat the puncheons and dies of the said coin, which broke,
and although I nearly always used the remainder of this puncheon to do the others, it will
be clearly seen that the first is always the best. This is in my possession, as the mintmaster
gave it to me, as he did at other times, not asking me for the payment of the metal, as I was
obliged to pay afterwards"* My grateful thanks to Glendining & Co for this appendix to
Herbert M. Lingford lot 486, Part I, Tuesday October 24ᵗʰ 1950 (M.B.)

Until an-depth die study is published to separate the genuine from Taylor's re-strikes, all
recorded varieties of both are listed and numbered. (M.B.)

PATTERN CROWNS

Obv. Y   Rev. 12

ESC	Type	Varieties, remarks etc	R	L&S	(Old ESC)
2057	**Y/12**	By **J.P. Droz**, dated **1820**, after **Monneron's pattern** by **Dupré** of 1792	R^5	211	243
	Obv	The figure of Hercules seated on a lion's skin, on the seashore, with his club by his right ankle, breaking a bundle of sticks across his left knee. Behind him is the base of an ornamented column: in front, the sea and four ships. The date, 1820, is in an unusually large exergue, above a wreath			
	Leg.	**VIS VNITATE FORTIOR** *'Strength is stronger through unity'*			
	Rev.	A crowned shield of arms of England and Scotland; France, Ireland and Hanover			
	Leg.	**DECVS ET TVTAMEN** *'An ornament and a safeguard'*			
	Edge	Plain [2] *(18 struck)*			
2058	—	*In gold* *(7 struck) (Not traced)*	R^5		243A
2059	—	*In copper*	R^2	212	244
2060	—	*In copper gilt*	R^6	213	245

2   This has been left under the reign of George III, where it is usually put, but Brooke gives it
To George IV, as he had found it assigned to that reign in a sale catalogue of 1828.
The type is hardly applicable to either reign, but one would expect to find it as a
suggestion for a new reign, as the king would naturally expect his portrait to be used:
maybe it should be classified as a medal rather than a coin. (P.A.R.)
The first public offering of this piece in the J.T. Brockett sale in June 1823 (H&R 1823.8)
lot 1199, where it says: *"No more than 25 having been struck in silver."* However, an MS
note in one copy of this catalogue says *"Only 18 copies of № 1199 were struck in silver-
7 were struck in gold, making the 25 above mentioned."* (P.A.R.)

BANK OF ENGLAND TOKENS

THREE SHILLINGS

FIRST BUST [1]

2 ties (A^{var})   A^{var} 1 tie (A^1)

Front leaf between DE   Front leaf to upright of E   Front leaf to end of E

A^2 A^3 A^4

1 - Wreath unbroken   2 - Wreath with a gap

BANK OF ENGLAND TOKENS

Obv.	**A**^{var}	Laureate draped bust in armour, right, front leaf points to end of **E** in **DEI** (No visible berries in wreath) Two tie ends protrude
Leg.		**GEORGIUS III DEI GRATIA REX**
	A^1	Similar, but smaller bust and changes to hair style, most noticeable at the back of neck, a single tie end protruding, five berries in wreath, front laurel leaf to end of **E**
	A^2	Similar, but front leaf between **D** and **E**
	A^3	Similar, but front leaf to back of **E**, four berries in wreath
Rev.	**1**^{1}	**BANK // TOKEN // 3 SHILL. // 1811** arranged low within oak wreath with twenty-seven acorns, top leaves touching. Large distinctive border and plain edge
	1^2	Similar, but with twenty-six acorns
	1^3	Similar, but with twenty-five acorns
	1^4	Similar, but with twenty-four acorns
	2	Similar, but with a gap between top leaves, dated **1812** to **1816**

First bust; laureate and draped in armour   Spink 3769

ESC	Date	Obv	Rev	Varieties		R	Davis	(Old ESC)
2061	**1811**	**A**^{var}	**1**^{1}					
2062	—	—	—	*Proof*	*(Not traced)*			
2063	—	**A**^{1}	—				D.49	407 A^1/1^1
2064	—	—	—	*Proof*		C^2	D.48	407A A^1/1^1
2065	—	—	**1**^{2}			C^2	D.48	408 A^1/1^2
2066	—	—	—	*Proof*	*(Not traced)*	R		409 A^1/1^2
2067	—	**A**^{2}	**1**^{1}	*Proof*		R^4		409A A^2/1^1
2068	—	—	**1**^{2}		*(Not traced)*	R^2	D.47	410 A^2/1^2
2069	—	—	**1**^{3}		*(Not traced)*	R^2	D.46	411 A^2/1^3
2070	—	—	—	*Proof*		R^2		412 A^2/1^1
2071	—	**A**^{3}	**1**^{1}	*Proof*		R^4		414A A^3/1^1
2072	—	—	**1**^{2}	*Proof*		R^4		414B A^3/1^3
2073	—	—	**1**^{4}			R^2	D.45	413 A^3/1^4
2074	—	—	—	*Proof*		R^2		414 A^3/1^4
2075	**1812**	**A**^{1}	**2**			C	D. 50	415 A^4/1^2
2076	—	—	—	*Proof*	*(Not traced)*			

GEORGE III, 1760-1820
BANK OF ENGLAND TOKENS

THREE SHILLINGS

SECOND BUST

Oak and laurel

B^1 3

B^1	Laureate, undraped bust, right, wreath with 2 long ties, no berries top leaf to centre of **D**, and legend as before in larger letters Plain edge and plain border (Not traced, but recorded by Rayner)
Var. B^2	Similar, but top leaf between **I** and **G**
Rev. 3	**BANK // TOKEN // 3 SHILL. // 1812, 13, 14, 15 & 16** Within a wreath of oak and olive; 16 acorns & 16 berries

Second bust; laureate and undraped, no beading   Spink 3770

ESC	Date	Obv	Rev	Varieties	R	Davis	(Old ESC)
2077	**1812**	**B**^{1}	3	*(Not traced)*	R^3	D. 55	419 B²/2
2078	—	—	—	*Proof in platinum (Not traced)*	R^6	D. 56	420 B²/2
2079	—	**B**^{2}	—		C	D. 52	416 B¹/2
2080	—	—	—	*Proof*	R		417 B¹/2
2081	—	—	—	*Proof in gold*	R^7	D. 53	418 B¹/2
2082	**1813**	—	—		C	D. 57	421 B¹/2
2083	**1814**	—	—		C	D. 58	422 B¹/2
2084	**1815**	—	—		C	D. 59	423 B¹/2
2085	**1816**	—	—		R^3	D. 60	424 B¹/2

1   All combinations have been allowed for; those with '*not traced*' are possibilities

GEORGE III, 1760-1820
LAST OR NEW COINAGE
HALFCROWNS

Trial striking by
Benedetto Pistrucci
after
Thomas Wyon
In copper on
Crown-size flan

D/T

WWP   W

Obv. A

Rev. 1

Type	**A.**	Large head *'Bull head'*, heavy looking features with a shoulder Laureate bust, right, long truncation, date below
Leg.		**GEORGIUS III DEI GRATIA**
		Top of head divides legend. *Edge,* Milled
Rev.	**1**	Baroque-style shield within the Garter and Collar of the Garter, St George pendant below, small crown above
Leg.		**BRITANNIARUM ♛ REX FID : DEF :**
		Small lettering on both sides **WWP** in left, **W** in right garniture (**W**illiam **W**ellesley **P**ole; Mint Master & William **W**yon)

Obv. B

E over E

W

Rev. 2

GEORGE III, 1760-1820
LAST OR NEW COINAGE
HALFCROWNS

B.   *'Small head'*, much neater looking, within legend
       Laureate bust, right, short truncation at neck, date below

Leg.   **GEORGIUS III DEI GRATIA**
       In larger letters, continuous overhead. *Edge,* Milled

Rev.   **2**   Plain scalloped shield, a large crown above overlays the
       Surrounding Garter (No Collar) and divides the legend.

Leg.   **BRITANNIARUM 👑 REX FID : DEF :**
       Large lettering both sides, only **W** (Wyon) on buckle
       Normal striking now *en medaille* ↑↑ i.e. both sides same way up

A/1.   Large head / *rev.* 1 - Irish harp with 6 strings   Spink 3788

ESC	Date	Varieties		R	(Old ESC)
2086	1816			C	613
2087	—	*Proof*	*wt. 14.13g*	R^2	614
2088	—	*Proof,* with plain edge	*wt. 14.20g*	R^2	615
2089	—	*Trial striking in copper on a crown size flan*		R^6	615A
		Edge DECUS ET TUTAMEN ANNO REGNI			
		QUINQUAGESIMO SEPTIMO	L&S 151		
2090	1817			C	616
2091	—	**D** over **T** in **DEI**		R	616A
2092	—	**I** over **S** in **PENSE**		R^3	616B
2093	—	*Proof*	*wt. 14.10g*	R^2	617
2094	—	*Proof in copper*		R^6	617A
2095	—	*Proof,* with plain edge		R^5	617B

B/2.   Small head / *rev.* 2 - Irish harp with 6 strings   Spink 3789

ESC	Date	Varieties		R	(Old ESC)
2096	1817			C^2	618
2097	—	*Proof*	*wt. 14.17g*	R^2	619
2098	—	*Proof,* with plain edge	*wt. 14.22g*	R	620
2099	1818			C	621
2100	—	Reversed Ƨ in Garter motto		R^5	621A
2101	—	*Proof*	*wt. 14.11g*	R^4	622
2102	1819			C	623
2103	—	**9** over **8**		$R^?$	623A?
2104	—	*Proof*	*wt. 14.13g*	R^3	624
2105	1820			S	625
2106	—	*Proof,* with plain edge		R^3	626
2107	—	*Proof,* with milled edge	*wt. 14.11g*	R^5	626A

GEORGE III, 1760-1820
LAST OR NEW COINAGE
HALFCROWNS
PATTERNS

WWP   W

		B¹	**Small head with 3ʳᵈ reverse**		
2108	**1817**	**B¹**	By **T. Wyon**, dated **1817**	R^4	
		Obv.	As the 'small head' but slightly different features. Struck ↑↓ Milled edge *wt. 14.11g*		
		Rev.	Three, similar to second, but different shape and garnished, the garnishing overlapping the Garter. **WWP** in left, and **W** in right garniture		

B¹

B²

Note alignment of leaves with DEI

		B²	**Small head variety with 3ʳᵈ reverse**		
2109	**1817**	**B²**	By **T. Wyon**, dated **1817**	R^4	627A
		Obv.	As B1, but slightly different spacing and		
		&	alignment of legend, most noticeable with date		
		Rev.	and truncation and subtle differences in		
			garniture on reverse *(6 strings) wt. 14.12g*		

GEORGE III, 1760-1820
LAST OR NEW COINAGE
HALFCROWNS

2110	181-		By **Benedetto Pistrucci** after **Thomas Wyon**	R^7	
			Unfinished date [1]		
			Uniface trial *in silver on a thin flan*		
		Obv.	Large laureate head		
			Incomplete date below **181**		
		Rev.	Plain and unworked *(Unique?) wt. 14.10g*		

	1	There are several small differences to the currency issue. The features are softer, the lowest curl is missing from in front of the ear and the curls behind the ear are less detailed Ex B. Pistrucci, died 1852, J.G. Murdoch, Sotheby 16 March 19014 (286 part), SNC December 1905, № 22458, H.M. Lingford, collection purchased en bloc by Baldwin 1951, Spink 177 (580) and M. Rasmussen 12/157

2111			By **Benedetto Pistrucci**, undated [2]	R^7	627B
		Obv.	Uniface trial in copper of the puncheon for the small laureate head incuse facing left with ribbon at back of head.		
		Rev.	Blank with a pair of small circles at centre		

	2	See *Spink Milled Silver Coinage 1925*, page 105, trial piece 5

GEORGE III, 1760-1820
LAST OR NEW COINAGE
HALFCROWNS

Arthur M. Fitts Collection, lot 2180
DNW Auction 124, 16 September 2014,
A group of five trials of the unfinished obverse
portrait for the second issue Halfcrown [181...

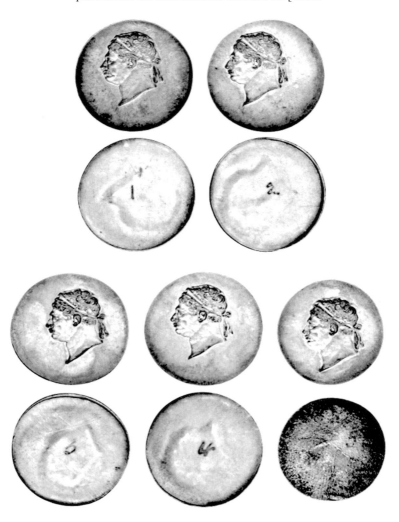

GEORGE III, 1760-1820
LAST OR NEW COINAGE
HALFCROWNS

Footnote to lot 2180.

Provenance: B. Pistrucci Collection; J.G. Murdoch Collection, Part III, Sotheby Auction, 15-19 March 1904, lot 283; Baron Philippe de Ferrari la Renotière Collection, Sotheby Auction, 27-31 March 1922, lot 88; An Important Collection of English Milled Silver Coins, Glendining Auct., 4 Oct. 1962, lot 132.Forrer (p.605), copying the Murdoch sale catalogue entry, states that originally there were six trials in the set, but the original document signed by Pistrucci that was sold with the trials in the 19th century stated that one (presumably numbered 6 on the back) had been sold 'evidently many years ago.' Forrer goes on to translate a portion of Pistrucci's notes on the pieces: 'To do this work (i.e. the Half Crowns) which was my second in steel I had from time to time incuse proofs made of the puncheon in order to verify the perfection of the flan before going on with the work. This I did with the permission of the Master of the Mint, because I did not want Mr Wyon to deceive me, as he had done previously in making me work on a false (uneven?) surface and I explained that I could not get along with the work which was quite lost, and that I was obliged to begin again three times, because I had been given a bad puncheon to work upon. At the end the mint master remonstrated with Mr Wyon, who was obliged to give me a good puncheon, which is the one with which I produced afterwards the Half Crowns of George III, showing the neck only.'

The background to the issue of a second type of halfcrown in the last coinage of George III, driven as it was by the internal Mint politics of the time, is amplified by Christopher Challis (A New History of the Royal Mint, 1992, pp.472-89) and Kevin Clancy ('The Reducing Machine and the last coinage of George III'), BNJ 2000, pp.118-23. With Benedetto Pistrucci's new portrait of the king for the halfcrown, copied by hand and transferred into steel coinage tools from a jasper model by the young Thomas Wyon (†22 September 1817), meeting hostility from within the Mint from the likes of William Wellesley Pole, the Master, and other contemporaries, Pole ordered that the new 'bull head' halfcrowns, which first saw the light of day in March 1817, were to be sent to the most distant parts of the country so they were not seen to be circulating in the metropolis. Meanwhile, the Mint had employed Soho's reducing machine to produce a new portrait and master tools for the obverse of what became the second type of halfcrown were available in February. Although it is undocumented as to exactly when the original halfcrown obverse gave way to the new type from the perspective of issued coin, it is known that royal approval of the new design was received on 26 April 1817.

This page is reproduced courtesy of Chris Webb. Director of DNW

GEORGE III, 1760-1820
BANK OF ENGLAND TOKENS

EIGHTEEN PENCE

Similar to Three shillings but, with subtle differences

Type A³   Type B²

Obv.	**A³**	First bust, wider spacing in legend due to smaller lettering, Front leaf to back of **E**
Rev.	**2.**	With a gap in wreath of oak leaves, small lettering. Value reads; **1 s. 6 D.**. Dates **1811 & 12**
	B²	Second bust, with berries in wreath, top leaf between **D** and **E**
Rev.	**3.**	With a wreath of oak and laurel leaves, larger lettering. Value reads; **1 s. 6 D.** Dates **1812, 13, 14, 15 & 16**

First bust; laureate and draped in armour / *rev.* 2   Spink 3771

ESC	Date	*Obv*	*Rev*	Varieties	*R*	Davis	(Old ESC)
2112	**1811**	**A³**	**2**		*C*	D.61	969
2113	—	—	—	*Proof*	*S*		970
2114	**1812**	—	—		*C*	D.63	971

Second bust; laureate and undraped / *rev.* 3   Spink 3772

2115	1812	**B²**	**3**		*C*	D.64	972
2116	—	—	—	*Proof*	*S*		973
2117	—	—	—	*Proof,* small lettering on *rev.*	*R⁷*		975
2118	—	—	—	*Proof in platinum*	*R⁷*		974
2119	**1813**	—	—		*C*	D.65	976
2120	—	—	—	*Proof in platinum*	*R⁷*	—	976A
2121	**1814**	—	—		*C*	D.67	977
2122	**1815**	—	—		*C*	D.68	978
2123	**1816**	—	—		*C*	D.69	979

SHILLINGS

'Northumberland'
A – 1st obv.

B – 2nd obv.
All stops

1 – Plain in angles

Rev. 3
No stops at date

Rev. 2 - No hearts

1 over inverted 1

Rev. 4 - With hearts

No stop above head

D – 4th obv.
Only stop after
GRATIA•

E – 5th obv.
No stops in *leg.*

307

SHILLINGS

Dorrien & Magens
F - 6th obv.

Only stop after
GRATIA •

5 - With hearts but
Dated •1798•

NEW COINAGE
Edge milling changed from oblique to straight with the introduction of this coinage
G – 3rd head

'Bull head'

Proof

Unbarred H

Rev. 6

High 8

9 over 3

9 over 9

I over S

Unbarred H & Stops in □s

R over E

GEORGE III 1760-1820
SHILLINGS

Type	**A.**	Young head, draped and laureate, right, laurel leaves protrude well above head. Known as the *'Northumberland Shilling'* [1]
Leg.		**GEORGIVS • III • DEI • GRATIA •** (Stop after **III** on leaf tip)

B. As before but, hair less defined and no leaf tips above hair line. The epaulette is more defined on his shoulder

Leg. As before but, with a clear stop after **III •** above head

C. As before but, no stop after **III** above head

D. As before but, **only** one **stop** in legend after **GRATIA •**

E. As before but, **no stops in legend**

F. Known as *'The Dorrien and Magens shilling'*, dated **• 1798 •** Similar to 'D' with only one stop after **GRATIA •** but, many subtle differences in hair style etc. and larger lettering

G. *'Bull head'*. Third bust, heavy looking features, laureate, right, Three tips of leaves protrude above, long straight ties hang down

Leg. **GEOR : III D:G: BRITT : REX F:D:** Top of head divides legend, date below. *Edge,* straight milling

Rev. **1.** As George II; crowned cruciform shields dividing legend Plain in angles, date in *leg.* at top divided by English/Sottish arms

Leg. ♛ **63·M·B·F·ET·** ♛ **H·REX·F·D·B·** ♛ **ET·L·D·S·R·I·** ♛ **A·T·ET·E·17**

2. Uncrowned cruciform shields with straight edges, Garter star in centre and crowns in the angles. Hanoverian shield without semée of hearts. *Leg.* As before but, date **•1787•**, with flanking stops below the Irish arms

3. As before but, no stops flanking date **1787**

4. As '2' but, **with semée of hearts** in the Hanoverian shield **•1787•**

5. As '4' but, larger lettering and dated **•1798•** *'Dorrien & Magens'*

6. Large baroque-style shield, crowned, within Garter with motto

309

SHILLINGS

A/1   *'Northumberland'* Young head with stop on tip of top laurel leaf
        Rev. 1- Plain in angles   Spink 3742

ESC	Date	Varieties	R	(Old ESC)
2124	**1763**	See note *wt. 6.02g (8s-7hts)*	S	1214

B/2.   Similar but, **with a clear stop after III •** above head
        Rev. 2 - No semée of hearts, with stops by date   Spink 3743

2125	1787		C^2	1216
2126	—	1 over inverted 1 in date	R^3	1216A
2127	—	*Proof.* Normal flan struck in a collar	R^2	1217

B/3.   As before but with,
        Rev. 3 - No semée of hearts, **no stops at date**   Spink 3745

2128	1787	Second **7** over **6** *(7 strings)*	N	1222

B/4.   As before but with,
        Rev. 4 - **With** semée of **hearts,** date with stops   Spink 3746

2129	1787	*(7 strings)*	N	1225
2130	—	Lower half of semée of hearts missing *(5 recorded)*	R^3	1225A
2131	—	**1** of date over inverted **1**	R^2	1225A
2132	—	*Pre-proof,* Plain edge *(Struck without a collar on a large heavy flan)*	R^4	1226

C/2.   As before but, **no stop after III** (therefore no stop above head)
        Rev. 2 - No semée of hearts, with stops by date   Spink 3744

2133	1787		N	1218
2134	—	*Proof*	R^2	1219
2135	—	*Proof,* Plain edge	R^3	1220
2136	—	*Proof,* Heavy flan *wt. 7.45g*	R^4	1221

D2.   As before but, **only** one **stop** in legend after **GRATIA •**
        Rev. 2 - No semée of hearts, with stops by date   Spink

2137	1787	*Proof,* plain edge	R^4	1224

E/2.   As before but, **no stops in legend**
        Rev. 2 - No semée of hearts, with stops by date   Spink 3745A

2138	**1787**		R^4	1223

SHILLINGS

F/3. *'Dorrien & Magens Shilling'*, with only stop after **GRATIA** •
Rev. 3 - **With semée of hearts** Spink 3747

ESC	Date	Varieties		R	(Old ESC)
2139	**1798**	*See note below**	*(< 20 known) (6 strings)*	R^5	1227

*In 1798. Dorrien & Magens and nine other banking firms sent (to the Mint) silver bullion
for coinage to the amount of upwards of £30,000. This was partly coined into Shillings, but
their issue was prohibited by order of the Lords of the Committee of Council. The name
given above is so rendered in the Mint book, but in Lowndes *London Directory* for 1798, the
firm is described as Dorrien, Magens, Mello, Martin and Harrison, 22 Finch Lane, Cornhill.
Dorrien & Magens expressed their sentiments in an anonymous publication of the same year
entitled, *'Thoughts upon a new Coinage of Silver.* 'Royal Mint Museum Cat., Vol. I, p. 158

LAST OR NEW COINAGE

G/6. *'Bull head'*, heavy looking features.
Rev. 6 – Crowned baroque shield within Garter Spink 3790

2140	**1816**		*(5 strings)*	C^2	1228
2141	—	*Proof*		R^3	1229
2142	—	*Proof* in gold	*wt. 7.97g*	R^7	1230
2143	—	*Proof*, plain edge		R^5	1231
2144	**1817**	*(Some have a broken B in BRITT – not to be mistaken for an R)*		C	1232
2145	—	**7** higher in date		$R^?$	1232C
2146	—	Unbarred **H** in **IIONI**		$R^?$	1232C
2147	—	Error **I** over **S** in **HONI**		R^3	1232B
2148	—	Error reads **GEOR** over **E:**		R^3	1232A
2149	—	*Proof*, plain edge	*wt. 5.64g*	R^2	1233
2150	**1818**			S	1234
2151	—	Date re-cut and second **8** higher	*(5 strings)*	R	1234A
2152	**1819**		*(5 strings)*	N	1235
2153	—	**9** over **3** *(Kevin Clancy, Director of R.M. Museum confirmed)*		R	1235A
2154	—	**9** over **6**		R	1235B
2155	—	**9** over **8**	*(5 strings)*	R	1235C
2156	—	**9** over **9**		R	1235D
2157	**1820**		*(5 strings)*	N	1236
2158	—	**20** over **19**			
2159	—	**20** over **20**			
2160	—	**I** over **S** in **HONI**		R^3	1236A
2161	—	**H** over ⊥ (horizontal) in **HONI**		R^3	1236B
2162	—	**Stops** in □s of **H□NI** & **S□IT**	*(5 strings)*	R^3	1236C
2163	—	*Proof*		R^2	1237

SHILLINGS

PATTERNS

D^1 D^3

2164	1764	D^1	By **Yeo**		1238
		Obv	Very similar to 'Type A', but with rather finer portrait and three curls instead of two on the shoulders. *Edge,* plain. *wt. 5.44g*		
		Leg.	**GEORGIVS · III · DEI · GRATIA**		
		Rev.	Crowned cruciform shields dividing leg.		
		Leg.	👑 **63·M·B·F·ET·**👑 **H·REX·F·D·B·** 👑 **ET·L·D·S·R·I·**👑 **A·T·ET·E·17**		
2165	—	—	Similar, but on heavier flan *wt. 6.52g*	$R^?$	1238A

2166	1775	D^2	Similar, but with a later date	R^5	1239

2167	1778	D^3	Similar, but older bust, stop after **GRATIA·**	R^3	1240
2168	—	—	Struck *en medaille* ↑↑ *wt. 6.50g*	R^3	1240B
2169	—	—	Similar, but heavier flan *wt. 6.52g*	R^3	1240A

 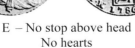  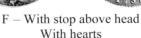

E – No stop above head
No hearts

F – With stop above head
With hearts

PATTERNS

2170	1786	E	By **Pingo** As type C, but dated **1786**, no stop over head, no stops flanking date and no semée of hearts. *Edge,* milled *(2 known – B.M.& R.M. Collections)*	R^6	1215

2171	1787	F	As type B; with a stop above head, dated 1787, but with a border of dots each side Stops flanking date, with semée of hearts *Edge,* plain *(7 struck)* wt. 5.7g	R^5	1241
2172	—	—	As before on a thicker flan *(168 struck)* wt. 6.0g	R	1241A

 G

2173	1787	G *Obv* *Leg* *Rev*	By **Droz**, dated **1787** Tall laureate head of the king, right, with long hair and **DF** on pointed truncation, date below *Edge,* milled **GEORGIUS III · D · G · MA · BR · F · ET · H · REX** No legend, the royal cipher *GR* crowned Within branches of laurel. *Edge,* milled	R^3	1242
2174	—	—	Similar, *In brass* *(B.M. Collection)*	R^5	1242A
2175	—	—	Uniface obverse. *In lead* wt. 4.41g	R^7	1242A

 H  I

SHILLINGS

PATTERNS

2176	1798	H	By **Milton**, dated **1798**	R^5	1243
		Obv	Very large head with short hair, laureate, right, with date below		
		Leg	**GEORGIVS · III · DEI ·**		
		Rev	**GRATIA · REX** *wt. 7.64g-8.02g*		
			Large plain shield crowned, with British and Hanoverian arms in six divisions		
		Leg	**M·B·F·ET·H·REX·F·D·B·ET· L·D·S·R·I·A·T·ET·E·** *Edge,* plain		
2177	—	—	*In silver gilt* *wt. 8.25g-8.54g*	R^5	1243A
2178	—	—	*In copper* *wt. 8.63g-10.09g*	R^5	1244
2179	—	—	Uniface obverse *In lead* *wt. 9.33g*	R^5	1244A

2180	1798	I	Uniface *obv.* as before, date below, but	R^5	1243
		Leg	reads **GEORGIVS · TER TIUS · D · G · REX · 1798** *wt. 5.66g*		
2181	—	—	*In gold with milled edge* *wt. 9.33g*	R^5	1244A

J

2182	(1816)	J	By **Thomas Wyon**, undated (1816)	R^6	1245
		Obv	Similar 'Bull head' to regular issue, but smaller. *Edge,* milled *(3 known)*		
		Leg	**GEORGIUS III DEI GRATIA**		
		Rev	Square shield, garnished and crowned, the colours of the arms are not indicated		
			BRITANNIARVM REX FIDEI DEFENSOR		
			(Uncertain if this is for a shilling or a sovereign)		
2183	—	—	*In gold with milled edge* *W&R 183, wt. 8.26g*	R^7	1245A

BANK OF ENGLAND TOKENS

PATTERNS

NINEPENCE
By T. Wyon Junior.

B² - 2 berries   B² ᵛᵃʳ· - 5 berries

B²/1   Second bust, laureate, undraped, right, 2 berries in King's wreath
Rev. 1 - **BANK** // **TOKEN** // **9 PENCE** // **1812**
Within a wreath of oak and laurel leaves   Spink 3773A

ESC	Date	Varieties		R	Davis	(Old ESC)
2184	**1812**		*wt. 3.53g*	R^6		1480

B² ᵛᵃʳ·/2   As before but die re-cut showing 5 distinct berries in wreath
Rev. 2 – Reads **BANK** // **TOKEN** // **9 D** // **1812**
Slightly larger lettering   Spink 3773

2185	1812	*Edge,* plain		R^3	D.71	1478
2186	—	*Edge,* plain *In copper*	*(Not traced)*	R^6	D.72	1479

xxxx	1825	Mule striking on a 2 mm flan *in Columbian platinum, wt. 9.43 gm*
	Obv.	George III Pattern Ninepence by **Thomas Wyon jnr** as before
	Rev.	George IV Farthing by **Benedetto Pistrucci** Britannia seated right on rock with shield, olive branch and trident, lion behind, date in exergue, toothed border. *Leg.* **BRITANNIAR: REX FID: DEF**
	Edge	Plain (Peck 1419) *(4 known. Recorded for interest sake)*

SIXPENCES

Rev. 1 – no hearts   Obv. A   Rev. 2 – with hearts

T over B

Obv. B – normal colons   2 stops no colons   bvRev. 3
                    (Filled die?)

9 over 8   Inverted 1   8 over 6   I over S

Type	**A.**	As type 'B' shillings
Leg.	1	**GEORGIVS · III · DEI · GRATIA ·**
Rev.	1	Cruciform shields, without semée of hearts in Hanoverian shield
Rev.	2	Similar, but with hearts in the Hanoverian shield

SIXPENCES

	B.	Last or new coinage. As type 'C' shillings with date below
Leg.	2	**GEO : III D:G:** **BRITT:REX F:D:**
Leg.	2a	**GEO . III D.G** **BRITT REX F D** (No colons [1])
Rev.	3.	Garnished shield, crowned, within the Garter

A/1. First bust with *rev.* 1 - **No hearts** Spink 3748

ESC	Date	Varieties		R	(Old ESC)
2187	**1787**			C^3	1626
2188	—	*Proof,* plain edge		R^5	1627
2189	—	*Proof,* plain edge heavy flan	*wt. 4.63g & wt. 4.64g*	R^4	1628

A/2. First bust with *rev.* 2 - **with hearts** Spink 3749

ESC	Date	Varieties	R	(Old ESC)
2190	**1787**		C^3	1629

B/3. **Second bust** with *rev.* 3 - **shield within Garter** Spink 3791

ESC	Date	Varieties		R	(Old ESC)
2191	**1816**			C^2	1630
2192	—	*Proof in gold*		R^7	1631
2193	—	**6 over 4**?		R^5	1631B?
2194	—	*Proof (not over date, wt. 2.81g)* **8 over 6**	*wt. 2.82g*	R^5	1631A
2195	**1817**		*(5 strings)*	C	1632
2196	—	*Proof,* plain edge	*wt. 2.84g*	R^2	1633
2197	—	*Proof,* milled edge	*wt. 2.84g*	R^4	1633A
2198	—	**X over B in REX** *(Die flaw?)*		R^9	1633B
2199	**1818**			S	1634
2200	—	*Proof,* milled edge	*wt. 2.81g*	R^3	1635
2201	**1819**			S	1636
2202	—	**8 of date very small**		R	1636A
2203	—	**9 over 8 and 1ˢᵗ T in BRITT over B**		R	1636B
2204	—	*Proof,* milled edge	*wt. 2.81g*	R^2	1637
2205	**1820**			S	1638
2206	—	**8 of date very small**			
2207	—	*Proof,* milled edge	*wt. 2.82g*	R^2	1639
2208	—	**1 of date inverted**		R^4	1639A
2209	—	**I of HONI over S**		R^3	1639B?
2210	—	No colons in obverse legend		R^3	1639C?

GEORGE III, 1760-1820
SIXPENCES

PATTERNS

C6

No stops by date

C7
border of dots

1 - with hearts

2 – no hearts
border of dots

2211	1786	C6	By **Pingo** As type B^2 shillings of 1787, but lacking stop at side of date, with stop over head, no semée of hearts. *Edge,* milled *(3 struck)*	R^6	

2212	1787	C7/1 *Obv*	By **Pingo** As the current sixpence of this date with semée of hearts, with border of dots each side. *Edge,* plain *(168 struck) wt. 3.07g-wt. 4.09g*	S	1640
2213	—	C7/2	As last, but without semée of hearts *wt.3.46g*	R^2	1640A

318

SIXPENCES

PATTERNS

D

See DNW 101, lots 721-2 for reasons for these

2214	**1787**	**D**	By **J. or F. Eginton** for **S. Garbett**, **1787**	R^5	1641
		Obv	Laureate bust, cuirassed, right, dot below		
		Leg	**GEO : III · D · G · REX ·** *Edge,* plain		
		Rev	No legend, star of the Garter type *wt.2.59g*		
2215	—	—	Similar, but a trial *in white metal*		

Obv. E

1   2   3

319

SIXPENCES

PATTERNS

2216	1788	E/1	By **Droz**, dated **1788**	*S*	1642
		Obv	No legend, the royal cypher, ***GR*** crowned within laurel branches. *Edge,* milled		
		Rev	Britannia seated divides legend **BRITAN NIA·**		
			Date **1788** in exergue *wt. 2.46g-2.54g*		
2217	—	—	*In gold* *wt. 3.55g-3.48g*	*R⁵*	1643
2218	—	—	*In copper* *(No traced)*	*R⁵*	1644

2219	1790	E/2	Similar, but rather smaller and date in *leg.*	*N*	1645
		Rev	Seated Britannia divides *wt. 2.62g*		
		Leg	**BRITANNIA 1790** *Edge,* plain		
2220	—	—	*In gold. Edge,* plain	*R⁷*	1646
2221	—	—	*In gold. Edge,* milled *wt. 2.60g*	*N*	1646A

2222	1791	E/3	Similar to last, but date in exergue *wt. 2.51g*	*R*	1647
			Smaller Britannia inside *leg. Edge.* plain		
2223	—	—	*In gold* *wt. 3.96g-3.99g*	*R⁶*	1648
2224	—	—	*In copper* *wt. 3.60g*	*R²*	1649
2225	No date	—	*In copper.* Undated, but mule composed of two obverses *wt. 2.42g-2.82g*	*R⁵*	1650

 F

2226	1816	F	By **T. Wyon**, dated **1816**	*R⁵*	1651
		Obv	Laureate head, right, rather as the current coin but a little smaller. *Edge,* milled.		
		Leg	**GEORGIVS III DEI GRATIA**		
		Rev	Shield in Garter crowned, date above the Garter divided by the crown. *Edge,* milled [2]		
		Leg	**BRITT · REX FID · DEF** · *wt.2.87g-3.21g*		
2227	—	—	As before. *Edge,* plain *wt. 2.66g*	*R⁵*	1652

SIXPENCES

PATTERNS

J. Barber

A B

2228	Undated	A	Uniface portrait trial by **J. Barber** [3] Laureate head right within solid circular border, signed **J. Barber F** below *In silver* wt 2·31g	R^6	?
2229	—	B	As last, but no border, initials **I B** below *In silver* wt 1·42g	R^6	?

Note
See the many notes regarding sixpences in DNW Auction 89, 2010/09/29

1   No colons (2 stops) or is this a case of a filled die?
2   The ESC rarity rating indicates five to ten examples known. Mrs Norweb did not own a silver pattern of this type, although she possessed one of the two known examples with a plain edge in gold. The handwritten note by Benedetto Pistrucci accompanying the gold proof in the Murdoch sale (1904) is perhaps worth quoting in part and states *'the workmen at the Mint were unable to strike this piece on account of its too high relief and would not give themselves the necessary trouble in order to please Mr Wyon, who could not bear with good grace that a work of his, retouched by me, should be issued'* (DNW 89, lot 1747)
3   *"Barber was a London-based medallist, active circa, 1809-1842, who worked for a time for the jewellers and medallists Rundell, Bridge & Rundell. His obverse portrait of the Prince Regent on the medallion for the Treaty of Paris, 1814, is paired with a reverse by T. Wyon Junior, whose family were involved with patterns for the new coinage of 1816. One might reasonably assume that the present pieces were Barber's attempt to produce an acceptable coinage portrait of his own"* (DNW 91)

GEORGE III, 1760-1820
MAUNDY MONEY

SETS of FOUR COINS

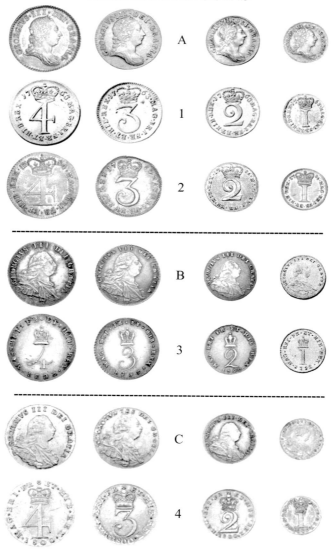

GEORGE III, 1760-1820
MAUNDY MONEY

NEW COINAGE

Type	**A.**	Young head; laureate bust, right, draped in armour
		Legend continuous over head
Leg.		**GEORGIVS · III · DEI · GRATIA ·**
Rev.	1	Value in Roman figures, crown above divides date
	2	As '1' but, new dies; similar type but flatter design, larger serifs
Leg.		**MAG · BRI · FR · ET · HIB · REX**
	B.	Known as *'Wire money'* on account of thin depression of values
Obv.		Older laureate and draped bust, cuirassed
Leg.		**GEORGIVS III DEI GRATIA** No stops
Rev.	3	Values *4*, *3* and *2* are in thin script and **I** in Roman, small crown
		above, within *leg.*, date below in *leg.*. Only issued in **1792**
	C.	*Obv.* as 'B' with
Rev.	4	Crowned value, larger Roman figures, date below in *leg.*
Leg.		**MAG · BRI · FR * ET · HIB · REX ·**
	D.	**Old head**, heavy looking features known as *'Bull head'*,
Obv.		Laureate bust, right, long truncation, date below
		Top of head divides legend. Laurel leaves protrude,
		long ties hanging down. *Edge,* plain
Leg.		**GEORGIUS III DEI GRATIA** (No stops)
Rev.	5	Value in Roman figures, large crown above divides legend
Leg.		**BRITANNIARUM REX FID: DEF:**

MAUNDY MONEY

A/1. Young head; laureate bust, right, draped in armour
Rev. 1 - Roman figure, crown divides date   Spink 3762

ESC	Date	Varieties, comments etc.	Robinson	R	(Old ESC)
2230	**1763**			S	2412
2231	—	*Proof* *(Not traced)*		R⁶	2413
2232	**1766**			S	2414
2233	**1772**			S	2415
2234	**1780**			S	2416

A/2. Young head
Rev. 2 – As '1', but new flatter design, larger serifs   Spink 3762

2235	**1784**			S	2417
2236	**1786**			S	2418

B/3. *'Wire money'*. Older laureate and draped bust, cuirassed
Rev. 3 – Values *4*, *3*, *2* in thin script & Roman **I**   Spink 3763

2237	**1792**		*p. 162,279*	R	2419

C/4. Older head; larger bust, cuirassed
Rev. 4 – Crowned value, larger Roman figures   Spink 3764

2238	**1795**	*1d, 2d, 3d & 4d*	*p. 163,283,4,5,6*	N	2420
2239	**1800**	*1d, 2d, 3d & 4d*	*p. 163,287,8,9,90*	C	2421

D/5. *'Bull head'*. Old head, laureate, long truncation, date below
Rev. 5 – Large crown above value divides legend   Spink 3792

2240	**1817**	*1d, 2d, 3d & 4d*	*p. 164,291,2,3,4*	S	2422
2241	**1818**	*1d, 2d, 3d & 4d*	*p. 164,295,6,7,8*	S	2423
2242	**1820**	*1d, 2d, 3d & 4d*	*p. 164,299,300,1,2*	S	2424

The following denominations are listed separately to highlight varieties

MAUNDY MONEY

GROATS or FOURPENCES

A/1. Young head; laureate bust, right, draped in armour
Rev. 1 - Roman 4, crown divides date   Spink 3750

ESC	Date	Varieties, comments etc.	Robinson	R	(Old ESC)
2243	**1763**		*p. 160,242*	N	1908
2244	—	*Proof*	*p. 160,246*	R^7	1908A
2245	**1765**		*p. 160,249*	R^5	1909
2246	**1766**		*p. 160,253*	S	1910
2247	**1770**		*p. 160,256*	R^3	1911
2248	**1772**		*p. 160,260(i)*	R^3	1912
2249	—	**2 over 0**		S	1913
2250	**1776**	Defective 6 looks like 5, see note [1]	*p. 160,264(i)*	N	1914
2251	**1780**	Large lettering on obverse	*p. 160,269*	N	1915

A/2. Young head
Rev. 2 – As '1', but new flatter design, larger serifs   Spink 3750

2252	**1784**		*p. 160,274*	S	1916
2253	**1786**		*p. 160,278(i)*	R	1917

C/4. Older head; larger bust, cuirassed
Rev. 4 – Crowned value larger Roman 3   Spink 3755

See sets	**1795**		*p. 163,286*	N	2420
See sets	**1800**		*p. 163,290*	C	2421

1   Dr G.H. Bullmore has kindly pointed out that this coin turns up with a defective **6**, appearing very much like a **5**. A genuine groat of 1775 has not yet been discovered. Collectors are warned. (P.A.R)

MAUNDY MONEY

THREEPENCES

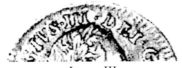 

Large III   5 over 3

A/1.   Young head; laureate bust, right, draped in armour
Rev. 1 - Roman 3, crown divides date   Spink 3753

ESC	Date	Varieties, comments etc.	Robinson	R	(Old ESC)
2254	**1762**	Over 30 different dies used	*p. 160,238*	C^3	2033
2255	**1763**		*p. 160,241*	C^2	2034
2256	—	*Proof*	*p. 160,245*	R^7	2034A
2257	**1765**		*p. 160,248*	R^4	2035
2258	—	**5 over 3**		R^5	2035A
2259	**1766**		*p. 160,252*	S	2036
2260	**1770**		*p. 160,255*	S	2037
2261	**1772**	Small lettering on obverse	*p. 160,259(i)*	N	2038
2262	—	Large lettering on obverse with very large **III**	*p. 160,259(ii)*	N	2039
2263	—	Large lettering on obverse with small **III**	*p. 160,259(iii)*	N	2040
2264	**1780**		*p. 160,268*	N	2041

A/2.   Young head
Rev. 2 – As '1', but new flatter design, larger serifs   Spink 3753

2265	**1784**		*p. 160,273*	S	2042
2266	**1786**		*p. 160,277*	N	2043

B/3.   *'Wire money'*. Older laureate and draped bust, cuirassed
Rev. 3 – Value **3** in thin script   Spink 3754

See sets	**1792**	Large letters on the reverse	*p. 162,281(i)*	R	2419

C/4.   Older head; larger bust, cuirassed
Rev. 4 – Crowned value larger Roman 3   Spink 3755

See sets	**1795**		*p. 163,285*	N	2420
See sets	**1800**		*p. 163,289*	C	2421
2267	**1818**	Unbarred As in **GRΛTIΛ**		R^2	

GEORGE III, 1760-1820
MAUNDY MONEY

PATTERNS

THREEPENCE
By Lewis Pingo

2268	1795	Obv.	Cuirassed bust to right	R^7	WR 153
		Leg.	**GEORGIVS III DEI GRATIA**		
		Rev.	Crowned **3** date below		
		Leg.	**MAG·BRI·FR ET·HIB·REX 1795**		
		Edge	Oblique milling,		
			Struck on a ⅓ Guinea size flan though		
			the weight is as ½ Guinea *wt. 4.21g*		
			In gold *(Huntarian Museum Collection)*		

TWOPENCE
By Lewis Pingo

2269	1795	Obv.	Cuirassed bust to right	R^7	WR 154
		Leg.	**GEORGIVS III DEI GRATIA**		
		Rev.	Crowned **2** date below		
		Leg.	**MAG·BRI·FR ET·HIB·REX 1795**		
		Edge	Oblique milling		
			Struck on a ⅓ Guinea flan *wt. 2.79g*		
			In gold *(Huntarian Museum Collection)*		

GEORGE III, 1760-1820
MAUNDY MONEY

HALFGROATS

72 over 62

A/1. Young head; laureate bust, right, draped in armour
       Rev. 1 - Roman 3, crown divides date   Spink 3756

2270	**1763**		*p. 160,240*	*S*	2238
2271	—	*Proof* *(2-3 known)*	*p. 160,244*	R^6	2238A
2272	**1765**	*Rev.* many re-entered letters	*p. 160,247*	R^3	2239
2273	**1766**	Pellet (•) on King's nose *(Do specimens exist without the pellet? R.B.)*	*p. 160,251*	*N*	2240
2274	**1772**			*N*	2241
2275	—	**72** over **62**	*p. 160,258(i)*	*N*	2242
2276	—	**2** over **6**	*p. 160,258(ii)*	*N*	2242
2277	**1776**			*N*	2243
2278	—	Unbarred **A** in **MAG**		*N*	2243A
2279	—	Wide space after A in **MA G**	*p. 160,263(i)*	*N*	2243A
2280	**1780**	Reads **BR-1**	*p. 160,267(i)*	*N*	2244

A/2. Young head
       Rev. 2 – As '1', but new flatter design, larger serifs Spink 3756

2281	**1784**		*p. 160,272*	*N*	2245
2282	**1786**		*p. 160,276*	*C*	2246
2283	—	Large lettering on *obv.*	*p. 160,194*	*C*	2247

B/3. *'Wire money'.* Older laureate and draped bust, cuirassed
       Rev. 3 – Value *2* in thin script   Spink 3757

See sets	**1792**			*R*	2419

C/4. Older head; larger bust, cuirassed
       Rev. 4 – Crowned value larger Roman 2   Spink 3758

See sets	**1795**		*p. 163,284*	*N*	2420
See sets	**1800**		*p. 163,288*	*C*	2421
2284	**1817**	Unbarred As **BRIT∧ NI ∧ RVM**	*p. 164,292(i)*	R^2	2424
2285	**1818**	Unbarred As **BRIT∧ NI ∧ RVM**	*p. 164,296(i)*	R^2	2424

328

MAUNDY MONEY

PENNIES

Thick Roman I   Thin Arabic 1
2nd 7 re-entered   *'Wire money'*

A/1.   Young head; laureate bust, right, draped in armour
              Rev. 1 - Roman I, crown divides date   Spink 3759

2286	**1763**		*p. 160,239(i)*	*S*	2353
2287	—	*Proof*	*p. 160,243*	R^7	2353A
2288	**1765**			R^7	2353B
2289	**1766**		*p. 160,250*	*N*	2354
2290	**1770**		*p. 160,254*	*C*	2355
2291	**1772**	**D** of **DEI** touches hair	*p. 160,257(i)*	*N*	2356
2292	**1776**	7 re-entered	*p. 160,262(i)*	*N*	2357
2293	—	**6** over **0**		*R*	2357
2294	**1779**		*p. 160,265*	*N*	2358
2295	**1780**		*p. 160,266*	*S*	2359
2296	**1781**		*p. 160,270*	*C*	2360
2297	**1784**		*p. 160,271*	*C*	2361
2298	**1786**		*p. 160,275*	*C*	2362

C/4.   Older head; larger bust, cuirassed
              Rev. 4 – Normal crowned Roman I   Spink 3761

See sets	**1795**	*Wire Money*		*N*	2420
2299	**1795**	No stop on obverse	*p. 163,283(i)*	*N*	2420
2300	—	Large letters, no stops?	*p. 163,283(ii)*	*N*	2420
See sets	**1800**		*p. 163,287*	*C*	2421

PATTERN CROWNS

Pistrucci and his assistant, Jean Baptiste Merlin, whom he introduced to the Mint in 1820, were together responsible for the greater part of the coinage of this reign. There are three main issues. The obverse, showing the King's laureate head, is combined with a reverse which shows a crowned floreate shield and emblems in the case of the first issue, and a square-topped shield crowned within the Garter on the second issue. The third issue consists of a bare head with, on the halfcrown, a coat-of-arms, and a crown surmounted by a crowned lion on the shilling and sixpence. The laureate King's head obverse was designed and engraved by Pistrucci. Merlin was responsible for the engraving of the reverse dies of all the silver coins. When the King's portrait was changed in 1825, Pistrucci was commissioned to engrave the obverse dies from a bust of George by Sir Francis Chantrey; but this he refused to do declaring that he would not degrade his art so far as to copy the work of another man. The result was that William Wyon produced his fine, bare head portrait. William Wyon was appointed Chief Engraver in 1828, Pistrucci being given the post of Chief Medallist at the same time. (P.A.Rayner, 1949)

FIRST BUST

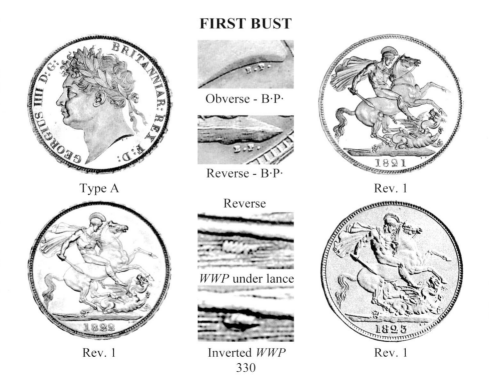

Type A

Obverse - B·P·

Reverse - B·P·

Rev. 1

Rev. 1

Reverse

WWP under lance

Inverted *WWP*

Rev. 1

330

PATTERN CROWNS

Type **A.** Large laureate bust, left, long ties hang down, engraver's initials
B.P. below truncation

Leg. **GEORGIUS IIII D : G : BRITANNIAR : REX F : D:**

Rev. **1.** St George and dragon on ground, date below, engraver's initials
B.P. below ground, right and ***WWP*** below broken lance (William
Wellesley Pole; Master of the Mint, (var. Shows ***WWP*** inverted)

Edge **DECUS ET TUTAMEN ANNO** followed by regnal year in
words, all in large raised letters.

1a. A long streamer of hair floating behind from beneath
St. George's helmet

Type **A/1.** Laureate bust / *rev.* 1 – St George and dragon   Spink 3805

ESC	Date	Edge	year	Varieties	R	L&S	(Old ESC)
2310	**1821**	**SECUNDO**	(2)	*(Beware of modern counterfeits)*	C^2		246
2311	—	—	—	Inverted initials ***WWP*** under lance	R		246A
2312	—	—	—	*Proof*	R	10	247
2313	—	—	—	*Matt Proof from sand blasted dies, held in a lunette or glass frame*	R^7	11	247A
2314	—	—	—	*Proof In copper* wt. 23.32g	R^6	12	248A
2315	—	Edge lettering very faintly struck and regnal year missing[1] *Proof in copper*				R^6	13	249A
2316	—	Edge completely plain, presumably filed off at the Mint[1] *Proof in copper*				R^6	14	249
2317	—	**TERTIO**	(3)	*Proof. Edge error*	R^3	15	250
2318	**1822**	**SECUNDO**	(2)		S		251
2319	—	—	—	*Proof*	R^4	16	251A
2320	**1822**	**TERTIO**	(3)		N		252
2321	—	—	—	*Proof*	R	17	253

PATTERN CROWNS

	B.	Bare head, left, date below
Leg.		**GEORGIUS IV DEI GRATIA** • (date) • smaller lettering
	2.	Square-topped shield of the royal arms heraldically shaded, encircled by the collar of the Garter with 18 links, the George pendant hanging below, all upon a richly decorated mantle of ermine with a crown above.
Rev.	**3.**	Square-topped shield garnished, surmounted by helmet crowned with lambrequins, motto on scroll **DIEU ET MON DROIT**
Leg.		**BRITANIARUM REX FID: DEF:**
Edge		As before, in rather small raised lettering

FIRST BUST

Engraver's centring spot	Rev 1a	W.W.P.
Long streamer of hair	Streamer of hair	under broken lance
from below helmet	Wide beading	B.P. in exergue right

ESC	Date	Type	Varieties	R	L&S	(Old ESC)
2322	1820	A/1a	By **Pistrucci**, dated **1820**	R^6	1	262
		Obv.	As the currency crown, first bust			
		Rev.	**1a.** - Similar to reverse 1, but there is a long streamer of hair floating behind from beneath St. George's helmet and a weak engraver's centring spot on the horse's body. Very small initials **W.W.P.** on ground below broken lance, and small initials **B.P.** in exergue far right			
		Edge	Plain. *In silver with narrow beading (see illustrations left & right above)*			
2323		—	*In lead*		2	

(continued)

PATTERN CROWNS

ESC	Date	Type	Varieties	R	L&S	(Old ESC)
2324	**1820**	A/1 a	*In lead.* Trial striking of reverse 1a, with a wide beading (see central illustration above) *(Unique) wt. 28.21g*	R^7	3	
2325	—	—	*In silver.* Trial striking of obverse A	R^7	4	
2326	—	—	*In brass.* Trial striking of obverse A	R^7	5	
2327	**182-**	—	Trial striking *in copper* of the currency reverse 1, but the last figure of date has been erased and the streamer deleted *(Linecar & Stone, p. 57 for illustration) (2 known)*	R^7	6	

Type	**A/1.**	Laureate bust / *rev.* 1 – St George and dragon		Spink 3805	
2328	**1823**	*Pattern.* Dated **1823**. As currency, *but not struck for general circulation, with plain edge (Sometimes described as a proof)* (3 or 4 known)	R^6	18	254
2329	—	*In white metal* (Unique?)	R^7	19	254a

Obv. A

Rev. 2

Type	**A/2.**				
2330	No date	By **Pistrucci** and **Merlin**, undated (1829) **A.** – First bust **2.** - Square-topped shield encircled by the collar of the Garter upon a richly decorated mantle of ermine with a crown above. **BRITANNIARUM REX FID: DEF: DECUS ET TUTAMEN ANNO REGNI NONO** (9) *In copper*	R^7	41	266

PATTERN CROWNS

SECOND BUST

Rosettes
flanking date

Obv. B   Rev. 3

Type **B/3.** Bare head – Plain edge
Rev.3. – Square-topped shield garnished   Spink 3806

ESC	Date	Edge	Varieties		R	L&S	(Old ESC)
2331	**1825**	Plain	*Pattern only* (9 strings) *wt. 27.77g*		R^3	20	255
2332	—	—	*Pattern, in Barton's metal* [2]		R^6	21	256
2333	—	—	*Trial striking of obverse In Barton's metal* [2]		R^6	22	
2334	—	—	*Trial striking of reverse In Barton's metal* [2]		R^6	23	
2335	—	—	*Trial striking of obverse in lead*		R^6	24	

Type **B/3.** Bare head – With edge legend
Rev.3. – Square-topped shield garnished   Spink 3806

ESC	Date	Edge year		Varieties	R	L&S	(Old ESC)
2336	**1826**	**SEPTIMO**	(7)	*Pattern (included in the sets of 1826)* *wt. 28.26g*	R	28	257
2337	—	—	(-)	*Pattern, Matt finish from sand blasted dies* [3]	R^7	29	257A
2338	—	Plain edge		*Pattern*	R^7	30	258
2339	—	**LVIII** [3]	(58)	*Pattern with edge error*	R^7	31	258A

1   ESC 248 this exists minus SECUNDO and with a plain edge having been
     probably removed at the Mint. See L&S p. 59 & 60

2   Barton's metal is a copper sheet on to which is rolled and pressed a thin sheet of
     gold; it is quite a different process to gilding, being more like Sheffield plating,
     and more gold is used. The copper core shows on the edge, but the process of
     cutting the blanks presses a little of the gold down over the edge

GEORGE IV, 1820-30
PATTERN CROWNS

| Obv. C | Rev. 3 | Obv. D |

Type **C/3**

ESC	Date		R	L&S	(Old ESC)
2340	?	Unfinished die. Slightly smaller bust Edge unfinished; **DECUS ET TUTAMEN ANNO REGNI** (without year) *In copper* [4]	R^7	32	258B

Type **D/3**

ESC	Date		R	L&S	(Old ESC)
2341	**1828**	As before, but head larger without initials on truncation, and new legend. *In copper* **GEORGIUS IV D: G: BRITANNIAR: REX F:D: 1828**	R^7	33	264
	Edge	**DECUS ET TUTAMEN ANNO REGNI SEPTIMO** (7) (incorrect for a coin of 1828)			

Type **D/3**

ESC	Date		R	L&S	(Old ESC)
2342	—	As before, but *Edge,* **DECUS**→→❁←←**ET**→→❁←← **TUTAMEN**→→❁←←**ANNO**→→❁←← **REGNI**→→❁←←**OCTAVO**→→❁←← (8th) two arrows and a rosette dividing words. *In copper*	R^7	34	265

3   Struck at a later date for the Great Exhibition. *"Having a matt finish unlike the normal coin, interesting and probably unique."* SNC 1974, 2362, p. 114

PATTERN CROWNS

| Obv. E | WW incuse on truncation | Rev.3 |

Type	**E/3**	Bare head with **W.W.** incuse on truncation			
ESC	Date	Varieties	R	L&S	(Old ESC)
2343	**1828**	**W. Wyon** and **J.B. Merlin**, dated **1828** Similar to the *proof* crown of 1826, but slightly larger head of king, **W.W.** incuse on truncation, minus the rosettes flanking date **GEORGIUS IV DEI GRATIA 1828**	R^7	35	263
	Edge	**DECUS ET TUTAMEN ANNO REGNI NONO** (9) Officially sheared by the Mint to prevent circulation *(2 Known)*			

| Rev. 3 | Obv. E | Rev. 4 |

W·W· in relief

PATTERN CROWNS

Type   **E/4.**   Bare head with **W.W.** in relief on truncation

ESC	Date		R	L&S	(Old ESC)
2344	**1829**	By **Wyon** and **Merlin**, dated **1829** Similar to proof crown of 1826, but with initials **W.W.** in relief on truncation, date below and a slight difference in the arrangement of the hair. *Rev.* **4.** - Square-topped shield within the Garter collar with 18 links, overlaying a crowned, richly decorated mantle of ermine **BRITANNIARUM REX FID: DEF:** *Edge,* plain *(3 known?)*	R^6	37	267
2345	—	Similar, but edge reads, in slightly raised letters; **DECUS ET TUTAMEN ANNO REGNI NONO (9)**	R^6	38	268
2346	—	*In copper*	R^7	39	269
2347	—	*In gold* *(Not traced)*	R^7	40	

Type   **E/3**

2348	**1829**	Obverse as before, but with reverse **3.**	R^7		270

Obv. F   *Pistrucci*

Type   **F/3.**   Laureate bust, left, **PISTRUCCI** below cloak buckle

2349	By **Pistrucci**, undated (1828 or 1829) *(Unique)* Uniface obverse, fourth bust laureate and draped, left **GEORGIUS IIII D:G:BRITANNIARUM REX F: D:** *Pistrucci* below cloak buckle Beaded border with inner circle. *Edge,* plain. *In lead*	R^7	L&S 42	

PATTERN CROWNS

FIFTH BUST

Obv. G – no collar   Rev. 5   Obv. F – with a collar

G. MILLS. F
MDCCCXX

PUB. BY R. WHITEAVES

MDCCCXX
MILLS. F

ESC	Date	Variety — No collar	R	L&S	(Old ESC)
2350	**1820**	By **Mills** for **Whiteaves**, dated **1820** Fifth bust; A very large bare head, left, little neck. **G. MILLS . F** on truncation Date **MDCCCXX** (1820) below **GEORGIUS IV DEI GRATIA** *Rev.* **5.** – Royal arms on square-topped shield within Garter with motto, crowned and with supporters, helmet, crest and mantling above, three badges of the Garter, Thistle and St Patrick below, **PUB. BY R . WHITEAVES** at edge beneath in small lettering. **BRITANNIARUM ET HAN : REX FIDEI DEFENSOR** *'King of Britain and Hanover, Defender of the Faith'.* *Edge,* plain *wt. 35.70g*	R^3	7	259
2351	—	*In gold*	R^7	8	260

PATTERN CROWNS

SIXTH BUST

ESC	Date	Variety	With a collar	R	L&S (Old ESC)
2352	**1820**	By **Mills** for **Whiteaves**, dated **1820** Similar to fifth bust, but King wears a collar and necktie, date **MDCCCXX** below truncation, **MILLS F**. Below date *Rev.* **7**. – As before	R^5	9 · 261

Rev. 6 with Ⓜ︎   Type A (No BP below)   Rev. 7 minus Ⓜ︎

2353	No date	By ?, undated (1828 or 1829) 1⅜ inches diameter[6] Laureate bust, left, similar to that of currency crown, but minus B.P. below **GEORGIUS IIII D:G: BRITANNIAR : REX F:D:** *Rev.* **6**. – Royal arms with supporters, no legend The letter Ⓜ︎ (Merlin) appears in Gothic script in the centre below the motto Plain. *In white metal* *wt. 16.46 g*	R^6	43 · 265a
2354	—	Plain. *In copper* *wt. 15.83 g*		
2355	—	As before, but minus letter M on reverse *wt.13.59 g*	R^7 · R^7	265b

4   Edge of the last reign incusely inscribed; an old flan has accidentally been used; Reads; **DECUS ET TUTAMEN ANNO REGNI LVIII**

5   Undated, edge reads **DECUS ET TUTAMEN** in large lettering.

6   These are considered by many to be medals and not intended for currency. However, since they have always been listed by ESC and sought after by collectors they are retained and numbered. (Note; slightly smaller than a crown)

GEORGE IV, 1820-30
HALFCROWNS

Obv. A

Rev. 1

Rev. 1a

a
b

W W P on shamrocks

JBM in beading

a – WWP on shamrocks
b – JBM in beading

Rev. 2

Thistle with more fronds

Thistle with less fronds
Heavier garnishing

The George below

Obv. B

Rev. 3

Pattern

340

HALFCROWNS

| Type | A. | As crown 'A'. Laureate bust, left, long ties |
| Leg. | | **GEORGIUS IIII D: G: BRITANNIAR: REX F: D:** |

| | B. | Bare head, left, date below |
| Leg. | | **GEORGIUS IV DEI GRATIA · (date) ·** |

| Rev. | 1. | Ornately garnished shield, crowned, surrounded by Emblems; Scottish thistle top left, Irish shamrocks top right and English rose below dividing the date. Single letters **WWP** on shamrocks (William Wellesley Pole – Mint Master) and **JBM** in border teeth (Jean Baptiste Merlin - Engraver) |
| Leg. | | **ANNO   1820** |

| | 1a. | As before, but heavier garnishing, fewer points on thistle leaves and diffrent arrangements of stalks on shamrocks and rose |

| | 2. | Crowned square-topped shield over Garter, with motto, and collar of the Garter, the George below divides date |

	3.	Square-topped shield garnished, surmounted by crowned helmet with lambrequins,
Motto		**DIEU ET MON DROIT** on scroll below.
Leg.		**BRITANNIARUM REX FID: DEF:**

A/1. Laureate bust
Rev. 1 - ornately garnished shield   *(10 harp strings)* Spink 3807

ESC	Date	Varieties		R	(Old ESC)
2356	(1820)	Uniface *obv.* trial *in copper*	*wt. 16.35g*	R^2	628A?
2357	**1820**			C^2	628
2358	—	*Proof*	*wt. 14.12g*	R	629
2359	—	*Proof* with plain edge		R^5	630
2360	**1821**	Light garnishing		C	631
2361	—	*Proof*	*wt. 14.03g*	R^2	632

A/1a.   Laureate bust
Rev. 1a - Heavier garnishing   *(8 harp strings)* Spink 3807

ESC	Date	Varieties	R	(Old ESC)
2362	**1821**		C	631A?
2363	—	*Proof*	R^2	632A
2364	**1823**	See note [1]	R^3	633

GEORGE IV, 1820-30
HALFCROWNS

A/2. Laureate bust
Rev. 2 - shield in Garter and collar   *(8 harp strings)* Spink 3808

2365	**1823**			C	634
2366	—	*Proof*	*wt. 14.16g*	R^3	635
2367	**1824**			S	636
2368	—	*Proof*		R^5	637
2369	—	*Proof in copper,* plain edge		R^5	638

B/3. Bare head
Rev. 3 – Shield with crowned helmet   *(10 harp strings)* Spink 3808

2370	**1824**			R^6	639
2371	**1825**			C	642
2372	—	*Proof*	*wt. 14.16g*	S	643
2373	—	*Proof* with plain edge	*wt. 13.93g*	R^2	644
2374	—	*Proof in Barton's metal* [3] Plain edge	*wt. 13.25g*	R^4	645
2375	**1826**			C^2	646
2376	—	*Proof,* issued in the sets	*wt. 14.09g*	S	647
2377	**1828**			S	648
2378	**1829**			N	649

PATTERNS

D^1

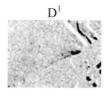

D^2

HALFCROWNS

PATTERNS

2379	1820	D¹	By **Pistrucci** and **Merlin**, dated **1820**	R⁵	649A
		Obv	D¹ - Almost as type 'A', but no engraver's initials (B.P.) below bust, and tie ends straighter. *wt. 14.08g*		
		Rev	**1** - Ornately garnished shield, etc. *(9 strings)* **WWP** incuse in centre of each shamrock		
2380	—	D²	Similar ¹ but, with engraver's initials (B.P.) below bust, hatch lettering and initials *wt. 14.11g* **WWP** raised in centre of each shamrock	R⁵	649B

1   The differences between D¹ and D² are very subtle; note alignment of letter **F** with king's neck and the end of upper tie with letter E

E

2381	1822	E	By **Pistrucci** and **Wyon**, dated **1822**	R⁷	650
		Obv	Similar to D¹ but with initials B.P. below bust and subtle differences in the bust (see note ²)		
		Rev	The Garter is slightly smaller in diameter and there is straight ground below under the dragon		
		1b	*Edge,* milled		
2382	—	—	*Edge,* plain	R⁷	651

2   Bust very slightly altered; see angle of truncation, and compare the base of the George with the currency issue

F (A)

PATTERNS

2383	**1823**	F	As type 'A' Laureate bust, but new and more deeply cut dies. *Edge,* milled *(8 strings) wt. 13.74g*	R^6	652

2384	**1824**	—	Similar, but for date *(8 strings) wt. 14.01g*	R^6	653

G^1

G^2

2385	**1824**	**G¹**	As currency type 'B-1' bare head, but new and more deeply cut polished dies; cf. truncation and cheek. *Edge,* milled *(10 strings) wt. 14.14g*	R^6	639A
2386	—	—	With plain edge *(10 strings) wt. 13.96g*	R^4	639B
2387	—	—	With plain edge *In gold*	R^7	640
2388	—	—	With plain edge *In copper* *(10 strings) wt. 13.07g*		641
2389	—	—	*Uniface obverse in lead* *wt. 20.80g*		641A
2390	—	—	*Uniface obverse in Barton's metal* *wt. 12.59g*	R^4	641B

2391	**1824**	**G²**	Similar, but, large toothed borders and *wt 14.13g* obliquely milled edge *(10 strings) (Unique?)*	R^7	639C

HALFCROWNS

PATTERNS

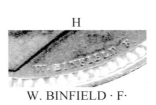

H

W. BINFIELD · F·

2392	No date	**H**	By **W. Binfield**, undated	R^7	654
		Obv	Large laureate head, left, artist's name in full beneath; **W·BINFIELD·F**		
		Rev	Value divided by a caduceus surmounted by trident, within laurel branches. *Edge,* plain		
2393	—	—	*In bronze or copper* (3 or 4 known)	R^6	655

JBM

6 over 8 or 2?

Obv. A

Arabic 1 & Roman I

Obv. B

Rev. 1

Rev. 2

Rev. 3

SHILLINGS

Obv.	**A.**	Laureate head, left, as half-crown 'A'		
	B.	Bare head, left, as half-crown 'B'		
Rev.	**1.**	Ornately garnished shield, as half-crown '1'		
	2.	Crowned square-topped shield over Garter, as half-crown '2'		
	3.	Lion standing on a crown with emblems below		
Leg.		**BRITANNIARUM REX FIDEI DEFENSOR**		

A/1.   Laureate head / *Rev.* 1 - Ornately garnished shield   Spink 3810

ESC	Date	Varieties		*R*	(Old ESC)
2394	**1820**	*Pattern.* No JBM in border		R^5	1246
2395	—	*Pattern.* With **JBM** in lower left border	*wt. 5.65g*	R^7	1246A
2396	**1821**	See note [1]		N	1247
2397	—	*Proof*	*(6 strings- 8 hearts)*	R^3	1248

A/2.   Laureate head / *Rev.* 2 – Square shield in Garter   Spink 3811

2398	**1823**			R	1249
2399	—	*Proof*	*(7 strings- 8 hearts)*	R^4	1250
2400	**1824**		*(7 strings- 8 hearts)*	N	1251
2401	—	*Proof* ↑↓	*wt. 5.66g*	R^4	1252
2402	**1825**	Some have a broken O in GEORGIUS	*(7 strings- 8 hearts)*	N	1253
2403	—	*Proof*		R^4	1253A
2404	—	**5** over **3**		R^3	1253B

B/3.   Bare head / *Rev.* 3 – Lion standing on a crown   Spink 3812

2405	**1825**			C	1254
2406	—	Roman **I** in date		R^5	1254A
2407	—	*Proof* ↑↓	*wt. 5.65g*	R^7	1255
2408	—	*Proof,* plain edge. *In Barton's metal* [2]		R^5	1256
2409	**1826**			C^2	1257
2410	—	**6** over **2** or is it an **8**?		R^3	1257A
2411	—	*Proof,* issued in the sets		S	1258
2412	**1827**			R	1259
2413	**1829**			S	1260
2414	—	*Proof* ↑↓	*wt. 5.63g*	R^3	1261

SHILLINGS

PATTERNS

C

2415	**1824**	C	By **W. Wyon** and **J.B. Merlin**, dated **1824**	R^6	1262
		Obv	Similar to 'C', but with an inner circle		
		Leg	**BRITANNIARUM REX FIDEI DEFENSOR**		
		Rev	**5;** Square-topped shield, crowned, motto on scroll below. *Edge,* milled **BRITANIARUM REX FID: DEF:** and spray; rose thistle and shamrock		
2416	—	—	Similar. *Edge,* plain. Struck *en medaille* ↑↑	R^6	1263

D

SHILLINGS

PATTERNS

2417	1825	D	By **W. Wyon** and **J.B. Merlin**, dated **1825**	R^5	1264
		Obv	Similar to '**C**'.		
		Rev	**6**; Similar to '4', but		
			Smaller; crown, lion and posy.		
			Much wider space in legend above lion.		
		Leg	**BRITANNIARUM REX FID: DEF:**		
			Edge, milled ↑↓ *wt. 5.64g*		
2418	—	—	*In Barton's metal* [2] ↑↓	R^6	1265

E

2419	1826	E	A trial striking in silver, struck without a collar, the flan slightly spread *Edge,* plain	R^6	1265A

Notes
1   Considerably scarcer in mint condition.
2   For Barton's metal see Crowns note 2

GEORGE IV, 1820-30
SIXPENCES

Rev. 1   Obv. A   Rev. 2

Obv. B   Rev. 3

BBITANNIAR

Obv.	**A.**	Bust A, laureate as the halfcrown
Leg.		**GEORGIUS IIII D: G: BRITANNIAR: REX F: D:**
	B.	Bust B, bare head, as the halfcrown
Leg.		**GEORGIUS IV DEI GRATIA · (date) ·**
Rev.	**1.**	Crowned garnished shield, surrounded by Emblems etc
	2.	Crowned square-topped shield over Garter etc.
	3.	Lion standing on a crown with emblems below.
Leg.		**BRITANNIARUM REX FIDEI DEFENSOR**

SIXPENCES

Type	**A/1.**	Bust A, laureate		
		Rev. 1 - Crowned garnished shield		Spink 3813

ESC	Date	Varieties	R	(Old ESC)
2420	**1820**	*Proof or pattern, edge milled.*	R^6	1653
		Initials **IBM** in border lower left *wt. 2.79g*		
2421	**1821**		C	1654
2422	—	*Struck without a collar, edge plain*	C	1654A
2423	—	*Proof,* edge grained *wt. 2.80g, wt. 2.86g*	R^2	1655
2424	—	Reads **BBITANNIAR** [1]	R^3	1656

	A/2.	Bust A, laureate		
		Rev. 2 - Crowned square-topped shield over Garter		Spink 3814

2425	**1824**		N	1657
2426	—	*Proof,* edge grained *wt. 2.83g*	R^3	1658
2427	**1825**		C	1659
2428	—	*Proof* *(Not traced)*	R^4	1659A
2429	—	*Proof. In Barton's metal* [2] *(Not traced)*	R^4	1659B
2430	**1826**		R^2	1660
2431	—	*Proof,* edge plain	R^3	1661
2432	—	*Proof,* edge grained *wt. 2.83g; wt. 2.85g*	R^3	1661 A

	B/3.	Bust B, bare head		
		Rev 3 - Lion standing on a crown		Spink 3815

2433	**1826**	See note [3]	C	1662
2434	—	Extra tuft of hair by ear (as on half sovereigns) [3]	R^2	1662A
2435	—	*Proof, issued in the sets,* edge grained *wt. 2.82g*	S	1663
2436	—	*Proof in pewter on a thick flan* *wt. 3.97g*	R^5	1663A
2437	**1827**		R^2	1664
2438	**1828**		S	1665
2439	**1829**		N	1666
2440	—	*Proof,* edge grained *wt. 2.88g*	R^4	1667

1   The first B was struck from a broken punch and when an attempt was made to strengthen it a new B was mistakenly struck over the second letter, giving the appearance of BBITANNIAR *Beware of some examples showing the second R with larger lower serifs which gives the appearance of a joined bottom line and often catalogued as the B over R variety when it is not! Caveat emptor.*

2   This may turn up as all other denominations of this date are known in Barton's metal

3   There are two varieties of bust on these third coinage sixpences.

SIXPENCES

PATTERNS

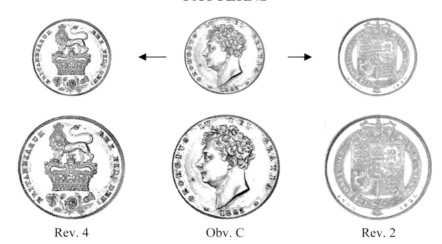

| Rev. 4 | Obv. C | Rev. 2 |

Obv.	**C.**	Bust C, bare head, similar to B but slightly smaller
Leg.		**GEORGIUS IV DEI GRATIA · (date) ·**
Rev.	**4.**	Lion standing on a crown, similar to 3 but narrower
Leg.		**BRITANNIARUM REX FID: DEF:**

C/4. Bust C, bare head
Rev 4 - Lion standing on a crown, narrower than 3   Spink 3815

ESC	Date	Varieties	R	(Old ESC)
2441	**1825**	By **W. Wyon**, dated **1825** *Obv.* **C**. - Bare head, left, smaller than B *wt. 2.84 g* *Leg.* **GEORGIUS IV DEI GRATI A · 1825 ·** *Rev.* **4** - As '3' but lion and crown narrower *Leg.* **BRITANNIARUM REX FID: DEF:**	R^7	1668
2442	—	As before *on thick flan,* *wt. 2.85g*	R^7	1668A

C/2. Bust C, bare head / *Rev* 2 - Lion standing on a crown

| 2443 | **1826** | *Obv.* As before
Rev. **2** – As currency   *(Not traced)* | R^6 | 1669 |

GEORGE IV, 1820-30
MAUNDY

SETS of FOUR COINS

Small head   1822

Obv. As larger coins of the first type

Rev. Value in the centre, dividing date, between two branches of oak,
tied together at the base with a bow. Plain edge   Spink 3816

ESC	Date	Varieties etc.	*Brian Robinson page 166*	R	(Old ESC)
2444	**1822**	3d - Small head[1]	*1d – 303; 2d – 304; 3d - 305; 4d - 306*	*N*	2425
2445	—	*Proof*	*1d – 307; 2d – 308; 3d – 309; 4d - 310*	*R⁴*	2426
2446	**1823**		*1d – 311; 2d – 312; 3d – 313; 4d - 314*	*N*	2427
2447	**1824**		*1d – 315; 2d – 316; 3d – 317; 4d - 318*	*R*	2428
2448	**1825**		*1d – 319; 2d – 320; 3d – 321; 4d - 322*	*N*	2429
2449	—	2d - **T** over **B** in **BRITANNIAR** *p. 166,320(i)*		*R³*	2429A
2450	**1826**		*1d – 323; 2d – 324; 3d – 325; 4d - 326*	*N*	2430
2451	—	2d - **T** over **B** in **BRITANNIAR** *p. 166,324(i)*		*R³*	2430A
2452	**1827**		*1d – 327; 2d – 328; 3d – 329; 4d - 330*	*N*	2431
2453	**1828**		*1d – 331; 2d – 332; 3d – 333; 4d - 334*	*N*	2432
2454	—	*Proof*	*1d – 335; 2d – 336; 3d – 337; 4d - 338*	*R⁵*	2433
2455	**1829**		*1d – 339; 2d – 340; 3d – 341; 4d - 342*	*N*	2434
2456	**1830**		*1d – 343; 2d – 344; 3d – 345; 4d - 346*	*N*	2435

1   The head of the threepence of 1822 is smaller than on the threepences of the other dates.
According to Hawkins the first punch broke and as there was no time to engrave another one
with the correct size head, a die was made up using the punch of the bust of the twopence.
Of the individual coins of this and the following reigns the threepence is the scarcest in
good condition as some of them apparently found their way into circulation after 1845.

WILLIAM IV, 1830-7
PROOF or PATTERN CROWNS (only)

The obverse of the coins of this reign was designed by W. Wyon who engraved the portrait from a bust by Sir William Chantrey. Merlin designed and engraved the reverses on the silver. There were no crowns struck for circulation during this reign, but proofs were issued in 1831 and 1834. These show the usual obverse portrait and on the reverse a crowned shield on a mantle of ermine. The design for the halfcrown is similar, but the shilling and sixpence have a new coinage type, the value in words with a crown above.

An interesting innovation in this reign was the reintroduction, as a denomination, of a fourpence or groat. These were first struck in 1836 and were also issued the following year.

The three-halfpenny pieces, first struck in 1834, were never current in this country, but were a special issue for use in the West Indies and Ceylon. They are usually collected under The English series however, and we have therefore included them in the present work. (P.A.Rayner, 1949)

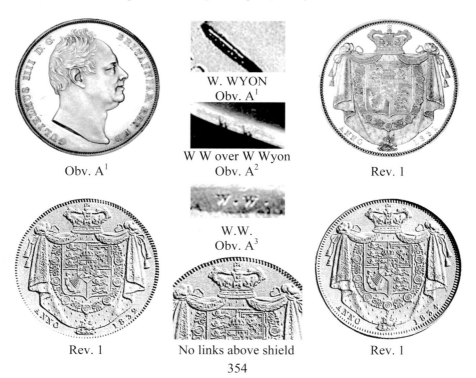

Obv. A¹

W. WYON
Obv. A¹

W W over W Wyon
Obv. A²

Rev. 1

Rev. 1

W.W.
Obv. A³

No links above shield

Rev. 1

354

WILLIAM IV, 1830-7
PROOF or PATTERN CROWNS (only)

ESC	Date	Type	Varieties	R	L&S	(Old ESC)
2460	**1831**	**A**^{1}	By **William Wyon**	R^4	3	273
		Obv	Bare head, right			
			W. WYON in relief on truncation.			
		Leg	**GULIELMUS IIII D: G:**			
			BRITANNIAR: REX F: D:			
		Rev.	**1 -** Square-topped shield within the			
			Garter, collar with 15 links,			
			overlaying a crowned richly			
			decorated mantle of ermine			
			Date **ANNO 1831** below divided			
			by the George facing left			
		Edge	Plain. *En medaille* ↑↑ *wt. 27.73g*			
2461	**1831**	**A**^{2}	As before, but initials **W. W.**	R^6		271A
			engraved incuse over **W. WYON** on			
			truncation. *Edge* Plain			
2462	**1831**	**A**^{3}	**W.W.** incuse on truncation *wt. 27.98g*	R^2	1	271
		Edge	Plain; issued in sets. Die axis ↑↓ *(7 str)*			
2463	—	—	*In gold* *wt. 40.45g*	R^5	2	272
2464	**1832**	**A**^{3}	As before, with	R^7	5	274
			W.W. incuse on truncation			
		Edge	**DECUS ET TUTAMEN ANNO**			
			REGNI TERTIO, the inscription			
			divided by a rose, shamrock, thistle			
			and a lion, the whole between an			
			ornamental border. *In lead*			
2465	**1834**	**A**^{3}	As before with	R^5	6	275
			W.W. incuse on truncation			
		Edge	Plain. *En medaille* ↑↓			
2466	—	**A**^{3}	As before with **W.W.** incuse, but	R^7	7	275A
		Edge	Grained and inscribed in incuse			
			lettering with rose-like stops;			
		Leg.	**DECUS ET TUTAMEN ❋ ANNO REGNI**			
		Error*	**QUINQUAGESIMO SEPTIMO** (57th)			

* This is an edge reading of George III's reign

WILLIAM IV, 1830-7
PROOF or PATTERN CROWNS (only)

B¹   links above shield   Rev. 2

2467	No date	**A³** *Obv* *Rev.*	By **W. WYON** and **J.B. Merlin**, undated As before, **W.W.** incuse on truncation **2** - Similar to '1', but a larger crown, the collar visible above shield, with 18 links, the mantle is more richly decorated, undated, initials **I.B.M.** in beading below the right facing George	R⁶	8	276
		Leg *Edge*	**BRITANNIARUM REX FID: DEF:** Plain *(9 strings)*			
2468	—	—	*In lead*	R⁷	9	277

W. WYON.

Rev. 2

2469	No date	**A¹** *Rev.*	As before, but **W. WYON.** in relief on truncation **2** - As before, but the initials omitted below the George.	R⁶	10	278
		Edge	Plain. *En medaille* ↑↑ *wt. 28.07g*			

WILLIAM IV, 1830-7
PROOF or PATTERN CROWNS (only)

Rev. 3

Rev. 3   Rev. 4

Rev. 4

2470	18(37)	Uniface reverse by **J.B. Merlin,** date unfinished *Rev.* 3 - Small ornate shield within the Collar and Garter, surmounted by helmet crowned with lambrequins and supporters motto on scroll below **DIEU ET MON DROIT** The George divides date **ANNO 18** Around the very wide border is written in Wyon's writing; *"Merlin's Crown good, but too good, too high L.C.W."* *Edge.* Plain. *In lead.* *(Unique)*	R^7	13	
2471	**1837**	Uniface reverse By **J.B. Merlin** Dated **ANNO 1837** *Rev.* **4** - Similar to last, but the shield of Hanover is superimposed in the centre of arms The George divides date **ANNO 1831** *Edge.* Plain. *In Barton's metal* *(2 known)*	R^6	12	

1   *"It would seem that chronologically the first die proposed for the new William IV*
Crown was the **W. Wyon** *version. It must have been considered far too bold of*
William Wyon to spell his surname in full, especially on the bust of the King's
coinage. Rather than waste a valuable obverse die with his enigmatic portrait of
the King, William Wyon must have re-filled the signature on the die's truncation
and re-engraved an incuse **W W** *over the top."*
(My thanks to Baldwin Fixed Price List Winter 2010-11, lot BM052)

WILLIAM IV, 1830-7
HALFCROWNS

Types as bare head crown

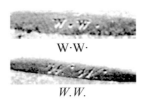

W·W·

W.W.

S re-entered

6 re-entered

6 over 5

Obv.	**A.**	**W.W.** in capitals, incuse on truncation	
	B.	**W.W.** in script, incuse on truncation	
Rev.	**1.**	Similar to crown, but only 5 links of Garter collar below shield	

A.   **W.W.** incuse in capitals on truncation   Spink 3834

ESC	Date	Varieties	R	(Old ESC)
2472	**1831**	*(A few were struck, but never put into general circulation)* *(Not traced)*	R^5	656
2473	—	*Proof* plain edge, issued in sets *wt. 13.99g*	S	657
2474	**1834**		R	660
2475	—	*Proof* *(Not traced)*	R^4	661

B.   **W.W.** incuse in script on truncation   Spink 3834A

2476	**1834**	*Proof only*	R^2	659
2477	—	*Proof only,* plain edge *wt. 14.03g* *(6 strings)*	R	658
2478	—	*(7 strings)*	C	662
2479	—	*Proof* *wt. 14.09g*	R	663
2480	—	*Proof,* plain edge *(Not traced)*	R^4	664
2481	**1835**		R	665
2482	**1836**	*(7 strings)*	C	666
2483	—	**6 over 5** (some with 6 double-entered)	R^3	666A
2484	—	**S over S in GULIELMUS**	R^3	
2485	—	*Proof,* plain edge *(Not traced)*	R^4	666B
2486	**1837**		S	667

358

WILLIAM IV, 1830-7
SHILLINGS

Only one type

Flat top **3**

Rounded 3

W·W·

Obv.	Type and legend as crown
Rev.	Value in the centre, between two branches; an olive left and oak right, tied together at the base with a ribbon, a large crown above and the date below. Milled edge
Note	Unless stated, the **3** of date has a flat top

Spink 3835

ESC	Date	Varieties	R	(Old ESC)
2487	**1831**	*Proof only* ↑↓	R^4	1267
2488	—	*Proof* with plain edge, issued in the sets	N	1266
2489	**1834**		C	1268
2490	—	*Proof* ↑↓	R^2	1269
2491	—	*Proof,* round top to **3** in date	R^5	1270
2492	**1835**		S	1271
2493	—	*Proof,* round top to **3** in date	R^6	1272
2494	**1836**		N	1273
2495	—	*Proof,* round top to **3** in date	R^6	1274
2496	—	*Proof,* plain edge. *In copper* (Not traced)	R^6	1275
2497	**1837**		R	1276
2498	—	*Proof* ↑↓	R^4	1277

WILLIAM IV, 1830-7
SIXPENCES

Obv. A

Obv. B
(Half-sovereign die)

Flat top   Round top

Obv.	**A**	Type and legend as crown
Rev.		Value in the centre, between two branches; an olive left an oak right, tied together at the base with a bow, large crown above and date below bow
		Milled edge
	B	Half-sovereign die: markedly smaller than on normal sixpence Larger gap above the head and below the truncation
Note		Flat-topped 3 of date unless stated

WILLIAM IV, 1830-7
SIXPENCES

Obv.		A		Spink 3836	
ESC	Date	Varieties		R	(Old ESC)
2499	**1831**			N	1670
2500	—	*Proof,* edge grained	*wt. 2.81g*	R²	1671
2501	—	*Proof only,* with plain edge, issued in the sets	*2.63g*	S	1672
2502	—	*Proof* on a very thin flan.	*wt. 1·82g & 1.94g*	R⁷	1672A
2503	—	*Proof,* plain edge. *In palladium*	*(Not traced)*	R⁷	1673
2504	**1834**			C	1674
2505	—	Date in large numerals		R	1674A
2506	—	*Proof*		R³	1674B
2507	—	*Proof,* round top to **3** in date	*(Not traced)*	R⁴	1675
2508	**1835**			S	1676
2509	—	*Proof,* round top to **3** in date	*wt. 2.81g*	R⁶	1677
2510	**1836**			R²	1678
2511	—	*Proof,* round top to **3** in date	*wt. 2.87g*	R⁶	1679
2512	**1837**			S	1680
2513	—	*Proof,* edge grained	*wt. 2.81g*	R⁶	1681

Obv.		B - Struck from a Half-Sovereign obverse die			
2514	**1837**		*wt. 2.81g*	R⁶	1681A

GROATS & MAUNDY

GROATS

		Only one type. *Edge,* milled
Obv.		Type and legend as crown
Rev.	**1**	Britannia seated, right, holding a trident in her left hand and resting her right hand on a shield. Date below in exergue.
Leg,		Value **FOUR** **PENCE** divided by Britannia

Spink 3837

ESC	Date	Varieties		R	(Old ESC)
2515	**1836**		*wt. 1·88g*	C^2	1918
2516	—	*Proof*		R^2	1919
2517	—	*Proof,* with plain edge, *en medaille* ↑↑	*wt. 1·88g*	S	1920
2518	—	*Proof in gold,* with plain edge	*wt. 3·37g*	R^5	1921
2519	—	*Proof in gold,* thinner flan	*wt. 1·32g*	R^6	1921A
2520	**1837**	See note [1]		C	1922
2521	—	*Proof*		R^4	1923
2522	—	*Proof,* with plain edge		R^4	1923A

Note

1   On later strikings, the obverse die appears to have been re-cut; the hair is finer, and the eyes more prominent.

GROATS & MAUNDY

PATTERN GROATS

2   3

Value FOUR PENCE

ESC	Date		Varieties	R	(Old ESC)
2523	**1836**		By **W. Wyon**. Dated **1836**	R^3	1924
		Obv	As current coin.		
		Rev	**2** - Smaller Britannia, within legend,		
			date below in a much lower exergue.		
		Leg	Value **FOUR PENCE** continuous over		
			Britannia. *Edge,* milled *wt. 1.84g*		
2524	—	—	*Edge*, plain *wt. 1.89g*	R^3	1925
2525	—	—	*Edge*, plain *In gold,* *wt 3.37g* WR 273	R^5	1925A
2526	—	—	*Edge*, milled. *In gold, thin flan,* 1.32g WR 274	R^6	1925B

Value 4 P

2527	**1836**	*Obv*	As before. *Edge,* milled *wt. 1.84g*	R^2	1926
		Rev	**3** – as '2' but Britannia between value **4 P**		
2528	—	—	*Edge*, plain *wt. 1.86g*	R^2	1927
2529	—	—	*Edge*, plain *In gold* *wt 3.37g* WR 271	R^5	1928
2530	—	—	*Edge*, milled. *In gold* *wt 3.37g* WR 272	R^6	1928A

GROATS & MAUNDY

THREEPENCES

Quantities of these dates were struck for use in the West Indies only
Being the same as the British currency they are numbered accordingly

Type A – Small head   Type B – Large head

	A.	Small head		Spink 3838	
ESC	Date	Varieties	R	(Old ESC)	
2531	**1834**		S	2044	
2532	**1835**		N	2045	
2533	**1836**		S	2046	
2534	**1837**		R	2047	

	B.	Large head[1]		Spink 3838A	
2535	**1834**		S	2044	
2536	**1835**		N	2045	
2537	**1836**		S	2046	
2538	**1837**		R	2047	

1   Uncertain if all these dates were struck and the rarity

GROATS & MAUNDY

THREE-HALFPENCE

This denomination was struck purely for use in some of the
British Colonies, which used the ordinary Imperial currency

Obv.　　　　　As groat
Rev.　　　　　Value **1½** crowned, date **1835** below within two oak branches

Spink 3839

ESC	Date	Varieties	R	(Old ESC)
2539	**1834**		*C*	2250
2540	—	*Proof*	*R⁵*	2250A
2541	**1835**	*(This without over-date unconfirmed)*	*R*	2251
2542	—	**5 over 4**	*N*	2251A
2543	**1836**		*N*	2252
2544	**1836**		*N*	2252
2545	**1837**		*R²*	2253
2546	—	*Proof*	*R⁶*	2253A

GROATS & MAUNDY

MAUNDY SETS
Only one type

Obv.	Type and legend as crown
Rev.	Crown above value in the centre, dividing date, between two branches; olive left and oak right, tied together with ribbon in a bow.
	Edge, plain

Spink 3840

ESC	Date	Varieties etc.	*Brian Robinson page 167*	R	(Old ESC)
2547	**1831**		*1d – 347; 2d – 348; 3d - 349; 4d - 350*	S	2436
2548	—	*Proof set*	*1d – 351; 2d – 352; 3d - 353; 4d - 354*	R	2437
2549	—	*Proof set in gold* WR 275 – weights; *1d 1.07g; 2d 1.97g; 3d 2.87g; 4d 3.89g;*	*1d – 355; 2d – 356; 3d - 357; 4d - 358*	R⁶	2438
2550	**1832**		*1d – 359; 2d – 360; 3d – 361; 4d - 362*	S	2439
2551	**1833**		*1d – 363; 2d – 364; 3d – 365; 4d - 366*	S	2440
2552	**1834**		*1d – 367; 2d – 368; 3d – 369; 4d - 370*	S	2441
2553	**1835**		*1d – 371; 2d – 372; 3d – 373; 4d - 374*	S	2442
2554	**1836**		*1d – 375; 2d – 376; 3d – 377; 4d - 378*	S	2443
2555	**1837**		*1d – 379; 2d – 380; 3d – 381; 4d - 382*	S	2444

VICTORIA
1837-1901
INTRODUCTION

As is only natural with a reign of this length, there were several changes in the coinage. There were three main issues known as *'Young head', 'Jubilee'* issue and *'Old' head'* issue respectively. There was also the so-called *'Gothic issue'* of crowns and florins.

'Young head'. This is the first issue and shows the Queen with a young head, usually with a fillet. The smaller denominations were issued in 1838. Crowns and halfcrowns were issued in the 1839 proof sets; a few of the latter being put into circulation, but crowns were not generally issued until 1844, and were again struck in 1845 and 1847. The *'Britannia'* groat was continued up to 1855, and was recalled from circulation in 1887. Threepences of the same type as the Maundy coin were issued for general circulation in 1845 and continued to be struck for nearly 100 years except for 1847 and 1848. Prior to 1845 however, they had sometimes been struck in quantities (as well as the twopences) for sending to some of the Colonies which used the British coinage. Wyon designed and engraved the so-called 'Young' head of the Queen, and the reverse designs were produced by Merlin, who retired in 1844. These designs, however, were engraved by Leonard Charles Wyon, who entered the service of the Mint on Merlin's retirement. He later succeeded W. Wyon, his father, as Chief Engraver, and is probably best known for his portrait of Victoria on the early bronze 'bun' pennies.

'Godless Florin'. In the early part of this reign, there was some strong opinion that the country should change over to a decimal coinage. A motion in favour of silver pieces of the value of one-tenth and one-hundredth of a pound was placed before Parliament, but was, however, withdrawn, on the understanding that the former piece be issued. Hence, the florin became a new denomination, and was first issued in 1849 with the Queen shown wearing a crown. Because D G or DEI GRATIA was omitted from the Queen's titles it has become popularly known as the *'Godless Florin'.* The Queen's portrait was designed and engraved by W. Wyon, and the reverse design for this and also for the Gothic florin, which superseded it, was by William Dyce.

'Gothic Issue'. The Gothic crown of 1847 was almost certainly issued to commemorate the Queen's 10th anniversary of her Coronation, and is regarded as one of the finest coins in the English milled series. Large numbers were struck and some undoubtedly did get into circulation, although it is somewhat unusual to find a worn piece. Why the much rarer 1853 Gothic crown was issued is unknown. A revised design for the florin was made in the Gothic style of the crown and first

367

VICTORIA
1837-1901
INTRODUCTION

used in 1851. The date on these pieces is in small Roman numerals in Gothic script at the end of the obverse legend.

Die numbers

Between 1863 and 1880 the Royal Mint conducted an experiment to study the life of its dies for currency gold and silver denominations, from the sovereign down to sixpence, with the exception of the halfcrown. (For gold see EMGC later) A sequential number was placed below the Queen's bust on the 'Gothic' florin, and above the date on the reverse of the shillings and sixpences. I have meticulously recorded all the numbers known to date, but am unable to allocate them to any specific die variety other than those few shown. Also the fact that some sequential numbers are missing does not prove they were never used but simply remain lost or undiscovered. For more information see; (1) SNC 1983, p. 119-120; (2) *Coins and Medals* August 1981; (3) *ON VICTORIAN DIE NUMBERS* by Gerald Sommerville C. Eng., M.I. Mech. E. S.C.M.B. 1990, pp. 99-101.

Mintage figures; these refer to the number of coins struck by the Mint in each year, but not necessarily with that date. Often dies remained in use into the following year (See appendix later)

VICTORIA, 1837-1901
CROWNS

Young head. First issue; 1839-1847 & 1879, shows the Queen with a young head, hair in the bun style tied with two ribbons, one or both either plain or ornate. Roman lettering and date below truncation.

Gothic . Second issue; 1847 & 1853, young portrait of the Queen wearing a crown and ornately decorated dress, hair plaited. Gothic lettering (date on rev.)

Jubilee Issue. Third issue; 1887-1892, a new coinage was introduced to celebrate the Queen's Golden Jubilee. The well-known Jubilee type head was engraved by L.C. Wyon from designs by Sir Joseph Boehm. Wyon designed the reverses himself, except of course for that of the crown, which shows Pistrucci's famous treatment of St. George and the Dragon. An innovation in this coinage was the issue of a double florin or four shilling piece, which did not prove popular, probably due to its being readily confused with the crown: this was discontinued in 1890. L.C. Wyon died in 1891 and was succeeded by George William de Saulles, who was appointed Chief Engraver in 1893.

Old Head. Fourth issue; 1893-1901, a new older looking portrait of the Queen wearing a coronet and veil, designed by Sir Thomas Brock and engraved by De Saulles. The reverse designs of the old head coins were by various artists. The crown still showed Pistrucci's St. George, the halfcrown was designed by Brock and the 'three shields' reverses of the florin and shilling by Sir Edward Poynter; the sixpence and threepence were modifications of Merlin's original designs.

EDGE LEGENDS

The punctuation on the Young head crowns is usually a stop (•)
but may also include either or both of these;

Cinquefoil   8 pointed star

Note;
Some minor die varieties exist for the Obverse of the Old head and Reverses of the Jubilee and Old head issues, beyond the remit of this edition - see Peter J Davis, pp 46-47

VICTORIA, 1837-1901
CROWNS

Obv. A
Small lettering

W.WYON.RA

Rev.1

Obv. B
large lettering

1847

1853

Obv. C

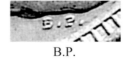

B.P.

Rev. 2

𝔫 over 𝔲 in unita

Rev. 3

𝔪 over inverted 𝔪

370

VICTORIA, 1837-1901
CROWNS

Obv.	**A.**	Young head, left, hair tied with ribbon in the 'Bun style'
		W.WYON.RA on truncation, date below
Leg.		**VICTORIA DEI GRATIA** in small lettering
		Letter **C** in **VICTORIA** in line with her mouth
Obv.	**B.**	Similar to A, but, **VICTORIA DEI GRATIA** in larger
		lettering with letter **T** in **VICTORIA** in line with her mouth
Obv.	**C.**	*'Gothic'* type bust;
		Crowned draped bust, left, wearing a richly embroidered bodice
Leg.		𝖁𝖎𝖈𝖙𝖔𝖗𝖎𝖆 𝖉𝖊𝖎 𝖌𝖗𝖆𝖙𝖎𝖆 𝖇𝖗𝖎𝖙𝖆𝖓𝖓𝖎𝖆𝖗. 𝖗𝖊𝖌: 𝖋: 𝖉· (Gothic lettering)
		Victoria by the Grace of God Queen, defender of the Faith
Rev.	**1.**	Crowned square-topped shield within branches of laurel
		Floral ornament below
Leg.		**BRITANNIARUM REGINA FID: DEF:**
Edge		**DECUS**, etc. incusely inscribed with ornament after
		TUTAMEN and the regnal year in Roman numerals
Rev.	**2.**	Cruciform shields crowned, quartering *leg.* Garter star in centre;
		rose, thistle, shamrock & rose in the angles within tressure of arcs
Leg.		𝖙𝖚𝖊𝖆𝖙𝖚𝖗 𝖚𝖓𝖎𝖙𝖆 𝖉𝖊𝖚𝖘 *May God guard these united*
		𝖆𝖓𝖓𝖔 𝖉𝖔𝖒 𝖒𝖉𝖈𝖈𝖝𝖑𝖛𝖎𝖎 (1847) or 𝖒𝖉𝖈𝖈𝖈𝖑𝖎𝖎𝖎 (1853)
Edge		As before, but in small raised Gothic characters, with rose &
		crown stops
Rev.	**3.**	St. George slaying the dragon, hair streaming from beneath his
		helmet, date and initials **B.P.** in exergue
Edge	*a.*	**DECUS ET TUTAMEN ANNO REGNI** followed by the regnal
		year in Roman numerals, in raised letters.
	b.	Milled

CROWNS

A/1. Young head, small lettering (letter **C** in line with her mouth)
Rev. 1 - Crowned square-topped shield   Spink 3882

ESC	Date	Edge year		Varieties, remarks etc *(Strings)*	R	L&S	Old ESC
2560	**1839**	None		*Proof plain edge*[1] wt. 28.32g (8)	R	38	279

B/1. Young head, large lettering (letter **T** in line with her mouth)
Rev. 1 - Crowned square-topped shield   Spink 3882

ESC	Date	Edge year		Varieties, remarks etc *(Strings)*	R	L&S	Old ESC
2561	**1844**	VIII	(8)	Edge stops; 8 point stars[2] wt. 28.22g (7)	C		280
2562	—	—	—	Edge stops; cinquefoils (8)	C		281
2563	—	—	—	*Proof.* Edge stops; cinquefoils	R⁶	42	280A
2564	**1845**	VIII	(8)	Edge stops; cinquefoils [2] (8)	C²		282
2565	—	—	—	Edge stops; cinquefoils Edge reads **AANNO** (7)	S		282B
2566	—	—	—	Edge stops are stars	C		282A
2567	**1847**	XI	(9)	Edge stops are cinquefoils [2]	C		286
2568	—	—	—	Edge stops are cinquefoils [2] Edge reads **FT** for **ET** *(Filled die?)*	R²		286A
2569	—	(XI omitted)	**DECUS** (with **U** not usual V)		R⁷		286A
2570	—	Milled (b)	*Pattern or trial piece* [3]		R⁷	68	287

C/2. 'Gothic' type bust, dated **mdccxlvii** (1847)
Rev. 2 - Cruciform shields crowned
With regnal years on edge   Spink 3883

ESC	Date	Edge year		Varieties, remarks etc	R	L&S	Old ESC
2571	**1847**	**undecimo**	(10)	*Proof only* [4] *(8,000 struck)* (9) *En medaille* ↑↓	S	57	288
2572	—	—	—	*Proof. Edge,* inscribed between two narrow grained borders with rose & crown stops	R⁶	60	342
2573	—	—	—	*Proof* with frosted bust	R⁵		289
2574	—	—	—	*Proof, totally frosted* Sealed in glass lunette	R⁶	63	289A
2575	—	—	—	*Proof struck en medaille* ↑↑ With a bevelled edge	R⁵		288/ 291
2576	—	**septimo**	(7)	*Proof* with *edge* error (should be **undecimo**)	R⁷	59	290

CROWNS

C/2.var. *'Gothic'* type as before, but with a plain edge   Spink 3883

2577	**1847**	*Proof in pure silver (0·999 fine)*	R^6	58	291
2578	—	*Proof in pure silver (0·999 fine) SG=10.5 ± 0.3* n over inverted n in **unita** *wt. 27.31g*	R^2		291B
2579	**1847**	*Proof in pure silver (0·999 fine)* m over inverted m in **dom**	R^2		291C
2580	—	*VIP proof All the design highly frosted* ↑↑ *In pure silver (0·999 fine) SG 10·47* *(3 known)*	R^6		291A
2581	—	*In gold* *wt. 53.55g*	R^7	61	292
2582	—	*In white metal*	R^7	62	292A
2583	—	*Proof* ↑↑ *Frosted bust and reverse* *wt. 27.76g*	R^5	70	294

C/2.   *'Gothic'* type bust, as before, but dated **mdccliii** (1853)
     Rev. 2 - Cruciform shields crowned
     With regnal years on edge   Spink 3884

2584	**1853**	**septimo**	(7)	*Proof only. In the sets* ↑↓	R^3	69	293

Note; One or two of the above old ESC 291A-C may be duplications

1   Only issued in the year sets. Obverse lettering is smaller than on later coins and starts at 8 o'clock instead of 7 o'clock.

2   Young head crowns are common in worn to average condition (F and below) but are difficult to obtain EF+ ; the rarity of an uncirculated specimen would perhaps be R^3

3   This piece which is in the British Museum does not have the appearance of a proof or pattern and is therefore possibly in the nature of a trial piece made from the old 1847 dies when the authorities were considering a milled edge for the 1887 issue.

4   Mr Stride, formerly Chief Clerk of the Royal Mint, says *'that the Gothic crowns were never issued for ordinary circulation and that all were struck in proof state. Some appear with the raised design heavily frosted, apparently early strikings.'*

CROWNS

JUBILEE HEAD

Obv. D

J.E.B.

B·P·

Rev. 3

Narrow date

Wide date

Obv.	**D.**	Jubilee head; Veiled and draped bust, left, wearing a small crown, two orders and necklace. **J.E.B.** on truncation
Leg.		**VICTORIA D: G: BRITT: REG: F: D:**
Rev.	**3.**	St. George slaying the dragon, hair streaming from beneath his helmet, date and initials **B.P.** in exergue
Edge	*b.*	Milled

D/3.   Jubilee head / *Rev.* 3 – St. George and the dragon   Spink 3921

ESC	Date		Varieties, remarks etc	R	L&S	Old ESC
2585	**1887**	Milled		C^2		296
2586	—	—	*Proof,* issued in the sets	R	74	297
2587	**1888**	—	Narrow date	S		298
2588	—	—	Wide date	S		298A
2589	**1889**	—		C^2		299
2590	**1890**	—		N		300
2591	**1891**	—		N		301
2592	**1892**	—		N		302

CROWNS

OLD HEAD

T.B.

| Obv. E | B.P. | Rev. 3 |

Obv.	**E.**	Old head; Coroneted, veiled and draped bust, left, wearing star and necklace
Rev.	**3.**	St. George slaying the dragon, hair streaming from beneath his helmet, date and initials **B.P.** in exergue
Edge	*a.*	**DECUS ET TUTAMEN ANNO REGNI** followed by the regnal year in Roman numerals, in raised letters.

E/3.   Old head / *Rev.* 3 – St. George and the dragon   Spink 3937

ESC	Date	Edge year		Varieties, remarks etc	R	L&S	Old ESC
2593	**1893**	**LVI**	(56)		*C*		303
2594	—	—	—	*Proof,* issued in the sets	*S*	109	304
2595	—	**LVII**	(57)		*R*		305
2596	**1894**	—	—		*S*		306
2597	—	**LVIII**	(58)		*S*		307
2598	**1895**	—	—		*S*		308
2599	—	**LIX**	(59)		*N*		309
2600	**1896**	—	—		*R*		310
2601	—	**LX**	(60)		*N*		311
2602	**1897**	—	—		*N*		312
2603	—	**LXI**	(61)		*C*		313
2604	**1898**	—	—		*R*		314
2605	—	**LXII**	(62)		*S*		315
2606	**1899**	—	—		*S*		316
2607	**1999**	**LXIII**	(63)		*S*		317
2608	**1900**	—	—		*S*		318
2609	**1900**	**LXIV**	(64)		*N*		319

Note, no crowns dated 1901 were issued

VICTORIA, 1837-1901
PATTERN CROWNS

'BONOMI PATTERN CROWN 1837'

This novel design by J. Bonomi was intended to protect the Royal portrait and legends from wear for as long as possible by being sunken below the field rather than in the traditional raised format, where the design and legend are the first to show wear in circulation. Another innovation was the reverse legend being at right angle and divided by Britannia. (NOT official Royal Mint issues, but since eagerly sought after by collectors when available are included in this publication) See Linecar & Stone, p. 76-80 for background information on these.

Type F/4a
Trial crown
<u>Design and
leg. in relief and
in mirror image</u>
Unfinished dies

ESC	Date	Type **F/4a** Comments	R	L&S	(Old ESC)
2610	**1837**	Designed by **J. Bonomi**. Dies sunk by **Theophilus Pinches** in 1893 for **Rochelle Thomas**[5] *Obv. & rev.* design and legend in relief, due to being in mirror fashion. *Obv.* Coroneted head right with no detail. *Rev.* Britannia standing left, holding Victory, no drapery detail, outline of shield only, no stars around circumference Plain edge. *In white metal. (Unique?)* wt. 38.40g*	R	4	321 B

   * *"Several uniface strikings of both obverse and reverse are recorded in Linecar and Stone the combination of both however escaped their notice. This is believed to be the only known specimen from both dies"* Mark Rasmussen, list 26/162, Summer 2014.
See also DNW 113, lot 229, 17 September 2013 for this same unique specimen.

Type F/4b
Design and
leg. incuse
Positive image
Semi-finished
dies

ESC	Date	Type **F/4b** Comments	R	L&S	(Old ESC)
2611	**1837**	*Obv.* As before but, only partially finished; no ear-ring, lacking hair detail and coronet ornamentation, with small stars around circumference, design and *leg.* incuse (sunken) as finished specimens *Rev.* Britannia standing right, holding Victory, drapery partially finished, as is the shield but, no stars around circumference. *In white metal. Edge.* Plain. *wt. 20.50g*	R^6	4	321A

Obv. F

Design and
leg. incuse
Positive image
Finished dies
F *rev.* design in relief

Rev. 4

Rev.5

PATTERN CROWNS

ESC	Date	Type **F/4** Comments	R	L&S	(Old ESC)
2612	**1837**	Finished dies. Design & *leg.* incuse; Coroneted head, left, with ear-ring, bun style hair, within an ornamented border of stars **VICTORIA REG DEI GRA** **18 37** below divided by truncation *Rev.* – Figure of Britannia as Minerva, standing, right, with trident holding Victory, half a shield showing behind with inscription **DECUS · ET · TUTAMEN** Vertical *leg.* across field reads **BRITT // MINERVA** behind Britannia and **VICTRIX // FID DEF** in front *In silver.* Weight inconsistent 3.076g-35.61g *Edge.* Plain but for a letter **T** followed by a number from 1-150 [5] (plus 2 for the Queen)	R^2	1	320
2613	—	*In gold (weight of 5 sovereigns)* (6 struck) (Numbered T1, T2, T3 T4, T5 & T6)	R^5	2	320A
2614	—	*In copper or bronze (numbered)* (10 struck)	R^4	3	321
2615	—	*In hard white metal (numbered)*	R^3	4	322
2616	—	*In white metal (no number)*	R^3	5	323
2617	—	*In tin (aluminium?) (no number)* (10 struck)	R^3	6	323a
2618	—	*In lead (pewter) (no number)*	R^3	7	324
2619	—	*In silver. Edge,* milled	R^5	8	325
2620	—	*In copper. Edge,* milled (10 struck)	R^3	9	326
2621	—	*In white metal. Edge,* milled	R^3	10	327
2622	—	*In lead. Edge,* milled	R^3	11	327A
2623	—	*In lead. Edge,* plain, thick flan	R^3	12	327B
2624	—	*In hard white metal,* thick flan *(numbered)*	R^3	12	327B

ESC	Date	Type **F/5** Comments	R	L&S	(Old ESC)
2625	—	*Obv.* F, as before but, with new *Rev.* **5.** – Royal arms with supporters, motto beneath; **DIEU ET MON DROIT** *'God and my right'* *In silver. Edge,* plain.	R^6	14A	328
2626	—	*In white metal. Edge,* plain	R^4	14	328A

VICTORIA, 1837-1901
PATTERN CROWNS

'UNA AND THE LION'
(This design was finally adopted for the gold Five-pound piece)
The following descriptions and table of numbers, L&S 15-33,
are by Linecar & Stone, pp. 81-3

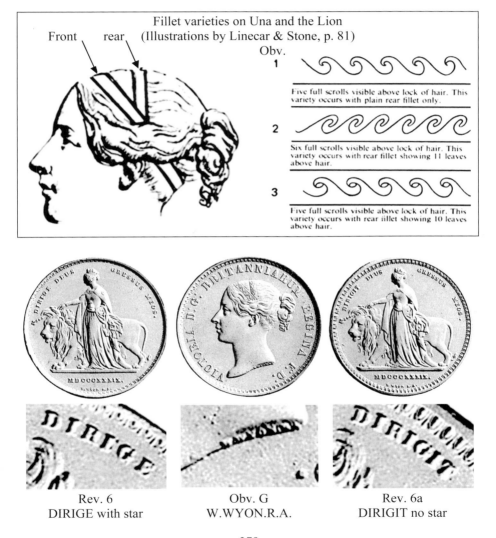

Fillet varieties on Una and the Lion
Front   rear   (Illustrations by Linecar & Stone, p. 81)

Obv.

1

Five full scrolls visible above lock of hair. This variety occurs with plain rear fillet only.

2

Six full scrolls visible above lock of hair. This variety occurs with rear fillet showing 11 leaves above hair.

3

Five full scrolls visible above lock of hair. This variety occurs with rear fillet showing 10 leaves above hair.

Rev. 6
DIRIGE with star

Obv. G
W.WYON.R.A.

Rev. 6a
DIRIGIT no star

VICTORIA, 1837-1901
PATTERN CROWNS

Obv. **G.** Small youg head of Queen Victoria facing left, surrounded by the legen d **VICTORIA D:G: BRITANIARUM REGINA F: D:** The Queen's hair is tied in two fillets; (L&S 1, 2 or 3)

Rev. Queen victoria standing facing left, representing Una, leading the British lion. The legend **DIRGE DEUS GRESSUS MEOS** *'May the Lord guide my footsteps'* . In the exurgue date and signature **MDCCCXXXIX** in Roman numerals and **W.WYON.R.A.** below The Queen is wearing the robes of the Garter with the star showing on her left arm near her shoulder. She is holding the orb in her left hand and the sceptre in her right hand.

Reverse varieties:
A. **(6).** As type description, **DIRIGE** and Garter star
B. **(6a).** As type description, **DIRIGIT** minus the Garter star

Edge varieties
U. Plain
V. **DECUS ET TUTAMEN ❋ ANNO REGNI TERTIO ❋** in large letters, in some cases overlapping edge of coin. Rose stops in line with bottom edge of lettering
W. **DECUS ET TUTAMEN ❋ ANNO REGNI TERTIO ❋** in small lettering between "wire edge" raised rims. Rose stops in centre of lettering.
X. As W but slightly off centre, giving raised edge on obverse side
Y. Incusely inscribed **PATTERN FOR A FIVE POUND PIECE**

Die positions, thickness and diameter
All the British Museums specimens have been inspected; the die positions are ↑↑ and the thickness is 2.3 mm. The diameter is 38 mm.

Table of Pattern Five pound pieces & Crowns
See Remarks and References pages 82-3

ESC	L&S	Metal	Obv.	Rev.	Edge	Remarks and References
2627	15	Gold	1	B	V	Old ESC 331. *R⁷* *wt.39.267g*
2628	16	Gold	1	B	U	B.M. specimen *wt.39.252g*
2629	17	Gold	2	A	W	B.M. specimen *wt.38.834g*
2630	18	Gold	3	A	W	B.M. specimen *wt.39.209g*
2631	19	Silver	2	A	U	Thin flan *wt.22.455g*
2632	19A	Silver	2	A	U	Normal flan

(continued)

380

PATTERN CROWNS

2633	20	Silver	3	A	X	B.M.col. *wt.29.257g* ^{Old ESC 332 *R7*}
2634	21	Copper	2	A	U	
2635	22	Copper	2	A	Y	
2636	23	Silver	3	A	W	
2637	24	Aluminium	3	A	W	*(2 known)*
2638	25	Tin	3	A	W	On a large flan
2639	26	Silver	3	A	U	Old ESC 331A. *R7*
2640	27	Pewter	2	B	U	
2641	28	Gold	1	B	V	Old ESC 330 *R7*
2642	29	Silver	1	B	V	Old ESC 29 *R7*
2643	30	White metal	3	A	U	
2644	31	Silver	2	B	X	
2645	32	Gold	3	A	U	Old ESC 331. *R7*
2646	33	White metal	2	B	U	

Obv. H   DIRIGE   Rev. 6

Hair flows down

ESC	Date	Type **H/6** Comments	R	L&S	(Old ESC)
2647	**1839**	By **W. Wyon**, dated **1839** obverse *Obv.* **H**, similar to G, but larger bust, and different curls in the hair, decorated fillets as before; front fillet leaning to the right **W.WYON.R.A.**in relief on truncation Small Arabic date **1839** below **VICTORIA DEI GRATIA** *Rev.* **6** – As before; **DIRIGE** etc. and star *Edge.* Plain	R^6	34	333

(continued)

PATTERN CROWNS

ESC	Date	Type **H/6** Comments	R	L&S	(Old ESC)
2648	**1839**	*In gold.*	R^7	35	334
2649	—	*In silver on a thin flan weighing 320 grains Edge,* inscribed (presumably **DECVS** etc.) but only faintly visible in parts	R^7	16	332

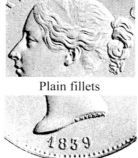

Plain fillets

Obv. I

Rev. 1

ESC	Date	Type **I/1** Comments	R	L&S	(Old ESC)
2650	**1839**	Smaller bust of the Queen, left, with two plain fillets **W. WYON. R.A.** in relief on truncation. Large Arabic date **1839** below **VICTORIA DEI GRATIA.** Legend starts opposite the queen's chin *Rev.* **1** - As adopted currency crowns of 1844, 1845 and 1847; Crowned shield of arms surrounded by branches of laurel with a floral emblem of a rose, shamrock and thistle below. Legend **• BRITANNIARUM REGINA FID: DEF: •** with rose type stops before and after legend *Edge,* plain	R^7	37	335

ESC	Date	Type **J/1** Comments	R	L&S	(Old ESC)
2651	**1839**	As the adopted proof of **1839**, but head much larger with smaller lettering. **1** - As adopted coin. *Edge,* plain *(Not traced)*	R^7		336

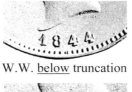

W.W. <u>below</u> truncation

W.WYON.R.A.
on truncation

Obv. K
Large date

Obv. L
Date Smaller than normal

Small bust
Fine hair small bun style

Rev. 1a
Similar to currency
minus rose stops

Large bust
Plait in large bun style

ESC	Date	Type **K/1a**	Comments	*R*	L&S	(Old ESC)
2652	**1844**	By **W. Wyon**, date **1844**		R^7	39	337
		Obv. **K.** Very small bust of Queen Victoria, left, hair tied with two plain fillets, **W.W.** in relief below truncation, legend small lettering **VICTORIA DEI GRATIA** date **1844** in large figures below Letter **I** in **VICTORIA** in line with her mouth *Rev.* **1a.** - As adopted coin 1 above, but minus the rose type stops before and after legend *Edge,* Plain				

(continued

PATTERN CROWNS

ESC	Date	Type **L/1a** Comments	R	L&S	(Old ESC)
2653	**1844** **VIII**	As currency issue, but date in smaller figures below, **W.WYON.R.A.** in relief on truncation Letter **T** in **VICTORIA** in line with mouth *Rev.* **1** - As adopted coin, with rose stops **DECUS ET TUTAMEN** (cinquefoil) **ANNO REGNI VIII** (cinquefoil) *(7 strings)*	R^7	40	338
2654	—	**DECUS ET TUTAMEN ANNO REGNI VIII** (Star stops)	R^6		
2655	**1845** **IX**	As before, but dated **1845.** *Edge.* **DECUS ET TUTAMEN ANNO REGNI IX** (9)	R^6		338A

Obv. M

W.WYON.R.A.

Rev. 1

ESC	Date	Type **M/1.** With plain edges	R	L&S	(Old ESC)
2656	**1845**	By **W. Wyon**, dated **1845** As the current coin, **W.WYON.R.A.** in relief on truncation, but smaller date and lettering, struck on a larger thinner flan. Letter **T** in **VICTORIA** in line with her upper lip Rev. **1** - As adopted coin. *Edge,* plain	R^6		
2657	—	As before, but there is a broad margin at the edge of the coin thus making the piece slightly larger in diameter	R^4	43	339
2658	—	As before, but struck on a heavy flan	R^6	49	
2659	—	*In gold* *WR 367 wt. 39.87*	R^7	44	339A

(continued)

384

PATTERN CROWNS

ESC	Date	Type **M/1.** With edge legend	*R*	L&S	(Old ESC)
2660	**1845 VIII**	Edge, **DECUS ET TUTAMEN ANNO REGNI VIII** (8) with cinquefoil stops	R^6	47	340
2661	—	As before but, edge legend incuse *wt.8.16g*	R^6	46	283
2662	**1845 IX**	*As before* but, regnal year 9, faintly inscribed **DECUS ET TUTAMEN ANNO REGNI IX**	R^7	48	340A

'GOTHIC CROWN'

Plain bodice
over shoulder

Obv. N   Rev. 2 - mɒcccxlvi
(1846)

ESC	Date	Type **N/2.** Comments	*R*	L&S	(Old ESC)
2663	**1846**	By **W. Wyon**, dated **1846** (unfrosted) *Obv.* **N**. As the 'Gothic' crown of 1847, but the Queen's bodice is plain below the border over her left shoulder *Rev.* **2.** – 👑 **tueatur** 👑 **unita** 👑 **deus anno dom** 👑 **mɒcccxlvi** *'May God guard these United'* *(Kingdoms)* *Edge*, plain	R^4	56	3 41
2664	—	Bust and the whole of reverse frosted	R^4		341A

PATTERN CROWNS

Decorated bodice

Obv. C

Rev. 2 - ᴍᴅᴄᴄᴄxʟᴠíí
(1847)

ESC	Date	Type **C/2.** As currency issue	R	L&S	(Old ESC)
2665	—	*Cliché of obverse on a thin copper blank*	R^6	64	
2666	—	*Cliché of reverse on a thin copper blank*	R^6	65	
2667	—	*Cliché of reverse in lead*	R^6	66	

W.WYON.R.A.

Obv. B

Rev. 1

ESC	Date	Type **B/1.** As currency issue, plain edge	R	L&S	(Old ESC)
2668	**1879**	By **W. Wyon**, dated **1845** *Obv.* **B.** As the currency coin, but not struck for circulation, **W.WYON.R.A.** in relief on truncation, small date *Rev.* **1** - As adopted coin *Edge,* plain *(3 known)*	R^6	71	295

PATTERN CROWNS

B.P.

Obv. O
(Unsigned)

Rev. 3

ESC	Date	Type **O/3.** Comments	R	L&S	(Old ESC)
2669	**1888**	**By L.C. Wyon**	R^6	99	357
		Obv. **O.** Large coroneted bust draped and veiled, left, wearing a necklace and earring, initials **L.C.W.** on truncation **VICTORIA D:G: BRITT : REG : F:D:** *Rev.* **3** - Pistrucci's St George and dragon, hair streaming from beneath helmet. Date **1888** in exergue *Edge.* Milled *(3 known)*			
2670	—	As before, but unsigned on truncation	R^7	100	

No illustration available for reverse 4

ESC	Date	Type **O/4.** Comments	R	L&S	(Old ESC)
2671	**1890**	**By L.C. Wyon**	R^7	101	358
		Obv. **O.** As before - Large coroneted bust *Rev.* **4** – Smaller St George and Dragon With value **FIVE SHILLINGS** above Date **1890** in exergue *Edge.* Milled *(Unique)*			

PATTERN CROWNS

No illustration available for
reverse 4

Rev. D

ESC	Date	Type **D/4.**	R	L&S	(Old ESC)
2672	**1890**	By **Joseph Edgar Boehm**, As currency crown D (Jubilee head type) with initials **J.E.B.** on truncation *Rev.* **4** –Smaller St George and Dragon, value **FIVE SHILLINGS** above Date **1890** in exergue *Edge.* Milled *(Unique)*	R^7	102	359

Obv. P

ESC	Date	Type **P/3.** Comments	R	L&S	(Old ESC)
2673	(1894)	By **Alexander Kirkwood** (Edinburgh) Undated uniface obverse. *Edge.* Plain Veiled bust left, small crown perched on top **VICTORIA : D : G : BRITT:REG:F:D:** *Rev.* Plain, but for wording in three lines **DESIGN / FOR / CROWN PIECE**	R^5	110	

PATTERN CROWNS

Obv. Q   REG   Rev. 3

No initials below

ESC	Date	Type **Q/3.** Comments	R	L&S	(Old ESC)
2674	**1892** **LVI**	By **T. Brock** initials T.B. omitted As the currency crown of 1893, but legend reads **REG** not REGINA *Rev.* **3** - Pistrucci's St George and dragon Date **1892** in exergue *Edge,* **DECUS ♔ ET TUTAMEN ♔ ANNO REGNI ♔ LVI** (56)	R^7	106	360
2675	—	Uniface obverse *in lead*	R^7		

Obv. R   Lis below B (pattern R)   cf. Lis over B (currency)

ESC	Date	Type **R/-.** Comments	R	L&S	(Old ESC)
2676	(1893)	Uniface obverse. *In lead* As currency crowns, but the lis in the Queen's crown does not cut the B in BRITT	R^7	107	360A

VICTORIA, 1837-1901
PATTERN CROWNS

The following group of coins were produced by **J. Rochelle Thomas for Spink & Sons Ltd in 1887** (therefore NOT official Royal Mint issues, but since eagerly sought after by collectors when available are included in this publication)

The following information is taken from Linecar & Stone, p. 93-4

Rev. 1 (Spink)

Type S (Spink)   Spink   & Son   Rev. 1a (Spink)

Obv. **Spink.** Bust of Queen Victoria facing three-quarters left, wearing a richly ornamented dress and veil, surmounted by a small crown, surrounded by the legend + **VICTORIA · BY · THE · GRACE · OF · GOD · QUEEN · OF · GREAT · BRITAIN · EMP · OF · INDIA** There is an outer circle with a floral motif

Rev. **1 (Spink)** The Royal Arms and supporters with **FIVE SHILLINGS** above and the date **MDCCCLXXXVII** (87) below. A floral motif is placed below the date. The whole is surrounded by an outer circle as on the obverse

Obv. 1. As type, but with plain truncation
        2. As type, but with **J.R.T.** on truncation
        3. As type, but with **SPINK & SON** on truncation

Rev. A. As type
        B. As type, but **SPINK & SON** added on reverse below the date

Edge a. Plain
        b. Milled
        c. Has words **MADE IN BAVARIA**

390

PATTERN CROWNS

ESC	L&S	Metal	Obv.	Rev.	Edge	(Old ESC)	Remarks and References
2677	75	Gold	1	B	a	347 R^5	*(6 struck) wt.746 grains*
2678	76	Gold	1	B	b	353 R^5	*(6 struck) wt.753grains*
2679	77	Gold	1	B	c	347 R^5	
2680	78	Silver	1	A	a	343 R^5	
2681	79	Silver	2	A	a	343 R^5	
2682	80	Silver	3	A	a	344 R^3	*(32 struck)*
2683	81	Silver	1	B	c	346 R^2	
2684	82	Silver	1	B	b	352 R^4	
2685	83	Copper	1	B	c	348 R^5	*(5 struck)*
2686	84	Bronze	1	B	a	348 R^5	*(5 struck)*
2687	85	Bronze	1?	B	c	348 R^5	
2688	86	Tin	1	B	c	348 R^5	
2689	87	Aluminium	1	B	a	349 R^5	*(10 = Total together*
2690	88	Aluminium	1	B	c	349 R^5	*struck in aluminium)*
2691	89	White metal	1	B	c	350 R^4	
2962	90	Pewter	1	B	a	350 R^4	
2693	91	Lead	1	B	a	351 R^4	
2694	92	Lead	2	B	b	351 R^4	

95 & 96 *"Numbers reserved for other Specimens which may exist"* (L&S)

DOUBLE FLORINS

J.E.B.

Arabic 1

Roman I

Second
I in VICTORIA*

1888
Full serifs

1889
Trace of
lower left serif

1888 & 1889
Lower left serif missing*
'Inverted I in VICTORIA'

*This variety is almost certainly the result of a filled die as, demonstrated with these illustrations, but since collectors like to own an example it is retained as a variety (A. Barr's specimens)

	Jubilee bust, left, **J.E.B.** on truncation (Joseph Edgar Boehm)
Leg.	**VICTORIA DEI GRATIA**
Rev.	Crowned cruciform shields, Garter star in centre, four sceptres in the angles. Outer beaded circle.
Leg.	**REG: 18 ♛ 87 FID: ♛ DEF: ♛ BRITT: ♛**
	Edge, milled

DOUBLE FLORINS

		Roman date		Spink 3922	
ESC	Date	Varieties, remarks, etc.	R	L&S	(Old ESC)
2695	**1887**		C		394
2696	—	*Proof*	R	97	394A

		Arabic date		Spink 3923	
2697	**1887**		C^2		395
2698	—	*Proof, issued in sets*	S	98	396
2699	**1888**		N		397
2700	—	Second **I** in **VICTORIA** inverted?	N		397A
2701	**1889**		C		398
2702	—	Second **I** in **VICTORIA** inverted?	C		398A
2703	**1890**		N		399

PATTERN

2704	**1890**	**By L.C. Wyon, 1890** Obverse as the currency coin *Rev.* Crowned cruciform shields, Garter star at centre, sceptres in angles, within beaded border *Leg* ♛ **DOUBLE** ♛ **FLORIN** ♛ sprig **18** ♛ **90** sprig Sprigs; rose, thistle and shamrock *Edge.* Milled	R^7	103	400
2705	—	Uniface reverse as illustration. *Edge,* plain	R^7		400B

DOUBLE FLORINS

PATTERN
Not struck in silver
Recorded for interest sake

 Gold

xxxx	**1868**	**Decimal trial, 1868**		R^5	401
	Obv	Coroneted bust left, hair tied with ribbon			
	Leg	**VICTORIA D:G: BRITANNIAR:REG:F:D:**			
	Rev	**DOUBLE** // **FLORIN** // **1868** within wreath			
		5 FRANCS // **INTERNATIONAL** surrounding			
	Edge	Milled. *In gold*	*wt. 1·62g*		
xxxx	—	Plain. *In gold* *W&R 372* *wt. 1·56g*		R^6	401A

HALFCROWNS

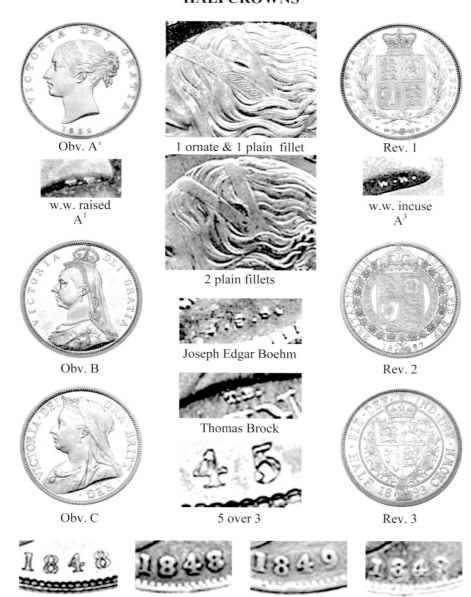

Obv. A¹

1 ornate & 1 plain fillet

Rev. 1

w.w. raised
A¹

w.w. incuse
A³

2 plain fillets

Obv. B

Joseph Edgar Boehm

Rev. 2

Thomas Brock

Obv. C

5 over 3

Rev. 3

1848 over 6

8 over 7

9 over 7

Small date

HALFCROWNS

Type   **A¹.**   Young head, left, one ornate and one plain fillet binding hair
            W.W. in relief on truncation (William Wyon)   (ESC. A¹)

Leg.   **VICTORIA DEI GRATIA** date below

      A².   Similar, but two ornate fillets   (ESC. A²)
      A³.   Similar, but two plain fillets   (ESC. A²/³)
      A⁴.   Similar, as last, but **W.W.** incuse   (ESC. A³)
      A⁵.   Similar to last, but no initials on truncation   (ESC. A⁴)
      A⁶.   Similar, but slightly coarser workmanship ¹   (ESC. A⁵)

      B.   Jubilee head. Tall bust, left, draped and veiled with a small crown
           J.E.B. on truncation (Joseph Edgar Boehm)

Leg.   **VICTORIA DEI GRATIA**

      C.   Old head. Large coroneted bust, left, veiled and draped

Leg.   **VICTORIA · DEI   GRA · BRITT · REG ·**

Rev.   **1.**   Crowned square-topped shield within laurel branches
            Thistle, rose and shamrock spray below.

Leg.   **REGINA FID: DEF: BRITANNIARUM**

Rev.   **2.**   Crowned square-topped shield within Garter and collar of the
            Order of the Garter. Date below divided by the George

Leg.   **REGINA FID: DEF: BRITANNIARUM**

Rev.   **3.**   Crowned spade-shaped shield within collar of the Garter.
Leg.   **· FID · DEF · IND · IMP ·**
          HALF 18 (the George) **93 CROWN**

      A¹/1.   **Young head, 1 ornate & 1 plain fillet, W.W. in relief** (ESC. A¹)
            Rev. 1 - Crowned square-topped shield   Spink 3885

ESC	Date	Varieties		R	(Old ESC)
2706	**1839**			R⁴	668
2707	**1839**	*Proof*	*wt. 14.11g*	R³	669
2708	**1839**	*Proof. Edge,* plain. Issued in sets	*wt. 13.51g*	S	670

HALFCROWNS

A²/1. Young head, **2 ornate fillets**, W.W. in relief (ESC. A²)
Rev. 1 - Crowned square-topped shield Spink 3886

2709	1839	*Proof or pattern. Edge,* plain	*(Not traced)*	R^4	671

A³/1. Young head, **2 plain fillets**, W.W. in relief (ESC. A²′³)
Rev. 1 - Crowned square-topped shield Spink 3886A

2710	1839	*Proof. Edge,* plain	*(Not traced)*	R^5	671A

A⁴/1. Young head, 2 plain fillets, **W.W. incuse** (ESC. A³)
Rev. 1 - Crowned square-topped shield Spink 3887

2711	1839			R^4	672
2712	—	*Proof*	*wt. 14.11g*	R^4	672A
2713	—	*Proof. Edge,* plain	*wt. 13.96g*	R^3	672B
2714	—	*Underweight flan (is this a genuine R.M. issue?)* (8 strings)		S	672C
2715	1840		*(8 strings)*	S	673

A⁵/1. Young head, 2 plain fillets. **No initials** on truncation (ESC. A⁴)
Rev. 1 - Crowned square-topped shield Spink 3888

2716	1841			R^3	674
2717	1842		*(7 strings)*	N	675
2718	1843			R	676
2719	—	**3 over 3**?		R	676A
2720	1844	(**4**s either with or without serifs)	*(8 strings)*	N	677
2721	—	Struck without a collar on large flan		R^4	678
2722	1845		*(7 strings)*	N	679
2723	—	**5 over 3**		$R^?$	679A
2724	1846			S	680
2725	—	**8 over 6**		R	680A
2726	1848	Date not altered from 1846 ²		R^3	681
2727	—	First **8 over 6**	*(7 strings)*	R^2	681A
2728	—	Last **8 over 6**		R^2	681B
2729	—	Last **8 over 7**		$R^?$	681C
2730	1849	Large date		S	682
2731	1849	Large date **9 over 7**		R	682A
2732	—	Small date		R	683
2733	1850			S	684
2734	—	*Proof*		R^4	685
2735	1851	*Does this date exist?*	*(Not traced)*	?	?
2736	1853	*Proof only.* Issued in sets	*wt. 14.13g (8 strings)*	R^3	687

HALFCROWNS

A¹/1. **Young head, 1 ornate & 1 plain fillet, W.W. in relief** (ESC. A¹)
Rev. 1 - Crowned square-topped shield Spink 3885

ESC	Date	Varieties	R	(Old ESC)
2737	**1862**	*Proof or pattern only*	R^5	688
2738	—	*Proof. Edge,* plain ↑↑ *weights vary 13.98g - 14.10g*	R^2	689
2739	**1864**	*Proof en medaille* ↑↑ *Edge,* milled ³ *wt. 14.06g*	R^2	690
2740	—	*Proof. Edge,* plain ³ *wt. 14.04g*	R^2	691

A⁶/1. Young head, plain fillets, no initials, inferior workmanship
Rev. 1 - Crowned square-topped shield (ESC. A⁵) Spink 3888

ESC	Date	Varieties	R	(Old ESC)
2741	**1874**	See note ⁴	N	692
2742	—	*Proof* *(Not traced)*	R^4	693
2743	—	*Proof* with plain edge	R^5	694
2744	—	*Proof In gold*	R^7	695
2745	**1875**		N	696
2746	—	*Proof en medaille* ↑↑ *wt. 13.99g*	R^3	697
2747	—	*Proof or pattern,* with plain edge ⁵ *(Not traced)*	R^7	698
2748	**1876**		S	699
2749	—	**6 over 5**	R^2	699A
2750	**1877**		S	700
2751	**1878**		S	701
2752	—	*Proof en medaille* ↑↑ *wt. 14.11g*	R^4	702
2753	**1879**		R	703
2754	**1879**	*Proof en medaille* ↑↑ *wt. 14.11g*	R^4	704
2755	—	*Proof* with plain edge *en medaille* ↑↑	R^5	704A
2756	**1880**		S	705
2757	—	*Proof en medaille* ↑↑ *wt. 14.11g*	R^4	706
2758	**1881**		N	707
2759	—	*Proof en medaille* ↑↑ *wt. 14.15g*	R^3	708
2760	—	*Proof,* with plain edge *(Not traced)*	R^7	709
2761	**1882**		N	710
2762	**1883**		N	711
2763	—	*Proof or pattern, en medaille* ↑↑ plain edge *14.12g*	R^6	711A
2764	**1884**		S	712
2765	**1885**		N	713
2766	—	*Proof en medaille* ↑↓ *wt. 14.11g*	R^3	714

(continued)

HALFCROWNS

ESC	Date	Varieties		R	(Old ESC)
2767	**1886**			N	715
2768	—	*Proof*	*(Not traced)*	R^7	716
2769	**1887**			N	717
2770	—	*Proof en medaille* ↑↑	*wt. 14.10g*	R^5	718

B/2.   Jubilee head
Rev. 2 - Crowned shield within Garter and collar   Spink 3924

2771	**1887**		C^3	719
2772	—	*Proof,* issued in the sets	S	720
2773	**1888**		N	721
2774	**1889**		S	722
2775	**1890**		S	723
2776	**1891**		S	724
2777	**1892**		S	725

C/3.   Old veiled head
Rev. 3 - Spade-shaped shield in collar of the Garter   Spink 3938

2778	**1893**		C	726
2779	—	*Proof,* issued in the sets	N	727
2780	**1894**		S	728
2781	**1895**		N	729
2782	**1896**		S	730
2783	**1897**		N	731
2784	**1898**		S	732
2785	**1899**		N	733
2786	**1900**		C	734
2787	**1901**		N	735

1   Dr G. Bullmore pointed out that there are really two types of A^5. The early coins show a narrower space between DEI and GRATIA and REGINA and FID; also the crown over shield is narrower. The back of the hair is slightly finer style. Dr Bullmore also indicates that the 1868 coins show all the features of post 1879 A^5 coins and suggests they were unofficial coins made perhaps in 1887 when the dies became obsolete on the introduction of the 1887 Jubilee issue. The official view expressed by the Royal Mint now is that the coins are all very clever forgeries, struck from false dies, probably around the turn of the century from Germany; they are all light weight and struck in silver around ·915 fine instead of ·925.

2   The obverse lettering on this die is irregularly spaced

3   Struck for the foundation ceremony of the Albert Memorial

HALFCROWNS

4   No halfcrowns for the U.K. were struck between 1850 and 1874. At various times, however, examples have been seen dated 1866, 1868 & 1871. A specimen dated 1861 brought £115 at a sale in the North in 1967, in about 'fair' condition. Also a coin sent in from Eire, although in very poor condition clearly showed the date, 1861. This was almost certainly a coin of type A^5. Three examples dated 1868 have been seen. One of these had a very broad second 8 in date. One specimen of 1871 was also seen. It would seem that 1861, 1866 and 1871 coins are extremely rare, but coins of 1868 are less rare than was at first thought (see note [1]) Graham Dyer, Librarian and Curator of the Royal Mint Collection, has researched these coins and proved them to have been struck from false dies in German around 1887. He confirms they are all of type A^5, and if the dates were genuine, they should be of type A^4.

5   A piece in the 'Nobleman' (Ferrari) Sale, ex Murdoch collection which H.A. Seaby catalogued; *'As the current coin but from a different die; believed to be a unique pattern from a die which fractured and was discarded'*

PATTERNS

Type D^1 Type D^2

ESC	Date	Varieties			R	(Old ESC)
2788	1839	**D^1** *Obv*	By **W. Wyon, 1839** below bust As current coin, but much smaller head with plain fillets, large date below; perhaps from the punch made for the halfpenny		R^6	736
		Edge	Plain			

2789	1839	**D^2**	Similar, but one ornamented fillet only		R^7	736A
		Edge	Plain	*(2 known)*		
2790	—	—	Similar. *Edge,* milled		R^6	737

HALFCROWNS

PATTERNS

Type E   Type F

ESC	Date	Varieties			R	(Old ESC)
2791	**1875**	**E**	By **W. Wyon** and **Pistrucci, dated 1875**		R^7	738
		Obv	As type A^5 (date both sides) *en medaille*↑↑			
		Leg.	**VICTORIA DEI GRATIA**			
		Rev	Pistrucci's St George and Dragon, date			
			1875 in exergue.			
			Edge, plain	*wt. 13.76g*		

2792	**1875**	**F**	By **L.C. Wyon**? and **Pistrucci**, dated **1875**		R^6	739
		Obv	Coroneted head, left, *en medaille* ↑↑			
		Leg	**VICTORIA DEI GRATIA**			
			BRITANNIAR: REG: F: D :			
		Rev	Pistrucci's St George and Dragon,			
			date **1875** in exergue.			
			Edge, plain	*wt. 13.72g*		

Type G

HALFCROWNS

ESC	Date		Varieties	R	(Old ESC)
2793	**1876**	**G**	**By L.C. Wyon, 1876**	R^5	740
		Obv	Coroneted head, left. **L.C.W.** below.		
		Leg	**VICTORIA D: G:**		
			BRITANNIAR: REG: F: D :		
		Rev	A fine equestrian figure of St George in		
			crested helmet about to transfix the		
			dragon, which is depicted unusually large,		
			ground beneath, no legend, **L.C.W.** below		
		Edge	Plain. *En medaille* ↑↑ *wt. 13.98g*		
2794	—	—	*In gold* 3 examples in the Royal Mint Collection	R^6	741
			respective weights: 15.63g; 15.68g & 15.73g		(WR 375)

PATTERNS
(C. Adam's sale[6])

Type H[1]/1

2795	**1884**	**H[1]**	**By L.C. Wyon (?), 1884** *(Unique?)*	R^7	742
			33mm flan. Necklace of 12 pearls		
		Obv	Similar to adopted issues, but smaller crown		
			above veiled bust, and no initials below bust		
			In small lettering, beaded border		
		Leg	**VICTORIA D:G: ♛ BRITT:REG:F:D:**		
		Rev	**1 -** Similar to currency issues, but smaller		
			square- topped shield and crown, the		
			George below facing <u>right</u>, divides date		
			in large lettering, toothed border		
		Leg	**BRITANNIARUM ♛ REGINA**		
			FID: DEF: 18 84		
			Edge. Milled. *En medaille* ↑↑ *wt. 14.11g*		
2796	—	—	*Edge.* Plain *(Some are hand numbered 1-12)*	R^7	742A

HALFCROWNS

PATTERNS

H²   2   H³

H⁴   H⁵   H⁶

ESC	Date	Varieties		R	(Old ESC)
2797	**1884**	**H²**	32mm flan. Necklace of 11 pearls	R²	742B
		Obv	Similar, but with medium lettering,		
			no stops, toothed border (both sides)		
		Leg	**VICTORIA ♔ DEI GRATIA**		
		Rev	**2 -** Baroque style shield encircled by		
			Garter and also collar of the Order.		
			The George below <u>facing left</u> divides date		
		Leg	**BRITANNIARUM ♔ REGINA**		
			FID:DEF: 18 **84** larger lettering		
		Edge	Milled. *En medaille* ↑↑ *wt. 13.72g*		
2798	—	—	Plain. *En medaille* ↑↑ *wt. 13.95g*	R⁷	742C

2799	**1884**	**H³**	As before, with large lettering (no stops)	R²	742D
		Leg	**VICTORIA DEI ♔ GRATIA**		
		Edge	Milled. *En medaille* ↑↑ *wt. 14.06g*		
2800	—	—	Plain. *En medaille* ↑↑ *wt. 14.06g*	R⁷	742E

HALFCROWNS

2801	**1884**	**H⁴**	As before, with large lettering (no stops)	$R^?$	742F
		Leg	**VICTORIA 👑 DEI GRATIA**		
		Edge	Milled. *En medaille* ↑↑		
2802	—	—	Plain. *En medaille* ↑↑	R^7	742G

2803	**1884**	**H⁵**	As before, with large lettering, one stop ↑↑	R^7	742H
		Leg	**VICTORIA · 👑 DEI GRATIA**		
		Edge	Milled. Note, stop after **VICTORIA ·**		-
2804	—	—	Plain. *En medaille* ↑↑ *wt.13.64g*	R^7	742I

2805	**1884**	**H⁶**	As before, with large lettering, one stop ↑↑	$R^?$	742J
		Leg	**VICTORIA 👑 DEI GRATIA.**		
		Edge	Milled. Note, stop after **GRATIA.** *wt.13.86g*		
2806	—	—	Plain. *En medaille* ↑↑ *wt.14.06g*	R^7	742K

I¹

J

2807	**1890**	**I**	By **Boehm** and **L.C. Wyon** (?), **1890**	R^7	743
		Obv	As ordinary Jubilee issue.		
		Rev	Square-topped shield, crowned and heraldically shaded within the Garter and also the collar of the Order, date below		
		Leg	**HALF 👑 CROWN 18 90**		
			George below <u>facing right</u>, divides date		
		Edge	Milled		
2808	—	—	Plain	R^7	743A
2809	—	—	Plain. Uniface reverse	R^7	743B

2810	**1890**	**J**	Diademed head of the Queen.	R^7	744
		Rev	As before *(Not traced)*		

HALFCROWNS

PATTERNS

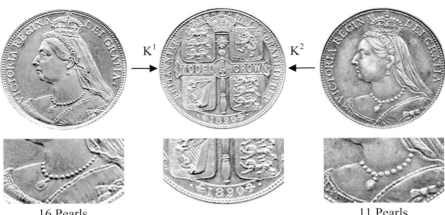

K^1 K^2

16 Pearls   11 Pearls

ESC	Date	Varieties		R	(Old ESC)
2811	**1890**	**K^1**	**By P.T.B., 1890**	R^4	745
		Obv	Head rather like the Jubilee type, but bust viewed more from the front. Necklace of 16 pearls. Faint initials **P.T.B.** below to the left of ribbon		
		Rev	Crown above four shields divided by sceptre and **MODEL ½ CROWN** below.		
		Leg	**BRITANNIAR: ˙REG˙♛ ˙ DEI˙ ˙GRAT:FID:DEF // ˙♣ 1890 ♣ ˙**		
		Edge	Plain. *En medaille* ↑↑ *wt. 14.03g* *In copper silvered* (full halfcrown size)		
2812	—	—	*In copper* on a thick flan. ↑↑ *wt. 19.77g*	R^4	745A

2813	**1890**	**K^2**	**By F.B., 1890**	R^5	745B
		Obv	Similar to 'K', but necklace of 11 pearls, and initials **F.B.** to right of ribbon.		
		Rev	As before.		
		Edge	Plain. *En medaille* ↑↑ *wt. 16.60g* *In copper silvered.*		

HALFCROWNS

PATTERNS

ESC	Date	Varieties		R	(Old ESC)
2814	**189-**	*Rev.*	**3** – Uniface, as current issue, *in lead* Date unfinished	R^7	
		Leg.	**· FID · DEF · IND · IMP ·** **HALF 18** (the George) **9 CROWN**		
		Obv.	Plain, but with inked words ***Single beads***		

6   Full details of this large series of rare 1884 patterns above, see the Colin Adams Collection Spink Auction 177, 2005/12/1, and page 203

FLORINS

"GODLESS"
D:G (DEI GRATIA) omitted from Queen's titles
3 pearls on central arch

Reverse 1
Central rose

Obverse A1 – w.w.
No inner circle (Pattern)

Reverse 2
Floriated cross

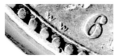

Obverse A2 – w.w.
With inner circle

A3 – trace of w w
With inner circle

A4 – (no w w)
With inner circle

GOTHIC DATES

No stop after

With a stop after

With a colon after

VICTORIA, 1837-1901
FLORINS

trefoil between **t :**

trefoil between **t .**

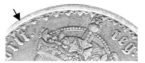

trefoil between **t .**

Obv. B1 & B2
brit: w w
(No die number)
48 trefoils 10 below

Obv. B3
brit. w w
(No die number)
48 trefoils 10 below

Obv. B4
brit. w w
With **die number**
48 trefoils 10 below

VARIETIES OF THE QUEEN'S CROWN

B
1851-1879, 1887
14 pearls on thin arches
8 pearls in centre of cross
3½ pearls on central arch

C
1877-1879
14 pearls on thick arches
8 pearls in centre of cross
5 pearls on central arch
(42 arcs)

D
1880-1886
14 pearls on thin arches
7 pearls in centre of cross
4½ pearls on central arch
(34 arcs)

VICTORIA, 1837-1901
FLORINS

trefoil between **t :**

t : between 2 trefoils

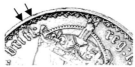

t : between 2 trefoils

B5 & B6
brit: w w
With **die number**
48 trefoils 10 below

B7
britt: w w
(No die number)
48 trefoils 10 below

B7 error
britt: w w
(No die number)
48 trefoils 10 below

1858

Widely spaced **ɾ ɾ ɾ**

Narrowly spaced **ɾɾɾ**

1885

Large trefoil on short arcs

Small trefoil on long arcs

409

FLORINS

 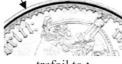 

t : between 2 trefoils	trefoil to :	trefoil to :

Obv. B8	Obv. C1 & C2	Obv. C3
britt: w w.	**britt:** (No ww)	**britt:**
With **die number**	With **die number**	(No ww or die number)
48 trefoils 10 below	**41 trefoils** 9 below	**41 trefoils** 9 below

un over **nu** in **pound**	**c** for **e** in **one**	**n** over **n** inverted	**m** over **m** inverted

Davies A
(Small design)

Davies B
(Large design)

The larger reverse design was introduced in 1868
The earlier small design was discontinued after 1872

Note; Reverse A in 1870 is R3, only known on die 4 at the present time
Minor variations of 2nd reverse are ignored to avoid complication (see Davies p.54)

VICTORIA, 1837-1901
FLORINS

trefoil to **t**

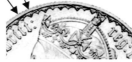

t : between 2 trefoils

No illustration

t : between 2 trefoils

No illustration
Available of E1

Obv. D1
britt:
(No ww or die number)
38 trefoils 8 below
Bust B with 3½ pearls

Obv. E2
britt:
(No ww or die number)
33 large trefoils 7 below
Bust D with 4½ pearls

Obv. E1 (hybrid)
britt:
(No ww or die number)
33 trefoils 7 below
Bust B with 3½ pearls

1 arc & 2 trefoils above
Cross. Equal number
arcs & trefoils

1874 die number 263

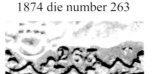

Highest die number
recorded to date

2 arcs only above cross
1 less trefoil than arcs

"I am indebted to Malcolm Lewendon for supplying most of the above illustrations and for his help and guidance over many weeks simplifying and proof reading this complicated series." (M.B.)

VICTORIA, 1837-1901
FLORINS

trefoil between **t** :

Obv. F1
britt:
(No ww or die number)
46 tall **trefoils** 10 below
Bust B with 3½ pearls

48 arcs & 48 trefoils
trefoil between **t** :

48 arcs & 48 trefoils
t : between 2 trefoils

46 arcs & 46 trefoils
trefoil between **t** :

42 arcs & 41 trefoils
t to arc & : trefoil

39 arcs & 38 trefoils
2nd **t** to trefoil

34 arcs & 33 trefoils
colon to trefoil

Quick calculation of arcs & trefoils in borders (see above)

The *"Lewendon"* method
48 arcs & 48 trefoils - bottom of arc points to the **t** in brit
48 arcs & 48 trefoils - bottom of arc points to a space between **t** : in britt
46 arcs & 46 trefoils - bottom of arc points to a space between **t** : in britt
42 arcs & 41 trefoils - bottom of arc points to the **t**
39 arcs & 38 trefoils - bottom of arc points to the :
34 arcs & 33 trefoils - bottom of arc points to the **t**

The *"Roger Shuttlewood"* method
Count the number of trefoils under the bust and multiply by 5

412

FLORINS

"GODLESS"

Obverse **A1.**		Young head, bust A, left; crowned (3 full pearls on central arch and 9 on cross), draped, hair plaited, small raised initials **w.w.** after date. Roman lettering. Beaded border. <u>No inner circle</u>
Leg.		**VICTORIA REGINA 1848** (Patterns only, see later**)**
	A2.	As 'A1', but with an inner circle, dated **1849**
Edge		Milled unless stated
	A3.	As before, but initials only half visible
	A4.	As before, but initials obliterated by the inner circle
Rev.	**1.**	Crowned cruciform shields; large rose in the centre, rose, thistle, rose and shamrock in the angles. Harp with 9 strings
Leg.		👑 + + **ONE** 👑 **FLORIN +** 👑 **ONE TENTH** 👑 **OF A POUND**

"GOTHIC"
(With many sub-varieties)

Obverse **B.**		**Bust B (3½ pearls on central arch and 8 in centre of cross) Ornate border consisting of 48 arcs & 48 trefoils** (10 below
(Old ESC.B1)		bust) Young head, similar to last, but with subtle differences in hair style which partially covers the ear, small raised **w w** below Legend and date in Gothic lettering
Leg.		𝔙𝔦𝔠𝔱𝔬𝔯𝔦𝔞 𝔡:𝔤: 𝔟𝔯𝔦𝔱: 𝔯𝔢𝔤: 𝔣: 𝔡· 𝔪𝔡𝔠𝔠𝔠𝔩𝔦. (date)
	B1.	Reads **𝔟𝔯𝔦𝔱:** (note; colon after a single **𝔱:**) **w w** below
Dates		**With a stop**; **1851., 1852., 1853., 1859.** & **1860.**
	B2.	As 'B1'- **𝔟𝔯𝔦𝔱: w w**, but
Dates		No stop; **1853, 1854, 1855, 1856, 1857, 1858, 1859** & **1863**
	B3.	Similar, but reads **𝔟𝔯𝔦𝔱.** (Note; stop after single **𝔱.**) **w w**,
Date		No stop; **1862**

FLORINS

B4. As 'B3'- **brit. w w**, but **with a die number**
Dates No stop; **1864** & **1865**

(ESC.B2) **B5.** As 'B2'- **brit:** (colon after single **t:**) **w w**, but **with a die number**
Dates No stop; **1864**, **1865**, **1866** & **1867**

B6. As 'B5'- **brit: w w**, and **die number**, but
Dates **With a colon; 1865:, 1866:** (?)

(ESC.B6) **B7.** Bust B, but reads **britt:** (note; double **tt:**) **w w**, no die number
Dates No stop; **1867**, **1878** & **1879**

(ESC.B3) **B8.** As 'B7'- **britt: w w**, but **with a die number**
Dates No stop; **1868**, **1869**, **1870**, **1871**, **1872**, **1873**, **1874**, **1875**, **1876**,
1877 (With only a trace of WW visible) & **1879**

Obverse **C.** **Bust C (5 pearls on central arch and 8 in centre of cross)**
Ornate border consisting of 42 arcs & 41 trefoils
(8 below bust) (Note; no trefoil between the two arcs above the
top of cross on crown)

(ESC.B5) **C1.** Reads - **britt:** no initials **with a die number**
Date **With stop; 1877.**

(ESC.B5) **C2.** As before - **britt:** no initials, **with a die number,** but
Dates No stop; **1867** & **1878**

(ESC.B5) **C3.** As before - **britt:** no initials or die number
Date No stop; **1877**

Obverse **D.** **Bust B (3½ pearls** on central arch and **8 in centre of cross),** but
Ornate border consisting of 39 arcs & 38 trefoils (8 below bust
No trefoil between the two arcs above top of cross on crown)

(ESC.B7) **D1.** Bust B - **britt:** no initials or die number
Date No stop; **1879**

FLORINS

Obverse **E.**		**Bust D (4½ pearls of varying sizes on central arch and 6 in centre of cross) Ornate border consisting of 34 arcs and 33 trefoils** (7 below bust). Note, no trefoil between the two arcs above the top of cross on crown on dates 1880 – 1885. In 1885 the border design was changed to longer arcs with small trefoils, giving 33 of each – there is now only 1 arc over the top cross on the crown. 1885 exists with both designs, 1886 all have longer arc design

	E1.	A hybrid; **Bust B - britt:** no initials or die number with
(Old ESC.B5/8)		**34 arcs & 33 trefoils** (7 below bust) *(Recorded but not proven)*
Date		No stop; **1880**

(ESC.B8)	**E2.**	As before, but **New Portrait**
		Bust D – britt: no initials or die number
Dates		**No stop; 1880, 1881, 1883, 1884, 1885 & 1886**

Obverse **F.**		**Bust 'B' (3½ pearls on central arch and 8 in centre of cross) Ornate border consisting of 46 arcs & 46 tall trefoils** (10 below bust)

(ESC.B9)	**F1.**	Reads **britt:,** but no initials or die number
Date		No stop; **1887**

Rev.	**2.**	Crowned cruciform shields; floriated cross in the centre, rose, thistle, rose and shamrock in the angles. Less ornate than before and smaller beaded border, with milled edge. Harp with 9 strings
Leg.		one ♔ florin
		♔ one tenth ♔ of a pound ♔

"GODLESS"

		With inner circle		Spink 3890	
ESC	Date	Varieties and remarks	R	(Old ESC)
2815	**1849**	A2.	Initials **w.w.** visible after date	C^2	802
2816	—	A3.	Initials half visible	N	802A
2817	—	A4.	Initial w w not visible *(slight trace possible)*	R^2	

VICTORIA, 1837-1901
FLORINS

"GOTHIC"
All with reverse **2** (minor sub-varieties see Davies pp. 54-6)

B1. Bust B - **brit:** (Note; colon after single **t:**) **w w** below
Border with **48 arcs** & **48 trefoils** (9 below bust) (Old ESC B1)
With stop after date Spink 3891

ESC	Date	Gothic date	Varieties and remarks	R	(Old ESC)
2818	(1851)	mdcccli.	*Proof*	R^5	804
2819	—	—	*Proof,* plain edge, *en medaille* ↑↑	R^6	805
2820	(1852)	mdccclii.		C	806
2821	—	—	*Proof*	R^2	807
2822	—	—	**ii.** second **i** over a stop	R^2	807A
2823	—	—	**n** over inverted **n** in **florin** *(3 seen*)*		
2824	—	—	*Leg.* reads **one tenth** *(1 seen*)*		
2825	(1853)	mdccccliii.		R^3	807B

B2. As 'B1'- **brit:** (colon after single **t:**) **w w**, but (Old ESC B1)
No stop after date Spink 3891

ESC	Date	Gothic date	Varieties and remarks	R	(Old ESC)
2826	(1853)	mdcccliii		C	808
2827	—	—	*Proof,* issued in the sets	R^2	809
2828	—	—	*Leg.* reads **one tenth** *(scarce*)*	R^3	811A
2829	(1854)	mdccccliv		R^3	811A
2830	—	—	*Leg.* reads **one tenth** *(4 seen*)*		
2831	(1855)	mdccclv		S	812
2832	—	—	*Leg.* reads **one tenth** *(5 seen*)*		
2833	(1856)	mdccclvi		S	813A
2834	—	—	*Leg.* reads **one tenth** *(7 seen*)*		
2835	(1857)	mdccclvii		S	814
2836	—	—	*Proof*	R^3	815
2837	—	—	*Leg.* reads **one tenth** *(6 seen*)*		
2838	(1858)	mdccclviii	*See note below* [1] Wide **c c c** in date[2]	N	816B
2839	—	—	*See note below* [1] Narrow **ccc** in date[2]	S	816B
2840	—	—	*Proof* *(Not traced)*	R^4	816A
2841	—	—	*Leg.* reads **one tenth** *(4 seen*)*		
2842	(1859)	mdccclix	*See note below* [1]	R	818

[1] *Minor differences occur on the obverse of 1858 & some 1859. See Davies pp 54-55*
[2] *See page 409*

416

FLORINS

B1. As before - **brit:** (colon after single **t:**) **w w**   (Old ESC B1)
With stop after date   Spink 3891

ESC	Date	Gothic date	Varieties and remarks	R	(Old ESC)
2843	(1859)	mdccclix.		N	817
2844	—	—	**m** over inverted **m**	R^4	
2845	(1860)	mdccclx.		R	819
2846	—	—	*Leg.* reads **one tenth** *(5 seen*)*		

B3. Bust B – **brit:** (Note; upper stop of colon after **t** very weak[1]) **w w**
No stop after date   (Old ESC B1) Spink 3891

2847	(1862)	mdccclxii		R^2	820
2848	—	—	*Proof,* milled edge *(2 in R.M.)*	R^6	821
2849	—	—	*Proof,* plain edge *(Not traced)*	R^5	

[1] See Seaby 1978, p.208. M.J. Dickenson explains why it must be a colon and not a stop, explaining that the two Proofs in the Royal Mint Collection exhibit faint traces of the upper stop on close inspection.

B2. As before - **brit:** (colon after single **t:**) **w w**   (Old ESC B1)
No stop after date   Spink 3891

2850	(1863)	mdccclxiii		R^3	822
2851	—	—	*Proof,* plain edge	R^4	823

B4. As B3 - **brit.** (Stop after single **t.**) **w w**, but with a **die number**
No stop after date

ESC	Date	Gothic date	Max die number *(Recorded die numbers)*	Varieties etc	R	(Old ESC)
2852	(1864)	mdccclxiv	30	*(20,22?,30)*	R^3	
2853	(1865)	mdccclxv	8	*(8)*	R^4	

B5. As B2 - **brit:** **w w**, but **with a die number**   (Old ESC B2)
No stop after date   Spink 3892

2854	(1864)	mdccclxiv	73	*(1,3,5,6-8,10-12,16-18,21,22?,23-26, 28,29,32-35,38-40,44-56,60,62-65, 67-69,71,73)*	N	824
2855	—	—	40	On heavy flan, *wt.14.77g (20 struck)*	R^4	824A
2856	—	—	47	*Proof on Piedfort flan*	R^4	825
2857	(1865)	mdccclxv	65	*(1-7,10-40,51?,53,54,65)*	S	826

(continued)

417

FLORINS

ESC	Date	Gothic date	Max die number *(Recorded die numbers)*	Varieties etc	R	(Old ESC)
2858	(1866)	mdccclxbi	32	*(1-5,8-32)*	R	828
2859	—	—	16	**un** over **nu** in **pound** *(2 seen*)*	R^4	
2860	(1867)	mdccclxbii	9	*(1-9)*	R^2	830

B6. As B5 - **brít: w w** and **die number**, but   (Old ESC B2)
With a colon after date   Spink 3892

| 2861 | (1865) | mdccclxb: | 51 | *(41,43-49,51?)* | R^2 | 827 |
| 2862 | (1866) | mdccclxbi: | ? | *(6,7 are possibilities)   (Not traced)* | R^3 | 829 |

B7. Bust B - **brítt:** (Note; colon after **tt:**) **w w**, no die number
No stop after date   (Old ESC B6) Spink 3897

| 2863 | (1867) | mdccclxbii | | *Proof or pattern   (1 seen*)* | R^5 | 831 |
| 2864 | — | — | | *Proof or pattern.* ↑↑ *Edge* plain | R^5 | 832 |

C2. Bust C (5 pearls) - **brítt:** no initials, but **with a die number**
Border with **42 arcs** & **41 trefoils** (9 below bust)   (Old ESC B5)
No stop after date   Spink 3895

| 2865 | (1867) | mdccclxbii | ? | Date error from 1877? | R^4 | 832A |

*Numbers seen - as recorded by Malcolm Lewendon, a Gothic Florin specialist

B8. Bust B - **brítt: w w**, but **with a die number and 48 arcs**
No stop after date   (Old ESC B3) Spink 3893

2866	(1868)	mdccclxbiii	30	*(1-9,11-30)*	R	833
2867	(1869)	mdccclxix	19	*(1-19)*	S	834
2868	—	—	14	**n/n** inverted in **florin** *(3 seen*)*		
2869	—	—	—	*Proof* *(Not traced)*	R^3	835
2870	(1870)	mdccclxx	24	*(1-11,13,15-24)*	S	836
2871	—	—	20	**m/m** inverted in date *(4 seen*)*		
2872	—	—	4	**u/u** inverted in **pound** *(3 seen*)*	R^3	
2873	—	—	35	*Proof (B.M. Collection)*	R^5	836A
2874	(1871)	mdccclxxi	68	*(1-5,7-36,38-51,53-60,62-68)*	S	837
2875	—	—	43	*Proof en medaille* ↑↑ *(43)*	R^4	838
2876	—	—	43	*Proof,* plain edge	R^4	839
2877	—	—		*Pattern struck in nickel*	R^2	

(continued)

FLORINS

ESC	Date	Gothic date	Max die number	Varieties etc (Recorded die numbers)	R	(Old ESC)
2878	(1872)	mdccclxxii	156	(1-4,6-17,19,21-107,109,111,113-123, 125-136,138-150,152-154,156)	C	840
2879	(1873)	mdccclxxiii	262	(2-7,9,10,12-31,33-42,44,46-80, 83-85,87,89-112,114-116,118-121, 124-129,131-135,137,138,140-154, 156-175,177-179,183-194-213, 215-223,225-235,237-241,243,244, 247-251,253-258,260-262) [1]	C	841
2880	—	—		Proof (Not traced)	R^5	842
2881	(1874)	mdccclxxiv	263	(1-6,8-18,20,23,25-28,31-35,38,39,41, 45,50-56,58-60,62 & 263)	N	843
2882	—		30	iv of date over iii (29,30)	R^2	843A
2883	(1875)	mdccclxxv	88	(9,11,13-20,22,24,26-28,30-34,36,37, 39,41-43,45,46,48,50-53,55-65,67,68, 70,72,74,76-79,82-84,86-88)	N	844
2884	(1876)	mdccclxxvi	50	(3-9,12,14,15,17-19,21-33,35-40, 42,43,45,47,49,50)	S	845
2885	(1877)	mdccclxxvii	61	(2-9,12,13,15,17,18,20,24,48,56, 59,61)*	R	846
2886	—	—	38	ww very feint (filled die?)	R^3	847

* (1877)   Additional dies (10,11,34,51-54,58,62,63,68), but indeterminate varieties

C1.   As 'C2' - britt: no initials, **with a die number and 42 arcs**
With a stop after date   (Old ESC B5) Spink 3895

2887	(1877)	mdccclxxvii.	68	(21,25-34,42,50-54,60,62,63,68)*	R	848

C3.   As 'C1' above, but no die number   Spink 3896

2888	(1877)	mdccclxxvii.		(Not traced)	R^4	848A

C2.   As 'C1'- britt: no initials, **with a die number,** but   (Old ESC B5)
No stop after date   Spink 3895

2889	(1878)	mdccclxxviii	95	(2-9,11-29,31-44,47,48,50,51, 53-58,60-68,71-79,81,82,85,86, 88-91,93-96)	N	849
2890	—	—	73	Proof (24,73)	R^6	849A

1   Specimens exist of; 1873 dies 129 and 131 with the bottom left of the 1st x in the date missing, making the date appear to be mdccclrxiii and specimens exist of 1881 with the bottom left of the 3rd x in the date missing, making the date appear to be mdccclxxri. Since these so-called errors are almost certainly due to filled dies they are disregarded as varieties

FLORINS

B7. Bust B - **britt:** (Note; **tt:**) **w w**, no die №. (Old ESC B6)
No stop after date Spink 3897

ESC	Date	Gothic date	Varieties and remarks	R	(Old ESC)
2891	(1878)	mdccclxxviii	(1 seen*)	R^7	
2892	(1879)	mdccclxxix		R^2	851
2893	—	—	Error: reads **briit:** See page 409		

C3. Bust C (5 pearls) - **britt:** no initials or die № (Old ESC B5/6)
No stop after date Spink 3896

2894	(1879)	mdccclxxix		R	850

D1. Bust C - **britt:** no initials or die № (Old ESC B7)
Border with **39 arcs** & **38 trefoils** (8 below bust) Spink 3898

2895	(1879)	mdccclxxix		R	852
2896	—	—	Proof	R^5	853
2897	—	—	Proof, en medaille ↑↑ Edge plain	R^5	853A

E1. Hybrid - earlier bust C, border as E2 - **britt:** no initials or die №
(Old ESC B3/8)

2898	1880	mdccclxxx		R^4	854A

E2. Bust D - **britt:** no initials or die №. (Old ESC B8)
Border with **34 arcs** & **33 trefoils** (7 below bust) Spink 3900

2899	(1880)	mdcccl·xxx	Is this pellet in date a flaw?		
2900	—	mdccclxxx	See note 1 page 419	S	854
2901	—	—	Proof	R^4	855
2902	(1881)	mdccclxxxi		C	856
2903	—	—	Proof	R^5	857
2904	—	—	Proof, plain edge	R^6	858
2905	(1883)	mdccclxxxiii		C	859
2906	—	—	Proof, plain edge	R^6	
2907	(1884)	mdccclxxxiv		C	860
2908	(1885)	mdccclxxxv	Short arcs (see page 409)	S	861
2909	—	—	Longer arcs (see page 409)	C	861
2910	—	—	Proof	R^6	862
2911	(1886)	mdccclxxxvi	Longer arcs (see page 409)	N	863
2912	—	—	Proof	R^6	864

FLORINS

F1. Bust B (3½ pearls) - **britt:** no initials or die № and
Border with **46 arcs** & **46 trefoils** (10 below bust) (Old ESC B9)
No stop after date Spink 3901

ESC	Date	Gothic date	Varieties and remarks	R	(Old ESC)
2913	(1887)	mdccclxxxvii		R	866
2914	—	—	Proof	R⁶	867

PATTERNS or PROOFS
By **WILLIAM WYON** - Dated **1848**
Struck *en medaille* ↑↑ with plain edges, unless stated,
Established classification retained; small lettering for obverse,
Large lettering for reverse, small Roman numerals for legend variety

a	b	c
A-i	A-v	B-i
B-ii	B-iii	B-iv

FLORINS

| C-i | C-vi | C-vii |

OBVERSES dated 1848

a. (A1) As the adopted 1849 'Godless' florin, crowned bust, left, but no inner circle

b. Similar, but large laureate head of Queen, left, date below with inner circle

c. Similar, but Queen's head with plain fillet, left, date below with inner circle

REVERSES

A. Cruciform shields, as adopted florin

B. Royal cypher **VR**, interlinked with rose, thistle and shamrock.
Prince of Wales's plumes with motto, all within quatrefoil

Ci. **ONE FLORIN** trident below within oak-wreath

Cvi. **ONE DECADE** trident below within oak-wreath

Cvii. **ONE CENTUM** trident below within oak-wreath

REVERSE LEGENDS

i. ONE FLORIN ONE TENTH OF A POUND

ii. ONE FLORIN TWO SHILLINGS

iii. ONE CENTUM ONE TENTH OF A POUND

iv. ONE DECADE ONE TENTH OF A POUND

FLORINS

| v. | ONE DIME | ONE TENTH | OF A POUND |

| vi. | ONE DECADE | 100 MILLES - ONE TENTH OF A POUND |

| vii. | ONE CENTUM | 100 MILLES - ONE TENTH OF A POUND |

ESC	Obv	Rev	Plain edges Reverse legend en medaille ↑↑	R	(Old ESC)
2915	a	Ai	ONE // FLORIN // ONE TENTH // OF A POUND // Milled edge. Struck with normal die axis ↑↓	R^5	801 or
2916	—	—	Milled edge. Struck *en medaille* die axis ↑↑	R^5	886B
2917	—	—		R^2	799
2918	—	—	*In gold, on a thick flan, no inner circle Obv.* (2 known) *Norweb 284, wt. 21.713g; 335.1grs*	R^2	800/ 886A
2919	b	—		R^2	887
2920	c	—		R^2	888
2921	a	Av	ONE // DIME // ONE TENTH // OF A POUND //	R^2	889
2922	b	—		R^2	890
2923	c	—		R^2	891
2924	a	Bi	ONE // FLORIN // ONE TENTH // OF A POUND //	R^2	892
2925	b	—		R^2	893
2926	c	—		R^2	894
2927	a	Bii	ONE FLORIN // TWO SHILLINGS //	R^2	895
2928	b	—		R^2	896
2929	c	—		R^2	897
2930	a	Biii	ONE CENTUM // ONE TENTH OF A POUND //	R^2	898
2931	b	—		R^2	899
2932	c	—		R^2	900
2933	a	Biv	ONE DECADE // ONE TENTH OF A POUND //	R^2	901
2934	b	—		R^2	902
2935	c	—		R^2	903
2936	a	Ci	ONE TENTH OF A POUND	R^2	904
2937	b	—		R^2	905
2938	c	—		R^2	906
2939	a	Cvi	100 MILLES // ONE TENTH OF A POUND //	R^2	907
2940	b	—		R^2	908
2941	c	—		R^2	909
2942	a	Cvii	100 MILLES // ONE TENTH OF A POUND //	R^2	910
2943	b	—		R^2	911
2944	c	—	Date, no stop	R^2	912

FLORINS

PATTERNS & PROOFS

MULES OF TWO REVERSES
With edge legend in raised lettering
★ **DECUS ET TUTAMEN** ★ **ANNO REGNI SEPTIMO**

ESC	Obv	Rev	Plain edges	Reverse legend	en medaille ↑↑	R	(Old ESC)
2945	**Bi**	**Bii**				R^5	913
2946	**Biii**	**Cvii**				R^5	914
2947	**Biv**	**Cvi**				R^5	915

Type D

2948	**1875**	**D**	By **Leonard Charles Wyon** (?) and **Benedetto Pistrucci**, **1875**	R^6	916
		Obv	Coroneted head, left		
		Leg	**VICTORIA DEI GRATIA BRITANNIAR : REG : F : D :**		
		Rev	Pistrucci's St George and dragon. *Edge,* plain		

Type E

2949	**1876**	**E**	By **L.C. Wyon, 1876** As the pattern halfcrown of this date, (Old ESC 740) but on a much lighter blank	R^6	917

VICTORIA, 1837-1901
FLORINS

Type F

2950	1887	F	By **Joseph Edgar Boehm, 1887**	R^7	918
		Obv	As the current Jubilee head, but very slightly smaller bust, further from the beaded border, eight beads to the left arch of crown		
		Rev	As the current coin.		
		Edge	Milled		

Type G
No illustration available
See matching pattern 1890 Double Florin

2951	1890	G	By **L.C. Wyon, 1890**	R^7	918A
			Uniface reverse as the current issue but		
		Leg.	♛ O N E ♛ FLORIN ♛		
			Sprig **18** ♛ **90** sprig		
			(Sprigs of rose-shamrock-thistle		
		Edge	Plain. *wt. 176.4grains, 11.43g. 30mm*		

Type H

2952	1891	H	By **L.C. Wyon, 1891**	R^7	918
			As the current Jubilee florin, but		
			FLORIN 1891 between two sprigs, and the shields lined.		
		Edge	Milled		

FLORINS

JUBILEE HEAD

Early - 1887 & 1888
Wide space
below truncation

3rd reverse[*]

[*]See P.J. Davies, p.56-7
for further sub-varieties
of obverses & reverses

Late - 1888 - 1892
narrow space
below truncation

Obv.   **J.**   *"Jubilee head"* Veiled and draped bust, left, wearing a small crown
Initials **J.E.B.** (Joseph Edgar Boehm) on truncation
Leg.   **VICTORIA   DEI   GRATIA**

Rev.   **3.**   Crowned cruciform shields, Garter star in centre, sceptres in angles
Leg.   **BRITT: ♛ REG: 18 ♛ 87 FID: ♛ DEF: ♛**

Jw/3. Early bust - **w**ide space below truncation   Spink 3925

ESC	Date	Varieties Note: All harps now have 10 strings	R	(Old ESC)
2953	**1887**		C^3	868
2954	—	*Proof,* issued in the sets	S	869
2955	**1888**		R	870

Jn/3. Late bust - **n**arrow space below truncation   Spink 3925

ESC	Date	Varieties	R	(Old ESC)
2956	**1888**		S	870A
2957	**1889**		S	871
2958	**1890**		R	872
2959	**1891**		R^2	873
2960	**1892**		R^2	874
2961	—	*Proof* *(7 struck but only one in private hands)*	R^6	875

FLORINS

OLD HEAD

T.B.

Obv. O   Rev. 4

Obv.	**O.**	*'Old head'.* Coroneted bust draped and veiled, left
		T.B. (Thomas Brock) below truncation
Leg.		**VICTORIA · DEI · GRA · BRITT · REGINA ·**
		FID · DEF · IND · IMP

Rev.	**4.**	Three shields of England, Scotland and Ireland, rose, shamrock and
		thistle between two sceptres within Garter, crown above,
		date below divided by the Garter buckle, harp with 9 strings
Leg.		**ONE · FLORIN +** 👑 **TWO SHILLINGS**

O/4. Old head [1]

Rev. 4 - Three shields within Garter, crown above   Spink 3939

2962	**1893**		*N*	876
2963	—	*Proof,* issued in the sets	*N*	877
2964	**1894**		*S*	878
2965	**1895**		*S*	879
2966	**1896**		*S*	880
2967	**1897**		*N*	881
2968	**1898**		*S*	882
2969	**1899**		*S*	883
2970	—	*Proof* *(Unique. Possibly struck at the Sydney mint [2])*	*R[7]*	883A?
2971	**1900**		*N*	884
2972	**1901**		*N*	885

---

1   See Davies pp. 57-58 for further sub-varieties of obverses & reverses.

2   See note in St James's Auction 2, 11th May 2005, lot 511 for theory about the origin of this
     coin.

SHILLINGS

YOUNG HEAD

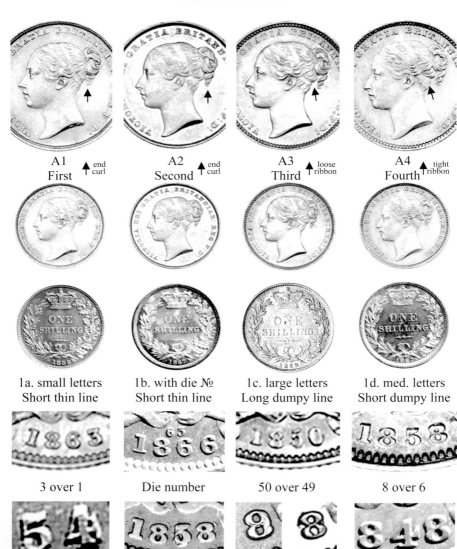

A1
First ↑ end curl

A2
Second ↑ end curl

A3
Third ↑ loose ribbon

A4
Fourth ↑ tight ribbon

1a. small letters
Short thin line

1b. with die №
Short thin line

1c. large letters
Long dumpy line

1d. med. letters
Short dumpy line

3 over 1

Die number

50 over 49

8 over 6

4 over higher 4

58 over 58

8 over 9

8 over 6

SHILLINGS

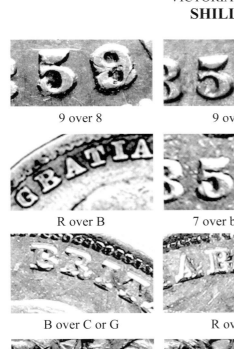

| 9 over 8 | 9 over 9 | 8 over 6 |

| R over B | 7 over broken 5 | Inverted V for 1st I |

| B over C or G | R over B | R over B |

| Die number | Pellet above die number | *Proof* no die number |

| Short line | Long line | Large lettering |

| Inverted G for D | Some As like triangles | 50 double struck? |

SHILLINGS

Obverse legends in abbreviated order
(Ignoring punctuation)

1	VICTORIA DEI GRA	BRITT REGINA FID DEF IND IMP
2	VICTORIA DEI GRATIA	BRITANNIAR REG F D
3	VICTORIA DEI GRATIA	BRITT REGINA F D
4	VICTORIA DEI GRATIA	REG F D
5	VICTORIA DEI GRATIA	
6	VICTORIA REGINA	

YOUNG HEAD

Obv. **A1.** First young head, bound with fillet, left, **W.W.** on truncation
Leg. 4 **VICTORIA DEI GRATIA: REG: F: D:** *Edge,* milled

A2. Second young head; similar, but slightly larger head and the back curl longer, with **W.W.** on truncation

A2var. As last, but without w.w. (Some of the earlier dates show traces of the w.w. having been removed from the die) (Old ESC. A^3)

A3. Third young head. A slight change of head; lower relief, slightly larger and hair at back is varied; the nose is more pronounced, the mouth fuller and the angle of truncation slightly altered.
Very pronounced border beads and rim (Old ESC A^5)

A4. Fourth young head; die has been re-cut, most noticeable in the wavy curls and hair above the ribbon at the back of the neck

Rev. **1a** Value in the centre, between two branches; an olive left and oak right, tied together at the base with a ribbon, a large crown above and the date below. Value in small letters in the centre
Leg. **ONE / SHILLING** / a thin line below (Old ESC. $A^{4\&6}$)

1b As '1a', but with a die number between wreath and date

1c Similar to '1a', but the words ONE SHILLING in larger letters and a long dumpy line below

1d Similar to '1c', but with subtle differences; the words are slightly smaller, although still larger than '1a', a short dumpy line below

SHILLINGS

A1/1a. First young head, with **w.w.** on truncation   (Old ESC A1)
Rev. 1a.   Spink 3902

ESC	Date	Varieties, remarks, etc.	R	(Old ESC)
2973	**1838**		S	1278
2974	—	*Proof* ↑↓ *weights vary 5.65g-5.88g*	R^4	1279
2975	**1839**		R	1280
2976	—	*Proof with plain edge struck en medaille* ↑↑	R^2	1281

A2/1a. Second young head, with **w.w.** on truncation   (Old ESC A2)
Rev. 1a.   Spink 3903

ESC	Date	Varieties, remarks, etc.	R	(Old ESC)
2977	**1839**	*Proof,* ↑↓ plain edge, from the set *wt. 5.66g*	S	1282

A2var./1a. Second young head, (no w.w.)   (Old ESC A3)
Rev. 1a   Spink 3904

ESC	Date	Varieties, remarks, etc.	R	(Old ESC)
2978	**1838**	Mule (Old ESC. A3/A1)	R^4	1278A
2979	**1839**		N	1283
2980	—	*Proof with plain edge struck normally* ↑↓	R	1284
2981	—	*Proof with plain edge struck en medaille* ↑↑	R	1284
2982	—	*Proof with milled edge*	R^6	1284A
2983	**1840**		R^2	1285
2984	—	*Proof*	R^5	1286
2985	—	Last **D** in legend over **F**	R^5	1286A
2986	**1841**		R	1287
2987	**1842**		S	1288
2988	—	*Proof*	R^5	1289
2989	**1843**		R	1290
2990	**1844**		S	1291
2991	**1845**		R	1292
2992	**1846**		S	1293
2993	**1848**		R^6	1294A
2994	—	Second **8** over **6**	R^2	1294
2995	**1849**		S	1895
2996	**1850**		R^3	1296
2997	—	**50** over **46**	$R^?$	1296A
2998	—	**50** over **49**	R^4	1297
2999	**1851**		R^2	1298
3000	—	*Proof*	R^2	1298A
3001	**1852**		S	1299

(continued)

SHILLINGS

ESC	Date	Varieties, remarks, etc.	R	(Old ESC)
3002	**1853**		S	1300
3003	—	*Proof,* only issued in the sets ↑↓ *wt. 5.66g*	R^2	1301
3004	**1854**		R^2	1302
3005	—	**4** over higher **4**	R^4	1302A
3006	**1855**		S	1303
3007	**1856**	Some letters **A** like triangles	S	1304
3008	**1857**		S	1305
3009	—	Inverted **G** for D : F:Ɔ :	R^4	1305A
3010	—	**7** over broken **5**	R^4	1305B
3011	**1858**		S	1306
3012	—	Second **8** over **6**	$R^?$	1306A
3013	—	**58** over **58**	R^4	1306B
3014	—	**8** over **9**	R^4	1306C
3015	**1859**		S	1307
3016	—	**9** in date is a damaged **8**	R^3	1307A
3017	—	*Proof*	R^5	1307B
3018	**1860**	**B** over **C** or **G** & 2nd **R** over **B** in **BRITANNIAR**	R	1308
3019	**1861**		R	1309
3020	—	**D** over **B** in **F : D :**	R^2	1309A
3021	**1862**		R^2	1310
3022	**1863**		R^2	1311
3023	—	**3** over **1**	R^4	1311A

A2/1b.   Second young head   (Old ESC A4)
         Rev. 1b – As before with a **die number** above date   Spink 3905

ESC	Date	Max number	*(Recorded die numbers)* Varieties etc	R	(Old ESC)
3024	**1864**	80	*(1-15,17-20,22-25,27-32,34,36-42(large),45,46,48,50, 51,55-59,62-68,72,75,77,78,80)*	N	1312
3025	**1865**	130	*(1,2,4-19,21-24,26-34,37-42,44-52,54,56-59,61-66, 68-70, 72,75,77-80,83,88,,89,92,94,97-101,103-110, 113-119,121,122,124,125,130)*	N	131 3
3026	—	29	**5** over **3** *(29)*		
3027	**1866**	70	*(1,3,4,6-10,13,15,17-20,22-62,65,66,68,70)*	N	1314
3028	—	63	Reads **BBITANNIAR** *(63)*	R^3	1314A
3029	—	30	Inverted **V** for **I** in **VICTORIA**	R^3	1314B
3030	**1867**	36	*(1-18,20,22,25-27,36,37)*	S	1315

SHILLINGS

A3/ 1a. Third young head   (Old ESC A5)
Rev. 1a. As before but, no die number above date   Spink 3906

ESC	Date	Varieties, remarks, etc.	R	(Old ESC)
3031	**1867**	*Does this exist as a non proof?* (Not traced)		1316
3032	—	*Proof* ↑↓ *wt. 5.61g*	R^4	1317
3033	—	*Proof, en medaille* ↑↑ *with plain edge*	R^5	1317A

A3/1b. Third young head   (Old ESC A6)
Rev. 1b - As before with **die number** above date   Spink 3906A

ESC	Date	Max number	*(Recorded die numbers)* Varieties etc	R	(Old ESC)
3034	**1867**	37	*(16,17,19-29,31,32,34-37 (& possibly 53,55)*	R^3	1317B
3035	—	18	*(17,18)* With a pellet above die numbers	R^3	1317C
3036	**1868**	51	*(1-3,5-19,21-38,40-42,44,47-51,54)*	N	1318
3037	**1869**	15	*(1-15)*	R	1319
3038	**1870**	20	*(1-20)*	R	1320
3039	**1871**	56	*(1,3,5-19,21,23-28,31-48,51-56)*	N	1321
3040	—	19	*Proof* ↑↓	R^5	1322
3041	—	19	*Proof, en medaille* ↑↑ *with plain edge*	R^6	1323
3042	**1872**	155	*(1-13,15,16,18,20-39,41,42,44-46,48-50,51-56, 61-63,65-68,70-78,80-88,90-103,105-108,113, 116,117,119,121,122,125-131,135,136,138,139, 148,150,151,153,155)*	C	1324
3043	**1873**	141	*(1-6,10-19,21,22,24,26,30,31,33-48,50,52-59, 61-67,69-71,73,75-77,79,83,84,86-89,92-94,96,100, 101,103,105-109,110,111,113-115,117-123,125, 127-129,131,132,135-137,141)*	C	1325
3044	**1874**	76	*(Crosslet 4): (1-15);(Plain 4): 16-19,21-23,25-28,30, 31,34-44,46-50,52,54-57,60-70,74,76 & 87?)*	N	1326
3045	**1875**	87	*(1-24,27-30,32-36,38,41-61,63-72,74,84,87)*	N	1327
3046	**1876**	36	*(1-7,9-18,20,21,23-29,33,35,36 & possibly 46,55,68)*	S	1328
3047	**1877**	70	*(1,3-15,17-19,22,24,25,28-35,37,38,40,41,43-45, 47-49,51,52,54-57,59,61,64,66,69,70)*	N	1329

A3/ 1a. Third young head   (Old ESC A5)
Rev. 1a. As before but, no die number above date   Spink 3906

3048	**1877**				1329A

SHILLINGS

A3/1b. Third young head (Old ESC A6)
Rev. 1b - As before with **die number** above date Spink 3906A

ESC	Date	Max number	*(Recorded die numbers)* Varieties etc	R	(Old ESC)
3049	**1878**	84	*(1877 type obverse): 1-5,7-18,20,23,25-29,31,32,33, 37,40,42 (switch may be at 40 rather than 44) (1879 type obverse): 44-60,62-69,72,74-76,84*	N	1330
3050	—	36	*Proof* ↑↓	R^6	1331

A4/1b. Fourth young head (Old ESC A7)
Rev. 1b - As before with **die number** above date Spink 3907A

3051	1878	47		R^3	
3052	—	36	*Proof* ↑↓	R^3	
3053	1879	26	*(1,2,4-6,8-12,14-16,17over16,22,26,28)*	R^2	1334
2054	—	9	**R** over **B** in **GRATIA**		
3055	—	13	**8** over **6**		
3056	—	26	*Proof* ↑↓	R^4	1333

A3/1a. Third young head (Old ESC A5)
Rev. 1a. As before, but no die number above date Spink 3907A

3057	1879			1334A
3058	—	*Proof, en medaille* ↑↑ *with plain edge*	R^3	1334B

A3/ 1a. Third young head (Old ESC A5)
Rev. 1a. As before, no die number above date Spink 3906

3059	1879			1316
3060	—	*Proof, with plain edge*	R^5	1317A

A4/1a. Fourth young head (Old ESC A7)
Rev. 1a. As before, no die number above date Spink 3907

3061	1879	Rev. small lettering, thin short line below value	N	1334
3062	—	*Proof*	R^5	1334A

Tower Hill shillings, up to 1879, were struck on Boulton presses using hand finished dies.
Each die was worked over by a die-improver who sharpened up on details of engraving,
over-punched indistinct letters and added the last two figures of the date.
This explains various errors.

A4/1d. Fourth young head (Old ESC A7)
Rev. 1d. Smaller letters, short dumpy line Spink 3907

3063	**1880**		N	1335A

SHILLINGS

A4/1c. Fourth young head   (Old ESC A7)
        Rev. 1c. Larger letters, long dumpy line   Spink 3907

ESC	Date	Varieties, remarks, etc.	R	(Old ESC)
3064	**1880**		N	1335
3065	—	*Proof* ↑↓	R^3	1336
3066	—	*Proof, with plain edge*	R^5	1337

A4/1d. Fourth young head   (Old ESC A7)
        Rev. 1d. Smaller letters, short dumpy line   Spink 3907

3067	**1881**		N	1335A

A4/1c. Fourth young head   (Old ESC A7)
        Rev. 1c. Larger letters, long dumpy line   Spink 3907

3068	**1881**			N	1338
3069	—	*Proof* ↑↓	*wt. 5.65g*	R^4	1339
3070	—	*Proof, with plain edge*		R^6	1340
3071	**1882**			S	1341
3072	**1883**			N	1342
3073	—	*Proof struck en medaille* ↑↑ *with plain edge*	*wt. 5.64g*	R^6	1342A

A4/1d. Fourth young head   (Old ESC A7)
        Rev. 1d. Smaller letters, short dumpy line   Spink 3907

3074	**1884**			N	1343
3075	—	*Proof*		R^5	1344
3076	**1885**			N	1345
3077	—	*Proof* ↑↓	*wt. 5.66g*	R^5	1346
3078	**1886**			N	1347
3079	—	*Proof*	*(Not traced)*	R^7	1348
3080	**1887**			S	1349
3081	—	*Proof* ↑↓	*wt. 5.67g*	R^5	1350

PATTERNS

No
illustration
available

Obv. D   Rev. 1e

SHILLINGS

PATTERNS

ESC	Date	Type	Varieties, remarks, etc.	R	(Old ESC)
3082	**1839**	**D**	By **W. Wyon, 1839**	R^5	1371
		Obv	As current young head shillings, but		
		Leg	**4 - VICTORIA DEI GRATIA REG F D**		
		Rev	**1e** - As the current design, but *rev.* is ruled with fine horizontal lines		

Obv. E   Rev. 1a   Obv. F

Plain on truncation   C.H.W. Raised

3083	**1863**	**E**	By **Ch. W. Wiener & Wyon, 1863**	R^3	1372
		Obv.	Head of Queen, left, wearing wreath composed of roses, shamrocks and thistles, two tie ends on neck.		
		Leg	**2 - VICTORIA DEI GRATIA BRITANNIAR : REG : F : D :**		
		Rev	**1a** - As current coin. *Edge,* plain ↑↓		

SHILLINGS

PATTERNS

3084	**1863**	F	Similar, but different features and without the tie ends, but with initials **C.H.W.** on neck in raised letters.	R^3	1373
		Rev	**1a** - As current coin. *Edge,* plain ↑↓		
3085	—	—	As before, but obverse uniface *(Unique?)*		

No
illustration

Obv. G

Rev. 1a

Obv. H

C H.W. Incuse

C H.W. Raised

3086	**1863**	G	Similar, but with coroneted head, back hair looped with pearls, **C.H.W.** incuse on neck	R^3	1374
		Rev	**1a** - As last. *Edge,* plain ↑↓		

3087	**1863**	H	Similar to 'G' but, **CH.W.** raised on neck	R^3	1375
		Leg	**5 - VICTORIA DEI GRATIA**		
		Rev	**1a** - As last. *Edge,* plain ↑↓		
3088	—	—	As before, but obverse uniface *(Unique?)*		

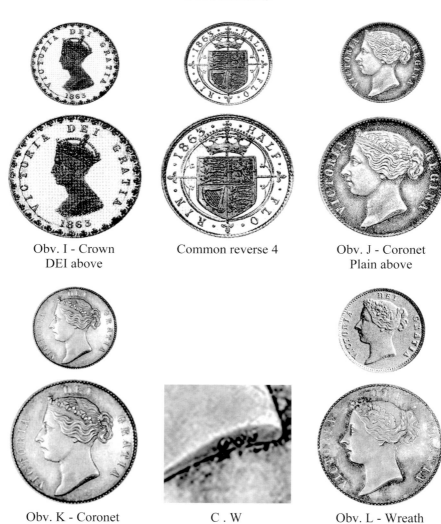

Obv. I - Crown
DEI above

Common reverse 4

Obv. J - Coronet
Plain above

Obv. K - Coronet
DEI above

C . W

Obv. L - Wreath
DEI above

SHILLINGS

PATTERNS

3089	**1863**	I	By **Wiener** and **Taylor**, **1863**	R	1376
		Obv	Small crowned bust draped, left, with ornamental border.		
		Leg	**5 - VICTORIA DEI GRATIA**		
		Rev	**4** - Square-topped shield, crowned, in tressure over cross. *Edge*, plain ↑↑		
		Leg	**· HALF · ♣ · FLO · ♣ · RIN · ♣ · 1863 · ♣**		
3090	—	—	*In gold* ↑↑ *(2 known) wt. 9.13g & 7.82g*	R^7	1376a

3091	**1863**	J	Similar, but	R	1377
		Obv	Coroneted head with **C.W** on truncation		
		Leg	**6 - VICTORIA REGINA**		
		Rev	**4** - As last. *Edge*, plain ↑↑		
3092	—	—	*In gold. Edge*, plain ↑↑ *wt. 9.2g*	R^7	1377a

3093	**1863**	J	*In copper. Edge*, plain ↑↑	R	1378
3094	—	—	*In silver. Edge*, milled ↑↑	R^2	1377A
3095	—	—	*In copper. Edge*, milled ↑↑	R^4	1378A

3096	**1863**	K	Similar with coroneted head, but	R	1380
		Leg	**5 - VICTORIA DEI GRATIA**		
		Rev	**4** - As last. *Edge*, plain ↑↑		
3097	—	—	*In gold. Edge*, plain ↑↑ *wt. 9.2g*	R^7	1380a
3098	—	—	*In copper. Edge*, plain ↑↑	R	1381
3099	—	—	*In silver. Edge*, milled ↑↑	R^3	1380A

3100	**1863**	L	Similar, but wreathed head	R	1382
		Leg	**5 - VICTORIA DEI GRATIA**		
		Rev	**4** - As last. *Edge*, plain ↑↑		
3101	—	—	*In gold. Edge*, plain ↑↑ *wt. 9.26g*	R^7	1382a
3102	—	—	*In copper. Edge*, plain ↑↑	R	1383

SHILLINGS

PATTERNS

Obv. M - Coronet   Obv. N - Wreath   Obv. O - Coronet

Common reverse 5   C.W.

3103	**1865**	**M** Leg Rev	Similar, but coroneted head, **C.W.** on neck **5 - VICTORIA DEI GRATIA** 5 - Square-topped shield, crowned, in tressure over cross. (Dated 1865) **HALF** (scroll) ✚ (scroll) **FLORIN** ♣ **M D C C** ♣ **C L X V** ♣ *Edge,* plain ↑↑ *wt. 6.73g*	*R*	1384
3104	—	—	*In gold.* *Edge,* plain ↑↑ *wt. 9.4g*	*R⁷*	1384A
3105	—	—	*In copper. Edge,* plain ↑↑	*R*	1385
3106	—	—	*In silver. Edge,* milled ↑↑	*R⁴*	1385A

SHILLINGS

PATTERNS

3107	**1865**	N	Similar, but wreathed head, **C.W** on neck	R	1386
		Leg	**5 - VICTORIA DEI GRATIA**		
		Rev	**5** - As last. *Edge,* plain ↑↑		
3108	—	—	*In gold.* *Edge,* plain ↑↑ *wt. 9.3g*	R^7	1386A
3109	—	—	*In copper. Edge,* plain ↑↑	R	1387
3110	—	—	Uniface obverse. *Silver gilt*	R^6	1387B

3111	**1865**	O	Similar, but coroneted head, **C.W** on neck.	R	1388
		Leg	**6 - VICTORIA REGINA**		
		Rev	**5** - As last. *Edge,* plain ↑↑		
3112	—	—	*In gold.* *Edge,* plain ↑↑ *wt. 8.9g*	R^7	1388A
3113	—	—	*In copper. Edge,* plain ↑↑	R	1389
3114	—	—	*In copper. Edge,* milled ↑↑	R	1390

C·W

No
illustration

Obv. P   Common reverse 6   Obv. Q

3115	No	P	By **C. Wiener** and **W.J. Taylor** (undated)	R	1391
	date	*Obv*	Similar, but coroneted head, **C.W** on neck		
		Leg	**5 - VICTORIA DEI GRATIA** *wt. 6.56g*		
		Rev	**6** - Shield in Garter, crowned. *Edge,* plain ↑↓		
3116	—	—	*In gold.* *Edge,* plain ↑↑ *wt. 9.1g*	R^7	1391A
3117	—	—	*In copper. Edge,* plain ↑↑ *(Not traced)*	R	1392

SHILLINGS

PATTERNS

3118	No date	Q Leg Rev	Similar, but wreathed head. **C.W** on neck **5 - VICTORIA DEI GRATIA** **6** - Shield in Garter crowned, undated	R	1393
3119	—	—	*In gold.* *Edge,* plain ↑↑ *wt. 9.3g*	R^7	1394
3120	—	—	*In copper.* *Edge,* plain ↑↑ *(Not traced)*	R	1394A

Obv. R   Common reverse 6   Obv. S

C·W

3121	No date	R Leg Rev	Similar, but coroneted head. **C·W** on neck. **6 - VICTORIA REGINA** **6** - As last. *Edge,* plain ↑↑	R	1395
3122	—	—	*In gold.* *Edge,* plain ↑↑ *(Unique?)* *wt. 9.4g*	R^7	1395A
3123	—	—	*In copper.* *Edge,* plain ↑↑ *(Not traced)*	R	1396

3124	No date	S Leg Rev	Similar coroneted head and **C.W** on truncation **5 - VICTORIA DEI GRATIA** **6** - As last. *Edge,* plain ↑↑	R	1397
3125	—	—	*Edge,* milled	R^2	1397A

SHILLINGS

PATTERNS

Obv. T

Rev. 7

3126	No date	**T**	Similar, but wreathed head, **C·W** on truncation	R^4	1398
		Leg	**5 - VICTORIA DEI GRATIA**		
		Rev	**7** - In imitation of engraving, small shield of arms within Garter, crowned, motto on ribbon beneath, scroll ornament in field, the whole on groundwork of horizontal lines		
		Edge	Plain ↑↑		

No illustrations available

Obv. U   Rev. 8   Obv. V

3127	No date	**U**	Similar, but coroneted head. **C·W** on truncation	R^4	1399
		Leg	**6 - VICTORIA REGINA**		
		Rev	**8 - ONE SHILLING** stamped incuse on a broad engine-turned and raised border, large figure **1** also engine-turned in centre, **W.J.T.** beneath. *Edge,* plain ↑↑ *(Not traced)*		

3128	No date	**V**	Similar, but coroneted head **CH.W.** incuse on truncation	R^4	1400
		Leg	**5 - VICTORIA DEI GRATIA**		
		Rev	**8** - As last. *Edge,* plain ↑↑		

SHILLINGS

PATTERNS

Rev. 9   Obv. A4   Rev. 10

3129	**1875**	**A4**	By **W. Wyon** and **Pistrucci, 1875**	R^6	1401
		Obv	As the current fourth young head shillings		
		Leg	**4 - VICTORIA DEI GRATIA: REG:F:D:**		
		Rev	**9** - Pistrucci's St George and dragon		
			Date **1875** in exergue.		
			Edge, plain ↑↑		
3130	—	—	*Edge,* milled *(Not traced)*	R^6	1402

3131	No	**A4**	As before, but undated. *Edge,* plain	R^5	1403
	date	*Rev*	**10** – as before, no beaded border		
3132	—	—	*In aluminium* ↑↑ *wt. 1.50g*	R^6	1403A

SHILLINGS

PATTERNS

Obv. W   Rev. 9

Obv. X   Rev. 11

3133	**1875**	**W**	By **L.C. Wyon, 1875**	R^6	1404A
		Obv	Coroneted head, left		
		Leg	**2 - VICTORIA DEI GRATIA BRITANNIAR: REG: F: D:**		
		Rev	**9** - Pistrucci's St George and dragon		
			Date **1875** in exergue		
			Edge, plain *(Not traced)*		
3134	—	—	*Edge,* milled ↑↑	R^6	1404

SHILLINGS

PATTERNS

3135	1880	X	By **W. Wyon & W.J. Taylor**, **1880**	R^6	1405
		Obv	As the current young head shillings, date below truncation		
		Leg	No*ne*		
		Rev	**11** - Crowned shield in Garter, as George III last issue shillings, but without the Hanoverian arms in centre.		
			Edge, plain ↑↑		

Obv. Y   Rev.

3136	No	**Y**	By **L.C. Wyon?** undated	R^6	
	date	*Obv*	Coroneted head, left, tied with ribbon		
		Leg	**VICTORIA QUEEN** beaded border		
		Rev	**JOHNSON MATTHEY & Co HATTON GARDENS** around **REFINERS** at centre		
		Edge	Plain, no border.		
			In aluminium		

SHILLINGS

JUBILEE HEAD

Obv. B1		Rev. 2a - wide date
Obv. B2		Rev. 2b - narrow date

Obv.	**B1.**	First Jubilee head; tall bust, left, draped and veiled, with a small crown perched on top of her head
Leg.	3	**VICTORIA DEI GRATIA BRITT: REGINA: F: D:**
Rev.	**2a**	Square-topped shield within Garter, crowned, date below divided by Garter buckle. No legend.
	B2.	Second Jubilee head; much larger bust
Rev.	**2b**	As before, but with many subtle differences; smaller date etc

SHILLINGS

B1/2a. Small Jubilee head / *Rev.* 2a - Wide date   Spink 3926

3137	1887		C^3	1351
3138	—	*Proof,* issued in the sets	S	1352
3139	1888		R^3	1353
3140	—	**8** over **7**	S	1353A
3141	1889		R^2	1354

B2/2b. Large Jubilee head / Rev. 2b - Narrow date   Spink 3927

3142	1889		N	1355
3143	—	*Proof*	R^3	1356
3144	1890		N	1357
3145	1891		N	1358
3146	—	*Proof*	R^5	1359
3147	1892		N	1360

PATTERNS

Obv. B2   Rev. 12

3148	1887	**B2**	**By L.C. Wyon, 1887**	R^7	1406
		Obv	As the usual Jubilee shillings (B²) but;		
		Rev	**12** - Date **1887** divided by the crown above the square-topped shield within a slightly different Garter, the value **ONE SHILLING** below. *Edge,* milled ↑↑		

SHILLINGS

PATTERNS

3149	1888	B2	By **L.C. Wyon, 1888**	R^7	1407
		Obv	As last, but		
		Rev	**13** - Square shield, crowned. Within the Garter. **ONE SHILLING** above in larger lettering than last, date below. *Edge,* milled *(Not traced)*		
3150	—	B2	*Obv.* As last	R^7	1408
		Rev	**14** - Plain square-topped shield, crowned. **ONE SHILLING** above and scroll with motto and date below. *Edge,* milled *(Not traced)*		
3151	—	B2	As the large head shillings	R^7	1409
		Rev	**15** - As *before* but **ONE SHILLING** in smaller letters *(Not traced)*		

(Uncertain which reign this may have been intended)

This unique (?) and previously unknown undated pattern has all the characteristics of C.H. Wiener and is now in the Royal Mint Collection

3152		Undated uniface reverse	R^7
		Similar basic design to the circulating issue; but the value in the centre, is between two branches consisting of roses, shamrocks and thistles tied together at the base with a ribbon, large crown above but, without any date below	
	Leg.	**BRITANNIARUM ♚ REX · FID : DEF :** **ONE** **SHILLING**	

SHILLINGS

OLD HEAD

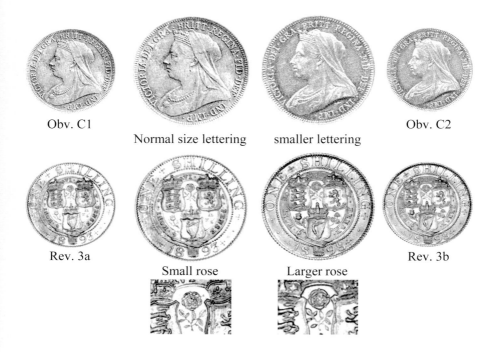

Obv. C1

Normal size lettering   smaller lettering

Obv. C2

Rev. 3a

Small rose

Larger rose

Rev. 3b

	C1.	Old head coroneted, left, veiled and draped
Leg.	1	**VICTORIA · DEI · GRA · BRITT ·**
		REGINA · FID · DEF · IND · IMP ·
Rev.	**3a.**	Three crowned shields in form of trefoil within the Garter.
		Small rose, shamrock and thistle in angles,
		Date below divided by Garter buckle
Leg.		**ONE + SHILLING / + · + 18 93 + · +**
	C2.	As last, but smaller lettering (Old ESC D)
Rev.	**3b.**	As before, but the rose is significantly larger

SHILLINGS

C1/3a. Old head, **large lettering**
Rev. 3a, with a **small rose**   Spink 3940

3153	**1893**		C	1361
3154	—	Smaller lettering on *obv.*	N	1361A
3155	—	*Proof,* issued in the sets	N	1362
3156	**1894**		N	1363
3157	—	Smaller lettering on *obv.*	N	1363A
3158	**1895**		R^2	1364
3159	**1896**		R^3	1365A

C2/3b. Old head, **smaller lettering**
Rev. 3b, with a **larger rose**   Spink 3940A

3160	**1895**		N	1364A
3161	**1896**		N	1365
3162	**1897**		N	1366
3163	**1898**		N	1367
3164	**1899**		N	1368
3165	**1900**		N	1369
3166	**1901**		N	1370

SHILLINGS

TENPENCE

3167	1867		By **L.C. Wyon, 1867**	R^3	1476
		Obv	Coroneted head, left, two long ties hanging down, date below		
		Leg	**VICTORIA D: G:** **BRITANNIAR: REG: F: D: 1867**		
		Rev	Square-topped shield, crowned, **W** below, All within a wreath of oak leaves		
		Leg	**ONE FRANC TEN PENCE**		

VICTORIA, 1827-1901
SIXPENCES

YOUNG HEAD
As shillings

First - A^1 plus
A^2 with die №

Second – A^4 plus
A^3 with die №

Third A^5
No lock on cheek

Rev. 1a

No die
number

Obv. A

With die
number

Rev. 1b

1a - early crown
Small letters

O over G

die number

1c - late crown
Large letters

Die number 6
double struck

453

SIXPENCES

| Small 6 | R over V | DRITANNIAR |

| 1848 over 6 | 5 over 3 | 8 over 6 | 8 over 7 | 9 over 8 |

| Roman I | large 44 | Small 44 | 1878 over 7 | 1847 |

Obv.	**A¹.**	First young head, bound with fillet, left. (Old ESC. A¹)
Leg.	2	**VICTORIA DEI GRATIA BRITANNIAR : REG : F : D :**
	A².	Second young head; similar, but head in lower relief (Old ESC. A³)
	A³.	Third young head, the Queen's hair is thinner and in longer waves, no lock on cheek. (Old ESC. A⁵)
Rev.	**1.**	Crown above value **SIX PENCE** between and an olive and oak branch tied with ribbon in a bow, date below (no die number)
	2.	As 1, but with a die number above the date under the bow

YOUNG HEAD

A¹/1a. First young head   (Old ESC. A¹)
       Rev. 1a - Early crown, no die number   Spink 3908

ESC	Date	Varieties		R	(Old ESC)
3168	**1838**			*N*	1682
3169	—	*Proof,* with milled edge	*wt. 2.83g*	*R³*	1683
3170	**1839**			*S*	1684
3171	—	*Proof,* with plain edge, in sets¹	*wt. 2.79g; wt. 2.79g*	*S*	1685
3172	—	*Proof,* with milled edge		*R⁵*	1685A
3173	**1840**			*R*	1686
3174	**1841**			*R*	1687

(continued)

SIXPENCES

ESC	Date	Varieties	R	(Old ESC)
3175	**1842**		R	1688
3176	**1843**		R	1689
3177	**1844**	Large **44** with serifs **C** over sideways **G** in VICTORIA	S	1690
3178	—	Small **44** no serifs & Roman **I** in date	R^2	1690A
3179	**1845**		R	1691
3180	**1846**		S	1692
3181	**1847**	See note ^{2}	R^6	1692A
3182	**1848**		R^3	1693
3183	—	**8** over **6**	R^3	1693A
3184	—	**8** over **7** ^{3}	R^3	1693B
3185	**1850**		R	1695
3186	—	**5** over **3** ^{4}	R^2	1695A
3187	**1851**		R	1696
3188	**1852**		R	1697
3189	**1853**		S	1698
3190	—	*Proof,* with milled edge (issued in the sets)	R^2	1699
3191	—	*Proof,* with plain edge	$R^?$	1699A
3192	**1854**		R^3	1700
3193	**1855**		S	1701
3194	—	**5** over **3**	R^2	1701A
3195	**1855**	*Proof*	R^3	1701B
3196	**1856**		S	1702
3197	—	Longer line below **PENCE**	S	1703
3198	**1857**		R	1704
3199	—	Longer line below **PENCE**	R	1705
3200	**1858**		R^2	1706
3201	—	*Proof, with milled edge* *wt. 2.82g*	R^5	1707
3202	—	**8** over **6**	R^3	1707A
3203	**1859**		S	1708
3204	—	**9** over **8**	R	1708A
3205	**1860**		R	1709
3206	—	Small **6** in date	R	1709A
3207	**1862**		R^3	1711
3208	—	*Proof*	R^3	1711A
3209	**1863**		R^2	1712
3210	**1866**		R^3	1716

SIXPENCES

A¹/1b. First young head   (Old ESC. A²)
Rev. 1b - Early crown, **with die number**   Spink 3909

ESC	Date	Max number	*(Recorded die numbers)* Varieties etc	R	(Old ESC)
3211	**1864**	58	*(1,3-15,17-20,22-24,27-31,33,34,36-38,40, 41,58)*	S	1713
3212	**1865**	32	*(1,3-19,21-24,32)*	R	1714
3213	**1866**	58	*(1-11,13,15-36,38-49,51,52,54-56,58,59)*	N	1715
3214	—	38	**8 over 6**	?	1715A

A²/1b. Second young head (in lower relief)   (Old ESC. A³)
Rev. 1b - Early crown, **with die number**   Spink 3910

ESC	Date	Max number	Varieties etc	R	(Old ESC)
3215	**1867**	23	*(1-15,17-21,23,26)*	R^2	1717
3216	—	2	*Proof with milled edge (2)* wt. 2.83g	R^5	1718
3217	—	24	*Proof, with plain edge (24 & 3)* wt. 2.78g	R^5	1718A
3218	**1868**	17	*(1-10,12-15,17)*	R^2	1719
3219	**1869**	17	*(1-17,19)*	R^2	1720
3220	—	7	*Proof with milled edge (7)* wt. 2.83g	R^5	1720A
3221	**1870**	19	*(2-10,12,19)*	R^2	1721
3222	—	10	*Proof with plain edge* wt. 2.84g	R^5	1722
3223	**1871**	54	*(1,2,6,7,9-13,15-18,20-29,31,32,34-39,41-43,45-48, 50,52,53,54)*	R	1723
3224	—	14	*Proof with plain edge* wt. 2.73g	R^5	1723B
3225	—	14	*Proof with milled edge (14)* wt. 2.81g	R^5	1723A
3226	**1872**	74	*(3-5,8,9,11-29,31-35,37-45,47,48,51-53,55-59,61-63, 67,69,70-74)*	R	1726
3227	—	11	*Proof with milled edge (11)* wt. 2.82g	R^5	1726A
3228	**1873**	124	*(1-6,8-21,24,26,29,31,34-45,47-49,51,52,53,59-63, 65-67,70,73-76,78,79,81,82,85-88,90-93,96,97,106, 115-118,120,121,124)*	S	1727
3229	**1874**	61	*(1-10,12-16,18-29,31-35,37,38,40-42,44,46,48,51-57, 59-61)*	S	1728
3230	**1875**	88	*(1,2,5,7-15,18,19,21-23,27-30-32,33-36,39,46,51-55, 57-59,62,63,65-67,69-75,77,78,84,88)*	S	1729
3231	**1876**	29	*(1,2,5-8,11,12,13,15,18-20,22,23,25,29)*	R^2	1730
3232	**1877**	34	*(1,2-5,8,11,13,14,16,18,20-22,24,25,27-29,31-35)*	S	1731
3233	**1878**	70	*(1,3,4-11,12,16,17,20-22,26-32,34,37-39,40,43,45, 47, 50,51-53,55-59,63,65,70)*	S	1733
3234	—	41	*Proof with milled edge (11)* ↑↓ wt. 2.75g-2.81g	R^5	1734
3235	—	30	Last **8 over 7**	R^4	1734A
3236	—	6	**D over B in DRITANNIAR**	R^3	1735
3237	**1879**	24	*(8,9,12,13,14,15,21)*	S	1736
3238	—	24	**9 over 8**	R^5	1736A

VICTORIA, 1827-1901
SIXPENCES

A²/1a. Second young head (in lower relief)　　(Old ESC. A⁴)
Rev. 1a - Early crown, no die number　　Spink 3911

ESC	Date	Varieties	R	(Old ESC)
3239	**1871**	See note ⁶	R^2	1724
3240	—		R^2	1718A
3241	—	*Proof*	R^6	1725
3242	**1873**		R^4	1727A
3243	**1877**		S	1732
3244	**1879**	122 teeth on *rev.*	R	1737
3245	—	No serif to **7**	R	
3246	—	*Proof*	R^5	1737A
3247	—	*Proof with plain edge struck en medaille* ↑↑	R^5	1737B

A³/1a. Third young head, no lock on cheek.　　(Old ESC. A⁵)
Rev. 1a - Early crown, no die number　　Spink 3912

3248	**1880**		R	1737C
3249	—	*Proof, milled edge*, with 1839 reverse die　*wt. 2.86g*	R^5	1738
3250	—	*Proof, milled edge*　*wt. 2.81g*	R^4	1739
3251	**1881**		S	1740
3252	—	*Proof with milled edge* ↑↑　*wt. 2.80g-2.83g*	R^4	1741
3253	—	*Proof with plain edge*	R^5	1742
3254	**1882**		R^2	1743
3255	**1883**		S	1744
3256	—	*Proof with plain edge*　*wt. 2.82g*	$R^?$	1744A
3257	**1884**		S	1745
3258	**1885**		S	1746
3259	—	*Proof with milled edge* ↑↓　*wt. 2.83g; wt. 2.84g*	R^6	1747
3260	**1886**		N	1748
3261	**1886**	*Proof*　*(Not traced)*	R^6	1749
3262	**1887**		C	1750
3263	—	*Proof with milled edge* ↑↓　*wt. 2.86g; wt. 2.87g*	R^5	1751

1　"Collectors could order 1839 proof sets, plus individual coins, until about 1851. After that you had to be a VIP or Royalty to obtain strikings until 1880's "(Steve Hill)
2　A sixpence dated 1847 was reported as having been found in Norfolk. It was apparently sent to both the Royal Mint and the B.M. who said they could find nothing wrong with it but were not prepared to say it was authentic *(Easter Daily Press, 17 July 1973)*
3　"Although mentioned by some authors, I have still not traced a coin dated 1849: probably those referred to in Mint records are dated 1848, but struck in 1849." (P.A.R.)
4　Ron Stafford says that the over struck figure is not typical of the period and might be struck from a broken punch.

457

SIXPENCES

JUBILEE HEAD

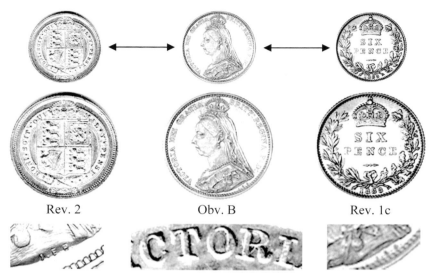

Rev. 2	Obv. B	Rev. 1c

J.E.B. on truncation	R over V	J.E.B. below truncation

Obv.	**B.**	Jubilee head; tall bust, left, draped and veiled, with a small crown perched on top of her head, initials **J.E.B** below truncation
Leg.	3	**VICTORIA DEI GRATIA BRITT: REGINA: F: D:**
Rev.	**2.**	Square-topped shield within Garter, crowned, date below divided by Garter buckle. No legend. *"Withdrawn type"* issued in one year only because if gilt would easily pass as half sovereigns

	B/2.	Jubilee head (withdrawn type reverse)	(Old ESC. B)
		Rev. 2 - Square-topped shield in Garter	Spink 3928

ESC	Date	Varieties	R	(Old ESC)
3264	**1887**		C^3	1752
3265	—	**R** of **Victoria** over **I**	R^3	1752A
3266	—	**R** of **Victoria** over **V**	R^3	1752C
3267	—	**J.E.B.** on truncation	R^3	1752B
3268	—	*Proof,* issued in the sets. **J.E.B.** on truncation *Edge,* milled *wt. 2.83g*	S	1753

(continued)

VICTORIA, 1827-1901
SIXPENCES

B/2. Jubilee head (withdrawn type reverse) (Old ESC. B)
Rev. 2 - Square-topped shield in Garter Spink 3928

ESC	Date	Varieties	R	(Old ESC)
3269	**1887**	*Proof,* issued in the sets. **J.E.B.** <u>below</u> truncation *Edge,* milled　　*wt. 2.84g*	R	1753A
3270	—	*Matt proof.* **J.E.B.** <u>below</u> truncation　*(Not traced)*	R⁶	1753B
3271	—	*Garter fills the whole interior of the crown?¹⁰*　*(Not traced)*	R⁷	1753C

B/1c. Jubilee head (Old ESC. C)
Rev. 1c - Late crown, large letters, no die number Spink 3929

ESC	Date	Varieties	R	(Old ESC)
3272	**1887**		C²	1754
3273	—	**R over I in VICTORIA & GRATIA**	R³	1754A
3274	—	**R over I over V in VICTORIA & GRATIA**	R³	1754B
3275	**1887**	*Proof struck en medaille ↑↑*　*wt. 2.81g; wt. 2.96g*	R³	1755
3276	—	*Matt proof from sand blasted dies*　*wt. 2.86g*	R³	1755A
3277	**1888**		N	1756
3278	—	*Proof struck en medaille ↑↑*　*wt. 2.81g; wt. 2.84g*	R⁶	1756A
3279	**1889**		N	1757
3280	**1890**		S	1758
3281	—	*Proof*　*(Not traced)*	R⁴	1758A
3282	**1891**		S	1759
3283	**1892**		S	1760
3284	**1893**		R³	1761

5　*"In 1863 the post of superintendent of the Coining Department became vacant and the Master, Thomas Graham, promoted his brother John to the position, despite the latter's inexperience. It was John Graham who introduced the practice of numbering the dies for denominations of sixpence and above* (excluding halfcrowns) *which passed through the Mint's Inspection Department. This was a way of enforcing quality control and monitoring the production of the machine operators or 'press boys'. For a few years all dies of a given annual date and denomination were numbered on strict numerical sequence, but following the death of both Graham brothers during the course of 1869 the system was relaxed somewhat, particularly on the gold coinage (Sommerville, SCMB May 1990, pp. 99-101)"* DNW 89, lot 1787

6　*"The decade between 1870 and 1880 saw much modernisation of the machinery at Tower Hill. From 1871 modern lever presses began to replace the old Boulton screw presses; by 1883 all old presses had been removed and replaced with 14 lever presses. During this transitional period, one would assume there would have to be a way to distinguish between the coins struck on the different types of press. It may well be that the 'no die number' sixpences of 1871, 1877 and 1879 were struck on new lever presses while those produced on the screw presses retained a die number (Sommerville, SCMB May 1990)"* (DNW 89, lot 1806)

SIXPENCES

OLD HEAD

Obv. C   Rev. 1c

Obv.	**C.**	Old head, coroneted, veiled and draped, left (Old ESC. D)
Leg.	1	**VICTORIA · DEI · GRA · BRITT ·**
		REGINA · FID · DEF · IND · IMP ·
Rev.	**1c.**	**SIX / PENCE** in wreath, similar to 1a, but larger lettering, late crown, no die number

(Old ESC. D)

C/1c. Old head / *Rev.* 1c   Spink 3941

ESC	Date	Varieties		R	(Old ESC)
3285	**1893**			N	1762
3286	—	*Proof,* issued in the sets	*wt. 2.82g*	N	1763
3287	**1894**			S	1764
3288	**1895**			S	1765
3289	**1896**			S	1766
3290	**1897**			N	1767
3291	**1898**			N	1768
3292	**1899**			N	1769
3293	**1900**			N	1770
3294	**1901**			C	1771

SIXPENCE
PATTERNS

No illustration of type E available

ESC	Date	Type	Varieties	R	(Old ESC)
3295	**1840**	E *Rev*	By **W. Wyon, 1840** As the current coin, but the *rev.* is ruled with fine horizontal lines *(Not traced)*	R^4	1772

Type
F

½ sov. die   Rev. 1c

| 3296 | **1841** | F
Obv
Leg
Rev | By **W. Wyon, 1841**
Head, left. From the half-sovereign die
VICTORIA DEI GRATIA
As the current sixpence. *In gold*   WR 377 | R^7 | 1773 |

Type
G

| 3297 | **1856** | G
Obv
Leg

Rev | By **W. Wyon & L.C. Wyon, 1856**
As the current coin, struck *en medaille* ↑↑
VICTORIA DEI GRATIA
BRITANNIAR : REG : F : D :
Similar to the current coin but reads
HALF / SHILLING in wreath, **1856**
date below, *Edge,* plain   *wt. 2.74g-2.83g* | R^4 | 1774 |

(continued)

SIXPENCE
PATTERNS

ESC	Date	Type	Varieties	R	(Old ESC)
3298	**1856**	**H** *Rev*	As before, but *rev.* reads ½ / **SHILLING** / **1856** date below *Edge,* plain *(Not traced)*	R^7	1775

 Type I

| 3299 | 1869 | I
 Obv
 Rev | By **T. Graham, 1869** [7]
 Young bust, left, no legend
 GRAHAM in centre, **PALLADIUM**
 HYDROGENIUM around, ✶**1869**✶ below
 Edge, plain. *Struck en medaille* ↑↑ *wt. 2.98g* | R^6 | |

 Type J

| 3300 | 1884 | J
 Obv
 Leg
 Rev | Unsigned (by **J.E. Boehm**), 1884
 Crowned veiled head, left
 VICTORIA DEI GRATIA 1884
 Crowned cruciform shields, with national <br> emblems in angles. *wt. 2.77g & wt. 2.88g*
 Edge, milled. *Struck en medaille* ↑↑ | R^6 | 1776 |

SIXPENCE
PATTERNS

Type
K

ESC	Date	Type	Varieties	R	(Old ESC)
3301	**1884**	**K**	Unsigned (*Obv.* after **L.C. Wyon**), **1884**	R^6	1776A
		Obv	Young bust, left, date below		
			(as on the half-sovereign)		
		Leg	**VICTORIA DEI GRATIA 1884**		
		Rev	Crowned oval shields cruciform in		
			cartouches *wt. 2.96g*		
			Edge, milled. *Struck en medaille* ↑↑		

Type
L

3302	1887	L	By **J.E. Boehm** & **L.C. Wyon, 1887**	R^7	1777
		Obv	As the Jubilee coin; **J.E.B.** below bust		
		Leg	**VICTORIA DEI GRATIA**		
			BRITT : REGINA F : D :		
		Rev	As the ordinary withdrawn Jubilee		
			sixpence, but date above divided by the		
			crown, **SIX PENCE** below.		
			Struck en medaille ↑↑		
			Edge, milled. *wt. 2.67g & wt. 2.78g*		

SIXPENCE
PATTERNS

 Type M

1   2

ESC	Date	Type	Varieties	R	(Old ESC)
3303	**1887**	**M¹/1**	By **J. Rochelle Thomas** for **Spink and Son**, dated **1887** As their *pattern* crown (ESC 342a) but beaded borders instead of ornate ones	R	1778
		Rev	**1** - Crowned arms, within the Garter, with lion and unicorn supporters with value **SIX PENCE** above and date *(64 struck)* **MDCCCLXXXVII** below, and below a spray of thisle, rose and shamrock *wt. 2.75g* dividing. **SPINK & SON** [8]. *Edge*, plain ↑↓		
3304	—	—	*In gold. Edge,* plain ↑↓ *(7 struck) wt. 4.65g*	R⁵	1779
3305	—	—	*In gold.* ↑↓ *wt. 4.61g* *WR380 wt. 4.63g* *Edge,* **MADE IN BAVARIA** (incuse)	R⁵	1779A
3306	—	—	*In copper.* *(10 struck) wt. 2.57g; 2.60g* *Edge,* **MADE IN BAVARIA** (incuse)	R⁵	1780
3307	—	—	*In aluminium.* *Edge,* plain ↑↓ *(20 struck) wt. 0.75g- 0.76g*	R⁴	1781
3308	—	—	*In tin. Edge,* plain ↑↓ *(9 struck) wt. 2.09g*	R⁵	1782
3309	—	—	*In silver. Edge,* milled *wt. 2.79g*	R²	1783
3310	—	—	*In copper. Edge,* milled *(Not traced)*	R⁴	1783A
3311	—	—	*In gold. Edge,* milled *(8 struck) wt. 2.61g-4.64g*	R⁴	1784
3312	—	—	*In nickel-bronze, en medaille*↑↑ *2.74g-2.79g*	R⁵	1784A

(continued)

SIXPENCE
PATTERNS

ESC	Date	Type	Varieties	R	(Old ESC)
3313	**1887**	**M¹/2** *Rev*	Similar, 2 - Without SPINK & SON below date	R	1784B

ESC	Date	Type	Varieties	R	(Old ESC)
3314	—	**M²/2** *Rev* *Edge*	Similar, but **JRT** on truncation 2 - Without SPINK & SON below date, Milled. *In nickel-bronze.*	$R^?$	1784C

ESC	Date	Type	Varieties	R	(Old ESC)
3315	—	**M³/2**	Similar, but with **S&S** on truncation 2 – Milled edge *wt. 2.82g*	$R^?$	1784D

ESC	Date	Type	Varieties	R	(Old ESC)
3316	—	**M⁴/2** *Rev* *Edge*	Similar, but S&S removed. 2 - Without SPINK & SON below date, Milled	$R^?$	1784E

7   *"Thomas Graham, master of the Mint from 1855 until his death in 1869, was an eminent chemist, renowned for his pioneering work on dialysis and the diffusion of gasses (Graham's Law). His interest in metallurgy prompted the striking of coins in various metals and establishing their reaction to gasses, including the absorption of hydrogen gas by palladium. According to his calculations this piece is said to contain 900 times its volume in hydrogen"* (DNW 89, lot 1800). Uncertain whether this is a Pattern Half Sovereign

8   Some of these coins have MADE IN BAVARIA lightly incuse on the edge. There are also Two reverse dies, with and without SPINK & SON. Are ESC 1783 & 1784d the same coin?

For sub-varieties of this series (beyond the remit of this publication) see Peter J. Davis, *BRITISH SILVER COINS SINCE 1816*, p. 64

GROATS

2 slanted   8 over 8 sideways

4 over ?   2 over 1   7 over 6   8 over 6   8 over 7

Type   **A**   Young head. *Edge*, milled
        B   Similar, but with Jubilee head *(Only issued for colonial use)*

Spink 3913

ESC	Date	Type	Varieties, comments etc.	R	(Old ESC)
3317	**1837**	A	*Proof. Edge* plain [1]	R^6	1929
			Obv. die is that of an early threepence		
3318	—	—	*Proof. Edge* milled ↑↓	R^6	1929A
3319	**1838**	—		C	1930
3320	—	—	*Proof. Edge* milled *(Not traced)*	R^4	1930A
3321	—	—	*Proof. Edge* plain *(Not traced)*	R^4	1931
3322	—	—	Second **8** of date over ∞ (**8** on its side)	R	1931A
3323	**1839**	—		N	1932
3324	—	—	*Proof. Edge* plain ↑↑ Issued in the sets	S	1933
3325	—	—	*Proof. Edge* plain ↑↓	R^2	1933A
3326	**1840**	—	Small **0**	C	1934
3327	—	—	Round **O** in date	S	1934A
3328	—	—	**0** over **9**	R	1934B
3329	**1841**	—		R	1935
3330	—	—	**4** of date over**?** and 2nd **1** out of line	R^3	1935A
3331	**1842**	—		N	1936
3332	—	—	*Proof. Edge* plain	R^3	1937
3333	—	—	**2** over **1**	R	1937A

(continued)

GROATS

ESC	Date	Type	Varieties, comments etc.	R	(Old ESC)
3334	**1843**	**A**		N	1938
3335	—	—	**4 over 5**	R^2	1938A
3336	**1844**	—		S	1939
3337	**1845**	—		N	1940
3338	**1846**	—		N	1941
3339	**1847**	—	**7 over 8**	R^4	1942
3340	**1848**	—		N	1943
3341	—	—	Second **8** over **6**	R	1944
3342	—	—	Second **8** over **7**	R	1944A
3343	**1849**	—		S	1945
3344	—	—	**9 over 8**	R	1946
3345	**1851**	—		R	1947
3346	**1852**	—	**2** of date slightly slanted	R^3	1948
3347	**1853**	—		R^5	1949
3348	—	—	*Proof,* issued in the sets. *Edge* milled	R^2	1950
3349	—	—	*Proof. Edge* plain	R^4	1951
3350	—	—	**5 over 3**	R^2	1951A
3351	**1854**	—		C	1952
3352	**1855**	—		N	1953
3353	**1857**	—	*Proof only. Edge* milled	R^5	1954
3354	**1857**	—	*Proof only. Edge* plain	R^5	1954A
3355	—	—	*Proof. Edge* milled. Late obverse die of threepence muled with normal reverse die	R^6	1955
3356	**1862**	—	*Proof. Edge* plain [2]	R^5	1955A
3357	—	—	*Proof. Edge* plain. Late obverse die of threepence muled with normal reverse die.	R^5	1955B
3358	—	—	*Proof. Edge* milled	R^5	1955C

ISSUED FOR COLONIAL USE ONLY

  Type B

3359	**1888**	**B**		N	1956
3360	—	—	*Proof*	R^4	1956A

1   See SCMB 784. December 1983, pp. 307-310 *"reason for the existence for this date"*

THREEPENCES

YOUNG HEAD

A^1 A^2 A^3 A^4

Twin arch crown   1   2   Single arch crown

1a   1b   2   RRITANNIAR

5 over 5   A^4 QED   1866   8 over 6

Proof

VICTORIA, 1837-1901
THREEPENCES

JUBILEE HEAD   OLD HEAD

B   Jubilee head   Old head   C

Type	A.	Young head with subtle differences;
Obv.	A^1.	First bust, young head, high relief, ear fully visible
	A^2.	First bust variety, slightly older portrait with aquiline nose, top left of ear covered by hair strands
	A^3.	Second bust, slightly larger, lower relief, the mouth fuller, nose more pronounced, rounded truncation
	A^4.	Second bust as before, but with reverse '1b' below
	A^5.	Third bust, older features, mouth closed, hair strands leading from 'bun' vary
	B.	Jubilee type as before; see note [1]
	C.	Old head as before; see note [2]
Rev.	**1a.**	Large wide crown with double arches. Subtle variations; space between cross on crown and tooth border; with *obv.* $A^{1, 2 \& 3}$
	1b.	As before, but tie ribbon further from tooth border, and cross on crown nearer to tooth border; with *obv.* $A^{3 \& 4}$
	2.	Smaller crown with a single arch

469

THREEPENCES

YOUNG HEAD

A¹/1a. First young head, high relief, ear fully visible
Rev. 1a – Space between cross on crown and border (Old ESC. A¹)
★Note; these were struck for Colonial use only   Spink 3914

ESC	Date	Varieties	R	Old ESC	ESC	Date	Varieties	R	Old ESC
3361	**1838**	*In gold*	R^6	2447a					
3362	**1838**	★	S	2048	3382	**1852**	★ Note [3]	R^4	
3363	—	BRITANNIA**B**	R^4		3383	—	**5 over 5**	$R^?$	
3364	**1839**	★	R	2049	3384	**1853**		R^2	2060
3365	**1839**	*Proof*	S		3385	—	*Proof* in sets	R^2	
3366	**1840**	★	S	2050	3386	**1854**		N	2061
3367	**1841**	★	R	2051	3387	**1855**		R	2062
3368	**1842**	★	S	2052	3388	**1856**		N	2063
3369	**1843**	★	N	2053	3389	**1857**		S	2064
3370	**1844**	★	S	2054	3390	**1858**		N	2065
3371	**1845**	Large date	C	2055	3391	—	BRITANNIA**B** **B**EGINA	R^2	
3372	—	Small date			3392	—	**8 over 6**	R^2	
3373	**1846**		R^3	2056	3393	—	**8 over 5**	R	
3374	**1847**	★	R^4		3394	**1859**		N	2066
3375	**1848**	★	R^4		3395	**1860**		S	2067a
3376	**1849**		R	2057	3396	**1861**		N	2068
3377	**1850**	Small **50**	N	2058					
3378	—	large **50**	N	2058					
3379	**1851**		N	2059					
3380	—	**5 over 8**	R^2						
3381	**1551**	(sic) Error*	R^6						

*Error recorded by P.J. Davis in *British Silver Coinage since 1816* (*Not traced. M.B.*)

A²/1a. First bust variety, older portrait with aquiline nose   Spink 3914A
Rev. 1a – Space between cross on crown and border   (Old ESC. A²)

ESC	Date	Varieties	R	Old ESC	ESC	Date	Varieties	R	Old ESC
3397	**1859**		N	2066A	3403	**1865**		S	2072
3398	**1860**		N	2067	3404	**1866**		N	2073
3399	**1861**		N	2068A	3405	—	*Proof*	R^6	
3400	**1862**		N	2069	3406	**1867**		N	2074
3401	**1863**		S	2070	3407	**1868**		N	2075
3402	**1864**		N	2071	3408	—	**B**RITANNIAR	R^3	

THREEPENCES

A³/1a. Second bust, larger, lower relief, mouth fuller, nose more
pronounced, rounded truncation   Spink 3914B
Rev. 1a – Space between cross on crown and border   (Old ESC. A³)

ESC	Date	Varieties	R	Old ESC	ESC	Date	Varieties	R	Old ESC
3409	1867		R						

A⁴/1b. Second bust as before   (Old ESC. A⁵)
Rev. 1b – Cross on crown close to border   Spink 3914C

ESC	Date	Varieties	R	Old ESC	ESC	Date	Varieties	R	Old ESC
3410	1866		R^6		3419	1875		C	2081
3411	1867		S	2074B	3420	1876		C	2082
3412	1868		R		3421	1877		N	2083
3413	1869		R	2075	3422	1878		N	2084
3414	1870		N	2076	3423	1879		N	2085
3415	1871		S	2077	3424	—	*Proof*	R^4	2086
3416	1872		S	2078	3425	—	**9 over 6**	R^5	
3417	1873		C	2079	3426	1884		C	2091
3418	1874		C	2080					

A⁵/1b. Third bust, older features, mouth closed,
hair strands leading from 'bun' vary   (Old ESC. A⁵)
Rev. 1b – Cross on crown close to border   Spink 3914D

ESC	Date	Varieties	R	Old ESC	ESC	Date	Varieties	R	Old ESC
3427	1880		N	2087	3431	1885		C	2092
3428	1881		C	2088	3432	—	*Proof*↑↓ ¹·⁴¹ᵍ	R^5	
3429	1882		S	2089	3433	1886		C	2093
3430	1883		C	2090	3434	1887		N	2094
					3435	—	*Proof*	R^4	2095

JUBILEE HEAD

B/1b. Jubilee head   (Old ESC. B)
Rev. 1b – Cross on crown close to border   Spink 3931

ESC	Date	Varieties	R	Old ESC	ESC	Date	Varieties	R	Old ESC
3436	1887	Note ¹	C^2	2096	3440	1890		C	2100
3437	—	*Proof*	S	2097	3441	1891		C	2101
3438	1888	Note ¹	S	2098	3442	1892		S	2102
3439	1889		C	2099	3443	1893	Note ¹	R^2	2103

THREEPENCES

OLD HEAD

C/1b. Old head   (Old ESC. C)

Rev. 1b – Cross on crown close to border   Spink 3942

ESC	Date	Varieties	R	Old ESC
3444	**1893**		C	2104
3445	—	*Proof*	N	2105
3446	**1894**		C	2106
3447	**1895**		C	2107
3448	**1896**		C	2108
3449	**1897**		C	2109

ESC	Date	Varieties	R	Old ESC
3450	**1898**		C	2110
3451	**1899**		C	2111
3452	—	**9 over 8**	R^5	
3453	**1900**		C	2112
3454	**1901**		C	2113

PATTERN

3455	1868		By **L.C. Wyon, 1868**	R^6	2113A
		Obv	As type A, but the head of the Queen is laureate as on the Maltese third-farthing		
		Rev	As currency issues		

1 The ordinary threepences of this and subsequently reigns can be distinguished from Maundy coins as they have a somewhat dull surface whereas the Maundy threepences look more like proofs with a highly polished field, the latter tone much more easily, and are often bluish or quite dark. The young head threepences are rather scarcer than marked in really first class condition.

2 It is possible that threepences were struck for Colonial use in 1847; a piece dated 1852 and undoubtedly a Colonial issue was shown to me by Mr. P. Mitchell in February 1990 (P.A.R)

3 The Jubilee type threepence was struck in 1887 for currency, but not until 1888 for inclusion in the Maundy sets. The rare Jubilee type threepence of 1893 differs from the Maundy threepence of that year as the coinage changed to the 'Old head 'before Easter.

4 For Colonial use only

VICTORIA, 1837-1901
TWOPENCE, THREE HALFPENCE & PENNY
(Issued for Colonial use)

TWOPENCE

Spink 3914E

ESC	Date	Varieties	R	(Old ESC)
3456	**1838**		C^2	2248
3457	—	Last **8** reads **S** *(is this due to a filled die?)**		
3458	**1848**		C	2249
3459	**1868**	*Proof, plain edge, struck en medaille ↑↑*	R^6	
3460	**1885**	*Proof ↑↓* wt. 0.95g	R^6	

*Error recorded by P.J. Davis in *British Silver Coinage since 1816, p. 72 (Not traced. M.B.)*

THREE HALFPENCE

2 over 2   1843 over?

TWOPENCE, THREE HALFPENCE & PENNY
(Issued for Colonial use)

Obv. Young head
Rev. Value 1½ crowned, date below within two oak branches

Spink 3915

ESC	Date	Varieties	R	(Old ESC)
3461	**1838**		*N*	2254
3462	—	*Proof* ↑↓ *wt. 0.70g*	R^3	2254A
3463	**1838**	**8 over 4**	R^2	2254B
3464	**1839**		*C*	2255
3465	**1840**		R^2	2256
3466	**1841**		*S*	2257
3467	**1842**		*S*	2258
3468	**1843**		C^2	2259
3469	—	*Proof*	R^5	2259A
3470	—	**43 over 34?**	R^2	2259B
3471	—	*Proof*	R^5	2259C
3472	**1860**		*R*	2260
3473	**1862**		*R*	2261
3474	—	*Proof*	R^5	2261A
3475	**1870**	*Proof or Pattern*	R^5	2262

PENNY

3476	**1868**	*Proof plain edge, struck en medaille* ↑↑	R^6	
3477	**1878**	*Proof plain edge*	R^3	

VICTORIA, 1837-1901
MAUNDY SETS

Type   **A**   **Young head** with standard rev.

B   **Jubilee head** with standard reverse [1]

C   **Old head** with standard reverse

VICTORIA, 1837-1901
MAUNDY SETS

YOUNG HEAD

A. Young head with standard reverse Spink 3916

ESC	Date	Varieties	Brian Robinson page 169	R	Old ESC
3478	**1838**		1d – 383; 2d – 384; 3d - 385; 4d - 386	N	2445
3479	—	*Proof*	1d – 387; 2d – 388; 3d - 389; 4d - 390	R^3	2446
3480	—	*In gold*	1d – 391; 2d – 392; 3d - 393; 4d - 394	R^5	2447
3481	**1839**		1d – 395; 2d – 396; 3d - 397; 4d - 398	N	2448
3482	—	*Proof*	1d – 399; 2d – 400; 3d - 401; 4d - 402	R	2449
3483	**1840**		1d – 403; 2d – 404; 3d - 405; 4d - 406	N	2450
3484	**1841**		1d – 407; 2d – 408; 3d - 409; 4d - 410	S	2451
3485	**1842**		1d – 411; 2d – 412; 3d - 413; 4d - 414	S	2452
3486	**1843**		1d – 415; 2d – 416; 3d - 417; 4d - 418	N	2453
3487	**1844**		1d – 419; 2d – 420; 3d - 421; 4d - 422	S	2454
3488	**1845**		1d – 423; 2d – 424; 3d - 425; 4d - 426	N	2455
3489	**1846**		1d – 427; 2d – 428; 3d - 429; 4d - 430	R	1456
3490	**1847**		1d – 431; 2d – 432; 3d – 433; 4d - 434	R	2457
3491	**1848**		1d – 435; 2d – 436; 3d - 437; 4d - 438	R	2458
3492	**1849**		1d – 439; 2d – 440; 3d - 441; 4d - 442	S	2459
3493	**1850**		1d – 443; 2d – 444; 3d - 445; 4d - 446	N	2460
3494	**1851**		1d – 447; 2d – 448; 3d - 449; 4d - 450	N	2461
3495	**1852**		1d – 451; 2d – 452; 3d - 453; 4d - 454	R	2462
3496	**1853**		1d – 455; 2d – 456; 3d - 457; 4d - 458	R	2463
3497	—	*Proof*	1d – 459; 2d – 460; 3d - 461; 4d - 462	R^2	2464
3498	**1854**		1d – 463; 2d – 464; 3d - 465; 4d - 466	N	2465
3499	**1855**		1d – 467; 2d – 468; 3d - 469; 4d - 470	S	2466
3500	**1856**		1d – 471; 2d – 472; 3d - 473; 4d - 474	N	2467
3501	**1857**		1d – 475; 2d – 476; 3d - 477; 4d - 478	N	2468
3502	—	2d - Reads; **BRITANNIAE EEGINA**	2d – 476(i)	R	2469
3503	**1858**		1d – 479; 2d – 480; 3d - 481; 4d - 482	N	2469A
3504	**1859**		1d – 483; 2d – 484; 3d - 485; 4d - 486	N	2470
3505	—	2d - Reads; **BEITANNIAE**	2d – 484(i)	R	2471
3506	**1860**		1d – 487; 2d – 488; 3d - 489; 4d - 490	N	2471A
3507	**1861**		1d – 491; 2d – 492; 3d - 493; 4d - 494	N	2472
3508	—	2d – **6 over 1**	2d – 492(i)	N	2473
3509	**1862**		1d – 495; 2d – 496; 3d - 497; 4d - 498	N	2473
3510	—	2d – No colons after **D G**	2d – 496(i)	N	2473A

(continued)

MAUNDY SETS

ESC	Date	Varieties	*Brian Robinson page 169*		R	Old ESC
3511	**1863**	4d – all with a flaw over **63**	*1d – 499; 2d – 500; 3d – 501; 4d –502*		*N*	2474
3512	**1864**		*1d – 503; 2d – 504; 3d – 505; 4d – 506*		*N*	2475
3513	**1865**		*1d – 507; 2d – 508; 3d – 509; 4d – 510*		*N*	2476
3514	**1866**		*1d – 511; 2d – 512; 3d – 513; 4d – 514*		*N*	2477
3515	—	2d - *Proof*	*2d – 515*		*R³*	2477A
3516	**1867**		*1d – 516; 2d – 517; 3d – 518; 4d – 519*		*N*	2478
3517	—	*Proof*	*1d – 520; 2d – 521; 3d – 522; 4d – 523*		*R³*	2479
3518	**1868**		*1d – 524; 2d – 525; 3d – 526; 4d – 527*		*N*	2480
3519	—	3d - Reads; **RRITANNIAR**	*3d – 526(i)*		*R⁶*	2480B
3520	—	*Proof*	*1d – 528; 2d – 529; 3d – 530; 4d – 531*		*R⁴*	2480A
3521	**1869**		*1d – 532 2d – 533; 3d – 534; 4d – 435*		*N*	2481
3522	**1870**		*1d – 536; 2d – 537; 3d – 538; 4d – 539*		*N*	2482
3523	**1871**		*1d – 540; 2d – 541; 3d – 542; 4d – 543*		*N*	2483
3524	—	*Proof* ²	*1d – 544; 2d – 545; 3d – 546; 4d – 547*		*R⁴*	2484
3525	**1872**		*1d – 548; 2d – 549; 3d – 550; 4d – 551*		*N*	2485
3526	**1873**		*1d – 552; 2d – 553; 3d – 554; 4d – 555*		*N*	2486
3527	**1874**		*1d – 556; 2d – 557; 3d – 558; 4d – 559*		*N*	2487
3528	**1875**		*1d – 560; 2d – 561; 3d – 562; 4d – 563*		*N*	2488
3529	**1876**		*1d – 564; 2d – 565; 3d – 566; 4d – 567*		*N*	2489
3530	**1877**		*1d – 568; 2d – 569; 3d – 570; 4d – 571*		*N*	2490
3531	**1878**		*1d – 572; 2d – 573; 3d – 574; 4d – 575*		*N*	2491
3532	—	*Proof*	*1d – 576; 2d – 577; 3d – 578; 4d – 579*		*R³*	2492
3533	**1879**		*1d – 580; 2d – 581; 3d – 582; 4d – 583*		*N*	2493
3534	—	*Proof*			*R³*	2493A
3535	**1880**		*1d – 584; 2d – 585; 3d – 586; 4d – 587*		*N*	2494
3536	**1881**		*1d – 588; 2d – 589; 3d – 590; 4d – 591*		*N*	2495
3537	—		*1d – 592; 2d – 593; 3d – 594; 4d – 595*		*N*	2495
3538	**1882**		*1d – 596; 2d – 597; 3d – 598; 4d – 599*		*N*	2496
3539	—	*Proof*			*R⁵*	2496A
3540	**1883**		*1d – 600; 2d – 601; 3d – 602; 4d – 603*		*N*	2497
3541	**1884**		*1d – 604; 2d – 605; 3d – 606; 4d – 607*		*N*	2498
3542	**1885**		*1d – 608; 2d – 609; 3d – 610; 4d – 611*		*N*	2499
3543	**1886**		*1d – 612; 2d – 613; 3d – 614; 4d – 615*		*N*	2500
3544	**1887**		*1d – 616; 2d – 617; 3d – 618; 4d – 619*		*S*	2501

MAUNDY SETS

JUBILEE HEAD

B. Jubilee head with standard reverse[1] Spink 3932

ESC	Date	Varieties	*Brian Robinson page 176*	R	Old ESC
3545	**1888**		*1d – 620; 2d – 621; 3d – 622; 4d – 623*	*S*	2502
3546	—	*Proof*	*1d – 624; 2d – 625; 3d – 626; 4d – 627*	*R³*	2503
3547	**1889**		*1d – 628; 2d – 629; 3d – 630; 4d – 631*	*S*	2504
3548	**1890**		*1d – 632; 2d – 633; 3d – 634; 4d – 635*	*S*	2505
3549	**1891**		*1d – 636; 2d – 637; 3d – 638; 4d – 639*	*S*	2506
3550	**1892**		*1d – 640; 2d – 641; 3d – 642; 4d – 643*	*S*	2507

1   The Jubilee bust was not used on the Maundy money of 1887 as the Maundy ceremony was some weeks prior to the Jubilee

OLD HEAD

C. Old head with standard reverse Spink 3943

ESC	Date	Varieties	*Brian Robinson page 177*	R	Old ESC
3551	**1893**		*1d – 644; 2d – 645; 3d – 646; 4d – 647*	*C*	2508
3552	**1894**		*1d – 648; 2d – 649; 3d – 650; 4d – 651*	*C*	2509
3553	**1895**		*1d – 652; 2d – 653; 3d – 654; 4d – 655*	*C*	2510
3554	**1896**		*1d – 656; 2d – 657; 3d – 658; 4d – 659*	*C*	2511
3555	**1897**		*1d – 660; 2d – 661; 3d – 662; 4d – 663*	*C*	2512
3556	**1898**		*1d – 664; 2d – 665; 3d – 666; 4d – 667*	*C*	2513
3557	**1899**		*1d – 668; 2d – 669; 3d – 670; 4d – 671*	*C*	2514
3558	**1900**		*1d – 672; 2d – 673; 3d – 674; 4d – 675*	*C*	2515
3559	**1901**		*1d – 676; 2d – 677; 3d – 678; 4d – 679*	*C*	2516

CROWNS

There was only one issue of coins during this reign, the obverse portrait of the King being engraved by George William De Saulles, as also were the new reverse designs for the halfcrown, florin and shilling. The florin of this reign is notable in that it shows the standing figure of Britannia. It was also during this reign that the practice of using a reducing machine was generally adopted and for this reason it would probably be more correct to refer to the engraver as the designer. (P.A.Rayner, 1949)

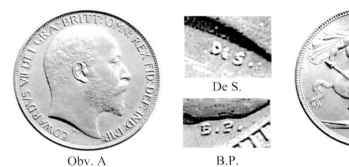

De S.

B.P.

Rev. 1

Obv. A

	Only the one issue, type and date
Obv.	His bare head facing right, engraver's initials **De S·** below
Leg.	**EDWARDVS VII DEI GRA : BRITT : OMN : REX FID : DEF : IND : IMP :**
Rev.	Pistrucci's St George and dragon, right, Date **1902** and initials **B.P.** in exergue
Edge	**DECUS ET TUTAMEN * ANNO REGNI II *** In raised letters

Spink 3978

ESC	Date	Varieties	R	L&S	(Old ESC)
3560	**1902**		C		361
3561	—	Words on edge in wrong order	R^5		361A
3562	—	*Proof,* matt surface; issued in the sets	N	2	362

Note

Rarities of all the following denominations as marked only apply to coins in EF condition – Fair specimens are not uncommon, apart from 1905, but uncirculated pieces are probably rarer than indicated

CROWNS

PATTERNS
£1, 10/- or 5/-

London
LONDONIA

Numbered
in exergue

ESC	Date	Varieties	R	L&S	(Old ESC)
3563	1902	**By Spink & Son, dated 1902**	R^3	4	363
		After the Tower crowns of Charles I			
	Obv	Crowned and robed equestrian figure of King to left, upright sword in right hand, ground line below, Anglo-Saxon monogram of London (Londonia) in field behind King, beaded inner circle			
	Leg	**EDWARD : VII . D : G : BRITT : ET TERRAR : TRANSMARIN : 1902 ·** *'Edward VII by the Grace of God King of Britain and territories beyond the seas'*			
	Rev	Oval garnished shield, beaded inner circle			
	Leg	**Q : I : D : S : BRITANNICA · REX · FID : DEF : IND : IMP :** (mintmark) **Sun** *'? ? Defender of the Faith, Emperor of India'*			
	Edge	Plain *Slaney, wt. 36.12g*			
3564	—	*In gold* *(6 known) W&R 413, wt. 79.98g*	R^6	5	364
3565	—	*In silver* on a thick flan of double weight to represent a half-pound or ten-shilling piece *(6 struck)* *wt. circa 75g?*	R^5	6	365
3566	—	*In silver* on a thicker flan to represent a one pound *(6 struck)* *wt. 128.5g*	R^5	7	366

HALFCROWNS

De S·

	Only one type, as the crown
Obv.	His bare head facing right, initials **De S·** below
Leg.	**EDWARDVS VII DEI GRA: BRITT: OMN: REX**
Rev.	Crowned spade-shape shield within the Garter
Leg.	**FID: DEF: IND: IMP:**
	· HALF · 19 02 · CROWN ·
Edge	Milled

Spink3980

ESC	Date	Varieties	R	(Old ESC)
3567	**1902**	See note [1]	C	746
3568	—	*Proof,* matt surface; issued in the sets	N	747
3569	**1903**	See note [2]	R^2	748
3570	**1904**		R	749
3571	**1905**		R^2	750
3572	**1906**		S	751
3573	**1907**		R	752
3574	**1908**		R	753
3575	**1909**		R	754
3576	**1910**		S	755

Note

[1]   During World War II, I received in change a very worn halfcrown mule – *obv.* Edward VII; *rev.* Victoria old head issue, dated 1901. (P.A. Rayner)

[2]   Halfcrown's of 1903, 1904 and 1905 are rare in any condition, particularly the last date (Beware of convincing modern fakes). Other dates are only as rare as marked if in EF state. This rule applies also to later reigns.

FLORINS

Only one type, as illustration

DES·

Obv.	His bare head facing right, engraver's initials **DE S·** below
Leg.	**EDWARDVS VII DEI GRA: BRITT: OMN: REX**
Rev.	Britannia[1] standing, three-quarters facing, on prow of a ship. Her right hand grasps a trident close below the prongs, her left hand rests on an oval shield, held slightly tilted, and heraldically inscribed with the flag of the Union. On her shoulders she wears a cloak which blows out behind her to her right. Behind, the sea, terminating in the horizon. On the prow of the ship the date, waves below. The legend is separated from the design by two linear half circles which spring from behind the prow of the ship and terminate to left and right of Britannia. (H.A. Greuber)
Leg.	**ONE FLORIN** **TWO SHILLINGS**
Edge	Milled

Spink 3981

ESC	Date	Varieties	R	(Old ESC)
3577	**1902**		C	919
3578	—	*Proof,* matt surface; issued in the sets	N	920
3579	**1903**		S	921
3580	**1904**		R	922
3581	**1905**		R^2	923
3582	**1906**		S	924
3583	**1907**		S	925
3584	**1908**		R	926
3585	**1909**		R	927
3586	**1910**		S	928

1   The figure of Britannia was modelled on the Chancellor of the Exchequer's second daughter Lady Susan Hicks-Beach

SHILLINGS

Only one type, as illustration

Obv.	His bare head facing right, engraver's initials **De S·** below
Leg.	**EDWARDVS VII DEI GRA: BRITT: OMN: REX**
Rev.	Crown surmounted by a standing lion, dividing date
Leg.	**FID: DEF: IND: IMP: ONE SHILLINGS**
Edge	Milled

Spink 3982

ESC	Date	Varieties	R	(Old ESC)
3587	**1902**		*N*	1410
3588	—	*Proof,* matt surface; issued in the sets	*N*	1411
3589	**1903**		*R*	1412
3590	**1904**		*R*	1413
3591	**1905**		*R²*	1414
3592	**1906**		*N*	1415
3593	**1907**		*S*	1416
3594	**1908**		*R*	1417
3595	**1909**		*S*	1418
3596	**1910**		*N*	1419

Note

Rarities indicated for coins of Edward VII only apply to EF specimens. Worn pieces are Fairly easy to obtain apart from 1904 and 1905, which are probably R even in low grade, and R³ in EF or better condition. Mint state examples of all dates other than 1902 or 1910 are becoming increasingly difficult to find

SIXPENCES

Only one type, as illustration

Obv.	His bare head facing right, engraver's initials **De S·** below
Leg.	**EDWARDVS VII DEI GRA: BRITT: OMN:**
	REX FID: DEF: IND: IMP:
Rev.	**SIX / PENCE** in wreath, crown above, date below
Edge	Milled

Spink 3983

ESC	Date	Varieties	R	(Old ESC)
3597	**1902**		*N*	1785
3598	—	*Proof,* matt surface; issued in the sets	*N*	1786
3599	**1903**		*S*	1787
3600	**1904**		*R*	1788
3601	**1905**		*S*	1789
3602	**1906**		*S*	1790
3603	**1907**		*S*	1791
3604	**1908**		*R*	1792
3605	**1909**		*S*	1793
3606	**1910**		*N*	1794

Rarities etc. as shillings

MAUNDY

SETS OF THE FOUR COINS
Only one type

Obv.	Type and legend as sixpence
Rev.	Crown above value in the centre, dividing date, between two branches; olive left and oak right, tied together with ribbon in a bow.
Edge	Plain

Spink 3985

ESC	Date	Varieties	*Brian Robinson page 179*	R	Old ESC
3607	**1902**		*1d – 680; 2d – 681; 3d - 682; 4d - 683*	C	2517
3608	—	*Matt proof*	*1d – 684; 2d – 685; 3d - 686; 4d - 687*	N	2518
3609	**1903**		*1d – 688; 2d – 689; 3d - 690; 4d - 691*	C	2519
3610	**1904**		*1d – 692; 2d – 693; 3d - 694; 4d - 695*	C	2520
3611	**1905**		*1d – 696; 2d – 697; 3d - 698; 4d - 699*	C	2521
3612	**1906**		*1d – 700; 2d – 701; 3d - 702; 4d - 703*	C	2522
3613	**1907**		*1d – 704; 2d – 705; 3d - 706; 4d - 707*	C	2523
3614	**1908**		*1d – 708; 2d – 709; 3d - 710; 4d - 711*	C	2524
3615	**1909**		*1d – 712; 2d – 713; 3d - 714; 4d - 715*	S	2525
3616	**1910**		*1d – 716; 2d – 717; 3d - 718; 4d - 719*	S	2526

MAUNDY

CURRENCY THREEPENCE

There is a subtle change in the style of the figure 3
on the reverse from 1904 onwards

Obvious difference

Compare the size and
shape of the bulbous end
of the figure 3

Maundy

Non Maundy

Obv.		As the florins			
Rev.		As the threepence in the Maundy set		Spink 3984	
ESC	Date	Varieties		R	Old ESC
3617	**1902**			N	2114
3618	—	*Matt proof*		N	2115
3619	**1903**			S	2116
3620	**1904**			S	2117
3621	**1905**			S	2118
3622	**1906**			S	2119
3623	**1907**			S	2120
3624	**1908**			N	2121
3625	**1909**			S	2122
3626	**1910**			S	2123

These coins are commoner than marked in worn state, but apart from 1902 and 1910, they
are probably at least *R* in mint state.
Note; a slight change in the style of the figure 3 on the reverse from 1904 onwards.

GEORGE V
1910-1935
INTRODUCTION

The coinage of this reign is usually considered to fall into four distinct issues, the first two being almost identical apart from fineness. The obverse portrait of George V used throughout the reign with small modifications was prepared from plaster casts made by Sir Bertram MacKennal and his initials B.M. appear on the truncation of the bust. The reverse designs for the halfcrown and shilling were modifications of De Saulles's design for Edward VII, but the sixpence no longer has the words SIX PENCE on the reverse and is a smaller version of the shilling, showing the crown surmounted by a lion crowned. The florin was designed after the style of the 1887 Jubilee issue piece, but was somewhat modified. The designer is not known and it was probably carried out by a staff engraver at the Royal Mint.

In 1920, after the First World War, for a few months the price of silver rose above 5/6d per ounce resulting in the metal price of the coinage being greater than its face value with the danger of profiteering. It was, therefore, resolved to debase the silver coinage for the first time since the reign of Edward VI

The new second (debased) issue was struck in metal of which 50% was silver and 50% alloy. At first great difficulty was experienced in finding a suitable alloy and the early coins in worn condition soon turned dull, almost a brownish colour. The authorities quickly improved the mixture and later coins do not become so discoloured. This second coinage appears to have been struck from new dies with the king's bust in lower relief, but the Mint informs us that the same bust was used, but that as the coins were in a different metal the resistance to the dies would be different. This would account for the apparent lower relief. Furthermore the engineers may have varied the striking pressure according to the alloy used and the rate of wear on the dies. Different dies do exist: there are a large number of minor varieties.

In 1926 the effigy of the king was slightly modified, the initials of the engraver's name were moved towards the rear of the truncation and the whole head slightly reduced in size; also a new beaded border was added. This type is often known as the *'modified effigy'* type or more correctly 'third coinage'.

In 1927 it was decided to change again the reverse types of the silver coins and two innovations occur. Up to this issue no crown had been struck for this reign, but through the efforts of Sir Charles Oman, then President of the Royal Numismatic Society and an M.P. for Oxford, this denomination was included.

GEORGE V
1910-1935
INTRODUCTION

However, there was so little demand for it that small numbers were struck at Christmas time for people to give as presents in the years 1927-36. The threepenny piece now had a reverse design of three acorns and can therefore be easily distinguished from the Maundy threepence. In 1930 the reverse dies of the Maundy were re-engraved but the design was not changed. All the new reverse types for the fourth coinage were designed by Kruger Gray.

The Royal Mint Museum Collection contains many patterns for this and later reigns, most of which are not available to collectors. However, from time to time some come on the market and are therefore included in this publication.

In 1935 the first true British commemorative coin was issued to mark the King's Silver Jubilee. The modernistic St. George reverse was designed by Percy Metcalfe. Twenty-five special Jubilee crowns were struck in gold[1] and two thousand five hundred were struck in sterling silver for the public and as the Mint received far more orders than they could supply, they were distributed by ballot[2]. These pieces had an edge inscription in relief whereas on the normal coins it is incuse.

PROOFS

Regular proof; design and field with a mirror finish
V.I.P. proof; the raised design is frosted[3] and the field has a mirror finish
Matt proof; the design and field has a matt finish to facilitate photography

Proofs usually have plain edges, but not always
(See *'Provenances'* for proven specimens of *V.I.P proofs*)

1	An extra five were struck for National Collections making a total of 30
2	1,329 applications for the gold examples
3	The incuse design on a die was treated with a mild acid solution to create the frosted effect

GEORGE V, 1910-36
CROWNS

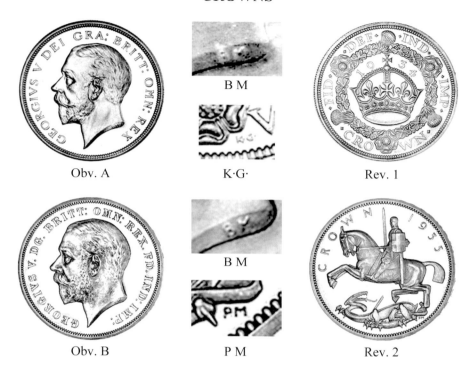

Obv. A	K·G·	Rev. 1

B M (top center crop), K·G· (bottom center crop), B M (lower center crop), P M (bottom center crop)

Obv. B	P M	Rev. 2

Type	**A.**	Bare head, left, **B M** on truncation (Bertram MacKennal)
Leg.	1	**GEORGIVS V DEI GRA: BRITT: OMN: REX**
Rev.	**1.**	Large crown and date above within wreath ornate with three roses and three thistles breaking the legend. **K·G.** above lower beading
Leg.		**·FID·✿·DEF· ·IND·✿·IMP· // ·CRO ✿ WN·**
Edge		Milled, in debased silver (·500) from now until 1947 (Cu.-Ni)
	B.	Head as last
Leg.	2	**GEORGIVS V. D G. BRITT: OMN:**
		REX. F D. IND: IMP:
Rev.	**2.**	St George and dragon of modernistic style, **P M** below dragon's tail (Percy Metcalfe)
Edge		Incusely inscribed **DECUS ET TUTAMEN ANNO XXV**

GEORGE V, 1910-36
CROWNS

A/1. Bare head, *leg.* 1 - **DEI   GRA**
  Rev. 1 – Crown, date above, within ornate wreath   Spink 4036

ESC	Date	Varieties, remarks, etc.	R	L&S	(Old ESC)
3630	**1926**	*Proof. Uniface reverse* [1] *Obv.* **MODEL**	R^7	50a	
3631	**1927**	*Proof only,* in sets *(15,030 struck)*	N	36	367
3632	—	Matt, sand blasted flan	R^7	37	367A
3633	**1928**	*(9,034 pieces struck)*	N		368
3634	—	*Proof*	R^5		368A
3635	—	*V.I.P. Proof*	R^6		368B
3636	**1929**	*(4,994 pieces struck)*	S	38	369
3637	—	*Proof*	R^5		369A
3638	**1930**	*(4,847 pieces struck)*	S	39	370
3639	**1931**	*(4,056 pieces struck)*	S		371
3640	—	*Proof*	R^6	40	371A
3641	**1932**	*(2,395 pieces struck)*	S		372
3642	—	*Proof*	R^5	41	372A
3643	—	*V.I.P. Proof*	R^6	41	372B
3644	**1933**	*(7,132 pieces struck)*	N		373
3645	—	*Proof*	R^5	42	373A
3646	—	*V.I.P. Proof*	R^5		373B
3647	**1934**	*(Only 932 pieces struck)*	R^2		374
3648	—	*Proof*	R^6	43	374A
3649	**1936**	Issued during the following reign of Edward VIII *(2,473 pieces struck)*	R		381
3650	—	*Proof*	$R^?$	50	381A

B/2. Bare head, *leg.* 2 - **D G**
  Rev. 2 – St George and dragon of modernistic style   Spink 4048

ESC	Date	Varieties, remarks, etc.	R	L&S	(Old ESC)
3651	**1935**	*(714,769 pieces struck)*	C^3		375
3652	—	Specimen issued in box [2]	N	44	376
3653	—	*Proof* in good silver (·925) [2]	R^5	45	377
3654	—	*Proof* in silver (·500)	R^6		377A
3655	—	*Proof or pattern* (·925) [2] Raised lettering on edge *(2,500 issued in boxes)*	R	46	378
3656	—	*Proof or pattern In gold* *(28 struck, 25 issued)*	R^3	47	379
3657	—	*Proof Edge* error (segments in wrong order) **DECUS ANNO REGNI ET TUTAMEN· XXV**	R^5	48	380

490

CROWNS

PATTERNS

A.G.WYON.

Obv. C   A.G.W.   Rev. 3

ESC	Date	Varieties, remarks, etc.	R	L&S	(Old ESC)
3658	C Obv. Leg Rev.	By **Allen G. Wyon,** undated (1910) Bare head, left, **A.G.WYON.** on truncation **GEORGIUS V D: G: BRITT: OMN: REX** **MDCDX** (1910) **3** - A fine conception of St George and the dragon left, filling the whole field. **A.G.W.** to lower right. Plain edge *(10 struck)*	R^5	1	382
3659	—	*In gold.* Plain edge *W&R 420*	R^6	2	383
3660	—	*In silver.* Milled edge ↑↑ *(10 struck)* *wt. 25.7g-28.95g*	R^5	3	384
3661	—	*In gold.* Milled edge *(2 known?)* *wt. 52.37g*	R^6	4	385
3662	—	*In plated copper, matt finish* Plain edge *(2 known)*	R^6	5	386
3663	—	*In copper.* Plain edge	R^6	6	386A
3664	—	*Lead impression of cancelled dies (obv/rev)*	R^7	7	386B

GEORGE V, 1910-36
CROWNS

PATTERNS

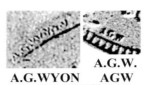

Obv. D² - A.G.WYON   Obv. D¹ - No initials   Rev. 4

ESC	Date	Varieties, remarks, etc.	R	L&S	(Old ESC)
3665	**D¹** *Obv.* *Leg* *Rev.*	**By Allen G. Wyon, dated 1910** Larger bare head, left (without initials) **GEORGIVS V D: G: BRITANNIARVM OMNIVM REX** **4 -** Smaller St George and dragon design on a straight ground line, **A.G.W.** in relief, behind horse's hind legs. **1910** in exergue. Plain edge *(10 Struck) wt. 32.47g*	R^5	8	387
3666	—	*In gold.* Plain edge *(2 known) W&R 422, wt. 55.83g*	R^6	9	388
3667	—	*In silver.* Milled edge *(10 struck) wt. 32.66g*	R^5		390A
3668	—	*In silver.* Milled edge. On smaller thinner flan *wt. 438 grs, 28.38g*	R^5	12	391
3669	—	*In silver.* Milled edge. Matt surface all over *(Unique?) wt. 425 grs, 27.54g*	R^7	13	391A
3670	**D²**	As before, but **A.G.WYON** incuse on truncation *In silver.* Milled edge *(10 Struck) wt. 30.91g -32.28g*	R^5	10	389
3671	—	*In gold.* Milled edge *(2 struck) W&R 423, wt. 56.04g*	R^6	11	390
3672	—	*In silver.* Plain edge *(10 struck) wt. 424 grs, 27.47g*			389A
3673	—	*In copper, edge?*		14	389B
3674	—	*In copper.* Plain edge		15	389C
3675	—	*Lead impression of cancelled dies (obv/rev)*	R^7	16	

GEORGE V, 1910-36
CROWNS

PATTERNS

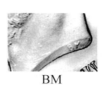

BM

Obv. A   Rev. 5

ESC	Date	Varieties, remarks, etc.	R	L&S	(Old ESC)
3676	**1935**	By **B. MacKennal & Kruger Gray**	R^6	49	391B
	Obv.	**A** - As current type with **B M** on truncation			
	Leg	**GEORGIVS V DEI GRA:**			
		BRITT: OMN: REX			
	Rev.	**5** - St George with lance piercing dragon; he is mounted on a very finely executed horse, quite unlike that on the current coin; date **1935** in front and value **CROWN** behind			
	Edge	**DECUS ET TUTAMEN**			
		ANNO REGNI XXV in relief.			
		In silver (3 or 4 known)			

Note
See Wilson & Rasmussen, pp. 481-4 for details of strikings in gold

Old ESC 375a is deleted because the edge error is undoubtedly due to collar slippage.

1   Part of a set 5s. to 3d, the Crown and halfcrown dated 1926 the remainder 1927, 1925, 1925 and 1927 respectively. (John Kromas Collection)

2   The mint had many more applications for the raised edge pattern than the 2,500 they had struck. The unlucky applicants were offered a specimen of the ordinary crown in a box; these were carefully struck and are superior to the ordinary coins. There are, however, a few very rare proofs of the incuse edge issue, №. 377, with highly polished field, actually better finished and more mirror-like than patterns.

GEORGE V, 1910-36
DOUBLE FLORINS
(UNOFFICIAL)
By John Pinches for **Reginald Huth**
Usually struck *en medaille* ↑↑
By **A.G. Wyon**?
Whenever these unofficial coins come on the market they are eagerly sought after.
For that reason they are included and numerated in this publication

Rampant dragon for
Wales

L&S 1
Both Silver (Ag) &
Copper (Cu)

Triskelion for
Isle of Man

Phosphor bronze (PB)

Anglesey Copper (AC)

Cornish Copper (CC)

Cadmium (Cd)

Iron (Fe)

Nickel (Ni)

Lead (Pb)

Tin (Sn)

Zinc (Zn)

GEORGE V, 1910-36
DOUBLE FLORINS
(UNOFFICIAL)

Platinum (Pt)
(No illustration)

A – Roman Is in date

B – Roman Is in date

C– curved 1s in date

5

D – curved 1s in date

Obv.	**1.**	Bare-headed bust draped, left, struck in silver unless stated*
Leg.		**GEORGIVS · V · DEI · GRATIA**

Location of metal type*; (s) above right s̲houlder; (t) below t̲runcation; (e) on e̲dge

Rev.		Crowned cruciform shields of England, Scotland, Ireland and Wales (rampant dragon), legs of Man ('triskeles') within star in centre, emblems in the angles; rose, thistle, leek and shamrocks.

Roman I's in date

Rev. leg.	**A.**	👑 REX · I9 👑 II · BRI 👑 TANI 👑 ARVM
—	**B.**	👑 REX · I9 👑 II · BRI 👑 DOUBLE 👑 FLORIN

Curved 1's in date

—	**C.**	👑 BRI · *J9* 👑 *JJ* · REX 👑 DOUBLE 👑 FLORIN
—	**D.**	👑 BRI · *J9* 👑 *J4* · REX 👑 TWELVE 👑 GROATS

DOUBLE FLORINS
(UNOFFICIAL)

Edges	i	Plain
	ii	Incuse name of metal in capitals; **SILVER, COPPER** or reads **SHIPS NAILS CALSHOT CASTLE MAY 1896** *(A device fort built by Henry VIII part of his defences of the Solent)*
	iii	Incuse in capitals **ON DEMAND IN LONDON LIVERPOOL OR ANGLESEY** *(As on the Anglesey Penny tokens of 1787)*
	iv	Milled

Roman figure **I**

Type 1/A.　♔ **REX · I9** ♔ **II · BRI** ♔ **TANI** ♔ **ARVM**

ESC	Date	Stamped incuse* Name of metal	Edge	R	L&S	Old ESC	Comments	Wt-gm
3677	**1911**		i	R^2	18	401	*In silver, thick flan*	22.69
3678	—		iv	R^2	19	401	*In silver*	
3679	—	(s) **LEAD**	i	R^6	?	402	*Thick flan*	26.27
3680	—	(s) **IRON**	ii	R^5	?	402	*Edge* **SHIPS NAILS** etc	27.21
3681	—	**PHOSPHOR** (t) **BRONZE**	i	R^6	23	402		20.10
3682	—	**ANGLESEY** (t) **COPPER**	iii	R^6	24	402	*4 mm thick flan* Edge. **ON DEMAND ....**	28.51
3683	—	**ANGLESEY** (t) **COPPER**	iii	R^6		402	*Silver plated. Edge.* **ON DEMAND ....**	26.87
3684	—	**CORNISH** (t) **COPPER**	i	R^6	25	402		18.14

Roman figure **I**

Type 1/B.　♔ **REX · I9** ♔ **II · BRI** ♔ **DOUBLE** ♔ **FLORIN**

ESC	Date	Stamped incuse	Edge	R	L&S	Old ESC	Comments	Wt-gm
3685	**1911**		i	R^2	20	402	*In silver*	22.61
3686	—	(s) **IRON**	ii	R^5	21	402	*Edge* **SHIPS NAILS** etc	27.22

Curved 1's in date

Type 1/C.　♔ **REX · J9** ♔ **JJ · BRI** ♔ **DOUBLE** ♔ **FLORIN**

ESC	Date	Stamped incuse	Edge	R	L&S	Old ESC	Comments	Wt-gm
3687	**1911**		i	R^7	?	402	*In silver. Struck without a collar*	20.60
3688	—	(s) **IRON**	i	R^6	?	402	*2.9mm thick flan.* *Obverse convex (dished bowl effect)*	19.35
3689	—	(s) **ZINC**	i	R^6	22	402	*5.8mm thick flan* *(Prone to corrosion)*	39.91

(continued)

DOUBLE FLORINS
(UNOFFICIAL)

ESC	Date	Stamped incuse* Name of metal	Edge	R	L&S	Old ESC	Comments	Wt-gm
3690	**1911**	(t) **CADMIUM**	i	R^6	?		*5.2mm thick flan* Warning; handle with care, poisonous if ingested!	38.75
3691	—	(t) **NICKEL**	i	R^6	?	402		
3692	—	(e) **SILVER**	ii	R^7	?	402	Note: **SILVER** on edge	22.70
3693	—		i	R^6			*In copper (not stated)*	16.55
3694	—	(e) **COPPER**	ii	R^6			*3mm thick flan* Note: **COPPER** on edge	22.56

Curved 1's in date

Type 1/D. ♛ **REX · J9** ♛ **J4 · BRI** ♛ **TWELVE** ♛ **GROATS**

ESC	Date	Stamped incuse* Name of metal	Edge	R	L&S	Old ESC	Comments	Wt-gm
3695	**1914**		i	R^6	26	403	*In silver. Thick flan*	22.69
3696	—		i	R^7	?	402	*In silver. Struck without a collar*	20.60
3697	—	(se) **NICKEL**	i	R^6	27	403		
3698	—	(s) **ZINC**	i	R^6	22	402	*Piedfort* (Prone to corrosion)	36.16
3699		**PLATINUM**	i	R^6	28	404	*(Not traced)*	
3700	—		iv	R^2	29	405	*In silver. Milled edge*	22.59
3701	—		iv	R^2	30	406	*In gold Milled edge*	22.55
3702	—	(s) **TIN**	i	R^7			*5mm thick flan*	36.18
3703	—	(s) **LEAD**	i	R^7			*4.5mm thick flan*	43.59
3704	—	(e) **COPPER**	ii	R^4			*3mm thick flan* Note: **COPPER** on edge	22.49
3705	—	(e) **SILVER**	ii	R^7	?	403	Note: **SILVER** on edge	22.79

(Mule) ♛ **REX · I9** ♛ **II · BRI** ♛ **DOUBLE** ♛ **FLORIN**
Type B/D. ♛ **REX · J9** ♛ **J4 · BRI** ♛ **TWELVE** ♛ **GROATS**

ESC	Date	Stamped incuse* Name of metal	Edge	R	L&S	Old ESC	Comments	Wt-gm
3706	**1911/1914**		i	R^5	31	406a	*In silver. Milled edge*	22.57
3707	— / —		i	R^6	32?	406a	*In silver. Piedfort Milled edge*	36.12

Curved 1's in date (Traces of under type very evident)

Type **D** . ♛ **REX · J9** ♛ **J4 · BRI** ♛ **TWELVE** ♛ **GROATS**
Muled with Pattern for **a Spanish 150 Peseta 1904**

ESC	Date	Stamped incuse* Name of metal	Edge	R	L&S	Old ESC	Comments	Wt-gm
3708	**1914**		iv	R^4	33?	405	*In silver. Milled edge*	

GEORGE V, 1910-36
HALFCROWNS

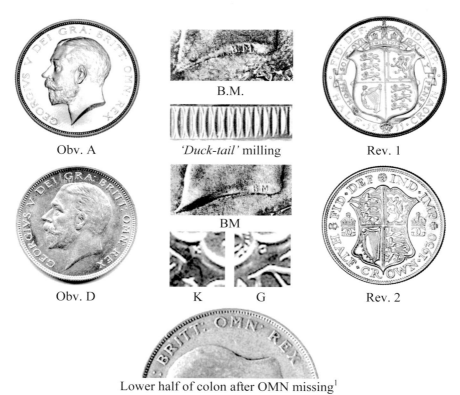

Obv. A

B.M.

'Duck-tail' milling

Rev. 1

Obv. D

K   G

BM

Rev. 2

Lower half of colon after OMN missing[1]

Type	**A.**	First coinage; deeply engraved in Sterling silver (·925 silver) Bare head, left, **B.M.** nearly central on deep truncation
Leg.		**GEORGIVS V DEI GRA: BRITT: OMN: REX**
Rev.	1	Crowned shield in Garter, date below divided by the buckle
Leg.		• **FID: DEF:** ♛ **IND: IMP:** • **HALF· 19 11 · CROWN**
	B.	Second coinage; deeply engraved, but in debased silver (·500 fine = 50% silver and 50% alloy) Bare head as before
	B¹.	Second coinage; re-cut shallow portrait in debased silver (·500 fine) Bare head as before

498

GEORGE V, 1910-36
HALFCROWNS

C. Third coinage. As before, but modified effigy; the initials **BM** are nearer to the back of a longer truncation (see front) and without stops, beading is more pronounced on both sides

D. Fourth coinage. Modified bare head as 'C' with a new reverse

Rev. **2.** Shield with concave sides (uncrowned), two interlinked **G**s crowned either side; beading more pronounced like obverse Initials **K - G** (George Kruger Gray) below shield

Leg. (Thistle) **FID · DEF ⊛ IND · IMP** (Shamrock) **HALF· CROWN ·** (date)

A/1. 1ˢᵗ Coinage; Bare head, **B.M.** nearly central on truncation ·925 ag
Rev. 1 - Crowned shield in Garter, date below   Spink 4011

ESC	Date	Varieties, remarks, etc.	R	(Old ESC)
3709	**1911**		*N*	757
3710	—	*Proof*	*S*	758
3711	**1912**		*S*	759
3712	**1913**		*R*	760
3713	**1914**		*S*	761
3714	**1915**		*N*	762
3715	**1916**		*N*	763
3716	**1917**		*N*	764
3717	**1918**		*N*	765
3718	**1919**		*S*	766

B/1. 2ⁿᵈ Coinage; Debased silver (·500 fine). Bare head as before
Rev. 1 - Crowned shield in Garter, date below   Spink 4021

3719	**1920**	Hollow neck	*S*	767

B¹/1. As before, but in lower relief
Rev. 1 - Crowned shield in Garter, date below   Spink 4021A

3720	**1920**		*S*	767A
3721	—	*Specimen with 'Duck-tail' milling*	*R⁵*	767B
3722	**1921**		*S*	768
3723	**1922**		*S*	769
3724	**1923**		*S*	770

(continued)

HALFCROWNS

ESC	Date	Varieties, remarks, etc.	R	(Old ESC)
3725	**1924**		*S*	771
3726	—	*Matt proof. Specimen finish* (2 known)	*R⁶*	771A
3727	**1925**		*S*	772
3728	**1926**		*R*	773

C/1. 3rd Coinage; 'Modified effigy' (silver ·500 fine). Bare head as before, **BM** without stops nearer the back of longer truncation
Rev. 1 - Crowned shield in Garter, date below Spink 4032

ESC	Date	Varieties	R	(Old ESC)
3729	**1926**	See note [2]	*S*	774
3730	**1927**		*N*	775
3731	—	*Proof in gold (4 struck) weights vary between 17.44-19.89g* See matching *gold* florin 1922 [3]	*R⁶*	775A

D/2. 4th Coinage; as 'C' with 'New type *rev.*' (silver ·500 fine)
Rev. 2 - Uncrowned shield with concave sides Spink 4037

ESC	Date	Varieties	R	(Old ESC)
3732	**1927**	*Proof only* [4]	*N*	776
3733	—	*Matt proof*	*R⁷*	776A
3734	**1928**		*N*	777
3735	—	*Proof*	*R*	777A
3736	—	*In bronze (flan officially cut, see below)* wt. 9.63g	*R⁶*	777B
3737	**1929**		*N*	778
3738	—	*Proof*	*R*	778A
3739	**1930**		*R²*	779
3740	—	*Proof*	*R²*	779A
3741	**1931**		*S*	780
3742	—	*Proof*	*R*	780A
3743	**1932**		*S*	781
3744	—	*Proof*	*S*	781A
3745	**1933**		*S*	782
3746	—	*Proof*	*R*	782A
3747	**1934**		*S*	783
3748	—	*Proof*	*R*	783A
3749	**1935**		*N*	784
3750	—	*Proof*	*R*	784A
3751	**1936**		*N*	785
3752	—	*Proof*	*R*	785A
3753	—	*V.I.P. proof*	*R*	785B

HALFCROWNS

PATTERN

3754	**1926**	Uniface model of new reverse, dated **1926** Type D Shield with concave sides (uncrowned), two interlinked **G**s crowned either side; beading more pronounced like obverse Initials **K - G** (George Kruger Gray) below shield	R^4	774A
	Leg.	(Thistle) **FID · DEF ✲ IND · IMP** (Shamrock) **HALF· CR OWN · 1926**		

Bronze trial
Officially cut at the Mint

1   *'No colon after OMN'* de-listed - This is not a true variety, but simply caused by a filled die. (See illustration)

2   Although the rarity has been reduced from *R* to *S* it is rarer than the 1927 coin; this 2nd coinage piece of 1926 is rarer than the following 3rd coinage piece of the same date

3   See Wilson & Rasmussen, pp. 487-8 for details of other unique strikings in gold
      See article *George V Florins and Halfcrowns in Gold,* SNC 1984, pp. 218-9

4   Many of the following dates were struck as *proofs* (not all are proven at present)

GEORGE V, 1910-36
FLORINS

As the halfcrown

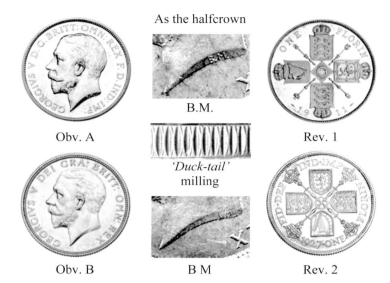

Obv. A

B.M.

Rev. 1

'Duck-tail'
milling

Obv. B

B M

Rev. 2

Type	**A.**	First coinage in high relief. Sterling silver (·925 silver) Bare head, left, **B.M.** nearly central on deep truncation
Leg.		**GEORGIVS V D. G. BRITT: OMN: REX F. D. IND: IMP:**
Rev.	**1.**	Crowned cruciform shields, star of Garter in centre, sceptre in each angle, date below
Leg.		♛ **ONE** ♛ **FLORIN** ♛ - **19** ♛ **11** -

B.   Second coinage; deeply engraved, but in debased silver (·500 fine = 50% silver and 50% alloy) Bare head as before

B¹.   Second coinage; recut shallow portrait in debased silver (·500 fine) Bare head as before

C.   Fourth coinage; as before, but modified effigy; the initials **BM** are nearer to the back of a longer truncation (see front) and without stops, beading is more pronounced on both *obv.* & *rev.*

FLORINS

Rev. **2.** Cruciform shields, **G** in centre, crowned sceptres in each angle
Leg. ♛ **FID · DEF** ♛ **IND · IMP** ♛
  1927· ONE ♛ **FLORIN**

A/1. 1st Coinage; Bare head, **B.M.** nearly central on truncation ·925 ag
  Rev. 1 - Crowned cruciform shields with sceptres   Spink 4012

ESC	Date	Varieties, remarks, etc.	R	(Old ESC)
3755	**1911**		N	929
3756	—	*Proof*	S	930
3757	**1912**		S	931
3758	**1913**		S	932
3759	**1914**		N	933
3760	**1915**		R^2	934
3761	**1916**		N	935
3762	**1917**		S	936
3763	**1918**		C	937
3764	**1919**		N	938

B/1. 2nd Coinage; Debased silver (·500 fine). Bare head as before
  Rev. 1 - Crowned cruciform shields with sceptres   Spink 4022

ESC	Date	Varieties, remarks, etc.	R	(Old ESC)
3765	**1920**		S	939

B¹/1. As before, but in lower relief
  Rev. 1 - Crowned cruciform shields with sceptres   Spink 4022A

ESC	Date	Varieties, remarks, etc.	R	(Old ESC)
3766	**1920**		S	939A
3767	—	*Specimen with 'Duck-tail' milling* [1]	$R^?$	939B
3768	**1921**		C	940
3769	**1922**		N	941
3770	—	*Proof in 24 ct gold on a thick flan (unique)* wt. 25.41g	R^7	941A
3771	—	*Proof in ·875 gold* alloyed with 150 silver & 100 copper See article SNC 1984 p.218 (2 struck) wt. 19.25g & wt. 17.44g	R^6	941B
3772	—	*Proof in ·750 gold alloy ag & cu* (1 struck) wt. 17.01g	R^7	941C
3773	—	*Proof in ·625 gold alloy ag & cu* (1 struck?) wt. 14.83g	R^7	941D
3774	**1923**		N	942
3775	**1924**		S	943
3776	—	*Matt proof specimen* (2 known)	R^6	943A
3777	**1925**		S	944
3778	**1926**		S	945

FLORINS

C/2. 4th Coinage; 'Modified effigy' (·500 fine). Bare head as before, **BM** without stops and nearer the back of longer truncation

Rev. 2 - Cruciform shields with crowned sceptres   Spink 4038

ESC	Date	Varieties, remarks, etc.		R	(Old ESC)
3779	**1927**	*Proof*		N	947
3780	—	*Matt Proof*		N	947A
3781	**1928**			N	948
3782	—	*Proof*	*(Not traced)*	R^6	948A
3783	**1929**			N	949
3784	—	*Proof*	*(Not traced)*	N	949A
3785	**1930**			N	950
3786	—	*Proof*		R^4	950A
3787	**1931**			S	951
3788	—	*Proof*	*(Not traced)*	R^6	951A
3789	**1932**			R	952
3790	—	*Proof*	*(5 known)*	R^4	952A
3791	**1933**			S	953
3792	—	*Proof*		R^5	953A
3793	**1935**			N	954
3794	—	*Proof*		R^4	954A
3795	—	*V.I.P. Proof*		R^6	954B
3796	**1936**			N	955
3797	—	*Proof*		R^4	955A
3798	—	*V.I.P. proof*		R^6	955B

1   *In addition to the half-crown and florin, once in my collection, other denominations, may have been struck to complete a set.* (M.B.)
2   "George V Florins and Halfcrown's in Gold" by G.P. Dyer, SNC 1984, pp. 218-9
3   See Wilson & Rasmussen, pp. 487-8 for details of other unique strikings in gold

SHILLINGS

Obv. A

Rev. 1

Obv. C

Rev. 2

K G

SHILLINGS

Obv.	**A.**	First coinage (·925 silver); as half-crown; his bare head, left, **B.M.** almost central on truncation
Leg.		**GEORGIVS V DEI GRA: BRITT: OMN: REX**
Rev.	**1.**	Crowned lion standing on a crown dividing date, all within an inner circle
Leg.		**FID: DEF: IND: IMP:** // **ONE SHILLING** (colons)
	B.	Second coinage; deeply engraved, but in debased silver (·500 fine = 50% silver and 50% alloy) Bare head as before
	B¹.	Second coinage; bare head as before, but re-cut shallow portrait in debased silver (·500 fine)
	C.	Third coinage; *'Modified effigy'* as other denominations
Leg.		**GEORGIVS V DEI GRA: BRITT: OMN: REX**
Rev.	**2.**	Similar, but no inner circle, larger crown, lion's crown and tail to outer beading dividing *leg.*, date in legend, **KG** above lion's tail.
Leg.		**FID · DEF** KG **IND · IMP** // **· ONE · SHILLING · 1927 ·**(stops)

A/1. 1St Coinage (·925 silver); Bare head, left, **B.M.** on truncation, *Rev.* 1 - Lion standing on crown, within circle   Spink 4013

ESC	Date	Varieties, remarks, etc.	R	(Old ESC)
3799	**1911**		*C*	1420
3800	—	*Proof*	*S*	1421
3801	**1912**		*N*	1422
3802	**1913**		*N*	1423
3803	**1914**		*N*	1424
3804	**1915**		*N*	1425
3805	**1916**		*N*	1426
3806	**1917**		*N*	1427
3807	**1918**		*N*	1428
3808	**1919**		*N*	1429

B/1. 2nd Coinage, debased silver (·500 fine), deeply engraved *Rev.* 1 - Lion standing on crown, within circle   Spink 4023

ESC	Date	Varieties, remarks, etc.	R	(Old ESC)
3809	**1920**		*N*	1430
3810	**1921**	King's nose to **S**	*S*	1431

SHILLINGS

B¹/1.   As before, but in lower relief
Rev. 1 - Lion standing on crown, within circle   Spink 4023A

ESC	Date	Varieties, remarks, etc.		R	(Old ESC)
3811	**1920**			N	1430
3812	—	*Specimen with 'Duck-tailed' milling* [1]	*(Not traced)*	R^2	1430A
3813	**1921**	King's nose to **SV**		S	1431
3814	—	*Proof*	*(Not traced)*		1431A
3815	**1922**			S	1432
3816	—	*Proof*	*(Not traced)*	S	1432A
3817	—	*Proof in gold*		R^6	1432B
3818	**1923**			N	1433
3819	—	*In nickel* [1]		R^4	1433A
3820	**1924**			R	1434
3821	—	*In nickel, struck en medaille* ↑↑ [2]	*wt. 5.68g*	R^4	1434A
3822	—	*Specimen with matt finish*	*(2 known)*	R^7	1434B
3823	**1925**			R	1435
3824	—	*Proof*	*(Not traced)*		1435A
3825	**1926**			S	1436
3826	—	*Proof*	*(Not traced)*		1436A

C/1.   3rd Coinage; 'Modified effigy' (silver ·500 fine). Bare head as
before, **BM** without stops, nearer the back of longer truncation
Rev. 1 - Lion standing on crown, within circle   Spink 4033

ESC	Date			R	(Old ESC)
3827	**1926**			S	1437
3828	**1927**			S	1438

C/2.   4th Coinage; as 'C' with 'New type *rev.*' (silver ·500 fine)
Rev. 2 - Lion standing on crown, no inner circle   Spink 4039

ESC	Date			R	(Old ESC)
3829	**1927**			S	1439
3830	—	*Proof*		N	1440
3831	—	*Matt proof*	*(Not traced)*	R^7	1440A
3832	**1928**			N	1441
3833	—	*Proof*		R^5	1441A
3834	—	*V.I.P. Proof*		R^6	1441B
3835	**1929**			N	1442
3836	—	*Proof*	*(Not traced)*	R^4	1442A
3837	**1930**			R	1443
3838	—	*Proof*		R	1443A

(continued)

SHILLINGS

ESC	Date	Varieties, remarks, etc.		R	(Old ESC)
3839	**1931**			*S*	1444
3840	—	*Proof*		*S*	1444A
3841	—	*V.I.P. Proof*		*S*	1444B
3842	**1932**			*N*	1445
3843	—	*Proof*		R^4	1445A
3844	—	*V.I.P. Proof*		R^4	1445B
3845	**1933**			*N*	1446
3846	—	*Proof*		*N*	1446A
3847	**1934**			*N*	1447
3848	—	*Proof*		R^4	1447A
3849	—	*V.I.P. Proof*		R^4	1447B
3850	**1935**			*N*	1448
3851	—	*Proof*	*(Not traced)*	R^4	1448A
3852	—	*V.I.P. Proof*		R^5	1448B
3853	**1936**			*C*	1449
3854	—	*Proof*		R^4	1449A
3855	—	*V.I.P. Proof*		R^5	1449B

PATTERNS

Obv. C

In nickel

Rev. 3

In nickel

3856	**1925**	As the fourth coinage, current coin. In nickel but the lion's tail slightly different style	R^7	1449A
3857	—	*In lead*	R^7	1449B

SHILLINGS

PATTERNS

Rev. 3
In pure nickel

ESC	Date	Varieties, remarks, etc.	R	(Old ESC)
3858	**1926**	By **Derwent Wood**	R^6	
	Obv	Uniface reverse, struck to a matt finish		
	Rev	**MODEL**		
	Leg	Stylised lion on crown, date **1926** below		
		FID: DEF: IND: IMP:		
		· ONE SHILLING ·		
	Edge	Milled		

1   See halfcrown and florin notes. V.I.P. proofs exist for many dates
2   Trial pieces, struck when the introduction of nickel coinage was being considered.

GEORGE V, 1910-36
OCTORINO or EIGHTPENCE

EIGHT ♔ PENCE   OCTO ♔ RINO

ESC	Date		Varieties		R	(Old ESC)
3859	**1913**		By **John Pinches** for **Reginald Huth**		R^4	1481
		Obv	Bare headed bust left, draped			
		Leg	**GEORGIVS · V · DEI · GRATIA**			
		Rev	1 - Crowned cruciform shields, clockwise			SPK 182
			in angles, a thistle, leek, shamrock & rose			
		Leg	♔ **BRI · 19** ♔ **13 · REX** ♔			
			EIGHT ♔ **PENCE**			
		Edge	Milled. *In silver*			
3860	—	—	*In nickel*		R^4	1481A
3861	—	—	*In gold*	*W&R 429*	R^4	1481B
3862	—	—	*In platinum, polished finish*		R^4	1481C
3863	—	—	*In platinum, matt finish*		R^4	1481D
3864	—	—	*In copper*		R^4	1481E
3865	—	—	*In iron*	*(Not traced)*	R^4	1481F
3866	—	—	*In iron. Piedfort*		R^7	1481G

ESC	Date		Varieties		R	(Old ESC)
3867	**1913**	*Obv*	As before with		R^3	1482
		Rev	2 - reads · **OCTO** ♔ **RINO** ·			
		Edge	Milled. *In silver*			
3868	—	—	*In gold*	*W&R 428*	R^4	1482B
3869	—	—	*In copper*		R^4	1482A
3870	—	—	*In lead*	*wt. 5.69g*	$R^?$	1482C

SIXPENCES

Type A – 1st coinage
(.925 silver)

B.M. central on
truncation - thin rim

1st reverse
Thin rim

Type B – 2nd coinage - As type A but in debased silver (.500 fine)

Type C
2nd coinage
(.500 fine silver)
New beading
Broader rim

B.M. central on
truncation - broader rim

2nd reverse
Broader rim

Modified effigy

Type D
2nd reverse

Slightly smaller bust
BM nearer the back of
neck – broader rim

Type E
3rd reverse

GEORGE V, 1910-36
SIXPENCES

1ˢᵗ coinage
B.M. almost central

Modified effigy
BM nearer back of neck

K G Kruger Gray

Obverse type as previous denominations

Obv.   **A.**   First coinage (·925 silver); His bare head, left, **B.M.** on truncation
Leg.   **GEORGIVS V DEI GRA: BRITT: OMN: REX**

Rev.   **1.**   As shilling; lion on crown dividing date, within inner circle
Leg.   **FID: DEF: IND: IMP: // SIXPENCE**

      B.   Second coinage; deeply engraved, but in debased silver
            (·500 fine = 50% silver and 50% alloy) Bare head as before

      C.   As 'B', but new beading and a broader rim

      D.   Modified effigy, as other denominations; slightly smaller bust,
            BM nearer the back of neck, with *rev.* 1

      E.   Similar, modified effigy, with *rev.* 2

      F.   Similar, but closer milling, 140 serrations
Leg.   **GEORGIVS V D. G. BRITT: OMN: REX F· D· IND: IMP:**

      2.   Three oak sprigs with 6 acorns dividing *leg.* **K G** in centre
Leg.   **🔒· SIX 🔒 PEN 🔒 CE ·🔒**
             · A ·🔒 1936 🔒· D ·

SIXPENCES

A/1. 1ˢᵗ Coinage (·925 silver); Bare head, left, **B.M.** on truncation,
Rev. 1 - Lion standing on crown, within circle   Spink 4014

ESC	Date	Varieties, remarks, etc.	R	(Old ESC)
3871	**1911**		C	1795
3872	—	*Proof* _____ wt. 2.81g	S	1796
3873	**1912**		N	1797
3874	**1913**		N	1798
3875	**1914**		N	1799
3876	**1915**		N	1800
3877	**1916**		N	1801
3878	**1917**		R	1802
3879	**1918**		N	1803
3880	**1919**		N	1804
3881	**1920**		N	1805

B/1. 2ⁿᵈ Coinage; deeply engraved, but in debased silver (·500 fine)
Rev. 1 - Lion standing on crown, within circle   Spink 4024

ESC	Date	Varieties, remarks, etc.	R	(Old ESC)
3882	**1920**		S	1806
3883	—	*Specimen with 'Duck-tailed milling* [1] (Not traced)	R[?]	1806A
3884	**1921**		S	1807
3885	**1922**		S	1808
3886	**1923**		R	1809
3887	—	*In pure nickel* [2]	R[4]	1809A
3888	**1924**		N	1810
3889	—	*Matt Proof or Specimen, edge* milled ↑↑ (2 known) wt. 2.84g	R[6]	1810A
3890	—	*Matt Proof or Specimen. In nickel* [2]	R[4]	1810B
3891	—	*Matt Proof or Specimen. In gold* W&R 430 wt. 2.89g (3 known, numbered 1, 2 or 3)	R[6]	1810C
3892	**1925**		N	1811

C/1. 2ⁿᵈ Coinage, as 'B', but with new beading and a broader rim
Rev. 1 - Lion standing on crown, within circle   Spink 4025

ESC	Date	Varieties, remarks, etc.	R	(Old ESC)
3893	**1925**		S	1812
3894	**1926**		S	1813

SIXPENCES

D/1. 3rd Coinage, 'Modified effigy' as other denominations

Rev. 1 - Lion standing on crown, within circle   Spink 4034

ESC	Date	Varieties, remarks, etc.		R	(Old ESC)
3895	1926			S	1814
3896	1927			S	1815
3897	—	*Proof, in nickel. Edge,* milled	*wt. 2.93g*	R^6	1815A
3898	—	*Proof, in silver. Edge,* milled	*wt. 2.82g*	R^6	1816
3899	—	*Matt Proof, in silver*		R^6	1816A

E/2. 4th Coinage, *'Modified effigy'* as 'D', but with a new reverse

Rev. 2 - Three oak sprigs, six acorns, **K G** in centre   Spink 4040

3900	1928			N	1817
3901	—	*Proof*		R^6	1817A
3902	—	*Matt proof. Edge,* milled	*wt. 2.81g*	R^6	1817B
3903	1929			N	1818
3904	—	*Proof*	*(Not traced)*		1818A
3905	1930			R	1819
3906	—	*Proof, Edge,* milled	*wt. 2.84g*	R^5	1819A

F/2 As 'E', but with closer milling   Spink 4041

3907	1931			N	1820
3908	—	*Proof. Edge,* milled	*wt. 2.82g*	R^6	1820A
3909	—	*V.I.P. Proof*		R^6	1820B
3910	1932			S	1821
3911	—	*Proof*	*wt. 2.84g*	R^6	1821A
3912	—	*V.I.P. Proof*		R^6	1821B
3913	1933			N	1822
3914	—	*Proof. Edge,* milled	*wt. 2.85g*	R^6	1822A
3915	1934			S	1823
3916	—	*Proof*	*wt. 2.83g*	R^6	1823A
3917	1935			N	1824
3918	—	*Proof. Edge,* milled	*wt. 2.82g*	R^5	1824A
3919	—	*V.I.P. Proof*		R^5	1824B
3920	1936			C	1825
3921	—	*Proof. Edge,* milled	*wt. 2.83g*	R^5	1825C
3922	—	*V.I.P. Proof*		R^6	1825D

SIXPENCES

PATTERNS

 G

ESC	Date	Varieties, remarks, etc.	R	(Old ESC)
3923	**1925** *Obv/ rev*	By **Percy Metcalfe** and **Kruger Gray** As the fourth coinage 1928, but *In nickel, struck en medaille* ↑↑ *wt. 2.80g*	R^7	1825A

| 3924 | **1925**
 Obv.
 Rev.
 Edge | Uniface reverse by **Kruger Gray**
 Reads **MODEL**
 As before
 Milled. *In silver*   *wt. 2.78g* | $R^?$ | 1825B |

 H

| 3925 | **1926**
 Rev

 Obv
 Edge | Uniface reverse trial by **F. Derwent Wood**
 Crowned full-blown rose, dividing <br> small date below **19   26**
 Legend between inner and outer circle reads
 FID : DEF · ♔ **IND : IMP :**
 · SIX · PENCE ·
 Reads **MODEL**
 Milled. *In silver*   *wt. 2.80g* | R^7 | |

1   This is assumed to exist to match the halfcrown and florin
2   Nickel shillings of 1923 and 1924 are trial pieces, struck when the introduction of nickel
      coinage was being considered. See also *pattern, 1925*

GEORGE V, 1910-36
THREEPENCES

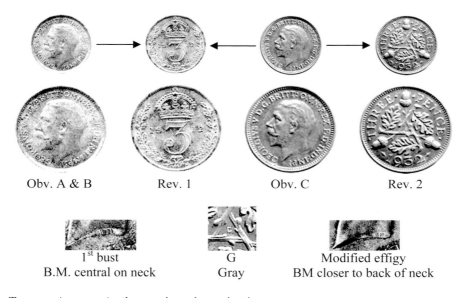

| Obv. A & B | Rev. 1 | Obv. C | Rev. 2 |

| 1ˢᵗ bust
B.M. central on neck | G
Gray | Modified effigy
BM closer to back of neck |

Type	**A.**	As the previous denominations
	B.	Similar, but metal changed to 50% silver and 50% alloy.
	C.	Modified effigy, as the sixpence. As the threepence in the Maundy sets except 1920
Rev.	**1.**	Large crown with a single arch above value
	D.	As the sixpence *obv. & rev.*
Rev. *Leg.*	2	Three oak sprigs with 3 acorns dividing *leg.* **G** in centre **THREE · 🌰 · PENCE ·** **🌰 - 1927 - 🌰**

516

THREEPENCES

A/1. 1st Coinage, as before (·925 silver), but with a dull finish
Rev. 1 - Large crown, single arch, above value   Spink 4015

ESC	Date	Var.	R	(Old ESC)
3926	**1911**		*N*	2124
3927	—	*Proof*	*S*	2125
3928	**1912**		*N*	2126
3929	**1913**		*N*	2127
3930	**1914**		*N*	2128
3931	**1915**		*N*	2129

ESC	Date	Var.	R	(Old ESC)
3932	**1916**		*C*	2130
3933	**1917**		*C*	2131
3934	**1918**		*C*	2132
3935	**1919**		*C*	2123
3936	—	**9** over **8**		2123A
3937	**1920**		*C*	2124

B/1. 2nd Coinage; as before, but debased silver (·500 fine)
Rev. 1 - Large crown, single arch, above value   Spink 4026

3938	**1920**		*N*	2135
3939	**1921**		*N*	2136
3940	—	Small **2**		2136A

3941	**1922**		*S*	2137
3942	**1924**	Matt proof	*R⁶*	
3943	**1925**		*R*	2138
3944	**1926**		*R*	2139

C. 3rd Coinage; *'Modified effigy'* as other denominations
Rev. 1 - Large crown, single arch, above value   Spink 40356

3945	**1926**		*S*	2140

D/2. 4th Coinage; *'Modified effigy'* as 'C', but with a new *rev.*
Rev. 2 - Three oak sprigs, three acorns, **G** in centre   Spink 4042

3946	**1927**	*Proof*	*S*	2141
3947	—	*Matt proof*	*R⁶*	2141A
3948	**1928**		*R*	2142
3949	**1930**		*R*	2143
3950	—	*Proof*	*R⁴*	2143A
3951	**1931**		*C*	2144
3952	—	*Proof*	*C*	2144A
3953	**1932**		*C*	2145
3954	—	*Proof*	*R⁴*	2145A

3955	**1933**		*C*	2146
3956	—	*Proof*	*R⁴*	2146A
3957	**1934**		*C*	2147
3958	—	*Proof*	*R⁴*	2147A
3959	**1935**		*C*	2148
3960	—	*Proof*	*R⁴*	2148A
3961	—	*V.I.P. Proof*	*R⁶*	2148B
3962	**1936**		*C*	2149
3963	—	*Proof*	*R⁴*	2149A
3964	—	*V.I.P. Proof*	*R⁴*	2149B

THREEPENCES

PATTERNS

First coinage

Gold

Rev. 1

A/1. 1st Coinage

ESC	Date	Varieties, remarks, etc.	R	(Old ESC)
3965	**1923**	*In pure nickel*	R^6	2149C
3966	**1924**	*Specimen matt finish, struck on sand blasted dies* *(2 known)*	R^6	2149D
3967	—	*In gold.* W&R 431 - *cross scratched in obverse field and a figure 4 scratched above **19** of date on reverse* wt. 2.49g	R^7	2149E

Modified effigy

Nickel

Rev. 2

D/2. 4th Coinage; *'Modified effigy'*

3968	**1925**	*In nickel*	R^6	2149B
3969	—	*In nickel. Matt proof struck on sand blasted dies*	R^6	2149C

GEORGE V, 1910-36
MAUNDY MONEY SETS

Standard design

Type   **A.**   Obverse as other denominations ·925 silver with standard reverse

         B.   Similar, but metal changed to ·500 silver

         C.   Modified effigy as other denominations with standard reverse

         D.   Similar, but reverse re-engraved

A.   ·925 silver   Spink 4016

ESC	Date	Varieties	*Brian Robinson page 179*	R	Old ESC
3970	**1911**		*1d – 720; 2d – 721; 3d - 722; 4d - 723*	S	2527
3971	—	*Proof*	*1d – 724; 2d – 725; 3d - 726; 4d - 727*	S	2528
3972	**1912**		*1d – 728; 2d – 729; 3d - 730; 4d - 731*	S	2529
3973	**1913**		*1d – 732; 2d – 733; 3d - 734; 4d - 735*	S	2530
3974	**1914**		*1d – 736; 2d – 737; 3d - 738; 4d - 739*	S	2531
3975	**1915**		*1d – 740; 2d – 741; 3d - 742; 4d - 743*	S	2532
3976	**1916**		*1d – 744; 2d – 745; 3d - 746; 4d - 747*	S	2533
3977	**1917**		*1d – 748; 2d – 749; 3d - 750; 4d - 751*	S	2534
3978	**1918**		*1d – 752; 2d – 753; 3d - 754; 4d - 755*	S	2535
3979	**1919**		*1d – 756; 2d – 757; 3d - 758; 4d - 759*	S	2536
3980	**1920**		*1d – 760; 2d – 761; 3d - 762; 4d - 763*	S	2537

MAUNDY MONEY SETS

B. Debased silver, ·500 fine   Spink 4027

ESC	Date	Varieties	*Brian Robinson page 179*	R	Old ESC
3981	**1921**		*1d – 764; 2d – 765; 3d - 766; 4d - 767*	*S*	2538
3982	**1922**		*1d – 768; 2d – 769; 3d - 770; 4d - 771*	*S*	2539
3983	**1923**		*1d – 772; 2d – 773; 3d - 774; 4d - 775*	*S*	2540
3984	**1924**		*1d – 776; 2d – 777; 3d - 778; 4d - 779*	*S*	2541
3985	**1925**		*1d – 780; 2d – 781; 3d - 782; 4d - 783*	*S*	2542
3986	**1926**		*1d – 784; 2d – 785; 3d - 786; 4d - 787*	*S*	2543
3987	**1927**	Note [1]	*1d – 788; 2d – 789; 3d - 790; 4d - 791*	*S*	2544

C. Modified effigy, silver ·500 fine   Spink 4043

3988	**1928**		*1d – 792; 2d – 793; 3d - 794; 4d - 795*	*S*	2545
3989	**1929**		*1d – 796; 2d – 767; 3d - 768; 4d - 769*	*S*	2546

D. Modified effigy, silver ·500 fine / re-engraved reverse Spink 4043

3990	**1930**		*1d – 800; 2d – 801 3d - 802; 4d - 803*	*S*	2547
3991	**1931**		*1d – 804; 2d – 805 3d - 806; 4d - 807*	*S*	2548
3992	**—**	Uniface obverse	*1d – 804(i)*	*S*	2548A
3993	**1932**	Note [2]	*1d – 808; 2d – 809; 3d - 810; 4d - 811*	*S*	2549
3994	**1933**		*1d – 812; 2d – 813; 3d - 814; 4d - 815*	*S*	2550
3995	**1934**		*1d – 816; 2d – 817; 3d - 818; 4d - 819*	*S*	2551
3996	**1935**	Note [3]	*1d – 820; 2d – 821; 3d - 822; 4d - 823*	*R*	2552
3997	**1936**		*1d – 824; 2d – 825; 3d - 826; 4d - 827*	*R*	2553

[1] When the type change took place in 1927/8 the design of the current threepence was altered but the Maundy threepence remained as before; so for the first time the Maundy and current threepences were of different design.

[2] Personally distributed by the reigning monarch. In 1932 it was the first time that this had been done for about two hundred and fifty years. In 1936 it was distributed by King Edward VIII but the coins still bore the portrait of George V.

[3] The King's Jubilee Year when most of the bags of Maundy coins were bought up by American visitors. (P.A.R. Old ESC, p. 210)

EDWARD VIII
1936

George V died in January of this 1936 and Edward VIII reigned until his abdication in December 1936. New dies were prepared for the reign; these were dated 1937 and coins were struck in fairly large quantities. Almost all the coins were melted down, and only a few examples survived. The 'commonest' of these is the 12-sided threepence (dodecagonal), some of which were sent to vending-machine manufacturers before the abdication, and were not returned when the pieces were recalled: a very few of this denomination found their way into circulation. A number of uniface trial pieces were publicly auctioned and I have seen a trial reverse for a florin which was found in circulation in the 1960s.

Coins of all denominations exist, except for half sovereigns and Maundy money of Edward VIII, but few are in private hands. The portrait on all these pieces, at the King's special request, was turned to the spectator's left, which if precedent had been followed, should have been the other way round.

During 1936 a full series of silver pieces was struck with the portrait and name of George V and many numismatists regard these as posthumous coins of George V struck during the reign of Edward VIII. A monograph *'The proposed coinage of King Edward VIII'* by Graham P. Dyer, Librarian and Curator, Royal Mint, has been published by H.M. Stationery Office, and gives full historical details of the background to the proposed coinage, describing all the patterns, trial pieces etc. which were submitted for consideration. (P.A. Rayner, 1949)

In *English Silver Coinage* (E.S.C) P.A. Rayner restricted mention to the finally accepted coinage, and omitted uniface patterns from his publications, however, for the sake of record, many uniface coins, which have passed through various auctions in recent times, are illustrated and numbered in this edition (M.B)

CROWN

HP

K G

Spink 4063

ESC	Date	Varieties	R	(Old ESC)
4000	**1937**	By **T. Humphrey Paget** & G. **Kruger Gray**	R^6	391c
		Proof en medaille ↑↑ *wt. 28.10g & 28.21g.*		
	Obv	Bare head, left, **HP** below truncation in relief		
	Leg	**EDWARDVS VIII D : G : BR : OMN : REX**		
	Rev	Crowned shield of arms with lion and unicorn		
		supporters, **K G** between their hind legs.		
	Leg.	**FID : DEF : ✝ : IND : IMP // CROWN : 1937 ·**		
4001	—	*In silver* Uniface reverse / **MODEL** in relief	R^6	
4002	—	*In tin[1]* Uniface obverse / **MODEL** in relief	R^6	
4003	—	*In tin[1]* Uniface reverse / **MODEL** in relief	R^6	

HALFCROWN

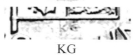

HP   KG   MCM

ESC	Date	Varieties	R	(Old ESC)
4004	**1937**	By **T. Humphrey Paget** & **G. Kruger Gray**	R^6	
	Obv	As before		
	Leg	**EDWARDVS VIII D : G : BR : OMN : REX**		
	Rev	The Royal arms as a Standard flag		
		Crowned **E8** monogram each side. **K G** below.		
	Leg	**FID : DEF : IND : IMP**		
		HALF · CROWN · 1937 ·		
	Edge	Milled. *Struck en medaille* ↑↑ *wt. 14.13g*		
4005	—	Uniface obverse / **MODEL** in relief	R^7	

4006		By **T. Humphrey Paget**, undated	R^7	
		Uniface obverse		
	Obv	Bust as before, **HP** in relief below truncation		
	Leg	**EDWARDVS VIII BY THE GRACE OF GOD**		
	Rev	In centre **MODEL** in relief (figure 4 scratched below)		
	Edge	Milled		

4007		By **McMillan**, undated	$R^?$	
		Uniface obverse		
	Obv	Bust as before, **MCM** in relief below truncation		
	Leg	**EDWARDVS ˇVIII ˇ DEI ˇ** (triangular stops)		
		GRA : BR : OMN : REX (colons)		
	Rev	In centre **MODEL** in relief (figure 7 scratched below)		
	Edge	Milled		

FLORIN

Proof   *Matt proof*

ESC	Date	Varieties	R	(Old ESC)
4008	**1937** *Obv* *Rev* *Leg*	**By T. Humphrey Paget & G. Kruger Gray** As crown. *Proof struck en medaille*↑↑ *wt. 11.34g* As the florin of George VI [2], but **E** below thistle, **R** below shamrock **KG** flanking the crowned rose stem **: FID : DEF : ✚ : IND : IMP :** **TWO SHILLINGS 1937**	R^6	
4009	—	*Matt Proof, from sand blasted dies* *wt. 11.31g*	R^6	
4010	—	Uniface obverse *trial piece*	R^6	

SHILLING

K   G

4011	**1937** *Obv* *Rev* *Leg*	**By T. Humphrey Paget & G. Kruger Gray** As crown. *Struck en medaille* ↑↑ *wt. 5.66g* As the Scottish shillings of George VI [3]; lion seated facing on crown, holding a sword and sceptre in each paw with **K G** below, dividing **19 37** and shields of Scotland & Ireland **FID : DEF ˙ IND : IMP** **ONE · SHILLING**	R^6	
4012	—	(Reserved for an English Shilling) *(Not traced)*	R^6	

SIXPENCE

ESC	Date	Varieties	R	(Old ESC)
4013	**1937**	By **T. Humphrey Paget** & **G. Kruger Gray**	R^6	
	Obv	As crown. *Struck en medaille* ↑↑　　*wt. 2.81g; wt. 2.82g*		
	Rev	Six rings of St Edmund intertwined **K G** below		
	Leg	**FID · DEF · IND · IMP · 1937**		
		SIXPENCE		
4014	—	Uniface obverse as before / **MODEL** *on reverse*	R^7	
		Struck in white metal　　　　　　　　　*wt. 2.86g*		

THREEPENCE

4015	**1937**	By **T. Humphrey Paget** & **G. Kruger Gray**	R^6	
	Obv	As crown. *Struck en medaille* ↑↑　　*wt. 1.41g*		
	Rev	Three rings of St Edmund entwined, **K G** below		
	Leg	**FID · DEF · IND · IMP · 1937**		
		THREE · PENCE		

Note
A full set of 13 coins in original case, Five Pound Piece down to Farthing sold to a private buyer in 2010 for £1·35 million. See Mark Rasmussen list 19, 2010, illustrated back cover.

1　　Spink auction 217, lot 864 *"According to Giordano the only pair of trial strikes in tin, the obverse being the only trial striking known in this metal, the reverse trial known also in silver"*

2　　The uniface trial piece referred to in the introduction appears on p. 12, plate C of Graham Dyer's monograph, and has the ER above the emblems

3　　No 'English' shilling of Edward VIII was struck. A pattern 'Scottish' shilling was offered in May 1992 for £20,000

GEORGE VI
1936-1952

A full complement of silver coins was issued in 1937 with new designs. There were two innovations. Shillings were issued concurrently with two reverse designs, one of these bearing the crest of the English and the other the crest of the Scottish version of the Royal Arms. The other change was the issue of a new 12-sided nickel-brass threepenny piece (dodecagonal) in addition to the small silver coin which was retained. This latter piece circulated chiefly in Scotland and the colonies; in fact complete issues of some years were sent overseas, hence their rarity in this country. The coin was not struck for circulation in the U.K. after 1941 and the last date of the denomination to appear was 1944.

A revolutionary change took place in 1947, when the silver coinage ceased to be issued and was replaced with a coinage in cupro-nickel. The designs were not changed, but the milling on the edge was made much closer. The change of metal was made in order to repay silver borrowed during the war from the United States. The Maundy coins were again struck in fine silver.

When India became independent in 1947 the King relinquished his title of Emperor (IND : IMP) and these titles were therefore omitted from 1949 onwards. This did not necessitate any major changes in design apart from re-spacing of words, with the exception of the sixpence, where the Royal cipher GRI was modified to GVIR. On the occasion of the National Exhibition in 1951 known as the Festival of Britain, a commemorative crown in cupro-nickel was struck. This year also marked the quarter centenary of the issue of the first silver crown by Edward VI in 1551. The dies for the reverse of this 1951 crown, which shows Pistrucci's St. George and the Dragon, were made from a punch manufactured for a crown of 1899, the date being added by hand. Over two million of these coins were struck, all from polished dies, but owing to the comparatively short time in which the Mint had to make them, the finish of the normal coins was not up to what we normally understand as proof standard. A few crowns were struck from specially prepared dies and these pieces have a more highly frosted portrait and a more brilliantly polished field. They have come to be known as 'VIP' proofs.

GEORGE VI, 1936-52
CROWNS

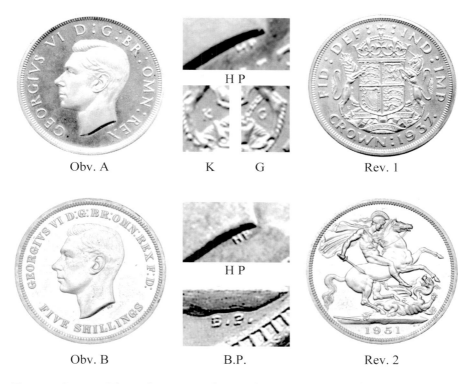

Obv. A   H P   K   G   Rev. 1

Obv. B   H P   B.P.   Rev. 2

Type	**A.**	First coinage; Royal arms, debased silver ·500 fine
Obv.		Bare head, left, **HP** below truncation
Leg.	1	**GEORGIVS VI D : G : BR : OMN : REX**
	B.	Festival of Britain commemoration issue, struck in *cupro-nickel*;
Obv.		Bare head, left, **HP** below truncation
Leg.	2	**GEORGIVS VI D:G:BR:OMN:REX F:D:**
		FIVE SHILLINGS
Rev.	**1.**	As Edward VIII; Crowned shield of arms with lion and unicorn supporters, initials **K G** between hind legs, motto on scroll on ground below
Leg.		**FID : DEF : ✝ : IND : IMP // CROWN : 1937 ·**
Edge		Milled

527

CROWNS

Rev. **2.** Pistrucci's St George and dragon, right, date **1951** in exergue
Edge ★**MDCCCLI CIVIUM INDUSTRIA**
 FLORET CIVITAS MCMLI
(1851 by the industry of its people the state flourishes 1951)

A/1. 1st Coinage; Bare head, left, **HP** below truncation, *leg.* 1
 Rev. 1 - Royal arms with supporters   Spink 4078/9

ESC	Date	Varieties, remarks etc.	R	L&S	(Old ESC)
4020	**1937**		*C*		392
4021	—	*Proof* from the sets *wt. 28.17g*	*N*	3	393
4022	—	*Proof* with more frosting on *rev.*	*R⁵*	5	393A
4023	—	*Matt proof from sand blasted dies*	*R⁷*	4	393B

B/2 '*Festival of Britain*' issue, bare head as before, in cupro-nickel
 Rev. 2 - St George and dragon, date in exergue   Spink 4111

4024	**1951**	Struck for the Festival of Britain Issued in small cardboard box, also issued in the proof sets	*C²*	8	393C
4025	—	*V.I.P. proof or pattern* with design frosted and the field more brilliant – crisper detail and initials **B.P.** very distinct	*R⁴*		393D
4026	—	*Matt proof from sand blasted dies giving a matt finish to whole coin* Struck en medaille ↑↑ *wt. 28.16g*	*R⁷*		393E
4027	—	*Trial.* Unfinished dies with heavier lettering	*R²*		393F
4028	—	*Trial.* Polished finish with lettering of finer style	*R²*		393G
4029	—	*Proof. Edge.* Plain ¹	*R⁴*		393H

1   The rare pieces with plain edge were unintentional strikings on un-edged blanks

GEORGE VI, 1936-52
CROWNS

TRIAL PATTERN CROWN

A/1. 1ˢᵗ Coinage; Bare head, left, **HP** below truncation, *leg.* 1
Rev. 1 - Royal arms with supporters   Spink 4078/9

ESC	Date	Varieties, remarks etc.	R	(Old ESC)
4030	**1937**	As currency issue, but with a lettered edge from the Maria Theresa Thaler ² *(2 known) wt. 24.87g & 25.55g*	R^7	393I
	Edge	**IUSTITIA ET CLEMENTIA** *In cupro-nickel.* Struck late in 1950-early 1951		

2   Examples of these coins were struck by the Royal Mint in the Forties, struck to experiment how many tons of pressure were required to make a lettered edge coin rather than a milled edge piece, experimental number "120" (tonnage) scratched in obverse field below. (Only 2 known, one in the R.M. Collection)
See full article by Steve Hill published in SNC October 1998

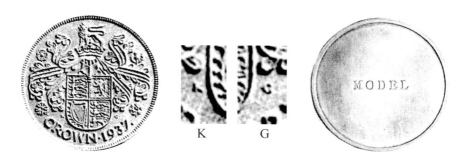

K   G

ESC	Date	Varieties, remarks etc.	R	L&S	(Old ESC)
4031	**1937**	Uniface reverse; Shield of arms, with helm crowned and lion over, with three strap-like leaves issuing from each side of helm and emblems rose, shamrock, thistle and leek flower. Initials **K** **G** at sides of shield	R^7	6	393J
	Leg	**CROWN · 1937 ·** below			
	Obv	Raised rim with **MODEL** in centre			
	Edge	Milled			

529

DOUBLE FLORINS

PATTERNS

ESC	Date	Varieties	R	L&S	(Old ESC)
4032	**1950**	By **T. Humphrey Paget, 1950**	R^6	7	406B
		Bare head bust, left, **HP** below truncation			
	Leg.	**GEORGIVS VI D: G: BR: OMN: REX**			
		FID: DEF: // · **1950** ·			
	Rev.	Pistrucci's St George and dragon within			
		Garter			
	Edge	Milled. *In cupro-nickel* *(4 struck)[1]*			
4033	—	Similar, but **FOUR SHILLINGS** stamped	R^5		406C
		incuse into the milled edge *(3 or 4 struck)[1]*			

1   Mintages revealed by G.P. Dyer at BNS lecture 22/01/2001

GEORGE VI, 1936-52
HALFCROWNS

Rev. 1 & 1a	Obv. A - silver (·500 fine)	Rev. 2
FID DEF IND IMP	Obv. B & C in cupro-nickel	FID DEF
Initials K· G below	Initials HP below	No initials

Type	**A.**	First coinage; as crown, struck in debased silver (·500 fine)
Obv.		Bare head, left, **HP** below truncation. Milled edge
Leg.	1	**GEORGIVS VI D : G : BR : OMN : REX**
Rev.	**1.**	First coinage; struck in debased silver (·500 fine)
		Shield, with concave sides, hanging from hook
		On each side, two interlinked **G**s crowned, initials **K· G** below
Leg.	1	**FID : DEF 🛡 IND : IMP**
		HALF CROWN 1937
	B.	Second coinage; as type A, but struck in cupro-nickel, with closer milling on edge
	1a.	Second coinage; as reverse 1, but struck in cupro-nickel, with closer milling on edge
	C.	Third coinage; obverse as type B, struck in cupro-nickel, with 'New type' reverse;
	2.	Similar to reverse 1a, but minus IND IMP, and engraver's initials
Leg.	2	♦ **FID** ♦ 🛡 ♦ **DEF** ♦
		HALF CROWN 1949

531

HALFCROWNS

Type **A/1.** 1st Coinage; debased silver (·500 fine), bare head, left, **HP** below, *Rev.* 1 – *Leg.* above shield; **FID:DEF IND:IMP** Spink 4080

ESC	Date	Varieties, remarks etc.	R	(Old ESC)
4034	**1937**		*N*	786
4035	—	*Proof*	*S*	787
4036	—	*Matt proof, from sand blasted dies* *wt. 14.05g*	*R*⁷	787A
4037	**1938**		*S*	788
4038	—	*Proof*	*R*⁴	788A
4039	**1939**		*S*	789
4040	—	*Proof*	*R*⁴	789A
4041	—	*V.I.P. Proof*	*R*⁶	789B
4042	**1940**		*C*	790
4043	—	*Proof*	*R*⁴	790A
4044	**1941**		*C*	791
4045	—	*Proof*	*R*⁴	791A
4046	**1942**		*C*	792
4047	—	*Proof*	*R*⁴	792A
4048	—	*Matt Proof, from sand blasted dies*	*R*⁶	792B
4049	**1943**		*C*	793
4050	—	*Proof*	*R*⁴	793A
4051	—	*Matt Proof, from sand blasted dies*	*R*⁷	793B
4052	—	*V.I.P. Proof*	*R*⁶	793C
4053	**1944**		*C*	794
4054	—	*Proof* (Not traced, but English & Scottish shillings known)	*R*⁴	794A
4055	**1945**		*C*²	795
4056	—	*Proof* (Not traced, but Scottish shilling known)	*R*⁴	795A
4057	**1946**		*C*²	796
4058	—	*Proof*	*R*⁴	796A

B/1a. 2nd Coinage; in cupro-nickel, closer milling on edge (Old ESC. B) *Rev.* 1a – *Leg.* above shield; **FID:DEF IND:IMP** Spink 4101

ESC	Date	Varieties, remarks etc.	R	(Old ESC)
4059	**1946**	*Proof or pattern* (Not traced)	*R*⁶	796B
4060	**1947**		*N*	797
4061	—	*Proof*	*R*⁶	797A
4062	—	*V.I.P. Proof*	*R*⁶	797B
4063	**1948**		*N*	798
4064	—	*Proof*	*R*⁴	798A

HALFCROWNS

Type **C/2.** 3rd Coinage; in cupro-nickel, bare head, as before (Old ESC. C)
Rev. 2 – Leg. above shield; ♦**FID**♦ ♦ **DEF** ♦ Spink 4106

ESC	Date	Varieties, remarks etc.		R	(Old ESC)
4065	**1949**			*N*	798A
4066	—	*Proof*		*R⁴*	798A?
4067	—	*V.I.P. Proof*		*R⁶*	
4068	**1950**			*N*	798B
4069	—	*Proof*		*N*	798C
4070	—	*Matt Proof, from sand blasted dies* ↑↑	*wt. 14.18g*	*R⁶*	798 ?
4071	**1951**			*N*	798D
4072	—	*Proof*		*N*	798E
4073	—	*Matt Proof, from sand blasted dies* ↑↑	*wt. 14.15g*	*R⁵*	798 ?
4074	**1952**	*Not issued for general circulation*	*(2 known)*	*R⁷*	798F
4075	—	*Proof*	*(Unique)*	*R⁷*	798F

Some coins dated 1942 & 1943 are termed "Specimen strikes" (Colin Adams 797 & 798) these have been carefully struck and handled showing no signs of contact with other coins. They are neither proofs nor patterns but may command a small premium in price

GEORGE VI, 1937-52
FLORINS

As the halfcrown

Rev. 1 & 1a
FID DEF IND IMP
Initials K· G below

Obv. A - silver (·500 fine)
Obv. B & C in cupro-nickel
Initials HP below

Rev. 2
FID DEF
No initials

Type	**A.**	First coinage; struck in debased silver (·500 fine)
Obv.		Bare head, left, **HP** below truncation. Milled edge
Leg.	1	**GEORGIVS VI D : G : BR : OMN : REX**
Rev.	**1.**	First coinage; struck in debased silver (·500 fine) Crowned rose between thistle and shamrock with **G R** below, Engraver's initials **K G** on either side of the rose stem
Leg.		**: FID : DEF : ✠ : IND : IMP : // TWO SHILLINGS 1937**
	B.	Second coinage; as type A, but struck in cupro-nickel, with closer milling on edge
	1a.	Second coinage; as reverse 1, but struck in cupro-nickel, with closer milling on edge
	C.	Third coinage; obverse as type B, struck in cupro-nickel, with 'New type' reverse;
	2.	Similar to reverse 1a, but minus IND IMP, and engraver's initials
Leg.		**: FID : ✠ : DEF : // TWO SHILLINGS 1951**

534

FLORINS

Type **A/1.** 1st Coinage; debased silver (·500 fine), bare head, left, **HP** below, *Rev.* 1 – Crowned rose, *leg.* **FID:DEF IND:IMP**   Spink 4081

ESC	Date	Varieties	R	(Old ESC)
4076	**1937**		N	956
4077	—	*Proof*	S	957
4078	—	*Matt proof, from sand blasted dies* ↑↑ *wt. 11.26g*	R⁷	957A
4079	**1938**		S	958
4080	—	*Proof*	R⁴	958A
4081	**1939**		C	959
4082	—	*Proof*	R⁴	959A
4083	—	*V.I.P. Proof*	R⁶	959B
4084	**1940**		C	960
4085	—	*Proof*	R⁴	960A
4086	**1941**		C	961
4087	—	*Proof*	R⁴	961A
4088	**1942**		C	962
4089	—	*Proof*	R⁴	962A
4090	—	*Matt Proof* (Not traced, but halfcrown known)	R⁴	962A
4091	**1943**		C	963
4092	—	*Proof*	R⁴	963A
4093	—	*V.I.P. Proof* (Not traced, but halfcrown known)	R⁶	963B
4094	—	*Matt Proof, from sand blasted dies*	R⁷	963B
4095	**1944**		C	964
4096	—	*Proof (Not traced, but English & Scottish shillings known)*	R⁴	964A
4097	**1945**		C²	965
4098	—	*Proof* (Not traced, but Scottish shilling known)	R⁴	965A
4099	**1946**		C²	966
4100	—	*Proof*	R⁴	966A

B/1a. 2nd Coinage; in cupro-nickel, closer milling on edge (Old ESC. B) *Rev.* 1a – Crowned rose, *leg.* **FID:DEF IND:IMP** Spink 4102

4101	**1946**	*Proof or Pattern (these were trials in cupro-nickel for the 1947 coinage, struck before 1947 dies were prepared.)*	R⁶	966B
4102	**1947**		N	967
4103	—	*Proof*	R⁴	967A
4104	—	*V.I.P. Proof*	R⁶	967B
4105	**1948**		N	968
4106	—	*Proof*	R⁴	968A
4107	—	*V.I.P. Proof* (Not traced, but E & S shillings known)	R⁶	968B

FLORINS

Type C/2. 3rd Coinage; in cupro-nickel, bare head, as before (Old ESC. C)

Rev. 2 – Crowned rose, *leg.* ♦**FID**♦ ♦ **DEF** ♦ Spink 4107

ESC	Date	Varieties	R	(Old ESC)
4108	**1949**		*N*	968A
4109	—	*Proof*	*R⁴*	968A
4110	—	*V.I.P. Proof*	*R⁶*	
4111	**1950**		*N*	968B
4112	—	*Proof*	*S*	968C
4113	—	*Matt proof, from sand blasted dies* ↑↑ *wt. 11.31g*	*R⁶*	
4114	**1951**		*N*	968D
4115	—	*Proof*	*R*	968E
4116	—	*V.I.P. Proof* (Not traced, but 2/-, E & S shillings known)	*R⁶*	
4117	—	*Matt proof, from sand blasted dies* ↑↑ *wt. 11.28g*	*R⁵*	968E
4118	**1952**	*Proof* (Not traced, but halfcrown & sixpence known)	*R⁶*	
4119	—	*V.I.P. Proof* (Not traced, but Sixpence known)	*R⁶*	

GEORGE VI, 1936-52
SHILLINGS

One obverse type as the larger denominations

K G

K   G

Rev. 1 – English
1 - silver (·500 fine)
1a – cupro-nickel

Rev. 2 – Scottish
2 - silver (·500 fine)
2a – cupro-nickel

Rev. 3 – English
Cupro-nickel

Standard obv. in
silver or cupro-nickel

Rev. 4 – Scottish
1a – cupro-nickel

SHILLINGS

Standard obverse:
Bare head, left, initials **HP** (T. Humphrey Paget) below
truncation, struck in debased silver (·500 fine) or cupro-nickel

Type	**A.**	Standard obverse struck in debased silver with -
Rev.	**1.**	*'English shilling'* - Large crowned lion standing on a large crown dividing date, initials **K G** at top divided by lion's tail
Leg.	1	**· FID · DEF** ᴷ ᴳ **IND · IMP ·** // ❀· **ONE· SHILLING ·**❀ (Punctuation; 6 lozenges & 1 stop after ONE· in value)

Type	**B.**	Standard obverse struck in debased silver with -
Rev.	**2.**	*'Scottish shilling'* - Small crowned lion sitting on a smaller crown flanked by two Scottish shields; left shield bearing the cross of St Andrew and right shield a thistle. The lion holding a sword in its right paw and a sceptre in left, initials **K G** below sword hilts, all dividing the date
Leg.	2	**FID : DEF ˙ IND : IMP** // **ONE· SHILLING** (Punctuation; 2 colons & a stop after DEF˙ & ONE· in value)

Type	**C.**	Second coinage; Obverse as before, but struck in cupro-nickel, closer milling on edge, with reverse **1a** – *English type,* as before

Type	**D.**	As type C, with reverse **2a** – *Scottish type,* as before

Type	**E.**	Third coinage: as type C, with 'New type' English reverse
Rev.	**3.**	*English,* as before minus IND : IMP in legend and initials
Leg.	3	**· FID · DEF ·** // **ONE· SHILLING** (Punctuation 5 lozenges)

Type	**F.**	Third coinage: as type C, with 'New type' Scottish reverse
Rev.	**4.**	*Scottish,* as before minus IND : IMP in legend and initials
Leg.	4	**· FID · · DEF ·** // **· ONE SHILLING ·** (Punctuation 6 round stops)

Edge		Milled, die axis ↑↑

SHILLINGS

Type A/1. **ENGLISH** reverse – Lion standing, struck in •500 silver

Leg. 1 – Reads • **FID • DEF** ᴷ ᴳ **IND • IMP** Spink 4082

ESC	Date	Varieties		R	(Old ESC)
4120	**1937**			*N*	1450
4121	—	*Proof*		*S*	1451
4122	—	*Matt Proof, from sand blasted dies*		*R⁶*	1451A
4123	**1938**			*S*	1454
4124	—	*Proof*		*R⁴*	1454A
4125	—	*V.I.P. Proof*		*R⁶*	1454B
4126	**1939**			*S*	1456
4127	—	*Proof*		*R⁴*	1456A
4128	—	*V.I.P. Proof*		*R⁷*	
4129	**1940**			*C*	1458
4130	—	*Proof*		*R⁴*	1458A
4131	**1941**			*C*	1460
4132	—	*Proof*		*R⁴*	1460A
4133	**1942**			*C*	1462
4134	—	*Proof*		*R⁴*	1462A
4135	—	*Matt Proof, from sand blasted dies* *(Not traced, but halfcrown known)*			1462B
4136	**1943**			*C*	1464
4137	—	*Die axis inverted*		*R³*	
4138	—	*Proof*		*R⁴*	1464A
4139	—	*Matt Proof, from sand blasted dies*		*R⁷*	1464B
4140	**1944**			*C*	1466
4141	—	*Proof*		*R⁴*	1466A
4142	—	*Matt Proof, from sand blasted dies*		*R⁶*	1466A
4143	**1945**			*C²*	1468
4144	—	*Proof*	*(Not traced)*	*R⁴*	1468A
4145	**1946**			*C²*	1470
4146	—	*Proof*		*R⁴*	1470A
4147	—	*V.I.P. Proof*		*R⁶*	1470A
4148	**1947**	*Proof or specimen¹*	*(B.M. collection)*	*R⁶*	1470B

1   A small number of these shillings were struck in ·500 silver. See B.M. collection.

SHILLINGS

Type **B/2.** **SCOTTISH** reverse – Lion sitting, struck in •500 silver
Leg. **2** – Reads **FID : DEF · IND : IMP**   Spink 4083

ESC	Date	Varieties		R	(Old ESC)
4149	**1937**			N	1452
4150	—	*Proof*		S	1453
4151	—	*Matt Proof, from sand blasted dies*		R^6	1453A
4152	—	Uniface rev. / Obv. reads **MODEL** *Matt Proof*		R^6	1453B
4153	**1938**			S	1555
4154	—	*Proof*		R^4	1455A
4155	—	*V.I.P. Proof*		R^6	1455B
4156	**1939**			S	1457
4157	—	*Proof*		R^4	1457A
4158	—	*V.I.P. Proof*		R^7	1457B
4159	**1940**			C	1459
4160	—	*Proof*		R^4	1459A
4161	**1941**			C	1461
4162	—	*Proof*		R^4	1461A
4163	—	*V.I.P. Proof*		R^6	1461B
4164	**1942**			C	1463
4165	—	*Proof*		R^4	1463A
4166	—	*Matt Proof* *(Not traced, but halfcrown known)*		R^4	
4167	**1943**			C	1465
4168	—	*Proof* *(Not traced)*		R^4	1465A
4169	—	*Matt Proof, from sand blasted dies*		R^7	1465B
4170	**1944**			C	1467
4171	—	*Proof*		R^4	1467A
4172	—	*Matt Proof, from sand blasted dies* *(Eng. 1/- known)*		R^6	1467B
4173	**1945**			C^2	1469
4174	—	*Proof* *(Not traced)*		R^4	1469A
4175	**1946**			C^2	1471
4176	—	*Proof* *(Not traced, but English known)*		R^7	1471A
4177	—	*V.I.P. Proof* *(Not traced, but English known)*		R^7	
4178	**1947**	*Proof or specimen[1]* *(Not traced)*		R^6	1471B

SHILLINGS

Type   C/1a.   **ENGLISH** reverse – Lion standing, struck in cupro-nickel

Leg. **1** – Reads **·** **FID · DEF** ᴷ ᴳ **IND · IMP**   Spink 4103

ESC	Date	Varieties	R	(Old ESC)
4179	**1946**	*Pattern* [2]	R^6	1470A
4180	**1947**		N	1472
4181	—	*Proof*	R^4	1472A
4182	—	*V.I.P. Proof*	R^4	1472B
		(Not traced, halfcrown, Scottish shilling and sixpence known)		
4183	**1948**		N	1474
4184	—	*Proof*	R^4	1474A
4185	—	*V.I.P. Proof*	R^6	1474B

Type   D/2a.   **SCOTTISH** reverse – Lion sitting, struck in cupro-nickel

Leg. **2** – Reads **FID : DEF ˙ IND : IMP**   Spink 4104

ESC	Date	Varieties	R	(Old ESC)
4186	**1946**	*Pattern* [2] *(Not traced)*	R^6	
4187	**1947**		N	1473
4188	—	*Proof*	R^4	1473A
4189	—	*V.I.P. Proof*	R^4	1473A
4190	**1948**		N	1475
4191	—	*Proof*	R^4	1475A
4192	—	*V.I.P. Proof*	R^6	

Type   E/3.   **ENGLISH** 'New type' reverse – Lion standing, in cupro-nickel

Leg. **3** - Reads **· FID   · DEF ·**   Spink 4108

ESC	Date	Varieties	R	(Old ESC)
4193	**1949**		N	1475A
4194	—	*Proof*	R^4	1475A
4195	—	*V.I.P. Proof*	R^6	1475A
4196	**1950**		N	1475C
4197	—	*Proof*	S	1475D
4198	—	*Matt Proof*	R^6	1475D
4199	**1951**		N	1475G
4200	—	*Proof* *(Not traced, halfcrown, florin and sixpence known)*	R	1475H
4201	—	*Matt Proof, struck on sand blasted dies*	R^6	1475H
4202	**1952**	*Proof* [3] *(Not traced, but sixpence known)*	R^7	1475?
4203	—	*Matt Proof* *(Not traced, but sixpence known)*	R^7	1475?

2   These coins were patterns, or trials in cupro-nickel for the 1947 coinage, struck
        before 1947 dies were prepared

3   Not issued for general circulation

SHILLINGS

Type **F/4.** **SCOTTISH** 'New type' reverse– Lion sitting, in cupro-nickel
Leg. **3** - reads **• FID** **• DEF •** Spink 4109

ESC	Date	Varieties	R	(Old ESC)
4204	**1949**		N	1475B
4205	—	*Proof*	R^4	1475B
4206	—	*V.I.P. Proof*	R^6	1475B
4207	**1950**		N	1475E
4208	—	*Proof*	S	1475F
4209	—	*V.I.P. Proof*	R^6	1475F
4210	—	*Matt Proof*	R^6	1475F
4211	**1951**		N	1475I
4212	—	*Proof*	R	1475J
4213	—	*Matt Proof, struck on sand blasted dies*	R^6	1475J
4214	**1952**	*Proof* [3] *(Not traced, but sixpence known)*	R^7	1475?
4215	—	*Matt Proof* *(Not traced, but sixpence known)*	R^7	1475?

PATTERNS

ENGLISH reverse – Lion standing, struck in pure nickel

4216	**1952**	*wt. 5.26g: 86.8grains*	R^7	

SCOTTISH reverse – Lion sitting, struck in pure nickel

4217	**1952**	*(Rumoured to exist but not traced)*	R^7	

Coins of George VI are only as rare as marked in uncirculated condition

Reverse 1 Initials KG in field FID DEF IND IMP	Standard obv. in silver or cupro-nickel	Reverse 2 No initials in field FID DEF

Obv.   One type, as the larger denominations. *Edge* milled, die axis ↑↑

Type **A.**   First coinage: bare head, left, initials **HP** below (T. Humphrey
Paget). Struck in debased silver (·500 fine) with

Rev. **1.**   Crowned **GRI** dividing date, small initials **K·G** (Kruger Gray)
below, legend above and value below

FID · DEF · + · IND · IMP

SIXPENCE

B.   Second coinage; as before, but struck in cupro-nickel, closer
milling on edge, with reverse **1**

C.   Third coinage: as B, in cupro-nickel, closer milling on edge, with
'New type' reverses

Rev. **2.**   Smaller crown, minus IND · IMP in legend and no initials
G^{VI}R crowned dividing date, legend above and value below

· FID + DEF ·

· SIXPENCE ·

SIXPENCES

Type **A.** First coinage: Bare head, debased silver (·500 fine)
Rev. **1** – *leg.* reads **FID : DEF : IND : IMP**   Spink 4084

ESC	Date	Varieties	R	(Old ESC)
4218	**1937**		N	1826
4219	—	*Proof, milled edge* wt. 2.77g	S	1827
4220	—	*Matt Proof, from sand blasted dies* wt. 2.84g	R^5	1827A
4221	**1938**		S	1828
4222	—	*Proof, milled edge* wt. 2.83g	R^5	1828A
4223	—	*V.I.P. Proof* (Not traced but, E & S shillings known)	R^7	1828B
4224	**1939**		S	1829
4225	—	*Proof, milled edge* wt. 2.82g	R^5	1829A
4226	—	*V.I.P. Proof* (Not traced but, 2/6, 2/-, & 1/-E&S known)	R^6	1829B
4227	**1940**		N	1830
4228	—	*Proof, milled edge* wt. 2.85g	R^5	1830A
4229	—	*V.I.P. Proof* (Not traced but, E & S shillings known)	R^7	1830B
4230	**1941**		C	1831
4231	—	*Proof, milled edge* wt. 2.82g	R^5	1931A
4232	—	*V.I.P. Proof* (Not traced but, E & S shillings known)	R^7	1931B
4233	**1942**		C	1832
4234	—	*Proof*	C	1833A
4235	—	*Matt Proof* (Not traced but, halfcrown known)	C	1833B
4236	**1943**		C	1833
4237	—	*Proof*	R^5	1833A
4238	—	*V.I.P. Proof*	R^5	1833B
4239	—	*Matt Proof, from sand blasted dies* (Not traced but, 2/6, 2/-, & 1/-E&S known)	R^5	1833C
4240	**1944**		C	1834
4241	—	*Proof* (Not traced, but English & Scottish shillings known)	R^6	1834A
4242	—	*Matt Proof* (Not traced, but English shilling known)	R^6	1834B
4243	**1945**		C^2	1835
4244	—	*Proof* (Not traced)	R^5	1835A
4245	**1946**		C^2	1836
4246	—	*Proof, milled edge* wt. 2.82g	R^5	1836B
4247	—	*V.I.P. Proof* (Not traced, but English shilling known)	R^6	1836B

SIXPENCES

Type **B.** Second coinage: Bare head, in cupro-nickel, closer milling
Rev. **1** – *leg.* reads **FID : DEF : IND : IMP**   Spink 4105

ESC	Date	Varieties		R	(Old ESC)
4248	**1946**	*Proof or pattern*		R^6	1836A
4249	**1947**			S	1837
4250	—	*Proof, milled edge*	*wt. 2.76g*	R^5	1837A
4251	—	*V.I.P. Proof*		R^5	1837B
4252	**1948**			S	1838
4253	—	*Proof, milled edge*	*wt. 2.83g*	R^5	
4254	—	*V.I.P. Proof*	*(Not traced but, E & S shillings known)*	R^6	

Type **C.** Third coinage: Bare head, in cupro-nickel, closer milling on edge
Rev. **2** – *'New type', leg.* reads · **FID + DEF** ·   Spink 4110

4255	**1949**			N	1838A
4256	—	*Proof, milled edge*	*wt. 2.85g*	R^5	1838A
4257	—	*V.I.P. Proof,*		R^6	
4258	**1950**			N	1838B
4259	—	*Proof* [1]		S	1838C
4260	—	*V.I.P. Proof*		R^5	
4261	—	*Matt proof, from sand blasted dies*	*wt. 2.84g*	R^5	
4262	**1951**			N	1838D
4263	—	*Proof*		S	1838E
4264	—	*V.I.P. Proof*		R^5	1838E
4265	—	*Matt proof, from sand blasted dies*	*wt. 2.74g*	R^5	1838E
4266	**1952**			R	1838F
4267	—	*Proof, milled edge*	*wt. 2.81g*	R^5	1838G
4268	—	*V.I.P. Proof*		R^5	1838G

SIXPENCES

PATTERNS

ESC	Date	Varieties	R	(Old ESC)
4269	**1937**	Uniface reverse trial in silver, with a milled edge *wt. 2.76g*	R^5	1827A

4270	**1938**	Die trial in aluminium *(Unique?)* *wt. 3.03g*	R^7	

SIXPENCES

PATTERNS

ESC	Date	Varieties	R	(Old ESC)
4271	**1949**	Uniface reverse trial in cupro-nickel, no initials with a milled edge *(6 struck) wt. 2.80g[1]*	R^6	cf.1453

> [1] This specimen was sold with a letter from T.H. Paget, dated 20 December 1948, enclosing the coin as a Christmas gift for the recipient's son (DNW Auction 91, Alfred Bole 203)

4272	(1949)	*Cu-Ni Pattern mule;* Double obverse *wt. 2.81g*	R^7	cf.1453

  Struck on small thin flans

4273	**1949**	Milled edge	*wt. 1.14g*		
4274	**1950**	Milled edge	*wt. 1.45g*		

Coins of George VI are only as rare as marked in uncirculated condition

THREEPENCES

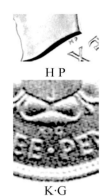

H P

K·G

Type	**A**	As the sixpence
Leg.		**GEORGIVS VI D : G : BR : OMN : REX**
Rev.		Shield of St George on a Tudor rose dividing date, **K·G** below
		Struck in ·500 silver
Leg.		**FID : DEF : IND : IMP**
		19 THREE · PENCE 41

Spink 4085

ESC	Date	Varieties	R	(Old ESC)
4275	**1937**		*N*	2150
4276	—	*Proof*	*S*	2151A
4277	—	*V.I.P. Proof*	R^6	2151B
4278	—	*Matt Proof, from sand blasted dies*	R^6	2151C
4279	**1938**		*N*	2152
4280	—	*Proof*	R^6	2152A
4281	—	*V.I.P. Proof*	R^6	2152B
4282	**1939**		*R*	2153
4283	—	*Proof*	R^6	2153A
4284	—	*V.I.P. Proof*	R^6	2153B
4285	**1940**		*N*	2154
4286	—	*Proof*	R^6	2154A
4287	—	*V.I.P. Proof*	R^6	2154B

(continued)

THREEPENCES

ESC	Date	Varieties	R	(Old ESC)
4288	**1941**		*N*	2155
4289	—	*Proof*	*R⁶*	2155A
4290	—	*V.I.P. Proof*	*R⁶*	2155B
4291	**1942**	Note ¹	*R*	2156
4292	—	*Proof*	*R⁶*	2156A
4293	—	*Matt Proof* *(Not traced, but halfcrown known)*	*R⁶*	2156B
4294	**1943**	Note ¹	*R*	2157
4295	—	*Proof* *(Not traced)*	*R⁶*	2157A
4296	—	*V.I.P. Proof* *(Not traced, but sixpence known)*	*R⁶*	2157B
4297	—	*Matt Proof, from sand blasted dies (Satin finish)*	*R⁶*	2157C
4298	**1944**	Note ¹	*R²*	2158
4299	—	*Proof* *(Not traced, but brass threepence known)*	*R⁶*	2158A
4300	—	*Matt Proof* *(Not traced, but English shilling known)*	*R⁶*	2158B
4301	**1945**	Note ²	*R⁶*	2159
4302	—	*Proof* *(Not traced)*	*R⁶*	2159A
4303	—	*V.I.P. Proof* *(Not traced)*	*R⁶*	2159B

Ordinary Proofs (design with mirror finish and usually, but not always, plain edges) and V.I.P. proofs (with frosted design) exist for most dates, so numbers are allocated. All are rare. (See *'Provenances'* for proven specimens)

1   Only struck in small quantities, and solely for use in the West Indies.

2   *At one time it was thought that this coin did not exist and that all specimens had been melted down. I have seen a genuine coin therefore one or two coins must have escaped destruction.* (P.A. Rayner)

In 1937 a twelve-sided aluminium-bronze threepence was struck and issued in large quantities at the same time as the silver threepence; these have been omitted here as they seem to be more applicable to the copper and bronze coinage.

GEORGE VI, 1936-52
MAUNDY MONEY

Type   **A.**   *Obv.* As other coins
Rev.   Normal, struck in debased silver ·500 fine (50% ag and 50% cu)
Leg.   **GEORGIVS VI D : G : BR : OMN : REX F: D : IND : IMP**

      B.   Similar, but struck in good silver ·925 fine[3]

      C.   As 'B', but without IND · IMP

      A.   In debased silver (·500 fine) reads **IND : IMP**

ESC	Date	Varieties	*Brian Robinson page 184*	R	Old ESC
4304	**1937**	Note[1]	*1d – 828; 2d – 829; 3d - 830; 4d - 831*	S	2554
4305	—	*Proof*	*1d – 832; 2d – 833; 3d - 834; 4d - 835*	R	2554A
4306	—	*Matt Proof from sand blasted dies*	*1d – 836; 2d – 837; 3d - 838; 4d - 839*	R	2554B
4307	**1938**		*1d – 840; 2d – 841; 3d - 842; 4d - 843*	R	2555
4308	**1939**		*1d – 844; 2d – 845; 3d - 846; 4d - 737*	R	2556
4309	**1940**	Note[2]	*1d – 848; 2d – 849; 3d - 850; 4d - 851*	R	2557
4310	**1941**		*1d – 852; 2d – 853; 3d - 854; 4d - 855*	R	2558
4311	**1942**		*1d – 856; 2d – 857; 3d - 858; 4d - 859*	R	2559
4312	**1943**		*1d – 860; 2d – 861; 3d - 862; 4d - 863*	R	2560
4313	**1944**	Note[2]	*1d – 864; 2d – 865; 3d - 866; 4d - 867*	R	2561
4314	**1945**	Note[2]	*1d – 868; 2d – 869; 3d - 870; 4d - 871*	R	2652
4315	**1946**	Note[2]	*1d – 872; 2d – 873; 3d - 874; 4d - 875*	R	2563

MAUNDY MONEY

B.   As type A, but in fine silver (·925) reads **IND : IMP**

ESC	Date	Varieties	Brian Robinson page 184	R	Old ESC
4316	**1947**		1d – 876; 2d – 877; 3d - 878; 4d - 879	R	2564
4317	**1948**	Note [2]	1d – 880; 2d – 881; 3d - 882; 4d - 883	R	2565

C.   As type B, in fine silver, but without IND : IMP

4318	**1949**		1d – 884; 2d – 885; 3d - 886; 4d - 887	R	2566
4319	**1950**	Note [2]	1d – 888; 2d – 889; 3d - 890; 4d - 891	R	2567
4320	**1951**	Note [2]	1d – 892; 2d – 893; 3d - 894; 4d - 895	R	2568
4321	**1951**	*Matt Proof from sand blasted dies*	1d – 896; 2d – 897; 3d - 898; 4d - 899	R[6]	2568A
4322	**1952**	Note [4]	1d – 900; 2d – 901; 3d - 902; 4d - 903	R	2569
4323	—	*In copper*	1d – 904; 2d – 905; 3d - 906; 4d - 907	R	2569A

1   Proofs of the Maundy were included in the 1937 specimen sets, but these cannot be distinguished from the ordinary Maundy coins which are of proof quality. In this reign also the Maundy threepence is of different design to the current silver threepences.

2   Personally distributed by the reigning monarch.

3   When the coinage was changed to cupro-nickel in 1947 it was decided that the Maundy pieces should not be struck in this metal, but should once again be made in good silver.

4   In 1952 it was distributed by Queen Elizabeth II, but the coins were of George VI

The Queen's Maundy are now the only coins struck regularly in ·925 silver

ELIZABETH II
1952-

Although Her Majesty ascended the throne in February, 1952, following usual practice no coins were issued bearing her portrait until about the time of the coronation in June 1953. Although striking of the new coins began late in 1952, denominations urgently needed were struck bearing the portrait of George VI exactly as his last coinage, and in fact sixpences, threepences, halfpennies and farthings were also struck early in 1953, but still dated 1952. A halfcrown with George VI's portrait dated 1952 turned up in the north of England in the late 1960s.

The only unusual feature of design which occurred on the new silver coinage of Elizabeth II was the equestrian figure for the crown, and this was the first official such representation since the reign of Charles I (apart from the patterns of Edward VII). The obverse, designed by Gilbert Ledward, shows Her Majesty, in uniform, seated on a police horse named Winston. The reverse is also unorthodox in that it bears no legend – the design consists of the national emblems radiating from a central crown, with uncrowned shields of England, Scotland, Ireland and England in saltire. It was designed by D.G. Fuller. Interestingly the edge inscription was in English language – first non-Latin inscription on a British coin since the Commonwealth!

The portrait of the Queen chosen for the coinage was by Mrs. Mary Gillick but the Mint found that it did not strike very well owing to its delicate treatment. A number of experiments were carried out late in 1953 in an attempt to sharpen the design and to ensure better wearing characteristics of the obverse. The Queen's portrait, especially when reduced to the size of the smaller denominations, appeared in very low relief and with insufficient detail. A number of different re-cut obverse dies were used for the later 1953 pieces and then for 1954 onwards: on these the portrait is shown in somewhat higher relief and much finer detail is visible. The reverse design for the halfcrown is reminiscent of that of the pound-sovereign of Elizabeth I, a crowned shield between E R. The florin and sixpence both show different treatments of the national emblems, with the leek of Wales appearing for the first time on a British coin. The traditional, dating from 1937, of striking two types of shilling, one English and one Scottish, was maintained, two coins depicting on the reverse the respective quartering of the royal arms, crowned.

In 1954, the Queen declared by proclamation a change in the royal style and titles. It was thought that the title 'BRITT : OMN :' (of all the Britons, i.e., overseas possessions) was no longer in keeping with status of the British

ELIZABETH II
1952-

Commonwealth, and the words were accordingly omitted from the legend on coins struck from that year onwards.

In 1960, on the occasion of the British Trade Exposition held in New York, the Royal Mint, who had a stand at the exhibition, struck commemorative medals at the site. A special crown was also issued at this time, but as U.K. coin may only be struck in this country, the crowns were struck at the Royal Mint. The pieces destined for sale in New York were struck from polished dies, the finish of the coin being somewhat similar to that of the 1951 Festival piece, though not of such high quality. The polished-die crowns were sold in special plastic cases at the Exhibition. When the Exhibition closed, surplus stocks were returned to the U.K. in bags, and most of the specimens from polished dies now on the market in the U.K. are more or less defaced by bag scratches. As it was thought desirable to make crowns available to collectors here, a limited quantity was struck from ordinary dies; these also are hard to obtain in perfect state, as they were supplied to dealers and banks in bags. The obverse of this crown is the normal coinage portrait of the Queen by Mary Gillick, and the reverse is identical with that of the 1953 crown apart from the date; the edge is milled. The value FIVE SHILLINGS appears below the head.

On the death of Sir Winston Churchill in 1965, it was decided to issue a commemorative crown. These coins have been widely criticised due to their poor standard of workmanship, which probably resulted from their having to be produced in very large quantities in as short a time as possible. This crown has the Gillick portrait with the date 1965 below the bust; the reverse shows the head of Churchill by the sculptor Oscar Nemon and the inscription CHURCHILL; the edge is milled. An unusual feature for a modern crown is that no mark of denomination appears. Interestingly Churchill was the first non-Royal personage to appear on a British coin, discounting Oliver Cromwell who refused the Royal title offered him.

Note; Proofs and V.I.P. Proofs are numerated for halfcrowns, florins, shillings and sixpences, even though untraced, when a specific denomination is recorded, in anticipation of discovery of the others in the set. The Mint usually struck one or two sets each year for internal reasons and the occasionally one finds its way on to the market.

Note; 1966 shillings are found with an inverted reverse. Since they were the last coins to be struck at Tower Hill it is most likely that they were struck unofficially as mementos

ELIZABETH II, 1952-
CROWNS

G L

Obv. A

Rev. 1

Obv. B

E F   C T

Rev. 1

M·G·

Obv. C

ON (monogram)

Rev. 2

Note

Reverse 2 is an illustration of the extremely rare <u>specimen</u> with artist's initials **ON** (Oscar Nemon) at 7 o'clock *(only 2 known)*. The standard coinage is similar but minus the initials

CROWNS

All coins struck in cupro-nickel with milled edges (unless stated)
(Maundy coins in ·925 silver being the exception)

Type	**A.**	Coronation issue. *In cupro-nickel*
Obv.		Queen in uniform seated on her favourite police horse Winston, left, horse standing on a pedestal, small wreath below, royal cipher, **EIIR**, each side of horse, initials **GL** (Gilbert Ledward) appear behind near hind hoof
Leg.		**ELIZABETH·II·DEI·GRATIA·BRITT OMN·REGINA·FIDEI·DEFENSOR** ✾**FIVE SHILLINGS**✾

Rev.	**1.**	Cruciform shields of England, Scotland, England and Ireland with emblems, thistle, rose, shamrock and leek, crown in centre, **1953** below. Initials **E.F.** (Edgar Fuller) appear below Irish shield and **C.T.** (Cecil Thomas) appear below English shield
Edge		✠ **FAITH AND TRUTH I WILL BEAR UNTO YOU**

	B.	Issued on the occasion of the British Trade Fair in New York
Obv.		Laureate bust, right, initials **M.G.** (Mary Gillick) on truncation
Leg.		**ELIZABETH II DEI GRATIA REGINA F· D· FIVE SHILLINGS**

	1.	As '1', but dated **1960**

	C.	Sir Winston Churchill commemorative issue
Obv.		As 'B', but with a new *legend;* **ELIZABETH II DEI GRATIA REGINA F· D· // 1965**

	2.	Bust of Churchill in 'Siren Suit' looking right
Leg.		**CHURCHILL**
Edge		Milled

TYPES OF PROOFS
(with plain edge unless stated)

Standard	Design and field with a mirror finish
V.I.P.	Raised design frosted, field with a mirror finish, sharper detail
Matt	Design and field with a matt finish from sand blasted dies to facilitate photography

ELIZABETH II, 1952-
CROWNS

A/1. *'Coronation issue';* Queen on horseback, left
Rev. 1 - Four shields in saltire, dated **1953**
Edge; ✠ **FAITH AND TRUTH I WILL BEAR UNTO YOU**   Spink 4136

ESC	Date	Varieties, remarks etc.	R	L&S	(Old ESC)
4330	**1953**	Currency issue *(5,962,621 issued in plastic case)*	C^3		393F
4331	—	*Proof* issued in sets* and at Maundy ceremony In 1953 and succeeding years *(*40,000 sets issued)*	N	2	393G
4332	—	*Proof (part matt)* First striking much sharper [1]	R^6		*393E*
4333	—	*V.I.P. Proof. Edge,* incusely inscribed [2]	R	3	393H
4334	—	*Matt Proof, from sand blasted dies*	R^7	4	393J

B/1. 2nd issue; Laureate bust, right. Milled edge
Rev. 1 - Four shields in saltire, dated **1960**   Spink 4143

4335	**1960**		N	7	393K
4336	—	*Edge,* plain; Unintentional striking without collar	R^3		?
4337	—	Struck from polished dies (not a proof) [3] *Struck in fine silver*	S	8	393L
4338	—	*V.I.P. Proof, with sharper detail (in cupro-nickel)*	R^4	10	393M

C/2. *'Sir Winston Churchill'*, commemorative issue
Obv. As 'B', but with a different legend
Rev. 2 - Bust of Churchill in 'Siren Suit', right   Spink 4144

4339	**1965**		C^3		393N
4340	—	*Edge,* plain; Unintentional striking without a collar	R^3	13	?
4341	—	*Specimen,* struck with a 'Satin' finish and underlying brilliance	R^5	14	393O
4342	—	*Specimen,* struck with a 'satin' finish. Initials **ON** (Oscar Neman) under bust near rim at 7 o'clock *(2 known)*	R^7		393P?
4343	—	Struck on a faulty light weight blank			

1   Confirmed by Royal Mint as an early striking from proof dies before the issue of proof sets: *"Sharper than the Crown normally found in the set, the raised parts are a little more matt"*

2   V.I.P. proofs* are known to have been struck from 1953-1963
Because the Mint would almost certainly have struck complete sets each year, and one or two individual specimens appear on the market from time to time, all the denominations are allocated a number. See under *'Provenances'* for known specimens to date

3   Struck on polished dies for sale at the British Trade Exposition in New York

CROWNS

PATTERNS

Type D

GL

Obv. A

Rev. 3

ESC	Date	Type **D**			R	L&S	(Old ESC)
4344	**1953**	By **Gilbert Ledward, 1953**			R^7	6	393P
		Obv. As the currency coin					
		Rev. **3.** - Similar to the currency coin, but in higher relief, the emblems are larger, the date is in larger figures and top of shields decorated					
		Edge ✠ FAITH AND TRUTH I WILL BEAR UNTO YOU. *In cupro-nickel* *(Unique?)*					

Types
E – legend raised
&
F – legend incuse

Type   **E**

ESC	Date	By **Arnold Machin** Undated	R
4345	E	*Obv.* Draped bust of the Queen, right, wearing a coronet	R^7
		Leg. **ELIZABETH · II D · G · REGINA · F · D**	
		Rev. a reduced impression of the 1847 *'Gothic'* Crown,	
		Leg. **tueatur unita deus** // **anno dom mdcccxlvii** (1847)	
		Edge. **DEI . GRATIA : DEF . REGINA** in raised lettering	
		Struck on a flan for the 1966 Irish 10/-, commemorating the Anniversary of the Irish Easter Rising	
		In cupro-nickel *(2 known)*	

CROWNS

Type	**F.**		
ESC			R
4346		By **Arnold Machin** Undated Similar to type E, but obverse lettering incuse and edge reading: **PATTERN TRIAL CROWN** *Struck in silver*	R^7

Proposed Crown size £5 & £25 denominations By Hunt/Foley
(Unofficial)

A.M. Foley obliged the British Treasury c.1965 to reform the coinage and make a much larger profit for the United Kingdom with his proposals for two crown-size coins; a silver £5 and a gold £25

A.M.F   K.C.HVNT. Sculp. D

A.M.FOLEY F.   K.C. HUNT.D

G

4

Type	**G.**			
ESC	Date		R	(Old ESC)
4347	**1966**	By **Anthony M. Foley & K.C. Hunt,** dated **1966** *Obv.* Conjoined busts of the Queen and Prince Philip, left, engravers initials on both truncations *Leg.* ❖ **ELIZABETH II : D : G : REGINA :** **F : D : + PHILIP DUKE OF EDINBURGH** *Rev.* **4. -** Britannia riding in a biga, left, hurling thunderbolts. Legend above and date in exergue **GREAT BRITAIN .** **1966** *Edge.* Plain. *In ·925 silver, as a £5 proposal* (100 struck)	R^2	393Q
4348	—	*In gold, as a £25 proposal*	R^6	393R

HALFCROWNS

| Obv. A | Rev. 1 | Obv. B |

Type	**A.**	First coinage; Laureate bust draped, right
		MG (Mrs Mary Gillick) incuse on truncation
Leg.	1	**✛ ELIZABETH II DEI GRATIA BRITT: OMN: REGINA**
	B.	Second coinage; as 'A', but BRITT OMN dropped from *leg.*
Leg.	2	**✛ ELIZABETH • II • DEI • GRATIA • REGINA**
Punc.		Lozenge stops
Rev.	**1.**	Square-topped shield crowned between **E R.** Initials below; left
		EF (Edgar Fuller) and right **CT** (Cecil Thomas)
Leg.		✠ **FID •** ♔ **• DEF** ✠
		HALF CROWN 1953

A/1. First coinage; Laureate bust draped, right, *leg.* **BRITT: OMN:**
Rev. 1 - Square-topped shield crowned between **E R** Spink 4137

ESC	Date	Varieties	R	(Old ESC)
4349	**1953**	Note	*N*	798G
4350	—	*Proof*	*S*	798H
4351	—	*V.I.P. Proof*	R^5	
4352	—	*Matt Proof, from sand blasted dies* ↑↑ *wt. 13.75g*	R^6	

ELIZABETH II, 1952-
HALFCROWNS

B/1.   Second coinage; As before, but minus BRITT: OMN:
Rev. 1 - Square-topped shield crowned between **E R** Spink 4145

ESC	Date	Varieties	R	(Old ESC)
4353	**1954**		C	798I
4354	—	*Proof*	R^4	
4355	—	*V.I.P. Proof*	R^6	
		(Not traced, but an English & Scottish shilling known)		
4356	—	*Matt Proof, from sand blasted dies*	R^6	
		(Not traced, but a Scottish shilling known)		
4357	**1955**		C	798J
4358	—	*Proof*	R^4	
4359	—	*Matt Proof, from sand blasted dies*	R^6	
		(Not traced, but an English shilling and Maundy set are known)		
4360	**1956**		C	798K
4361	—	*Proof*	R^4	
4362	—	*V.I.P. Proof*	R^6	
4363	**1957**		C	798L
4364	—	*Proof*	R^4	
4365	—	*V.I.P. Proof* *(Not traced, but florin & shillings E&S known)*	R^6	
4366	**1958**		C^2	798M
4367	—	*Proof*	R^4	
4368	—	*V.I.P. Proof*	R^6	
4369	**1959**		C^2	798N
4370	—	*Proof* *(Not traced)*	R^4	
4371	**1960**		C^2	798Q
4372	—	*Proof*	R^4	
4373	—	*V.I.P. Proof* *(Not traced, but crown & Scottish 1/- known)*	R^6	
4374	—	*Struck in bronze*	R	
4375	**1961**	Notes [1,2]	C^3	798P
4376	—	*Struck on blanks originally prepared for proofs*	S	
4377	—	*Proof*	R^4	
4378	—	*V.I.P. Proof* *(Not traced, but shillings E&S known)*	R^6	
4379	**1962**		C^3	798S
4380	—	*Proof*	R^4	
4381	—	*V.I.P. Proof*	R^5	
4382	**1963**		C^3	798T
4383	—	*Proof* *(Not traced)*	R^4	

(continued)

HALFCROWNS

ESC	Date	Varieties		R	(Old ESC)
4384	**1964**			C^3	798U
4385	—	*Proof*	*(Not traced, but a sixpence known)*	R^4	
4386	**1965**			C^3	798V
4387	—	*Proof*	*(Not traced)*	R^4	
4388	**1966**			C^3	798W
4389	—	*Proof*	*(Not traced)*	R^4	
4390	**1967**			C^3	798X
4391	—	*Proof*	*(Not traced)*	R^4	
4392	**1970**	*Proof*		C^3	798Y

1   The coin listed in previous editions as '798Q'; engraver's initials E.F. omitted, has been deleted because this so-called error is almost certainly due to a filled die.

2   St James Auction 6 lot 444 *"struck on a thin flan wt. 9.78g VAS"*

ELIZABETH II, 1952-
FLORINS

   E.F      C.T

Obv. A   Rev. 1   Obv. B

Type	**A.**	As halfcrown
Obv.		First issue; Laureate bust draped right.
		MG (Mrs Mary Gillick) incuse on truncation
Leg.		**✚ ELIZABETH II DEI GRATIA BRITT: OMN: REGINA**

| | **B.** | Second issue; as 'A', but BRITT OMN dropped from *leg.* |
| *Leg.* | | **✚ ELIZABETH · II · DEI · GRATIA · REGINA** |

Rev. A double rose in the centre within a circle of radiating thistles, shamrocks and leeks, **E·F** and **C·T** beside lowest leek

Leg.

FID: DEF:

TWO   SHILLINGS   1953

A/1. First coinage; Laureate bust draped, right, *leg.* **BRITT: OMN:**
Rev. 1 - Double rose within a circle   Spink 4138

ESC	Date	Varieties	R	(Old ESC)
4393	**1953**		N	968F
4394	—	*Proof*	S	968G
4395	—	*V.I.P. Proof*	R^6	
4396	—	*Matt Proof, from sand blasted dies* wt. 11.26g	R^5	

B/1. Second coinage; As before, but minus BRITT: OMN:
Rev. 1 - Double rose within a circle   Spink 4146

4397	**1954**		C	968H
4398	—	*Proof*	R^6	
4399	—	*V.I.P. Proof* (Not traced, but Eng. & Scot. shillings known)	R^5	
4400	**1955**		C	968I
4401	—	*Proof*	R^4	
4402	**1955**	*Matt Proof* (Not traced but shillings E & S known)	R^5	

(continued)

562

FLORINS

ESC	Date	Varieties	R	(Old ESC)
4403	**1956**		C	968J
4404	—	*Proof*	R^4	
4405	—	*V.I.P. Proof*	R^5	
4406	**1957**		C	968K
4407	—	*Proof*	R^4	
4408	—	*V.I.P. Proof*	R^5	
4409	**1958**		C	968L
4410	—	*Proof*	R^4	
4411	—	*V.I.P. Proof* *(Not traced but 2/-,1/-E&S known)*	R^5	
4412	**1959**		C^2	968M
4413	—	*Proof* *(Not traced)*	R^4	
4414	**1960**		C^2	968N
4415	—	*Proof* *(Not traced but a halfcrown known)*	R^6	
4416	—	*V.I.P. Proof* *(Not traced but crown & Scot. shilling known)*	R^5	
4417	**1961**		C^2	968O
4418	—	*Proof*	R^4	
4419	—	*V.I.P. Proof* *(Not traced but E & S shillings known)*	R^4	
4420	**1962**		C^3	968P
4421	—	*Proof* *(Not traced but halfcrown known)*	R^5	
4422	—	*V.I.P. Proof* *(Not traced but halfcrown known)*	R^6	
4423	**1963**		C^3	968Q
4424	—	*Proof* *(Not traced but halfcrown known)*	R^6	
4425	—	*V.I.P. Proof in gold* *(Trials. 3 known in B.M. Collection)*	R^6	
4426	**1964**		C^3	968R
4427	—	*Proof* *(Not traced but a sixpence known)*		
4428	**1965**		C^3	968S
4429	—	*Proof* *(Not traced)*	R^4	
4430	—	*Nickel-Brass* (flan was prepared for Iceland, nickel-brass 2-Kronur ? (1966 halfpenny)	R^5	
4431	**1966**		C^3	968T
4432	—	*Proof* *(Not traced)*	R^4	
4433	**1967**		C^3	968U
4434	—	*Proof* *(Not traced)*	R^4	
4435	**1970**	*Proof*	S	968V

Note; see 'Introduction'
Proofs *not traced* are listed when considered a possibility
V.I.P. Proofs are listed when a single other denomination is known

FLORINS

PATTERNS

4436	**1955** *Struck in pure nickel, plain edge. № 5 stamped in obv. field (unique)*

TRIAL STRIKINGS OF PATTERN FLORINS UNDATED

Five types of trial pieces were produced by the Royal Mint in October 1961 for a
Royal Mint advisory committee towards an eventual Decimal Coinage under
Sir Francis Meynell and Mr Milner Gray, investigating the most suitable
type of lettering for the coinage (Spink Auction 134, lot 465)

4437	As the accepted obverse design but with different lettering fonts, with wording below chin : **TRIAL ALB** (Albertus) *Rev.* blank except for the Royal Mint logo. *In Cupro-nickel*	R^6
4438	As before, but wording below chin : **BAS** (Baskerville) *Rev.* blank except for **TRIAL DIE**	R^6
4439	As before, but wording below chin : **POL** (Poliphilus)	R^6
4440	As before, **ALBERTUS LIGHT**	R^6
4441	As before, **ION** (Ionic)	R^6

See more examples under PATTERNS FOR DECIMAL COINAGE

ELIZABETH II, 1952-
SHILLINGS

Obv. A
First issue

Obv. B
Second issue

Rev. 1
English

Rev. 2
Scottish

Obv.	**A.**	First issue; laureate and draped bust, right
		M.G. (Mary Gillick) incuse on truncation
Leg.	1	✠ **ELIZABETH II DEI GRATIA BRITT: OMN: REGINA**
	B.	Second issue; as before but, minus BRITT OMN in *leg.*
Leg.	2	✠ **ELIZABETH · II · DEI · GRATIA · REGINA**

565

ELIZABETH II, 1952-
SHILLINGS

Rev. **1.**   *'English shilling'*; crowned shield bearing the three leopards of
England dividing date and **W G** (William Gardner)

Leg.   ✦ **FID** + **DEF** ✦
              ONE SHILLING

Rev. **2.**   *'Scottish shilling'*, crowned shield bearing the Scottish lion
rampant dividing date and initials **W G** (William Gardner)

Type **A/1.**   First issue with **'ENGLISH'** reverse   Spink 4139

ESC	Date	Varieties	R	(Old ESC)
4442	**1953**		N	1475K
4443	—	*Proof*	S	1475L
4444	—	*V.I.P. Proof*	R^6	
4445	—	*Matt Proof, from sand blasted dies*	R^6	

       A/2.   First issue with **'SCOTTISH'** reverse   Spink 4140

4446	**1953**		N	1475M
4447	—	*Proof*	N	1475N
4448	—	*V.I.P. Proof*	R^6	
4449	—	*Matt Proof, from sand blasted dies (Not traced, but halfcrown, florin, English shilling and sixpence known)*	R^6	

       B/1.   Second issue with **'ENGLISH'** reverse   Spink 4147

4450	**1954**		C	1475O
4451	—	*Proof*	R^6	
4452	—	*V.I.P. Proof*	R^6	
4453	—	*Matt Proof, from sand blasted dies (Not traced, but Scottish shilling known)*	R^6	
4454	**1955**		C	1475Q
4455	—	*Proof*	R^6	
4456	—	*Matt Proof, from sand blasted dies*	R^6	

(continued)

SHILLINGS

ESC	Date	Varieties		R	(Old ESC)
4457	**1956**			C	1475S
4458	—	*Proof*		R^6	
4459	—	*V.I.P. Proof*		R^6	
4460	**1957**			C^2	1475U
4461	—	*Proof*		R^6	
4462	—	*V.I.P. Proof*		R^6	
4463	**1958**			C^2	1475W
4464	—	*Proof*		R^6	
4465	—	*V.I.P. Proof*		R^5	
4466	**1959**			C^2	1475Y
4467	—	*Proof*	*(Not traced)*	R^6	
4468	**1960**			C^2	1475A
4469	—	*Proof*	*(Not traced, but halfcrown known)*	R^6	
4470	—	*V.I.P. Proof*	*(Not traced, but Scottish shilling known)*	R^7	
4471	**1961**			C^3	1475C
4472	—	*Proof*		R^6	
4473	—	*V.I.P. Proof*		R^6	
4474	**1962**			C^3	1475E
4475	—	*V.I.P. Proof*	*(Not traced, but halfcrown known)*	R^6	
4476	**1963**			C^3	1475G
4477	—	*Proof*	*(Not traced, but halfcrown known)*	R^6	
4478	**1964**			C^3	1475I
4479	—	*Proof*	*(Not traced, but sixpence known)*	R^6	
4480	**1965**			C^3	1475K
4481	—	*Proof*	*(Not traced)*	R^6	
4482	**1966**			C^3	1475M
4483	—	*Proof*	*(Not traced)*	R^6	
4484	**1970**	*Proof*		R	1475O

B/2. Second issue with **'SCOTTISH'** reverse   Spink 4148

			R	(Old ESC)
4485	**1954**		C	1475P
4486	—	*Proof*	R^6	
4487	—	*V.I.P. Proof*	R^6	
4488	—	*Matt Proof, from sand blasted dies*	R^6	

SHILLINGS

(continued)

ESC	Date	Varieties	R	(Old ESC)
4489	**1955**		*C*	1475R
4490	—	*Proof*	*R⁶*	
4491	—	*Matt Proof, from sand blasted dies*	*R⁶*	
4492	—	*In pure nickel, plain edge.* № 30 stamped in obverse field	*R⁷*	
4493	**1956**		*C*	1475T
4494	—	*Proof*	*R⁶*	
4495	—	*V.I.P. Proof*	*R⁶*	
4496	**1957**		*C²*	1475V
4497	—	*Proof*	*R⁶*	
4498	—	*V.I.P. Proof*	*R⁶*	
4499	**1958**		*C²*	1475X
4500	—	*Proof*	*R⁶*	
4501	—	*V.I.P. Proof*	*R⁶*	
4502	**1959**		*R*	1475Z
4503	—	*Proof* *(Not traced)*	*R⁶*	
4504	**1960**		*C²*	1475B
4505	—	*Proof* *(Not traced)*	*R⁶*	
4506	—	*V.I.P. Proof*	*R⁶*	1475BB
4507	**1961**		*S*	1475D
4508	—	*Proof*	*R⁶*	
4509	—	*V.I.P. Proof* *(Not traced, but English shilling known)*	*R⁶*	
4510	**1962**		*C³*	1475F
4511	—	*V.I.P. Proof* *(Not traced, but halfcrown known)*	*R⁶*	
4512	**1963**		*C³*	1475H
4513	—	*Proof* *(Not traced, but halfcrown known)*	*R⁶*	
4514	**1964**		*C³*	1475J
4515	—	*Proof* *(Not traced, but sixpence known)*	*R⁶*	
4516	**1965**		*C³*	1475L
4517	—	*Proof* *(Not traced)*	*R⁶*	
4518	**1966**	See note in 'Introduction' regarding mementoes	*C³*	1475N
4519	—	*Proof* *(Not traced)*	*R⁶*	
4520	**1970**	*Proof*	*R*	1475P

ELIZABETH II, 1952-
SIXPENCES

Obv. A	Rev. 1	Obv. B
First coinage		Second coinage

Type   **A.**   First coinage: Laureate and draped bust, right, *in cupro-nickel*
           MG (Mary Gillick) incuse on truncation

Leg.   **✚ ELIZABETH II DEI GRATIA BRITT: OMN: REGINA**

Rev.   A garland of interlaced rose, thistle, shamrock and leek, the rose
           at the top between two leaves, the leek on the left, the thistle on
           the right, the shamrock at the bottom between small shamrock
           and leaf, **EF** and **CT** in lower field

Leg.   **FID ·✺ DEF ·**
                  SIX PENCE · 1953

          B.   Second coinage: As before, but with a change to *legend,*
                 BRITT OMN omitted

Leg.   **✚ ELIZABETH · II · DEI · GRATIA · REGINA**

A.	**BRITT: OMN: REGINA** (cupro-nickel)			Spink 4141
ESC	Date	Varieties	R	(Old ESC)
4521	**1953**		N	1838G
4522	—	*Proof*	S	798H
4523	—	*V.I.P. Proof* *(Not traced, but other denominations known)*	R^5	
4524	—	*Matt Proof, from sand blasted dies*	R^6	

569

ELIZABETH II, 1952-
SIXPENCES

B. BRITT OMN omitted (cupro-nickel) Spink 4149

ESC	Date	Varieties	R	(Old ESC)
4525	**1954**		C	1838I
4526	—	*Proof, milled edge* wt. 2.85g	R^5	
4527	—	*V.I.P. Proof* (Not traced, but shillings known)	R^6	
4528	—	*Matt Proof* (Not traced, but Scottish shilling known)	R^6	
4529	**1955**		C	1838J
4530	—	*Proof*	R^5	
4531	—	*Matt Proof* (Not traced, but English shilling, Maundy known)	R^6	
4532	**1956**		C	1838K
4533	—	*Proof* (Not traced, but other denominations known)	R^5	
4534	**1957**		C	1838L
4535	—	*Proof, milled edge* wt. 2.81g	R^5	
4536	**1958**		C^2	1838M
4537	—	*Proof*	R^5	
4538	—	*V.I.P. Proof* (Not traced, but halfcrown known)	R^6	
4539	**1959**		C^2	1838N
4540	—	*Proof, milled edge* wt. 2.70g	R^5	
4541	**1960**		C^2	1838O
4542	—	*Proof* (Not traced, but halfcrown known)	R^5	
4543	**1961**		C^2	1838P
4544	—	*Proof, milled edge* wt. 2.81g	R^5	
4545	**1962**		C^2	1838Q
4546	—	*Proof* (Not traced, but halfcrown known)	R^5	
4547	**1963**		C^2	1838R
4548	—	*Proof*	R^5	
4549	**1964**		C^3	1838S
4550	—	*Proof, milled edge* wt. 2.85g	R^5	
4551	**1965**		C^3	1838T
4552	—	*Proof* (Not traced)	R^5	
4553	**1966**		C^3	1838U
4554	—	*Proof* (Not traced)	R^5	
4555	**1967**		C^3	1838V
4556	—	*Proof* (Not traced)	R^5	
4557	—	*Brass*	R^5	
4558	**1970**	*Proof*	S	1838W

MAUNDY MONEY

A   B

Type	**A.**	As halfcrown, *in ·925 fine silver. Edge,* plain
Obv.		Laureate bust draped right
Leg.		**✛ ELIZABETH II DEI GRA BRITT: OMN: REGINA F:D:**
Rev.		As established design
	B.	As before with change to *leg.,* BRITT OMN omitted
Leg.		**✛ ELIZABETH II DEI GRATIA REGINA F:D:**
		Struck to the usual proof standard

Spink 4126

ESC	Date	Type	Maundy Ceremony Venue	*R*	(Old ESC)
4559	**1953**	A	St Paul's Cathedral	R^2	2570
4560	—	—	*Matt proof, from sand blasted dies*	R^5	
4561	—	—	*In gold*	R^7	
4562	—	—	*Proof struck in nickel bronze*	R^7	

Spink 4131

ESC	Date	Type	Maundy Ceremony Venue	*R*	(Old ESC)
4563	**1954**	B	Westminster Abbey	R	2571
4564	**1955**	—	Southwark Cathedral	R	2572
4565	—	—	*Matt proof with a milled edge*	R^6	2572
4566	**1956**	—	Westminster Abbey	R	2573
4567	**1957**	—	St Alban's Cathedral	R	2574
4568	**1958**	—	Westminster Abbey	R	2575
4569	**1959**	—	Windsor, St George's Chapel	R	2576
4570	**1960**	—	Westminster Abbey	R	2577
4571	**1961**	—	Rochester Cathedral	R	2578
4572	**1962**	—	Westminster Abbey	R	2579
4573	**1963**	—	Chelmsford Cathedral	R	2580
4574	**1964**	—	Westminster Abbey	R	2581
4575	**1965**	—	Canterbury Cathedral	R	2582
4576	**1966**	—	Westminster Abbey	R	2583
4577	**1967**	—	Durham Cathedral	R	2584
4578	**1968**	—	Westminster Abbey	R	2585
4579	**1969**	—	Selby Abbey	R	2586
4580	**1970**	—	Westminster Abbey	R	2587

Note; after decimalisation these denominations were re-valued as 'New' pence.

A SMALL SELLECTION OF PATTERNS FOR DECIMAL COINAGE. MANY MORE ARE KNOWN

These patterns are for information only

P.D.S. 1.

Edward VII, Pattern Set for a proposed Decimal Coinage, dated 1901, made for Thomas Parker, Aluminium 1 (One Mille), 2 (Two Milles), 3 (Three Milles), and 5 (Five Milles) "THOUSANDTHS OF A £ STERLING", and Silvered-bronze 10 (One Cent) and 25 (Two and a Half Cents) "THOUSANDTHS OF A £ STERLING", each with KING / EDWARD/ VII in three lines at centre, metal above, date below, *rev* value in four lines, toothed border and rim each side, edge plain, respective weights 0.90g, 1.41g, 2.00g, 2.35g, 1.82g, 2.48g (Rogers 900, 902, 904, 910, 915, 920, all rated RRR). *The aluminium pieces brilliant as struck, the latter two toned, generally good extremely fine or as struck, extremely rare.* (6)

These coinage patterns were sent to Members of Parliament by Thomas Parker (1843-1915), who was a prominent Wolverhampton based businessman and inventor. He had actively campaigned for a decimal system of weights (based on the quarter of a grain) and measures (based on the inch), as well as for a coinage based on a Pound Sterling. Parker was a chemist and engineer, who made a small steam engine at the age of 14, developed an electric car from 1884 and was heavily involved with electrolytic process and the distribution of electricity in the Midlands He later invented Coalite, a smokeless fuel. He died 5 December 1915.

A SMALL SELLECTION OF PATTERNS FOR
DECIMAL COINAGE. MANY MORE ARE KNOWN

Many of the following groups of trial coins struck in the Winter and Spring of 1962-63 were struck for the "Decimal Currency Committee" which had been appointed in December 1961 to advise on the most convenient and practical form that a decimal currency might take. The Chairman of the Committee was the Rt. Hon. Earl of Halsbury FRS. The Secretary was Mr N.E.A. Moore, who subsequently became secretary of the Decimal Currency Board. The Assistant Secretary was Mr John Rimington. The Trial coins were circulated at the meetings by the Deputy Master of the Mint, Mr J.H. James CB. (Spink 124, lots 2263-2265)

P.D.S. 1. **PATTERN DECIMAL SET DATED 1961**
Standard obverse: Laureate and draped bust, right

	50 Cents, *in silver*
Leg	**+ ELIZABETH · II · DEI · GRATIA · REGINA · F:D:**
Rev	Una and the lion, left
	50 CENTS
	date **1961** in exergue
Edge	in raised letters
	PATTERN DECIMAL COINAGE

	20 Cents, *in cupro-nickel*
Leg	**+ ELIZABETH · II · DEI · GRATIA · REGINA**
Rev	Britannia standing on a plinth
	sea in the background
Leg	date **1961** on plinth
Edge	**TWENTY CENTS**
	Milled

	10 Cents, *in cupro-nickel*
Leg	**+ ELIZABETH · II · DEI · GRATIA · REGINA**
Rev	Shield in crowned garter with
Leg	**10 CENTS** both left & right
	Date **19 61** below
	divided by strap
Edge	Milled

A SMALL SELLECTION OF PATTERNS FOR
DECIMAL COINAGE. MANY MORE ARE KNOWN

P.D.S. 1. continued

	5 Cents, *in cupro-nickel*
Leg	**+ ELIZABETH · II · DEI · GRATIA · REGINA**
Rev	Lion standing on a crown
Leg	**5 CENTS** both left and right Date **1961** below
Edge	Milled

Bronze
2 & 1 cent
illustrated for
completeness

(SNC 2005, p. 140, MS6357 & Norweb 1168)

P.D.S. 2.   (Spink 124, lot 2263 – Plain on obverse)

20-Pence – milled edge Cupro-nickel, 36mm *wt. 22.74g*	10-Pence – milled edge Cupro-nickel, 28.5mm *wt. 11.38g*	5-Pence – milled edge Cupro-nickel, 24mm *wt. 6.01g*

Half-penny – plain edge Bronze, 17mm - *wt. 1.99*	Penny – plain edge Bronze, 20mm - *wt. 3.56g*	2-Pence – plain edge Bronze, 26mm - *wt. 7.09g*

574

P.D.S. 3   (Spink 124, lot 2265)

Obv. Draped figure of Britannia, seated on stool facing two-thirds right at coin striking pedestal, striking hammer in right hand, coin die in left hand, newly minted coins by foot, **BRITANNIA MONETA** around, terminating with dolphin. *Rev.* mark of numerical value, *edge* **DECUS ET TUTAMEN** incusely inscribed

50-Pence	20-Pence	10-Pence	5-Pence
edge legend	edge legend	milled edge	milled edge
Cupro-nickel	Cupro-nickel	Cupro-nickel	Cupro-nickel
32mm, *wt. 16.23g*	25mm, *wt. 6.69g*	28mm, *wt. 11.01g*	23.5mm, *wt. 5.58g*

Quarter-penny	Half-penny	Penny	2-Pence
plain edge	plain edge	plain edge	milled edge
Bronze 20mm,	Bronze 19mm,	Bronze 21.5mm,	Cupro-nickel
wt. 1.15g	*wt. 2.20g*	*wt. 4.56g*	18mm, wt. 2.25g

Note: With this set is an extra blank possibly for a Pound coin,
32mm diameter, 3.5mm thickness, *wt. 22.55g*

A SMALL SELLECTION OF PATTERNS FOR
DECIMAL COINAGE. MANY MORE ARE KNOWN

P.D. 4.   (Spink 124, lot 2264 – Mint mark on obverse)
Missing the Halfpenny, *in bronze* and Quarter-penny, *in aluminium*

| 50-Pence – plain edge Cupro-nickel – 32mm *wt. 16.15g* | *Obv.* Tower mintmark plain border at centre Cupro-nickel | 20-Pence – plain edge Cupro-nickel – 25mm *wt. 6.40g* |

| Penny plain edge Bronze 28mm, *wt. 21.5g* | 2-Pence milled edge Cupro-nickel 18mm, *wt. 2.23g* | 5-Pence milled edge Cupro-nickel 23.5mm, *wt. 5.58g* | 10-Pence milled edge Cupro-nickel 28mm, *wt. 11.19g* |

P.D. 5.   (Spink 62, lot 461)
These patterns were produced for submission to the Royal Mint Advisory
Committee who had concluded that the current reverse designs were unsuitable

461

576

A SMALL SELLECTION OF PATTERNS FOR
DECIMAL COINAGE. MANY MORE ARE KNOWN

P.D. 5. Continued		
	Pattern set of reverses in silver, 1926, by Derwent Wood (Models by T.A. Paget). All but the crown bearing the word **MODEL** on the reverse	
Crown	Peace seated right, legend around **GIVE PEACE IN OUR TIME O LORD**, edge milled	*wt. 25.69g*
Halfcrown	crowned shield within Garter, edge milled	*wt. 14.08g*
Florin	three roses, one in bloom, edge milled	*wt. 11.27g*
Shilling	large crown surmounted by a crowned lion, edge milled	*wt. 5.53g*
Sixpence	crowned Tudor rose, edge milled	*wt. 2.80g*
Threepence	large thistle, edge plain	*wt. 1.42g*
	(See G.P. Dyer, Numismatic Chronicle "Thomas Humphrey Paget" Pages 167/8, for some background to these pieces)	

P.D.S. 6.

Elizabeth II, A group of Decimal Trials for a new decimal coinage, undated (c.1961), no unit of currency stated but denominated as 50 and 20, struck in cupro-nickel with lettered edges DECUS ET TUTAMEN, 10, 5, and 2, struck in brass with milled edges, 1, ½ and ¼ struck in bronze with plain edges; all with common obverse, Britannia seated striking hammered coins, BRITANNIA MONETA, followed by dolphin, *rev* each with denominational Arabic number. *All as struck and extremely rare.* (8)

A SMALL SELLECTION OF PATTERNS FOR DECIMAL COINAGE. MANY MORE ARE KNOWN

P.D.S. 7.　　　　Baldwin F.P.L. Winter 2012-13, lot BM105
FLORINS / TEN NEW PENCE
Rare group of Pattern Florins Trialling Various Font Styles

An assemblage of five undated trial pieces struck in cupro-nickel, on Florin size Blanks with Florin type obverses, produced for the purpose of testing new font styles in legends for a proposed decimal coinage of Ten Pence size, each with a different font for lettering as follows:- Albertus 11.34g, Albertus Light 11.28g, Poliphilus 11.33g, Baskerville 11.24g, Ionic 11.31g each with the same design, young laureate head right engraved by Mary Gillick, MG incuse on truncation, legend surrounding **+ELIZABETH.II.DEI.GRATIA.REGINA** beaded border and raised rim surrounding, incuse letters in field in front of neck denote each font style upon trial piece respectively, **TRIAL / ALB, ALB.L, BAS, ION.**, reverse **TRIAL DIE** in two lines at centre, raised outer rim, edge milled

Milner Connorton Gray, graphic designer, CBE 1968, born 8th October 1899, died 29th September 1997.
Sir Francis Meredith Wilfrid Meynell, British poet and printer at Nonesuch Press, knighted 1946, born 12th May 1891, died 10th July 1975.

UNOFFICIAL REPRODUCTIONS
NOT ROYAL MINT ISSUES
Illustrated purely as a warning not to be fooled
'PATINA' CROWNS[1]

Type A

Obv.	Small coroneted young head of Victoria, left, date below. Engraver's initials **DRG** (Donald R. Golder) below truncation
Leg	**VICTORIA DEI GRATIA 1879**
Rev	Square-topped shield, crowned within two laurel branches (Similar to the first official reverse, but without the posy below)
Leg.	**BRITANNIARUM REGINA FID: DEF:**
Edge	Plain. *Struck in aluminium*

Type. B   Type. C

Obv.	B - Bare head, right, initials **DRG** below truncation (Donald R. Golder)
Leg	**EDWARDVS VII D:G: BRITT: OMN:REX F:D:IND:IMP:MDCDX** (Date 1910 in Roman NUMERALS)
Rev	St George, left, slaying the dragon (no legend)
Obv.	**C** - Uniface as before but Arabic date **1910**

UNOFFICIAL REPRODUCTIONS
NOT ROYAL MINT ISSUES
Illustrated purely as a warning not to be fooled
DOUBLE-FLORIN

Type D

Obv.	**D.** - King, bare-headed, wearing a collar and tie, right
Leg	**EDWARDVS VII · DEI GRATIA ·IND : IMP :**
Rev	As Victoria issue; Cruciform crowned shields, star of the Garter in centre, four sceptres in the angles
Leg	**REX: 19 ♛ 02 FID: ♛ DEF: ♛ BRITT: ♛**

Type. E

Obv.	**E.** - Bare head, left, initials **DRG** below truncation
Leg	**GEORGIVS V D G: BRITT: OMN:REX F:D:IND:IMP:1911**
Rev	St George, left, slaying the dragon (no legend)

1   Produced by the International Numismatic Agency, Birmingham in 2001[1]
Just a small sellection, go on line to discover a whole range of these. Commonly struck in aluminium with plain edges

EDWARD VII, 1901-10
UNOFFICIAL REPRODUCTIONS
NOT ROYAL MINT ISSUES
Illustrated purely as a warning not to be fooled
FANTASY PATTERNS CROWNS [2]
Many varieties of these fantasy pieces have continued to be struck over the years, with reverses for various dominions and colonies, e.g. Australia, Bermuda, Ceylon, Hong Kong and New Zealand as well as Great Britain, in the original series, and others in more recent strikings. These are just a few. See 8 more examples sold in St James' Auction 5, 2006, circa £30 -40 each

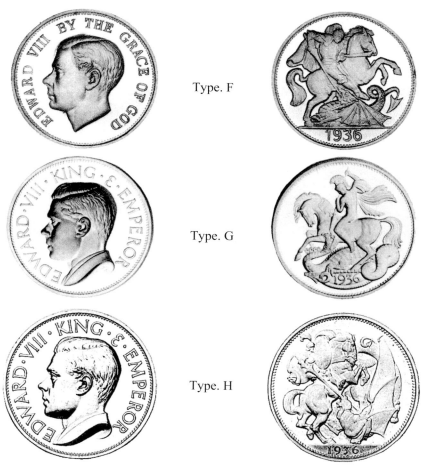

Type. F

Type. G

Type. H

2   Some struck in 1948 and others circa 1972 by the Pobjoy Mint. (Included out of interest)

UNOFFICIAL REPRODUCTIONS
NOT ROYAL MINT ISSUES
Illustrated purely as a warning not to be fooled

1936		F. - By **G. Hearn, 1936**		391
	Obv	Small truncated bare head, left. Unsigned		
	Leg	**EDWARD VIII BY THE**		
		GRACE OF GOD		
	Rev	St George right, slaying the dragon		
		Very large date in exergue.		
		In gold		

1936		**G.** - Small draped bust, left. Unsigned *(L&S, p. 110)*		
	Leg	**EDWARD · VIII · KING · & · EMPEROR**		
	Rev	St George left, slaying the dragon		
		Larger date above dragon's tail. *(50 struck)*		
—	—	*In gold* *(25 struck)* *wt. 38·44g*		

1936		**H.** - Large draped bust, left. Unsigned		
	Leg	**EDWARD · VIII · KING · & · EMPEROR**		
	Rev	St George on rearing horse, right, spearing dragon at		
		close range. Small date in exergue.		
—	—	*In silver gilt*		
—	—	*In gilt bronze*		

1937	C/4	By **Pobjoy Mint c. 1937**	
	Obv	Large draped bust, right. Unsigned	
	Leg	**EDWARD · VIII · KING · AND · EMPEROR**	
	Rev	St George left, slaying the dragon	
		Very large date in exergue.	
—	—	*In gold* *wt. 42.88g*	

PROVENANCES

Entries **in bold** signify **illustrated** in the main body of this edition

METAL ABBREVIATIONS

Ag (Silver, *Argentum*); Al (Aluminium, *Alumen*); Au (Gold, *Aurum*); Cu (Copper, *Cuprum*)
Cd (Cadmium, *Cadmia*); Fe (Iron, *Ferrum*); Ni (Nickel, *Kupfernickel*); Pb (Lead, *Plumbum*)
Pt (Platinum, *Platina*); Sn (Tin, *Stannum*); U (Uranium, *Uranus*); Zn (Zinc, *Zink*)
Wm (White metal, an alloy made from 93% tin, 1% copper & 6% antimony)
Pw (Pewter, an alloy of 85–99% tin, with copper, antimony & bismuth)
Nb (Nickel-brass, an alloy of 60% copper, 30% zinc & 10% nickel)
Cu-ni (An alloy of Copper and nickel – post 1947 coins)

NAMED COLLECTIONS

Adams. Colin	Halfcrowns - high quality	Spink 177. Dec. 2005. Most comprehensive collection
Asherson. N	All denominations	Spink 6. Oct. 1979 Very comprehensive collection
Barr. Alan	High quality crowns	Sold through M. Rasmussen c. 2008 Most comprehensive
L.B.	Quality on line stock	Lloyd Bennett. Dealer: Web page *Coins of Britain*
Besly. E	Commonwealth	BNJ 64. Plate 13, № 5
Bole. Alfred	Sixpences Part I	DNW 89. 29/9/2010, lots 1448-1870 Very
— —	— — II	DNW 90. 9/12/2010, lots 1-183 comprehensive
— —	— — III	DNW 91. 16/3/2011, lots 1-203 collection
— —	— — IV	DNW 92. 21/6/2011, lots 1-65
— —	— — V	DNW 93. 26/9/2011, lots 1355-1542
Bull. Maurice	Halfcrowns (complete)	Private collection sold through Mark Rasmussen 2010-14
Bruno	High Quality crowns	Dr Bruno Mantegazza. Spink Auction 113. 1996.
Bonhams	Quality selection	Auction on 17/10/2006
Christies	Various	Auction on 28/5/1992
Graham. K.V	Pattern crowns	Auction Glendining 12/6/1963
Hamilton	Comprehensive collection	Hamilton. Lord. Spink 3, 21/2/1979
Hughes. Martin	Shillings & Sixpences	Spink 139. 16/11/1999 Henry VIII – GIII
Karon. Paul W	Crowns etc	Spink 129. 17/11/1998
Kent. E.R.	William III etc (Study)	Jackson-Kent. Glendining 26/5/1965
La Riviere	Quality collection	La Riviere and Kaufman Spink 124. 18/11/1997
Lingford	Comp. Bank $ & Crowns	Lingford. H.M. Glendining 24/10/1950
RCL	Comprehensive collection	Lockett. R.C. Glendining 1956-1960.
Magnus	English & Forein Coins	Spink 212, 2012/3/28&29
Manville	Comprehensive collection	Manville. H.E. Spink 9, 4/6/1980
Montagu	Comprehensive collection	Montagu. Hyman. Sotheby 13/11/1896
Morrieson	Comprehensive collection	Morrieson. Colonel. Sotheby 20/11/1933
Norweb	Select high grade rarities	R. Henry Norweb. Spink Auctions; 45, 48, 56 & 59
Paget. T.H.	Edward VIII patterns	Glendining 12/3/1970. Lots 235-248
Parsons	Comprehensive collection	Parsons. H.A. Glendining 11/5/1954

PROVENANCES

Rashleigh	Comprehensive collection	Rashleigh. Glendining, 1953
M.R. (list №)	High quality illustrated list	Mark Rasmussen (Quarterly publication - A4)
— 4	Collection of halfcrowns	Rasmussen Spring 2003
— 6	Collection of halfcrowns	Rasmussen Winter 2008
— 21	Collection of halfcrowns	Rasmussen Summer 2011 'Frogmore Collection'
— 22	Shillings, very comp.	Rasmussen. Mark. List № 22. Winter 2011/12
— 22	Crowns, very comp.	Rasmussen. Mark. List № 22. Winter 2011/12
— 25	Crowns down, comp.	Rasmussen. Mark. List № 25. Winter 2013/14
Rees-Jones. D.	Crowns. Comprehensive	Spink 117. 19/11/1996
Richardson. R.	High quality illustrated list	Richardson. Roderick (Quarterly publication – A5)
Rowlands. J.F.	Crowns	Spink Auction 4. 22/2/1979
Selig. Herman	Comprehensive George III	Spink Auction 131. 2/3/1999
Slaney	High quality collection	The Slaney Collection. Spink Auction 163, 15/5/2003
Scothern. Andr.	Comprehensive milled	DNW 111, 12&13/6/2013
Sommerville. G	Comp. Shillings 1816-date	DNW. 102, 18/9/2012
Roekel	High quality silver crowns	Van Roekel. E.D. Spink Auction 156. 15/11/2001
Whetmore	Comprehensive Crowns	A.H. Glendining 14/7/1961
Willis.Frederick	Comprehensive collection	Parts I & II. Glendining's 5/6/1991
Willis. Frederick	Complete Maundy collect.	Parts II. Glens 1991/6/5. Lot 825 (Not illustrated)
W&R	*Trials & proofs in gold*	Alex Wilson & Mark Rasmussen, Alexander 2000

DEALER'S LISTS ETC

Baldwin			Baldwins. Fixed Sales List issued bi- annually
—		G.V. Pat Double Florins	Baldwins. Fixed Sales List Summer 2011
CoE		Coins of England & UK	Priced Standard Catalogue by Spink. Annual publication
EMC		Silver Coinage (reference)	English Milled Coinage, 1st edition, 1975
ESC		Silver Coinage (reference)	English Silver Coinage, 5th revised edition, 1992
SCMB	1954		Seaby's Coin & Medal Bulletin. *William III, 2nd bust 6d*
SNC		Illustrated lists (A4)	Spink Numismatic Circular. As dated
—	1997	Maundy (not illustrated)	Spink Numismatic Circular, pp. 556-7
—	1999	Pattern & proof shillings	Spink Numismatic Circular, pp. 332-335
—	2001	Comp. Maundy odds	Spink Numismatic Circular, April 2001 (not illustrated)
—	2003	2/6, 1/-, 6d, 4d, 3d & 1½d	Spink Numismatic Circular. April 2003
—	2003	Patterns & proof Florins	Spink Numismatic Circular. April 2003
—	2005	Maundy sets 1670-2010	Spink Numismatic Circular, August 2005, pp. 278-284
—	2011	Maundy sets 1670-2010	Spink Numismatic Circular, March 2011, pp. 41-47
—	2011	Maundy sets 1670-2010	Spink Numismatic Circular, July 2011, pp. 122-3
Spink		Spink Annual publication	Up-to-date price list (Originally a Seaby publication)

SELECTION OF IMPORTANT AUCTION CATALOGUES

Baldwin	14	Commonwealth	13/10/1997
—	17		5/5/1998
—	18	Countermarked dollars etc	13/10/1998. Clipped and countermarked dollars
—	48		26/9/2006
—	52		25/9/2007
—	57	Halfcrowns	23 & 24/9/2008. Large collection
—	80		13/5/2013
DNW	64	Dix Noonan Web.	14/12/2004
—	82	—	18/6/2009
—	85	—	17/3/2010

PROVENANCES

DNW	86	—	16/7/2010
—	?	—	22/10/2009
—	97	—	7/12/2011
DNW	101	—	21/6/2012
—	107	—	21/3/2013
—	113	Countermarked dollars etc	17/9/2013
Glens	1962	Pattern Florins	4/10/1962
—	1968	Pattern shillings	19/6/1968
—	1972	Crowns struck in gold	13/4/1972 Plus other patterns in gold
—	1973	Crowns of Charles II	24/10/1973
—	1974	Countermarked dollars etc	19/6/1974, lots 384-412
—	1992	Countermarked dollars etc	9/12/1992, lots 620-667
—	2000	Comp. Commonwealth	9/2/2000
—	2000		7/2/2000
Plym. A		Plymouth Auction Rooms	18/4/2008 – Evan Roberts Col. (Ex. J.G. Murdoch Col.)
SJA	4	St James's Auction	8/5/2006
—	6		8/6/2007
—	9	Countermarked coins	18/6/2008. Including Spanish French & USA
—	12	Maundy sets	5/11/2009, lots 788-859
—	18	Comp 2/6 & BoE Dollars	27/9/2001. Large collection
—	23	Reddite crown etc	4/2/2013. Choice selection
Seaby 1			23/4/1986 (Their one and only auction)
SMB			Seaby Mail Bid Sale 22/10/1982(the only one)
Spink	12	Assortment	19/11/1980
—	14	Auction	19/3/1981
—	38	Patterns and proofs	10/10/1984 (Gold & silver 1746-1936)
—	46	Sixpences 1547-1952	9/2/2000 Includes Edward VIII, lots 819-21
—	55	Commonwealth	8/10/1986
—	101	Pat. shillings & sixpences	24/11/1993. Small selection of Victorian
—	113	Quality crowns	5/3/1996. Dr. Bruno Mantegazza collection
—	125	Quality crowns, Proof sets	3/3/1998
—	140	Gothic Florins	16/11/1999. Very comprehensive collection
—	145	Hammered & milled	12-14/7/2000. Large comprehensive collection
—	154	Commonwealth	12/7/2001. Very comprehensive collection
—	157	Comp. Milled proofs	15/11/2001. Very comprehensive collection
—	183	Comprehensive Maundy	26/9/2006, lots 128-391
—	207	Selection all denoms	23 & 24/3/2011
—	210	Selection of Maundy	6/10/2011, lots 516-564
—	214	Small quality collection	26/9/2012. Ancient British & Foreign Coins
—	215	Good run of Florins	4 & 5/12/2012. Ancient British & Foreign Coins

Web sites

Neville Eilbeck Commonwealth, Cromwell *http://cromwellcoins.com*

Note

PC = Private collector (initials only for identification and privacy)

PROVENANCES

COMMONWEALTH - CROWNS

ESC	Variety	Provenance	(Old ESC)	ESC	Variety	Provenance	(Old ESC)
1	1649 ^{Obv}	**Montagu 678**	1	1	1649 ^{Rev}	**Montagu 678**	1
2	1649 ^{Wire}	**Roekel** 76 *(AVF)*	2	3	1651	Rasmussen$^{16/69(AEF)}$	3
4	1652	Norweb 1455 ^{EF}	4	5	1652/1	**Spink 117** 39 *(EF)*	5
6	1653	Norweb 413 *(EF)*	6	7	1653 $^{N/Ns}$	**PC (DT)** *(VF)*	6A
8	1654	Willis 378 *(EF)*	7	9	A for V in VS	**PC (DT)** *(VF)*	7A
10	1656	Willis 379 *(GVF)*	8	11	1656/4	**PC (DT)** *(GVF)*	8A
12	1656/4 A for V	**PC (DT)** *(GVF)*	8A	13	1656/4	**Asherson 128**	9
14	1656/^{6}/4	**Spink 125** 693 *(EF)*	9A	XXX	1660^{Anchor}	**Barr 221** Fabrication	

COMMONWEALTH - HALFCROWNS

ESC	Variety	Provenance	(Old ESC)	ESC	Variety	Provenance	(Old ESC)
15	1649 $^{-IIVI-}$	**Montagu 684**$^{(VAS)}$	425	16	1649 $^{-IIVI-}$	**PC (DT)** *(GVF)*	425
17	1651 $^{-IIVI-}$	**Spink 154** 10 *(VF)*	426	18	1651 $^{-IIVI-}$	**Asherson130**$^{(AEF)}$	425A
18	1651 $^{-IIVI-}$	**Spink 170** 583 *(EF)*	425A	19	Mule 1/- / 2/6	**Spink 154** 11 *(GVF)*	428
	WE·ALTH	**L. Bennett**	426B	21	GOD WITH		426A?
22				23	1651 P		427
24	1652 $^{-IIVI-}$	**Adams 254** *(AEF)*	429	25	165$_2$ ^{large}$_2$	**SNC1991**·6586*(GVF)*	429A?
26	1652/1	**Spink 55,** 12 *(VF)*	430			**PC (DT)** *(GVF)*	430B?
28	1653	**Spink 154**$^{13(AEF)}$	431	29			
30				31			
32	THE $^{No stp}$	**Adams 259** *(F)*	431A	33			
34	Only stps ·mm·	**Glens 2000** 261 *(AF)*	431C?	35	5/4	**PC (DT)** *(GVF)*	
35	No stops rev.	**Glens 2000** 264 *(F+)*	431D?	36	Stop date only	**Adams 260** *(GF)*	431B
37	1653/1	**Adams 261** *(GVF)*	432	38	3/2	**Baldwin 17,** $^{lot 613}$	433
39	1665/56	**SNC 2012** ·4921/GF	433A?	39	1654 no stops	**SNC 1991,** 6590	434A?
40	1654	**Spink 154** 14 *(GVF)*	434		E/P	**Spink 208,** $^{lot 757}$	?
	· mm ·	**Baldwin 17,** 613	?		N/G	**PC (DT)** *(GVF)*	
	IIVI	**Bonham's** 1532	?	42			
43	1654/3	**Glens** 2000,266 *(Fr)*	435	44			
45	1654 $^{O/M}$	**Adams 263** *(GVF)*	435A	46	WEALH	**PC (DT)** *(GVF)*	
47				48	1655	**Adams 264** *(GF)(3rd)*	436
48	1655	**PC (DT)** *(GF)* *(4th)*	436	49	1656	**Asherson 131**	437
50	1656 P?	**Spink 154**$^{16(AEF)}$	437B	51	Only stps ·mm·	**PC (DT)** *(GVF)*	437F
51	1656 ·mm·	**Baldwin 14** 481 *(F)*	437F	52	1656 ^{THE}	**Baldwin 14,** 479(Fr)	437E
53	1656 $^{TH·E}$	**Spink 55,**24 *(NVF)*	437A		MMON·WEAL		437C
54	1656/4	**Adams 267** *(AVF)*	437B	55	1656/5	**Glens 2000**268 *(NVF)*	438
56	56/5$^{TH·E}$	**Adams 269** *(AVF)*	438A?	57	1657	**BNJ 64,** pl. 13-5	438B
57	1657	**Adams 270** *(AVF)*	438B?	57	1657	**PC (DT)** *(GF)*	438B?
58	1658 ^{rev} B	**Spink 154** 18 *(VF)*	439	59	1658/7	**Adams 272** *(GF)*	440
60	1659	**Adams 273** *(VF)*	441	61	1660	**Spink 154** 20 *(VF)*	442
62	1651$^{Pat.}$ C	**Spink 139,**206 *(GEF)*	443	63	1651$^{Pat.}$D	**Glens**1962/10/4, 2*(VF)*	444
64	'51^{Pat}C^{Cu}	(Montagu 712 Fine)	444A	65	Pattern E	**Spink 55,** lot 86	444B
66	Pattern F	**Montagu 708**	445		Pattern F^{Bead}		445A
67	Pattern F Pln	(Montagu 709)	445B		Pattern F Thin	Norweb 959$^{(NEF)}$	445C
68	Pattern G	**ESC** 445D	445D				

COMMONWEALTH - SHILLINGS

ESC	Variety	Provenance	(Old ESC)	ESC	Variety	Provenance	(Old ESC)
69	1649	Glens 2000, 276 (EF)	982	70	F/D in OF	PC (DT) (VF)	982D
71	No stop OF		982B	72	ENGLND no st	Spink 154, 24 (AEF)	982A
73				74	1649 N/G	PC (DT) (VF)	982C
75				76	No stpTHE/XII	DNW 82, 310(GF)	982D?
77				78			
79	1651 THE·	Spink 154, 25 (Mint)	983	80			
81				82			
83				84	No stops obv	Baldwin 40 249 (EF)	983B
85	1651 N/invt.N	Neville Eilbeck		86			
87				88	51/49 ·mm·	Spink 139 191 (VF)	983A
89	No stops obv	PC (DT) (GVF)	983B	90	No stp THE	Spink 55, 31 (VF)	984
91	1651 P	SJA 10, 480 (GEF)		92	Only stps ·mm·	Spink 55, 28 (VF)	984A
93				94			
95	ENGLND no st	Glens.2000, 276 (EF)	984B	96			
97	COMONWEA	Spink 154 27 (VF)	984C	98	1/- / 2/6		984D
99	No stops mm	SJA 10, 481 (VAS)	984E	100			
101	Vlue/inverted	PC (DT) (VF)		101	XII/IIX	PC (DT) (VF)	984F
102				103	1652	Spink 170, 585 (AEF)	985
104				105			
106	No stops obv	Glens 2000, 291(AVF)	986D	107	·1652 No stp af	Glens 2000 301 (VF)	986A
108	No stp THE	Asherson 136		109	ENGLAND		986B
110				111			
112	2/1	DNW 91 519 (NVF)	985A	113			
114	No stops rev	Glens 2000 287 (VF)	985B	114	No stops rev	PC (DT) (GVF)	985B
115				116	COMMON·W	Spink 117 392(VF)	986C
116	2/2 side	Spink 55, 36 (F)	985C	116	2/2 side	PC (DT) (VF)	985C
117	1652	SNC2011, 4736 (VF)	986H				986
118	1652/1 V/O	Spink 55, 34 (VF)	986E	118	1652/1 V/O	PC (DT) (VF)	986E
119				120			
121	No stops mm	(Glens.2000, 294 (F))	986F	122	ON·WEALTH	Glens 2000, 293 (F)	986G
123	Colon in COM		986I	124	1653	Asherson 137	987
125	1653 N/invt.N	Neville Eilbeck		126	No T	Baldwn 14 539(NVF)	988C
127	D/P	Glens 2000 296 (VF)	987A	128	1653 T/G	PC (DT) (VF)	
129	No stp THE	(Baldwin 14 567 (F+))	988A	130	1653 No T?	Spink 154 31 (GF)	988B
130	1653 No T?	PC (DT) (VF)	988B	131			
132	ENGLAND	DNW 90 499 (NEF)	988	133	No stop @ mm	Baldwin 14 540 (VF)	989B
134	1653/2		989C	135	Only stps ·mm·	Baldwin 14 542 (VF)	989E
136	Only stop date		989D	136	1653· only		898D
137	1654	Norweb 1459	990	138			
139	1654/3	Spink 55, 48 (VF)	991	139	1654/3	PC (DT) (VF)	991
140	ENGLND	Glens 2000 302 (AVF)	990A	141	1654 E/A	Bonham 1546(VF)	991A?
142	ENGLND	Spink 154 34 (AVF)	992	143	No sotp OF	Baldwin 14 559 (F)	992A
144	No stops rev	DNW 107 368 (GF)		145	1655	Glens 2000 305 (GVF)	993
146				147	ENGLAND	Baldwin.14 561 (VF)	993A
148	1655/4		994	149	1655/4/3	Spink 55, lot 52(F)	994A
150	1656	Spink 139 193 (AEF)	995	151			
152	ENGLAND	Baldwin14 574(NVF)	995A	153	No stops mm	Glens 2000 307(AVF)	995B

(continued)

PROVENANCES

ESC	Variety	Provenance	(Old ESC)	ESC	Variety	Provenance	(Old ESC)
154	O·F	**Bonham** [1549] *(NVF)*	995C	155	No stops *obv*	Baldwin 14 [577] *(F)*	995D
156	No stp *ob+valu*	DNW 85, [487] *(AF)*	985E	157	Only stps value	**Glens 2000** [311] *(Fr)*	995F
158	1657	Spink 154 [38] *(GVF)*	996	159	No stop OF	**PC (DT)** *(VF)*	996A
160	No stops *obv*		997	161	1658	Spink 145 [2221] *(GVF)*	998
162				163	No stops *obv*	**PC (DT)** *(F)*	999C
163	No stops *obv*	Baldwin14 [585] *(F)*	999C	164	No stop THE		
165	ENGLAND	**Glens 2000,** [309] *(AF)*	998A	166	O/M + M/O	Spink 55, [59] *(AF)*	999B
	Colon	**Bonham's** [1541]	?	166	O/M + M/O	**PC (DT)** *(VF)*	999B
167	1658/7 [G/L]	**DNW 85,** [488] *(F+)*	999	167	8/7ENGLAND	**Glen. 2000,** [308] *(F)*	999A
168	1658 G/L	**PC (DT)** *(VF)*	999	169	1659	Spink 154, [40] *(GF)*	1000
170	1660	Spink 139, [196] *(VF)*	1001	171	No stops *mm*	**DNW 82,** [31] *(Fr-F)*	1001 A
172							
173	1651 [Pat] C	Norweb 1548	1002	173	1651 [Pat] C	**PC (DT)** *(VAS)*	1002

COMMONWEALTH - SIXPENCES

ESC	Variety	Provenance	(Old ESC)	ESC	Variety	Provenance	(Old ESC)
177	1649	Spink 145 [2314] *(GVF)*	1483	178	ENGLAND	Bole 3, [83] *(VF)*	1483A
179	1651	Norweb 1461 *EF*	1484	180			
181	No stops *@mm*	**Baldwn 382** [595] *(EF)*	1484A	182	ENGLAND		1484B
182	1654/49	Bole 3, [84] *(NVF)*	1485B	183	1651/49	**Norweb 1462**	1485
184	No stops *rev*		1486A	185	1652 ·	Bole 1, [1636] *(NVF)*	1486B?
186	1652	Spink 145 [2316] *(GVF)*	1486	187	1652 N inv	Spink 154, [45] *(GVF)*	1486C?
188				189			
190				191	1652 ·	**Glens 2000,** [325]	?
192	52/49	Glens 2000, [326] *(F)*	1487	193	1652/1	Bole 1, [1635] *(VF+)*	1487A
194	1652/49	**Bole 1,** [1634] *(GF)*	1487B	195	52/1/49	Bole 3, [185] *(Fair)*	1487D
196	1652	Bole 2, [110] *(GF)*	1487C?				
197	1653	Spink 154 [48] *GVF*	1488	198	No stop THE	Bole 1, [1638] *(F)*	1488A
	V1/O	**DNW 85,** [493]	1488B	199	1653/1	Bole 1, [1635] *(F)*	1488C?
200	1654	Spink 154 [49] *(VF)*	1489	201			
202	1654/3	**Bole 1,** [1639] *(NVF)*	1490	203	1655	Bole 1, [1636] *(F)*	1491
204	1656	SNC 2011 [4737] *(GVF)*	1492	205	Only stp · mm·	Spink 154 [52] *(GVF)*	1492A
206				207	1657	**Spink 55,** [58] *(Fr-F)*	1493
208	1657/6	Spink 154 [53] *(VF)*	1493A	209	1658	**Asherson 146**	1494
210	C	**Spink 210,** [271]	1495	210	1658/7	Bole 4, [1445] *(NVF)*	1495
					Stops	**Spink 139,** [197]	
211	D/O	Spink 55, [lot 78]	1495A	211	D/O	**PC (DT)** *(GVF)*	1495A
212				213	1659	DNW 119 [2365] *(VF)*	1496
213	1659	**Bole 1,** [1646] *(F)*	1496	214	No stp COMM		1496A
215	1660	Spink 154 [56] *(GVF)*	1497	216	No stop THE	**PC (DT)** *(GVF)*	1497A
217	1651 [Pat] C	**Glens** [1962/10/4, 4] *(VF)*	1498	217	1651 [Pat] C	**DNW 89** [1632] *(VF)*	1498
217	1651 [Pat] C	**PC (DT)** *(EF)*	1498	218	1651 [Thin fl]	*(Not traced)*	1498A
219	1651 [Pat] D	**Montagu 711**	1499	219	1651 [Pat] D	**DNW 89** [1633] *(AVF)*	1499
220	1651 [Au]	Wilson+Rasm 37	1500	221	[Pat] D [Cu]		1501
222	[Pat] D [Stars]	**DNW 89**	1502	223	D [plated Cu]		1503
	3/?	**DNW 82,** [324]	?		53/?	**DNW 89,** [1637]	?
	8/?	**Morrieson** [705]	?				

PROVENANCES

COMMONWEALTH
HALFGROATS, PENNIES & HALFPENNIES

ESC	Variety	Provenance	(Old ESC)	ESC	Variety	Provenance	(Old ESC)
224	2d	Spink 55, lot 82	2160	224	2d	Spink 145 2387(AEF)	2160
225				226			
227				227			
228	1d	Spink 154 60 (EF)	2263	229	No stps value	Glens 2000, 326 (VF)	2263A
230	½d	Spink 154 61(Unc)	2363		2, 1, ½d	Spink 206, 966 (AVF)	

CROMWELL - CROWNS

240	1658/7Obv	Lingford 259	10	241	1658/7 Au	Norweb 424 (EF)	10A
242	1658Pewter	(R.E. Ockenden Collection)	10B	243	1658	Roekel 85 (GEF)	11
243	Dutch copy Gilt	Spink 117, 46 (GVF)	11	244	Dutch copy Gilt	Spink 117, 47 (GEF)	11A
245				246	1658Tanner	Roekel 87 (GEF)	13
247	1658 Pln	Spink 117, 49 (EF)	14	248	Sim/Tan mule	Huntarian Museum, Glasgow	14A
249	Tan/Sim mule		14B	250	Crom/Louis 14	Spink 117, 50 (EF)	14C

CROMWELL - HALFCROWNS

251	1656	SNC2010, 9177 (AEF)	446	252	1658	DNW 113 83 (AEF)	447
253	1658 Au	Spink 107 404(EF)	447A	XXX	1657forgery	Spink 15481(GVF)	

CROMWELL - SHILLINGS

254	1658	DNW 86 660 (VAS)	1005	255	1658 Au	Wilson & Ras 47	1005A
256	Dutch copy Pln	Norweb 1465 EF	1006	257	1658	Bonhams 1573	1006A
258	Dutch copy mil		1006B	259	Dutch Bronze		1007
XXX	Swan cmk	Spink 204 248	1005B?				

CROMWELL - SIXPENCES

260	1658HIB&c	Manville 5 (F)	1504	261	1658 Pewtr		1504A
262	1658 HIB·	M.R. 12/ 106 (AFDC)	1505	263	HIB PRO	Bald.48 5032 (GEF)	1506
264	1658 Bronze		1506A	XXX	Liberty cap	SJA 2 157 (F)	1506B

CHARLES II – 1st HAMMERED - HALFCROWNS

270	A/1obv.rev	Asherson 156	448	270	A/1obv.rev	Spink 154, 64 (GVF)	448
271	Rev. 1a	DNW 64, 229	448A				

CHARLES II – 1st HAMMERED - SHILLINGS

272	Rev. 1	Norweb 1466 EF	1010	272	Rev. 1	M.R. 7 124 (VF)	1010
273	A – obv.	Asherson 157	1009	273	Rev. 1a	M.R. 7 125 (VF)	1009

CHARLES II – 1st HAMMERED - SIXPENCES

274	A / 1a	Spink 139, 204 (VAS)	1507	274	BRIT FRAN	Norweb 1469EF	1507

CHARLES II – 1st HAMMERED - HALFGROATS

275	A-3	DNW 75, 35 (AEF)	2161	275	Rev. 1a	Norweb 1471	2161
276	BRIT FR ET H		2162	278	BR FR ET H	Spink 124, 1787(GVF)	2163

CHARLES II – 1st HAMMERED - PENNY

279	A1 BRIT FR	Esc A (VAS)	2264	279	Rev. 1a	Esc A (VAS)	2264
282	A2 BRF ET	Esc B (VAS)	2265	283	Type A2	Spink 154 78 (AVF)	2266

PROVENANCES

CHARLES II - 2nd HAMMERED - HALFCROWNS

ESC	Variety	Provenance	(Old ESC)	ESC	Variety	Provenance	(Old ESC)
285	BRIT FRAN	**Adams 280** *(AVF)*	449	286	BRIT FRA	**Adams 281** *(AF)*	450
287	BRI FRA	**Adams 282** *(AVF)*	451	288	Large XXX	DNW 119,[2370(NVF)]	451A
				289	S/S	**Bull**	451B?

CHARLES II - 2nd HAMMERED - SHILLINGS

290	B[6] BRI HIB	Spink 145 [2223 (F)]	1011	291	B[7] BRI HI	Spink 154 [68(AVF)]	1012
292	B[8] BR HIB	**DNW 106,** [563]	1013	292	*Rev.* 1a	**DNW 106,** [563]	
293	B[9] BR HI	**Asherson 160** *(GF)*	1014				

CHARLES II - 2nd HAMMERED - SIXPENCES

294	B[6] BRI HIB	Bole 5, [1446 *(NVF)*]	1508	295	B[7] BRI HI		1509

CHARLES II - 2nd HAMMERED - HALFGROATS

296	B[10]	Spink 154, [76 (F+)]	2164	296	*Rev.* 1a	**Seaby 3316**	2164

CHARLES II – 3rd HAMMERED - HALFCROWNS

297	BRIT FRA	**Adams 283** *AVF*	452	298	BRI FRA	**M.R. 7/123** *(GVF)*	453
299	CAROLV	**Adams 285** *(AVF)*	454	300	BR FR	Adams 286 *(VF)*	455
301	BR FR	**Spink 154** [66] *(GEF)*	456	302			
303	A/R	**Adams 287** *(GF)*		304	V/A	**PC (M. Bull)** *(NVF)*	?
305	c6 Bust lower	**SNC 2007,**[HC025]	456B	306	MA BR FR HI		456A

CHARLES II – 3rd HAMMERED - SHILLINGS

307	BRIT FRA		1015	308	BRIT FR	**DNW 106,** [566]	1016
309	BRI FRA	**Norweb 1468**[vas]	1019	310	BRI FR		1018
311	Small XII		1019A	312	CARLVS	**M.R. 10, 187**	1019B?
313	BRI FR HI	(Glens16/1968, 317 *(AEF)*)	1021A	314	BR FR HIB		1020
315	BR FR HI		1021		*Rev.* 2	**DNW 106,** [566]	

CHARLES II – 3rd HAMMERED - SIXPENCES

316	mm no stops	**Norweb 1470**	1510	316	*Rev.* 2	**M.R. 10, 188**	1510
316		**M.R. 7, 126** *(EF)*	1510	316		Bole 2, [112] *(NVF)*	1510
317				318	Stop mm	Bole 4 [43] *(NVF)*	1510A
319	C[3] ·mm·	**DNW 90.** [Bole 112]	1510B	320	Thicker flan	**British Museum**	1511

CHARLES II – 3rd HAMMERED - MATCHING SET

321	UNDATED	SNC 2005[6609 (GVF)]	2364	321	Type A	Spink 210 [516(VF)]	2364

CHARLES II – 3rd HAMMERED - GROATS

322	*Rev.* 2	**Bonham's** [1587]	1839	322	C[8] mm no stps	**DNW 104,** [304]	1839
					C[8] · mm ·		1839A?

CHARLES II – 3rd HAMMERED - THREEPENCES

325	C[14] mm	Spink 124, [1794 (AEF)]	1957		*Rev.* 2	**L. Bennett**	1957
	C14 · mm ·		1957A?				
	1676/5	DNW 97 [283 (VAS)]		1679		SNC 2003,[7234 (NEF)]	1970

PROVENANCES

CHARLES II – 3rd HAMMERED - HALFGROAT

ESC	Variety	Provenance	(Old ESC)	ESC	Variety	Provenance	(Old ESC)
	C[5]	Spink 124,[1795 (AEF)]	2165		Rev. 2	DNW 104, [306]	2165
	BRI FRA	SNC2011,[4491 (GF)]	2165		BR FR		2166

CHARLES II – 3rd HAMMERED - PENNY

ESC	Variety	Provenance	(Old ESC)	ESC	Variety	Provenance	(Old ESC)
332	MAG BR FR		2267		MAG B F		2268
	M BR F ET		2269				
	C[16] M B F	Bonham's [1590]	2270		Rev. 2	Bonham's [1590]	2270

CHARLES II – CROWNS

ESC	Variety	Provenance	(Old ESC)	ESC	Variety	Provenance	(Old ESC)
339	A & B ✪	Roekel 88 [(EF)]	15	340	1662 ✪	Roekel 89 [(EF)]	15A
341	1662 P [Mil]	(Montagu 835 (EF))	15B	342			
343	1662 P [Pln]	Spink 31·[304 (EF)]	16	344			
345	1662	Barr 224 [(GVF)]	17	346	1662 II	Barr 222 [(F)]	16A
347	1662	Roekel 92 [(AEF)]	18	348			
349	Rev. 1	Manville 6 [(GEF)]	20	350	1662	Slaney 135 [(NEF)]	20A
351	C, D & E	Barr 225 [(EF)]	19		Obv. A[1]	Barr 222 [(F)]	?
352	1663	Barr 227 [(GF)]	22A	353	1663 [XV]	SNC 2002,[2703 (EF)]	22
354	1663 [XV]	Barr 69 [(GVF-EF)]	23	355	1663 P	DNW 111,[573 (NEF)]	24
356	1663 [Au]	Glens 4/1972, [371]	25	356	1663 [Au]	R. Richardson	25
357	1663 [Frost]	Barr 228 [(GVF)]	26	358	1663 [Rev.2]	Barr C558 [(VF)]	27
358	1663 [JR]	Spink 156 [98 (GVF+)]	27	359	No stops on rev	Glen[11/1973, 116 (GVF)]	27A
360	No stop II	Spink 117 [69 (Fair)]	26A	361			
362	1664 [XVI]	Manville 6 [(VAS)]	28	362	1664 small flan	Glens [11/1973, 119 (EF)]	28A
363	1664 P[XVI]	Bald [FPL. Sum 2009 (32)]	29	364	1665 [XVI]	Hamilton 10 [(AVF)]	30
365	1665 [XVII]	Spink 145,[2396 (GF)]	31	366	1666 [XVIII]	Barr 72 [(GVF)]	32
367	[1666] RE·X	Bald [11/1973, 123 (Fair)]	32A	368	1666 [Eleph]	Roekel 102 [(GEF)]	33
369	[Eleph]RE·X	Spink 85 [503 (GVF)]	34	370	1667 [XVIII]	Spink 117 [77(Fr/F)]	34A
371	'67 [AN.REG]	Spink 117 [78(Fr/F)]	35	372	AN.·REG··	Roekel 104 [(GEF)]	35A
373	1668 [20th]	Roekel 105 [(EF)]	36	374	1668 [invert]	Spink 117, 81[(Fair)]	36A
375	MAG[no stp]	(P.C.) M.Shaw [(VF)]		376	1668/7	Roekel 106 [(AVF)]	37
377	[1668/5] B/R	(P.C.)[M. Lewendon]	37A	378	1669	Spink 117, 83 [(F)]	38
379	1669/8	Spink 85 [506 (EF)]	39	380	1670 [22nd]	Spink 189,[66 (GVF)]	40
381	1670/69	Barr 424 [(GF)]	41	382	1671 [23rd]	Bruno 34 [(GEF)]	42
383	T/R	SNC 1998, [6993]	42A	383	[1671] T/R	(P.C.)[M. Lewendon]	42A
384	1671 [ET/FR]	Roekel 112 [(EF)]	42B	385			
386	1671 [23rd]	Bruno 35 [(EF)]	43	386	HIB [no stop]	Willis 35 [(GVF)]	43
387	1671 [24th]	Spink 104 [254 (AVF)]	44	388	1672 [24th]	Bruno 36 [(EF)]	45
389	1673 [24th]	(Glens16/1968, 69 (AEF))	46	390	1673 [25th]	DNW 86 [665 (EF)]	47
391	B/R [in BR]	SNC 1999, [1459]	47A?	391	R/B [in FRA]	(P.C.)[M. Lewendon]	47A?
392	1673 [I/O]	Barr 239 [(GF-VF)]	47B	393	1673/2	SNC 2002,[4272 (EF)]	48
394	1674 [26th]	Spink 117, 93[(Fair)]	49	395	1675 [27th]	Spink 117, 94[(GVF)]	50
396	1675/3[27th]	Spink 156 [120 (EF)]	50A	397	1676 [28th]	Bruno 37 [(EF)]	51
	HIB [no stop]	(P.C) M.Shaw[(NEF)]		398	1677 [29th]	Roekel 122[(GEF)]	52
399	1677/6[29th]	Roekel 123 [(AEF)]	53	xxx	1677 [Boar's]	Barr 74 [(GVF)] Delisted	54
400	1677/6[A/G]	Barr C564 [(GF)]	53A	401	1678/6	Barr 242 [(VF)]	55A
402	1678/7[30th]	Manville 21 [(AVF)]	55	403	1679 [Bust 3]	Spink 85 [514 (VAS)]	56

(continued)

PROVENANCES

ESC	Variety	Provenance	(Old ESC)	ESC	Variety	Provenance	(Old ESC)
404	**1679/8**	P.C. M. Lewendon		405	**1679** Bust 4	**Roekel 127** (GEF)	57
406	1679 HIBR-EX		57A	407			
408	1680 Bust 3	Roekel 128 (GEF)	58	409	1680/79 3	**Barr 427** (GF)	59
410				411			
412	1680 Bust 4	Barr 82 (EF)	60	413	1680/79 4	Hamilton 39 (VF)	61
414	1681 33rd	**Spink 214** 681 (EF)	64	415	1681 Eleph	**SNC2003,** 4717 (VF)	63
416	1682 34th	Spink 124 1840 (Mint)	65	417	1682/1	**Roekel 134** (EF)	65A
418	1662 Pattern	Roekel 95 (EF)	21	418	1682QVRRTO	Roekel 114 (GVF)	65B
419	1683 35th	Roekel 136 (EF)	66	420	1684 36th	Roekel 137 (EF)	67
421				422			
423	1662 Rb dated	**Lingford 282**	18A	424	1662 S Ar	**Slaney 134** (EF)	68
425	1662 Sa Pln	Richardson Sum '07,2 (GEF)	70	425	1662 Sa Pln	**Lingford 266**	70
426	1662 SAu	**Spink 107** 405 (VAS)	69	427	1662 Sa Au	**Lingford 265**	71
428	1663T Wm	**SNC 2003,** 5664 (EF)		428	1663 Pw Pln	**SNC 2003,** 5664 (EF)	
429	1663 Pat U	**Slaney 136** (VAS)	72	430	1663 Pat U Pln	Glens 6/1963 159	72A?
431	Reddite V Ag	Willis 269 (Mint)	73	432	Reddite V Pw	**Asherson 169** (EF)	74
433	Render W Ag		74A	434	Pat W Pln Pw	Spink 69, 308 (FDC)	75
435	Cliche Petition	**Spink 124,** 26 & 27		436			
437	Lead squeeze	**La Riviere 27**			Cliche. rev	**Glens 3/1981** 148	
XXX	Electro Pat U	**P.C.(M.Bull)** GVF)	CF 72		Petition legend	**Spink 190, 503**	

CHARLES II – HALFCROWNS

ESC	Variety	Provenance	(Old ESC)	ESC	Variety	Provenance	(Old ESC)
438	1663 XV	**Slaney 138** (GEF)	457	439			
440	1663 V/S	**Adams 293** (NVF)	457A				
441	1663 R/B	**(P.C.)** M. Lewendon		442	1663 A/?	Adams 290 (VF)	457B
443	1663 P	(Montagu 838 (EF))	458	444	No stops	**Adams 294** (NEF)	459
445	1664 obv E	**Manville 28** (GEF)	460	446	1666/4	**Adams 296** (VF)	461
447	1666/4 ele	Spink 124 1844 (VAS)	462	448	1667/4	**Adams 299** (Fr-F)	463
449	1668/4	Adams 300 (VF)	464	450	1669	Hamilton 52 (VF)	465
451	1669 obv F	**Adams 302** (GVF)	465A	452	1669/4	SNC 2007, 027 (VF)	466
453	1670 22nd	DNW 111, 13 (AEF)	467	454			
455	MRG	**Adams 308** (GF)	467A	456	LV/SV	Adams 307 (GVF)	467B?
457	1671 23rd	Adams 311 (VF)	468	458	1671/0	**Adams 312** (GF)	469
459	1672 24th	**Adams 313** (GVF)	471	460	1672 24th	**Adams 315** (NEF)	472
461	1673 Plu obv	SNC 1979 7067 (Fair)	474	462	1673 25th	Adams 316 (NEF)	473
462	1673 Plu o/r	**Adams 323** NVF	475				
463	1673 A/R	**Adams 321** (GF)	473A	464	1673 B/R	**Adams 322** (F)	473B
465	1673 F/M	**Adams 318** (NVF)	473C		EGNI	**Adams 320** (GF)	
466	1674 26th	Adams 324 (VF)	476	467	1674/3	**Adams 325** (NVF)	476A
468	1675 27th	Adams 326 (VF)	477	469	1675 retro 1	Adams 327 (GVF)	477A
470	1676 28th	Adams 328 (GVF)	478	471	1676 retro 1	DNW 72, 175(VAS)	478A
472				473	1676 F/H,	**Adams 335** (NVF)	478C
474				475	1677 29th	Adams 336 (GVF)	479
476				477	1678 30th	DNW 111, 17(AEF)	480
478	1678 30th	Adams 340 (GVF)	480A	479	1679 31st	Adams 341 (NEF)	481
480	GRATTA	**Adams 345** (Fair)	481A	481	FRA HIB no st	**Adams 343** (NVF)	481?
482	1679 31st	Adams 344 (GVF)	481B?	482	Re-entered S	**Adams 334** (GF)	478B?
483	REGRI	**Adams 347** (Fr)	482	483	1679 31st	Adams 347 (GVF)	482

(continued)

PROVENANCES

ESC	Variety	Provenance	(Old ESC)	ESC	Variety	Provenance	(Old ESC)
484	DECNS	DNW 99.461(GVF)	483				
485	DNCVS	P.C.(M.B) (NVF)	483A	486	PRICESIMO	Bull (NVF) Adams 350	484
487	1679 31st	Adams 352 (VF)	484A	488	1680 32nd	Spink 124 1848 (EF)	485
489	1680 32nd	Adams 355 (EF)	485A	490	1681 33rd	Adams 357 (GF)	486
491	1681 E&C	Bald 57, 463 (NVF)	488	491	Eleph. & castle	Bald 57, 463 (NVF)	488
492	1682 34th	Adams 359 (VF)	489	493	1682/1		489A
494	1682/79	Adams 361(Fr-F)	489B	495	1683 plume	Manville 48 (Pr)	491
496	1683 35th	Spink 124 1850 (VAS)	490	497			
498	1684/3 36th	Adams 363 (VF)	492				

CHARLES II – SHILLINGS

ESC	Variety	Provenance	(Old ESC)	ESC	Variety	Provenance	(Old ESC)
500	D	Spink 11008, 516	1022	500	Std rev	Spink 11008, 516	1022
500	1663	SNC 2011 9715 (GEF)	1022	500	1663	Spk 216 820 (GVF)	1022
501				502			
503	GARTIA	SNC 2000 221	1023	503	GARTIA	PC (RF/NP)	1023
504	Transposed	DNW 79 3062 (GF)	1024	504	Transposed	PC (RF/NP) (EF)	1024
505	1663 A/G	SNC 2000 2373(F)	1024A	505	1663 A/G	PC (RF/NP) (GVF)	1024A
506	1663	M.R. 22 102 (AEF)	1025	507	1666 Eleph	Spk 216 827 (VF)	1026
508	1666	Spink 124 1853(GVF)	1028	509	1666 Eleph	Hamilton 78 (GF)	1027
510	1668	Hamilton 80 (F+)	1029				
511	1668	SNC 2004 6167 (GEF)	1030	511	1668 No stop II	M.R. 22 105 (GVF)	
513	1668/7	Spink 196, 927	1030A	512			
515	1669/6	Spink 9, 54	1031	515	1669/6	Man. 54 (GVF+)	1031
516	1669	(Montagu 810 (F))	1032	517	1670	Hamilton 83 (GVF)	1033
518	1671	Norweb 1482 AEF	1034	519	1671 MAG	M.R. 22 109 (GF)	1034A
520	1671 Plume	M.R. 22 110(GVF)	1035	520	1671 Plume	Spink 139, 220 (EF)	1035
521	1672	Spink 124 1854 (EF)	1036	522	1673	Hamilton 87 (VF)	1037
523	1673/2	(SNC 2001,MSO787(GF+))	1037A	524	1673 E/R ET	M.R. 22 112 (VF)	1037B
525	1673 Plume	Hamilton 88 (VF)	1038	526	1674 plume	Norweb 225 (VAS)	1040
	1674	(Not traced)	1039	527	1674/3	M.R. 22 114 (EF)	1039A
528	1674 Plume	Hamilton 91 (VF)	1041	529	1674	Hamilton 92 (VF+)	1042
530	1675	M.R. 22 119	1043	531	K	M.R. 22 120	1043A
532	1675 Plume	Manville 64 (VAS)	1046	533	1675	Hamilton 940 (VF+)	1044
534	1675/4	M.R. 22 118 (VF)	1045	535	1675/3	M.R. 6/233	1043A
536	1676	SNC 2004 6169 (GEF)	1047	537			
538				539	1676/5	Hamilton 98 (VF+)	1048
540	1676 Plume	DNW 104 465 (VF)	1049	541	1677 Plume	Manville 6 (AEF)	1051
542	1677	Manville 67 (EF)	1050	543	1678	Hamilton 102 (VF)	1052
544	1678/7	(Not traced)	1053	545	1679	Hamilton 103(GVF)	1054
546	1679/7	(Hamilton104 (GF))	1055	547	1679 Plume	Spink 139, 224 (GVF)	1057
548	1679 Plume	SNC 2003 5465A (GEF	1056	549	1680 Plume	Hamilton 108 (VF+)	1059
550	1680/79	(Not traced)	1060	551	1680	Manville 72(NEF)	1058
552				553	1681	Spink 145, 2470 (GVF)	1061
554	1681/0	Hamilton 110 (GF+)	1061A	555	1681/0 Ele	Hamilton 111 (VF)	1062
556	1682/1	Spink 9, 75	1063	557	1683	Spink 145, 2472 (GF)	1064
558	1683	M.R. 22 130 (EF)	1065	559	1684	Spink 139, 224 (GEF)	1066
560	O rev. 1	SNC 2000 222	1067	561	P rev. 2	M.R. 15, 110	1067A
561	1663 Pat pCu	Spink 139, 226 (GVF)	1067A	562	1663 Mule revs	SNC 2000, 1571 (EF)	1067B
563				564	1676 Mule revs	M.R.16/C285(VAS)	

PROVENANCES

CHARLES II – SIXPENCES

ESC	Variety	Provenance	(Old ESC)	ESC	Variety	Provenance	(Old ESC)
566	1674	SNC 1987 $^{5248\ (Mint)}$	1512	567	1675	Hamilton 117$^{(\ EF)}$	1513
568	1675/4	Hamilton 118 $^{(EF)}$	1514	568	1675/4	**Bole 1,** $^{1655\ (VF)}$	1514
569	1676	Spink 46 $^{247\ (AF)}$	1515	570	1676/5	**Spink 139,**$^{230\ (GEF)}$	1515A
571	1677	Spink 124 $^{1864\ (VAS)}$	1516	572	G/O	SNC 2001,$^{0853\ (VF)}$	1516A
				573	1678/7	Manville 82 $^{(EF)}$	1517
574	1679	Bole 1,$^{1660\ (GVF)}$	1518	575	1679/7	**Bole 1,**$^{1659\ (GVF)}$	1518A
576	1680	Manville 84 $^{(EF)}$	1519	577	1681	DNW 111,$^{29\ (VAS)}$	1520
578	1682	Norweb 449 ^{EF}	1522	579	1682/1	**Bole 1,**$^{1663\ (GVF)}$	1521
580	1683	Spink 139,$^{233\ (GEF)}$	1523	580	1683	SNC 2004,$^{6235(EF)}$	1523
580	1683	Bole 1,$^{1664\ (GVF)}$	1523	581	1684	DNW 75,$^{368(GEF)}$	1524

CHARLES II – UNDATED MAUNDY

ESC	Variety	Provenance	(Old ESC)	ESC	Variety	Provenance	(Old ESC)
582	2d ^{Type} C		2167	**583**			
584	1d ^{Type} C		2271	585	1d ^{AVSPCE}	**Spink 154** $^{79\ (VF)}$	2271A
586	2d ^{Type} D	**Spink 124**$^{1790\ (GVF)}$	2168	587	1d ^{Type} D	**Spink 154** $^{80\ (EF)}$	2272
588	2d ^{Type} F		2169	589	1d ^{Type} F	DNW 75,$^{370(GVF)}$	2273
590	^{Type} B - 4, 3, 2 & 1d		2365				
591	4d ^{Type} B		1840	592	3d ^{Type} B		1958

CHARLES II – MILLED MAUNDY SETS – TYPE C - DATED

ESC	Variety	Provenance	(Old ESC)	ESC	Variety	Provenance	(Old ESC)
593	1670	SNC 2009· $^{8938\ (VF)}$	2366	594	1671	SNC 2002· $^{4432\ (EF)}$	2367
595	1672/1	SNC 2008 $^{8555\ (GVF)}$	2368	596	1673	SNC 2005,$^{6615\ (GVF)}$	2369
597	1674	SNC 2005,$^{6617\ (NEF)}$	2370	598	1675	SNC 2005,$^{6618\ (GVF)}$	2371
599	1676	**SNC 2007** $^{,8351(GF)}$	2372	600	1677	SNC 2005,$^{6620(GVF)}$	2373
601	1678	SNC 2005,$^{6621\ (EF)}$	2374	602	1679	SNC 2005,$^{6622\ (EF)}$	2375
603	1680	SNC 2005 $^{6621\ (GVF)}$	2376	604	1681	(SNC2001,0283 (VF))	2377
605	1682	Spink 200,$^{383\ (VF)}$	2378	606	1683	Spink 183 $^{131\ (VF)}$	2379
607	1684	Spink 124,$^{1798\ (AEF)}$	2380				

CHARLES II – MAUNDY GROATS – TYPE C

ESC	Variety	Provenance	(Old ESC)	ESC	Variety	Provenance	(Old ESC)
608	1670	(SNC 2003, 4972 (F))	1841	609	1671	(SNC 2001, MS1313 (AVF)	1842
610	1672/1	(SNC 2001, 1315 (GF))	1843	611	1673	(SNC 2001, MS1316 (NF))	1844
612	1674	(SNC 2001, MS1317 (VF))	1845	613	1674		1845A
614	74/63	SNC 2005 $^{6617\ (NEF)}$	1845B	615	4/6		1845C
616	1675	Spink 200,$^{376\ (GVF)}$	1846	617	1675/4	SNC 2005,$^{6618\ (VF)}$	1846A
618	1676	(SNC 2001, MS1320 (AVF))	1847	619	1676 7/6		1847A
620	1676/5		1847B	621			1847C
622			1847D	623			1847E
624	1677	SNC 2006,$^{7200\ (EF)}$	1848	625	1678		1849
626	^{1678}8/7		1850	627	1678/6	(SNC 2001, MS1322 (VF))	1850A
628	1679	(SNC2006,7200 (GVF))	1851	629			1851A
630			1851B	631			1851C
632	1680	(SNC 2006,7203 (VF))	1852	633	1681	(SNC 2001, MS1326 (VF)	1853
634	B/R	(SNC 2001, MS1327 (F)	1853A	635	1681/0		1854
636	1682	(SNC 2001, 1328 (GF))	1855	637	1682/1	(SNC 2003, 4974 (Fr-F))	1856
638	2/1		1856A	639	1683	(SNC2006,7203 (VF))	1857
640	1684		1858	641	1684/3	SNC 1998·$^{7234\ (VF)}$	1859

PROVENANCES

CHARLES II – MAUNDY THREEPENCES

ESC	Variety	Provenance	(Old ESC)	ESC	Variety	Provenance	(Old ESC)
642	1670	(SNC 2001, MS1398 (AVF))	1959	643	1671	(SNC2006,7268 (GF))	1960
644	1671		1961A	645	1671		1961
646	1671		1961B				
647	1672/1	(SNC 2001, MS 1400 (GF))	1962	648	1673	(SNC 2001, MS1401 (GF))	1963
649	1674	(SNC 2001, MS 1402 (GF))	1964	650	1674 7/4	SNC 2005,6617 (NEF)	1964A
651	1675	Spink 200,376 (GVF)	1965	652	1675/4	SNC 2005,6618 (GVF)	1965
653	1676	(SNC 2001, MS 1404 (GF))	1966	654	1676/5	(SNC 2003, 5016 (F))	1966A
656	1676 4d fla	(SNC 1973, 9004 (AEF))	1967	655	1676 ERA	(SNC 2001, MS 1405 (VF))	1967
657	1677	(SNC 2001, MS 1406 (F))	1968	658	1678	SNC 2005,6621 (EF)	1969
659	1678 large		1969A				
660	1679	SNC 2006,7234 (NEF)	1970	661	1679 O/A	P.C.(M. Lew.)(GF)	1971
662	Broken die		1971A	663	1680	(SNC 2001, MS 1411 (VF))	1972
664	Double 6/6		1972A	665	Cracked die		1972B
666	1681	(SNC 1977,13407 (AEF))	1973	667	1681/0		1974
668	1682	(SNC2006,7235 (GF))	1975	669	1682/1		1976
670	1683	(SNC 2001, MS 1413(F))	1977	671	Large 3		1997A
672	Large 4d flan		1977B				
673	1684	(SNC 1977,13410 (AVF))	1978	674	1684/3	SNC 1998,7234 (VF)	1979

CHARLES II – MAUNDY HALFGROATS

ESC	Variety	Provenance	(Old ESC)	ESC	Variety	Provenance	(Old ESC)
675	1668	(SNC 2001, MS1490 (VF))	2170	676	1670	(SNC 2001, MS1491 (VF))	2171
677	1671	(SNC 2001, MS1492 (AVF))	2172	678	1672/1	DNW 114 1385(EF)	2173
679	1672		2173A	680	1673	(SNC 2001, MS1494 (VF))	2174
681	1674	(SNC 2003, 5128 (Poor))	2175	682	1674 7/4	SNC 2005,6617 (NEF)	2175A
683	1675	Spink 200,376 (GVF)	2176	684	1676	(SNC 2001, MS1496(F))	2177
685	1677	(SNC 2001, MS1497(VF))	2178	686	CAROLVS II·		2178A
687	1678	(Not traced)	2179	688	1678/6	SNC 2005,6621 (EF)	2180
689	CAROLVS II·		2180A	690	1679	(SNC 2001, MS1499 (F))	2181
691	1679 HIB/FRA	SNC 2006,7271 (GVF)	2181A	692	HIB/FRA		2181B
693	DEI		2181C	694	Large flan		2181D
695	1680	SCMB 843,G302(GF)	2182	696	1680/79	(SNC 2006,7272 (VF))	2183
697	1681	(SNC 2006,7273 (GVF))	2184	698	1682	(Not traced)	2185
699	1682/1	(SCMB843,G304(F))	2186	700	ERA	(SNC 2001, MS1504 (GVF))	2187
701	1683	(Not traced)	2188	702	1683/1		2189A
703	1683/2	(SNC 2001, MS1505 (GVF))	2189	704	1684		2190
705	No stop DEI		2190A				

CHARLES II – MAUNDY PENNIES

ESC	Variety	Provenance	(Old ESC)	ESC	Variety	Provenance	(Old ESC)
706	1670	(SNC 2001, MS1619 (VF))	2274	707	Blundered 0		2274A
708	1671	(SNC 2001, MS1620 (VF))	2275	709	1672/1	SNC 2010 9388 (F)	2276
710	1673	(SNC 2001, MS1622(GVF))	2277	711	1674		2278
712	1674	SNC2005,6617 (NEF)	2279	713	1674		2279A
714	1675	Spink 200,376 (GVF)	2280	715	1675 ERA	SNC2005,6618 (GVF)	2280A
716	1675		2280B	717	1676	(SNC 2001, MS1624 (F))	2281
718	1676		2281A	719	1677		2282
719	1677	(SNC 2001, MS1625(GVF))	2282	720	1677 5 RATIA	S&B Coins G395 (AEF)	2283

(continued)

PROVENANCES

ESC	Variety	Provenance	(Old ESC)	ESC	Variety	Provenance	(Old ESC)
721	RE·X		2283A	722	1678		2284
723	1678	SNC 2005,6621 (EF)	2285	724	1679	(SNC 2001, MS1627 (F))	2286
725	No stop DEI		2286A	726	1680	(SNC 2001, MS1628(VF))	2287
727	1680		2287A	728	1681		2288
729	1682		2289	730	1682/1		2289
731			2289B	732	1682ERA		2289A
733	1683		2291	734	CAROLVS		2291
735	1683/2		2291A	736	1684		2292
737	1684/3		2292A	738	CAROLVS		2292B

JAMES II - CROWNS

740	1686 2nd	Slaney 142 (EF)	76	741	1686 No stop	Spink 170, 596 (EF)	77
742				743	1687 3rd	Slaney 143 (VAS)	78
743	1687 Rev.	Barr 251 (AEF)	78	744	1687 3rd	Norweb 228	79
745	Sm edge leters	Hamilton 131(EF)	79A	746	1688 4th	Roekel 142 (GEF)	80
747	1688/7 4th	Glens 1962/10/4, 43(EF)	81	xxx	GRATIA	(Glens 15/1974,20(F))	80A

JAMES II - HALFCROWNS

ESC	Variety	Provenance	(Old ESC)	ESC	Variety	Provenance	(Old ESC)
748	1687 1st	M.R. 11/101 (EF)	493	749	1688 2nd	M.R. 11/102 (EF)	494
750	1686/5 2nd	DNW 71 254 (AEF)	495	751	1686 3rd	Adams 368 (VF)	496
752	1686 V/S	Adams 369 (EF)	496A	xxx	1686 V/B	Hamilton 137 (EF)	497
753	1687 3rd	Adams 372 (EF)	498	754	1687/6	Adams 373 (VF)	499
755	1687/6 6/8	Adams 374 (F)	499A	756	1687 Bust 2	DNW 59 65 (EF)	500
757	1687 A/R	Adams 376 GVF	500A?	758	1687 P	(Not traced)	501
759	1688 4th	Adams 378 (GVF)	502				

JAMES II - SHILLINGS

760	1685	M.R. 22/135 (EF)	1068	761	1685 Lge star	SNC1999/4 1548(F)	1068A
762	1685 No stops	M.R. 22/135 (EF)	1069				
763	Rev. B	Spink 139,238 (Fr)	1069A	764	1686 E/T	Spink 215, 293 (GVF)	1070C
765	1686	SNC 20035466A/GEF	1070	766	V/S	SPINK 217 761	1070A
767	1686/5	Spink 139,240 (GVF)	1070B	768	1687	(Hamilton 144 (VF))	1071
768	1687	PC (RF/NP) (VF)	1071	769	Rev. A	SNC 2001, 0797	1072
769	1687/6	PC (RF/NP) (EF)	1072	769	1687/6	M.R. 22/140 (EF)	1072
770	1687/6 G/A	PC (RF/NP) (EF)	1072A	770	1687/6 G/A	M.R. 22/140 (EF)	1072A
771	1688	Hamilton 146 (GVF)	1073	772	1688/7	Spink 139 245 (NEF)	1074

JAMES II - SIXPENCES

773	1686	M.R. 6/248 (UNC)	1525	773	Rev. A	M.R. 11/103 (EF)	1525
773	1686 ES	SNC 2003,5558 (Mint)	1525				
774	1686 8/6	Spink 139 248 (NEF)	1525a	775	1687 ES	Hamilton 149 (EF)	1526
776	1687/6 ES	Spink 145,2567 (EF)	1526a	777	Rev. B	Bole 1,1668 (GVF)	1526B
777	Late shields	Norweb 229 (VAS)	1526b	778	1687 L/E	DNW 59 72 (VAS)	1526C
779	1687/6 LS	(Not traced)	1527	780	1688 B/R	Manville 110 (EF)	1528

PROVENANCES

JAMES II - MAUNDY SETS

ESC	Variety	Provenance	(Old ESC)	ESC	Variety	Provenance	(Old ESC)
781	1686	Spink 124,[1799 *(VAS)*]	2381	782	1687	DNW 111,[583 *(VF+)*]	2382
783	1688	SNC 2006,[7803*(VF)*]	2383				

JAMES II - MAUNDY GROATS

784	1686	(SNC 2001, 1334 *(VF)*)	1860	785	1686	*(Not traced)*	1861
786	1687/6	**SNC 2005**,[6628 *(VF)*]	1862	787	1688		1863
788	3d die		1863A	789	No stop FRA		1863B
790	1688 1/8	SNC 2001,[1337 *(AVF)*]	1863C	791	1688/7	(Spink 200,383 *(NVF)*)	1864

JAMES II - MAUNDY THREEPENCES

792	1685	(SNC 2001, MS1415 *(AEF)*)	1980	793	1685		1980A
794	Rev sideways		1980B	795	1686	(SNC 2001, MS1417 *(EF)*)	1981
796	Small o		1981A	797	1686 mule	(SNC 2001, MS1418 *(GF)*)	1981B
798	1687	(SNC 2001, MS1419 *(VF)*)	1982	799	1687/6	**SNC 2005**,[6628 *(VF)*]	1983
800	2.4 diam		1983A	801	1688	(SNC 2001, MS1421 *(F)*)	1984
802	1688	(SNC 2001, MS1423 *(F)*)	1985				

JAMES II - MAUNDY HALFGROATS

803	1686	ESC 2191	2191	804	Small o		2191A
805	V for A	(SNC 2001, MS1509 *(Fr-F)*)	2192	806	1687	(SNC 2001, MS1510 *(GVF)*)	2193
807	1687/8	**SNC 2005**,[6628 *(VF)*]	2193A	808	ERA		2193B
809	1688/7	**S&B** Coins G397*(AEF)*	2195				

JAMES II - MAUNDY PENNIES

810	1685	(SNC 2001, MS1629 *(AVF)*)	2293	811	1686	(SNC 2001, MS1630*(EF)*)	2294
812	E/I REX		2294A	813	1687	(SNC 2001, 1632 *(VF)*)	2295
814	1687/8	**SNC 2005**,[6628 *(VF)*]	2295A	815	7/6		2295B
816	1688/7	SJA 12, 803 *(VF)*	2297				

WILLIAM & MARY - CROWNS

820	1691 I/E	**Barr 252** *(AEF)*	82	820	1691 3rd	Roekel 145 *(GEF)*	82
821	1691 I/E	**Spink 214** 686 *(GVF)*	82B?	822	1692	Spink 140,[906 *(EF)*]	83
823	1692/2 4th	**SNC 2002**,[4289 *(EF)*]	84	824	1692/2 5th	**M.R. 11/105** *(EF)*	85
825	1692 5th	*Does this exist?*	85A	825	1692/25th G/R	M.R. 17, 339 *(VF)*	85A

WILLIAM & MARY - HALFCROWNS

XX	crowns	**PC (M. Bull)**		XX	Shields	**PC (M. Bull)**	
XX	*Obv. A*	**DNW86,**[702 *(GEF)*]	510	XX	*Rev. 1*	**PC (M. Bull)**	
826	1689 1st	Adams 379 *(EF)*	503	827	1689 L/M	**Bull** NEF Adams[382]	503A
828	1689 1st	Adams 383 *(NVF)*	503B	829	1689 FRA	**Bull** NEF Adams[391]	507B
830	1689 1st	Adams 384 *(NEF)*	504	831	1689 1st	Adams 385 *(VF)*	505
832	Inverted N		505A	833	1689 V/A	**Adams 386** *(EF)*	505B
834	1689 1st	Adams 387 *(GVF)*	506	835	1689 1st	Adams 388 *(NEF)*	507
836	No stops obv	**Adams 390** *(GF)*	507A	837	1689 1st	Adams 392 *(GVF)*	508
838	*Obv. B*	**Adams 393**[*(GVF)*]	509	838	*Rev. 2*	**Adams 393**[*(GVF)*]	509
839	1689 1st	DNW 86,[702 *(GEF)*]	510	840	Inverted N	**PC** (M.Lewendon) *(VF)*	
841	1889 No stop	**PC** (M.Lewendon) *(VF)*		842	Defined caul	**PC** (M.Lewendon) *(GVF)*	

(continued)

PROVENANCES

ESC	Variety	Provenance	(Old ESC)	ESC	Variety	Provenance	(Old ESC)
843	1689 1st	Adams 396 (Fr-F)	510B	844	Int fros. no pls	(Not traced)	510A
845	1689 1st	Adams 397 (GVF)	511	846	1689 1st	Adams 399 (VF)	512
847	1690 2nd	Adams 401 (VF)	513	848	1690 V/A	Bull (VF) Adams402	514
848	GRETIA + V/S	**Adams 402 GVF**	514A	849	1690 3rd	**Adams 403** (EF)	515
850	1691Ob. C	SNC 2007, 041 (GEF)	516	850	1691 Rv. 3	**Adams 404**(NEF)	516
851	Inv edge error	(Bald Argentum June 2006)	516A	852	No stop BR		516B
853	1692 4th	Manville 118 (EF)	517	854	1692 R/G	Adams 406 (VF)	517A
855	1692 5th	Adams 407 (NVF)	518	856	1693/3	**Adams 410 NVF**	520
857	1693/3	**Manville 119VAS**	521	858	No stp GRATIA		521A
859	F/E in FRA		521B	860	'REX		519A
861	1693 5th	Adams 408 (EF)	519	862	1693 FR/A	**Adams 409** (VF)	519A?
				XXX	Dates	**P.C.(M.Bull)**	

WILLIAM & MARY - SHILLINGS

863	1692	**M.R. 22, 142** (GEF)	1075	864	Inverted 1		1075A
865	1692	**M.R. 22, 142** (GEF)	1075B	865	RE/ET in REX	**M.R. 22, 142** (GEF)	1075B
866	GRAT/TI A	(Rasmussen 22/143(GF))	1075C	867	No stop BR		
868	Obv.	**M.R. 22, 142** (GEF)	1076	868	1693	**M.R. 22, 144** (AEF)	1076
XX	1693 9/0	**M.R. 22, 145** (AEF)	1076A	XXX	E/T	**DNW 102, 2542**	1076A

WILLIAM & MARY - SIXPENCES

869	1693	**Manville 122** (EF)	1529	869	1693	Hamilton177 (Mint)	1529
870	Inverted 3		1530	871	1694	**DNW 59 88 (VAS)**	1531

WILLIAM & MARY - SETS

872	1689	SNC 2005,6629(EF)	2384	873	1691	SNC 2011,9794 (GVF)	2385
874	1692	SNC 2005, 6945(GVF)	2386	875	1693	(Spink 200,392 VF))	2387
876	1694	Spink 214, 794 (GVF)	2388				

WILLIAM & MARY - GROATS

ESC	Variety	Provenance	(Old ESC)	ESC	Variety	Provenance	(Old ESC)
877	1689	SJA 8, 264 (NVF)	1865	878	1689 G	SNC 2006, 7204 (F)	1866
878	Ob/rev A	**Spink 214, 794**	1866	879	· G	**SJA 21, 226**	1867
880				881	Berries wreath		1868
882	1689 G	SNC 20011341 (VF)	1868A	883	1690	SJA 5, 365 (AEF)	1869
884				885	1690 6/5	SNC 2001·1343 (EF)	1869A
886	1691	(SNC 2001, MS1346 (GF))	1870	887	1691/0	SNC 2001·1347 (EF)	1871
888	1694 small lets		1878A	889	1692	SNC 2001·1348 GEF)	1872
889	GV	**Spink/Sby 3440**	1872	890	1692/1	SNC 2001· 1349, (F)	1873
xxx	MAR·IA	**SNC 2001· 1349 (F)**	1873A	891	MARIA		1874
892	Small lets o/r			893			
894				895			
896	1692 Lg let	SNC 2006 7205 (NEF)	1875	897	1693		1876
898	1693/2	(SNC 2001, MS1351 (AVF))	1877	899	1694		1878
900	1694 Sm	(SNC 2001, 1352 (AVF))	1878A	901	MARIA	(SNC 2001, 1355 (F))	1879

PROVENANCES

WILLIAM & MARY - THREEPENCES

ESC	Variety	Provenance	(Old ESC)	ESC	Variety	Provenance	(Old ESC)
902	1689^Roman	SJA 8, 264 (NVF)	1986	903-908			
909-15				916	Arabic 1	DNW 79 ^3079 (EF)	1986A
917	1689	(SNC 2001, MS1424 (GVF))	1987	918	LMV/LVS	SNC 2006' ^7236 (GF)	1987A
921	1689^No stps	(SNC 2001, MS 1426 (EF))	1988	918	LMV/LVS	London coins 2014, 16290	1987A

ESC	Variety	Provenance	(Old ESC)	ESC	Variety	Provenance	(Old ESC)
923	1690	(SNC 2001, MS1427 (EF))	1989	926	1691 no ties		
927	1691	(SNC 2001, MS1430 (F))	1990	928	1691 type B	(SNC 2001, MS1431(AVF))	1990A
930	1692 G	(SNC 2001, MS1433 (F))	1991	931	1692 GV	(SNC 2001, MS1434 (F))	1992
934	1692 GVL		1993	935	1693 G		1994
936	1693/2	(SNC 2001, MS1435 (GVF))	1994A	937	1693 GV		1995
938				939	1694 G	SNC 1994, ^5897	1996
940	1694	(SNC 2001, MS1437 (Fr-F))	1997	941	1694 GV		1998
942	1694 GVL		1999				

WILLIAM & MARY - HALF GROATS

ESC	Variety	Provenance	(Old ESC)	ESC	Variety	Provenance	(Old ESC)
943	1689	(SNC 2001, MS1512 (AEF))	2196	944	Blundered leg.		2196A
945	1691	(SNC 2001, MS1513 (GVF))	2197	946			
947	1692	(SNC 2001, MS1515 (GF))	2198	948	1693		2199
	1693 GV		2200	949	1693/2	(SNC 2001, MS1517 (AEF))	2200A
951	1694		2201	952	1694/3		2201A
	1684/3^G/D	(SNC 2001, MS1518 (F))	2201B	954	1694 GVLI		2202
955	1694 HI		2203	958	1694 GVL	(SNC 2001, MS1519 (VF))	2204
959	MARLA	SNC 2003, ^5672 (EF)	2205	960			

WILLIAM & MARY - PENNIES

ESC	Variety	Provenance	(Old ESC)	ESC	Variety	Provenance	(Old ESC)
961	1 not visible			962	1689	Spink/Sby ^3444	2298
				964	GVIELMVS	SJA 1 494 ^(GVF)	2299
965-70				971	1691/0	(SNC 2001, MS1638 (GVF))	2301
972-4							
975	1690	SNC 2001, ^1637(EF)	2300	975	B	Spink/Sby ^3445	2300
976	1692		2302	977			
978	1692/1	SNC 2005,^6945(GVF)	2303	979	1693	S&B Coins G400 (AEF)	2304
980				981			
982	1694		2305	983			
984	No stops	SJA 21, ^736	2306	985	1694 HI	SNC 2006 ^7245 (GVF)	2306A
986	1694/6		2306B				

WILLIAM III - CROWNS

ESC	Variety	Provenance	(Old ESC)	ESC	Variety	Provenance	(Old ESC)
990	1695 7th	SNC 2002^2729(Mint)	86	991	1695 8th	SNC 2002 ^2732(Mint)	87
992	1695 OCAVO	(Lingford 411 (VF))	87B	993	1695 OCTAO	(Spink 1973, 7831 (VAS))	87C
994	1695 P^Pln	Norweb 997 ^VAS	88	995	A	Spk/Sby ^3470 (VAS)	89
995	1696 ^Rev. 1	Spk/Sby ^3470 (VAS)	89	996	1696 No stops		89A
996	No stops G/D	DNW 90, ^530 (EF)	89C	997	G/D unbard. A	Barr 255 ^(F)	89B
998	1696/5	Roekel 156 ^(GVF)	90	999			
1000	1696 GEI	Roekel 157(GVF/EF)	91	1001			
1002	96 OCCTAVO			1003	1696P Pln	Willis 418 ^(AFDC)	92
1004	1696 8th	Norweb 474 ^VAS	94	1004	1696 8th	Norweb 474 ^VAS	94

(continued)

PROVENANCES

ESC	Variety	Provenance	(Old ESC)	ESC	Variety	Provenance	(Old ESC)
1005	No stops Obv			1006	No stops Rev	P.C. (M.S.)	
1007	TRICESIMO		94A	1008	1696P ^{Pln}	Roekel 159 $^{(VAS)}$	
1009	1697 ^{9th}	**Roekel 160** $^{(EF)}$	96	1010	1700 ^{12th}	Roekel 161/2 $^{(Mint)}$	
1011	1700 $^{Rev.3}$	**Manville** $^{130(GEF)}$	98	1012	Pat. 1	**ESC B2**	93
1013	Pat. 2	**Spk/Sby** ^{3471} $^{(NEF)}$	93A	XXXX	1696 P2 Electro	**Spink 117** $^{139\ (BM)}$	

WILLIAM III - HALFCROWNS – LONDON

ESC	Variety	Provenance	(Old ESC)	ESC	Variety	Provenance	(Old ESC)
1014	1696 ^{8th}	SNC2007.^{046} $^{(VAS)}$	534	1015	A inv DECVS	**M.R. 6,** $^{257\ (GEF)}$	534A
1016	1696 ^{8th}	Adams 412 $^{(NEF)}$	522	1017	1696 P ^{Pln}	Adams 414 $^{(FDC)}$	523
1018	1696^{piedfor}	**Montgu 929** $^{20.403g}$	523A	1019	96 P Pln Thk		523B
1020	1696 ^{8th}	Adams 423 $^{(GVF)}$	530	1021	1697 ^{9th}	Adams 439 $^{(GVF)}$	541
1022				1023	**1697** $^{M/M}$	**PC** $^{(M.\ Lewendon)}$	
1024	1697/6	**Adams 447** $^{GF)}$	541A	1025	GRR	**Adams 448** $^{(Fr)}$	541B
1026				1027	1697 ^{9th}	Adams 438 $^{(VF)}$	541C
1028	1697 $^{V/A}$		541D	1029	M·AG	**Adams 443** $^{GF)}$	541E
1030	GVLIELMVS	**Adams 445**$^{(GVF)}$	541F?	1031	MAG/A	**Adams 446** $^{(F)}$	541G
1032	1697 P ^{Pln}	Adams 450 $^{(FDC)}$	542	1033	1698 ^{8th}	Adams 472 $^{(VF)}$	553
1033	*Rev.* 5i	**Bull**	553	1034	1698 ^{10th}	SNC 2007$_{049}$ $^{(VAS}$	554
1035	1698/7	**Adams 475** $^{(Fair)}$	554A	1036	1698 ^{11th}	Adams 476 $^{(VF)}$	555
1037	1699 ^{11th}	Manville $^{138\ (EF)}$	556	1038	1699 ^{11th}	Adams 478 $^{(F)}$	557
1038	1699 ^{11th}	Adams 479 $^{(VF)}$	557A	1039			
1040				1041	Scot arms	**Adams 480** $^{(F)}$	559
1042	Inverted lion	**Spink** $^{140},\ ^{624\ (F)}$	560	1043	1700 ^{12th}	**Manville 139**	561
1043	1700 $^{A/V}$		561A	1044	1700 ^{13th}	Adams 484 $^{(EF)}$	562
1045	1700 ^{13th}	Adams 485 $^{(VF)}$	563	1046	1701 ^{13th}	Adams 486 $^{(EF)}$	564
1047	1701 ^{13th}	Adams 487 $^{(VF)}$	564A	1048	E/N ^{DECVS}		564B
1049	No stops	**Adams 488** ^{NVF}	565	1050	1701 $^{El\ Cas}$	Hamilton $^{223\ (AF)}$	566
1051	Taller E & C	Adams 489 $^{(F)}$	566A?	1052	1701 ^{Plunes}	**Manville** $^{142\ (F+)}$	567
1102	Bust 2	**ESC 540**	540				

WILLIAM III - HALFCROWNS – BRISTOL

ESC	Variety	Provenance	(Old ESC)	ESC	Variety	Provenance	(Old ESC)
1053	1696B ^{Obv}	**Adams 430** $^{(NEF)}$	535	1054	1696B P	Spink 140$^{619(FDC}$	535B
1055	1696B ^{Rev}	**Adams** $^{431(Pr-Fr)}$	535A	1056	1696B ^{8th}	Adams 415 $^{(VF)}$	524
1057	1696B $_{REGNE}$	M.R. 25, 115 $^{(GVF)}$		1058	1696^{piedfor}		524A
1059	1696 $^{rev\ 4}$		530A	1060	1697B ^{9th}	Adams 451 $^{(VAS)}$	543
1061	1697B?	Spink 140 $^{620\ (FDC)}$	543A	1061	1697 ^{Proof}	Spink 65, $^{1074\ (VF)}$	543A
1062	No stops ^{rev}	Adams 453 $^{(GF)}$	544	1063	No strings	**Bull**	
	1696 $^{rev\ 1}$		535C				

WILLIAM III - HALFCROWNS - CHESTER

ESC	Variety	Provenance	(Old ESC)	ESC	Variety	Provenance	(Old ESC)
1064	1696C ^{8th}	Adams 432 $^{(VF)}$	536		Chester c	**Adams 432**$^{(NVF)}$	525A
1065	1696C ^{8th}	**Adams 417** $^{(VF)}$	525	1066	1696C ^{8th}	**Adams 424** $^{(GF)}$	531
1067				1068	1697C ^{9th}	Norweb 236 $^{(EF)}$	545

WILLIAM III - HALFCROWNS – EXETER

ESC	Variety	Provenance	(Old ESC)	ESC	Variety	Provenance	(Old ESC)
1069	SS-EH ^{8th}		537	1070	1696E ^{8th}	**Adams 418** $^{(VF)}$	526
1071	1696E ^{8th}	Adams 426 $^{(VF)}$	532	1072	1696E ^{9th}	Adams 427 $^{(F)}$	532A
1073	1697E ^{9th}	Adams 456 $^{(F)}$	546	1074	1697E ^{9th}	M.R. 6, 260 $^{(EF)}$	547

(continued)

(continued)

PROVENANCES

ESC	Variety	Provenance	(Old ESC)	ESC	Variety	Provenance	(Old ESC)
1075				1076	Inverted A	Adams 463 $^{(GVF)}$	547A?
1077				1078	1697E/C	Adams 460 $^{(F)}$	548
1079				1080	1697E/B	Adams 461 $^{(GVF)}$	548B
1081	1697E/B	Adams 462 $^{(GVF)}$	548C	1082	1697E ^{9th}	Adams 463 $^{(P-Fr)}$	548D?

WILLIAM III – HALFCROWNS – NORWICH

ESC	Variety	Provenance	(Old ESC)	ESC	Variety	Provenance	(Old ESC)
1083	1696N ^{8th}	Manville 132 $^{(EF)}$	538	1084	1696 Small N	Adams 434 ^{NVF}	538A?
1085	1696 med shld	(Spink 3, Manville 195)	538B	1086			
1087				1088	1696 $^{rev\,3}$	(Not traced)	527
1089	Normal N	(Not traced)	533	1090	1697N ^{8th}	Adams 464 $^{(GF)}$	549
1091	1697N ^{9th}	Adams 465 $^{(GVF)}$	550	1092	Scot arms date	Adams 467 $^{(F)}$	550A
1093	HIB·	Adams 466 $^{(F)}$	550B				

WILLIAM III – HALFCROWNS – YORK

ESC	Variety	Provenance	(Old ESC)	ESC	Variety	Provenance	(Old ESC)
1094	1696Y ^{8th}	Adams 437 $^{(NVF)}$	539	1095	1696Y ^{8th}	Adams 419 ^{GEF}	528
1096	MAG FRA		528B	1097		(Not traced)	528A
1098	1696Y/E	Adams 421 $^{(GF)}$	529	1099	1697Y ^{8th}	Adams 468 $^{(NVF)}$	550B
1100	1697Y ^{9th}	Manville 136 $^{(EF)}$	551	1102	1697 $^{Lg\,shld}$	(Glens15/1974, 168(NVF))	552

WILLIAM III - SHILLINGS – LONDON

ESC	Variety	Provenance	(Old ESC)	ESC	Variety	Provenance	(Old ESC)
1103	1695	M.R. 22, 146 $^{(EF)}$	1077	1104	1696	DNW 90, $^{534\,(GEF)}$	1078
1105	1696 $^{no\,stps}$		1078A	1106	1044	Spink ^{140} 626 $^{(AF)}$	1078B
1107	1696 ^{piedfor}	SNC 1977, $^{357\,(VF)}$	1079	1108	GVLIEMVS	SNC $^{2001,\,0799(VF)}$	1080
1109	2nd V/A	SNC 2001, $^{2382\,(F)}$	1080A	1109	1696 $^{A/V}$		1080A
1110	1st V/A	SNC 1993, ^{7234}	1080A?	1111	Colon		1080B
1112				1113			
1114	1669 ^{error}	Hamilton 228 $^{Fr)}$	1080D	1115	1696 ^{copper}	Spink140$^{637(VAS)}$	
1116	2nd Bust	PC(RF/NP)$^{257\,(VF)}$	1088A	1116	2nd Bust	Spink 139 $^{257\,(VF)}$	1088A
				1117	1697 $^{Bust\,1}$	Hamilton 239	1091
1118	E-I-F-S	SNC $^{2001,\,1963\,(GF)}$	1091A	1118	E-I-F-S	PC(RF/NP) ^{GVF}	1091A
1119	Irish shield		1091B	1120	1697 L/E	SNC $^{1995,\,3485(EF)}$	1091C
1121	2nd V/A	SNC 2001, $^{0802(Fr-F)}$	1091D	1122	No stops rev	M.R. 22, $^{156\,(AEF)}$	1092
1123	GVLELMVS	PC (RF/NP) $^{(GF)}$	1093	1123	GVLELMVS	SNC $^{2000,\,2389\,(GF)}$	1093
1124	E/A $^{in\,DEI}$	SNC $^{2001,\,0803\,(F)}$	1094A	1125	^{1697} GRI	M.R. 22,155$^{(EF)}$	1094
1126	1697 ^{copper}	Spink140 $^{639\,(GF)}$		1127	1697 $^{Bust\,3}$	M.R. 22,163$^{(EF)}$	1102
1128				1129			
1130	Large lettering		1102A	1131			
1132	1697 ^{3var}	Spink 139 $^{260\,(GEF)}$	1108	1133	1697$^{3rd\,bst}$		1108A
1134	No stops rev		1108B	1135	2nd L/M	SNC 1997, ^{5890}	1108C?
1136	1698 ^{3var}	M.R. 22, 172 $^{(EF)}$	1112	1137	1698 P ^{Pln}	SNC ^{2000,} 224 $^{(GEF)}$	1113
1138	1698 ^{Plume}	M.R. 22, 173 $^{(EF)}$	1114		4th Obv	Kent 164	
	4th Ob x2	Kent 164			4th Rev	Kent 164	
1139	1698 $^{No\,stp}$	M.R. 22/175 $^{(EF)}$	1115B	1140	1698 P	(SNC 1987, 1419)	1115A
1140	1698 P ^{Pln}	PC $^{(RF/NP)\,(VAS)}$	1115A	1141	1698	Manville 156 $^{(EF)}$	1115
1141	1698 ^{Flame}	Norweb 239$^{(VAS)}$	1115	1142	1699 $^{Bust\,4}$	Norweb 999 $^{(EF)}$	1116
1143	1698^{piedfor}	PC $^{(RF/NP)\,(VAS)}$	1116A	1144			
1145	1699	Hamilton 260 ^{EF}	1117	1146	1699 P ^{Pln}	Spink ^{140} 636 $^{(VAS)}$	1118
1147				1148	1699 ^{Roses}	M.R. 22/179 $^{(VF)}$	1120

(continued)

PROVENANCES

ESC	Variety	Provenance	(Old ESC)	ESC	Variety	Provenance	(Old ESC)
1149	Plumes sm lion	**M.R. 22, 178** *(AEF)*	1119	1150	Large letters	SNC2010.9209VAS	1121
1151	1700 sm o	SNC 2003,5473 (VAS)	1121A	1152	3rd Bust v	**M.R. 22/181**GEF	1122
1153	No stops tall 0	**M.R. 22/181**	1122A	1154	1700 Plume	**Manville 265**	1123
1155	1701	DNW 79,3093 (EF)	1124	1156			
1157	1701Plumes	Norweb 482 (EF)	1125		5th Obv	**Montagu 933**	
1200	1699 Pat	*(Not traced)*	1127		5th Rev.	**Montagu 933**	
1302	1696P 2nd			1303	1697P 2nd		
1304	1696P 3rd						

WILLIAM III - SHILLINGS – BRISTOL

1158	1696B	**M.R. 22/148** *(GEF*	1081	1159	REx		
1160	Lge GMAG			1161	1697B	SNC 2011,9718 (EF)	1095
1162	3rd B	**DNW 102** 2554	1103				
1163	Sm lettering		1103A	1164	1697 3var	**M.R. 22, 170** *(AEF)*	1109

WILLIAM III - SHILLINGS – CHESTER

1165	1696C	**M.R. 22/149** *(GVF)*	1082	1166	R/Vin GRA	**SNC 2004,** 6175 (EF)	1082A
1167	1696 Ppied		1083	1168	1697 C	Glen.15/1974,315(EF)	1096
1169	Mule?			1170	1697Cno st	SNC 2000, 2391 (VF)	1104A
1171	1696C	Hamilton 237 (EF)	1089	1172			
1173					3rd C	**Spink/Sby** 3507	
1174	E-I-F-S	**SNC 2001** 0805	1097	1174	E-I-F-S	Hamilton 243 (AF)	1097
1175	1697C	M.R. 22/164 (EF)	1104	1176	FR·A·ET		1104C
1177	Scot arms		1104B	1178	3rd C, var	**M.R. 22/171** *(GVF)*	1110
1179	1697 3var	Hamilton 255 AVF	1111				

WILLIAM III - SHILLINGS - EXETER

1180	1696E 1st	Hamilton 231 (EF)	1084	1181	1696E 3rd	Spink 124,1888 (F)	1089A
1181	1696Emule	SNC 1993 6250 (GF)	1089A	1182	1697E	Manville 150 (AEF)	1098
1183	3rd E	**M.R. 22/165** *(EF*	1105	1183	1697E	Spink 145,2493 (GEF)	1105

WILLIAM III - SHILLINGS - NORWICH

1184	1696N	**Slaney 157**(GEF)	1085	1185	1697N	SNC 2000.0095 (NVF)	1099
1186	No stops Obv			1187	Small 7		
1188	1696N	Hamilton 233 (VF)	1106				

WILLIAM III - SHILLINGS - YORK

1189	1696Y	SNC 2004 6167 (GEF)	1087	1190	1696Y/Y	Hamilton 23 6 (AVF)	1088
1190	1696Y/Y	**PC (RF/NP)** *(AVF)*	1088	1191	1st Y	**Manville 146** *(EF)*	1086
1192				1193	1696V	**Hamilton 238** NF	1090
1194	1697Y	Spink 145,2491 (VF)	1101	1195	Double obv. P	Spink 140 625 (VF)	1101A
1196	1697Y	**M.R. 22, 161** *(AEF)*	1100	1197	Scot↔Ireland		1100B
1198	France↔Irelan		1100a	1199	1697Y	DNW 86,723 (GVF)	1107

WILLIAM III - SIXPENCES – LONDON

1201	1695	Bole 1,1672 (GVF)	1532	1202	D/I in DEI		1533B
1202	1696 Bust 1	**DNW 76,**107 (Mint)	1533	1202	Rev. 1	**Bole 1,1674** *(GEF)*	1533
1202	1st B x 2	**DNW 89**1957 (VAS)	1533	1203			

(continued)

PROVENANCES

ESC	Variety	Provenance	(Old ESC)	ESC	Variety	Provenance	(Old ESC)
1204							
1205	No stops *obv*		1533A	1205	No stops *rev*	(P.C)	1533A
XXX	1696 DFI	SNC 2000, 239*(NVF)*	1534D	1207	1696/5	**Bole 1,1673** *(NEF)*	1534
1208	2^GVLIEMVS	**DNW 91,** 122		1208	L/M	**Bole 96** DNW 91,	1534?
1209	1696P^Hevy	Bole 1,1676 *(NVF)*	1534A		E/R		
1210	1696 P^CU	Bole 1,1677 *(NVF)*	1534	1210	1696 P^CU	Spink 140,640 *(VF)*	1534
1211	1696	Norweb 1509 *(EF)*	1543	1212			
1213							
1214	4^Scot. at date	**Bole 1,1678** *(NEF)*	1534B	1215	5 French date	**Spink/Sby** 3520	1534C
1216	lion^inverted	Bole 3,102 *(GF)*	1545	1216	1696	Spink 46 270 *(GVF)*	1545
1217	1696 2a	**Bole 1,**1687 *(AEF)*	1550	1217	1696	Norweb 483 *VF*	1550
1217	Bust 2a	**Norweb 483**	1550	1217	Pattern 2c	**SCMB 1954**	1550?
1218	GVLELMVS	**DNW 89,** 2137	1551	1218	GVLELMVS	**DNW 89,** 2137	1551
	Pattern 2b				1696 L E	Bole 3,96 *(NEF)*	1552
1219	*Rev. 3*	**M.R. 23/**94	1552	1219	*Rev. 3*	**M.R. 23/94**	
1219	1697 L S	DNW 86,729 *(GEF)*	1552	1220			1553
1221				1222	Shilling flan	**Bole** 1690 DNW 89,	1552A
1222	1/- flan	**DNW 89,** 1690	1552A	1222	1697	Bole 1,1690 *(AVF)*	1552A
1223	1697^transp	SNC 2010,9076 *(F)*	1552B	1223	*Rev* 8 transpos	**Bole 3,108** *(GF)*	1552B
1224	1697	Hamilton 286 *(VF)*	1564	1225	No stop		1564B
	Pattern 2d	**SCMB 1954**	1550?		Thick flan		1545A
1226				1227			
1228	GR/DE		1564A	1229	GVLELMVS	Bole 2, 137 *(VF+)*	1565
1229	1697	Spink 140 649 *(EF)*	1565	1230	G/I	**Bole 1,1697** *(AVF)*	1565B
1230	1st V/A	Bole 1,1698 *(EF)*	1565B	1231			
1232	2nd V/A	(SNC 2001,1077 *(Poor)*)	1565A	1233	*Rev. 2*	**DNW89** 1958 *(VAS)*	1566
1234			1566A	1235			
1236	1697 Bust 3	SNC 2010,9080 *(VF)*	1566B	1237	1697 Bust 3	Bole 2, 139 *(VAS)*	1566C
1238	1697 Bust 3	Spink 46 283 *(VAS)*	1567	1239			
1240	D/E in DEI		1567A	1241	G/D in GRS		1567B
1242	1697 G/I	SNC 2001,0863 *(EF)*	1576C	1243	1698	DNW 111,83 *(EF)*	1574
1244	1698^Plumes	Manville 179 *(GEF)*	1575	1244	7 Plumes	**DNW 86,** 731	1575
1245	1699^Plumes	Norweb 241 *VAS*	1577	1246	1699 Roses	Spink 139 288 *(EF)*	1578
1247	1669 Roses	DNW 86,732 *(NVF)*	1578A	1248	1699	Hamilton 299 *Mint*	1576
1249				1250	1700 Bust 3	DNW 111,85 *(VAS)*	1579
1251	1st V/A	**Bole 1,**1705 *(VAS)*	1579A	1252	1701	Hamilton 302*(VAS)*	1581
1253	1700^Plume	**Spink/Sby** 3548 *(EF)*	1580		VLIEMVS		

WILLIAM III - SIXPENCES – BRISTOL

1254	1st B	**Norweb 240** *VAS*	1535	1254	1696B	Bole 1,1680 *(GVF)*	1535
1255	3rd B/E	DNW 71,684 *(AEF)*	1535A	1256	1696B L L		1546
1257	No stops *obv.*		1546A	1258	1696B	Hamilton 276 *(EF)*	1547
1259	1696B	(SNC2006,7817 *(AVF)*)	1548	1260			
1261	1697B	**Norweb 483** *VAS*	1555	1262	1697↑↑		
1263	B/E	SNC 2011,9733 *(VF)*	1555A?	1263	1697 B/E	DNW 111,81 *(AEF)*	1555A
1264	M·AG	**Bole 3,110** *(VF+)*	1555C	1265	Inverted lion		
1266	1697B	Bole 1,1699 *(VF+)*	1568	1267	1697 B/E		1568A

PROVENANCES

WILLIAM III - SIXPENCES – CHESTER

ESC	Variety	Provenance	(Old ESC)	ESC	Variety	Provenance	(Old ESC)
1268	1696C $^{E\,L}$	Bole 1,1682 $^{(GVF)}$	1536	1269	1696C $^{L\,S}$	Bole 3,103 $^{(AVF)}$	1548A
1270	1697C $^{L\,L}$		1556	1271	1697C	DNW $^{111,82\,(GEF)}$	1557
1272	No collar	Bole 1,$^{1692\,(AEF)}$	1557B?	1273	No stps MAG		1557A
1274	6 $^{Irish\,at\,date}$	Bole 1,1693 $^{(AEF)}$	1558	1274	1st C	DNW 89, ^{1693}	1558
1275	1697C	Spink 46 $^{287\,(EF)}$	1569	1276	1697C	Spink 46 $^{288\,(EF)}$	1570
1276	1697C	Bole 1,1700 $^{(GVF)}$	1570				

WILLIAM III - SIXPENCES – EXETER

ESC	Variety	Provenance	(Old ESC)	ESC	Variety	Provenance	(Old ESC)
1277	1696E	Bole 1,1683 $^{(GVF)}$	1537	1278	1696E/Y	Bole 1,$^{1689\,(AEF)}$	1548B
1279	1696E $^{E\,L}$	Bole 3,106 $^{(NVF)}$	1542A	1280	1697E	Spink 46 $^{279\,(GVF)}$	1559
1281	1 697E	Bole 1,$^{1694\,(GVF)}$	1560	1282	1697E/B	Spink 46 $^{280\,(AEF)}$	1560A
1282	1st E/B	SNC 1995, ^{4368}	1560A				
1283	1697 ^{Sm} 7		1560C	1284	E/M	DNW91 Bole^{115}	1560B
1285	E/C in GVLIELMVS			1286	1697E	Bole 1,1701$^{(AVF)}$	1571
1286	1697E	(Spink 3, Manville 294)	1571	1287	1697E	Bole 3,127 $^{(VF+)}$	1572

WILLIAM III - SIXPENCES – NORWICH

ESC	Variety	Provenance	(Old ESC)	ESC	Variety	Provenance	(Old ESC)
1288	1696N	Spink 145,$^{2575\,(VAS)}$	1538	1289	1697N	Bole 1,1695 $^{(EF)}$	1549
1290	1697N	SNC 2010$^{,9078\,(AEF)}$	1561	1291	No stop BR		
1292	Large lets Rev			1292	Large lettering	Bole 3,117 $^{(NEF)}$	1561
1293	GVLIEMVS	Bole 3,118 $^{(GF)}$	1561A	1293	1 ^{GVLIEMVS}	DNW 91, ^{118}	1561A

WILLIAM III - SIXPENCES – YORK

ESC	Variety	Provenance	(Old ESC)	ESC	Variety	Provenance	(Old ESC)
1294	1st Y	Slaney 168	1540	1295	No stops	SNC 2010$^{,9075\,(EF)}$	1541
1296	1696Y	SNC 2010,$^{9074\,(EF)}$	1539	1297	1696Y	Bole 1,1688 $^{(Fair)}$	1542
1298	1697Y$^{sm\,7}$	DNW 86,$^{730(GVF)}$	1562	1299	Irish at date	Bole 1,1696 $^{(GVF)}$	1563
1300	(1696Y mule)	(Spink 3, Manville 273)	1542A	1301	1696Y	SNC 2004 $^{6241\,(GEF)}$	1573
	Unbarred H	Bole 1695 $^{DNW\,89,}$	1561				

WILLIAM III - SIXPENCES – LONDON -2nd Bust

ESC	Variety	Provenance		ESC	Variety	Provenance	
1302	1696 B^{1}	B.M. collection		1303	1697 B^{1}	B.M. collection	
1304	1696 B^{2}	B.M. collection		1304	1696 B^{2}	Bald. FPL$^{.Wint.'14/15}$ $_{BM119}$	

WILLIAM III – MAUNDY SETS

ESC	Variety	Provenance	(Old ESC)	ESC	Variety	Provenance	(Old ESC)
1305	1698	Spink 124,$^{1800\,(VAS)}$	2389	1306	1699	Spink 183$^{162\,(VF)}$	2390
1307	1700	SNC 2005$^{,6631(EF)}$	2391	1308	1701	SNC 2005$^{,6632(EF)}$	2392

WILLIAM III - MAUNDY GROATS

ESC	Variety	Provenance	(Old ESC)	ESC	Variety	Provenance	(Old ESC)
1309	1697		1880	1310	1698 ^{MAG}	SNC 2001$^{,\,1359\,(VF)}$	1881
1311	1699 $^{Ob/rv}$	Spink/Sby ^{3549}	1882	1312	1700 $^{no\,stp}$	(SNC 2001, MS1362 $^{(F)}$	1883A
	1700	(SNC 2001, MS1361 $^{(VF)}$	1883				
1313	1701 ^{Rev}	SNC 2007 $^{8354(GF)}$	1884	1314	1702	Baldwin 48$^{,4398(VF)}$	1885

WILLIAM III - THREEPENCES

ESC	Variety	Provenance	(Old ESC)	ESC	Variety	Provenance	(Old ESC)
1315	1698 ^{Obv}	SNC 2001$^{,\,1438\,(EF)}$	2000	1315	1698 ^{Rev}	SNC 2001 ^{1438}	2000
1316	1699	(SNC 2001, MS1440 $^{(F)}$)	2001	1317	1700	(SNC 2001, MS1441(AVF))	2002
1318	1701 $^{z-type}$	SJA 8, 286 $^{(NVF)}$	2003	1319	1701 ^{Rev}	Spink/Sby ^{3553}	2004
1319	1701 ^{rev}	SNC 12, ^{2007}	2004	1320	1701 ^{GBA}	Spink 1 $^{225\,(VAS)}$	2003A

PROVENANCES

WILLIAM III - HALF GROATS

ESC	Variety	Provenance	(Old ESC)	ESC	Variety	Provenance	(Old ESC)
1321	1698 A/1	SNC 2001, 1522 *(EF)*	2206		1698 A/1a	SNC 2001, 1523 *(VF)*	2206A
1323	1699 B/2	(SNC 2001, MS1524 (EF))	2007	1324	1700 B/2	(SNC 2001, MS1525 (GVF))	2008
1325	1701 B/2	SNC 12, 2007	2209				

WILLIAM III - PENNIES

1326	1698	Baldwin 48 -4398(VF)	2307	1327	1698	(SNC 2001, MS1642 (VF))	2308
1328	1698		2309	1329	1698 IRA		2310
1330	1698	(SNC 2001, MS1643 (EF))	2311	1332	1699 Obv	Spink/Sby 3549	2312
1333	1700	(SNC 2001, MS1645 (GVF))	2313	1334	1701 Rev	Spink/Sby 3553	2314

ANNE - CROWNS

1340	1703- A 3rd	M.R. 17/357 *(AEF)*	99	1340	B.U. Pln Rev	M.R. 7 184 *(EF)*	99
1341	1705 Plume 5th	Spink 125 709(EF)	100	1341	Busts B+C	Barr 259 *(EF)*	100
1341	1705 R&P 5th	Hamilton305 *Mint*	100	1342	1706	Willis 207 *(EF)*	101
1342	1706 RP 5th	DNW 90, 539 *(GEF)*	101	1343	1707 RP6th	Norweb 1522 *AEF*	102
1344	1707- D 7th	Barr 262 *(EF)*	104	1345			
1346	1708-G 7th	Roekel 170 *(GEF)*	105	1347	1708 Plume 7th	Roekel 172 *(GEF)*	108
1348				1349	1713 R&P	Roekel 173 *(Mint)*	109
1350				1351			
1352	1707E SEXTO	Spk 163 174 *(Mint)*	103	1353			
1354	SEPTIMO	Willis 430 *(VAS)*	103A	1355	1708/7 7th	Barr 264 *(AEF)*	107
1356	1707E 7th	Roekel 171 *(EF)*	106		Busts E+F	Barr 261 *(GVF)*	103

ANNE - HALFCROWNS

1357	1703 3rd	Spink 124 1894 *(GVF)*	568	1358	B.U. Pln Rev	Adams 492 *(EF)*	569
1358	Vigo	Adams 492 *(EF)*	569				
1359	1704 Plume	Manville 199 *VAS*	570	1360	1705 Plume	Adams 494(NVF)	571
1361	1706 R&P	DNW 111, 97(AEF)	572	1362	1707 R&P	Adams 497(EF)	573
1363				1364	Roses+ plumes	Adams 498 *(EF)*	573
1365	A.U. Pln Rev	Adams 502 *(NEF)*	575	1366	1707 7th	Adams 500 GEF	574
1367				1368	1707 Pied.	Adams 501(EF)	574B
1369	1st bust	Adams 508 *(EF)*	578	1369	1708 Plume	Adams 508 *(EF)*	578
1370	1708 7th	Adams 507 *(EF)*	577	1371	1709 8th	Adams 509 *(EF)*	579
1372	1710 R&P	Adams 512(EF)	581	1372	Roses+ plumes	Adams 514 NEF	581
1373				1374	1712 R&P	Adams 515(EF)	582
1374	2nd bust	Bull	582	1375	1713 R&P	Adams 518(EF)	584
1376	1713 12th	Adams 517(NVF)	583	1377	1714 R&P	Adams 521 *(VF)*	585
1378	1714/3 RP	Adams 522 *(VF)*	585A	1379	Edge ★for V	Adams 504 *(F)*	575
1379	1707E 6th	DNW 86, 746 *(EF)*	575	1380	T★TAMEN	Adams 504 *(F)*	
1381	1707E 7th	Hamilton 323 *(Mint)*	575A	1382	1708 Z type	James 18, 160 *(VF)*	576
1382	1708E Z type	Adams 506 *(EF)*	576	1382	Z type 1	PC (M. Bull)	576
1383				1384	1709E Z type	Adams 511 *(NVF)*	580

ANNE - SHILLINGS

1385	1702 Plain	M.R. 6/186 *(GEF)*	1128	1386	1st bust	Norweb 236 *UNC*	1129
1386	B.U. Plumes	Spk 216 963 *(NEF)*	1129	1387	1702 VIGO	SNC 2010, -9026(EF)	1130
1388	1703 VIGO	Norweb 494 *VAS*	1131	1389	1704	M.R. 22/191 *(EF)*	1132

(continued)

PROVENANCES

ESC	Variety	Provenance	(Old ESC)	ESC	Variety	Provenance	(Old ESC)
1390	1704 Plumes	Manville 217 (VAS)	1133	1391	1705	M.R. 22/193 (EF)	1134
1392	2nd bust	Norweb 496 VAS	1135	1393	1705 R&P	M.R. 6/188 (EF)	1136
1394	1707 R&P	M.R. 22/196 (EF)	1137	1395	1707 AU	Spink 139 300 (Mint)	1141
1396	1707 Plume	M.R. 22/200 (EF)	1142	1397			
1398	1708 R&P	Hamilton 348 (EF)	1146	1399	1708 R&P	Spink 139 304 (VAS)	1147
1400	1708 Plume	Hamilton 350 (EF)	1148	1401	1708 R&P	M.R. 22/206 (EF)	1149
1402	1709 3rd bus	Manville 228 (EF)	1154	1403	1710	Spink 139 311(EF)	1155
1403	1710 R&P	DNW 111, 109 (EF)	1155	1404	1710 P Pln	Montagu 988	1155A
1405	1710 R&P	Manville 229 (AEF)	1156	1445	1708E	Hamilton 355 (EF)	1153
1406	1710 P B4		1156A	1407	1711 3rd bus	Spink 139 313 (NEF)	1157
1408	1711 4th bu	Spink 139 314 (EF)	1158	1409			
1410	1712 R&P	Spink 139 311(GEF)	1159	1410			
1411	1713/2 RP	Spink 139 316(EF)	1160	1411	1713/2	DNW86, 756 (AEF)	1160
1412	1714 R&P	M.R. 22/215 (EF)	1161	1413	1714/3	Spink 139 317 (NEF)	1161A
1414	1707E	M.R. 22 197 (AEF)	1138	1415			
1416	1707E P Pln	SNC 1982 7535 (FDC)	1139	1417	No stops rev.	SNC 2001, 0816 (VF)	1138A
1418				1419	E★ local die	Kent 187	1140
1420				1421			
1422				1423			
1424	E local die	DNW 89 1960 (GEF)	1140A	1425			
1426	E below bust	M.R. 22/201 (EF)	1143		1707E★	SNC 2001, 0977 (F)	1143A
	1708E	(SNC 2001, MS0978 (AF))	1144		1708E★	DNW 79, 3123(AVF)	1145
	8/7	PC (RF/NP)	1145A		E below bust	(SNC 2001,MSO819(F+))	1145B
1432	No rays to star	SNC2001, 0820 (F)	1145C	1433			
1434	E★ local die	(SNC2001, 0819 (AF/F))	1145D	1435			
1436	1708E	Spink 139 307 (GVF)	1150	1437	1708/7	(Glen.15/1974,334 (EF))	1150A
1438				1439	1708E★	SNC 2001, 0822 (VF)	1151
1440				1441			
1442				1443			
1444	1709E★	Hamilton 354 (EF)	1152	1445			

ANNE - SIXPENCES

ESC	Variety	Provenance	(Old ESC)	ESC	Variety	Provenance	(Old ESC)
1446	1703 VIGO	Norweb 497 UNC	1582				
1447	A&B (1)	Bole 1, 1707 (NEF)	1583	1447	Bust A	Bole 1, 1707 (NEF)	1583
1448	Rev C¹ (2)	M.R. 17,192 (EF)	1584	1448	Busts B & E	Bole 3,132 (NEF)	1584
1449	Rev C² (3)	Bole 1, 1709 (NEF)	1584A	1450	1705 RP	DNW 86, 758 (EF)	1585
1451	Rev D (4)	Norweb 498 VAS	1586	1452	BR FRA	Bole 3, 137 (VF)	1587A
1453	1707 E & B	Bole 1, 1711 (EF)	1587	1454	Rev E (8)	Bole 1, 1711 (EF)	1587
1454	Rev E (5)	Bole 1, 1711 (EF)	1587	1455	1707 Plume	Bole 1, 1715 (NEF)	1590
1456	1708	DNW 111, 115(GEF)	1591	1457	1708E	Bole 1, 1717 (VF)	1592
1458	Rev I (6)	Spink 139 324(VAS)	1594	1459	Rev J (7)	Spink 139 325 (GEF)	1595
1460	Small lis	SNC 2006, 7047(GEF)	1596	1460	Small lis	SNC 2010, 9235 (VAS)	1596
1461	1711 Lge lis	Bole 3,144/5 (GVF)	1596A	1461	Large lis	Bole 1, 1711 (EF)	1596A
1462	1707E	Bole 1, 1713 (NEF)	1588	1463			
1464				1465	1707E P Pln	Bole 1, 1714 (GEF)	1589
1465	After Union	Bole 1, 1714 (GEF)	1589	1466	Obv F Lge E	Bole, 137 DNW 91	1588A
1467				1468	Obv G	Bole 1, 1719 (VF+)	1593
1469				1470			
1471	1708/7	Bole 1, 1718 (AVF)	1593A	1472	Obv H	Bole 1, 1720 (NVF)	1593B

PROVENANCES

ANNE - MAUNDY SETS

ESC	Variety	Provenance	(Old ESC)	ESC	Variety	Provenance	(Old ESC)
1473	1703	SNC 2008 ^{8560} (NVF)	2393	1474	1705	SNC 2011 $^{.9464}$ (AVF)	2394
1475	1706	SNC 2010 $^{.9390}$ (NEF)	2395	1476	1708	DNW 78. ^{325} (AEF)	2396
1477	1709	**DNW 86,** ^{1050} **(GVF)**	2397	1478	1710	Spink 124 $^{1801(EF)}$	2398
1479	1713	SNC 2011 $^{.9740}$ (GVF)	2399				

ANNE - GROATS

ESC	Variety	Provenance	(Old ESC)	ESC	Variety	Provenance	(Old ESC)
1480	1703	(SNC 2001, MS1365 (F))	1886	1481	1704	(SNC 2001, MS1366 (AVF))	1887
1482	No stops Obv		1887A	1483	1705	(SNC 2001, MS1367 (AVF))	1888
1484	1706 ^{FRA}	(SNC 2001, MS1368 (AVF))	1889	1485	1708 ^{BRI}	(SNC 2001, MS1369 (VF))	1890
1486	1709	SNC 2001 $^{1370 (EF)}$	1891	1487	1710 $^{B-2a}$	SNC 2001, $^{.1372(AEF)}$	1892
1488	1710 $^{C-2a}$	SNC 2001 $^{1372 (EF)}$	1892A	1488	1710 $^{C-2a}$	SNC 2001 $^{1372(AEF)}$	1892A
1489	1713 $^{B-2a}$		1893	1490	1713 $^{C-2a}$	(SNC 2001, MS1374 (VF))	1893A
1491	1713 Close		1893B				
1492	1711 Pat silver			1492	1711 Pat cu		

ANNE - THREEPENCES

ESC	Variety	Provenance	(Old ESC)	ESC	Variety	Provenance	(Old ESC)
1494	1703	(SNC 2001, MS1445 (GF))	2005	1495	1701		2006
1496	1704	(SNC 2006, 7238 (GF))	2007	1497	1705	(SNC 2001, MS1447 (F))	2008
1498	1706	(SNC 2001, MS1448(F))	2009	1499	1707	SNC 2001, $^{1447(Mint)}$	2010
1500	1708	(SNC 1972, 5521 (EF))	2011	1501	1708/7	(SNC 2001, MS1450(VF))	2011A
1502	1709	(SNC 2001, MS1452 (GF))	2012	1503	No stop af date		2012A
1504	1710	(SNC 2001, MS1453 (VF))	2013	1505	1713	(SNC 2001, MS1455 (GVF))	2014
1506	Curls over head		2014A	1507	1713	(SNC 2001, MS1457 (VF))	2014B

ANNE - HALF GROATS

ESC	Variety	Provenance	(Old ESC)	ESC	Variety	Provenance	(Old ESC)
1508	1703 $^{A/1b}$		2210	1509	1704 $^{A/1b}$	S&B ^{Coins} G402 (EF)	2211
1510	1704 $^{A/1b}$		2212	1511	1704 $^{A/1b}$		2213
1512	1705 $^{A/1b}$	(SNC 2001, MS1530 (VF))	2214	1513	1706 $^{A/1b}$	(SNC 2001, MS1531 (F))	2215
1514	N o stop DEI		2215A	1515	1707 $^{A/1b}$	(SNC 2001, MS1532 (EF))	2216
1516	1703 $^{B/2a}$	(SNC 2001, MS1528(VF))	2210A	1517	1708 $^{B-2a}$	Rich. $^{Sum 2006,141(EF)}$	2217
1518	1709 $^{B/2a}$	(SNC 2001, MS1584 (AVF))	2218	1519	N o stop DEI		2218A
1520	1710 $^{B/2a}$	(SNC 2076, 7208 (EF))	2219	1521	1713 $^{B/2a}$	SJA 6, 238 $^{(AVF)}$	2220
1522	1713/0	(SNC 2001, MS1588 (VF))	2220A	X1.5	SNC 12, ^{2007}		2398
	B	**SNC 12,** ^{2007}	2398	1b	**Spink/Sby** ^{3599}		2399
	A	**Spink/Sby** ^{3599}	2399	2a	**SNC 12,** ^{2007}		2398

ANNE - PENNIES

ESC	Variety	Provenance	(Old ESC)	ESC	Variety	Provenance	(Old ESC)
1523	1703	(SNC 2001, MS1647 (VF))	2315	1524	1705	(SNC 2001, 1648 (EF))	2316
1525	1706		2317	1526	1706	(SNC 2001, MS1648 (EF))	2318
1527	1708		2319	1528	1709	S&B ^{Coins} G401 (EF)	2320
1529	M A G		2320A	1530	M AG		2320B
1531	1710		2321	1532	1713/0	(SNC 2001, MS1652 (EF))	2322
1532	N o stop DEI		2322A				

PROVENANCES

GEORGE I - CROWNS

ESC	Variety	Provenance	(Old ESC)	ESC	Variety	Provenance	(Old ESC)
1540	1716 2nd	Willis 283 (GEF)	110	1541	1718	Roekel 175 (VAS)	111
1542	1718/6 5th	**Roekel 176** (GEF)	111A	1543	1720/18	**Barr 267** (GEF)	113
1544	1723 10th	**SNC 2003** 4731 (VAS)	114	1545	1720 R&P	Roekel 177 (AEF)	112
1546	1726 13th	Roekel 180 (VAS)	115	1547	1726 EGNO	Dr Rees Jones 163	115B
1548	Inverted Ns	Spink 124 1900 (EF)	115A				

GEORGE I - HALFCROWNS

ESC	Variety	Provenance	(Old ESC)	ESC	Variety	Provenance	(Old ESC)
1549	1715 Pat	**Norweb 251** FDC	586	1549	1715 Pat	Adams 523 (NEF)	586
1550	*Rev.* B	**Bull.** Adams 524 (EF)	587	1550	1715 R&P	Baldwn 48 5033(GEF)	587
1551	1715 NNO	Adams 525/526 (NF)	588B	1552	1715 R&P	Adams 527 (GVF)	588C
1553	1715 R&P	Adams 528 (VF)	588A	1554	1717 R&P	Adams 527 (VF)	589
1555	1720/17	**Adams 530** (EF)	590	1556	1720 R&P	Adams 531 (GVF)	591
1557	1723 SSC	**Adams 532** GEF	592	1557	*Rev.* C	**Adams 532** GEF	592
1558			592A	1559	1726 R&P	SNC 1977 5660 (EF)	593
	Rev. D	**PC (M. Bull)**	593	Z-type 1		**Adams 531** (GVF	591

GEORGE I - SHILLINGS

ESC	Variety	Provenance	(Old ESC)	ESC	Variety	Provenance	(Old ESC)
1560	1715 R&P	M.R. 12/129	1162	1561			
1562	1716 R&P	SNC 2008 .8675 (EF)	1163	1562	2. R-P	**Spink 139** 328 (EF)	1163
1563	1716 V/L		1163A	1564	1717 R&P	Hamilton 389 (GEF)	1164
1565	Obv leg lets		1164A	1566	1718	Manville 263 (VAS)	1165
1567	1719 R&P	**M.R. 22/223** (GVF)	1166	1568	1. Plain	**M.R. 22/228** (GVF)	1167
1569	Large 0 in date		1167A	1570	1720/18		1167B
1571	1720/19		1167C	1572	1720	SNC 2001 .0829 (EF)	1168
1572	1720	SNC 2011, 9721(VAS)	1168	1573	1720	Manville 266 (GEF)	1169
1574	1720O/G	DNW 114 1409 (NVF)	1169A	1575	1721	Norweb 517 GVF	1170
1576			1170A	1577	1721	M.R. 22/229 (EF)	1171
1578	1721/0	M.R. 22/228 (GVF)	1172	1578	1721/0	**PC (RF/NP)** (GVF)	1172
1579	1721/18	**DNW 85,** 571	1173	1580	21/18 P&R	**SNC 2000,** 226 (VF)	1171A
1581	1722 R&P	Spink 139 339 (EF)	1174	1582			1174A
1583	1723 R&P	Spink 139 340 (EF)	1175	1584			1175A
1585			1175B	1586	1723 SS-C	**Spink 139** 341 (VAS)	1176
1586	1723 SSC	Spink 139 341 (VAS)	1176	1587	4. C/SS	**DNW 93** 1640 (EF+)	1176A
1588	C/SS	**DNW 85,** 575	1176A	1589	France at date	**M.R. 22/235** (GVF)	1177
1589	French arms	**SNC 2003** .5680 (EF)	1177	1590	C/SS		1176A
1591	1723 SS C	Spink 139 344 (GEF)	1178	1592	1723 WCC	Spink 126 512 (EF)	1180
1593	1723 R&P	M.R. 22/237 (GEF	1179	1594	1724 R&P	Manville 273 (EF)	1181
1595	F	SNC 1998, 6967	1182	1595	1724 WCC	**Hamiltn 404** (EF)	1182
1596	1725 WCC	**M.R. 22/242** (GEF)	1185	1596	1725 WCC	M.R. 12/132 (GEF)	1185
1597	1725 R&P	SNC 2012 .9859 (EF)	1183	1598	1725/4		1183A
1599	1725 no stp	Spink 139 350 (EF)	1184	1600			1184A
1601	1726 R&P	Hamilton 407 AEF	1186	1602			1186A
1603			1186B	1604	1726 WCC	Hamilton 408 (EF)	1187
1605				1606	1727 R&P	Manville 279 (GF)	1188
1607	No stops Obv	M.R. 22/244 (EF)	1188A	1608	No stops Rev		1188B

PROVENANCES

GEORGE I - SIXPENCES

ESC	Variety	Provenance	(Old ESC)	ESC	Variety	Provenance	(Old ESC)
1609	1717 R&P	SNC 2010,^{9094} (EF)	1597	1610	1717 Pln ed		1598
1611	A R&P	**DNW 91, ^{146}**	1599	1611	2170/17	**Spink 139** ^{355} (VAS)	1599
1612	B SSC	SNC 2011^{9433} (UNC)	1600	1612	Small letters	Bole 2, ^{156} (GVF)	1600
1613	1613/0		1601	1614	Large letters	**Bole 1, 1724** (EF+)	1601A
1615	Lge let. B/R	**DNW 91 149** (VF+)	1601	1616	C sm R&P	**Spink 139** ^{358} (EF)	1602

GEORGE I - MAUNDY SETS

1617	1723	SNC 2011 ^{9470} (VF)	2400	1618	1727	SNC 2003^{,5630} (AEF)	2401

GEORGE I - GROATS

1619	1717	**SNC 2001,** ^{1376} (EF)	1894	1620	1721	(SNC 2001, MS1377 (VF))	1895
1621	1723	M.R. 10/224 (EF)	1896	1622	1727	(SNC 2001, MS1379 (VF))	1897

GEORGE I - THREEPENCES

1623	1717	SNC 2001 ^{1452} (Mint)	2015	1624	1721	(SNC 1977, 13611(VF))	2016
1625	1723		2017	1626	F.R		2017A
1627	1727	(SNC 2001, MS1460 (EF))	2018	1628	Leg ends bust		2018A

GEORGE I - TWOPENCES

1629	1717	(SNC 2001, MS1589 (VF))	2221	1630	1721	**DNW 101,^{699}**	2222
1631	1723	ESC 2223	2223	1632	1726	(SNC 2001, MS1592(VF))	2224
1633	Large O		2225	1634	Norm. O		2225A
1635	Small lets Rev		2225B				

GEORGE I - PENNY

1636	•1716•	(SNC 1977, 13607 (VF))	2323	1637	•1716		2323A
1638	1718	(SNC 2006, 7246 (VF))	2324	1639	No stop GEORGIVS		2324A
1640	1720	(SNC 2006, 7247 (VF))	2325	1641	1720^{HIPEX}	**DNW 101,^{699}**	2326
1642	1723	(SNC 2006, 7248 (VF))	2327	1643	GEORGIVS•		2327A
1644	GEORGI$_V$S		2327B	1645	1725	(SNC 2001, MS1658 (GVF))	2328
1646	FR· $_E$T		2328A	1647	1726	(SNC 2001, MS1660 (AEF))	2329
1648	1727	(SNC 2001, MS1661 (VF))	2330				

GEORGE II - CROWNS

1660	1732 RP6th	Hamilton 415 (Mint)	117	1661	1732 P Pln	SNC 2012^{,9812} (VAS)	118
1662	1734-A ^{7th}	Spink 124,^{1919} (VAS)	119	1662	1734 R&P	**Barr 270** (GEF)	119
1663	1735$^{RP\ 8th}$	Roekel 184 (VAS)	120	1664	1736 RP9th	DNW 97 ^{301} (GEF	121
1665	1739 ^{12th}	DNW 102^{2589}(GEF	122	1666	1741 R ^{14th}	**Asherson 190** VAS	123
1667	GEORGIUS	**Spink 111** ^{179} (EF)	124	1668	1746 LIMA	SNC 2002 ^{2758} (GEF)	125
1669	1746 P	Roekel 190 (FDC)	126	1670	1750 ^{14th}	Roekel 191 (GEF)	127
1671	1751 ^{14th}	**Spink 163** ^{194} (VAS)	128	1670	Obv. D	**Barr 273** (GVF)	127
1672	1731 P	(Not traced)	116				

PROVENANCES

GEORGE II - HALFCROWNS

ESC	Variety	Provenance	(Old ESC)	ESC	Variety	Provenance	(Old ESC)
1673	Busts A-C	PC (M. Bull) $^{(FDC)}$	594	1673	Rev·1	PC (M. Bull) $^{(FDC)}$	594
1674	1731 P	Adams 534 $^{(GVF)}$	595	1674	1732$^{RP\ 6th}$	Adams 537 $^{(EF)}$	595
1674	1731 ^{RP5th}	Adams 535 $^{(EF)}$	595	1675	1732 ^{RP6th}	Manville 297 $^{(EF)}$	596
1676	1734$^{RP\ 7th}$	Adams 535 $^{(EF)}$	597	1677	1735$^{RP\ 5th}$	Adams 540 $^{(EF)}$	598
1678	1736 ^{RP9th}	Spink 124,$^{1923\ (VAS)}$	599	1678	Rev·2	Adams 541$^{(EF)}$	599
1679	Rev·3	Adams 543 $^{(VF)}$	600	1679	1739 Roses	Manville 290$^{(VAS)}$	600
1680	1739 Inver N^s	Bald.55 $^{2396\ (EF)}$	600A	1681	1741 R 14th	Spink 124,$^{1924\ (VAS)}$	601
1682	1741/39 ^{R}	Spink 124,$^{1925\ (VAS)}$	601A	1683	1741 R 14th	Adams 546 $^{(VF)}$	602
1684	1743 R 17th	Adams 547 $^{(EF)}$	603A	1684	Bust D	Adams 547 $^{(EF)}$	603A
1685	1745 R 19th	Adams 548 $^{(EF)}$	604	1686	1745/5	PC (M. Bull) $^{(EF)}$ (delisted)	604A
1687	1745 Lima	Adams 550 $^{(EF)}$	605	1687	Bust E^1	DNW 104, ^{504}	605
1688	1745 Lima	Adams 551 $^{(GEF)}$	606		Bust E^2	DNW 86, ^{797}	
1689	1746/5^{Lim}	Adams 551 ^{GEF}	607	1690	1745 V/U	Adams 552 $^{(GEF)}$	607A
1691	Bust F	PC (M. Bull) $^{(FDC)}$	608	1691	1746P 20th	DNW 86,$^{798(FDC)}$	608
1692	1750 24th	Adams 555 $^{(VAS)}$	609	1693	1751 24th	Manville 306 $^{(VAS)}$	610

GEORGE II - SHILLINGS

ESC	Variety	Provenance	(Old ESC)	ESC	Variety	Provenance	(Old ESC)
1694	1727^{Plumes}	M.R. 22/250 $^{(EF)}$	1189	1695	A-D	Spink 101, ^{707}	1190
1695	1727 $^{R\&P}$	SNC 2011,$^{9723\ (VAS)}$	1190	1695	1727 $^{R\&P}$	M.R. 22/251 $^{(EF)}$	1190
1696	1728 $^{R\&P}$	Spink 139 $^{362\ (EF)}$	1192	1697	E/R		
1698	1728	M.R. 22/252 $^{(EF)}$	1191	1699	1729 $^{R\&P}$	Spink 139 $^{363\ (GEF)}$	1193
1700	Regular 9 date			1701	·DEI		
1702	1731^{Plumes}	Manville 313 $^{(EF)}$	1195	1703	1731$^{R\&P}$	Manville 312 $^{(AEF)}$	1194
1704	A·T / E·ET·E			1705	1732$^{R\&P}$	M.R. 22/255 $^{(VAS)}$	1196
1706	1734 $^{R\&P}$	Manville 315 $^{(AEF)}$	1197	1707	1735 $^{R\&P}$	Norweb 1550 $^{(EF)}$	1198
1708	173 5/5 $^{R\&P}$	M.R. 16/86 $^{(EF)}$	1198A	1709	1736 $^{R\&P}$	DNW 111,$^{166\ (GVF)}$	1199
1710	1736/5	M.R. 22/258 $^{(EF)}$	1199A	1711	1737 $^{R\&P}$	SNC 1980·$^{3694\ (VAS)}$	1200
1712	Unbarred As		1200A	1713	1739 Roses	Spink 139 $^{371\ (EF)}$	1201
1714	1739/7		1201A	1715	1739$^{sm\ star}$	M.R. 22/262 $^{(EF)}$	1201B
1716				1717	1741 Roses	Spink 139 $^{373\ (EF)}$	1202
1718	1741/39	Spink 139 $^{374\ (GVF)}$	1202A	1719	1741Ros.G's	M.R. 8, 252 $^{(VF)}$	1202B
1720	1743 Roses	M.R. 22/264 $^{(AEF)}$	1203	1721	1743/1	SNC 2001 ^{0838}	1203A
1722	1745 Roses	Spink 139 $^{377\ (NEF)}$	1204	1723	1745/3	M.R. 22/265 $^{(EF)}$	1204A
1724	1745 Lima	Spink 139 $^{379\ (VAS)}$	1205	1725	1746 LIMA	Spink 139 $^{380\ (GEF)}$	1206
1726	1746/5	Spink 139 $^{381\ (EF)}$	1207	1727	1746 P	Norweb 258 $^{(FDC)}$	1208
1727	G	SNC 2000, ^{230}	1208	1728	1747 Roses	SNC 2011·$^{9724(GEF)}$	1209
1728	Thin 0	SNC 2001, ^{1976}	1209	1729	1750$^{Thin\ 0}$	Spink 139 $^{384\ (EF)}$	1210
1730	E	Spink 101, ^{709}	1210A	1730	1750/6	Spink 139 $^{385\ (NEF)}$	1210A
1731	Thin 0/7			1732	1750/47	M.R. 22/273 $^{(EF)}$	1211
1732	5/4 Wide O	SNC 2010, $^{9037(EF)}$	1211	1733	1751	Spink 145,$^{2552\ (VAS)}$	1212
1734	1758	Manville 327 $^{(VAS)}$	1213	1735	1758$^{sm\ 58}$		1213A?

GEORGE II - SIXPENCES

ESC	Variety	Provenance	(Old ESC)	ESC	Variety	Provenance	(Old ESC)
1736	Obv A-D	Bole 1, 1726 $^{(GEF)}$	1603	1737	1728 P ^{Pln}	SNC 2005$^{6338\ (AFDC}$	1604
1737	Rev 1 Plain	Bole 1726 $^{DNW\ 89}$	1604	1738	Rev 4 ^{Plumes}	Spink 124,$^{1933(VAS)}$	1605
				1740	1728	Spink 139 $^{391(GEF)}$	1606
1741	1731$^{R\&P}$	Spink 109 $^{486\ (GEF)}$	1607				

(continued)

PROVENANCES

ESC	Variety	Provenance	(Old ESC)	ESC	Variety	Provenance	(Old ESC)
1743	1732	Norweb 1556^{VAS}	1608	1744	1734 $^{R\&P}$	Spink 139 $^{394(EF)}$	1609
1745	1735	Bole 3,152 $^{(NEF)}$	1610	1746	1635/4	**Spink 139 $^{395(EF)}$**	1610A
1747	1736 $^{R\&P}$	Hamilton 463^{Mint}	1611	1748	GEORGV	**Bole 153, $^{DNW\ 91}$**	1610B
1749	1739 ^{Roses}	DNW 91 $^{550\ (GEF)}$	1612	1750	^{GE}O/R^{GIVS}	Spink 139 $^{398(EF)}$	1612A
1751	1741 ^{Roses}	Spink 139 $^{399(EF)}$	1613	1752	1743 ^{Roses}	SNC 2006$^{7144\ (UNC)}$	1614
1753	1745 ^{Roses}	SNC 2006$^{7145\ (UNC)}$	1615	1754	1645/3	**Bole 1, 1730 $^{(VF+)}$**	1616
1754	^{Obv} E	**Bole 1730 $^{DNW\ 89}$**	1616	1754	^{Rev} 3 ^{Roses}	**Bole , 1730 $^{DNW\ 89}$**	1616
1755	1645/4	**DNW $^{74B\ 754\ (VF)}$**	1616A	1756	1745 ^{Lima}	Spink 139 $^{402\ (EF)}$	1617
1757	1746 ^{Lima}	DNW 97 $^{312\ (VAS)}$	1618	1758	1746/5	**Bole 1, 1731 $^{(AEF)}$**	1618A
1759	1746 P	DNW 86,$^{809(FDC)}$	1619	1760	1750 ^{Lge} 0	Spink 139 $^{405\ (EF)}$	1620
1761	1751	Manville 343 $^{(AEF)}$	1621	1762	1757	Spink 139 $^{406\ (EF)}$	1622
1763	1758	**Bole 1, 1734 $^{(VAS)}$**	1623	1764	1758/7	DNW 85, $^{600\ (VAS)}$	1624
XXX	Stop in D	**Bole 1, 1735 $^{(GEF)}$**	1624A				

GEORGE II - MAUNDY SETS

1765	1729	SNC 2008$^{.8562\ (GF)}$	2402	1766	1731	SNC 2008$^{.8638(AEF)}$	2403
1767	1732	SNC 2005$^{.6946\ (EF)}$	2404	1768	1735	SNC 2005$^{.6635\ (GEF)}$	2405
1769	1737	SNC 2011$^{.9741\ (VF)}$	2406	1770	1739	SNC 2008$^{.8564\ (VF)}$	2407
1771	1740	DNW 86,$^{1063\ (EF)}$	2408	1772	1743	SNC 2010,$^{9316\ (VF)}$	2409
1773	1746	SNC 2005$^{.6641(EF)}$	2410	1774	1760	SNC 2007$^{.8276\ (GVF)}$	2411

GEORGE II - MAUNDY GROATS

1775	1729	(SNC 2001, MS1382(VF))	1898	1776		Stop over head	
1777	1731	(SNC 2001, MS1383(AVF))	1899	1778	1732	(SNC 2001, MS1384 (VF))	1900
1779	1735	(SNC 2001, MS1385 (AEF))	1901	1780	1737	(SNC 2001, MS1386 (F))	1902
1781	1739	(M.R. 8/258,259 (EF))	1903	1782	1740	(SNC 2001, MS1387(EF))	1904
1783	1743	(SNC 2001, MS1388 (EF))	1905	1784	174/3		
1785	1746	(SNC 2001, MS1389 (EF))	1906	1786	1760	(SNC 2001, MS1390 (AEF))	1907

GEORGE II - MAUNDY THREEPENCES

1787	1729 sm crown	*(Not traced)*	2019	1788	1729	(SNC 2001, MS1462 (VF))	2019A
1789	1731	(SNC 2001, MS1464 (GVF))	2020	1790	1731^{Sm}		2021
1791	1732		2022	1792	1732 ^{Stop}	SNC 2005$^{.6933(EF)}$	2023
1793	1735		2024	1794	1743	(SNC 2001, MS1469(EF))	2028
1795	1743/0		2028A	1796	1743 ^{Stop}		2030
1797	1737	(SNC 2001, MS1466 (VF))	2025	1798	1739	(SNC 2001, MS1467 (GF))	2026
1799	1740/39	(SNC 2001,MS1468 (EF)	2027	1800	1743 ^{Lge}		2029
1801	1746/3	(SNC 2001, MS1470(VF))	2031	1801	1746/3	London coins 2014, 20944	2031
1801	1746/3	(SNC 2006, 7239(GF))	2031	1802	1746/5		
1803	1760	(SNC 2001, MS1471 (VF))	2032				

GEORGE II - MAUNDY HALFGROATS

1804	1729	(SNC 2001, 1594 (VF))	2226	1805	1731	(SNC 2001, MS1595 (GVF))	2227
1806	1732	(SNC 2001, MS1596 (VF))	2228	1807	1735	(SNC 2001, MS1598 (GVF))	2229
1808	1737	(SNC 2006, 7279(VF))	2230	1809	1739	(SNC 2001, MS1600 (EF))	2231
1810	1740	(SNC 2001, MS1602(AVF))	2232				
1811	1743		2233	1812	1743/0	(SNC 2001, MS1603(AEF))	2233A
1813	1746	(SNC 2006, 7281(GEF))	2234	1814	1756	(SNC 2001, MS1607(AEF))	2235
1815	1759	(SNC 2001, MS1608 (GVF))	2236	1816	1760	(SNC 2001, MS1609 (GVF))	2237

PROVENANCES

GEORGE II - MAUNDY PENNIES

ESC	Variety	Provenance	(Old ESC)	ESC	Variety	Provenance	(Old ESC)
1817	1729	(SNC 2001, MS1662 (AEF))	2331	1818	GRATIA		2331A
1819	1818P thick flan		2331B	1820	1731	(SNC 2001, MS1664 (EF))	2332
1821	1732		2333	1822	1732	(SNC 2001, MS1665(GVF))	2234
1823	1735	(SNC 2001, MS1666 (AEF))	2335	1824	1737	(SNC 2001, MS1667 (GVF))	2336
1825	1739	(SNC 2001, MS1668 (AEF))	2337	1826	1740	SNC 1973 $^{.9084(GVF)}$	2338
1827	1743	(SNC 2001, MS1670 (EF))	2339	1828	1743/0	SNC 2010 $^{9316\,(VF)}$	2339A
1829	1746	(SNC 2002, 4442 VF+))	2340	1830	1746/3		2341
1831	1750	(SNC 2001, MS1674 (EF))	2342	1832	1752	(SNC 1977, 13615 (VF))	2343
1833	1752/0	(SNC 2001, MS1675 (VF))	2344	1834	1753	(SNC 1977, 13616 (VF))	2345
1835	1753/2	(SNC 2001, MS1676 (VF))	2345A	1836	1754	(SNC 2001, MS1677 (AEF))	2346
1837	1755	(SNC 2001, MS1678 (EF))	2347	1838	1756	(SNC 2001, MS1679(EF))	2348
1839	1757	(SNC 1977, 13620 (VF))	2349	1840	1758	(SNC 2001, MS1680 (EF))	2350
1841	1759	(SNC 2001, MS1682 (Mint))	2351	1842	1760	(SNC 2001, MS1683(AEF))	2352
1843	GRATIA:	Colon die flaw de-listed	2349A	1843	GEOR G IVS		2352A

SPANISH COUNTERMARKED DOLLARS (8 Reales)

ESC	Variety	Provenance	(Old ESC)	ESC	Variety	Provenance	(Old ESC)
	Type A	**Oval cmk**			**Type B**	**Octagonal cmk**	
1850	Madrid	Whetmore 197	135	1866	Madrid	Whetmore 214	141
1851	Seville	Whetmore 199	135	1867	Seville	Whetmore 216	143
1852	Mexico	Barr 274 (AEF)	129	1868	Mexico	Bruno 82 (EF)	138
1856	Mexico Pillar	Barr 101 (AEF)	129		Mexico Pillar	?	
1853	Santiago	Barr 439 (EF)	134	1869	Santiago	Bruno 86 (EF)	
1854	Nueva Granada	Whetmore 202	132	1870	Nueva Granada	Bruno 85 (GVF)	140
1855	PoTosI	Whetmore 210	131	1871	PoTosI	Spink 175 ^{1685}	139
1857	PoTosI Pillar	Bruno 72 (GVF)	131		PoTosI Pillar	?	
1858	LIMÆ	Barr 276 (EF)	133	1872	LIMÆ	Selig 1091 (GVF)	140A
1858	LIMÆ Pillar	SNC 2004 $^{.6015}$	133		LIMÆ Pillar	?	
1865	USAS Sm eagle	B.M. Collection		1873	USAS Sm eagle	Bruno 87 (GVF)	
1859	France Bayonne	M.R. 13/206	136	1874	USAS L eagle	Hamilton 480	143
1860	— Constitutional	Bruno 81 (NEF)	136	1874	USAS L eagle	M.R. 17/ 416(GVF)	143
1861	France Toulous	Glens $^{5/1976,139\,(VF)}$	136		France counterfeit	BOE Collection	
1860	France PAU	M.R.17/ 414 (GVF)	136				
1862	France A Paris	Whetmore 197	136				
1863	France M 1792	SJA 9 376 (VF)					
1864	France Tuscany	SJA 9, 377 (GVF)			Trial cmk	SJA 18, 282 (VF)	

GEORGE III - HALF DOLLARS (4 Reales)

	A	Oval cmk			B	Octagonal cmk	
1875	Madrid 1792	M.R. 7/226(VF)	611	1886	Madrid 1791	Adams 578 (VF)	611
1875	Madrid 1792	M.R. 7/226(VF)					
	Inverted cmk	James 11, 193 (EF)	611				
1877	Mexico	Adams 568 (VF)	611	1889	Mexico 1802	DNW 2002 ^{1270}	
1880	PoTosI	Adams 558 (VF)	611	1891	PoTosI 1780	SJA 18,276(VF)	
	— (Pillar)	SNC1971 $^{5916(GF)}$			PoTosI 1776	DNW 101 $^{.441(F)}$	
1879	Nueva Granada	?		1890	Nueva Granada	?	
1878	Santiago	Adams 486a GF	611		Santiago	?	

(continued)

PROVENANCES

ESC	Variety	Provenance	(Old ESC)	ESC	Variety	Provenance	(Old ESC)
1876	Seville	Adams 570^(GVF)	611		Seville	?	
1887	— (Pillar)	M.R. 17/417	611				
1882	LIMÆ	Adams 572 (VF)	611		LIMÆ	?	
1892	USA ½$	BoE Collection					

GEORGE III - 2 Reales

ESC	Variety	Provenance		ESC	Variety	Provenance	
1893	Madrid	Glens 5/1981,509 (VF)		1896	M^adrid Forgery?	(SNC 1971, 5916 (GF))	
1894	Mexico	Spink 174 157(AEF)		1897	LIMÆ	Spink 55, 398 (VF)	

GEORGE III - 1 reale

ESC	Variety	Provenance	
1898	Madrid	BoE Collection	
1899	Mexico	SJA 18, 278 (VF)	
1900	LIMÆ	Glens 1992/10/1, 507(VF)	

GEORGE III - ½ reale

ESC	Variety	Provenance	
1901	Madrid	BoE Collection	
1902	Mexico	DNW 38, 94 (F)	
1902	—(Pillar)	SJA 18,280 (VF)	

1798 CROWNS

ESC	Variety	Provenance	(Old ESC)	ESC	Variety	Provenance	(Old ESC)
1904	1798 A/1		171	1905	1798 A/1 Cu	Lingford 641 VAS	172
1906	1798 C/1		168	1907	1798 C/1 Au	Wils & Ras 143	169
1908	1798 C/1 Cu	Selig 1235 (VAS)	170	1909	1798 C/1 Cu thick	Spk 117, 196 (EF)	170A
1909	1798 C/1 Cu tk	Willis 438 (VAS)	170A	1910	F/1 Cu. Hearts	Lingford 644 EF	173
1911	1798 F/1 Cu		174	1912	1798 G/1	SJA 18,284,(EF)	175
1913	1798 G/1 Cu	Glens 1972, 47 (Mint)	175A	1914	G/1	Lingford 644 EF	175B
	G/1 Cu gilt		175C		I/1. P AG	Lingford 645 EF	
1915	1798 H/1 Sn	Norweb 265 VF/EF	176	1916	1798 I/1 Cu		177
1917				1918	1798 I/1 Cu		178
1919	1798 J/1 Cu	Glen, 1964,382 (EF)	178A	1920	1798 J/1 Sn	Selig 1236 (VAS)	178B
1921	1798 J/1 Pew	SNC 2003, 5687 (VAS)	178C	1922	1798 K/1 Left	Whetmore 191VAS	179
1923	1798 K/1 Cu	Glen 3/1984,258(VAS)	180	1924	1798 K/1 Au	Wils & Ras 145	180A

GEORGE III - BANK OF ENGLAND DOLLARS

ESC	Variety	Provenance	(Old ESC)	ESC	Variety	Provenance	(Old ESC)
1925	1804 A/2	DNW 79 3985(VAS)	144	1926	1804P A/2	SNC 2004,6018 (VAS)	145
1927	1804P A/2 Cu	(Lingford 651 (EF))	146	1928	1804 A/2b		147
1929	1804 B/2	Norweb 266 VAS	148	1929	A-D REX..	Barr 278 (GEF)	148
1930	1804P B/2	Selig 1237 (VAS)	148A	1931	1804 C/2	SNC 2011,9419 (NEF)	149
1932	1804P C/2	Spink 31, 374 (EF)	150	1933	1804P Cu gilt	Lingford 648 (FDC)	151
1933	1804P Cu gilt	DNW 43 1017 (VAS)	151	1934	1804P C/2 Cu	Spink 136 1475(EF)	152
1937	C/2 Cu+Ni	SJA 18, 296 (VAS)	152A	1936	1804P C/2 Ni	SNC2000 3146FDC	152B
1938	1804 C/2a	SNC 2007,8146 (GEF)	153				
1939	1804P C/2a	Selig 1238 (FDC)	154	1940	1804P C/2a Cu	Barr 280 (EF)	155
1941	1804P C/2b	SNC 2002, 2883(GEF)	156	1942	1804P C/2b	(SNC2001, 1874(FDC))	156A
1944	1804P D/2	Willis 443 (AEF)	158	1945	1804P D/2a	Spink 1 258 (VAS)	159
1946	1804P D/2a	Roekel 204 (VAS)	160	1947	1804P D/2a gilt	DNW113 169 (EF)	160A
1948	1804P D/2a Cu	Willis 444 (GEF)	161	1949	1804 D/2b		162
1950	1804P D/2b Cu		163	1951	1804 E/2	Willis 445 (AEF)	164

(continued)

PROVENANCES

ESC	Variety	Provenance	(Old ESC)	ESC	Variety	Provenance	(Old ESC)
1952	1804P E/2	James 18, 307 (VAS)	165	1953	1804 E/2 Thick	Willis 447 (VAS)	165A
1954	1804P E/2 Cu	SNC 2001,3054 (EF)	166	1956	1804P E/2 Cu tk	R-Jones 191 (EF)	164A
1955	1804P E/2 Cu tk	Selig 1239 (VAS)	167	1955	1804P E/2 Cu tk	DNW 89 2171 (VAS)	167
1957	1804 E/3 Mule	Lingford 657 FDC	167B	1958	1804 C/3 Cu	Selig 1242 (FDC)	???
1959	1804 G/3		188	1960	1804 G/3 Cu	Lingford 644 EF	189
1961	1804 H/3	SNC 1981,3964 (GEF)	181	1962	1804 H/3	SNC 1980,7284 (FDC)	181A
1963	1804 I/3	Selig1243/4 (VAS)	182	1964	1804 I/3 Cu		183
1965	1804 I/3 Sn		184	1966	1804 J/3	Spink 46, 739 (EF)	185
1967	1804 J/3 /Oct cmk	SCMB 1982,p 223(EF	186	1967	1804 J/3	Selig 1245 (FDC)	186
1968	1804 J/3 Cu	Selig 1246 (VAS)	187	1969	1804 K/3 Cu	Selig 1247 (VAS)	189X
1970	1804 I/2		190	1971	1804 J/2		191
1972	1804 K/2 Cu	Selig 1241 (VAS)	193	1973	1804 L/2 Cu	Lingford 673 EF	192
1974	1811 C/4	Spk 156 206 (VAS)	194	1975	1811 C/4 Cu	Lingford 664 EF	194A
1976	1811 C/4 Cu	SNC 2002, 4347(VAS)	195	1977	1811 C/4 Cu gilt	Spink 119 182 (VF)	195A
	1811Mule C/5	Lingford 674 VAS	195B				
1978	1811 D/4		196	1979	1811 D/4 Cu		197
1980	1811 C/5 Pln	Lingford 674 VAS	208	1981	1811 C/5 Cu		209
1982	1804 Mule K/2	Lingford 673 EF	199B	1983	1811 K/4	Lingford 658 VAS	198
1984	1811 K/4 Cu	Selig 1249 (VAS)	199	1985	K/4 Cu thick flan	Spink 119 184 (EF)	199A
1986	1811 L/4	Selig 1248 (VAS)	200	1987	1811 L/4 Cu	Spink 38 108 (VAS)	201
1988	1811 L/4 Sn	Lingford 661 VAS	202	1989	Washed flan		202A
1990	1811 L/5	SJA 12,538(FDC)	203	1991	1811 L/5a Cu	Barr 284 (GEF)	204
1992	1811 L/5a Ag	SJA 17,323(FDC)	204A	1993			
1994	1811 K/5a	Lingford 666 VAS	205	1995	Ag Thick flan		
1996	1811 K/5 Cu	Spink 1.260 (VAS)	206	1997	1811 K/5Cu	Willis 449 (VAS)	206A
1998	1811 K/5 Cu thin			1999	1811 K/5Cu Tk		
2000	K/5 Cu piedfort	Selig 1253 (NVF)	206B	2001	1811 K/5Brass	SJA 10,868(GEF)	207
2002	1811 D/5		210	2003			
2004							

GEORGE III – CROWNS

ESC	Variety	Provenance	(Old ESC)	ESC	Variety	Provenance	(Old ESC)
2005	1818 LVIII	Spk 156 194 (Mint)	211	2006	1818 P	DNW89 2183 (VAS)	212
2007	1816 Pat	Glens 1962/10/4,124	213	2008	1818 LVIII	Hamiltn 504 (EF)	213A
2009	Pistrucci	DNW 97, 342	214	2009	1818	Roekel 195 (GEF)	214
2010	1819 LIX	Asher. 201 (Mint)	215	2010	1819 Rev.	DNW 97, 342	215
2011	1819LIX no stp	SNC 2002,4359(GEF)	215A	2012	1819/8	SNC 2002, 4361 (EF)	215B
2012	H - N	Barr 445	215B	2012	M - Y	Barr 445	215B
2013	1819 LX	SNC 2002, 4363(GEF)	216	2014	1819 P		217
2015	1819 P Pln	Whetmore 123	218	2016	1820 LX	SNC 2002, 4394(VAS)	219
2017	1820 P		220	2018	1820/19	Barr 113 (GEF)	220A

GEORGE III – PATTERN - CROWNS

ESC	Variety	Provenance	(Old ESC)	ESC	Variety	Provenance	(Old ESC)
2020	Pa M/1 Ag Pln	Selig 1187& 88	223	2020	B rev. 1	Lingford 459	223
2021	Pattern M/1 Au	Selig 1186 (FDC)	224	2022	Pattern M/1 Cu	DNW102 2643(VAS)	225
2023	Peidfort M/1 Sn	Selig 1189 (VAS)	226		Patn M/1 Sn	Selig 1190 (VAS)	226A
	3x B/1 Ag & Sn	SNC1984 435			Uniface patterns	(Selig 1193-1211)	
2025	Uni 1817Cu	DNW 89 2180 (EF)	225				

(continued)

PROVENANCES

ESC	Variety	Provenance	(Old ESC)	ESC	Variety	Provenance	(Old ESC)
2026	Pattern N/2 ^{Pb}	Selig 1191 $^{(EF)}$	227	2027	Patn N/3 ^{Pb}	Lingford 464	228A
2028				2029	Pattern O ^{Ag}$_{Pln}$	Selig 1184 $^{(FDC)}$	229
2030	Pattern O ^{Au}	Selig 1183 $^{(FDC)}$	230	2031	Pattern P ^{Ag}	Selig 1179 $^{(EF)}$	231
2032	Ob Pat O ^{Sn}	Selig 1185 $^{(VAS)}$	230B	2033			
2034				2035	Pattern Q	Willis 471 $^{(Mint)}$	233
2036	Pattern R	Willis 470 $^{(Mint)}$	232		Pattern Cu	Selig 1180 $^{(VAS)}$	???
2037	Pattern S ^{Ag}	Selig 1199 $^{(VAS)}$	234	2038	Pattern S ^{Pb}	Norweb 1064 ^{EF}	235
2039				2040	Pattern S ^{Au}	Glens 4/1972 ^{377}	234A
2041	Pattern S ^{Sn}	(Lingford 484 $^{(VAS)}$)	234B	2042			
2043	Pattern T ^{Lge}	Willis 467 $^{(GEF)}$	236	2044	Pattern T ^{inc}	Lingford $^{489(VAS)}$	238
2045	Pattern T ^{Small}	Glens 7/1962 $^{-118}$	237	2046	Pattern T ^{Pb}	Lingford $^{485 (EF)}$	239
2047				2048	Pattern S ^{Lge}		240
2049	Pat U Uni. obv			2050	Pat U Uni. obv Pb		244
2051	PatternV rose stps	Lingford $^{488(VAS)}$	241	2052	Pattern V stars	Selig 1204 $^{(VAS)}$	241A
2053	Pattern V Pln edge	Lingford $^{491 (F)}$	242	2054	Pattern W Sn	Lingford $^{490(VAS)}$	242A
	Ob.Pat J ^{Pb}	Selig 1181 $^{(VAS)}$	?		Rv.Pat J ^{Pb}	Selig 1182 $^{(VAS)}$	?
	Pattrn K1 ^{Pb}	Lingford $^{476 (EF)}$	233		Patrn K2 ^{Pb}	Selig 1196 $^{(VAS)}$	
	Ob pat L1 ^{Pb}	Lingford $^{466 (VF)}$			Ob pa L2 ^{Pb}	Lingford467$^{(VAS)}$	
2055	Pat X ^{Ag}$_{Pln}$	SNC$^{2001,3060 (VAS)}$	221	2056	Rev Patn X ^{Pb}	Selig 1211 $^{(VAS)}$	222
2057	Pattern Y ^{Ag}	Selig 1208 $^{(VAS)}$	243	2058	Pattern Y ^{Au}		
2059	Patrn Y ^{Cu}	Barr 116 $^{(AFDC)}$	244		Ob Pat N ^{Cu}	Lingford468$^{(VAS)}$	
2060	Pattern YAu/Cu		245		Ob Pat P ^{Ag}	SNC 1978, ^{9550}	
	Rev Pat O ^{Pb}	Barr 291 (EF)					

LAST OR NEW COINAGE

GEORGE III - BANK TOKENS - THREE SHILLINGS

ESC	Variety	Provenance	(Old ESC)	ESC	Variety	Provenance	(Old ESC)
2061	1811 A^{var}/1^1	**Bull**		2062	1811P A^{var}/1^1	*(Not traced)*	
2063	1811 A^1/1^1	DNW 91 $^{562 (EF+)}$	407	2064	1811P A^1/1^1		407A
2065	1811 A^1/1^2	SJA 24,192$^{(FDC)}$	408	2066	1811P A^1/1^2		409
2067	1811 A^2/1^1	SJA 24,190$^{(FDC)}$	409A				
2068	1811 A^2/1^2		410				
2069	1811 A^2/1^3		411	2070	1811P A^2/1^3		412
	1811 A^3/1^1			2071	1811P A^3/1^1	SJA 24,191(FDC)	414A
	1811 A^3/1^2			2072	1811P A^3/1^2	DNW ^{124}$_{2171}$	414B
2073	1811 A^3/1^4	Baldwin FPL '13/14,140	413	2074	1811P A^3/1^4		414
2075	1812 A^1/2	SJA 24,191 $^{(FDC)}$	415		1812P A^1/1^2		
2077	1812 B^1/3		419	2078	1812P^{Pt}B^1/3		420
2079	1812 B^2/3	SNC $^{2006 7073(GEF)}$	416	2080	1812P B^2/3	SNC 19847483(FDC)	417
2081	1812 ^{Au} B^2/3	Wils & Ras 149					
2082	1813 B^2/3	DNW89 $^{2172 (VAS)}$	421				
2083	1814 B^2/3	(DNW 59,312 (EF))	422				
2084	1815 B^2/3	SNC$^{2006 7075(GEF)}$	423				
2085	1816 B^2/3	SNC$^{2003 5386 (GEF)}$	424				

PROVENANCES

GEORGE III - HALFCROWNS

ESC	Variety	Provenance	(Old ESC)	ESC	Variety	Provenance	(Old ESC)
2086	1816 ^{BH}	Adams 582 $^{(GEF)}$	613	2087	1816 P ^{Milled}	Adams 583 $^{(VAS)}$	614
2088	1816 P ^{Plain}	SNC^{2000,4306} $^{(Mint)}$	615	2088	1816 P ^{Pln}	Adams 584 $^{(VAS)}$	615
2089	1816 $^{Trial Cu}$	Selig 1178 $^{(VAS)}$	?		B/2 ^{1817}	PC (M. Bull)	
2090	1817	Adams 585 $^{(VAS)}$	616	2091	1817 $^{D/T}$	Bull $^{GEF\ (Adams\ 590)}$	616A
2092	$^{I/S\ in}$ PENSE	SNC 2001^{G3068}	616B	2093	1817 P ^{Milled}	Adams 591 $^{(VAS)}$	617
2094	1817 P ^{Cu}	Adams 589 $^{(GVF)}$	617A	2095	1817 P ^{Pln}	(Glens16/1968,252(FDC))	617B
2096	1817 SH	DNW83,$^{3119(GEF)}$	618	2097	1817 P ^{milled}	Adams 594 $^{(GEF)}$	619
2098	1817 P ^{Pln}	Adams 595 $^{(GEF)}$	620	2099	1818	Adams 598 $^{(GEF)}$	621
2100	^{Reversed} S	Spink 109$^{285(AEF)}$	621A	2101	1818 P	Adams 599 $^{(FDC)}$	622
2102	1819	Adams 600 $^{(GEF)}$	623	2103	1819/8	Adams 602 $^{(EF)}$	623A?
2104	1819 P	Adams 603$^{(FDC)}$	624	2105	1820	Adams 604 $^{(GEF)}$	625
2106	1820 P ^{Pln}	Spink 55,$^{383(FDC)}$	626	2107	1820 P ^{Mil}	Adams 606 $^{(FDC)}$	626A
2108	1817^{Pat}B^1$_{Mil}$	Adams 596 $^{FDC)}$	627	2109	$^{Pat.}$ B^2	Adams 597 $^{(Mint)}$	627A
2110	181 ^{unfinished}	M.R. 12, 157		2111	$^{Uniface\ obv.}$	Adams 592 $^{(GEF)}$	627B

GEORGE III - EIGHTEEN PENCE

ESC	Variety	Provenance	(Old ESC)	ESC	Variety	Provenance	(Old ESC)
2112	1811 A	SNC 2012^{9850} $^{(UNC)}$	969	2112	1811 A	SNC ^{1998,}$_{1988(Mint)}$	969
2113	1811 P	SNC$^{2006,7090(FDC)}$	970	2114	1812 A	SNC ^{2006,}$_{7091\ (UNC}$	971
2115	1812 B	SNC^{2006,7092} $^{(UNC)}$	972	2116	1812 P B	SNC ^{2003}$_{,5691\ FDC}$	973
2116	1812 P	Selig 1257 $^{(VAS)}$	973	2117	1812 P $^{sm\ lets}$	SNC $^{2005,6332(FDC)}$	975
2118	1812 P ^{Pt}	SJA 24,211 $^{(FDC)}$	974	2119	1813	DNW 59,$^{320(GEF)}$	976
2120	1813 P ^{Pt}	(Cokayne Sale)	976A	2121	1814 B	DNW 102, ^{2636}	977
2121	1814	SNC 2006,^{7095} $^{(UNC)}$	977	2122	1815	SNC^{2006,7096} $^{(UNC)}$	978
2123	1816	SNC 2006,^{7097} $^{(UNC)}$	979				

GEORGE III - SHILLINGS

ESC	Variety	Provenance	(Old ESC)	ESC	Variety	Provenance	(Old ESC)
2124	$^{North-ber-land}$	M.R. 22, 297 $^{(GVF)}$	1214	2124	^{1663} A &B	M.R. 22, $^{297(GVF)}$	1214
2125	1787$_{No\ hts}$	DNW 85 $^{609\ AEF)}$	1216	2125	1787 ^{hearts}	SNC2010$^{9219(EF)}$	1216
2126	1/1787$_{n\ ht}$	DNW 85 $^{609\ AEF)}$	1216A	2127	1787 P $_{n\ h}$	Spink 6 $^{743\ (VF)}$	1217
2128	1787/6	DNW 86, ^{1097}	1222	2129	1887 ^{hearts}	DNW 97, ^{328}	1225
2129	^{1787}A & B	DNW 97, ^{328}	1225	2130	1/1787	SNC ^{2012}$_{9862(UNC)}$	1225A
	1787 P$_{coll}$	Spink 14, $^{405\ (AFDC)}$	1225B				
2132	1787 No collar	SNC ^{2011,9730} $^{(VAS)}$	1226	2132	No collar$_{heavy}$	Spink55,$^{387(AFDC)}$	1226
2133	1787 $^{no\ hts}$	SNC2010^{9220} $^{(EF)}$	1218	2134	No stop P$_{mil}$		1219
2135	No stop P $_{Pln}$		1220	2136	^{1787}P $_{heavy}$	SNC ^{2001,3086} GEF	1221
2137	1787P ^{Stop}	Norweb 1036 ^{EF}	1224	2138	1787 $^{No\ stp}$	SNC ^{2001,3085} (VF)	1223
2139	1798D&M	Selig 1223 $^{(VAS)}$	1227	2140	1816	Sommer ^{2770} Mint	1228
2141	1816 P $_{milled}$		1229	2142	1816 P ^{Au}	Spk 157,$^{547(AFDC)}$	1230
2143	1816 P $_{Plain}$	Spink 55,^{390} (FDC)	1231	2144	1817	Sommer ^{2771} GEF	1232
2145				2146			
2147	$^{1817\ HON}$I/S	SNC ^{2002} 3885 (VF)	1232B				
2148	GEOE	PC(RF/NP)$^{(VAS)}$		2148	GEOE	SCMB1987$_{p\ 144\ (NEF)}$	1232A
2149	1817 P ^{Pln}	PC(RF/NP)$^{(FDC)}$	1233	2149	1817 P ^{Pln}	SNC^{2006,7134} (FDC)	1233
2150	1818	SNC 2001 $^{0843\ (GEF)}$	1234	2151	1818 $^{high\ 8}$	Sommer ^{2773} VAS	1234A
2152	1819	Sommer ^{2774} $^{(VAS)}$	1235	2153	1819/3	Spink 228, lot783	
2154				2155	1819/8	M.R. 22, $^{313(VAS)}$	1235A
2156	1820	Sommer ^{2775} $^{(VAS)}$	1236	2157			

(continued)

PROVENANCES

ESC	Variety	Provenance	(Old ESC)	ESC	Variety	Provenance	(Old ESC)
2158				2159	$_{1820}$ HONI/S	SNC^{2010,9043} (VAS)	1236A
2160	H /⌐	M.R. 22/317 (EF)	1236B	2161	$^H_{\ominus}$NI $^S_{\ominus}$IT	M.R.22/315 (UNC)	1236C
2162	1820 P	Norweb 589 (FDC)	1237	2163	^{1764}D^1 rev	M.R. $^{17/403}$(GEF)	1238
2164	^{1764}D^{1Heavy}		1238A	2165	1775 D^2		1239
2166	1778$^P_{D1}$ ^{Pln}	SNC 2001^{3081} (FDC)	1240	2166	1778$^P_{D1}$ ^{Pln}	PC(RF/NP)$^{(VAS)}$	1240
2166	$^{Pat.}$D $^{obv/rev}$	M.R. 22, ^{298} (EF)	1240	2167			
2168	$^{1778P}_{D1}$ ^{heavy}	SNC1995$^{5610(EF)}$	1240A	2169			
2169	^{1786} ^{Pat}E6	Glens$^{1962,138(FDC)}$	1215	2170	^{1787} ^{Pat}E	Glen$^{1962/10/4}$ 138	
2170	^{1787} ^{Pat}E	M.R. 22, 299 $^{(GEF)}$	1241	2171	^{Pat}F ^{Thicker}	Selig 1221 $^{(VAS)}$	1241A
				2172	1787 ^{Pat}F	DNW93 $^{1665(GEF)}$	1242
2173	G $^{Droz\ obv}$	Selig 1222	1242A	2173	G $^{Droz\ rev}$	ESC 1242a	1242A
2175	H ^{Obv}	PC(RF/NP) $^{(VAS)}$	1243	2175	H ^{Obv}	M.R. 19, ^{179} (FDC)	1243
2176	1798 $^{Au/Ag}$	Selig 1224 $^{(VAS)}$	1243A	2177	1798$^{Cu}_{Thk}$	Selig 1225 $^{(VAS)}$	1244
2178	1798 ^{Pb}	Selig 1226 $^{(VAS)}$	1244A	2179	1798 ^{P}I $_{obv}$	,380 (VAS)	
	$^{Fullerton}_{1799Thk}$	Dolph$^{in\ 2.\ 626\ (FDC)}$		2180			
2181	1816 ^{Pat}I	Glen $^{1962/10/4,13}$ (EF)	1245	2182	$^{(1816)}$J $_{Au}$	W&R 183	

GEORGE III - NINEPENCE

ESC	Variety	Provenance	(Old ESC)	ESC	Variety	Provenance	(Old ESC)
2183	1812 P ^{B1}	Selig 1259 $^{(FDC)}$	1480	2184	1812 P ^{B2}	SNC$^{2003, 5694(FDC)}$	1478
2185	1812 P ^{Cu}		1479	XXX	1825 Mule 9d/¼d?	Bald. 52 ^{620} (EF)	1479A

GEORGE III - SIXPENCES

ESC	Variety	Provenance	(Old ESC)	ESC	Variety	Provenance	(Old ESC)
2186	1/A	SNC^{2006,7152} (GEF)	1626	2187	1787 P ^{Pln}		1627
2188	1787P$_{Hevy}$	SNC^{2006,7153} (GEF)	1628	2189	1787$^{with\ ht}$	SNC ^{2011,9791} (VAS)	1629
2189	2/A	Bole 165 $^{,DNW\ 89}$	1629	2190	1816	SNC 2006^{,7158} (UNC)	1630
2191	1816 P ^{Au}		1631	2192	1816/4?	Bole 5, 1459 $^{(EF)}$	1631B
2193	1816P8/6	Bole 4, 50 $^{(EF+)}$	1631A	2193	B/3	Bole 15 $^{DNW\ 92}$	1631A
2194	1817	SNC^{2005,6762} (GEF)	1632	2195	1817 P ^{Pln}	Bole 3,162 $^{(AFDC)}$	1633
2196	1817 P ^{Mil}	Bole 1,1748$^{(FDC}$	1633A	2197			
2198	1818	SNC 2006^{,7160} (UNC)	1634	2199	1818 P ^{Mil}	Bole 1,1749$^{(FDC}$	1635
2200	1819	SNC 2006^{,7162} (EF)	1636	2201	1819 $^{sm\ 8}$	SNC $^{2010,9244(UNC)}$	1636A
2202	1819/8	Bole 167 $^{DNW\ 90}$	1636B	2202	T/B	Bole 167 $^{DNW\ 90}$	1636B
2203	1819 P ^{Mil}	Bole 1, 1750 $^{(EF+)}$	1637	2204	1820	SNC2005$^{6765(GEF}$	1638
2205				2206	1820 P ^{Mil}	Bole 1, 1751 $^{(FDC)}$	1639
2207	^{Inverted}1	SPK 201,^{370} $^{(EF)}$	1639A	2208	HONI/S	Bole 3,165 $^{(EF+)}$	1639B?
2209	$^{No\ colons}$	Bole 3,166 $^{(NEF)}$	1639C?	2210	1786 Pat	Glens$^{1962,138(FDC}$	1625
2211	^{Pat}C/1 ^{Pln}	Selig 1228 $^{(VAS)}$	1640	2212	^{Pat}C/2	Bole 1, 1737$^{(EF+}$	1640A
2213	^{Patt}D ^{Plain}	DNW 101 ^{722} $^{(EF)}$	1641	2213	^{Trial}D ^{Pb}	DNW 101$^{721(EF)}$	1641
				2215	^{Pat}E/1 ^{Mill}	M.R. 19, 181$^{(EF)}$	1642
2216	^{Pat}E/1 ^{Au}	DNW 89$^{1740(AVF)}$	1643	2216	^{Pat}E/1 ^{Au}	Bole 1, 1738 $^{(AVF)}$	1643
2217	^{Pat}E/1 ^{Cu}		1644	2218	$^{Pat.}$E/2 ^{Pln}	Bole 1, 1741 $^{(GEF)}$	1645
2219	$^{Pat.}$E/2 ^{Mill}	Bole 1, 1742 $^{(AE)}$	1646	2220	$^{Pat.}$E/2Mill $_{Au}$		1646A
2221	^{Pat}E/3 ^{Pln}	Bole 1, 1743 $^{(AEF)}$	1647	2222	^{Pat}E/3$^{Au}_{Pl}$	Bole 1,1745$^{(AEF)}$	1648
2223	^{Pat}E/3 ^{Cu}	Bole 1, 1745 $^{(GEF)}$	1649	2224	$^{2\ x\ obvs\ Cu}$	Bole 1,1746$^{(EF+)}$	1650
2225	^{Pat}F ^{Milled}	Bole 1, 1747 $^{(EF)}$	1651	2226	^{Pat}F ^{Plain}	Bole 5, 1457$^{(GEF}$	1652
2227	Barb.^{Pat}A	Bole 3,167 $^{(EF)}$	?	2228	Barb.^{Pat}B	Bole 3, 168 $^{(EF)}$	?

PROVENANCES

GEORGE III - MAUNDY SETS

ESC	Variety	Provenance	(Old ESC)	ESC	Variety	Provenance	(Old ESC)
2229	1763	SNC 2010 $^{9392\ (GEF)}$	2412	2230	1763 P		2413
2231	1766	SNC 2008 $^{8568\ (EF)}$	2414	2232	1772	SNC 2005 $^{6631(EF)}$	2415
2233	1780	SNC 2005 $^{6646\ (GEF)}$	2416	2234	1784	DNW 79 $^{3196\ (VAS)}$	2417
2235	1786	SNC 2005 $^{6647(NEF)}$	2418	2236	1792 ^{Wire}	SNC 2005 $^{6648\ (EF)}$	2419
2237	1795	SNC 2005 $^{6651\ (EF)}$	2420	2238	1800	**SNC 2011**$^{9797\ (AEF)}$	2421
2239	1817	SNC 2005 $^{6657\ (EF)}$	2422	2240	1818	SNC 2011 $^{9492\ (GEF)}$	2423
2241	1820	SNC 2005 $^{6658\ (EF)}$	2424				

GEORGE III - MAUNDY GROATS

2242	1763		1908	2243	1763 P		1908A
2244	1765	SNC 2000, $^{252\ (EF)}$	1909	2245	1766		1910
2246	1770	(SNC 1977, 13623 (VF))	1911				
2247	1772		1912	2248	1772/0	(SNC2006,7176 (AVF))	1913
2249	1776	SNC $^{2001\ MS1391\ (VF)}$	1914	2250	1780		1915
2251	1784		1916	2252	1786		1917

GEORGE III - MAUNDY THREEPENCES

2253	1762	SNC 2010 $^{.9138\ (UNC)}$	2033				
2254	1763	(SNC 2006, 7241(VF))	2034	2255	1763 P	SJA 7, 395 $^{(AEF)}$	2034A
2256	1765	SNC 2001 $^{.3120\ (AEF)}$	2035	2257	1765/3	**DNW 80,** $^{166(VF)}$	2035A?
2258	1766		2036	2259	1770	(SNC 2001, MS1475 (GVF))	2037
2260	1772 ^{Small}	(SNC 2001, MS1475 (GF))	2038	2261	1772 $^{v\ lge}$	(SNC 2001, MS1477 (EF))	2039
2260	1772 $^{v\ sm}$		2040	2263	1780		2041
2264	1784	SJA 14, 244 $^{(UNC)}$	2042	2265	1786	(SNC 2001, MS1479 (F))	2043
2266	1818 ʌ			2267	1795 ^{Au}	Wilson & Ras 153	2043A

GEORGE III - MAUNDY HALFGROATS

2269	1763		2238	2270	1763 P	SNC 1987 $^{6646(VAS)}$	2238A
2271	1765	**M.R. 7/225** $^{(VF)}$	2239	2272	1766		2240
2273	1772	(SNC 2001, MS1611 (VF))	2241	2274	1772 7/6	(SNC 2001, MS1612 (VF))	2242
2276	1776		2243		1776 ^{MAG}	(SNC 2001, MS1613 (GF))	2243A
2279	1780	(SNC 1970, 7351 (EF))	2244	2280	1784	SJA 14, 245 $^{(UNC)}$	2245
2281	1786	Rich. $^{Sum\ 2006,142(EF)}$	2246	2282	1786 $^{Lg\ lets}$		2247
	1816			2283	1817	(SNC 2006, 7284(VF))	
2284	1818	(SNC 2006, 7285(VF))			1819		
	1820	(SNC 2006, 7286(EF))		2268	1795 ^{Au}	Wilson & Ras 154	2047A?

GEORGE III - MAUNDY PENNIES

2285	1763	(SNC 2003, 5208 (AEF))	2353	2286	1763 P		2353a
2287	1765			2288	1766		2354
2289	1770	(SNC 1977, 13623 (VF))	2355	2290	1772	(SNC 2001, MS1686 (EF))	2356
2291	1776 $^{7/7}$	(Bald Arg1/6/13,239(EF)	2357	2293	1779	(SNC 1977, 13625 (VF))	2358
2294	1780	(SNC 1977, 13626 (VF))	2359	2295	1781	(SNC 1977, 13627 (VF))	2360
2296	1784	(SNC 2003, 5210 (AEF))	2361	2297	1786	(SNC 2006, 77355(AVF))	2362
2298	1795No st obv		2420	2299	1795 lage lets		2421

Maundy odds are found easily so ignored from this reign onwards

PROVENANCES

GEORGE IV - CROWNS

ESC	Variety	Provenance	(Old ESC)	ESC	Variety	Provenance	(Old ESC)
2310	1821 ^{2nd}	SNC 2001,$^{1875\ (VAS)}$	246	2311	$^{WWP\ inverted}$	Barr 292 $^{(EF)}$	246A
2312	1821 P^{2nd}	SNC 2002, $^{4370(FDC)}$	247	2313			
2314	1821 P^{Cu}	Spink 69,$^{359\ (FDC)}$	248	2315			
2316	1821 P^{Cu}	Norweb 1067 ^{EF}	249	2317	1821 ^{obv}A	DNW 89, ^{2203}	250
2317	1821 ^{rev} 1	DNW 89,$^{2203(VAS)}$	250	2317	1821 P ^{3rd}	Willis 515 $^{(VAS)}$	250
2318	1822 ^{2nd}	Spink 1, 276 ^{Mint}	251	2319	1822 P^{2nd}		251A
2320	1822 ^{3rd}	Roekel 211 $^{(Mint)}$	252	2321	1822 P ^{3rd}	Spink 31$^{404(AFDC)}$	253
2322	$^{1820\ P}$A/1a	Lingford 507	262	2323			
2328	1823 P ^{Pln}	Lingford $^{514\ (FDC)}$	254	2329	1823P ^{Wm}	SNC 1993 ,^{2624a}	254A
2330	1829^{P}A/2	Lingford 507	266	2331	1825^{P}B/3	Willis 515 $^{(VAS)}$	255
2332	1825^{Barton}	Spink 1 $^{277\ FDC}$	256	2333			
2334				2335			
2336	1826 P ^{7th}	Norweb 275 ^{FDC}	257	2337			
2338	1826 P ^{Pln}	Willis 5185 $^{(VAS)}$	258	2339	1826 ^{LVIII}	Glens 1962, $^{158\ (EF)}$	258A
2340	P ^{Cu} C/3		258B	2341	^{1828}D/3$_{Cu}$	Norweb 595 ^{EF}	264
2342	^{1828}D/3$_{Cu}$	Norweb 1645 ^{EF}	265	2343	^{1828Pat}D/3	Spink 96 $^{284\ (VAS)}$	263
2344	^{1829P}E/4	SNC1969, $^{9989\ (FDC)}$	267	2345	^{1829P}E/4	Lingford 527$^{(FDC)}$	268
2346	^{1829}E/4 ^{Cu}	Spink 38$^{135\ (AFDC)}$	269	2348	1829	Lingford 530	270
				2350	^{Pat} G/5	Glens 1961,^{130}	259
2350	^{Pat} G/5	DNW 89 $^{2202\ (VAS)}$	259	2351	G/5 ^{Au}	Wilson & Ras 255	260
2352	^{Pat} F/5	Glens 1961, ^{131}	261	2352	^{Pat} F/5	Glens 1961,^{130}	261
2353	Tooth beading	Lingford 506	262A	2353	^{Pat} A/6^{Wm}	DNW 113 $^{213\ (EF)}$	265A
	'22 uni ob. pb	Rees-Jones 222^{VAS}			Uni Cu	Glens $^{11/}$1979 ^{349}	
2355	Patt G/6^{Wm}	DNW 113 $^{214\ (EF)}$	265B	2355	^{Pat} G ^{rev} 6	DNW 113 $^{214\ (EF)}$	265B
	Uni Ag	Glens $^{11/}$1979 ^{348}			182? P ^{8th}		258C
	Uni Pln	Lingford 529					

GEORGE IV - HALFCROWNS

ESC	Variety	Provenance	(Old ESC)	ESC	Variety	Provenance	(Old ESC)
2356	$^{Obv.}$ Trial	Adams 607 $^{(EF)}$	628A?	2357	1820	Adams 608 $^{(GEF)}$	628
2358	$^{Obv.}$ A	Bull	629	2358	$^{Rev.}$ 1	Bull	629
2358	1820 P	Bull $^{(FDC)\ Adams\ 609}$	629	2359	1820 P ^{Pln}	Norweb 276 ^{FDC}	630
2360	1821$^{Light\ g}$	Bull $^{(VAS)\ Adams\ 612}$	631	2360	$^{Rev.}$ 1a	Bull	631
2361	1821$_{Light}$	Spink 147$^{623(GEF)}$	632	2362	1821^{Heavy}	Adams 614 $^{(VF)}$	631A
2363	1821$_{P\ hevy}$	Bull^{FDC} Adams ^{615}	632A	2364	1823^{Heavy}	Adams 617 $^{(EF)}$	633
2365	1823	DNW 83,$^{3145(GEF)}$	634	2365	$^{Rev.}$ 2	Bull	634
2366	1823 P	Adams 619 $^{(VAS)}$	635	2367	1824	Adams 620 $^{(EF)}$	636
2368	1824 P		637	2369	1824 P ^{Cu}	Norweb 1068 ^{VAS}	638
2370	1824	SNC 1975, $^{5543(Mint)}$	639	2371	1825	Adams 629 $^{(GEF)}$	642
2372	1825 P$_{Mill}$	Adams 631 $^{(FDC)}$	643	2372	$^{Rev.}$ 3	Bull	643
2373	1825 P ^{Pln}	Adams 632 $^{(FDC)}$	644	2374	1825P ^{Bart}	Adams 633 $^{(FDC)}$	645
2375	1826	DNW 83,$^{3149(GEF)}$	646	2376	1826 P	Adams 636 $^{(FDC)}$	647
2377	1828	Adams 637 $^{(GEF)}$	648	2378	1829	Adams 638 $^{(GEF)}$	649
2379	$^{1820\ Pat}$D^{1}	Adams 611 $^{(FDC)}$	649A	2380	$^{1820\ Pat}$D^{2}	Adams 610$^{(VAS)}$	649B?
2381	$^{1822\ Pat}$E	SNC 1991, ^{3691}	650	2382	$^{1822\ Pat}$E^{Pln}		651
2383	$^{1823\ Pat}$F	Adams 616 $^{(FDC)}$	652	2384	$^{1824\ Pat}$F	Adams 621 $^{(FDC)}$	653
2385	$^{1824\ P}$G$^{1}_{Mill}$	Adams 623 $^{(FDC)}$	639A	2385	1824 P ^{Pln}	Norweb 1068	639B
2386	^{1824Pat}G$^{1}_{Pln}$	Adams 624 $^{(GEF)}$	639B	2387	1824 P ^{Au}	Spink 38 $^{135(EF)}$	640

(continued)

PROVENANCES

ESC	Variety	Provenance	(Old ESC)	ESC	Variety	Provenance	(Old ESC)
2388	1824 P^{Cu}	Adams 626 *(VAS)*	641	2389	1824 P^{Pb}	Adams 627 *(VF)*	641A
2390	1824P Uni$_{Bart}$	Adams 628 *(VAS)*	641B	2390	Pat G^{Bartons}	Adams 628 *(VAS)*	641B
2391	1824 P G$^2_{obli}$	**Adams 625** *(FDC)*	639C	2392	Binfield H^{Ag}	**Norweb 596** *FDC*	654
2393	Binfield H^{Cu}	Adams 639 *(FDC)*	655				

GEORGE IV – SHILLINGS

ESC	Variety	Provenance	(Old ESC)	ESC	Variety	Provenance	(Old ESC)
2394	1820 P	**Norweb 597** *VAS*	1246	2395	1820P^{JBM}	SNC 2002 $^{2537(FDC)}$	1246A
2396	1821	Sommer $^{2776\ (VAS)}$	1247	2397	1821 P^{Mil}	Spink 12 339 *(FDC)*	1248
2398	1823	Sommer $^{2777\ GEF}$	1249	2399	1823 P	SNC 2000· $^{2407(FDC)}$	1250
2400	1824	Sommer $^{2778\ (VAS)}$	1251	2401	1824 P	SNC 2002·$^{2538(FDC)}$	1252
2402	1825	DNW 89,$^{1993(GEF)}$	1253	2402	2	**DNW 102,** ^{2658}	1253
2403	1825 P	SNC 2003· $^{5504(VAS)}$	1253A	2404	1825/3	SNC 1978 $^{11989(VAS)}$	1253B
2405	1825	SNC 2006,$^{7796\ (VAS)}$	1254	2406	Roman I date	**DNW104** $^{548\ (AF)}$	1254A
2407	1825 P	SNC 2010$^{9223\ (FDC)}$	1255	2408	1825P^{Bartn}	SNC 1975·$^{218\ (FDC)}$	1256
2409	1826	SNC 2011· $^{9731\ (EF)}$	1257	2409	1826	**SNC 2010**$^{9370\ (AEF)}$	1257
2410	1826/2^{or}8	**SNC 2010**·$^{9047\ (VF)}$	1257A	2411	1826 P	SNC 2010·$^{9371\ (FDC)}$	1258
2412	1827	M.R. 22/345 *(VAS)*	1259	2413	1829	Sommerville $^{2784\ (EF)}$	1260
2414	1829 P	SNC 2002· $^{2541(FDC)}$	1261	2415	C	**Glens 1968** ^{265}	1262
2416	1824 ^{Pat} C	SNC 2003· $^{5727(VAS)}$	1263	2417	1825 ^{Pat} D	Baldwn.44 $^{979\ (FDC)}$	1264
2418	1825$^{Pat}_{Bart}$	SNC 2000·$^{2411\ (FDC)}$	1265	2419	1826 Trial E	**Spink 203,** $^{356\ (VF)}$	1265A

GEORGE IV - SIXPENCES

ESC	Variety	Provenance	(Old ESC)	ESC	Variety	Provenance	(Old ESC)
2420	1820 P ^{Mil}	Norweb 498 *(EF)*	1653	2420	A/1	Bole 1752 $^{DNW\ 89}$	1653
2421	1821	DNW 89 $^{1996(GEF)}$	1654	2422	1821 ^{Plain}	Bole 1, 1753 *(EF+)*	1654A
2423	1821 P ^{Mil}	SNC 2002·$^{3369\ (FDC)}$	1655	2424	BBITANNIAR	**SNC 2010**$^{9109\ (GEF)}$	1656
2425	1824	SNC 2010·$^{9245\ (UNC)}$	1657	2426	1824 P ^{Mil}	**Bole 1, 1754** *(EF+)*	1658
2427	1825	DNW 83,$^{3166(VAS)}$	1659	2428	1825 P	*(Not traced)*	1659A
2429	1825 ^{Barton}	*(Not traced)*	1659B	2430	1826	DNW 83,$^{3167(AEF)}$	1660
2431	1826 P ^{Pln}	Bole 1, 1757 *(GEF)*	1661	2432	1826 P ^{Mil}	Bole 3, 172 *(EF+)*	1661A
2433	1826	DNW 86·$^{1144\ (GEF)}$	1662	2434	Extra tuft hair		1662A
2435	1826 P ^{Mil}	SNC 2010·$^{9246\ (FDC)}$	1663	2436	1826P ^{Pew}	Bole 3, 1738 $^{(NVF)}$	1663A
2437	1827	DNW 83,$^{3169(AEF)}$	1664	2438	1828	**Bole 1, 1759** *(VAS)*	1665
2439	1829	**Spk 224, 771** *(GEF)*	1666	2440	1829 P ^{Mil}	Bole 1, 1760 $^{(AFDC)}$	1667
2441	1825 P ^{Mil}	**Bole 1, 1756** *(EF+)*	1668	2442	1825 thick flan		1668A
2443	1826 ^{Pat} C		1669				

GEORGE IV - MAUNDY SETS

ESC	Variety	Provenance	(Old ESC)	ESC	Variety	Provenance	(Old ESC)
2444	1822	DNW 79 $^{3255\ (Mint)}$	2425	2445	1822 P		2426
2446	1823	SNC 2006 $^{7179\ (AEF)}$	2427	2447	1824	SNC 2011 $^{9496\ (EF)}$	2428
2448	1825	DNW 83 $^{3173\ (GVF)}$	2429	2449	2d - T/B		2429A
2450	1826	SNC 2008 $^{8577\ (AEF)}$	2430	2451	2d - T/B		2430A
2452	1827	**SNC 2011** $^{9499(EF+)}$	2431	2453	1828	SJA 12, 836 $^{(EF+)}$	2432
2454	1828 P		2433	2455	1829	SNC 2008 $^{8579\ (AEF)}$	2434
2456	1830	SNC 2011 $^{9798(AFDC)}$	2435		1822 Sm head	**Esc 2425** $^{(EF)}$	2425

PROVENANCES

WILLIAM IV - CROWNS

ESC	Variety	Provenance	(Old ESC)	ESC	Variety	Provenance	(Old ESC)
	A $^{W.W.incus}$	Slaney 229 $^{(FDC)}$		2460	A$^{1\ W.W.WYON}$	Glens 1961,^{138}	273
2460	1831 P ^{Pln}	Lingford 535	273	2461	WW/W Wyon	Bald FPL $^{Wintr\ 2010}$	271A?
2462	1831 P ^{Pln}	Spk 85 119 $^{(GEF)}$	271	2462	1831 P ^{Pln}	Norweb 278 $^{(FDC)}$	271
2463	1831 P ^{Au}	Glens 4/1972, ^{378}	272	2464	1832$^{Pat\ Pb}$	Lingford 536	274
2465	1834 P ^{Pln}	SJA 6, 315 $^{(FDC)}$	275	2466			275A
2467	B^{1}/2	Glens 1961,^{136}	276	2467	B^{1}/2	SJA 23,239 $^{(VAS)}$	276
2467	B^{1}/2	Glens 1961,^{136}	276	2468	B^{1}/2 $^{Pln\ Pb}$	Glens. $^{5/1974,192\ (EF)}$	277
2469	A^{1}/2	SNC 1997 $^{5647(FDC)}$	278	2470	18-- ^{Pat} 3	Lingford 542	
2471	1837 ^{Pat} 4	Lingford 541					

WILLIAM IV - HALFCROWNS

ESC	Variety	Provenance	(Old ESC)	ESC	Variety	Provenance	(Old ESC)
2472	1831	(Not traced)	656	2473	1831 P ww	Adams 640 $^{(FDC)}$	657
	Rev.	PC $^{(M.\ Bull)\ (FDC)}$		2473	Obv.	Bull ^{FDC} Adams ^{640}	657
2474	1834 ^{WW}	Adams 643 $^{(GEF)}$	660	2475	1834 P $^{W.W.}$	(Not traced)	661
2476	1831P ^{WW}	Adams 642 $^{(FDC)}$	659	2477	1831 P ^{WW}	Adams 641 $^{(FDC)}$	658
2478	1834 ^{WW}	Adams 644 $^{(GEF)}$	662	2479	1834 P ww	Adams 646 $^{(FDC)}$	663
2480	1834 P ^{Pln}	(Not traced)	664	2481	1835 ^{WW}	Adams 647 $^{(GEF)}$	665
2482	1836 ^{WW}	Adams 648 $^{(EF)}$	666	2483	1836/5	PC $^{(M.\ Bull)\ (GEF)}$	666A
2484	S/S	Bull		2485	1836 P ^{Pln}	(Not traced)	666B
2486	1837 ^{WW}	Adams 650 $^{(GEF)}$	667				

WILLIAM IV - SHILLINGS

ESC	Variety	Provenance	(Old ESC)	ESC	Variety	Provenance	(Old ESC)
2487	1831 P ^{mil}	SNC 2005 $^{6325\ (FDC)}$	1267	2488	1831 P ^{Pln}	Sommerville $^{2785\ FDC}$	1266
2489	1834 $^{obv.rv}$	SNC 2005,$^{6720(VAS)}$	1268	2489	1834	Sommer $^{2786\ (AEF)}$	1268
2490	1834 P	SNC 2003,$^{5513\ (VAS)}$	1269	2491	1834P ^{rnd3}	SNC 1977,$^{394\ (UNC)}$	1270
2492	1835	Sommer 2787 $^{(VAS)}$	1271	2493	1835P ^{rnd3}	SNC 1977,$^{394\ (UNC)}$	1272
2494	1836	SNC 2001,$^{1988\ (UNC)}$	1273	2495	1836P ^{rnd3}	SNC 1977,$^{394\ (UNC)}$	1274
2496	1836 P ^{Cu}		1275	2497	1837	Sommerville $^{2789(GEF)}$	1276
2498	1837 P	SNC 2000 $^{2415\ (FDC)}$	1277				

WILLIAM IV - SIXPENCES

ESC	Variety	Provenance	(Old ESC)	ESC	Variety	Provenance	(Old ESC)
2499	1831	DNW 101 $^{743(VAS)}$	1670	2500	1831P ^{Mil}	DNW 59,$^{367\ (FDC)}$	1671
2501	1831P ^{Pln}	Spink 12 343 $^{(FDC)}$	1672	2502	1831P $^{Pln}_{thin}$	Bole 2, 170 $^{(AFDC)}$	1672A
2503	1831P ^{Pall}		1673				
2504	1834	SNC 2010$^{9247\ (UNC)}$	1674	2505	1834 ^{large}	SNC 2010,$^{9112\ (EF)}$	1674A
2506	1834 P		1674B	2507	1834P ^{rnd3}		1675
2508	1835	Bole 1, 1763 $^{(VAS)}$	1676	2508	A	Bole 1763 $^{DNW\ 89}$	1676
2509	1835 P ^{Mil}	Bole 1, 1764 $^{(FDC)}$	1677	2510	1836	Bole 3, 179 $^{(VAS)}$	1678
2511	1836 P ^{Mil}	Bole 1, 1765 $^{(AFDC)}$	1679	2512	1852	SNC 2007,$^{2974\ (GVF)}$	1680
2513	1881 P ^{Mil}	Bole 1, 1766 $^{(GEF)}$	1681	2514	B $^{obv/rev}$	Bole 3, 180 $^{(VF)}$	1681A?

WILLIAM IV - GROATS

ESC	Variety	Provenance	(Old ESC)	ESC	Variety	Provenance	(Old ESC)
	2 $^{obv/rev}$	SNC 1998, ^{2122}	1925		3 $^{rev.}$	SNC 1998, ^{2123}	
2515	1836	SNC 1998,$^{2119\ (VAS)}$	1918	2516	1836 P	SNC 1998,$^{2121\ (FDC)}$	1919
2517	1836 P ^{Pln}	M.R. 20,160 $^{(AFDC)}$	1920	2518	1836 P ^{Au}	M.R. 11/166 $^{(AFDC)}$	1921
2519	1836 P ^{Au}	Glens 5/1974 $^{(195e)}$	1921A	2520	1837	SNC 2008 $^{8629\ (GEF)}$	1922

(continued)

PROVENANCES

ESC	Variety	Provenance	(Old ESC)	ESC	Variety	Provenance	(Old ESC)
2521	1837 P	Norweb 1669 $^{(VAS)}$	1923	2522	1837 P	DNW 43,$^{857\ (VAS)}$	1923A
2523	1836 P^{Mill}	M.R. 20,161 $^{(AFDC)}$	1924	2524	1836 P ^{Pln}	M.R. 20,162 $^{(AFDC)}$	1925
2525	1836 P Pln Au	W&R 273	1925A	2526	Pln Au thin flan	W&R 274	1925B
2527	1836 P	M.R. 20,163 $^{(AFDC)}$	1926	2528	1836 P ^{Pln}	Norweb $^{1071\ (VAS)}$	1927
2529	1836 P ^{Au}	Glens 5/1974 $^{(196d)}$	1928	2530	1836 P ^{Au}	Wilson & Ras 272	1928A

WILLIAM IV - THREEPENCES

2531	1834 SH	M.R. 21/267 $^{(Unc)}$	2044	2531	1834	SNC 2002,$^{2578\ (AEF)}$	2044
2532	1835 SH	M.R. 21/268 $^{(Unc)}$	2045	2532	1835	SNC 2002,$^{2580\ (EF)}$	2045
2533	1836 SH	SNC 2002.$^{2581(EF)}$	2046	2534	1837 SH	(SNC 2002,2582 (Min))	2047
2535	1834 LH		2044	2536	1835 LH		2045
2537	1836 LH		2046	2538	1837 LH		2047

WILLIAM IV - THREE-HALFPENCES

ESC	Variety	Provenance	(Old ESC)	ESC	Variety	Provenance	(Old ESC)
2539	1834	SNC 1998.$^{3741(FDC)}$	2250	2540	1834 P	SNC 2000.$^{3166\ (FDC)}$	2250A
2541	1835	(SNC 1987, 4561 (GEF))	2251	2542	1835/4	Baldwin 55 $^{2447\ (EF)}$	2251A
2543	1836	(SNC 2003, 5192 (EF))	2252	2545	1837	(SNC 2001, 1298 (GF))	2253
2546	1837P	(SNC 2001, 1298 (GF))	2253A				

WILLIAM IV - MAUNDY SETS

2547	1831	DNW 76,$^{141\ (VAS)}$	2436	2548	1831 P	Spink 171,$^{137\ (VAS)}$	2437
2549	1831 P ^{Au}	Spink 120 $^{644\ (FDC)}$	2438	2550	1832	Spink 183.$^{228\ (EF)}$	2439
2551	1833	DNW 79 .$^{3270\ (VAS)}$	2440	2552	1834	SNC 2008 $^{8582\ (EF)}$	2441
2553	1835	SNC 2011 $^{9507\ (EF)}$	2442	2554	1836	SNC 2011 $^{9799\ (GEF)}$	2443
2555	1837	SNC 2011.$^{9509\ (EF)}$	2444				

VICTORIA - CROWNS

2560	1839 P ^{Pln}	Norweb 281 ^{VAS}	279	2560	A ^{Small}	DNW, 97,^{379}	279
2560	1839 P ^{Pln}	SJA 23 251 $^{(FDC)}$	279	2561	1844 ^{VIII}	Norweb 1076^{VAS}	280
2562	1844 ^{VIII}	SNC 2002.$^{4378\ (EF)}$	281	2563	1844 P	Whetmore158$^{(FDC)}$	280A
2564	1845 ^{VIII}	Spink 1 $^{284\ (Mint)}$	282	2565	1845ANNO	P.C. (A.H.)	282B
2566	1845	Bruno 118 $^{(EF)}$	282A	2567	1847 ^{XI}	Roekel 219 $^{(VAS)}$	286
2568	1847 DEC U^{S}	Glens. 1972, $^{61\ (VF)}$	286A	2569			
2570	1847 Pat		287	2571	1847 P ^{Pln}	Bald.48 $^{5039\ (FDC)}$	288
2571	2	DNW, 97,^{385}	288	2571	1847 P^{11th}	Norweb 282 ^{FDC}	288
2572				2573	1847^{Frosted}	Whetmore162 $^{(EF)}$	289
2574				2575	1847P ^{11th}	Barr 123 $^{(VAS)}$	288/291
2576	1847 P ^{7th}	Norweb 617 $^{(VAS)}$	290	2577	1847 P ^{Pln}	Bruno 124 $^{(FDC)}$	291
2578	1847 P ^{Pln}	P.C. (M.L.)	291B	2579	1847 P ^{Pln}	P.C. (M.L.)	291C
2580	1847 VIP	Bald $^{FPL.Winter\ 2008,\ 51}$	291A	2581	1847 P ^{Au}	Wilson & Ras 368	292
2582	1847 P^{wm}	Lingford 568^{FDC}	292A	2583	1853 P ^{Pln}	Roekel 223 $^{(FDC)}$	294
2584	1853 P ^{7th}	Norweb 1072 $^{(VAS)}$	293	2585	1887 ^{JH}	Roekel 224 $^{(UNC)}$	296
2586	1887 P ^{JH}	SNC 2011.$^{9404(FDC)}$	297	2587	1888 ^{narrow}	DNW 104$^{574\ (VAS)}$	298
2588	1888 ^{wide}	Barr 454 $^{(VAS)}$	298A	2589	1889 ^{wide}	Barr 455 $^{(GEF)}$	299
2590	1890	DNW 111.$^{279/(GEF)}$	300	2591	1891 $^{obv\ C}$	DNW, 97,^{392}	301
2592	1892	SNC 2002 $^{2797(UNC)}$	302	2593	1893 ^{LVI}	DNW 111.$^{281(GEF)}$	303
2594	1893P ^{LVI}	SNC 2002$^{2800(AFDC)}$	304	2595	1893 ^{LVII}	Barr 309 $^{(AEF)}$	305

(continued)

PROVENANCES

ESC	Variety	Provenance	(Old ESC)	ESC	Variety	Provenance	(Old ESC)
2596	1894 ^{LVII}	Barr 310 $^{(GEF)}$	306	2597	1894 ^{LVIII}	**Barr 311** $^{(GEF)}$	307
2598	1895 ^{LVIII}	Barr 312 $^{(GVF)}$	308	2599	1895 ^{LIX}	Barr 314 $^{(VAS)}$	309
2600	1896 ^{LIX}	Barr 315 $^{(AEF)}$	310	2601	1896 ^{LX}	Barr 316 $^{(UNC)}$	311
2602	1897 ^{LX}	DNW 111,$^{285(VAS)}$	312	2603	1897 ^{LXI}	Barr 318 $^{(VAS)}$	313
2604	1898 ^{LXI}	Roekel 242 $^{(UNC)}$	314	2605	1898 ^{LXII}	Barr 320 $^{(UNC)}$	315
2606	1899 ^{LXII}	DNW 97 $^{406 (VAS)}$	316	2607	1899 ^{LXIII}	Barr 322 $^{(GEF)}$	317
2608	1900 ^{LXIII}	Barr 323 $^{(VAS)}$	318	2609	1900 ^{LXIV}	DNW 97$^{409 (VAS)}$	319
2610	1837 Unfinished in WM		321B	2611	1837^{Pat}F^1 White metal		321A
2612	F *obv*	**Glens 1961,** ^{156}	320	2612	F *rev* 4	**Glens 1961,**^{156}	320
2612	1837 ^{Pat} F	**Spink 163** $^{233 (VAS)}$	320	2613	1837p F^{Au}	Glens 4/1972, ^{379}	320A
2614	1837 F ^{Cu}	Norweb 1078 $^{(VAS)}$	321	2615	1837F ^{Wm}	Norweb 1079 $^{(VAS)}$	322
2616	1837F ^{Wm}	Spink 4 $^{674 (AEF)}$	323	2617	1837F ^{Al}	Norweb 1080 $^{(VA)S}$	323A
2618	1837 P ^{Pb}	(Willis 587 *(EF)*)	324	2618	1837 P^{Pew}	(Willis 589 *(EF)*)	324A
2619	1837 P ^{Mil}		325	2620	1837 P ^{Cu}		326
2621	1837 P ^{Sn}	(Lingford 548)	327	2622	1837 P ^{Pb}	Spink 119 $^{203 (VAS)}$	327A
2623				2624			
2625	1837 P		328	2626	1837P ^{Wm}	**Lingford 550**	328A
2627	L&S 15			2628	L&S 16		
2629	L&S 17			2630	L&S 18		
2631	L&S 19			2632	L&S 19A		
2633	L&S 20			2634	L&S 21		
2635	L&S 22			2636	L&S 23		
2637	L&S 24			2638	L&S 25		
2639	L&S 26			2640	L&S 27		
2641	L&S 28			2642	L&S 29		
2643	L&S 30			2644	L&S 31		
2645	L&S 32			2646	L&S 33		
2647	1839 P ^{Pln}		333	2647	1839 P ^{Pln}	Spink 117 $^{230 (VF)}$	333
2647	1839 P ^{Pln}		333	2648	1839 P ^{Au}		334
2649	DIRIGE $_{small}$	Whetmor 144$^{(FDC)}$	332				
2650	I^1 *ob/rev*	**Glens 1961,** ^{143}	335	2650	1839 P ^{Pln}	Whetmor 145$^{(FDC)}$	335
2651	1839 ^{Pat} J		336	2652	*Rev.*	**Glens 1961,**^{146}	337
2652	1844 ^{Large}	**Glens 1961,** ^{146}	337	2653	1844 ^{Small}	**Roekel 215** $^{(Mint)}$	338
2654	1844 Star stops			2655	1845 ^{Pat} L	**Willis 595** $^{(FDC)}$	338A
2656	1845 ^{Thin}	**Willis 596** $^{(VAS)}$	338	2657	1845 Patt M^2	**M.R. 16/115** $^{(VAS)}$	339
2658	1845 ^{Heavy}			2659	1845 P ^{Au}	Wilson & Ras 367	339A
2660	1845 ^{VIII}	Lingford 563	340	2661	1845 P ^{Pln}	Glens$^{1962, 221 (FDC)}$	283
2662	1845 ^{IX}	Lingford 564	340A	2663	1846^{Pat} M	**Willis 598** $^{(VAS)}$	341
2664	^{Pat}M^{frosted}	Whetmore 151$^{(EF)}$	341A	2665	C $^{thin Ob.Cu}$		
2666	C $^{thin Rv.Cu}$			2667	C $^{thin Rv.Pb}$		
2668	1879 P ^{Pln}	Lingford 573$^{(VAS)}$	295	2669	1888^{Pat} T^1	**Slaney 235** $^{(FDC)}$	357
2670	^{Pt}O ^{unsigned}			2671	1890 ^{Pat} O		358
2672	1879 ^{Pat} D		359	2673	^{Pat} P $^{(1894)}$		
2674	1892^{Pat}Q	**Lingford 580**	360	2675	Pat Q ^{Pb}		
2676	(1893 P) ^{Pb}R	**Lingford 581**	360A				
	1839 DIRIGE	**Lingford 551**	331		1839 P $^{Pln}_{Ag}$		331A
	^{Patn} ^{Wm}	Spink 6 $^{793 (FDC)}$	331B		1839^{PlnWm}	Norweb 280 $^{(VAS)}$	331B

(continued)

PROVENANCES

ESC	Variety	Provenance	(Old ESC)	ESC	Variety	Provenance	(Old ESC)
	1839^Pat	Lingford 554	329		DIRIGIT	**Glens 1961,^152**	329
	1839 P ^Au		330		1839 P ^Au_Pln		331
	rev	**DNW 113 ^236 (VAS)**	339		1847 ^Pln	(Lingford 567)	
	1847^Pat	**Lingford 570**	342		1853 Pt Au	Baldwin 80 ^.2409 (GF)	
	1847^Pln_Wm	(Lingford 568)			Pat. P ^Au	James 15,^554(FDC)	342A
	1879 P ^Pln	Whetmore153^(FDC)	295		1879 ^Pat	**DNW 65^. 429 (FDC)**	
	Pln belo_Pat Obv.	**Glens 1963,^213**	343		1887^Pat	Spink 4 ^687 (VAS)	344
	Obv.	**Glens 1962,^230**	346		Q^4 Rev.	**Rashleigh 401**	346
	1887 P ^Au	**Lingford 574**	347		1887 P ^Cu	Spink 4 ^688 (EF)	348
	1887 P ^Al	Norweb 1081^VAS	349		1887 P ^Pb	(Lingford 576)	351
	1887 P ^Cn		351A		1887 P ^Mil		352
	1887 P ^Au	Wilson & Ras 370	353		1887 P^Wm	(Lingford 576)	353A
	1887^Bavaria	Glens ^7/1962, 231 (EF)	354				
	1 obv/ rev	**Lingford 578**	357A		1888^Pat	Whetmor 151 ^(FDC)	357A
	(1847 proof)	(SNC 1993, 7216)	unique		Pattern X ^Pln	Glens ^11/1964,398 (EF)	

VICTORIA - DOUBLE FLORINS

ESC	Variety	Provenance	(Old ESC)	ESC	Variety	Provenance	(Old ESC)
2695	I 887^Roman	Barr 459 ^(EF)	394	2696	I 887 P	Spink 157,^569 (AFDC)	394A
2697	1887 ^Arabic	**SNC 2001^1896 (UNC)**	395	2698	1887 P	Barr 462 ^(EF)	396
2699	1888 ^Arabic	Barr 463 ^(EF)	397	2701	1889	SNC 2001^1896 (UNC)	398
2703	1890 ^Arabic	Barr 467 ^(AEF)	399	2704	1890 ^pattern	**SNC 1998^6951 (FDC)**	400
xxxx	1868 P Mil Au	Bald. 52 ^663 (AFDC)	400	xxxx	1868 P Pln Au	Spink 55,^461(FDC)	400A

VICTORIA - HALFCROWNS

ESC	Variety	Provenance	(Old ESC)	ESC	Variety	Provenance	(Old ESC)
2706	1839 ^relief	Adams 651 ^(Poor)	668	2707	1839 P	Adams 652 ^(FDC)	669
2708	1839 P ^Pln	**DNW 113 ^261 (VAS)**	670	2708	A ^obv/rev	**DNW 113 ^261 (VAS)**	670
2709	1839 P ^A2	*(Not traced)*	671	2710	1839P^A2/3	*(Not traced)*	671A
2711	1839 currency	Adams 655 ^(EF)	672	2712	1839 P	Adams 657 ^(GEF)	672A
2713	1839 P ^Pln	**Adams 658 ^(VAS)**	672B	2714	1839 Lt wt	Adams 656 ^(Fr-F)	672C
2715	1840	Adams 659 ^(GEF)	673	2716	1841	DNW 111,^295(GEF)	674
2717	1842	Adams 661 ^(GEF)	675	2718	1843	DNW 111,^298 (EF)	676
2719	1843	Adams 663 ^(VF)	676A	2720	1844 ^Serifs	Adams 664 ^(UNC)	677
2720	1844 ^no ser	**Norweb 494 ^VAS**	677	2721	1844 ^Serifs	Adams 667 ^(EF)	678
2722	1845	Adams 668 ^(UNC)	679	2723	1845/3	**Spink 204,^283 (NVF)**	679A
2724	1846	Adams 671 ^(UNC)	680	2725	1846 8/6	Adams 673 ^(GVF)	680A
2726	1848	Adams 675 ^(EF)	681	2727	18/648	M.R. 9/244 ^(Unc)	681A
2728	1848/6	**Adams 675 ^(EF)**	681B	2729	1848/7	Adams 674 ^(GEF)	681C
2730	1849 L date	Adams 678 ^(GEF)	682	2731	1849/7	**Adams 680^(Fr)**	682A
2732	1849 S date	DNW 83,^3236(AEF)	683	2733	1850	Adams 683 ^(EF)	684
2734	1850 P	Adams 684 ^(GEF)	685	2735	1851	*(Not traced)*	???
2736	1853 P	**Bull^FDC Norweb1072**	687	2737	1862 P		688
2738	1862 P ^Pln	Adams 686 ^(FDC)	689	2739	1864 P_mill	Adams 687 ^(FDC)	690
2740	1864 P ^Pln	Adams 688 ^(FDC)	691	2741	1874	Adams 690 ^(UNC)	692
2742	1874 P	*(Not traced)*	693	2743	1874P^Frost	Glens^1962, 247 FDC	694
2744	1874 P ^Au	Wils & Ras 374	695	2745	1875	Adams 691 ^(GEF)	696
2746	1875 P	**Adams 692 ^FDC**	697	2747	1875 P ^Pln	*(Not traced)*	698
2748	1876	Adams 696 ^(EF)	699	2749	1876/5	Adams 697 ^(GEF)	699A
2750	1877	Adams 698 ^(EF)	700	2751	1878	Adams 699 ^(GEF)	701

(continued)

PROVENANCES

ESC	Variety	Provenance	(Old ESC)	ESC	Variety	Provenance	(Old ESC)
2752	1878 P	Adams 700 $^{(FDC)}$	702	2753	1879	Adams 701 $^{(GEF)}$	703
2754	1879 P	Adams 704 $^{(FDC)}$	704	2755	1879 P ^{Pln}	Spink 107 $^{440\,(FDC)}$	704A
2756	1880	Adams 705 $^{(GEF)}$	705	2757	1880 P	Adams 707 $^{(FDC)}$	706
2758	1881	Adams 709 $^{(UNC)}$	707	2759	1881 P	Adams 710 $^{(FDC)}$	708
2760	1881 P ^{Pln}	*(Not traced)*	709	2761	1882	Adams 711 $^{(GEF)}$	710
2762	1883	Adams 712 $^{(GEF)}$	711	2763	1883 P	Spink 157, $^{581\,(FDC)}$	711A
2764	1884	Adams 724 $^{(GEF)}$	712	2765	1885	Adams 725 $^{(UNC)}$	713
2766	1885 P	Adams 726 $^{(FDC)}$	714	2767	1886	Adams 727 $^{(UNC)}$	715
2768	1886 P		716	2769	1887 YH	DNW 111 $^{317(VAS)}$	717
2770	1887 P ^{YH}	Adams 729 $^{(FDC)}$	718	2771	1887 JH	Adams 730 $^{(UNC)}$	719
2772	B $^{obv/rev}$	**DNW 113** $^{286\,(VAS)}$	720	2772	1887 P ^{JH}	**DNW 113** $^{286\,(VAS)}$	720
2773	1888	Adams 733 $^{(UNC)}$	721	2774	1889	Adams 736 $^{(UNC)}$	722
2775	1890	Adams 740 $^{(GEF)}$	723	2776	1891	Adams 741 $^{(GEF)}$	724
2777	1892	Adams 742 $^{(GEF)}$	725	2778	1893	Adams 744 $^{(GEF)}$	726
2779	1893 P	**DNW 113** $^{293\,(VAS)}$	727	2780	1894	Adams 747 $^{(UNC)}$	728
2781	1895	Adams 748 $^{(UNC)}$	729	2782	1896	Adams 749 $^{(UNC)}$	730
2783	1897	Adams 751 $^{(UNC)}$	731	2784	1898	Adams 752 $^{(GEF)}$	732
2785	1899	Adams 753 $^{(UNC)}$	733	2786	1900	Adams 754 $^{(GEF)}$	734
2787	1901	Adams 755 $^{(GEF)}$	735	2788	$1839^{Pat}D^1$	**Glens** $^{1962/10/4,\,242}$	736
2789	$1839^{Pat}D^2$		736A	2790	$^{Pat}D^2 P^{Mill}$	**Glens** $^{1963/10/4,\,242}$	737
2791	$^{1875Pat}E_{Pln}$	**Adams 693** $^{(FDC)}$	738	2792	$^{1875\,Pat}F_{Pln}$	**Adams 694** $^{(VAS)}$	739
2793	$^{1876\,Pat}G_{Pln}$	**Glens** $^{1962/10/4,\,249}$	740	2794	1876 P ^{Au}	Wilson & Ras 375	741

VICTORIA - PATTERN – H - HALFCROWNS dated 1884

ESC	Variety	Provenance	(Old ESC)	ESC	Variety	Provenance	(Old ESC)
2795	H^1 ^{Milled}	**Norweb 622** ^{VAS}	742	2796	H^1 ^{Plain} ?	**Adams 713** $^{(Mint)}$	742A
2797	H^2 ^{Milled}	**Adams 719** $^{(Mint)}$	742B	2798	H2 ^{Plain} ?		742C
2799	H^3 ^{Milled}	**Adams 718** $^{(Mint)}$	742D	2800	H^3 ^{Plain}	**Adams 715** $^{(Mint)}$	742E
2801	H^4 ^{Milled}		742F	2802	H^4 ^{Plain}	**Adams 717** $^{(Mint)}$	742G
2803	H^5 ^{Milled}	**Adams 714** $^{(Mint)}$	742H	2804	H^5 ^{Plain} ?		742I
2805	H^6 ^{Milled} ?		742J	2806	H^6 ^{Plain}	**Adams 716** $^{(Mint)}$	742K
2807	1890 ^{Pat} I	**SNC 1998,** ^{6965}	743	2808	^{Pat} I ^{Plain}	SNC 1998 $^{6965\,(FDC)}$	743A
2809	$^{Uniface\,rev}$ I	Adams 737 $^{(VAS)}$	743B	2810	1890 ^{Pat} J		744
2811	$1890^{Pat}K^1$	**Adams 738** $^{(Mint)}$	745	2812	$^{Pat}K^1$ $^{Cu}_{Pln}$	**Adams 738** $^{(Mint)}$	745A
2813	$1890^{Pat}K^2$	**Adams 739** $^{(EF)}$	745B	2814	Uniface rev.	**Adams 743**	745C

VICTORIA - FLORINS

ESC	Variety	Provenance	(Old ESC)	ESC	Variety	Provenance	(Old ESC)
2815	1849 ^{milled}	**DNW 101,** ^{760}	802	2816	$^{1849\,milled}A^2$	**DNW 90,** ^{672}	802A
2817	1849 $^{no\,ww}$	**P.C. (M.L.)**	802B		1851 ^{Stop}	*Believed not to exist*	803
2818	$1851P_{stp\,Mil}$	SNC 1990 $^{4369\,(FDC)}$	804	2819	$1851P_{Pln}{}^{st}$	Spink 140 $^{723\,(AFDC)}$	805
				2819	$1851P_{Pln}{}^{st}$	SJA 2, 458 $^{(AFDC)}$	805
2820	1852^{Stop}_{B1}	**SNC 2003** $^{4537(UNC)}$	806	2821	$1852P_{Mil}{}^{st}$	DNW 43, $^{1070\,(VAS)}$	807
2822	$1852/1^{Stop}$	**SNC 2003** $^{4538\,(VAS)}$	807A	2823	u/u ^{inverted}	**P.C (M.L)**	
2824	1852 onc			2825	1853 ^{Stop}	**P.C.(M.L)**	808A
2826	1853	**DNW 83,** $^{3445\,(GEF)}$	808	2827	1853 P	M.R. 8 300 $^{(VAS)}$	809
	1854	DNW 83, $^{3446\,(GVF)}$	811	2829	1854	Spink 140 $^{733\,(AEF)}$	811A
2830	1854 onc	**P.C (M.L)**		2831	1855	SNC 2003 $^{4544\,(UNC)}$	812
2832	1855 onc	**P.C (M.L)**		2833	1856 ^{B1}	SNC 2010 $^{8991(UNC)}$	813A
2834	1856 onc	**P.C (M.L)**		2835	1857	DNW 111, $^{331\,(VAS)}$	814

(continued)

PROVENANCES

ESC	Variety	Provenance	(Old ESC)	ESC	Variety	Provenance	(Old ESC)
2836	1857 P	SNC 1980,3689 (AFDC)	815	2837	1857 onc	P.C (M.L)	
2838	1858 B1	DNW 111.332(VAS)	816B	2839	1858 P		816A
2840	1858 onc	P.C (M.L)		2841	1859	DNW 83.3451 (EF)	818
2842	1859 Stop	DNW 111.333 (VAS)	817	2843	m/m inverted	DNW 30.317 (VF+)	818A
2844	1860 Stop	DNW 111.334 (EF)	819	2845	1860 onc	P.C (M.L)	
2846	1862 B1	M.R. 8 301 (VAS)	820	2847	1862 P Mil	SJA 2, 459 (AFDC)	821
2848	1862 P Pln	M.R. 19 215 (FDC)	821A	2849	1863	DNW 111,336 (EF+)	822
2850	1863 P Pln	SNC 2004.6147 (GEF)	823	2851	1864	P.C (M.L)	
2852	1865	P.C (M.L)		2853	1864BRIT	SNC 2003 4548(UNC)	824
2853	B2	DNW 83, 3454	824	2854	1864P Hvy	SNC 2000,0070 (GVF)	824A
2855	1864 P	(SNC 1993, 2642)	825	2856	1865	P.C (M.L)	
2857	1866 B2	SNC 2003, 4551(VAS)	828	2858	1866 un/nu	SNC 2003, 4551(VAS)	828A
2859	1867 (1)	DNW 111.340 (AEF)	830	2860	1865 colon	SNC 2003 4550 (UNC)	827
2860	1865: B2	SNC 2011.9430 (GEF)	827	2861	1866 colon	(Not traced)	829
2862	1867P Mil	Spink 89 185 (FDC)	831	2863	1867 P Pln	Norweb 285(FDC)	832
2864	1867 B5		832A	2865	1868 B3	SNC 2010,8996 (GEF)	833
2866	1869 (17)	DNW 111 341 (GEF)	834	2867	n over invert n	P.C (M.L)	834A
2868	1869 P	(Not traced)	835	2869	1870 (2)	Spink 203, 389 (UNC)	836
2870	m/m inverted	P.C (M.L)		2871	1870 P	B.M. Collection	836A
2872	1871 (48)	DNW 111.343 (GEF)	837	2873	1871 P	SNC 2000 212 (AFDC)	838
2874	1871 P Pln	SNC 2000 213 (AFDC)	839	2875	1871 P nickel		839A
2876	1872 (62)	SNC 2003 4556 (VAS)	840	2877	1873B3(6)	SNC 2003 4557 (UNC)	841
2878	1873 P	(Not traced)	842	2879	1874 (55)	DNW 111.346 (GEF)	843
2880	1874/3 B3	SNC 2003 4558 (EF)	843A	2881	1875 (45)	SNC 2009 8840 (GEF)	844
2882	1876 (23)	SNC 2006 7471 (AEF)	845	2883	1877B5	Spink 140 793(FDC)	846
2884	1877 Stop	Spink 199, 155 (GEF)	847	2885	1877B5 stop	SNC 2010 8998 (GEF)	848
2886	1877 Stop	Spink 140 796 (GEF)	848A	2887	1878 (55)	DNW 111, 348 (VAS)	849
2888	1878 P	(SNC 1994, 7251)	849A	2889	1878	P.C (M.L)	
2890	1879 B3/6	DNW 83,3468(VF)	851	2890	1879 B6	Spink 140 801 (GEF)	851
2891	1879			2892	1879 B5/6	Spink 120, 566 (EF)	850
2893	1879 B7	SNC 2003 4559 (VAS)	852	2894	1879 P Pln	Spink 107 440 (FDC)	853
2895	1879 P Pln	Spink 107 440 (FDC)	853A	2896	18·80	SNC 2010 9002 (GEF)	
2897	1880 B8	SNC 2010 9002 (GEF)	854	2898	1880 P	Norweb 1084(VAS)	855
2899	1881 B8	SNC 2010 9003 (VAS)	856	2900	1881 P	Spink 6 815 (FDC)	857
2901	1881 P Pln	Spink 140 812 FDC)	858	2902	1883 B8	Spink 140,841 (UNC)	859
2903	1883 P Pln	Spink 157 585 (FDC)	859A		a-v	SNC 2002 3081	860
2904	1884 B8	SNC 2008 8537(GEF)	860	2905	1884/2	(Not traced)	860A?
2906	1885 B8	DNW 111.351(VAS)	861	2907	1885 P	Spink 157 586 (FDC)	862
2908	1886 B8	DNW 111.352 (VAS)	863	2909	1886 P	(Spink55,485 (AFDC))	864
2910	1887	SNC 2003 5445 (UNC)	866	2910	1887 B9	SNC 2002 3115 (UNC)	866
2911	1887 P3/8	SNC 1992 7703 (FDC)	867	2911	1887 P	SNC 1998 1977 (FDC)	867

VICTORIA - 1848 PATTERN FLORINS
Struck en medaille ↑↑with plain edges (unless stated otherwise)

ESC	Variety	Provenance	(Old ESC)	ESC	Variety	Provenance	(Old ESC)
2924	a. B-ii		895	2925	b. B-ii	SNC 2002 3083(FDC)	896
2926	c. B-ii	Norweb 625 (FDC)	897	2927	a. B-iii	Spink 157 593 (FDC)	898
2928	b. B-iii	DNW 89 2246 (VAS)	899	2929	c. B-iii	DNW 78.412 (AFDC)	900
2930	a. B-iv	Spink 109 348 (FDC)	901	2931	b. B-iv	Baldwn 80 2403(GEF)	902

(continued)

PROVENANCES

ESC	Variety	Provenance	(Old ESC)	ESC	Variety	Provenance	(Old ESC)
2932	c. B-iv	Spink 157 $^{594\ (FDC)}$	903	2933	a. C-i	Spink 38 $^{162\ (FDC)}$	904
2934	b. C-i	Baldwn 80 $^{2404\ (VAS)}$	905	2935	c. C-i	**SNC 2003** $^{4528(FDC)}$	906
2936	a. C-vi	Spink 109 $^{354\ (FDC)}$	907	2937	b. C-vi	**Norweb 628** $^{(FDC)}$	908
2938	c. C-vi	Spink 157 $^{597\ (FDC)}$	909	2939	a. C-vii	**SNC 2003** $^{4532\ (VAS)}$	910
2940	b. C-vii	**Norweb 629** $^{(FDC)}$	911	2941	c. C-vii	SNC 2005 $^{6314\ (FDC)}$	912
2942	b^i.B-ii SEPTIMO	Bald 80 2406 VAS	913	2943	b^{iii}.C-vii SEPTIMO	SNC 2003,4534	914
2944	B^{iv}.C-vi		915	2944	Mule 2 $rev.$	SNC 1977 $^{8345\ (VAS)}$	915
2945	1875 P ^{Pln}	**Norweb 630** ^{FDC}	916	2946	1876 ^{Pat} E		917
2947	1887 ^{Pat} F	SNC 1999 $^{1541\ (FDC)}$	918	2948	1890^{Pat}G		918A
2949	1891^{Pat}H		918				

VICTORIA JUBILEE HEAD FLORINS

2950	1887 JH	SNC 2010 $^{9006\ (VAS)}$	868	2951	1887P JH	SNC 2010 $^{9007\ (VAS)}$	869
2952	1888	SNC 2007 $^{8097\ (GEF)}$	870	2953	Narrow space	**P.C (M.L)**	870A
2954	1889	SNC 2009, $^{8779\ (VAS)}$	871	2955	1890	SNC 2002 $^{3119\ (UNC)}$	872
2956	1891	SNC 2002 $^{3121\ (UNC)}$	873	2957	1892	SNC 2002 $^{3122\ (UNC)}$	874
2958	1892 P	Norweb 286 ^{FDC}	875	2958	1892 P	Bald. FPL $^{Win'11/12.105}$	875

VICTORIA OLD HEAD FLORINS

2959	1893	SNC 2008 $^{8612\ (VAS)}$	876	2960	1893 P	**SNC 2010** $^{9008(FDC)}$	877
2961	1894	SNC 2007 $^{8178\ (GEF)}$	878	2962	1895	SNC 2007 $^{8179\ (EF)}$	879
2963	1896	SNC 2008 $^{8613(UNC)}$	880	2964	1897	SNC 2010 $^{9009\ (EF)}$	881
2965	1898	SNC 2008 $^{8614\ (UNC)}$	882	2966	1899	SNC 2008 $^{8615\ (UNC)}$	883
2967	1899 P	SJA 2, 511 $^{(GEF)}$	883A	2968	1900	SNC 2009 $^{8780\ (VAS)}$	884
2969	1901	SNC 2008 $^{8617\ (VAS)}$	885				

VICTORIA - SHILLINGS

ESC	Variety	Provenance	(Old ESC)	ESC	Variety	Provenance	(Old ESC)
2970	A^1/1	**SNC 2003** $^{4562(UNC)}$	1278	2970	1838	DNW 111, $^{359\ (GEF)}$	1278
2971	1838 P	SNC 1999 $^{5239\ (FDC)}$	1279	2972	1839	Sommerville $^{2791\ (GEF)}$	1280
2973	1839 P		1281	2974	1839 P ^{Pln}	Spink 157 $^{601\ (FDC)}$	1282
2975	Mule A^3/A^1		1278A	2976	1839	SNC 2003 $^{4564\ (UNC)}$	1283
2977	1839P ↑↓			2978	1839 P ^{Pln}	Norweb 1689 $^{(FDC)}$	1284
2979	1839 P	Sommer 2794 $^{(AFDC}$	1284A	2980	1840	M.R. 22/419 $^{(Unc)}$	1285
2981	1840 P	SNC 1992 $^{912\ (FDC)}$	1286	2982	D over F		1286A
2983	1841	Sommer $^{2796\ (VAS)}$	1287	2984	1842	SNC 2003 $^{4570\ (UNC)}$	1288
2984	1842 D/F	(P.C. $^{C.\ Tasker}$)	1288	2985	1842 P	DNW 83 $^{3257(GEF)}$	1289
2986	1843	M.R. 22/422 $^{(Unc)}$	1290	2987	1844	SNC 2003 $^{4571\ (UNC)}$	1291
2988	1845	SNC 2003 $^{4572\ (UNC)}$	1292	2989	1846	SNC 2003 $^{4573(UNC)}$	1293
2990				2991	1848/6	**SNC 2003** $^{4574(UNC)}$	1294
2992	1849	Sommer 2803 $^{(VAS)}$	1295	2993	1850	Sommerville2805^{GVF}	1296
2994	1850/46	$^{(SNC\ 1986,\ 6200)}$	1296A	2995	1850/49	Sommerville$^{2804\ (AEF)}$	1297
2996	1851	SNC 2003 $^{4577\ (UNC)}$	1298	3997			
2998	1852	**SNC 2006**$^{7799\ (UNC)}$	1299	2998	$A^{3\&4}$	**SNC 104** ^{588}	1299
2998	1852	Sommer 2807 $^{(VAS)}$	1299	2999	1853	Norweb 1072 $^{(VAS)}$	1300
3000	1853 P ^{Mil}	Spink 12 $^{350\ (FDC)}$	1301	3001	1854	DNW 111, $^{370\ (EF+)}$	1302
3002	1854/4	SNC 2003 $^{4581\ (UNC)}$	1302A	3003	1855	Sommerville$^{2810\ (VAS)}$	1303
3004	1856	DNW 75, $^{546\ (VAS)}$	1304	3005	1857	Sommerville $^{2812\ (VAS)}$	1305

(continued)

PROVENANCES

ESC	Variety	Provenance	(Old ESC)	ESC	Variety	Provenance	(Old ESC)
3006	Invert. G for D	**SNC 1998,** 2041	1305A	3007	1857/5	**Rax 21/437** (EF)	1306B
3008	1858	Sommer 2813 (VAS)	1306	3009	1858/6	**Spink 201** 513 (GVF)	1306A
2010				3011			
3012	1859	SNC 2003 4586 (UNC)	1307	3013	1859/8	SNC 2001 0850 (GEF)	1307A
3014	1859 P	SNC 1999 5243 (FDC)	1307B?	3015	1860	Sommerville2816 VAS	1308
3016	1861	Sommer 2817 (VAS)	1309	3017	1861 D/B		1309A
3018	1862	Sommer 2818 (VAS)	1310	3019	1863	SNC 2003 4592 (UNC)	1311
3020	1863/1	**Sommr 2819**(GEF)	1311A	3021	1864 № 11	Sommer 2820 (VAS)	1312
3022	1865 № 116	Sommer 2821 (VAS)	1313	3023			
3024	1866 № 29	Sommer 2822 (VAS)	1314	3025	1866 BBIT	M.R. 22/449 № 63	1314A
3026	Inverted V for I	**SNC 2001** 0851	1314B?	3027	1867 № 6	Sommer 2823(GEF)	1315
3028	1867 ???	*(Not traced)*	1316	3029	1867 P	SNC 1999 5244(FDC)	1317
3030	1867 P Pln	SNC 1999· 5245(FDC)	1317A	3031	1867 № 17	M.R. 22/451 (Unc)	1317B
3032	Pellet die numb		1317C	3033	1868	**DNW104** 591 (VAS)	1318
3033	A 5&6	**DNW 104,** 591	1318	3033	1868 № 32	Sommer 2825 (EF)	1318
3034	1869 № 11	DNW 83, 3281(GEF)	1319	3035	1870 № 3	Sommer 2827 (EF)	1320
3036	1871 № 13	Sommer 2828 VAS	1321	3037	1871 P	SNC 1999 5246(FDC)	1322
3038	1871 P Pln	SNC 1999· 5247(FDC)	1323	3039	A4&6 Rev.	**SNC 2005** 6893	1324
3039	1872 № 23	Sommer 2829 (VAS)	1324	3040	1873 № 47	Sommerville 2830 (EF)	1325
3041	1874 № 38	Sommer 2831 (EF)	1326	3042	1875 № 60	Sommerville 2832 (EF)	1327
3043	1876 № 25	Sommer 2833 (VAS)	1328	3044	1877 № 28	Sommerville 2834 (VAS)	1329
3045	1877		1329A	3046	1878 № 9	Sommerville 2835 (VAS)	1330
3047	1878 P	SNC 2002 2545(FDC)	1331	3048			
3049	1879 № 18?	Sommer 2836 (EF)	1332	3050	1879	Sommerville 2838 GEF	1334
3050	A 7	**DNW 102,** 2837	1334	3051	1879 R/B	**DNW 114,** 1560 (NF)	
3052	1879 8/6	**DNW 114,** 1561 (NF)		3053	1879 P Pln	Spink 107 440 (FDC)	1333
3054				3055	1879 P Pl	**PC (RF/NP)** (FDC)	1334B
3055	1879 P Pl	SNC 2002 2546 (FDC)	1334B	3056			
3057				3058			
3059				3060			
3061	1880	SNC 2003 4610 (GEF)	1335	3062	1880 P	SNC 1999 5250(FDC)	1336
3603				3604			
3065	1881	Spink 196, 1137 (AEF)	1338		1881	(SNC2002,3951(GF))	1338A
3066	1881 P	SNC 2002 2547 (FDC)	1339	3067	1881 P Pln		1340
3068	1882	SNC 2003 4612 (UNC)	1341	3069	1883	DNW 89 2034 (VAS)	1342
3070	1883 P Pln	Spink 157 613 (FDC)	1342A	3071	1884	SNC 2003 4613 (UNC)	1343
3072	1884 P		1344	3073	1885 small	**SNC 2003** 4615 (UNC)	1345
3074	1885 P	SNC 1999 5252 (FDC)	1346	3075	1886	M.R. 23/189 (UNC)	1347
3076	1886 P		1348	3077	1887	Spink 199, 169 ((EF)	1349
3078	1887 P YH	Norweb 1699	1350	3079	1878 P	(SNC 1992, 940)	1371
3079	D obv/rev	**SNC 2002** 6329	3271	3080	1863 Pat E	**M.R. 19, 218** (VAS)	1372
3081	1863 Pat F	**Norweb 1692**	1373	3082			
3083	1863 Pat G	Norweb 1085 VAS	1374	3084	1863 Pat H	**M.R. 19, 219** (VAS)	1375
3084	Uniface Pat H	**M.R. 19, 220** (VAS)	1375	3085	Uniface Pat H	**M.R. 19, 220** (VAS)	1373
3086	1863 Pat I	SNC 1999· 5307(FDC)	1376	3087	1863 P I au	Spink 157, 616 (AFDC)	1376A
3088	1863 Pat J	SNC 1999· 5308(FDC)	1377	3089	1863 P J Au	Plym.A 2008 27(vas)	
3090	1863 Pat J cu		1378	3091	1863 Pat J	SNC 1999 5309 (FDC)	1377A
3092				3093	1863 Pat K	DNW 89 2248 (FDC)	1380

(continued)

ESC	Variety	Provenance	(Old ESC)	ESC	Variety	Provenance	(Old ESC)
3094	1863^{P}K^{Au}	Plym.A 2008 $^{26(vas)}$	1380A	3095	1863^{P}K^{Cu}		1381
3096	1863^{Pat}K	SNC 1999 $^{5311 (FDC)}$	1380A	3097	1863^{Pat}L	DNW 89 $^{2249 (VAS)}$	1382
3098	1863^{P}L^{Au}	Plym.A 2008 $^{28(vas)}$	1382A	3099	Pattern L ^{Cu}	SNC 1999 $^{5313 (FDC)}$	1383
3100	1865^{Pat}M	Spink 157, $^{617(AFDC)}$	1384	3101	1863^P MAu	Plym.A 2008 $^{29(vas)}$	1384A
3102	1865^{Pat}M		1385	3103	1865^{Pat}M	SNC 2002 $^{3273 (UNC)}$	1385A
3104	1865 ^{Pat}N	Norweb 1693$^{(GEF)}$	1386	3105	1863^{P}N^{Au}	Plym.A 2008 $^{31(vas)}$	1386A
3106	Pattern N ^{Cu}	SNC 1999 $^{5316 (FDC)}$	1387	3107			
3108	1865 ^{Pat}O	SNC 1999 $^{5317(FDC)}$	1388	3109	1865^{P}O^{Au}	Plym.A 2008 $^{30(vas)}$	1388A
3110	Pattern O ^{Cu}	**Norweb 1694**	1389	3111	Pat O $^{Cu}_{thick}$		1390
3112	No date Pat P	**Norweb 1695**$^{(FDC)}$	1391	3113	1863^{P}P^{Au}	Plym.A 2008 $^{32(vas)}$	1391A
3114	Pattern P ^{Cu}		1392	3115	No date Pat Q	**Norweb 1696**	1393
3116	1863^{P}Q^{Au}	Plym.A 2008 $^{34(vas)}$	1394	3117	Pattern Q ^{Cu}		1394A
3118	No date Pat R	SNC 2002 $^{3276 (FDC)}$	1395	3119	Pattern R ^{Au}	**Bald** $^{FixPL. Win.2008,37}$	1395A
3120	Pat. R $^{Cu}_{Mill}$	DNW 59, $^{386 (GVF)}$	1396	3121	No date Pat S	SNC 1999$^{5321 (FDC)}$	1397
3122	Pattern S ^{Pln}	SNC 1975, $^{8799 (VAS)}$	1397A	3123	No date Pat T	Norweb 1088$^{(VAS)}$	1398
3124	No date Pat U		1399	3125	No date Pat V		1400
3126	Uniface Rev			3127	1875^P A4	Norweb1697 $^{(FDC)}$	1401
3128	Pat A4 ^{Pln}		1402	3129	1875^P A4	**M.R. 19, 221** $^{(VAS)}$	1403
3130	Pat A4 Pln Al	Norweb 1698	1403A	3131	Patt W ^{Pln}		1404A
3132	1875 ^{P} W	Norweb 631 $^{(Mint)}$	1404	3133	1880^P X	SNC 1999 $^{5324 (FDC)}$	1405
3134	No date P Y	**SNC 1998,** ^{3750}	?????	3135	1887 JH	SNC 2010 $^{9055 (UNC)}$	1351
3136	1887 P $_{sm}$	SNC 2010 $^{9227 (FDC)}$	1352	3137	B$^{1 obv}$	**DNW 85,**$^{694(FDC)}$	1353
3138	1888/7	**DNW 85,** ^{694}	1353A	3139	1889 ^{B1}	SNC 2002, $^{3279 (UNC)}$	1354
3140	1889 ^{B2}	**SNC 2010** $^{9056(GEF)}$	1355	3141	1889 P	Spink 12 $^{352 (FDC)}$	1356
3142	1890	SNC 2007, $^{8105 (VAS)}$	1357	3143	1891	SNC 2007, $^{8106 (VAS)}$	1358
3144	1891 P	(SNC2002,3283(VAS))	1359	3145	1892	Spink 199 $^{171 (VAS)}$	1360
3146	1887^P B2	Norweb 632 $^{(Mint)}$	1406	3147	1888^P B2		1407
3148	1888^P B2		1408	3149	1888^P B2		1409
3150	Normal letters	**SNC 2007** $^{8107(GEF)}$	1361	3150	C $^{Obv.}$	**SNC 2007** ^{8104}	1361
3150	C $^{Rev.}$	**SNC 2007** ^{8104}	1361	3151	Large letters	**SNC 2005** ^{6901}	1361A
3152	1893 P ^{OH}	Spink 12 $^{354 (FDC)}$	1362	3153	1894	SNC 2010 $^{9059 (VAS)}$	1363
3154				3155	1895	SNC 2006, $^{7037(GEF)}$	1364
3156	1895	SNC 2006 $^{7038 (VAS)}$	1364A	3157			
3158	1896	SNC 2007 $^{8108 (VAS)}$	1365	3159	1897	SNC 2007 $^{8073 (VAS)}$	1366
3160	1898	(SNC 2003,5543 (UNC))	1367	3161	1899	SNC 2007$^{8109 (UNC)}$	1368
3162	1900	SNC 2007 $^{8110 (VAS)}$	1369	3163	1901	Spink 199 $^{173 (VAS)}$	1370

VICTORIA - TENPENCES

ESC	Variety	Provenance	(Old ESC)	ESC	Variety	Provenance	(Old ESC)
3164	No date A	SNC 1998 $^{3750 (VAS)}$		3164	1867A ^{Pln}	**SJA 24,** $^{336 (EF)}$	1476
3164	1867 A	SNC 2008, $^{8624 (VAS)}$					

VICTORIA - SIXPENCES

ESC	Variety	Provenance	(Old ESC)	ESC	Variety	Provenance	(Old ESC)
3165	1838	Bole 3, 181 $^{(GEF)}$	1682	3166	1838 P ^{Mil}	Bole 1, 1767 $^{(AFDC)}$	1683
3167	1839	Bole 3, 182 $^{(VAS)}$	1684	3168	1839 P ^{Pln}	Bole 1, 1768 $^{(AFDC)}$	1685
3169	1839 P ^{Mil}	Bole 1, 1769 $^{(FDC)}$	1685A	3170	1840	Bole 3, 184 $^{(GEF)}$	1686
3171	1841	DNW 85, $^{699 (VAS)}$	1687	3172	1842	(Rasmussen 20/214 (EF))	1688
3173	1843	Spink 175 $^{1537(GEF)}$	1689	3174	Large 44	**SNC 2010** $^{9248(UNC)}$	1690
3175	Small 44	SNC 2010, $^{9113 (VAS)}$	1690A	3176	1845	SNC 2003 $^{4619 (UNC)}$	1691

(continued)

PROVENANCES

ESC	Variety	Provenance	(Old ESC)	ESC	Variety	Provenance	(Old ESC)
3177	1846	SNC 2003 [4620] (UNC)	1692	3178	1847	Bole 1, 1773 (Poor)	1692A
3179	1848	SNC 2010 [9114] (GEF)	1693	3180	1848/6	**Bole 1, 1774** (AEF)	1693A
3181	1848/7	(Spink 109 514 (NEF))	1693B	3182	1850	SNC 206, [78916](AEF)	1695
3183	1850 5/3	**Bole 1, 1775** (VAS)	1695A	3184	1851	DNW2002/10/8.1324	1696
3185	1852 Bust 1	**Bole 1, 1776** (VAS)	1697	3186	1853	SNC 2003 [4621](UNC)	1698
3187	1853 P Mil	SNC 2003 [4622] (FDC)	1699	3188	1853 P Pln	SNC 2005 [9349](FDC)	1699A
3189	1854	DNW 83, [3299](EF)	1700	3190	1855	Bole 1, 1779 (VAS)	1701
3191	1855/3	Spink 109 [519] (AEF)	1701A	3192	1855 P		1701B
3193	1856	SJA 17, 242 (UNC)	1702	3194	1856	Bole 1, 1780 (GEF)	1703
3195	1857	M.R. 20/228 (GEF)	1704	3196	1857 long line		1705
3197	1858	Bole 1, 1783 (UNC)	1706	3198	1858 P Mil	Bole 1, 1784 (EF+)	1707
3199	1858/6		1707A	3200	1859	SNC 2010 [9116] (GEF)	1708
3201	1858/6	**Bole 1, 1782** (VAS)	1707A	3201	1859/8	SNC 2003 [4627] (UNC)	1708A
3202	1860	DNW 83, [3302](VAS)	1709	3203	Small 6 in date		1709A
3204	1862	SNC 2003 [4628] (UNC)	1711	3205	1862 P	Baldwin 40 [343](EF)	1711A
3206	1863	DNW 83, [3305](EF)	1712	3207	1866	Spink 109 [526] (GF)	1716
3208	1864	DNW 83, [3306](VAS)	1713	3209	1865 (22)	SNC 2007, [2976] (EF)	1714
3210	1866	SNC2010, [9249] (UNC)	1715	3211	1866 8/6	Bole 1, 1792 (EF+)	1715A
3212	1 sm.letters	**DNW 104,** [603]	1717	3212	2nd bust	**DNW 104, 603**	1717
3213	1867 P Mil	**Bole 1, 1794** (AFDC)	1718	3214	1867 P Pln	Bole 3, 191 (AFDC)	1718A
3215	1868 № 10	M.R. 19, 229 (UNC)	1719	3216	1869	M.R. 23/189 (GEF)	1720
3217	1869 P Mil	Bole 1, 1799 (AFDC)	1720A	3218	1870	Spink 157, [623] (UNC)	1721
3219	1870 P Pln		1722	3220	1871 (14)	SNC 2002 [2563] (FDC)	1723
3221	1871 P Pln	Spink 157 [624] (FDC)	1723B	3222	1871 P Mil	**Bole 1, 1804** (AFDC)	1723A
3223	1872	Bole 5, 1469 (VAS)	1726	3224	1872 P Mil	Bole 1, 1810 (AFDC)	1726A
3225	1873	SNC 2003 [4632] (UNC)	1727	3226	1874	SNC 2003, [4633] (EF)	1728
3227	1875	SJA 2, 494 (VAS)	1729	3228	1876	Bole 1, 1475	1730
3229	1877 (3)	Spink 195, [1090] (VAS)	1731	3230	1878	SNC 2006, [7916] (AEF)	1733
3231	1878 P Mil	Bole 1, 1828 (AFDC)	1734	3232	1878/7	Bole 1, 1825(VAS)	1734A
3233	DRITANNIAR	**SNC 2010** [9119](GEF)	1735	3233	DRITANNIAR	Spink 199 [180] (EF)	1735
3234	1879	(Rasmussen 20/251 (VF))	1736	3235	1879/8	**Bole 1, 1829** (NEF)	1736A
3236	1871	Bole 1, 1806 (GEF)	1724	3237	1867 P		1718A
3238	1871 P Mil	**Bole 1, 1805** (GEF)	1725	3239	1873		1727A
3240	1877	SNC 2006 [7915] (AEF)	1732	3241	1879	SNC 2006 [7917] (GEF)	1737
3242	1879 No ser		1737	3243	1879 P Pln	Spink 107 [440] (FDC)	1737A
3244	1879 P Pln	M.R. 6/360 (FDC)	1737B	3245	1880	SNC 2006, [7918] (AEF)	1737C
3246	1880 P Mil		1738	3247	1880 P Mil	**Bole 1, 1831** (AFDC)	1738
				3248	1881	SNC 2010, [9120] (EF)	1740
3249	1881 P Mil	**Bole 1, 1832** (AFDC)	1741	3250	1881 P Pln	Glen.1962, [294] (FDC)	1742
3251	1882	SNC 2006 [7920] (GVF)	1743	3252	1883	SNC 2003 [4637] (GEF)	1744
3253	1883P Pln	**Bole 1, 1883** (AFDC)	1744A	3254	1884	SNC 2003, [463] (UNC)	1745
3255	1885	SNC 2005 [6775] (GEF)	1746	3256	3rd bust	**Bole 1838** DNW 89	1747
3256	1885 P Mil	**Bole 1, 1838** (FDC)	1747	3257	1886	Spink 180, [90] (NEF)	1748
3258	1886 P		1749	3259	1887 YH	SNC 2003 [4640] (UNC)	1750
3260	1887 P Mil	**Bole 1, 1839** (FDC)	1751	3261	1887 wit dra	SNC 2010 [9121] (GEF)	1752
3262	1887	SNC 2002, [3401] (EF)	1752A	3263	1887 R/V		1752C
3264	1887 withdra	SNC 2010, [9122] (EF)	1752B	3265	1887P W D	SNC 2010, [9123] (GEF)	1753

(continued)

PROVENANCES

ESC	Variety	Provenance	(Old ESC)	ESC	Variety	Provenance	(Old ESC)
3266	1887 P ^{Set}		1753A	3267	1887 MP		1753B
3268	Large garter		1753C	3269	1887 JH	SNC 2010,$^{9124\ (VAS)}$	1754
3270	R/I		1754A	3271	R/V	**P.C.(M. Lew.)**$^{(VF))}$	1754B
3272	1887 P	SNC 2002, $^{2567(FDC)}$	1755	3273	1887 MP	Norweb 633 ^{FDC}	1755A
3274	1888	(SNC2002,3405 (UNC))	1756	3275	1888P- ^{1c}	**Bole 1, 1850** $^{(EF)}$	1756A
3276	B	**DNW 104,** ^{610}	1757	3276	C	**SNC 2005** ^{6933}	1757
3276	*Rev.* 1c	**DNW 104,** ^{610}	1757	3277	1890	(SNC2002,3407(GEF))	1758
3278	1890 P		1758A	3279	1891	(SNC2002,3408 (GEF))	1759
3280	1892	(SNC2002,3409 (UNC))	1760	3281	1893 JH	Norweb $^{1089(VAS)}$	1761
3282	1893 OH	SNC 2010 $^{9125\ (GEF)}$	1762	3283	1893 P	Bald.F.P.L.Sum.'13, BM258	1763
3284	1894	(SNC2005,6779 (GVF))	1764	3285	1895	(SNC2005,6780 (VAS))	1765
3286	1896	(SNC2005,6781(VAS))	1766	3287	1897	SNC 2005, $^{6933(EF)}$	1767
3288	1898	(SNC2005,6783 (VAS))	1768	3289	1899	(SNC2005,6784 (GEF))	1769
3290	1900	(SNC2005,6785 (GEF))	1770	3291	1901	SNC 2005, ^{6934} 3(EF)	1771
3292	Pat. E		1772	3293	1841 P ^{Au}	Glens 4/1972, ^{402}	1773
3294	1856 ^{Pat} G	**Bole 1, 1781** $^{(AFDC)}$	1774	3295	Pat. H		1775
3296	Pat. $_I$ ^{Graham}	**M.R. 12/178**	1775A	3297	Pat. J	**Bole 1, 1836** $^{(AFDC)}$	1776
3298	Pat. K	**Bole 1, 1837** $^{(AFDC)}$	1776A	3299	1887 ^{Pat} L	**Norweb 288** ^{FDC}	1777
3299	1887 ^{Pat} L	Bole 5 1488 $^{(GEF)}$	1777	3300	1887 M^1	Bole 1, 1842 (GEF)	1778
3301	Pat. M^1 ^{Au}	**Bole 1, 1843** $^{(GEF)}$	1779	3302	M1 ^{Au} $_{Bavaria}$	**Bole 5, 1490** $^{(EF+)}$	1779A
3302	^{Pat} M^1 ^{Au}	**Bole 1, 1843** $^{(GEF)}$	1779A	3302	M1 ^{Au} $_{Bavaria}$	**Bole 5, 1491** $^{(EF+)}$	1779A
3303	^{Pat} M^1 ^{Cu}	**Bole 1, 1844** $^{(GEF)}$	1780	3304	^{Pat} M^1 ^{Al}	DNW 71,$^{868\ VAS)}$	1781
3305	^{Pat} M^1 ^{Sn}	**Bole 1, 1846** $^{(GEF)}$	1782	3306	^{Pat} M^1 ^{Mill}	**Bole 1, 1847** $^{GEF)}$ ↓	1783
3307	1887 Pat M Cu		1783A	3308	M^1 Mill Au	**Bole 1, 1848** $^{(EF+)}$	1784
3309	M^1 ^{Ni}	**Bole 1, 1849** $^{(NEF)}$	1784A	3310	Pat. M^1	**Bole 5, 1493** $^{(EF+)}$	1784B
3311	M^2 JRT$_{Ni}$		1784C	3312	M^3 S&S		1784D
3313	M^4		1784E		M^1 Mill $_{JRT}$	Bole 5, 1495 $^{(GVF)}$	1784E
	^{Pat} M^1 ^{Mill}	Bole 5, 1494 $^{(EF+)}$↑	1784D				

VICTORIA - GROATS

ESC	Variety	Provenance	(Old ESC)	ESC	Variety	Provenance	(Old ESC)
3314	1837	SCMB $^{784,\ p.309\ (VF)}$	1929	3315	1837 P	DNW 43,$^{858\ AEF)}$	1929A
3316	1838	SNC 2003 $^{4641(UNC)}$	1930	3317	1838 P	*(Not traced)*	1930A
3318	1838 P	*(Not traced)*	1931	3319	1888/∞	SNC 2003 $^{4643\ (UNC)}$	1931A
3320	3195	SNC 2003 $^{4645(UNC)}$	1932	3321	1839 P	Spink 12 358 $^{(FDC)}$	1933
3322	1839 P ^{Pln}	DNW 64,$^{409\ (FDC)}$	1933A	3323	1840	SNC 2003 $^{4651\ (UNC)}$	1934
3324	1840	SNC 2003 $^{4653\ (UNC)}$	1934A	3325	1840/9	SNC 2003 $^{4652(UNC)}$	1934B
3326	1841	SNC 2003 $^{4655(UNC)}$	1935	3327	1841 $_{(1)}$	DNW 43,$^{868\ (EF)}$	1935A
3328	1842	SNC 2003 $^{4656(UNC)}$	1936	3329	1842 P ^{Pln}	Spink 157 $^{634\ (FDC)}$	1937
3330	1842/1	(DNW43,871 (EF))	1937A	3331	1843	SNC 2003 $^{4657(UNC)}$	1938
3332	1843 4/5		1938A	3333	1844	SNC 2003 $^{4659(UNC)}$	1939
3334	1845	SNC 2003 $^{4661\ (UNC)}$	1940	3335	1846	SNC 2003, $^{4663(GEF)}$	1941
3336	1847/6	Spink 67,$^{288\ (EF)}$	1942	3337	1848	(SNC2002, 4251(EF))	1943
3338	1848/6	Spink 168 $^{295\ (GEF)}$	1944	3339	1848/7	SNC 2003 $^{4664(UNC)}$	1944A
3340	1849	SNC 2003 $^{4671\ (UNC)}$	1945	3341	1849/8	**SNC 2003** $^{4672(UNC)}$	1946
3342	1851	DNW 83,$^{3323\ (VAS)}$	1947	3343	1852	SNC 2003 $^{4675\ (AEF)}$	1948
3344	1853		1949	3345	1853 P ^{mil}	SNC 2000, $^{268\ (FDC)}$	1950
3346	1853 P ^{Pln}		1951	3347	1853 5/3	DNW 111,$^{414\ (EF)}$	1951A

(continued)

PROVENANCES

ESC	Variety	Provenance	(Old ESC)	ESC	Variety	Provenance	(Old ESC)
3348	1854	SNC 2007, 8032 (EF)	1952	3349	1855	SNC 2003 4678 (UNC)	1953
3350	1857 P Mil	DNW 43, 900 (VAS)	1954	3351	1857 P Pln		1954A
3352	1857 P	Bald. FPLSum2012,89	1955	3353	1862 P Pln	Norweb 1091	1955A
3354	1862 P	Norweb 1091 VAS	1955B	3355	1862 P		1955C
3356	1888	SNC 2007. 8033 (VAS)	1956	3357	1888 P	SNC 1998 2130 (FDC)	1956A

VICTORIA - THREEPENCES

ESC	Variety	Provenance	(Old ESC)	ESC	Variety	Provenance	(Old ESC)
3358	1838 P Au	Spink 107 442 (FDC)	2447A	3359	1838	SNC 2003 4684 (UNC)	2048
3360	1838 error		2048A	3361	1839	SNC 2002 2584 (UNC)	2049
3362	1839 P		2049A	3363	1840	SNC 2003 4685 (UNC)	2050
3364	1841	SNC 2001. 1217 (GF)	2051	3365	1842	SNC 2002 2587 (GEF)	2252
3366	1843	SNC 2002, 2588 (EF)	2053	3367	1844	DNW 74B. 1017 (Mint)	2054
3368	1845	SNC 2002 2590 (UNC)	2055	3369			
3370	1846	SNC 2002 2591 (UNC)	2056	3371	1847	SNC 1998 2132 (Mint)	2056B
3373	1849	M.R. 21/309 (UNC)	2057				
3374	1848	SNC 2002 2593 (UNC)	2056A	3374	1850	SNC 2003 4687 (UNC)	2058
3375				3376	1851	SNC 2003 4688 (UNC)	2059
3377	5/8	(SNC 1973, 5038 (GVF)	2059A	3378			
3379	1852	DNW 86, 1203 (VAS)	2059B	3380	5/5	DNW 86, 1203	2059C?
3380	Rev. a	DNW 86, 1203	2059C/?	3381	1853	SNC 2002 2599 (UNC)	2060
3382	1853 P	SJA 6, 389 (AFDC)	2060A				
3383	1854	SCMB 1988. p284 (EF)	2061	3384	1855	SNC 2001 2030 (UNC)	2062
3385	1856	SCMB 834, G481(GEF)	2063	3386	1857	(SNC 1999, 1629 (EF))	2064
3387	1858	SNC 2003 4690 (UNC)	2065	3388	1858 error		2065A
3389	1858/6	SNC 2007 8034 (GEF)	2065B	3390	1858/5		2066C
3391	1859 A^1	M.R. 21/320 (UNC)	2066	3392			
3393	1860 A^1	SNC 1999 1631 (AEF)	2067A	3393	1860 A^1	M.R. 21/321 (EF)	2067A
3394	1861 A^1	(Spink 199,199 (GEF))	2068	3394	1859 A^2	SNC 2001 1223 (GVF)	2066A
3395	1860 A^2		2067	3396	1861 A^2	SNC 2002 2607(UNC)	2068A
3397	1862	(SNC2001, 1224 (EF))	2069	3398	1863	SNC 2002 2609 (UNC)	2070
3399	1864	Spink 199 200 (VF)	2071	3399	1864	SNC 2002 2610 (GEF)	2071
3400	1865	SNC 2002. 2611(EF)	2072	3401	1866 A^2	M.R. 5/345	
3402	1866 P	DNW102 2727(VAS	2073A?	3403	1867	Spink 199 200 (VAS)	2074
3404	1868	SNC 2002. 2615 (AF)	2075	3405	RRITANNIAR	**Spink 199, 201 (F)**	2075A
3406	1867 A^3	(SNC 2002 2614 (Mint))	2074A	3407	1866 A^4	M.R. 5/345	
3408	1867 A^4		2074B	3409	1868 A^4		
3410	1869 A^4	SNC 1999, 1637(GEF)	2075C	3410	1869 A^4	SNC 2002 2616 (UNC)	2075C
3411	1870	SNC 2002 2617 (UNC)	2076	3412	1871	SNC 2002 2618 (UNC)	2077
3413	1872	DNW 71, 832 (VAS)	2078	3414	1873	SNC 2003 4693 (UNC)	2079
3415	1874	SNC 2003 4695 (UNC)	2080	3416	1875	SNC 2002 2622 (UNC)	2081
3417	1876	SNC 2002 2623 (UNC)	2082	3418	1877	SNC 2002 2624 (UNC)	2083
3419	1878	(SNC 1999,1645 (EF))	2084	3420	1879	SNC 2002 2626 (UNC)	2085
3421	1879 P	SNC 1977 3382 (FDC)	2086	3422	1879/9 inv	Glens '94/6/2.420 (VAS)	2086A
3423	1884	SNC 2003 4696 (UNC)	2091	3424	1880	SNC 2002 2627 (UNC)	2087
3425	1881	(SNC2002, 2628(UNC))	2088	3426	1882	(SNC 1999,1649(EF))	2089
3427	1883	(SNC2002, 2630(UNC))	2090	3428	1885	SNC 2003 4697 (UNC)	2092
3429	1885 P	**M.R. 6, 348 (FDC)**	2092A	3430	1886	SNC 2003 4699 (UNC)	2093
3431	1887	SNC 2002 2634 (UNC)	2094	3432	1887 P	SNC 2003 4701 (FDC)	2095

(continued)

PROVENANCES

ESC	Variety	Provenance	(Old ESC)	ESC	Variety	Provenance	(Old ESC)
3433	1887	(SNC 2003, 5051 *(VAS)*	2096	3434	1887 P	SNC 2010 ^{9140} *(FDC)*	2097
3435	1888	(SNC2002, 2636*(GEF)*)	2098	3436	1889	(SNC 2003, 5063 *(GEF)*	2099
3437	1890	SNC 2006 ^{7622} *(UNC)*	2100	3438	1891	(SNC2002, 2639*(UNC)*)	2101
3439	1892	(SNC 2003, 5069*(VF)*	2102	3440	1893 $^{Jub\ hd}$	SNC 2002, ^{2641}*(UNC)*	2103
3441	1893 $^{Old\ hd}$	SNC 2010 ^{9141} *(AEF)*	2104	3442	1893 P	SNC 2010 ^{9142}*(FDC)*	2105
3443	1894	(SNC2002, 2644*(UNC)*)	2106	3444	1895	(SNC2002, 2645*(UNC)*)	2107
3445	1896	(Spink 199,206*(EF)*)	2108	3446	1897	(SNC 2003, 5078 *(UNC)*	2109
3447	1898	(SNC 2003, 5080 *(UNC)*)	2110	3448	1899	(SNC2002, 2649 *(UNC)*)	2111
3449	1899/8	Spink 168, ^{296} *(AEF)*	2111A	3450	1900	SNC 2006 ^{7623} *(GEF)*	2112
3451	1901	SNC 2010 ^{9143} *(GEF)*	2113	3452	1868 ^{Pat}	**Spink129** ^{208} *FDC)*	2113A

VICTORIA - HALFGROATS - TWOPENCES

ESC	Variety	Provenance	(Old ESC)	ESC	Variety	Provenance	(Old ESC)
3453	1838	SNC 2003 ^{4702} *(EF)*	2248	3455	1848		2249
3456	1868 P ↑↑	**Bald.** ^{FPLSum2012,090}		3457	1885 P↑↓	Spink 157 ^{638} *(FDC)*	3456A

VICTORIA - THREE-HALFPENCE

ESC	Variety	Provenance	(Old ESC)	ESC	Variety	Provenance	(Old ESC)
3458	1838	**SNC 2003** ^{4703}*(UNC)*	2254	3459	1838 P↑↓	SNC 2000 ^{3191}*(FDC)*	2254A
3460	1838/4	(SNC 1978, 1984 *(GEF)*)	2254B	3461	1839	SNC 2003 ^{4706} *(GEF)*	2255
3462	1840	(SNC 2003, 5197 *(AEF)*)	2256	3463	1841	(SNC 2001, 1302 *(GF)*)	2257
3464	1842	SNC 2003, ^{4707}*(UNC)*	2258	3465	1843	SNC 2003 ^{4708} *(UNC)*	2259
3466	1843 P		2259A	3467	1843/34	**M.R. 20/297** ^{GEF}	2259B
3468	1843	Spink 36 ^{1130} *(FDC)*	2259C	3469	1860	(Rasmussen 20/298 *(UNC)*)	2260
3470	1862	(SNC 2003, 4710 *(GVF)*	2261	3471	1862 P	SCMB $^{1990.\ p92}$ *(AFDC)*	2261A
3472	1870 P	**SNC 1989** $^{2662(GEF)}$	2262				

VICTORIA - PENNIES

ESC	Variety	Provenance	(Old ESC)	ESC	Variety	Provenance	(Old ESC)
3473	1868 P↑↑	**Bald.** ^{FPLSum2012,097}		3474	1878 P	DNW 97, 427 $^{(VAS)}$	2492

VICTORIA - MAUNDY SETS

ESC	Variety	Provenance	(Old ESC)	ESC	Variety	Provenance	(Old ESC)
3475	1838	Spink 183, $^{243\ (UNC)}$	2445	3476	1838 P	SJA 4, 605 $^{(AFDC)}$	2446
3477	1838 P ^{Au}	Wilson & Ras 382	2447	3478	1839	Spink 183, $^{245\ (UNC)}$	2448
3479	1839 P	SNC 2002 $^{4450\ (FDC)}$	2449	3480	1840	Spink 183, $^{245\ (UNC)}$	2450
3481	1841	Spink 183, $^{246\ (UNC)}$	2451	3482	1842	Spink 183, $^{247\ (UNC)}$	2452
3483	1843	Spink 183, $^{248\ (GEF)}$	2453	3484	1844	Spink 183, $^{249\ (GEF)}$	2454
3485	1845	SNC 2011 $^{9517\ (GVF)}$	2455	3486	1846	Spink 183, $^{251\ (UNC)}$	2456
3487	1847	Spink 199, $^{431\ VAS}$	2457	3488	1848	Spink 199, $^{432\ (VAS)}$	2458
3489	1849	Spink 201, $^{624\ (UNC)}$	2459	3490	1850	Spink 183, $^{252\ (UNC)}$	2460
3491	1851	SNC 2006, $^{7180\ (EF)}$	2461	3492	1852	(SNC2001, 0335*(GEF)*)	2462
3493	1853	Spink 199, $^{433\ (VAS)}$	2463	3494	1853 P		2464
3495	1854	SNC 2011 $^{9746\ (VF+)}$	2465	3496	1855	Spink 201, $^{630\ (GEF)}$	2466
3497	1856	SNC 2008, $^{8639\ (EF)}$	2467	3498	1857	SNC 2011 $^{9529\ (GEF)}$	2468
3499	2d $_{leg.\ errors}$			3500	1858	SNC 2008. $^{8640\ (EF)}$	2469A
3501	1859	SNC 2011. $^{9531\ (EF)}$	2470	3502	2d $_{leg.\ errors}$		2471
3503	1860	SJA 12, 851 $^{(GEF)}$	2471A	3504	1861	Baldw.77 $^{2830\ (Unc)}$	2472
3505				3506	1862	Spink 210, $^{551\ (EF)}$	2473
3508	1863	Spink 199, $^{434\ VAS)}$	2474	3509	1864	Spink 199, $^{436\ VAS}$	2475
3510	1865	SNC 2005 $^{6949\ (GEF)}$	2476	3511	1866	Spink 201, $^{635\ (VAS)}$	2477
3513	1867	(Spink 183,266 *(UNC)*)	2478	3514	1867 P		2479

(continued)

PROVENANCES

ESC	Variety	Provenance	(Old ESC)	ESC	Variety	Provenance	(Old ESC)
3515	1868	Baldw.77 ^{2832} (Unc)	2480		1868 P	Assumed based on 1d, above	
3516				3516			
3518	1869	Spink 195^{1094} (UNC)	2481				
3519	1870	Spink 199,^{440} VAS)	2482	3520	1871	SNC 2007, ^{8277} (VAS)	2483
3521	1871P $^4_2{}^1$	Spink 157, ^{636} (FDC)	2484	3522	1872	Spink 210, ^{553} (EF)	2485
3523	1873	SNC 2011 ^{9545} (GEF)	2486	3524	1874	SJA 30, 151$^{(VAS)}$	2487
3525	1875	Spink 210, ^{554} (EF)	2488	3526	1876	Spink 195^{1095} (GEF)	2489
3527	1877	DNW 97 ^{423} (VAS)	2490	3528			
3528	1878	Spink 210, ^{555} (GEF)	2491	3529	1878 P		2492
3530	1879	(SNC2001, MS0354(GEF)	2493	3531	1879 P	Spink 107 ^{440} (FDC)	2493A
3532	1880	Spink 210, ^{556}(EF)	2494	3533	1881	SNC 2005 ^{6951} (GVF)	2495
3535	1882	SNC 2011 ^{9554} (GEF)	2496	3536	1882 P	Spink 157, ^{635} (FDC)	2496A
3537	1883	(SNC2001, 0357(UNC)	2497	3538			
3538	1884	Spink 210, ^{557} (GEF)	2498	3539	1885	SNC 2011 ^{9557} (GEF)	2499
3540	1886	Spink 201 ^{559} (VAS)	2500	3541	1887	SNC 2007 ^{8019} (GEF)	2501
3542	1888	Baldwin77 $^{2838(Unc)}$	2502	3543	1888 P		2503
3544	1889	Spink 208,^{1165} (GEF)	2504	3545	1890	**SNC 2011 $^{9562(UNC)}$**	2505
3546	1891	Spink 216,^{1026} (GEF)	2506	3547	1892	SNC 2006, ^{7183} (EF)	2507
3548	1893	SNC 2011 ^{9749} (GEF)	2508	3549	1894	Baldw.77 ^{2844} (Unc)	2509
3550	1895	SNC 2011 $^{9567(UNC)}$	2510	3551	1896	Baldw.77 $^{2845(Unc)}$	2511
3552	1897	**SPINK 216, ^{1028}**	2512	3553	1898	Baldw.77 ^{2846} (Unc)	2513
3554	1899	SNC 2010 ^{9396} (EF)	2514	3555	1900	SNC 2009 ^{8803} (UNC)	2515
3556	1901	SNC 2007 ^{8021} (VAS)	2516		1838-1901 Col	SJA 30, 151$^{(VAS)}$	

EDWARD VII - CROWNS

ESC	Variety	Provenance	(Old ESC)	ESC	Variety	Provenance	(Old ESC)
3560	1902	Barr 468 $^{(VAS)}$	361	3561	Edge wrong		361A
3562	1902 MP	Barr 469 $^{(VAS)}$	362				
3563	1902 P $^{5/-}$	**Slaney 243 $^{(EF)}$**	363	3563	1902 P $^{5/-}$	Spink 163 ^{243} (EF)	363
3564	1902 P ^{Au}	SJA 15, 560 $^{(VAS)}$	364	3565	1902 P$^{10/-}$		365
3566	1902 P $^{£1}$	**Lingford 588**	366				

EDWARD VII - HALFCROWNS

ESC	Variety	Provenance	(Old ESC)	ESC	Variety	Provenance	(Old ESC)
3567	1902	Adams 757 $^{(UNC)}$	746	3567	1902 MP	Adams 756 $^{(UNC)}$	747
3569	1903	DNW 111,^{482} (VAS)	748	3570	1904	DNW 111,^{483} (VAS)	749
3571	1905	Adams 760 $^{(VAS)}$	750	3572	1906	Adams 761 $^{(GEF)}$	751
3573	1907	Adams 762 $^{(UNC)}$	752	3574	1908	Adams 763 $^{(UNC)}$	753
3575	1909	Adams 764 $^{(UNC)}$	754	3576	1910	DNW 111,^{489} (VAS)	755

EDWARD VII - FLORINS

ESC	Variety	Provenance	(Old ESC)	ESC	Variety	Provenance	(Old ESC)
3577	1902	Spink 199 ^{305} (VAS)	919	3578	1902 P	SNC 2010 ^{9010} (FDC)	920
3579	1903	DNW 89 ^{2261} (EF+)	921	3580	1904	DNW 91 ^{372} (EF+)	922
3581	1905	Norweb 294 ^{VAS}	923	3582	1906	DNW 111,^{494} (VAS)	924
3583	1907	DNW 91 ^{375} (VAS)	925	3584	1908	**DNW 91 ^{376} (EF+)**	926
3585	1909	DNW 91 ^{377} (EF+)	927	3586	1910	SNC 2007 ^{8057} (GEF)	928

EDWARD VII - SHILLINGS

ESC	Variety	Provenance	(Old ESC)	ESC	Variety	Provenance	(Old ESC)
3587	1902	Sommer 2850$^{(GEF)}$	1410	3588	1902 P	Sommerville $^{2850(GEF)}$	1411
3589	1903	Sommer 2850$^{(GEF)}$	1412	3590	1904	Sommerville $^{2851(GEF)}$	1413

(continued)

PROVENANCES

ESC	Variety	Provenance	(Old ESC)	ESC	Variety	Provenance	(Old ESC)
3591	1905	**Somr 2852** *(GEF)*	1414	3592	1906	SNC 2005,6903 *(GEF)*	1415
3593	1907	**Norweb 295** *VAS*	1416	3594	1908	M.R. 22/618 *(Unc)*	1417
3595	1909	M.R. 32/261 *(GEF)*	1418	3596	1910	SNC 2006 7743 *(GEF)*	1419

EDWARD VII - SIXPENCES

ESC	Variety	Provenance	(Old ESC)	ESC	Variety	Provenance	(Old ESC)
3597	1902	SNC 2005, 6935 *(EF)*	1785	3598	1902 MP	SNC 2010 9126 *(GEF)*	1786
3599	1903	(SNC 2001, 0589 *(EF)*)	1787	3600	1904	DNW 91 385 *(VAS)*	1788
3601	1905	**DNW 89** 2057 *(GEF)*	1789	3602	1906	(SNC 2002, 4166 *(VF)*)	1790
3603	1907	(SNC 2002, 4167(GEF))	1791	3604	1908	Spink 199 314 *(VAS)*	1792
3605	1909	SNC 2006 7949 *(GVF)*	1793	3606	1910	Spink 199, 199 *(VAS)*	1794

EDWARD VII - MAUNDY SETS

ESC	Variety	Provenance	(Old ESC)	ESC	Variety	Provenance	(Old ESC)
3607	1902	SNC 2007,8022 *(GEF)*	2517	3608	1902 MP	Spink 216 1030 *(GEF)*	2518
3609	1903	SNC 2007 8370 *(GEF)*	2519	3610	1904	SNC 2006, 7809 *(VAS)*	2520
3611	1905	Spink 214, 806 *(UNC)*	2521	3612	1906	Baldwin 68 3687 *(Unc)*	2522
3613	1907	**SNC2011** 9580 *(UNC)*	2523	3614	1908	SNC 2007 8279 *(UNC)*	2524
3615	1909	(SNC 2001, 0382 *(UNC)*)	2525	3616	1910	Spink 199 316 *(VAS)*	2526

EDWARD VII – THREEPENCES

ESC	Variety	Provenance	(Old ESC)	ESC	Variety	Provenance	(Old ESC)
3617	1902	SNC 2006, 7624 *(VAS)*	2114	3618	1902 P		2115
3619	1903	(SNC 2002, 2653(GEF))	2116	3620	1904	(SNC 2003, 5096(F))	2117
3621	1905	(SNC 2002, 2655(UNC))	2118	3622	1906	(SNC 2002, 2657(GEF))	2119
3623	1907	(SNC 2002, 2658(UNC))	2120	3624	1908	(SNC 2002, 265(EF))	2121
3625	1909	(SNC 2002, 2660(UNC))	2122	3626	1910	(SNC 2002, 2661(UNC))	2123

GEORGE V - CROWNS

ESC	Variety	Provenance	(Old ESC)	ESC	Variety	Provenance	(Old ESC)
3630	1926 Uni Obv			3631	1927 P.925	Barr 470 *(FDC)*	367
3632	1927 MP	Norweb 297 *(FDC)*	367A	3633	1928	DNW 97 469 *(VAS)*	368
3634	1928 P	Spink 117 277 *(EF)*	368A	3635	1928 VIP		368B
				3636	1929	Roekel 253 *(UNC)*	369
3637	1929 P	Spink 117 280 *(FDC)*	369A	3638	1930	Roekel 254 *(VAS)*	370
3639	1931	Roekel 255 *(UNC)*	371	3640	1931 P	Norweb 1121 *(FDC)*	371A
3641	1932	Spink 117, 284 *(VAS)*	372	3642	1932 P	Norweb 1122 *(VAS)*	372A
3643	1932 VIP		372B				
3644	1933	Norweb 706 *(VAS)*	373	3645	1933 P		373A
3646	1933 VIP	Spink 166 87 *(VAS)*	373B	3647	1934	**SNC 2001** 1894(UNC)	374
3648	1934 P	Norweb 707 *(VAS)*	374A	3649	1936	DNW 97 490 *(VAS)*	381
3650	1936 P	Spink 12 362 *(FDC)*	381A	3651	1935	Barr 478 *(UNC)*	375
3652	1935 Speci	**SNC 2004** 6067 *(GEF)*	376	3653	1935 P.925	Norweb 1125 *(FDC)*	377
3654	1935P .500	Barr 326 *(FDC)*	377A	3655	1935 P	SNC 2011,9416(FDC)	378
3655	2	**Spink 156** 261 *(Mint)*	378	3656	1935 P Au	Norweb 1124 *(FDC)*	379
3657	1935 P.925	Barr 327 *(FDC)*	380	3658	1910 Pat C	Norweb 1120	382
3659	1910 P Au	Wilson & Ras 420	383	3660	1910 Pat C	**Glen.**7/1962, 306 *(FDC)*	384
3661	1910 P Au	Glens 4/1972, 382	385	3662	Undate MP Pln	Spink 16 783 *(FDC)*	386
3663	1910 P Cu	Spink 4 705 *(AFDC)*	386A	3664	1910 P Pb		386B
3665	1910 P D1	**DNW 89,**2275 *(VAS)*	387	3665	1910 P D1	**Graham 218**	387
3665	1910 P D1	DNW 89 2275 *(FDC)*	387	3666	D1 Plain Au	Norweb 296	388
3667	1910 P D1	(Lingford 593)	390A	3668	1910P D1 thin	(Lingford 593)	391

(continued)

PROVENANCES

ESC	Variety	Provenance	(Old ESC)	ESC	Variety	Provenance	(Old ESC)
3669	Pat D¹ Mat	Willis 800 (VAS)	391A	3670	1910 P D²	Slaney 244 (FDC)	389
3671	D² Milled Au	Norweb 296 (FDC)	390	3672	1910 P D²	(Lingford 597)	389A
	1910 P D¹	(Lingford 598)	390B	3676	1935 P Ag	Norweb 298 (FDC)	391B
xxxx	Patina Al	DNW 65, 433 (FDC)					

GEORGE V – PROOF DOUBLE FLORINS (Unofficial)

ESC	Variety	Provenance	L&S	ESC	Variety	Provenance	L&S
3677	1911 *in silver*	Barr 124 (UNC)	18				
3678			19	3679	LEAD		?
3680	IRON	Baldwin 13 2049	?	3681	PHOS. BRONZE	Spink 119 227 (EF)	23
3682	ANGLESEA.COPPER	Spink 147 696 (GEF)	24	3683	COPPER Plated		?
3684	CORNISH COPPER	Glen 14-1988, 205 (EF)	25	3685	1911 *in silver*	Lingford 638	20
3686	1911 IRON		21	3687	*1911 silver*	Glen 14-1988, 201 VAS	?
3688	*1911* IRON		?	3689	*1911* ZINC	SNC 1977, 8330 (EF)	22
3690	*1911* CADMIUM		?	3691	NICKEL	Glen 15/1974, 114(EF)	?
3692	*1911 in silver*	Barr 126 (UNC)	?	3693	*1911* copper	DNW 75, 582 (EF)	?
3694	COPPER on edge		?	3695	*1914* silver	Glen 14-1988,202 (EF)	26
3696	*1914* Silver no collar		?	3697	*1914* NICKEL	SNC 1978, 6455 (EF)	27
3698	*1914* ZINC	SNC 1977, 8330 (EF)	22	3699	*1914* PLATINUM		28
3700	*1914 in silver* Milled	Barr 127 (UNC)	29	3701	*1914*	Norweb 1127(FDC)	30
3702	*1914* TIN		?	3703	*1914* LEAD		?
	1911 in silver Milled	?????	?	3705	*1914 in silver*	Barr 128 (UNC)	?
3706	Mule 1911/1914		31	3707	Mule 1911/1914 piedfort		32
3708	Spanish 150 pesetas	SNC 2000 3193(FDC)	33				

GEORGE V - HALFCROWNS

ESC	Variety	Provenance	(Old ESC)	ESC	Variety	Provenance	(Old ESC)
3709	1911	Adams 767 (UNC)	757	3710	1911 P	DNW 101, 508 (FDC)	758
3711	1912	Adams 768 (GEF)	759	3712	1913	Adams 768 (GEF)	760
3713	1914	Adams 769 (GEF)	761	3714	1915	Adams 769 (GEF)	762
3715	1916	Adams 770 (GEF)	763	3716	1917	Adams 770 (GEF)	764
3717	1918	Adams 771 (GEF)	765	3718	1919	Adams 771 (GEF)	766
3719	1920	(Adams 772 (GEF))	767	3720	1920 low		767A
3721	1920 Sp	PC (M. Bull) (FDC)	767B?	3722	1921	(Adams 772 (UNC))	768
3723	1922	(Adams 773 (NEF))	769	3724	1923	SNC 2006, 7550 (VAS)	770
3725	1924	(Adams 774 (UNC))	771	3726	1924 MP	Adams 775 (FDC)	771A
3727	1925	Adams 776 (UNC)	772	3728	1926	Adams 777 (UNC)	773
3729	1926 mod	Adams 779 (GEF)	774	3730	1927 ty C	Adams 779 (GEF)	775
3731	1927 P Au	Spink 107, 451 (FDC)	775A?	3731	1927 P Au	Spink 107 451/2 (FDC)	775A?
3731	1927 P Au	Spink 107, 452 (FDC)	775A?	3732	1927 P	Adams 782 (FDC)	776
3733	1927 MP	Norweb 297 (FDC)	776A	3734	1928	Adams 784 (UNC)	777
3735	1928 P	Adams 783 (FDC)	777A?	3736	1928 bronze	Adams 785 (UNC)	777B
3737	1929 (2 var)	(Adams 786 (UNC))	778	3738	1929 P		778A?
3739	1930	DNW 101, 514 (EF)	779	3740	1930 P	Norweb 709 (FDC)	779A?
3741	1931	Spink 199 334 (VAS)	780	3742	1931 P	Adams 787 (FDC)	780A?
3743	1932	(Adams 792 (UNC))	781	3744	1932 P	Adams 788 (FDC)	781A
3745	1933	(Adams 792 (UNC))	782	3746	1933 P	Adams 789 (FDC)	782A
3747	1934	SNC 2006, 7551 (VAS)	783	3748	1934 P	Adams 790 (FDC)	783A
3749	1935	(Adams 792 (UNC))	784	3750	1935 P	Norweb 1131	784A

(continued)

PROVENANCES

ESC	Variety	Provenance	(Old ESC)	ESC	Variety	Provenance	(Old ESC)
3751	1936	(Adams 792 (UNC))	785	3752	1936 P	Adams 791 (FDC)	785A
3754	1936 VIP	SJA 21, 427 (FDC)	785B	3754	1926 model	Adams 780 (EF)	774A?

GEORGE V - FLORINS

ESC	Variety	Provenance	(Old ESC)	ESC	Variety	Provenance	(Old ESC)
3755	1911	SNC 2010, 9012 (EF)	929	3756	1911 P	SNC 2010 9013 (FDC)	930
3757	1912	SNC 2005 6477 (UNC)	931	3758	1913	SNC 2009 8784 (GEF)	932
3759	1914	SNC 2006 7560 (VAS)	933	3760	1915	(SNC 2005, 6477 (AEF))	934
3761	1916	SNC 2009 8784 (GEF)	935	3762	1917	(SNC 2005, 6482 (UNC))	936
3763	1918	Spink 199, 337 (GEF)	937	3764	1919	SNC 2007 8058 (VAS)	938
3765	1920	(SNC 2005, 6485 (UNC))	939	3766	1920 low relief		939A
3767	1920 Specimen	PC (M.B.)	939B	3768	1921	(SNC 2005, 6486 (UNC))	940
3769	1922	(SNC 2005, 6487 (UNC))	941	3770	1922P 24ct Au	Norweb 1132	941A
3771	1922P .875 Au	Spink 107 454(FDC)	941B	3772	1922 P .750 Au	See article SNC 1984 p.218	941C
3773	1922 P .625 Au	See article SNC 1984 p.218	941D	3774	1923	SNC 2006 7561 (VAS)	942
3775	1924	(SNC 2005, 6489 (UNC))	943	3776	1924 MP		943A
3777	1925	SNC 1986 5281 (VAS)	944	3778	1926	SNC 2010 9014 (GEF)	945
3779	1927 P	DNW 13/6/12	947	3780	1927 MP	Norweb 297 (FDC)	747A
3781	1928	SNC 2010, 9016 (VAS)	948	3782	1928 P	SNC 1979 9047 (FDC)	948A
3783	1929	(SNC 2005, 6493 (UNC))	949	3784	1929 P		949A
3785	1930	(SNC 2005, 6494 (UNC))	950	3786	1930 P	Norweb 711 (VAS)	950A
3787	1931	Spink 199, 338 (UNC)	951	3788	1931 P	SNC 1998, 1985 (FDC)	951A
3789	1932	DNW 111, 533(GEF)	952	3790	1932 P	Glens 6/1986,163 (FDC)	952A
3791	1933	Spink 195, 1175 (VAS)	953	3792	1933 P	Norweb 1133	953A
3793	1935	(SNC 2005, 6498 (UNC))	954	3794	1935 P	Norweb 1131	954A
3795	1935 VIP		954B	3796	1936	SNC 2006 7562 (UNC)	955
3797	1936 P	Spink 12 369 (FDC)	955A	3798	1936 VIP	SJA 21, 428(FDC)	955B

GEORGE V - SHILLINGS

ESC	Variety	Provenance	(Old ESC)	ESC	Variety	Provenance	(Old ESC)
3799	1911	SNC 2009 8796 (VAS)	1420	3800	1911 P	SNC 2010 9062(FDC)	1421
3801	1912	SNC 2009 8797 (UNC)	1422	3802	1913	SNC 2010 9063 (VAS)	1423
3803	1914	SNC 2007 8074 (UNC)	1424	3804	1915	SNC 2009 8798(UNC)	1425
3805	1916	Spink 199, 341 (GEF)	1426	3806	1917	SNC 2006 7587 (GEF)	1427
3807	1918	Spink 199, 341 (GEF)	1428	3808	1919	SNC 2009 8800 (VAS)	1429
3809	1920deep	(SNC 2005, 6520 (EF))	1430	3810	1921deep	DNW 44, 446 VAS)	1431
3811	1920 low	(SNC 2005, 6520 (EF))	1430	3812	1920 Specimen	(Not traced)	1430A?
3813	1921	DNW 44, 446 VAS)	1431	3814	1921 P	(Not traced)	1431A
3815	1922	(SNC 2005, 6522 (UNC))	1432	3816	1922 P	(Not traced)	1432A
3817	1922 P Au	Spink 107 454 (AFDC)	1432B	3818	1923	SNC 2010 9064 (UNC)	1433
3819	1923 P Ni	Norweb 1880 (EF)	1433A	2820	1924	(SNC 2005, 6524 (GVF))	1434
3821	1924 P Ni	Norweb 1881 (EF)	1434A	3822	1924 Specimen	SNC 1999 5256 (FDC)	1434B
3823	1925	(SNC 2005, 6525 (EF))	1435	3824	1925 P	(Not traced)	1435A
3825	1926	Spink 199, 341 (GEF)	1436	3826	1926 P	(Not traced)	1436A
3827	1926 mod f	SNC 2006, 7589 (VAS)	1437	3828	1927 mod f	SNC 2010 9066 (UNC)	1438
3829	1927 new	SNC 2010, 9067(GEF)	1439	3830	1927 P	SNC 2008, 8447	1440
3831	1927 MP	(Not traced)	1440A	3832	1928	(SNC 2005, 6530 (UNC))	1441
3833	1928 P	SNC 1999 5257 (FDC)	1441A	3834	1928 VIP		1441B
3835	1929	(SNC 2005, 6531 (UNC))	1442	3836	1929 P	(Not traced)	1442A
3837	1930	Spink 199, 342 (GEF)	1443	3838	1930 P	Norweb 713	1443A

(continued)

PROVENANCES

ESC	Variety	Provenance	(Old ESC)	ESC	Variety	Provenance	(Old ESC)
3839	1931	Spink 199,^{341} *(GEF)*	1444	3840	1931 P	Norweb 1134	1444A
3841	1931 VIP		1444B	3842	1932	*(SNC 2005, 6534 (UNC))*	1445
3843	1932 P	Spink 32 ^{519} *(FDC)*	1445A	3844	1931 VIP		1444B
3845	1933	*(SNC 2005, 6535 (GEF))*	1446	3846	1933 P	Spink 12 ^{370} *(FDC)*	1446A
3847	1934	Spink 199,^{341} *(GEF)*	1447	3848	1934 P	Norweb 714 $^{(VAS)}$	1447A
3849	1934 VIP		1447B	3850	1935	*(SNC 2005, 6537 (UNC))*	1448
3851	1935 P	Norweb 1131	1448A	3852	1935 VIP	SJA 21, 429$^{(FDC)}$	1448B
3853	1936	*(SNC 2005, 6538 (UNC))*	1449	3854	1936 P	Spink 12 ^{371} *(FDC)*	1449A
3855	1936 VIP	SNC 2002, $^{4044(VAS)}$	1449B	3856	1925 $^{Pat\ Ni}$	Norweb 712 $^{(VAS)}$	1449A
3857	1925P Pb	Spink 153,^{1056}	1449B	3858	1926 ^{Model}	SNC 1999, $^{5330(VAS)}$	

GEORGE V - EIGHTPENCES

ESC	Variety	Provenance	(Old ESC)	ESC	Variety	Provenance	(Old ESC)
2859	1913 P ^{Ag}	**SJA 24,** ^{336} *(EF)*	1481	3860	1913 ^{Ni}	Norweb 1138 ^{EF}	1481A
3861	1913 P ^{Au}	Wilson & Ras 428	1481B	3862	1913 P ^{Pt}	*(SNC 1973, 5005 (FDC))*	1481C
3863	1913MP^{Pt}	*(SNC 1973, 5005 (FDC))*	1481D	3864	1913 P ^{Cu}	Baldwin 1,^{553} *(FDC)*	1481E
3865	1913 P ^{Fe}		1481F	3866	1913P$^{Fe}_{Pie}$	Norweb 1139 *(EF)*	1481G
3867	1913 P	**SNC 1998** $^{3762(FDC)}$	1482	3868	1913 P ^{Au}	Wilson & Ras 429	14842B
3869	1913 P ^{Cu}	Norweb 1137 *(EF)*	14842A	3870	1913 P ^{Pb}	SNC 1998, ^{3763} *(VF)*	14842C

GEORGE V - SIXPENCES

ESC	Variety	Provenance	(Old ESC)	ESC	Variety	Provenance	(Old ESC)
3871	1911	SNC 2010 ^{9127} *(UNC)*	1795	3872	1911 P	SNC 2010 ^{9128} *(FDC)*	1796
3873	1912	SNC 2006 ^{7952} *(UNC)*	1797	3874	1913	Spink 199,^{345}*(VAS)*	1798
3875	1914	*(SNC 2002, 4176 (EF))*	1799	3876	1915	Spink 199 ^{345}*(VAS)*	1800
3877	1916	*(SNC 2002, 4179 (GEF))*	1801	3878	1917	Spink 199,^{345}*(VAS)*	1802
3879	1918	Spink 199,^{344} *(VAS)*	1803	3880	1919	*(SNC 2002, 4183(GEF))*	1804
3881	1920	*(SNC 2001, 0606 (EF))*	1805	3882	1920 ^{debase}	*(SNC 2002, 4185 (GEF))*	1806
3883	1920 Specimen		1806A	3884	1921	*(SNC 2002, 4186 (UNC))*	1807
3885	1922	*(SN C2002, 4187(UNC))*	1808	3886	1923	Spink 199,^{346} *(EF)*	1809
3887	1823 ^{Ni}		1809A	3888	1924	*(SNC 2002, 418 8 (UNC))*	1810
3889	1924 P	Bole 1, 1855 $^{(AFDC)}$	1810A	3890	1924 ^{Nil}		1810B
3891	1924 ^{Au}	**Bole 1, 1854** / **Bole 5, 1501**	1810C	3892	1925	*(SNC 2001, 0612 (GEF))*	1811
3893	1925 ^{mod}	SNC 2010 ^{9130} *(GEF)*	1812	3894	1826 ^{mod}	*(SNC 2001, 0614 (UNC))*	1813
3895	1926 ^{new}	CoE $^{47th\ ed.\ p.\ 488}_{4025}$	1814	3896	1927	SNC 2010 ^{9131} *(UNC)*	1815
3897	1927P ^{Nicl}	Bole 5, 1504 $^{(AFDC)}$	1815A	3898	1927 P ^{Ag}	Bole 5, 1505 $^{(AFDC)}$	1816
3899	1927MP		1816A	3900	1928	SNC 2010 ^{9133} *(UNC)*	1817
3901	1928 P	Bole 5, 1507 $^{(AFDC)}$	1817A	3902	1928 MP		1817B
3903	1929	Spink 199,^{346} *(EF)*	1818	3904	1929 P		1818A
3905	1930	*(SNC 2002, 4199 (EF))*	1819	3906	1930 P	Norweb 717 ^{FDC}	1819A
3907	1931	Spink 199,^{346} *(EF)*	1820	3908	1931 P	Bole 5, 1508 $^{(AFDC)}$	1820A
3909	1931 VIP		1820B	3910	1932	Spink 199 ^{346} *(VAS)*	1821
3911	1932 P	Bole 1, 1858 $^{(AFDC)}$	1821A	3912	1932VIP		1821B
3913	1933	*(SNC 2002, 4201 (EF))*	1822	3914	1933 P	Bole 5, 1509 $^{(AFDC)}$	1822A
3915	1934	Spink 199,^{346} *(EF)*	1823	3916	1934 P	Norweb 718 $^{(FDC)}$	1823A
3917	1935	*(SNC 2002, 4204 (GEF))*	1824	3918	1935 P	Bole 4, 58 $^{(AFDC)}$	1824A
3919	1935 VIP	SJA 21, 431 $^{(FDC)}$	1824B	3920	1936	*(SNC 2002, 4205 (GEF))*	1825
3921	1936 P$_{mill}$	SJA 21, 432$^{(FDC)}$	1825C	3922	1936 VIP		1825D
3923	1925 P ^{Ni}	Bole 1, 1856 $^{(AFDC)}$	1825A	3924	1925 Uni. Rev	Bole 5, 1503 $^{(AFDC)}$	1825B
3924	1925 P	Bole 1, 1857 $^{(EF)}$	1825B	3925	1926 Uni. Rev		

PROVENANCES

GEORGE V - THREEPENCES

ESC	Variety	Provenance	(Old ESC)	ESC	Variety	Provenance	(Old ESC)
3926	1911	(SNC 2003, 5103 (UNC)	2124	3927	1911 P		2125
3928	1912	**SNC 2006** 7560(UNC)	2126	3929	1913	SNC 2011 9584 (UNC)	2127
3930	1914	(SNC 2003, 5104 (VF)	2128	3931	1915	(SNC 2003, 5105 (GVF)	2129
3932	1916	(SNC 2003, 5106 (EF)	2130	3933	1917	(SNC 2003, 5110 (EF)	2131
3934	1918	(SNC 2003, 5113 (UNC)	2132	3935	1919	(SNC 2003, 5116 (GEF)	2123
3936	1919/8		2123A	3937	1920	CoE 47th ed. p. 488 4026	2124
3938	1920 debase	(SNC 2003, 5117 (AEF)	2135	3939	1921	(SNC 2003, 5119 (AEF)	2136
3940	1921sm 2		2136A	3941	1922	**SNC 2006** 7626(GEF)	2137
3942	1924MP						
3943	1925	(SNC 2002, 2674 (UNC))	2138	3944	1926	(SNC 2002, 2639 (GEF))	2139
3945	1926 mod	(SNC 2002, 2676 (UNC))	2140	3946	1927P new	Spink 199, 347 (VAS)	2141
3947	1927 MP		2141A?	3948	1928	Spink 199, 348 (VAS)	2142
3949	1930	CoE 47th ed. p. 491 4042	2143	3950	1930 P	Norweb 720 (FDC)	2143A?
3951	1931	(SNC 2003, 5122 (EF)	2144	3952	1931 P	SNC 2006 7513 (VAS)	2144A
3953	1932	(SNC 2002, 2682 (UNC))	2145	3954	1932 P	Norweb 1144	2145A?
3955	1933	(SNC 2002, 2683 (UNC))	2146	3956	1933 P Pln	SNC 1994 8130 (FDC)	2146A
3957	1934	(SNC 2002, 2684 (UNC))	2147	3958	1934 P	Norweb 721	2147A
3959	1935	**SNC 2006** 7627(UNC)	2148	3960	1935 P	Norweb 1131	2148A
3961	1935 VIP	SJA 21, 433 (FDC)	2148B	3962	1936	(SNC 2002, 2686 (UNC))	2149
3963	1936 P	SNC 1984 7547(FDC)	2149A	3964	1936 VIP	SJA 21, 434 (FDC)	2149B
3965	1923 P Ni	SNC 1998 2135 (VAS)	2149C	3966	1924 MP	**SNC 1997,** 5989	2149D
3967	1924 Av	W&R 431	2149E	3967	1924 P Au	SNC1998 6920 (VAS)	2149E
3968	1925 P Ni	Norweb 719 (FDC)	2149B	3969	1925 MP	SNC1998 2119 (VAS)	2149C

GEORGE V - MAUNDY SETS

ESC	Variety	Provenance	(Old ESC)	ESC	Variety	Provenance	(Old ESC)
3970	1911	**SNC 2009** 8806 (GEF)	2527	3971	1911 P	(SNC 2011, 9585 (VAS))	2528
3972	1912	Spink 202, 341 (EF)	2529	3973	1913	(SNC 2001, 0386 (UNC))	2530
3974	1914	(SNC 2005, 6674 (VAS))	2531	3975	1915	SNC 2006 7810 (AEF)	2532
3976	1916	Baldw.77 2921 (Unc)	2533	3977	1917	SNC 2011 9591 (UNC)	2534
3978	1918	**SNC 2009** 8807 (GEF)	2535	3979	1919	Baldw.77 2922 (Unc)	2536
3980	1920	SJA 10, 976 (FDC)	2537	3981	1921 debase	(SNC 2001, 0392 (UNC))	2538
3982	1922	(SNC 2001, 0393 (UNC))	2539	3983	1923	SJA 10, 980 (FDC)	2540
3984	1924	(SNC 2002, 4487 (UNC))	2541	3985	1925	(SNC 2001, 0396 (UNC))	2542
3986	1926	(SNC 2002, 4488 (UNC))	2543	3987	1927	(SNC 2003, 5657 (AEF))	2544
3988	1928 debase	CoE 47th ed. p. 491 4043	2545	3989	1929	Spink 201, 661(VAS)	2546
3990	1930 new	SNC 2011 9604(UNC)	2547	3991	1931	(SNC 2001, 0400 (UNC))	2548
3992	Uniface Obv.		2548A	3993	1932	(SNC 2001, 0401 (UNC))	2549
3994	1933	(SNC 2001, 0402 (UNC))	2550	3995	1934	(SNC 2001, 0403 (UNC))	2551
3996	1935	Spink 201, 663 (VAS)	2552	3997	1936	Spink 202, 348 (VAS)	2553

EDWARD VIII

ESC	Variety	Provenance	(Old ESC)	ESC	Variety	Provenance	(Old ESC)
4000	5/- Obv / rev	**Spink 149** 346	391C	4000	5/- Obv / rev	Spink 124 2262 (VAS)	391C
4000	5/- Obv / rev	Spink 149 346 (FDC)	391C				
4002	5/- Uni Ob. tin	Spink 217 864 (VAS)		4001	5/- Model obv	SNC 1997, 214	?
4002	5/- Uni Ob. tin	Glens 3/1970 236 (VAS)		4003	5/- Uni Rv tin	Spink 217 864 (VAS)	
4003	5/- Uni Rv. tin	Glens 3/1970 236 (VAS)		4004	2/6	Spink 46 819 (FDC)	785A
4005	2/6 Uni. obv	Adams 794 (EF)	785C	4006			

(continued)

PROVENANCES

ESC	Variety	Provenance	(Old ESC)	ESC	Variety	Provenance	(Old ESC)
4007				4008			
4009	2/- MP	SNC 2000, 3194 (FDC)	955B		2/- Rev	CoE 47th ed. p. 494 4063	955A
	2/- Model	(DNW 107, 616)	?	4011	1/- Pat Scot	SNC 1992 3625(VAS)	1449
4011	1/-	Spink 46 820 (FDC)	1449B	4012			
4013	6d	Bole 1, 1861 (FDC)	1825B	4014	6d model obv	Bole 5, 1510 (AFDC)	1825C
4015	3d rev	CoE 47th ed. p. 494 4063	2149D				

GEORGE VI - CROWNS

ESC	Variety	Provenance	(Old ESC)	ESC	Variety	Provenance	(Old ESC)
4020	1837	Spink 190, 739 (VAS)	392	4021	1937 P	Spink 4 716 (FDC)	393
4022	1937 VIP	SJA 21, 444 (FDC)	393A	4023	1937 MP	Barr 127 (AFDC)	393B
4024	1951 VIP	Barr 483 (FDC)	393C	4025	1951 VIP	SNC 2010 8953 (FDC)	393D
4026	1951 MP	Barr 130 (FDC)	393E	4027	1951 Trial	Barr 484 (EF)	393F
4028	1951 Trial	**Barr 485 (EF)**	393G	4029	1951 P Pln	Norweb 1907 (EF)	339H
4030	1937 Trial cn	**SNC 2003 5780 (FDC)**	393I	4031	1937 Uni, Rev.	L&S 6	393J

GEORGE VI - DOUBLE FLORINS

ESC	Variety	Provenance	(Old ESC)	ESC	Variety	Provenance	(Old ESC)
4032	1950 P Mil	Barr 131 (UNC)	406B	4033	1950 P 4 Shills	SJA 15, 562 (VAS)	406C

GEORGE VI - HALFCROWNS

ESC	Variety	Provenance	(Old ESC)	ESC	Variety	Provenance	(Old ESC)
4034	1937	(Rasmussen 9/430 (UNC))	786	4035	1937 P	Adams 795 (FDC)	787
				4036	1937 MP	Norweb 729 FDC	787A
4037	1938	Spink 199 356 (VAS)	788	4038	1938 P	Adams 795 (FDC)	788A
4039	1939	(Rasmussen 9/432 (UNC))	789	4040	1939 P	Spink 107 457 (FDC)	789A
				4041	1939 VIP	Spink 166 90 (AFDC)	789B
4042	1940	(Commonly found)	790	4043	1940 P	Norweb 1898	790A
4044	1941	(Rasmussen 9/433 (UNC))	791	4045	1941 P	Norweb 1899	791A
4046	1942	(Commonly found)	792	4047	1942 P	Spink 69, 409 (FDC)	792A
4046	1942 Specimen strike	Adams 797 (UNC)	792	4048	1942 MP		792B
4049	1943 Specimen strike	Adams 798 (UNC)	793				
4049	1943	(Rasmussen 9/434 (UNC))	793	4050	1943 P	Spink 199 385 (FDC)	793A
4051	1943MP	SNC 1998, 448 (FDC)	793B	4052	1943 VIP	Spink 166 91 (AFDC)	793C
4053	1944	(Rasmussen 9/435 (UNC))	794	4054	1944 P		794A
4055	1945	(Rasmussen 9/435 (UNC))	795	4056	1945 P		795A
4057	1946 1st	(Commonly found)	796	4058	1946 P	Norweb 1902	796A
				4059	1946 P2nd	Very rare	796B
4060	1947	(Rasmussen 9/436 (UNC))	797	4061	1947 P	Adams 800 (FDC)	797A
				4062	1947 VIP	Spink 1171 159 (FDC)	797B
4063	1948	(Rasmussen 9/436 (UNC))	798	4064	1948 P	Spink 12 385 (FDC)	798A
4065	1949	Adams 803 (UNC)		4066	1949 P	Spink 107 458 (FDC)	
				4067	1949 VIP	Bald. Sum. 14, BM162	
4068	1950	Adams 803 (UNC)		4069	1950 P	Adams 803 (FDC)	
				4070	1950 MP	Norweb 1161	
4071	1951	Adams 803 (UNC)		4072	1951 P	Adams 803 (FDC)	
				4073	1951 MP	SJA 20, 172 (FDC)	
4074	1952			4075	1952 P	Baldwin 125yr sale 1997	

PROVENANCES

GEORGE VI - FLORINS

ESC	Variety	Provenance	(Old ESC)	ESC	Variety	Provenance	(Old ESC)
4076	1937	Spink 215, 469 (UNC)	956	4077	1937 P	Spink 199, 340 (FDC)	957
				4078	1937 MP	Norweb 729 FDC	957A
4079	1938	Spink 199, 357 (VAS)	958	4080	1938 P	Norweb 1157	958A
4081	1939	(SNC 2002, 3793 (UNC))	959	4082	1939 P	Spink 107 457 (FDC)	959A
				4083	1939 VIP	SNC 1998 3766 (FDC)	959B
4084	1940	(SNC 2002, 3796 (UNC))	960	4085	1940 P	Norweb 1898	960A
4086	1941	**Bull**	961	4087	1941 P	Norweb 1899	961A
4088	1942	(SNC 1994, 4278 (VAS))	962	4089	1942 P	Norweb 1900	962A
4090	1942 MP		962A	4091	1943	(SNC 1994, 4279 (VAS))	963
4092	1943 P		963A	4093	1943 VIP		963B
4094	1943 MP	SNC 1998 3768 (FDC)	963B				
4095	1944	(SNC 1994, 4280 (UNC))	964	4096	1944 P		964A
4097	1945	(SNC 1994, 4281 (UNC))	965	4098	1945 P		965A
4099	1946	SNC 1998 945 (UNC)	966	4100	1946 P		966A
4101	1946 P Cu	*Very rare*	966B	4102	1947 cu	SNC 1998 946 (UNC)	967
4103	1947 P	Norweb 1159	967A	4104	1947 VIP		967B
4105	1948	(Rasmussen 9/441 (UNC))	968	4106	1948 P	Spink 12 388 (FDC)	
4107	1948 VIP			4108	1949 new	(Rasmussen 9/441 (UNC))	968A
4109	1949 P	Spink 107 458 (FDC)		4110	1949 VIP	Bald. FPLSum'14 BM166	
4111	1950	(Rasmussen 9/441 (UNC))	968B	4112	1950 P	Spink 216, 1009 (FDC)	968C
4113	1950 MP	Norweb 1161	968F	4114	1951	(Rasmussen 9/441 (UNC))	968D
4115	1951 P	**SNC 2005** 6117 (FDC)	968E	4116	1951 VIP		
4117	1951 MP	SJA 13, 830 (FDC)	968G	4118	1952 P		
4119	1952 VIP						

GEORGE VI - SHILLINGS

	English				Scottish		
4120	1937	(Rasmussen 9/442 (UNC))	1450	4149	1937	(Rasmussen 9/442 (UNC))	1452
4121	1937 P	(Rasmussen 9/442 (UNC))	1451	4150	1937 P	Spink 199, 347 (VAS)	1453
4122	1937 MP	Norweb 729 (FDC)	1451A	4151	1937 MP	Norweb 729	1453A
				4152	1937 Obv. unifa	Spink 199, 347 (VAS)	1453B
4123	1938	Spink 199, 358 (VAS)	1454	4153	1938	Spink 199, 358 (VAS)	1455
4124	1938 P	Norweb 1157	1454A	4154	1938 P	Norweb 1157	1455A
4125	1939	(Rasmussen 9/443 (UNC))	1456	4155	1938 VIP		
4126	1939 VIP			4156	1939	(Rasmussen 9/444 (UNC))	1457
4127	1939 P	Spink 107 457 (FDC)	1456A	4157	1939 P	Spink 107 457 (FDC)	1457A
4128	1939 VIP			4158	1939 VIP	SNC 1998 3768 (FDC)	
4129	1940	(Rasmussen 9/443 (UNC))	1458	4159	1940	(Rasmussen 9/444 (UNC))	1459
4130	1940 P	Norweb 1898	1458A	4160	1940 P	Norweb 1898	1459A
4131	1941	(Rasmussen 9/443 (UNC))	1460	4161	1941	(Rasmussen 9/444 (UNC))	1461
4132	1941 P	Norweb 1899	1460A	4162	1941 P	Norweb 1899	1461A
				4163	1941 VIP	Norweb 1899	1461A
4133	1942	CoE 47th ed. p. 497 4082	1462	4164	1942	(Rasmussen 9/444 (UNC))	1463
4132	1942 P	Spink 69, 409 (FDC)	1462A	4165	1942 P	Spink69, 409 (FDC)	1463A
4135	1942 MP		1462B	4166	1942 MP		
4136	1943	(Rasmussen 9/443 (UNC))	1464	4167	1943	(Rasmussen 9/444 (UNC))	1465
4137	1943	*Die axis inverted*					

(continued)

PROVENANCES

ESC	Variety	Provenance (English)	(Old ESC)	ESC	Variety	Provenance (Scottish)	(Old ESC)
4138	1943 P	SNC 1999 $^{5268(FDC)}$	1464A	4168	1943 P		
4139	1943 MP		1464B	4169	1943 MP	M.R. 14/185 $^{(FDC))}$	1465B
4140	1944	(Rasmussen 9/443 (UNC))	1466	4170	1944	(Rasmussen 9/444 (UNC))	1467
4141	1944 P	SNC ^{1999,} $_{5269(FDC)}$	1466A	4171	1944 P	SNC ^{1999,} $_{5282(FDC)}$	1467A
4142	1944 MP			4172	1944 MP		
4143	1945	(Rasmussen 9/443 (UNC))	1468	4173	1945	CoE $^{47th\ ed.\ p.\ 497}$ $_{4083}$	1469
4144	1945 P		1468A	4174	1945 P		1469A
4145	1946.500 ag	(Rasmussen 9/443 (UNC)	1470	4175	1946.500 ag	(Rasmussen 9/444 (UNC)	1471
4146	1946 P ag	Norweb 1903	1470 A	4176	1946 P ag		1471A
4147	1946 VIP			4177	1946 VIP		
4148	1947 P ag	B.M. collection	1470B	4178	1947 P ag		1471B
4179	1946P cu-ni	SNC ^{1979} $_{11463(FDC)}$	1470A	4186	1946P cu-ni	Reserved	
4180	1947		1472	4187	1947	(Rasmussen 9/446 (UNC))	1473
4181	1947 P	Norweb 1159	1472A	4188	1947 P	Norweb 1159	1473A
4182	1947 VIP		1472B	4189	1947 VIP	M.R. 14/186 $^{(FDC)}$	1473
4183	1948	**Bull**	1474	4190	1948	**Bull**	1475
4184	1948 P	SNC ^{1999} $_{5272\ (FDC)}$	1474A	4191	1948 P	SNC ^{1999} $_{5284\ (FDC)}$	1475A
4185	1948 VIP			4192	1948 VIP		
4193	1949	(Rasmussen 9/445 (UNC))	1475A	4204	1949	(Rasmussen 9/446 (UNC))	
4194	1949 P	Spink 107 $^{458\ (FDC)}$	1475AA	4205	1949 P	Spink 107 $^{458\ (FDC)}$	
4195	1949 VIP	B.F.P.L. $^{2014.\ BM186}$		4206	1949 VIP	B.F.P.L. $^{2014.\ BM185}$	
4196	1950	(Rasmussen 9/445 (UNC))	1475C	4207	1950	(Rasmussen 9/446 (UNC))	1475E
4197	1950 P	**Bull**	1475D	4208	1950 P	**Bull**	1475F
				4209	1950 VIP		
4198	1950 MP	Norweb 1161	1475DD	4210	1950 MP	Norweb 1161	1475H
4199	1951	(Rasmussen 9/445 (UNC))	1475G	4211	1951	(Commonly found)	1475I
4200	1951 P			4212	1951 P		
4201	1951 MP	SNC 1999 $^{5275\ (GEF)}$	1475H	4213	1951 MP	SJA 13, 831 $^{(FDC)}$	1475J
4202	1952 P Ni		1475?	4214	1952 P Ni	Norweb 731 ^{FDC}	
4203	1952 MP			4215	1952 MP	Spink 199, $^{347\ (VAS)}$	cf.1453
4216	1952 P Ni	**Norweb 731**		4217	1952 P Ni		

GEORGE VI - SIXPENCES

ESC	Variety	Provenance	(Old ESC)	ESC	Variety	Provenance	(Old ESC)
4218	1937	(Rasmussen 9/448 (UNC))	1826	4266	1937 P		
4219	1937 MP	Bole 1, 1862 $^{(AFDC)}$	1827	4220			
4221	1938	(SNC 2002, 4208 (UNC))	1828	4222	1938 P	Bole 1, 1863 $^{(FDC)}$	1828A
4223	1938 VIP			4224	1939	(SNC 2002, 4209 (UNC))	1829
4225	1939 P	Spink 107 $^{457\ (FDC)}$	1529A	4226	1939 VIP	SNC 1998 $^{3768\ (FDC)}$	
4227	1940	(Rasmussen 9/448 (UNC))	1830	4228	1940 P	Bole 1, 1864 $^{(FDC)}$	1830A
4229	1940 VIP			4230	1941	(SNC 2002, 4210 (EF))	1831
4231	1941 P	**Bole 4, 60** $^{(AFDC)}$	1831A	4232	1941 VIP		
4233	1942	Spink 69, $^{409\ (FDC)}$	1832	4234	1942 P	Spink 69, $^{409\ (FDC)}$	
4235	1942 VIP			4236	1943	(SNC 2002, 4212 (UNC))	1833
4237	1943 P	SNC 1998 $^{3772\ (AFD)}$	1833A	4238	1943 VIP		1833B
4239	1943 MP		1833C	4240	1944	(SNC 2002, 4213 (UNC))	1834

(continued)

PROVENANCES

ESC	Variety	Provenance	(Old ESC)	ESC	Variety	Provenance	(Old ESC)
4241	1944 P			4242	1944 MP		
4243	1945	(SNC 2002, 4214 (UNC))	1835	4244	1945 P		
4245	1946	(SNC 2002, 4215 (UNC))	1836	4246	1946 P	Bole 1, 1865 (AFDC)	1836B
4247	1946 VIP			4248	1946 Pat cu-ni		1836A
4249	1947	(SNC 2002, 4216 (UNC))	1837	4250	1947 P	Bole 5, 1514 (FDC)	1837A
4251	1947 VIP	SJA 20, 173 (FDC)		4252	1948	(Rasmussen 9/448 (UNC))	1838
4253	1948 P	Bole 1, 1866 (FDC)		4254	1948 VIP		1838A?
4255	1949 new	(SNC 2002, 4217 (UNC))	1838A	4256	1949 P	Spink 107 458 (FDC)	1838A
4257	1949VIP	B.F.P.L. 2014. BM204		4258	1950	(Commonly found)	1838B
4259	1950 P	(Rasmussen 9/448 (UNC))		4260	1950 VIP		1838C
4261	1950 MP	Bole 5, 1516 (AFDC)	1838C?	4262	1951	(Commonly found)	1838D
4263	1951 P	SJA 13, 832 (FDC)	1838E	4264	1951 VIP		1838E?
4265	1951 MP	Bole 5, 1517 (AFDC)		4266	1952	(SNC 2002, 4212 (GVF))	1838F
4267	1952 P	Bole 1, 1867 (FDC)		4268	1952 VIP		1838G
4269	1937 model	Bole 5, 1511 (EF)	1827A	4270	1938 T Al	Bole 5, 1512 (VF)	1828B
4271	1949 Pat	Bole 5, 1515 (VF)	1838A	4271	1949 Uni .Rev	DNW 91 203 (EF)	
4272	Double obv. mule			4273	1949 Thin flan		
4274	1950 Thin flan						

GEORGE VI - THREEPENCES

ESC	Variety	Provenance	(Old ESC)	ESC	Variety	Provenance	(Old ESC)
4275	1937	(SNC 2002, 2687 (UNC))	2150	4276	1937 P	(SNC 2003, 5124 (GEF))	2151A
4277	1937 VIP	SNC '89. 4808	2151B	4278	1937 MP	Norweb 729 FDC	2151C
4279	1938	(SNC 2002, 2688 (UNC))	2152	4280	1938 P	Norweb 1157	2152A
4281	1938 VIP	SNC 1998 5558 (FDC)		4282	1939	(SNC 2002, 2689 (UNC))	2153
4283	1939 P	Spink 107 457 (FDC)		4284	1939 VIP	SNC 1998 3768 (FDC)	2153A
4285	1940	(SNC 2002, 2690 (UNC))	2154	4286	1940 P	Norweb 1898	2154A
4287	1940 VIP	SNC 1989, 4809		4288	1941	SNC 2006 7628(UNC)	2155
4289	1941 P	Norweb 1899		4290	1941VIP	SNC 1989, 4810	2155A
4291	1942	(SNC 2002, 2692 (UNC))	2156	4292	1942 P	Spink 69, 409 (FDC)	2156A
4293	1942 MP			4294	1943	(SNC 2002, 2693 (UNC))	2157
4295	1943 P			4296	1943VIP		2157A
4297	1943 MP	SNC 1998 3771 (FDC)		4298	1944	SNC 2002 2639 (UNC)	2158
4299	1944 P			4300	1944 MP		2158A
4301	1945		2159	4302	1945 P		2159A
4303	1945 VIP						2159B

GEORGE VI - MAUNDY SETS

ESC	Variety	Provenance	(Old ESC)	ESC	Variety	Provenance	(Old ESC)
4304	1937	SNC 2011. 9611(UNC)	2554	4305	1937 P		2554A
4306	1937 MP	Norweb 729 FDC	2554B	4307	1938	(SNC 2001, 0407 (GEF))	2555
4308	1939	Spink 201, 664 (VAS)	2556	4309	1940	Spink 202, 349 (VAS)	2557
4310	1941	(SNC 2005, 6678(VAS))	2558	4311	1942	(SNC 2001, 0411 (UNC))	2559
4312	1943	(SNC 2001, 0412 (UNC))	2560	4313	1944	Spink 202, 350 (VAS)	2561
4314	1945	SNC 2011 9619(UNC)	2652	4315	1946	(SNC 2001, 0415 (UNC))	2563
4316	1947	(SNC 2001, 0416 (UNC))	2564	4317	1948	Spink 215, 469 (EF)	2565
4318	1949	SNC 2006, 7812 (VAS)	2566	4319	1950	Spink 199, 444 VAS	2567
4320	1951	Spink 217 866 (Unc)	2568	4321	1951 MP	SJA 13, 833 (FDC)	2568A
XXXX	1951 Full issue	Spink 221 1031 22coins)	2568				
4322	1952 Cu-ni	Norweb 733 FDC	2569	4323	1952 copper		2569A?

PROVENANCES

ELIZABETH II - CROWNS

4330	1953	SNC 2006 $^{7194\,(GEF)}$	393F	4331	1953 P	Barr 486 $^{(GEF)}$	393G
4332	1953P early strk	Spink 4 $^{717\,(FDC)}$	393E	4333	1953 VIP	Norweb 1912 $^{(FDC)}$	393FF
4333	1953 VIP	**Barr 328** $^{(FDC)}$		4334	1953 MP	Barr 132 $^{(FDC)}$	393J
4335	1960 milled	Barr 487 $^{(UNC)}$	393K	4336	1960Plain edge	Barr 488 $^{(EF)}$	393K?
4337	1960 P Pol	Barr 489 $^{(AFDC)}$	393L	4338	1960 VIP	**Norweb 745** ^{FDC}	393M
4339	1965	(Commonly found)	393N	4340	1965Plain edge	Barr 492 $^{(EF)}$	
4341	1965Sp ^{Sat}	DNW104 $^{574\,(VAS)}$	393O	4342	1965 ON	**SJA 23,** $^{307\,(VAS)}$	393P
4343	1965 light wt	Barr 493 $^{(EF)}$		4344	1953P $_{cn\text{-}ni}$	SJA 23, 307 $^{(VAS)}$	393P?
4345	Machin pattern	SNC 1994 $_{1112}$ $^{(VAS)}$		4346	Machin pattern	SNC 2000 $_{3197}$ $^{(VAS)}$	
4347	1966 Pat.	**Barr 494** $^{(AFDC)}$	393Q	4348	1966P av		393R

ELIZABETH II - HALFCROWNS

4349	1953	CoE $^{47th\,ed.\,p.\,506}$ $_{4137}$		4350	1953 P	Adams 806 $^{(FDC)}$	798H
4351	1953 VIP	DNW 114,1584		4352	1953 MP	Norweb 744 $^{(FDC)}$	
4353	1954	(Commonly found)		4354	1954 P	Spink 107 $^{460\,(FDC)}$	
4355	1954 VIP			4356	1954 MP		
4357	1955	(Commonly found)		4358	1955 P	Adams 807 $^{(FDC)}$	
4359	1955 MP			4360	1956	(Commonly found)	
4361	1956 P	Adams 808 $^{(FDC)}$		4362	1956 VIP		
4363	1957	(Commonly found)		4364	1957 P	Adams 809 $^{(FDC)}$	
4365	1957 VIP			4366	1958	Spink 199 $^{356\,(VAS)}$	
4367	1958 P	Adams 810 $^{(FDC)}$		4368	1958 VIP	SJA 20, 176 $^{(FDC)}$	
4369	1959	(Commonly found)		4370	1959 P		
4371	1960	(Commonly found)		4372	1960 P	SNC 1986 $^{7005\,(VAS)}$	
4373	1960 VIP			4374	1960 ^{Bronze}	Spink 6 $^{872\,(VF)}$	
4375	1961	(Commonly found)		4376	1961Polished	(Commonly found)	
4377	1961 P	Adams 811 $^{(FDC)}$		4378	1961 VIP		
4379	1962	(Commonly found)		4380	1962 P	SNC 1978 $^{.8288\,(FDC)}$	
				4381	1962 VIP		
4382	1963	(Commonly found)		4383	1963 P		
4384	1964	Adams 812 $^{(UNC)}$		4385	1964 P		
4386	1965	Adams 812 $^{(UNC)}$		4387	1965 P		
4388	1966	Adams 812 $^{(UNC)}$		4389	1966 P		
4390	1967	Adams 812 $^{(UNC)}$		4391	1967 P		
				4392	1970 P	Adams 812 $^{(FDC)}$	

ELIZABETH II - FLORINS

4393	1953	CoE $^{47th\,ed.\,p.\,506}$ $_{4138}$	968F	4394	1953 P	Norweb 744 ^{FDC}	968G
4395	1953 VIP	DNW 114,1584		4396	1953 MP		
4397	1954	(Commonly found)	968H	4398	1954 P	Spink 107 $^{460\,(FDC)}$	
4399	1954 VIP			4400	1955	(Commonly found)	968I
4401	1955 P	Norweb 746 ^{FDC}		4402	1955 MP		
4403	1956	(Commonly found)	968J	4404	1956 P	Norweb 1165	
4405	1956 VIP			4406	1957	CoE $^{47th\,ed.\,p.\,508}$ $_{4146}$	968K
4407	1957 P	SNC 1998 $^{3779(FDC)}$	968K	4408	1957 VIP		
4409	1958	(Commonly found)	968L	4410	1958 P	**Spk 216** $^{1014\,(FDC)}$	
4411	1958 VIP			4412	1959	Spink 199, $^{357\,(VAS)}$	968M
4413	1959 P			4414	1960	(Commonly found)	

(continued)

PROVENANCES

ESC	Variety	Provenance	(Old ESC)	ESC	Variety	Provenance	(Old ESC)
4415	1960 P			4416	1960 VIP		
4417	1961	(Commonly found)	968N	4418	1961 P	Norweb 1167	968O
4419	1961 VIP			4420	1962	(Commonly found)	968P
4421	1962 P			4422	1962 VIP		
4423	1963	(Commonly found)	968Q	4424	1963 P		
4425	1963 P ^{Au}	Wilson & Ras 455					
4426	1964	(Commonly found)	968R	4427	1964 P		
4428	1965	(Commonly found)	968S	4429	1965 P		
				4430	1965$^{Ni\text{-}bras}$	Glens.1992/12/9738 (EF)	
4431	1966	(Commonly found)	968T	4432	1966 P		
4433	1967	(Commonly found)	968U	4434	1967 P		
4435	1970 P	(Commonly found)	968V	4436	1955$^{P.\ cu\text{-}ni}$	Sovereign 2000/11, p.30.142	
4437	1961 Pat	**ALB Spk 134,** ^{465}		4438	1961 Pat	**BAS Spk 134**	
4439	1961 Pat	**POL Spk 134**		4440	1961 Pat	ALBERTUS	
4441	1961 Pat	**ION (IONIC)**					

ELIZABETH II – SHILLINGS

English				Scottish			
ESC	Variety	Provenance	(Old ESC)	ESC	Variety	Provenance	(Old ESC)
4442	1953	CoE $^{47th\ ed.\ p.\ 507}_{\ 4139}$	1475K	4446	1953	CoE $^{47th\ ed.\ p.\ 507}_{\ 4140}$	1475M
4443	1953 P	SNC 1999 $^{5289\ (FDC)}$	1475L	4447	1953 P	SNC 1999 $^{5296\ (FDC)}$	1475N
4444	1953 VIP	DNW 114,1584		4448	1953 VIP	DNW 114,1584	
4445	1953 MP	Norweb 744 ^{VAS}		4449	1953 MP		
4450	1954	**Bull**	1475O	4485	1954	**Bull**	1475P
4451	1954 P	Spink 107 $^{460\ (FDC)}$		4486	1954 P	Spink 107 $^{460\ (FDC)}$	
4452	1954 VIP	Spk 115, 2150		4487	1954 VIP	Spk 115, 2150	
4453	1954 MP			4488	1954 MP	SNC $^{1979,11644\ (FDC)}$	
4454	1955	(Commonly found)	1475Q	4489	1955	(Commonly found)	1475R
4455	1955 P	Norweb 746 ^{FDC}		4490	1955 P	Norweb 746 ^{FDC}	
4456	1955 MP	Norweb 744 ^{FDC}	1475Q	4491	1955 MP		
				4492	1955Pat. nickel	Sovereign 2000/11, p.30.142	
4457	1956	(Commonly found)	1475S	4493	1956	(Commonly found)	
4458	1956 P	Norweb 1165	1475S	4494	1956 P	Norweb 1165	
4459	1956 VIP	SNC. 2003 ^{MS5784}		4495	1956 VIP	SNC. 2003 ^{MS5784}	
4460	1957	(Commonly found)	1475U	4496	1957	(Commonly found)	1475V
4461	1957 P	Norweb 1166		4497	1957 P	Norweb 1166	
4462	1957 VIP			4498	1957 VIP		
4463	1958	(Commonly found)	1475W	4499	1958	(Commonly found)	1475X
4464	1958 P	SNC 1999 $^{5293\ (FDC)}$		4500	1958 P	SNC 1986 $^{8427\ (GEF)}$	1475X?
4465	1958VIP	SNC. 2003 ^{MS5784}		4501	1958VIP	SNC. 2003 ^{MS5784}	
4466	1959	(Commonly found)	1475Y	4502	1959	Spink 199, $^{358\ VAS)}$	1475Z
4467	1959 P			4503	1959 P		
4468	1960	(Commonly found)	1475AA	4504	1960	(Commonly found)	1475BB
4469	1960 P			4505	1960 P		
4470	1960 VIP	*(Not traced)*		4506	1960 VIP	Bald.FPL Summer 2012,BM079	
4471	1961	(Commonly found)	1475CC	4507	1961	(Commonly found)	1475DD
4472	1961 P	Norweb 1167		4508	1961 P	Norweb 1167	
4473	1961 VIP			4509	1961 VIP		

(continued)

PROVENANCES

ESC	Variety	English Provenance	(Old ESC)	ESC	Variety	Scottish Provenance	(Old ESC)
4474	1962	(Commonly found)	1475EE	4510	1962	(Commonly found)	1475FF
4475	1962 VIP			4511	1962 VIP		
4476	1963	(Commonly found)	1475GG	4512	1963	(Commonly found)	1475HH
4477	1963 P			4513	1963 P		
4478	1964	(Commonly found)	1475II	4514	1964	(Commonly found)	1475JJ
4479	1964 P			4515	1964 P		
4480	1965	(Commonly found)	1475KK	4516	1965	(Commonly found)	1475LL
4481	1965 P			4517	1965 P		
4482	1966	(Commonly found)	1475M	4518	1966	(Commonly found)	14755N
4483	1966 P			4519	1966 P		
4484	1970 P	(Commonly found)	1475OO	4520	1970 P	(Commonly found)	1475PP

ELIZABETH II - SIXPENCES

ESC	Variety	Provenance	(Old ESC)	ESC	Variety	Provenance	(Old ESC)
4521	1953	CoE 47th ed. p. 507 4141	1838G	4522	1953 P	Bald 80 2435(GEF)	1838H
4523	1953 VIP			4524	1953 MP	Norweb 744 VAS	????
4525	1954	**Spink/Sby 4041**	1838G	4526	1954 P	Spink 107 460 (FDC)	1838H
4527	1954 VIP			4528	1954 MP		
4529	1955	(Commonly found)	1838G	4530	1955 P	Norweb 746 FDC	1838G
				4531	1955 MP		
4532	1956	(Commonly found)	1838H	4533	1956 P	(SNC 2002 2575 (FDC))	
4534	1957	(Commonly found)	1838G	4535	1957 P	SNC 2002, 3423 (FDC)	1838L
				4535	1957 P	Bole 5, 1519 (FDC)	1838G
4536	1958		1838H	4537	1958 P	Bole 1, 1869 (FDC)	1838G?
				4538	1958 VIP		
4539	1959	(Commonly found)	1838H	4540	1959 P		
4541	1960	(Commonly found)	1838G	4542	1960 P		
4543	1961	(Commonly found)	1838P	4544	1961 P	Norweb 1167	
4545	1962	(Commonly found)	1838Q	4546	1962 P		
4547	1963	(Commonly found)	1838R	4548	1963 P		
4549	1964	(Commonly found)	1838S	4550	1964 P	Bole 1, 1870 (FDC)	1838SS
4551	1965	(Commonly found)	1838T	4552	1965 P		
4553	1966	(Commonly found)	1838U	4554	1966 P		
4555	1967	(Commonly found)	1838V	4556	1967 P		
4557	1967 Brass	Bole 5, 1523 (VAS)	1838V?	4558	1970 P	(SNC 2002, 4225 (FDC))	1838W

ELIZABETH II - MAUNDY SETS

ESC	Variety	Provenance	(Old ESC)	ESC	Variety	Provenance	(Old ESC)
4559	1953	**SNC 2007** 8023 (VAS)	2570	4572	1962	SJA 12, 871 (FDC)	2579
4560	1953 MP	Norweb 1169	2570A	4573	1963		
4561	1953 P Au	Norweb 747 FDC	2570B	4574	1964	Spink 202, 355 (VAS)	2581
4562	1963P cu-ni	(SNC 2005, 6683(Mint))	2580	4575	1965	SNC 2007 8024 (UNC)	2582
4563	1954	Spk 221,1033	2571	4576	1966	SNC 2006 7813 (GEF)	2583
4564	1955	Spink 202, 353 (VAS)	2572	4577	1967	(SNC 2001, 0436 (UNC))	2584
4565	1955 MP	SNC 2005 6356 (FDC)	2572A	4578	1968	SJA 12, 872 (FDC)	2585
4566	1956	(SNC 2001, 0425 (UNC))	2573	4579	1969	SJA 17, 288 (FDC)	2586
4567	1957	Spink 208, 1226(UNC)	2574	4580	1970	(SNC 2001, 04395 (UNC))	2587
4568	1958	SJA 11, 350 (FDC)	2575			**See under Decimal coinage**	

(continued)

PROVENANCES

ESC	Variety	Provenance	(Old ESC)	ESC	Variety	Provenance	(Old ESC)
4569	1959	SJA 12, 869$^{(FDC)}$	2576	xxxx	1971	SNC 2011 $^{9645\ (UNC)}$	2588
4570	1960	SJA 17, 287 $^{(FDC)}$	2577	xxxx	1972$^{Full\ iss}$	(SNC 2005, 6971 (EF))	2589
4571	1961	Spink 214, $^{794\ (UNC)}$	2578	xxxx	1973	(SNC 2001, 0442 (UNC))	2590

ELIZABETH II
PROPOSED DECIMAL PATTERNS 1961
50, 20, 10, 5, 2 & 1 cents

PDS.1			PDS.2	SNC 2005, p.140, MS6357	
PDS.3	Spink 124, lot 2263		PDS.4	Spink 124, lot 2264	
PDS.5	Spink 62, lot 461		PDS.6		
PDS.7	Bald. F.P.L.W2012/13,BM105			Spink 124, lot 2265	
PDS.1	Spink 130, $^{379\ (FDC)}$		PDS.1		

Note
Commonly found = rarely illustrated in catalogues because easily collected

UNOFFICIAL 'PATINA' CROWNS

				xxxx	*Patina* A ^{Al}	DNW 65, $^{430\ (FDC)}$	
xxxx	*Patina* B ^{Uni}	DNW 65, $^{430\ (FDC)}$		xxxx	*Patina* C $^{4/-}$	DNW 65, $^{430\ (FDC)}$	
xxxx	^{1936}A/1 ^{Au}	Spink 31$^{474\ (FDC)}$	391	xxxx	^{1936}B/2	DNW 77 $^{354\ (FDC)}$	
xxxx	B/2 $^{Au/Ag}$	DNW 74B$^{1054(FDC)}$		xxxx	B/2 $^{Au/}$	Glen '94/6.441 (VAS)	
xxxx	^{1936}B/3	Glen '95/10.365 (VAS)	391E	xxxx	^{1936}B/3 ^{Au}	SJA 16, 237 $^{(FDC)}$	391F
xxxx	^{1937}C/4 ^{Ag}	(Spink 6, 858 (EF))		xxxx	^{1937}C/4 ^{Av}	Spink 21, $^{863\ (FDC)}$	

APPENDIX I

SILVER AND CUPRO-NICKEL COINAGE TABLES FROM 1816
(Reproduced from the fifth edition of E.S.C by P. Alan Rayner)

Collectors have frequently commented that a list of the numbers of coins issued each year by the Mint would provide a useful addition to this work. Detailed records of seventeenth and eighteenth century minting are incomplete but the tables below give the issues from **1816-1966** inclusive. However, we have some reservations in mind regarding these figures, as they are frequently misinterpreted. The amounts given are the numbers of coins issued by the Mint in a particular calendar year, not the number of coins that bear a particular date. In many instances dies of one year continued to be used the following year, and it is only since **1950** that totals of particular dates can be computed with accuracy. Also in some years coins have been struck with the following year's date, but have been included in the total of coins issued in the year they were made. The figures given below have been compiled from Mint records but some amounts may require amendment following current research.

TABLE I — REGULAR DENOMINATIONS

Year	Crowns	Halfcrowns	Florins	Shillings	Sixpences	Groats	Threepences
1816[1]	—	—	—	—	—	—	—
1817	—	8,092,656	—	23,031,360	10,921,680	—	—
1818	155,232	2,905,056	—	1,342,440	4,284,720	—	—
1819	683,496	4,790,016	—	7,595,280	4,712,400	—	—
1820	448,272	2,396,592	—	7,975,440	1,488,960	—	—
1821	437,976	1,435,104	—	2,463,120	863,280	—	—
1822	124,929	—	—	—	—	—	—
1823	—	2,003,760	—	693,000	—	—	—
1824	—	465,696	—	4,158,000	633,600	—	—
1825	—	2,258,784	—	2,459,160	483,120	—	—
1826	—	2,189,088	—	6,351,840	689,040	—	—
1827	—	—	—	574,200	166,320	—	—
1828	—	49,890	—	—	15,840	—	—
1829	—	508,464	—	879,120	403,920	—	—
1830	—	—	—	—	—	—	—
1831	—	—	—	—	1,340,195	—	—
1832	—	—	—	—	—	—	—
1833	—	—	—	—	—	—	—
1834	—	993,168	—	3,223,440	5,892,480	—	—
1835	—	281,952	—	1,449,360	1,552,320	—	—
1836	—	1,588,752	—	3,567,960	1,987,920	4,253,040	—
1837	—	150,526	—	479,160	506,880	962,280	—
1838	—	—	—	1,956,240	1,607,760	2,150,280	—
1839	—	—	—	5,666,760	3,310,560	1,461,240	—
1840	—	386,496	—	1,639,440	2,098,800	1,496,880	—
1841	—	42,768	—	873,160	1,386,000	344,520	—
1842	—	486,288	—	2,094,840	601,920	724,680	—
1843	—	454,608	—	1,465,200	3,160,080	1,817,640	—
1844	94,248	1,999,008	—	4,466,880	3,975,840	855,360	—
1845	159,192	2,231,856	—	4,082,760	3,714,480	914,760	1,314,720
1846	140,976	1,539,648	—	4,031,280	4,268,880	1,366,200	47,520
1847	75,706[2]	367,488	—	847,440	586,080	225,720	—
1848	—	91,872	—	194,040	—	712,800	—

648

APPENDIX I

Year	Crowns	Halfcrowns	Florins	Shillings	Sixpences	Groats	Threepences
1849	—	261,360	413,820	645,480	205,920	380,160	126,720
1850	—	484,613	—	685,080	498,960	594,000	950,400
1851	—	—	1,540	470,071	2,288,107	31,300	479,065
1852	—	—	1,014,552	1,306,574	904,586	—	—
1853	—	—	3,919,950	4,256,188	3,837,930	11,880	31,680
1854	—	—	550,413	552,414	840,116	1,096,613	1,467,246
1855	—	—	831,017	1,368,499	1,129,084	646,041	383,350
1856	—	—	2,201,706	3,168,000	2,779,920	95,040³	1,013,760
1857	—	—	1,671,120	2,562,120	2,233,440	—	1,758,240
1858	—	—	2,239,380	3,108,600	1,932,480	—	1,441,440
1859	—	—	2,568,060	4,561,920	4,688,640	—	3,579,840
1860	—	—	635,580	1,671,120	1,100,880	—	3,405,600
1861	—	—	839,520	1,382,040	601,920	—	3,294,720
1862	—	—	594,000	954,360	990,000	—	1,156,320
1863	—	—	938,520	859,320	491,040	—	950,400
1864	—	—	1,861,200	4,518,360	4,253,040	—	1,330,560
1865	—	—	1,580,040	5,619,240	1,631,520	—	1,742,400
1866	—	—	914,760	4,989,600	5,140,080	—	1,900,800
1867	—	—	423,720	2,166,120	1,362,240	—	712,800
1868	—	—	896,940	3,330,360	1,069,200	—	1,457,280
1869	—	—	297,000	736,560	388,080	—	—
1870	—	—	1,080,648	1,467,471	479,613	—-	1,283,218
1871	—	—	3,425,605	4,910,010	3,662,684	—	999,633
1872	—	—	7,199,690	8,897,781	3,382,048	—	1,293,271
1873	—	—	5,921,839	6,489,598	4,594,733	—	4,055,550
1874	—	2,188,599	1,642,630	5,503,747	4,225,726	—	4,427,031
1875	—	1,113,483	1,117,030	4,353,983	3,256,545	—	3,306,500
1876	—	633,221	580,034	1,057,487	841,435	—	1,834,389
1877	—	447,059	682,292	2,980,703	4,066,486	—	2,622,393
1878	—	1,466,323	1,786,680	3,127,131	2,624,525	—	2,419,975
1879	—	901,356	1,512,247	3,611,507	3,326,313	—	3,140,265
1880	—	1,346,350	2,167,170	4,842,786	3,892,501	—	1,610,069
1881	—	2,301,495	2,570,337	5,255,332	6,239,447	—	3,248,265
1882	—	808,227	—	1,611,786	759,809	—	472,965
1883	—	2,982,779	3,555,667	7,281,450	4,986,558	—	4,369,971
1884	—	1,569,175	1,447,379	3,923,993	3,422,565	—	3,322,424
1885	—	1,628,438	1,758,210	3,336,527	4,652,771	—	5,183,653
1886	—	891,767	591,773	2,086,819	2,728,249	—	6,152,669
*1887	273,581	1,438,046	1,776,903	4,034,133	3,675,607	—	2,780,761
*1888	131,899	1,428,787	1,547,540	4,526,856	4,197,698	—	518,199
*1889	1,807,223	4,811,954	2,973,561	7,039,628	8,738,928	—	4,587,010
*1890	997,862	3,228,111	1,684,737	8,794,042	9,386,955	—	4,465,834
1891	566,394	2,284,632	836,438	5,665,348	7,022,734	—	6,323,027
1892	451,334	1,710,946	283,401	4,591,622	6,245,746	—	2,578,226
1893	497,845	1,792,600	1,666,103	7,039,074	7,350,619	—	3,067,293
1894	144,906	1,524,960	1,952,842	5,953,152	3,467,704	—	1,608,603
1895	252,862	1,772,662	2,182,968	8,880,651	7,024,631	—	4,788,609
1896	317,599	2,148,505	2,944,416	9,264,551	6,651,699	—	4,598,442
1897	262,118	1,678,643	1,699,921	6,270,364	5,031,498	—	4,541,294
1898	161,450	1,870,055	3,061,343	9,768,703	5,914,100	—	4,597,177
1899	166,300	2,863,872	3,996,953	10,965,382	7,996,804	—	6,246,281
1900	353,356	4,479,128	5,528,630	10,937,590	8,984,354	—	10,644,480
1901	—	1,516,570	2,648,870	3,426,294	5,108,757	—	6,098,400
1902	256,020	1,316,008	2,189,575	7,809,481	6,367,378	—	8,268,480
1903	—	274,840	1,995,298	2,061,823	5,410,096	—	5,227,200
1904	—	709,652	2,769,932	2,040,161	4,487,098	—	3,627,360
1905	—	166,008	1,187,596	488,390	4,235,556	—	3,548,160
1906	—	2,886,206	6,910,128	10,791,025	7,641,146	—	3,152,160
1907	—	3,693,930	5,947,895	14,083,418	8,733,673	—	4,831,200
1908	—	1,758,889	3,280,010	3,806,969	6,739,491	—	8,157,600
1909	—	3,051,592	3,482,829	5,664,982	6,584,017	—	4,055,040

APPENDIX I

1   The coins dated 1816 were not issued until 1817, so they are included in the figures for 1817
2   This includes 8,000 'Gothic' crowns

Year	Crowns	Halfcrowns	Florins	Shillings	Sixpences	Groats	Threepences
1910	—	2,557,685	5,650,713	26,547,236	12,490,724	—	4,563,380
1911	—	2,914,573	5,951,284	20,065,901	9,155,310	—	5,841,084
1912	—	4,700,789	8,571,731	15,594,009	10,984,129	—	8,932,825
1913	—	4,090,169	4,545,278	9,011,509	7,499,833	—	7,143,242
1914	—	18,333,003	21,252,701	23,415,843	22,714,602	—	6,733,584
1915	—	32,433,066	12,367,939	39,279,024	15,694,597	—	5,450,617
1916	—	29,530,020	21,064,337	35,862,015	22,207,178	—	18,555,201
1917	—	11,172,052	11,181,617	22,202,608	7,725,475	—	21,662,490
1918	—	29,079,592	29,211,792	34,915,934	27,558,743	—	20,630,909
1919	—	10,266,737	9,469,292	10,823,824	13,375,447	—	16,845,687
1920	—	17,982,077	15,387,833	22,825,142	14,136,287	—	16,703,597
1921	—	23,677,889	34,863,895	22,648,763	30,339,741	—	8,749,301
1922	—	16,396,724	23,861,044	27,215,738	16,878,890	—	7,979,998
1923	—	26,308,526	21,546,533	14,575,243	6,382,793	—	—
1924	—	5,866,294	4,582,372	9,250,095	17,444,218	—	
1925	—	1,413,461	1,404,136	5,418,764	12,720,558	—	3,731,859
1926	—	4,473,516	5,125,410	22,516,453	21,809,621	—	4,107,910
1927	15,030[4]	6,825,872	116,497	9,262,344	68,939,873	—	15,022[4]
1928	9,034	18,762,727	11,087,186	18,136,778	23,123,384	—	1,302,106
1929	4,994	17,632,636	16,397,279	19,343,006	28,319,326	—	
1930	4,847	809,051	5,753,568	3,137,092	16,990,289	—	1,319,412
1931	4,056	11,264,468	6,556,331	6,993,926	16,873,268	—	6,251,936
1932	2,395	4,793,643	717,041	12,168,101	9,406,117	—	5,887,325
1933	7,132	10,311,494	8,685,303	11,511,624	22,185,083	—	5,578,541
1934	932	2,422,399	—	6,138,463	9,304,009	—	7,405,954
1935	714,769[5]	7,022,216	7,540,546	9,183,462	13,995,621	—	7,027,654
1936	2,473	7,039,423	9,897,448	11,910,613	24,380,171	—	3,238,670
1937	418,699	9,106,440	13,006,781	15,107,997	22,302,524	—	8,148,156
1938	—	6,426,478	7,909,388	9,631,288	13,402,701	—	6,402,473
1939	—	15,478,635	20,850,607	21,316,569	28,670,304	—	1,355,860
1940	—	17,948,439	18,700,338	21,012,215	20,875,196	—	7,914,401
1941	—	15,773,984	24,451,079	19,477,913	23,086,616	—	7,979,411
1942	—	31,220,090	39,895,243	31,130,402	44,942,785	—	4,144,051
1943	—	15,462,875	26,711,987	21,228,427	46,927,111	—	1,379,220
1944	—	15,255,165	27,560,005	22,576,918	37,952,600	—	2,005,553
1945	—	19,849,242	25,858,049	30,249,674	39,939,259	—	
1946	—	22,724,873	22,300,254	33,861,645	43,466,407	—	
1947	—	21,911,484	22,910,085	25,449,132	29,993,263	—	
1948	—	71,164,703	67,553,636	90,928,860	88,323,540	—	
1949	—	28,272,512	28,614,939	40,571,479	41,355,515	—	
1950	—	28,335,500	24,357,490	33,543,473	32,741,955	—	
1951	2,003,540[4]	9,003,520	27,411,747	20,918,104	40,399,491	—	
1952	—	—	—	—	1,013,477	—	
1953	5,962,621	3,883,214	11,958,710	61,606,422	70,323,876	—	
1954	—	11,614,953	13,085,422	57,033,767	105,241,150	—	
1955	—	23,628,726	25,887,253	73,210,814	109,929,554	—	
1956	—	33,934,909	47,824,500	87,760,647	109,841,555	—	
1957	—	34,200,563	33,071,282	60,734,205	105,654,290	—	
1958	—	15,745,668	9,564,580	55,214,862	123,518,527	—	
1959	—	9,028,844	14,080,319	20,455,766	93,089,441	—	
1960	1,024,038	19,929,191	13,831,782	41,404,846	103,288,346	—	-
1961	—	25,887,897	37,735,315	42,579,465	111,284,384	—	
1962	—	23,998,112	35,129,903	54,165,689	158,355.270[6]	—	
1963[7]	—	17,572,800	25,580,000	78,520,000	124,860,000	—	
1964[8]	—	4,576,800	16,313,000	18,864,000	137,352,000	—	
1965[9]	12,080,000	8,124,800	48,723,000	11,236,000	149,948,000	—	
1966[10]	7,560,000	14,811,200	84,574,000	31,364,000	171,636,000	—	
1967	—	33,058,400	39,718,000	—	240,788,000	—	
1968	Decimal Coinage Struck						

APPENDIX I

*   Doubleflorins issued only in: 1887, 483,347; 1888, 243,340; 1889, 1,185,111; 1890, 782,145
3   No groats known of this date, so they were probably dated 1855
4   Proof coins
5   Includes 2,500 raised edge proofs
6   Includes 3,767,633 sixpences dated 1961
7   Figures include the following number dated 1962: 2/6, 15,200; 2/-, 18,000; 1/-, 1,506,000
      6d, 11,896,000
8   Figures include the following number dated 1963: 2/6, 77,600; 2/-, 909,000; 1/-, 5,038,000;
      6d, 7,092,000
9   Figures include the following number dated 1964: 2/6, 1,474,400; 2/-, 1,135,000; 1/-, 4,000;
      6d, 22,076,000
10   Figures include the following number dated 1965: 5/-, 7,560,000; 2/6, 3,228,000;
      2/-, 575,000; 1/-, 758,000

TABLE II — ENGLISH & SCOTTISH SHILLINGS

Year	English	Scottish	Total
1937	8,359,122	6,748,875	15,107,997
1938	4,833,436	4,797,852	9,631,288
1939	11,052,677	10,263,892	21,316,569
1940	11,099,126	9,913,089	21,012,215
1941	11,391,883	8,086,030	19,477,913
1942	17,453,643	13,676,759	31,130,402
1943	11,404,213	9,824,214	21,228,427
1944	11,586,751	10,990,167	22,576,918
1945	15,143,404	15,106,270	30,249,674
1946	18,663,797	16,381,501	35,045,298
1947	12,120,611	12,283,223	24,403,834
1948	45,576,923	45,351,937	90,928,860
1949	19,328,405	21,243,074	40,571,479
1950	19,243,872	14,299,601	33,543,473
1951	9,956,930	10,961,174	20,918,104
1952	—	—	—
1953	41,942,894	20,663,528	62,606,422
1954	30,262,032	26,771,735	57,033,767
1955	45,259,908	27,950,906	73,210,814
1956	44,907,008	42,853,639	87,760,647
1957	42,774,217	17,959,988	60,734,205
1958	14,392,305	40,822,557	55,214,862
1959	19,442,778	1,012,988	20,455,766
1960	27,027,914	14,376,932	41,404,846
1961	39,816,907	2,762,558	42,579,465
1962	36,395,179	17,470,510	54,165,689
1963[1]	44,723,200	33,796,800	78,520,000
1964[2]	13,617,440	5,246,560	18,864,000
1965[3]	9,218,900	2,017,100	11,236,000
1966[4]	15,002,000	16,362,000	31,364,000

[1] Figures include the following coins dated 1962: English 1/-, 9,200; Scottish 1/-, 1,496,800.
[2] Figures include the following coins dated 1963: English 1/-, 5,029,440; Scottish 1/-, 8,560.
[3] Figures include the following coins dated 1964: English 1/-, 2,900; Scottish 1/-, 1,100.
[4] Figures include the following coins dated 1965: English 1/-, NIL; Scottish 1/-, 758,000.

651

APPENDIX I

TABLE III — MAUNDY MONEY

Year	Fourpence	Threepence	Twopence	Penny
1816	1,584	1,584	2,376	4,752
1817	1,386	1,584	2,376	10,296
1818	1,188	1,584	2,376	9,504
1819	792	1,320	1,980	6,336
1820	990	1,320	1,584	7,920
1821	990	1,320	1,980	3,960
1822	2,970	3,960	5,940	11,880
1823	1,980	2,640	3,960	12,672
1824	1,584	2,112	3,168	9,504
1825	2,376	3,432	3,960	8,712
1826	2,376	3,432	3,960	8,712
1827	2,772	3,168	3,960	7,920
1828	2,772	3,168	3,960	7,920
1829	2,772	3,168	3,960	7,920
1830	2,772	3,168	3,960	7,920
1831	3,564	3,960	4,752	10,296
1832	2,574	2,904	3,564	8,712
1833	2,574	2,904	3,564	8,712
1834	2,574	2,904	3,564	8,712
1835	2,574	2,904	3,564	8,712
1836	2,544	2,904	3,564	8,712
1837	2,574	2,904	3,564	8,712
1838	4,158	4,312	4,488	8,976
1839	4,125	4,356	4,488	8,976
1840	4,125	4,356	4,488	8,976
1841	2,574	2,904	3,960	7,920
1842	4,125	4,356	4,488	8,976
1843	4,158	4,488	4,752	7,920
1844	4,158	4,488	4,752	7,920
1845	4,158	4,488	4,752	7,920
1846	4,158	4,488	4,752	7,920
1847	4,158	4,488	4,752	7,920
1848	4,158	4,488	4,752	7,920
1849	4,158	4,488	4,752	7,920
1850	4,158	4,488	4,752	7,920
1851	4,158	4,488	4,752	7,920
1852	4,158	4,488	4,752	7,920
1853	4,158	4,488	4,752	7,920
1854	4,158	4,488	4,752	7,920
1855	4,158	4,488	4,752	7,920
1856	4,158	4,488	4,752	7,920
1857	4,158	4,488	4,752	7,920
1858	4,158	4,488	4,752	7,920
1859	4,158	4,488	4,752	7,920
1860	4,158	4,488	4,752	7,920
1861	4,158	4,488	4,752	7,920
1862	4,158	4,488	4,752	7,920
1863	4,158	4,488	4,752	7,920
1864	4,158	4,488	4,752	7,920
1865	4,158	4,488	4,752	7,920
1866	4,158	4,488	4,752	7,920
1867	4,158	4,488	4,752	7,920
1868	4,158	4,488	4,752	7,920
1869	4,158	4,488	4,752	7,920
1870	4,569	4,488	5,347	9,002
1871	4,627	4,488	4,753	9,286
1872	4,328	4,488	4,719	8,956
1873	4,162	4,488	4,756	7,932
1874	5,937	4,488	5,578	8,741
1875	4,154	4,488	5,745	8,459
1876	4,862	4,488	6,655	10,426
1877	4,850	4,488	7,189	8,936
1878	5,735	4,488	6,709	9,903
1879	5,202	4,488	6,925	10,626
1880	5,199	4,488	6,247	11,088
1881	6,203	4,488	6,001	9,017
1882	4,146	4,488	7,264	10,607
1883	5,096	4,488	7,232	11,673

652

APPENDIX I

Year	Fourpence	Threepence	Twopence	Penny
1884	5,353	4,488	6,042	14,109
1885	5,791	4,488	5,958	12,302
1886	6,785	4,488	9,167	15,952
1887	5,292	4,488	8,296	17,506
1888	9,583	4,488	9,528	14,480
1889	6,088	4,488	6,727	14,028
1890	9,087	4,488	8,613	13,115
1891	11,303	4,488	10,000	21,743
1892	8,524	4,488	11,583	15,525
1893	10,832	8,976	14,182	21,593
1894	9,385	8,976	12,099	18,391
1895	8,877	8,976	10,766	17,408
1896	8,476	8,976	10,795	17,380
1897	9,388	8,976	11,000	16,477
1898	9,147	8,976	11,945	16,634
1899	13,561	8,976	14,514	17,402
1900	9,571	8,976	10,987	17,299
1901	11,928	8,976	13,539	17,644
1902	10,117	8,976	14,079	21,278
1903	9,729	8,976	13,386	17,209
1904	11,568	8,876	13,827	18,524
1905	10,998	8,976	11,139	17,504
1906	11,065	8,800	11,325	17,850
1907	11,132	8,760	13,238	18,388
1908	9,929	8,760	14,815	18,150
1909	2,428	1,983	2,695	2,948
1910	2,755	1,440	2,998	3,392
1911	1,768	1,991	1,635	1,913
1912	1,700	1,246	1,678	1,616
1913	1,798	1,228	1,880	1,590
1914	1,651	982	1,659	1,818
1915	1,441	1,293	1,465	2,072
1916	1,499	1,128	1,509	1,647
1917	1,478	1,237	1,506	1,820
1918	1,479	1,375	1,547	1,911
1919	1,524	1,258	1,567	1,699
1920	1,460	1,399	1,630	1,715
1921	1,542	1,386	1,794	1,847
1922	1,609	1,373	3,074	1,758
1923	1,635	1,430	1,527	1,840
1924	1,665	1,515	1,602	1,619
1925	1,786	1,438	1,670	1,890
1926	1,762	1,504	1,902	2,180
1927	1,681	1,690	1,766	1,647
1928	1,642	1,835	1,706	1,846
1929	1,969	1,761	1,862	1,837
1930	1,744	1,948	1,901	1,724
1931	1,915	1,818	1,897	1,759
1932	1,937	2,042	1,960	1,835
1933	1,931	1,920	2,066	1,872
1934	1,893	1,887	1,927	1,919
1935	1,995	2,007	1,928	1,975
1936	1,323	1,307	1,365	1,329
1937	1,325	1,351	1,472	1,329
1938	1,424	1,350	1,374	1,275
1939	1,332	1,234	1,436	1,253
1940	1,367	1,290	1,277	1,375
1941	1,345	1,253	1,345	1,255
1942	1,325	1,325	1,231	1,243
1943	1,335	1,335	1,239	1,347
1944	1,345	1,345	1,345	1,259
1945	1,355	1,355	1,355	1,367
1946	1,365	1,365	1,365	1,479
1947	1,375	1,375	1,479	1,387
1948	1,385	1,491	1,385	1,397
1949	1,503	1,395	1,395	1,407
1950	1,515	1,405	1,405	1,527
1951	1,580	1,468	1,580	1,480
1952	1,064	1,012	1,064	1,024
1953	1,078	1,078	1,025	1,050
1954	1,076	1,076	1,020	1,088

653

APPENDIX I

Year	Fourpence	Threepence	Twopence	Penny
1955	1,082	1,082	1,082	1,036
1956	1,088	1,088	1,088	1,100
1957	1,094	1,094	1,094	1,168
1958	1,100	1,100	1,164	1,112
1959	1,106	1,172	1,106	1,118
1960	1,180	1,112	1,112	1,124
1961	1,118	1,118	1,118	1,200
1962	1,197	1,125	1,197	1,127
1963	1,205	1,205	1,131	1,133
1964	1,213	1,213	1,137	1,215
1965	1,221	1,221	1,221	1,143
1966	1,206	1,206	1,206	1,206
1967	986	986	986	1,068
1968	964	964	1,048	964
1969	1,002	1,088	1,002	1,002
1970	1,068	980	980	980
1971	1,108	1,018	1,018	1,108
1972	1,118	1,026	1,118	1,026
1973	1,098	1,098	1,004	1,004
1974	1,138	1,138	1,042	1,138
1975	1,148	1,148	1,148	1,050
1976	1,158	1,158	1,158	1,158
1977	1,138	1,138	1,138	1,240
1978	1,178	1,178	1,282	1,178
1979	1,188	1,294	1,188	1,188
1980	1,306	1,198	1,198	1,198
1981	1,288	1,178	1,178	1,288
1982	1,330	1,218	1,330	1,218
1983	1,342	1,342	1,228	1,228
1984	1,354	1,354	1,238	1,354
1985	1,366	1,366	1,366	1,248
1986	1,378	1,378	1,378	1,378
1987	1,390	1,390	1,390	1,512
1988	1,402	1,528	1,526	1,402
1989	1,353	1,353	1,353	1,353
1990	1,523	1,523	1,523	1,523
1991	1,514	1,384	1,384	1,514
1992	—	—	—	—
1993	—	—	—	—

TABLE IV — PROOF SETS

These figures are included in the preceding tables and the number given
includes both the silver coins issued with and without gold

Year	Silver sets with gold*		Silver sets without gold
1826	c.400		
1831	c.200		
1839	c.300		
1853	c.20-50		
1887	797		287
1893	c.650		556
1902	Long set	8,066	
1902	Short set	7,057	
1911	Long set	2,812	2,243
1911	Short set	952	
1927			15,000
1937			20,901

Year	Cupro-nickel (No gold)
1950	17,513
1951	20,000
1953	40,000
1970	750,000

*Until the end of the nineteen century it was possible for collectors and institutions to purchase
individual proof coins from the Mint in addition to complete sets, unfortunately no records exist.
The popular **1839 Five Pounds** was sold singularly and the mintage must be in the order of 700-800

A SELECT BIBLIOGRAPHY

Amstell, M.	*A Start to Coin Collecting, English Coins.* W. Foulsham & Co Ltd., London. 1966
Ansell, George F.	*The Royal Mint, with suggestions for its better managenent.* London, 1870
B.N.J.	*Various papers in* The British Numismatic Journal (the journal of the British Numismatic Society. All journals available on line at www.britnumsoc.org
Brooke, George C.	*English Coins, from the Seventeenth Century to the present day.* Methuen & Co. Ltd, London. 3rd Edition 1966
Cope, & Rayner	*The Standard Catalogue of English Milled Coinage in Silver, Copper and Bronze.1662-1972.* London, 1978
Challis, C.E.	*a New History of the Royal Mint from 600.* Cambridge, 1992
Craig, Sir John.	*The Mint. A History of the London Mint from A.D.287-1948* Cambridge, 1953
Crowther, G.P.	*A Guide to English Pattern Coins.* London, 1887
Davis, Peter J.	*British Silver Coins since 1816.* London, 1982. ISBN 0 9507613 0 X
Davis, W.J.	*The Nineteenth Century Token Coinage* B.A. Seaby Ltd
Dyer, G.P.	*The Proposed coinage of King Edward VIII.* H.M.S.O. 1973
Farey, Roderick	*The Royal Mint at Tower Hill.* Coin News March 2015, p. 47-50
Feaveryear, Sir A.	*A Pound Sterling.* 2nd edition. Oxford, 1963
Grueber, H.A.	*Handbook of the Coins of Great Britain and Ireland in the British Museum.* London, 1989
Hawkins, E.	*The Silver Coins of England.* 3rd edition. London, 1887
Hocking, W.J.	*Catalogue of the Coins, Tokens, Medals, Dies and Seals in the Museum of the Royal Mint,* 2 vols. London, 1966
Hsun, L. Ming	*The Great Re-coinage of 1696-1699.* London, 1966
Kelly, E.M.	*Spanish Dollars and Silver Tokens* Spink & Son Ltd
Linecar, H.W.A.	*The Crown Pieces of Great Britain and the British Commonwealth.* London, 1962
Linecar, H.W.A.	& Stone A.G. (L&S) *English Proof and Pattern Crown-size Pieces 1658-1960.* Spink & Son Ltd., 1968
Nathanson, Alan. J.	*Thomas Simon his life and work 1618-1665*
Oman, Sir Charles	*The Coinage of England.* Oxford, 1931
Phillips, M.	*The Token Money of the Bank of England.* London, 1900
Rayner, P. Alan	*The Designers and Engravers of the English Milled Coinage.* London, 1954
Robinson, Brian	*Silver Pennies & Linen Towels – Story of the Royal Maundy* Spink, London, 1992 (Note; B.R for Maundy varieties)

A SELECT BIBLIOGRAPHY

Royal Mint.   *Annual Report of the Deputy Master and Controller.*
                     London, 1870-1977 etc.
Ruding, The Rev. Rogers. *Annals of the Coinage of Great Britain and its*
                     Dependences. 3rd edition (3 vols.) London, 1840
The N.C   *Various papers in* The Numismatic Chronicle (Journal of the
                     Royal Numismatic Society)
Seaby, Peter.   *The Story of the English Coinage.* London. Revised ed. 1990
Spink & Son   *Standard Catalogue of British Coins.* Issued annually
Spink & Son   *Catalogue of a collection of Milled English Coins, including*
                     Patterns and Proofs, formed by H. Montagu. London, 1891
Spink & Son   *Spink's Numismatic Circular.*
Spink & Son   *The Milled Coinage of England, 1662-1946* (gold & silver)
                     Robert Stockwell Ltd., London, S.E.1, 1950
Stride, H.G.   *The Royal Mint: its evolution and development.* In Seaby's
                     Coin and Medal Bulletin, 1954-60

PROOF SETS & SINGLE COINS

Year	Denominations in set	№ of coins in set	Provenance
1746	Crown, Halfcrown, Shilling & Sixpence	4	Baldwin's Fixed Price List Summer 2012, PF001
1879	Halfcrown, Florin, Shilling, Sip pence, Maundy set, Halfpenny & Farthing	10	Spk107, 440 Rasmussen 6/360
1826	*"New issue"* Five Pounds to Farthing in a contemporary maroon rectangular fitted original case	11	Baldwin's Fixed Price List Summer 2009, BM024
1831	*Presentation Set in embossed case* Gold Five Pounds to Farthing	14	Baldwin's Fixed Price List Summer 2009, BM025 & Spk 72, 144
1831	*"Coronation"* Two Pounds to Farthing		
1839	*"Young Head"* Una and the Lion Five Pounds and Sovereign to Farthing	14	
1853	*Presentation Set in early Spink case* Gold Five Pounds to Farthing	16	Spk 72, 156
1853	Sovereign to Farthing including Gothic type Crown	16	
1853	Sovereign, Half-Sovereign, Crown, Halfcrown, Florin, Shilling, Sixpence, Groat, Penny, Halfpenny, Farthing and Half-Farthing	12	Norweb 1072
1879	2/6, 2/-, 1/-, 6d, Maundy, ½d & ¼d, all with plain edges	10	Spk 107, 440
1887	Jubilee bust for *Golden Jubilee* Five Pounds to Threepence	11	
1887	*Presentation Set in original case* Gold Five Pounds to Sixpence	10	Spk 72, 227
1887	Silver Crown to Threepence	7	
1893	*Presentation Set in original case* Gold Five Pounds to Threepence	10	Spk 72, 233
1893	Old bust, Five Pounds to Threepence	10	
1893	Silver Crown to Threepence		
1902	*"Coronation"*. Five Pounds to Maundy Penny. Struck with a Matt finish	13	
1911	*"Coronation"*. Five Pounds to Maundy Penny.	12	Spk 115, 2145
1911	Silver Halfcrown to Maundy Penny.	8	
1927	*"New Coinage"* Wreath type Crown to Threepence	6	

PROOF SETS & SINGLE COINS

Year	Denominations in set	№ of coins in set	Provenance
1927	Sand blasted set comprising Crown, Halfcrown, Florin, Shilling, Sixpence and Threepence	6	Norweb 297
1928	V.I.P. Halfcrown to Threepence		Spk 115, 2146
1929			
1930			
1931			
1932			
1933			
1934			
1935	Halfcrown to Threepence	5	Spk 69, 402
1935	Halfcrown to Farthing	8	Norweb 1131
1935	V.I.P. Shillings to Farthing	6	SJA13, 822
1935	Crown to Threepence	6	Spk 67, 296
1935	Crown to Farthing (cased)	9	Spk 64, 383
1936	Halfcrown to Threepence	5	Spk 69, 403
1937	Edward VIII, A full set of 13 coins in original case, Five Pound Piece down to Farthing sold to a private buyer in 2010 for £1·35 million. See Mark Rasmussen list 19, 2010, illustrated on back cover.	13	
1937	*"Coronation"*. Crown to Farthing, including Maundy Set	15	Spk 107, 457
1937	*"Coronation"*. Gold Five-pounds to Farthing, including Maundy Set	18	Spk 115, 2147
1937	Sand blasted set comprising Crown, Halfcrown, Florin, Shillings (E&S), Sixpence, silver Threepence, Maundy set, brass Threepence, Penny, Halfpenny and Farthing	15	Norweb 729
1938	Halfcrown to Farthing	10	Norweb 1157
1938	Halfcrown to Threepence	6	Spk 69, 405
1939	Halfcrown to Farthing	10	Norweb 1158
1939	Halfcrown to Threepence	6	Spk 69, 406
1940	Halfcrown to Threepence	6	Spk 69, 407
1940	Halfcrown to Halfpenny	8	Norweb 1898
1941	Halfcrown to Threepence	6	Norweb 1899
1942	Halfcrown to Threepence	6	Spk 69, 409

658

PROOF SETS & SINGLE COINS

Year	Denominations in set	№ of coins in set	Provenance
1943	Halfcrown to Threepence	6	Spk 69, 410
1943	Specimen set Halfcrown to Threepence	6	Spk 89, 311
1944			
1945			
1946			
1947	V.I.P. Halfcrown to Sixpence	5	Spk 115, 2148
1947	Halfcrown to Sixpence	5	Norweb 1159
1948	Halfcrown to Sixpence	5	Spk 69, 412
1949	Halfcrown to Sixpence	5	Spk 69, 412
1949	Halfcrown to Farthing	9	Norweb 1160
1949	V.I.P. Halfcrown, Florin, Shillings (E&S), Sixpence,	5	Baldwin's F.P.L. Sum'14 BM162,166,185,186,204
1949	V.I.P. Halfcrown, Florin, Shillings (E&S), Sixpence, brass Threepence, Halfpenny & Farthing	8	Spk 115, 2149
1950	*"Mid Century"*, Halfcrown to Farthing	9	*(Commonly found)*
1950	Sand blasted *"Mid Century"* Halfcrown to Farthing	9	Norweb 1161
1951	*"Festival of Britain"*, Crown to Farthing	10	*(Commonly found)*
1952	Halfcrown to Sixpence	5	Spk 69, 414
1953	*"Coronation"*, Crown to Farthing	10	*(Commonly found)*
1953	Sand blasted set comprising Crown, Halfcrown, Florin, Shillings (E&S), Sixpence, brass Threepence, Penny, Halfpenny and Farthing	10	Norweb 744 Baldwin 68, lots 3711-20
1954	Halfcrown, Florin, Shillings (E&S), Sixpence, brass Threepence, ~~Penny~~, Halfpenny and Farthing	8	Spk 107, 460
1954	V.I.P. Halfcrown, Florin, Shillings (E&S), Sixpence, brass Threepence, Halfpenny and Farthing	8	Spk 115, 2150
1954	Halfcrown to Farthing	8	Norweb 1913
1955	Halfcrown, Florin, Shillings (E&S), Sixpence, brass Threepence, Penny, Halfpenny and Farthing	10	Norweb 746
1956	V.I.P. Halfcrown to Farthing	8	SNC. 2003 MS5784
1956	Halfcrown to Farthing	8	Norweb 1165
1957	Halfcrown to Halfpenny	7	Norweb 1166

PROOF SETS & SINGLE COINS

1958	V.I.P. Halfcrown to Sixpence	4	SNC. 2003 MS5784
1958	Gold Sovereign, silver Halfcrown, Florin, Shillings (E&S), Sixpence, bronze Halfpenny and twelve-sided nickel brass Threepence	8	Norweb 1162
1959			
1960			
1961	Halfcrown to Penny	7	Norweb 1167
1961	Pattern Decimal set, Fifty Cents-One Cent	6	Norweb 1168
1970	*"Last Sterling" set.* Halfcrown to Halfpenny plus medallion	8	*(Commonly found)*

SINGLE PROOF COINS - 1902-1970
P = Proof; M = Matt, S = Specimen, V = V.I.P.[1]

Date	5/-	2/6	2/-	1/-	E 1/-	S 1/-	6d	3d silver	3d brass	1d	½d	¼d
1902	M	M	M	M			M					
1908										M		
1911		P	P	P			P					
1920		M	M									
1924			M	M			M	M				
1925			P Ni				P Ni	P Ni				
1926										P	P	
1927	P	P		P			P P Ni M			P V	P V	P V
1928	V	P		P V						P V	P V	
1929	P V			P						P	P V	P V
1930		P	P	P			P	P		P	P V	P
1931	P	P		P V			P V	P		P	P	P V
1932	P V	P	P	P V			P V	P		P	P V	P
1933	P V	P	P	P			P	P		P	P	P

660

PROOF SETS & SINGLE COINS

Date	5/-	2/6	2/-		E 1/-	S 1/-	6d	3d silver		3d brass	1d	½d	¼d
1934	P	P		P V			P	P			P V	P V	P
1935	P S	P	P V	V			V	P V			V	V	V
1936	P	P V	P V	P V			P V	P V			P	P	P
Ed. 8 1937	P	P	P M		P		P			P M			
G. VI 1937	V M	M	M		P Ni M (uniface)	M	P M	M		M	P		
1938		P	P		P V	P V	P	P			P		
1939		P V	P V		P V	P V	P	P			P	P	P
1940		P	P		V	V	P	P					
1941		P	P		P V	V	P	P					
1942		P M	P		P	P	P	P					
1943		P S V M	P S M		P S M	P S M	PS V	P S M					
1944					M			P		P			
1945													
1946		P			P V		P			P V			
1947		P V	P V		P V	P V	P V				P		
1948		P	P		P V	P V	P			P	P	P	P
1949		P V	P V		P V	P V	P V				P	P V	

PROOF SETS & SINGLE COINS

Date	5/-	2/6	2/-		E 1/-	S 1/-	6d	3d silver		3d brass	1d	½d	¼d
1950		P	P		P	P	P			P	P	P	P
1951	P V	P	P		P	P	P			P	P	P	P
1952		P	P		P	P	P V			P V	P	P	P V
1953	P V M	P V	P M		P V M	P V M				P M	P M	P	P
1954		P V	P V		P V	P V	P V			P	P	P	P
1955		P	P		P M	P M	P			P	P	P	P
1956		P V	P V		P V	P V	P			P V	P	P V	P V
1957		P	P V		P V	V	P			P V	P	P	
1958		P V	P		P V	P V	P V			P V	P	P V	
1959													
1960	V					V				P V		P	
1961		P	P		P V	P V	P			P	P	P	
1962		P V								P			
1963		P											
1964							P						
1965	P Churchill S												
1966													
1967													
1970		P	P		P	P	P			P	P	P	

1   Some Proofs may be wrongly described as V.I.P. in catalogues